RESISTING GENOCIDE

THE CERI COMPARATIVE POLITICS
AND INTERNATIONAL STUDIES SERIES

Series editor, Christophe Jaffrelot

This series consists of translations of noteworthy manuscripts and publications in the social sciences emanating from the foremost French researchers, from Sciences Po, Paris.

The focus of the series is the transformation of politics and society by transnational and domestic factors—globalisation, migration, and the postbipolar balance of power on the one hand, and ethnicity and religion on the other. States are more permeable to external influence than ever before and this phenomenon is accelerating processes of social and political change the world over. In seeking to understand and interpret these transformations, this series gives priority to social trends from below as much as to the interventions of state and non-state actors.

RESISTING GENOCIDE
The Multiple Forms of Rescue

Editors
Jacques Semelin
Claire Andrieu
Sarah Gensburger

Translated by
Emma Bentley and Cynthia Schoch

UNIVERSITY PRESS

In Association with the Centre d'Etudes et de Recherches Internationales (CERI), Paris

OXFORD
UNIVERSITY PRESS

Oxford University Press, Inc., publishes works that further
Oxford University's objective of excellence
in research, scholarship, and education.

Oxford New York
Auckland   Cape Town   Dar es Salaam   Hong Kong   Karachi
Kuala Lumpur   Madrid   Melbourne   Mexico City   Nairobi
New Delhi   Shanghai   Taipei   Toronto

With offices in
Argentina   Austria   Brazil   Chile   Czech Republic   France   Greece
Guatemala   Hungary   Italy   Japan   Poland   Portugal   Singapore
South Korea   Switzerland   Thailand   Turkey   Ukraine   Vietnam

Copyright © 2013 C. Hurst & Co. (Publishers) Ltd.

Oxford is a registered trade mark of Oxford University Press in the UK
and certain other countries.

Published by Oxford University Press, Inc
198 Madison Avenue, New York, New York 10016

Published in the United Kingdom in 2013 by C. Hurst & Co. (Publishers) Ltd.

www.oup.com

Oxford is a registered trademark of Oxford University Press

All rights reserved. No part of this publication may be reproduced,
stored in a retrieval system, or transmitted, in any form or by any means,
electronic, mechanical, photocopying, recording, or otherwise,
without the prior permission of Oxford University Press.

Library of Congress Cataloging-in-Publication Data
Résistance aux génocides. English.
Resisting genocide : the multiple forms of rescue / editors, Claire Andrieu, Sarah Gensburger, Jacques
Semelin ; translated by Emma Bentley and Cynthia Schoch.
p. cm.
"First edition published in 2010."

"This volume is the outcome of a conference entitled "Rescue Practices Facing Genocides. Comparative
Perspectives" that took place at CERI (the Centre for International Studies and Research, CNRS/Sciences
Po) in Paris in December 2006, in association with Sciences Po's Centre d'histoire."

Includes bibliographical references and index.
ISBN 978-0-19-933349-3 (alk. paper)
1. Genocide—History—Congresses. 2. Crimes against humanity—History—Congresses.
3. Holocaust, Jewish (1939-1945)—Influence—Congresses. 4. Genocide—Prevention—Congresses.
I. Andrieu, Claire, 1952- editor of compilation. II. Gensburger, Sarah, editor of compilation. III. Semelin,
Jacques, editor of compilation. IV. Title.
HV6322.7.R4713 2013
364.151—dc23
2013017003

1 3 5 7 9 8 6 4 2

Printed in India
on Acid-Free Paper

CONTENTS

Acknowledgments	ix
Notes on Contributors	xi
Maps	xix

Introduction: From Help to Rescue   *Jacques Semelin*   1

PART I

BETWEEN HISTORY AND MEMORY: RESCUE AS A NOTION

Introduction to Part I   15

1. From the Memory of Rescue to the Institution of the Title of "Righteous"   *Sarah Gensburger*   19
2. In Search of "the Righteous People": The Case of the Armenian Massacres of 1915   *Fatma Müge Göçek*   33
3. Assistance to Jews and to Allied Soldiers and Airmen in France: a Comparative Approach   *Claire Andrieu*   51
4. Researching the Survival and Rescue of Jews in Nazi Occupied Europe: A Plea for the Use of Quantitative Methods   *Marnix Croes*   65
5. Anti-Semitism and the Rescue of Jews in France: An Odd Couple?   *Renée Poznanski*   83
6. Who Dared to Rescue Jews, and Why?   *Nechama Tec*   101
7. Rescue and Self-Interest. Protecting Property to Save People?   *Florent Le Bot*   113
8. Italian Jews and the Memory of Rescue (1944–1961)   *Paola Bertilotti*   127
9. Rescuers and Killer-Rescuers during the Rwanda Genocide: Rethinking Standard Categories of Analysis   *Lee Ann Fujii*   145

CONTENTS

PART II

THE STATE, ITS BORDERS AND THE CONDITIONS FOR AID

Introduction to Part II	159
10. Rescue Practices During the Armenian Genocide *Hasmik Tevosyan*	163
11. Ottoman Officials against the Armenian Genocide: A Comparative Approach to Turkish Towns *Raymond Kévorkian*	183
12. Conversion and Rescue: Survival Strategies in the Armenian Genocide *Ugur Ümit Üngör*	201
13. Humanitarianism and Massacres: The Example of the International Committee of the Red Cross *Irène Herrmann and Daniel Palmieri*	219
14. The Swiss Reaction to the Nazi Genocide: Active Refusal, Passive Help *Ruth Fivaz-Silbermann*	231
15. The OSE and the Rescue of Jewish Children, from the Postwar to the Prewar Period *Katy Hazan and Georges Weill*	245
16. The Context of Rescue in Nazi-Occupied Western Europe *Bob Moore*	265
17. The "Brunner Aktion": A Struggle against Rescue (September 1943–March 1944) *Tal Bruttmann*	279
18. "Guide and Motivator" or "Central Treasury"? The "Joint" in France, 1942–1944 *Laura Hobson Faure*	293
19. The BBC Hungarian Service and Rescue of Jews of Hungary, 1940–1945 *Frank Chalk*	313
20. From "Rescue" to Violence: Overcoming Local Opposition to Genocide in Rwanda *Scott Straus*	331
21. Crossing a Border to Escape: Examples from the Gishamvu and Kigembe Communities of Rwanda *Charles Kabwete Mulinda*	345

PART III

NETWORKS, MINORITES AND RESCUE

Introduction to Part III	363
22. Beatrice Rohner's Work in the Death Camps of Armenians in 1916 *Hans-Lukas Kieser*	367

CONTENTS

23. The Impossible Rescue of the Armenians of Mardin:
 The Sinjar Safe Haven *Yves Ternon* 383
24. Was the UGIF an Obstacle to the Rescue of the Jews? 395
 Michel Laffitte
25. Roundups, Rescue and Social Networks in Paris (1940–1944) 411
 Camille Ménager
26. Protestant Minorities, Judeo-Protestant Affinities and Rescue
 of the Jews in the 1940s *Patrick Cabanel* 433
27. Nieuwlande, Land of Rescue (1941/1942–1945) 447
 Michel Fabréguet
28. Surviving Undetected: The "Bund," Rescue and Memory
 in Germany *Mark Roseman* 465
29. Social Cohesion State of Exception: The Muslims of Mabare
 during the Genocide in Rwanda (April 1994) 481
 Emmanuel Viret
Conclusion: Rescue, A Notion Revisited *Claire Andrieu* 495

Bibliography 507
Index of Names 525
Index of Places 535

The translations of the French chapters have been written by:

Emma Bentley: Chapters 3, 11, 13, 14, 17, 21, 24, 26, 27, 29.

Cynthia Schoch: All introductions, chapters 1, 5, 7, 8, 15, 23, 25 and the conclusion.

ACKNOWLEDGMENTS

This volume is the outcome of a conference entitled 'Rescue Practices Facing Genocides. Comparative Perspectives' that took place at CERI (the Centre for International Studies and Research, CNRS/Sciences Po) in Paris in December 2006, in association with Sciences Po's Centre d'Histoire. This conference was organized thanks to the financial support of the Foundation for the Memory of the Shoah, the French Ministry of Defence, the City of Paris, the Resistance Foundation, Air France and Sciences Po's Graduate School. It brought together about fifty scholars coming from a variety of countries including Armenia, the Republic of Belarus, Belgium, Britain, Canada, France, Germany, Hungary, Israel, Italy, the Netherlands, Poland, Rwanda and the United States.

The debate immensely benefited from the panels discussants' work: Marc-Olivier Baruch, Hamit Bozarslan, Nancy Green, Pieter Lagrou, Marie-Claire Lavabre and René Lemarchand. The editors are also very grateful to Odette Christienne, Philippe Joutard, Lucien Lazare, Gilles-Pierre Lévy, Michel Marian, Michael R. Marrus, Esther Mujawayo, Karen Murphy, Richard Prasquier, Paule René-Bazin, Anne-Marie Revcolevschi, Valérie Rosoux, Paul Thibaud and Michel Wieviorka, whose participation in the conference was crucial. The editors would like to extend their warm thanks to Christian Jaffrelot for his help, to Cynthia Schoch and Emma Bentley for their translations, and finally to Jonathan Derrick, Laura Hobson Faure, Miriam Perier and Irina Vauday for their wonderful work on the finished version of the manuscript.

NOTES ON CONTRIBUTORS

Editors

Claire Andrieu is Professor of Contemporary History at Sciences Po, Paris. She co-edited the *Dictionnaire De Gaulle* with Philippe Braud and Guillaume Piketty (Paris, Robert Laffont, 2006) and contributed to the *Dictionnaire historique de la Résistance* edited by François Marcot (Paris, Robert Laffont, 2006). Her books about the French Resistance deal with its political project (*Le programme commun de la Résistance*, Editions de l'Erudit, 1984, and a co-edited work: *Les nationalisations de la Libération*, Paris, Presses de Sciences Po, 1987). As a former member of the Fact-Finding Mission on the Spoliation of Jews in France, she published several books on spoliations and restitutions. Her current research is on the behaviour of European civilians towards fugitives in World War II.

Sarah Gensburger obtained a PhD in Sociology from EHESS, on the expression of memories through the title "Righteous." Her publications include "De Jerusalem à Kigali. L'émergence de la catégorie de 'Juste' comme paradigme mémoriel" in Caroline Hähnel-Mesnard *et al.* (eds), *Cultures et mémoire. Représentation contemporaines de la mémoire dans les espaces mémoriels, les arts du visuel, la littérature et le théâtre* (Paris, Editions de l'Ecole Polytechnique, 2008); with Agnizeszka Niewiedzial, "Figure du Juste et politique publique de la mémoire en Pologne: entre relations diplomatiques et structures sociales," *Critique Internationale*, 1, 2007; and "Les figures du 'Juste' et du résistant et l'évolution de la mémoire historique française de l'Occupation," *Revue Française de Sciences Politiques*, 52 (2–3), 2002.

Jacques Semelin is Professor of Political Science and Modern History and Senior Researcher at CERI Sciences Po-CNRS, Paris. He holds a

PhD in contemporary history from the Sorbonne (1986) and a postgraduate degree in psychopathology from Université Paris V. A former post-doctoral fellow at the Harvard University Center for International Affairs (1986–88), he is the founder (in 2008) and editor in chief of massviolence.org. Semelin is member of the editorial boards of the *European Review of History*, the *Journal of Genocide Research* and *Vingtième Siècle*. Member of the International Genocide Scholars Association (IGSA) and of the International Network of Genocide Scholars (INOGS). His publications include *Purify and Destroy. The Political Uses of Massacre and Genocide* (London, Hurst & Co. and New York, Columbia University Press, 2007); "Taking Mann Seriously?," *Political Studies Review* 4(3), September 2006; "What is Genocide?" *European Review of History*, 12(1), March 2005.

Contributors

Paola Bertilotti is finishing her PhD in Contemporary History at Sciences Po, Paris. Supervised by Prof. Marc Lazar, Paola is working on Fascist and Nazi anti-Semitic persecutions in Italy ("Les persécutions antisémites fascistes et nazies en Italie: mémoires et représentations entre 1944 et 1967").

Tal Bruttman is researcher at the city of Grenoble Commission of Inquiry on Spoliation of Jews and is currently preparing a PhD on the French World War II Vichy *milice* at EHESS. His publications include *La logique des bourreaux* (Paris, Hachette Littératures, 2003) and *Au bureau des affaires juives. L'administration française et l'application de la legislation antisémite, 1940–1944* (Paris, La Découverte, 2006).

Patrick Cabanel is Professor of Contemporary History at the University of Toulouse-Le Mirail, France. He is the editor of the journal *Diasporas. Histoire et Sociétés*. His publications include: *Juifs et protestants en France, les affinités électives XVIe-XXIe siècle*, Paris, Fayard, 2004; (ed., with L. Gervereau) *La Deuxième Guerre mondiale, des terres de refuge aux musées*, Le Chambon-sur-Lignon, Sivom Vivarais-Lignon, 2003; (ed., with Ph. Joutard and J. Poujol), *Cévennes terre de refuge 1940–1944*, Presses du Languedoc, 2006 [1987]).

Frank Chalk (PhD, History, University of Wisconsin) is Professor of History and Director of the Montreal Institute for Genocide and Human

NOTES ON CONTRIBUTORS

Rights Studies, Concordia University. Prof. Chalk served as President of the International Association of Genocide Scholars (1999–2001), and is a past president of the Canadian Association of African Studies. Prof. Chalk's publications include chapters on "Hate Radio in Rwanda," published in *The Path of A Genocide: The Rwanda Crisis from Uganda to Zaire*, ed. Howard Adelman and Astri Suhrke (New Brunswick, NJ: Transaction Press, 1999): with Dinah Shelton, Howard Adelman, Alexander Kiss and William Schabas, he was an editor of the three-volume Macmillan USA (Thomson Gale) *Encyclopedia of Genocide and Crimes Against Humanity*, 2004. Recent publications include, with Danielle Kelton, "Mass Atrocity Crimes in Darfur and The Response of Government of Sudan Media to International Pressure," Chap. 5 in *Crisis in Darfur*, ed. Amanda Grzyb (Montreal, McGill-Queens University Press, 2009).

Marnix Croes holds MA degrees in modern history and political science from the University of Amsterdam. He is a researcher at the WODC, the Research and Documentation Centre of the Dutch Ministry of Justice. Among his publications are "The Holocaust in the Netherlands and the Rate of Jewish Survival," *Holocaust and Genocide Studies*, 20 (3), 2006; and "Gentiles and the Survival Chances of Jews in The Netherlands, 1940–1945: A Closer Look," in Beate Kosmala and Feliks Tych (eds), *Facing the Nazi Genocide: Non Jews and Jews in Europe* (European Science Foundation-Metropol Verlag, 2004).

Michel Fabréguet is Professor of Contemporary History, with a focus on Nazism, at the Institut d'études politiques, Strasbourg, France. He has published several books, including *Mauthausen. Camp de concentration national-socialiste en Autriche rattachée, 1938–1945* (Honoré Champion, 1999). He is a member of the editorial board of the journal *La revue d'Allemagne et des pays de langue allemande*.

Ruth Fivaz-Silbermann is a historian and teaches at the School of Translation and Interpretation at the University of Geneva. In 1998 she started working on Swiss asylum policies during the Second World War, particularly on French Jews fleeing to Switzerland, their trajectories and their strategies to escape extermination.

Lee Ann Fuji is Assistant Professor of Political Science and Program Coordinator of the politics cohort of the Women's Leadership Program at George Washington University (USA). She is the author of *Killing*

NOTES ON CONTRIBUTORS

Neighbors: Webs of Violence in Rwanda (Cornell University Press, 2009). She has also written articles on mass killing, ethnicity, and conducting fieldwork in post-war zones.

Fatma Müge Göçek is Associate Professor in Sociology at the University of Michigan in the Program for Women's Studies. Her publications include three edited volumes (*Social Constructions of Nationalism in the Middle East*, Albany, SUNY Press, 2002; *Political Cartoons in the Middle East*, Princeton, Markus Wiener Publishers, 1998, *Reconstructing Gender in the Middle East: Tradition, Identity and Power*, with Shiva Balaghi, New York, CUP, 1994); two single authored books (*Rise of the Bourgeoisie, Demise of Empire: Ottoman Westernization and Social Change*, New York, OUP, 1994; *East Encounters West: France and the Ottoman Empire in the Eighteenth Century*, New York, OUP, 1987); and numerous articles in academic journals.

Katy Hazan holds an *Agrégation* in history and a doctorate in literature and arts. She is the Director of the Department of Archives and History of the Oeuvre de Secours aux Enfants (OSE). She is a member of the editorial board of the journal *Revue d'Histoire de la Shoah*. Her publications include *Les orphelins de la Shoah. Les maisons de l'espoir* (Paris, Les Belles Lettres, 2000) and with Eric Ghozlan, *A la vie! Les enfants de Buchenwald, du Shtetl à l'OSE* (Paris, Le Manuscrit, 2005). She has also contributed to the series "Témoignage de la Shoah" published by the Fondation pour la Mémoire de la Shoah (Paris, Le Manuscrit).

Irène Herrmann is Associate Professor of Modern History at the University of Fribourg and lecturer in Swiss history at the University of Geneva. She currently leads a research project on "The making of Swiss citizens' political responsibility"; she also works on humanitarianism and political uses of the past in post-Soviet Russia. She has published more than seventy articles, several edited books and two monographs: *Les cicatrices du passé* (Berlin, Berne etc., Peter Lang, 2006) and *Genève entre république et canton* (Geneva and Quebec, Editions Passé-Présent and Presses de l'Université Laval, 2003).

Laura Hobson Faure (PhD) is Assistant Professor at the Ecole Polytechnique (Paris). She has recently completed a doctorate thesis on the role of American Jewish organizations in the reconstruction of the French Jewish community after the Shoah, supervised by Professor Nancy L.

NOTES ON CONTRIBUTORS

Green. Her recent publications include "Renaître sous les auspices américains et britanniques. Le mouvement libéral juif en France après la Shoah (1944–1970)," *Archives Juives*, October 2007.

Raymond Kévorkian is Senior Researcher at the Institut Français de Géopolitique, at Paris VIII-St-Denis University, and curator of the Nubar Armenian library. His publications include *Le Génocide des Arméniens* (Paris, Odile Jacob, 2006) and *Les Arméniens, 1917–1939, la quête d'un refuge* (co-edited, RMN, 2007).

Hans-Lukas Kieser is *Privatdozent* in Modern History at the University of Zurich, specializing in the late Ottoman and post-Ottoman world and its interaction with Europe and the USA. Among his books are *Die armenische Frage und die Schweiz/La question arménienne et la Suisse (1896–1923)*, Zurich, Chronos, 1999; *Der Völkermord an den Armeniern und die Shoah/The Armenian Genocide and the Shoah*, Zurich, Chronos, 2002; *A Quest for Belonging. Anatolia beyond Empire and Nation (19th-21st c.)*, Istanbul, Isis, 2007; *Nearest East. American Mission and Millennialism in the Middle East (1810s–1970s)*, Philadelphia, Temple University Press, 2010.

Michel Laffitte holds an *Agrégation* and a doctorate in History at EHESS and is member of the Fondation pour la Mémoire de la Shoah. He has published *L'Union générale des israélites de France face aux réalités de a Shoah* (Paris, Liana Levi, 2003), Winner of the Henri-Hertz prize in 2004; *Juif dans la France allemande* (Tallandier, 2006); and, with Georges Bensoussan, a special issue of the journal *Revue d'Histoire de la Shoah* on Jewish councils.

Florent Le Bot holds a PhD in History and is a researcher at CNRS (IDHE ENS Cachan, France). His publications include *La fabrique réactionnaire. Antisémitisme, spoliations et corporatisme dans le cuir (1930–1950)*, Paris, Presses de Sciences Po, 2007. His research focuses on companies, territories and the globalization process (eighteenth–nineteenth centuries), especially during severe economic and political crises. He manages the electronic research space www.mondesenmouvements.e-monsite.com

Camille Ménager holds a research Master's in History and Political Theory from Sciences Po, Paris. She is currently a researcher for historical documentary films.

NOTES ON CONTRIBUTORS

Bob Moore is Professor of Twentieth Century European History at the University of Sheffield and has published extensively on the Netherlands, Prisoners-of-War and World War II, Major works include *Victims and Survivors: The Nazi Persecution of the Jews in the Netherlands 1940–1945* (1997) and *Resistance in Western Europe* (2000). His most recent publication is *Crises of Empire* (2008) co-authored with Martin Thomas and Larry Butler, and he has just completed a monograph, *The Rescue of Jews in Nazi-occupied Western Europe*, for Oxford University Press.

Charles Kabwete Mulinda is Lecturer at the National University of Rwanda. He is also a PhD student at the University of the Western Cape (South Africa); his PhD topic is "A Space for Genocide: Local Authorities, Local Population and Local Histories in Gishamvu and Kibayi (Rwanda)." He is a Doctoral Fellow at the University of Minnesota (USA).

Daniel Palmieri is Historical Research Officer at the International Committee of the Red Cross; his work deals with humanitarian history and the history of conflicts. Among his latest publications is "Crossing the Desert—the ICRC in Iraq: Analysis of a Humanitarian Operation," *International Review of the Red Cross*, Cambridge University Press, vol. 90, no. 869, 2008.

Renée Poznanski is Professor at the Department of Political Science, Ben Gurion-Negev University (Israel), where she holds the Yaakov and Poria Avnon chairs of Holocaust studies. She has edited Jacques Biélinky's diary, *Un journaliste juif à Paris sous l'occupation* (Cerf, 1992) and is the author of *Jews in France during World War II* (Lebanon, NH, University Press of New England & US Holocaust Memorial Museum, 2001) and *Propagandes et Presécutions. La résistance et le 'problème juif', 1940–1944* (Fayard, 2008), among other publications.

Mark Roseman is Pat M Glazer Chair of Jewish Studies, Indiana University. A historian of modern Europe, with particular interests in the history of the Holocaust and modern German history, his recent publications include *The Past in Hiding*, London, Penguin Press, 2000; *The Villa, the Lake, the Meeting. The Wannsee Conference and the 'Final Solution'*, London, Penguin, 2002.

Scott Straus is Associate Professor of Political Science and International Studies at the University of Wisconsin, Madison, where he also serves as

NOTES ON CONTRIBUTORS

the faculty director of the Human Rights Initiative. His primary research and teaching interests lie at the intersection of large-scale violence, human rights, and African politics. His publications include *The Order of Genocide: Race, Power, and War in Rwanda* (Ithaca, Cornell University Press, 2006); with Robert Lyons, *Intimate Enemy: Images and Voices of the Rwandan Genocide* (New York, MIT/Zone Books, 2006); with David Leonard, *Africa's Stalled Development: International Causes and Cures* (Boulder, Lynne Rienner, 2003). He has published articles on violence and genocide in *World Politics*, *Politics & Society*, *Foreign Affairs*, *Genocide Studies and Prevention*, the *Journal of Genocide Research*, *Patterns of Prejudice*, and the *Wisconsin International Law Journal*. Prior to entering academia, Straus was a freelance journalist based in Nairobi.

Nechama Tec, Professor Emerita of Sociology, University of Connecticut, Stamford, received her PhD from Columbia University. A Holocaust scholar for years, she has concentrated her research and publications on the intricate relationships between self-preservation, compassion, altruism, rescue, resistance, cooperation and gender. Her publications include *Resilience and Courage: Women, Men and the Holocaust*, Yale University Press, 2003; *Defiance: The Bielski Partisans*. Oxford University Press, 1993; as well as more than seventy scholarly articles.

Yves Ternon holds a PhD in history from Université Paris IV-Sorbonne and an accreditation to direct research from Université Paul Valéry-Montpellier-3. His publications include *L'Etat criminel* (Paris, Seuil, 1995), *Les arméniens. Histoire d'un génocide* (Seuil, 1996) and *Guerres et génocides aux XXe siècle* (Paris, Odile Jacob, 2007).

Hasmik Tevosyan is a recipient of the Academic Fellowship Program award by the Open Society Institute. She designed and taught courses in International Development and Security and in Human Rights and Humanitarian Law at the Russian-Armenian State University in Yerevan. She worked with the UN mission in Armenia and is currently consulting for the Open World Leadership Center at the Library of Congress. Her published works include articles on motivational and behavioural patterns of the migrant labourer (Institute of Economic Forecasting of the Russian Academy of Sciences, Moscow, 2001) and on socio-psychological transformation of the labour migrant's self-conception (Yerevan State University Press, 2001).

NOTES ON CONTRIBUTORS

Uğur Ümit Üngör is Lecturer in International History at the University of Sheffield and fellow at the Centre for the Study of Genocide and Mass Violence. He studied Sociology and History at the Universities of Groningen, Utrecht and Toronto, and finished his PhD thesis entitled "Young Turk Social Engineering: Genocide, Nationalism, and Memory in Eastern Turkey, 1913–1950" at the University of Amsterdam. His main area of interest is the historical sociology of mass violence and nationalism. He has published on genocide in general, and on the Rwandan and Armenian genocides in particular.

Emmanuel Viret is a PhD candidate at Sciences-Po in Paris. His research, for which he did nineteen months of fieldwork, focuses on patronage relations and peasant mobilisation in rural Rwanda.

Georges Weill is an archivist, paleographer, general honorary curator of national heritage, and former curator of the Universal Israelite Alliance (UIA) library and archives. He is the author of numerous articles on archival work, the history of Jews in Alsace and of the UIA, in particular *Emancipation et progrès, l'AIU et les droits de l'Homme* (Paris, Nadir, 2000). His personal story (he was saved and hidden by OSE) allowed him to contribute to the reconstitution of facts through analysis of archives of French and foreign institutions that took part in the rescue of children.

MAPS

The maps on the following pages are intended to serve as a pedagogical guide to the reading. They only show a schematic diagram of the events. The map of the Armenian genocide is more detailed than that of the genocide of the Jews. To achieve a similar degree of precision for the Jewish genocide, such a map would stretch over several pages (in particular, concentration camps where Jews were held along with other prisoners are not shown). The victims of the three genocides number over 1.2 million Armenians, about 6 million Jews, and approximately 800,000 Tutsis (according to UNO sources). Sources: Jacques Semelin (ed.), *Online Encyclopedia of Mass Violence*; Raymond Kévorkian, *Le Génocide des Arméniens* (Paris, Odile Jacob, 2006); Martin Gilbert, *Atlas de la Shoah* (La Tour d'Aigues, Editions de l'Aube, 2005, reed.); Republic of Rwanda, Ministry of Local Government, *Census of Victims of Genocide*, 2000.

THE SPATIAL SCALE OF THREE GENOCIDES

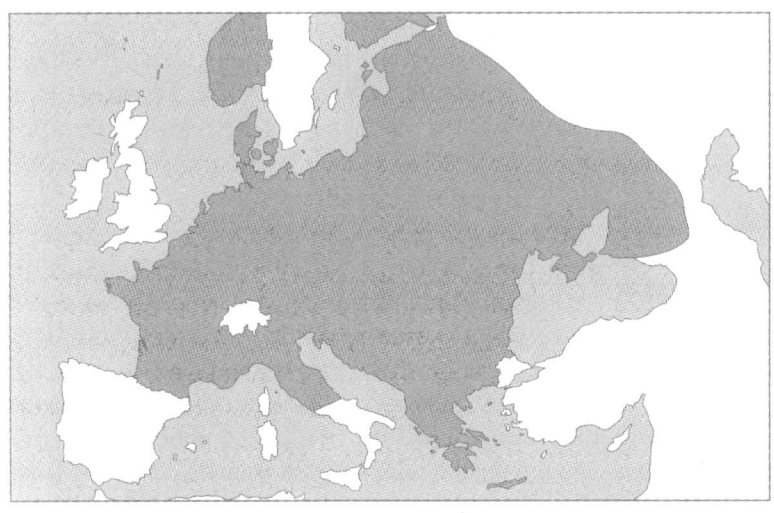

1. The Geographic Spread of the Genocide of the Jews

2. The Geographic Spread of the Genocide of the Armenians

3. The Geographic Spread of the Genocide of the Tutsis

Scale
0   500   1000 km

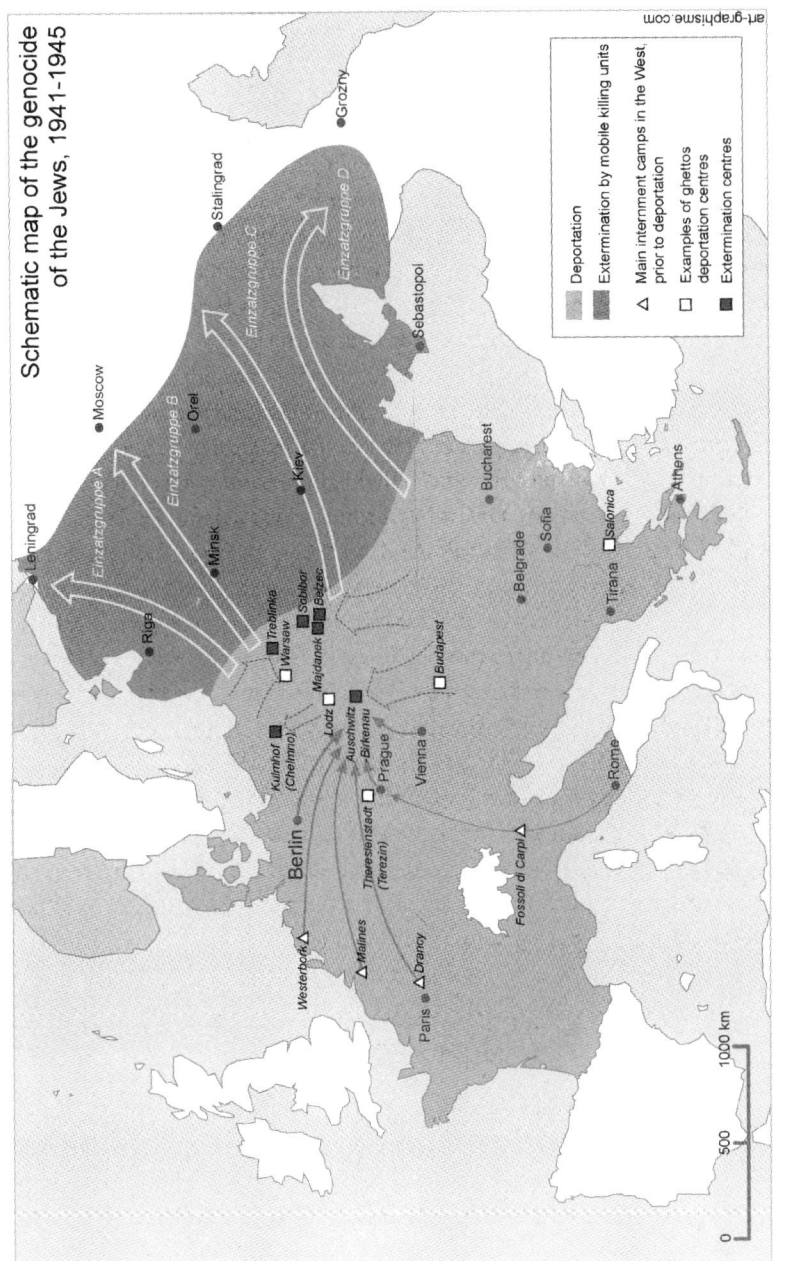

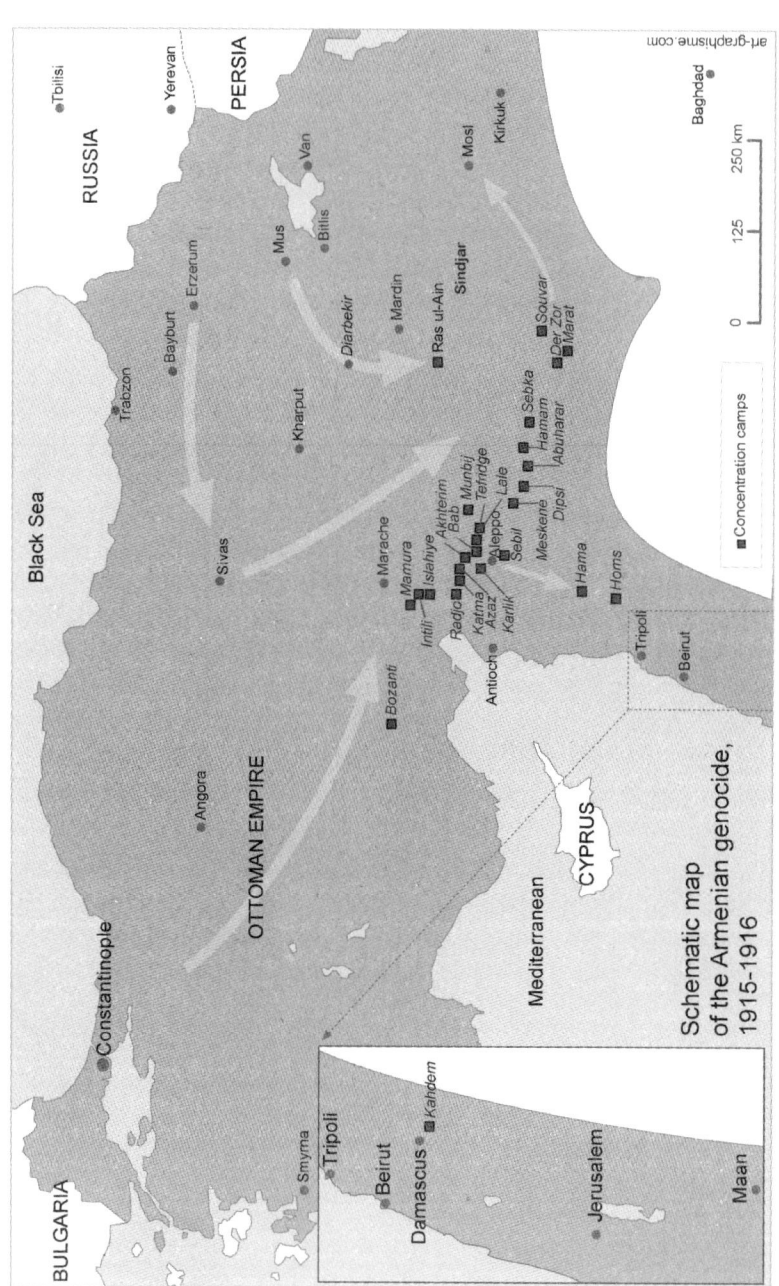

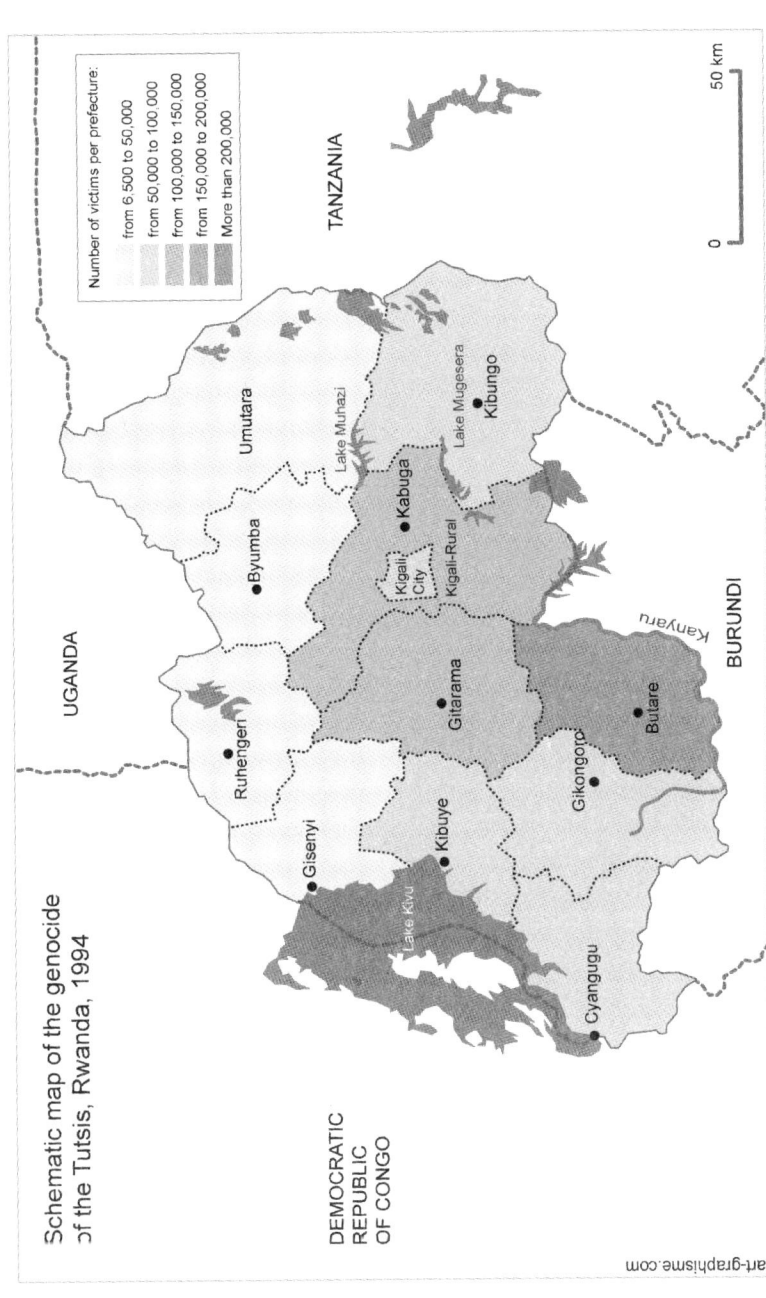

Schematic map of the genocide of the Tutsis, Rwanda, 1994

INTRODUCTION
FROM HELP TO RESCUE

Jacques Semelin

When a country is overcome by hatred and fear, when war and massacres spread like the plague, there are nevertheless always a few men and women who do not join the pack. Without a word, they step aside. In secrecy and in danger, they prefer to help rather than denounce, protect rather than destroy. Who knows if even some of those who take part in a slaughter don't also sometimes attempt rescues? It would not be the first time that human beings display their surprising faculty to conduct themselves in an ambiguous, even contradictory fashion.

Aside from a handful of groundbreaking studies, scholarly research has taken little interest in such behaviour, in what we refer to here as acts of rescue in genocidal situations. Take for example the genocide of the Jews. Compared with the impressive bibliography dealing with the phases of their persecution, deportation and extermination, rare are the studies that have been devoted to rescue operations. In this book, we do not discuss the exceptional story of Danish Jews evacuated in October 1943 to Sweden, or even the less well-known case of the rescue of Bulgarian Jews.[1] We also set aside such well-known emblematic figures as the Swedish diplomat Raoul Wallenberg in Budapest or the American Varian Fry

---

[1] It should not be forgotten that Bulgaria deported the Jews in Macedonia (annexed by Sofia in 1941). But Bulgarian Jews escaped deportation thanks to protest from members of parliament, intellectuals and Orthodox Church officials who put pressure on the Sofia government not to deport Bulgarian Jews.

operating in Marseilles. Foremost in our mind was the action of those "ordinary people" who, in the secrecy of their own homes, one day agreed to harbour one or more people who were hunted down because they were Jewish. The fact that these were scattered initiatives which moreover, for obvious reasons, generated no documentary evidence may well be what has hampered the development of scholarly research on them. This often happens with civic action undertaken outside the framework of established society, all the more so when it is performed in secret; by comparison, the masses of archives produced by persecuting states provide endless research opportunities.

The history of rescue has long suffered from another handicap, that of being often characterized by ordinary everyday gestures that lack the drama of armed struggle or the intrigue of military espionage. Yet placed back in their context, such protective acts are indeed extraordinary gestures in the consequences they entail for both their authors and their beneficiaries. Despite the apparent banality of such gestures of mutual aid, they preserve, even momentarily, a corner of civilization in a world of barbarity. This is moreover what the most recent historiography tends to reflect, which now considers these acts of rescue as a specific form of civil resistance. Such resistance does not involve causing harm to the enemy's physical and political forces, but saving lives that the enemy would like to see disappear.

So even if archives pertaining to rescue initiatives are rare, we nevertheless have several testimonials from rescued people recorded by the Yad Vashem Institute in Jerusalem, whose mission includes awarding the title of "Righteous among the Nations" to non-Jews who selflessly saved Jews.[2] Investigations conducted by this Israeli Institute have resulted in a rich corpus of thousands of life stories, all equally poignant, collected in all the countries that were occupied by Nazi Germany. They go to show that human solidarity is not a vain word, even when barbarity has the upper hand. Rescuers in fact come from all social and occupational categories, as Mordecai Paldiel's research has shown in general[3] and Lucien Lazare's has

---

[2] This distinction is awarded by the state of Israel in the form of a medal to pay tribute to the person for his or her act of rescue. The medal bears these words from the Talmud: "Whoever saves a single life, saves an entire universe."

[3] Mordecaï Paldiel, *The Path of the Righteous, Gentile Rescuers of the Jews During the Holocaust*, Hoboken (NJ), Ktav, 1993. Lucien Lazare, *Le Livre des Justes*, Paris, Hachette, 1995.

also demonstrated in the particular case of France. The banality of good is now mentioned in this context, in response to the disputed notion of the banality of evil suggested by philosopher Hannah Arendt.[4]

The title of "Righteous," however, poses serious difficulties for the researcher because it is primarily a religiously inspired moral category and not a concept that can be used in the social sciences. One might recall in this regard the debates that preceded the definition of this award in Israel. For Justice Moshe Landau, who presided over the tribunal in charge of trying Adolf Eichmann, only a non-Jew who had saved a Jew in a selfless manner should be declared "Righteous." The "Righteous" could thus only be defined according to strict rules, taking into consideration only a person who had acted with no ulterior motives whatsoever, whether political, economic, sexual, etc. But by that definition, a man who was rescued by the German entrepreneur Oskar Schindler, Moshe Bejski, has retorted that there would be very few "Righteous." Bejski thus reproached Landau for having a far too abstract and elitist representation, having not been confronted with the genocide, because Landau had left Germany just before the war broke out. Debates around Schindler's case thus brought to light the matter of "judging" the one who rescues: either in the name of moral purity predefined from the outside, or according to human criteria that are inseparable from the historic context in which the rescue takes root. However, it was the definition of Moshe Landau, the most famous judge in Israel at the time, that was accepted.

Afterward, the notion of "Righteous" met with growing success throughout the 1990s and even more in the 2000s.[5] It is also been introduced in other contexts of massacres and genocides, such as those in Rwanda and in Bosnia,[6] to the point that the Italian Gabriele Nissim intends to work towards the creation of "a world garden of righteous."[7] The internation-

---

[4] Enrico Deaglio, *La Banalità del bene. Storia di Giorgio Perlasca*, Milan, Feltrinelli, 1993.

[5] Sarah Gensburger, "Les Justes de France. Politiques publiques de la mémoire," Paris, Presses de Sciences Po, 2010.

[6] Cf., on Rwanda, *Tribute to Courage*, Kigali and London, African Rights, 2002, as well as the symposium on the "Righteous" organized in Kigali in December 2007 by Gerd Ankel (Hamburger Institut für Sozialforschung). Regarding Bosnia, see the testimonials collected by Marshal Tito's granddaughter, Svetlana Broz, *Good People in an Evil Time: Portraits of Complicity and Resistance in the Bosnian War*, New York, Random House, 2005.

[7] Gabriele Nissim, *Le Jardin des justes. De la liste de Schindler au tribunal du Bien*,

alization of the notion of "Righteous," which thus transcends the case of the Holocaust alone, tends to make it a universal figure of Good, as if we had an imperious need to honour the most laudable human conduct to offset the most abject moral disaster. The result is a hagiographic literature that tends to idealize the rescuers, whom some even go so far as to call "saviours." The religious resonance of this last word certainly reflects a rescued person's immense gratitude towards the person to whom he or she owes his or her life. From the victims' point of view, such idealization is perfectly understandable, even if it may make the honored person rather uncomfortable, as the rescuers often believe that they merely did their duty.

In any event, the attribution of the "Righteous among the Nations" award by the state of Israel, which has arguably been used in some cases to influence foreign policy,[8] draws the historian's attention to the study of these mutual aid behaviours. There is indeed no doubt that historians have neglected its importance, busy as they have been trying to grasp the extraordinary monstrosity of the Nazi crimes. Now that the process of the extermination of European Jews is much better known, it becomes easier to look back at events that sometimes may have obstructed, and even prevented, this process of death. In this aim, while taking into account the considerable remembrance efforts undertaken by Yad Vashem, it is up to researchers to forge their own analytical tools regarding rescue practices. Such is the ambition of this work, which aims to understand the decision to perform an act of rescue, as we have already attempted to understand the decision to indulge in massacre. How can this moral question thus be turned into a true object of research?

Making rescue an object of research

The present book marks the completion of several years of collective research, from a conference in 2002 in Chambon-sur-Lignon[9] to the

---

Paris, Payot, 2007 (Italian original: *Il tribunale del bene. La storia di Moshe Beskj dalla lista di Schindler al Giardino dei giusti*, Milan, Mondadori, 2003.)

[8] See Sarah Gensburger's chapter in this volume.

[9] The most significant having been the 2002 symposium organized by Patrick Cabanel and Laurent Gervereau (eds), *La Deuxième Guerre mondiale, des terres de refuge aux musées*, Saint-Agrève, Sivom Vivarais-Lignon, 2003.

preparation of an international symposium at Sciences-Po in Paris in 2006, for which the chapters assembled here were produced. Our approach hopes to be innovative in that it begins by offering a historiographic overview of research on the rescue of Jews in Nazi Europe, without making claims to be exhaustive. Research in this field is indeed the most advanced and the reader will see that it occupies the lion's share of this volume. However, we wanted to broaden our inquiry by also taking a look at efforts to protect victims of other mass murders. What about acts of rescue during the Armenian genocide in 1915–16? The question is rarely asked and is fairly unconventional with respect to the commemoration struggle of Armenian organizations that are constantly working toward international recognition of the genocide. It will appear obvious here that it is nevertheless worth exploring. What about acts of rescue during the Rwandan genocide of the Tutsis in 1994? Even if such incidents were rare, a few examples are known, so why not give them a closer look? During our symposium, we wanted to hear testimonials relating to these three cases in order to compare the narratives, beyond their specific contexts.[10]

For our scholarly ambition is also to lay the foundation for a possible comparative analysis. Certainly the exercise of comparison is always risky, given the very problem of establishing parallels between very different historical situations. However, the advantage is to stimulate reflection and enable knowledge to circulate. Comparison can then suggest new analytical perspectives and also suggest cross-disciplinary questions for the cases studied, constantly keeping in mind that comparing amounts to differentiating.

That established, let us attempt to better define our object of research. In an initial approach, we will define rescue as a set of actions, whether covert or not, that aim to legally or physically conceal the identity of wanted persons and/or organize their escape to a place where they will

---

[10] To achieve this, our symposium ended with two roundtable discussions: the first on "Witnesses and Memories of Rescue," with Odette Christienne (Paris City Hall), Lucien Lazare (Yad Vashem Israel), Richard Prasquier (Yad Vashem France), Esther Mujawayo (Rwanda), Paul Thibaud (Amitié Judéo-Chrétienne); the second on "What Lessons Can be Drawn for the Present and the Future?" with Anne-Marie Revcolevschi (Fondation pour la Mémoire de la Shoah), Karen Murphy (Facing History and Ourselves), Valérie Rosoux (FNRS, Université Catholique de Louvain), Michel Marian (Les Nouvelles d'Arménie).

find safety. Depending on the country and the period, such operations have taken very different forms. However, the notion of rescue, which seems self-evident, is not as obvious as it may seem. It only has genuine significance with respect to the period of genocide, the time during which an absolute death threat hangs over the designated victims. There is thus a great risk of falling into anachronism, since we know how the story ends. Hence, it is impossible to speak of saving Jews *per se* in 1940 when the Final Solution was not yet decided in Berlin. In that regard, we must clearly distinguish between immigration and rescue. The flow of German or Austrian Jews leaving their country in the 1930s is not part of this field of study. Until the autumn of 1941, Nazi policy in fact aimed to drive the Jews out of the Reich, not to exterminate them. For the same reason, transports of Jewish children from Czechoslovakia to England in 1939 are not part of our subject matter either. These humanitarian operations indeed had the very positive consequence of giving shelter to Jewish children who, we now know, ran the risk of being rounded up later by the Nazis. Organized migration to England nonetheless did not constitute an act of rescue in 1939, because these children were not in danger of death at their date of departure.

This book does not deal either with the role of specifically military operations. We know that genocide usually occurs in wartime. So if a war ends, from the very fact of military defeat of those who organized the massacres, the slaughter perforce ends. Thus the last death camp in Poland at Auschwitz ceased to function owing precisely to the advance of the Soviet army at the end of 1944. But in the West, gas chambers where prisoners of all origins were exterminated remained in operation, the last attested gassing having occurred in Ravensbrück on 23 April 1945 and in Mauthausen on 28 April—ten days away from Germany's military surrender on 8 May 1945. It was thus indeed the defeat of the Third Reich that definitively and at the last moment put an end to the extermination of European Jews. Likewise, the victory of Paul Kagame's Rwandan Patriotic Front (RPF) in July 1994 put an end to the gruesome series of genocidal massacres of Tutsis. This military approach to rescue, which could be extended to international military-humanitarian intervention, is not part of our field of investigation either.

Rather, what this volume examines is the social distinction of acts of sheltering and aiding a person who is persecuted and perhaps marked for destruction. Such acts are not only discreet, in that they are often conducted under cover, but also discrete, as they are often unrelated to one another, carried out separately in a totally disconnected manner. While the social climate is characterized by killing, this aid relationship seems, if we dare say so in writing, almost abnormal in that it is so far removed from this new societal norm. In a way, it is this peculiarity of "goodness" that subsists in the interstices of a universe of social war that we seek to explain.

For the genocidal process is based on the breakdown, worse, the destruction of the social tie with the group described as an enemy, towards which what sociologist Helen Fein calls "the universe of obligations" is no longer applied. According to this pioneer of genocide studies, the notion can be defined as "that circle of people with reciprocal obligations to protect each other whose bonds arose from their relation to a deity or sacred source of authority (the state constituting one of the current forms of this authority to which individuals swear allegiance)."[11] But, she says, to make the inhumanity of these victims perceptible, you only have to place them outside this universe of obligations. This "other" enemy therefore becomes completely "other," that is to say disengaged totally from any reciprocal relationship of identification. It is in effect a process of de-identification (or even of deculturation, as psychologists might say) that expels individuals from the community to which they belong. At that point anything becomes possible against this "other/enemy" banned from society and doomed to be annihilated. So in the face of this destructive stigmatization, who still manages to resist? Who holds fast? Who act as a refuge? What enables us to understand why some continue to perceive this other/enemy as a human being?

An initial response can be found in pioneer studies on rescuing conducted by Nechama Tec[12] and Samuel and Pearl Oliner.[13] The act of rescue can, it is suggested, be explained by the rescuers' personality. They come from a wide variety of social backgrounds, as shown by the files of Yad Vashem, but they apparently have an essential common feature, that of being driven by moral values and thereby being open to others, in

---

[11] Helen Fein, *Accounting for Genocide. Victims and Survivors of the Holocaust. National Responses and Jewish Victimization During the Holocaust*, New York, The Free Press, 1979, p. 4.

[12] Nechama Tec, *When Light Pierced the Darkness: Christian Rescue of Jews in Nazi-Occupied Poland*, Oxford, Oxford University Press, 1986.

[13] Samuel P. and Pearl M. Oliner, *The Altruistic Personality: Rescuers of Jews in Nazi-Europe*, New York, The Free Press, 1988.

short, of having a basically altruistic disposition. This approach, which thus emphasizes psychological and ethical traits, does not enable us to apprehend easily other profiles of rescuers whose motivations are less noble. What are we then to think of those who requested payment or were even anti-Semitic? It is to Nechama Tec's credit to have agreed to reconsider her early research with a critical eye and integrate such profiles for the purposes of this book. She also includes the case of Jews who themselves participated in the organization of rescue networks.

The psychological approach, however, leaves aside other social and political parameters which are also useful for explaining the rescue act. The person who aids and protects usually does not act alone. To manage to save even a single life requires, for instance, finding more food than one needs for oneself, possibly getting forged papers, counting also on the absolute silence of one's immediate entourage, etc. In this regard, the definition of "Righteous among the Nations," here again, rests on too narrow a representation of the person who rescues. As a moral category, it defines the rescuer as "a hero of Good," making him a sort of brave lone knight, surrounded by passive if not anti-Semitic individuals. This elitist representation of the rescuer, which implies an actor struggling against a totally hostile environment, does not really stand up to socio-historical analysis. Despite the existence of this dangerous social universe, the rescuer indeed must benefit from some degree of complicity, be it passive or active, among his immediate family or social or professional entourage. That means that to understand the act of rescue, the context of the act must be taken into account as well as the history of this context. Such is the approach used here, which hopes to be more global than the mere study of the rescuers' personalities. Along these lines, we will be less interested here in the rescuer than in the rescue itself, as a social act performed in an extreme crisis situation. What we are investigating here are acts or operations rather than actors.

This perspective then helps to open up the pioneering research on rescue to bring it closer to studies on the Resistance iself. By underscoring the role of social background, we in fact share a set of issues that are familiar to historians of the Resistance—that resistance is only possible and enduring thanks to a social environment that protects it, an environment of at least partial complicity. In this sense, the distinction between people who resist and those who do not is often too artificial. Many studies have in fact shown that in a situation of domination and persecution, the subjected individuals react in varying degrees of submissive or unsubmissive behaviour. This is what I attempted to describe through the notion of civil resistance, to refer to the everyday aspect of the resistance state of mind within a society that is occupied or dominated by a foreign power.[14] In general, it is what is called "anonymous resistance," unspectacular by definition, made of thousands of little acts of refusal, often symbolic, sometimes very concrete indeed, various forms of challenge to the authorities or solidarity toward the victims of those in power. Rescue acts fall much more into this category of civil resistance than into that of so-called humanitarian resistance, which induces too artificial a separation between what relates to a political dynamic of conflict and to the protection of victims.

Conceptualizing rescue thus necessarily requires breaking free from the notion of organized resistance to attempt to grasp these thousands of little everyday gestures in a country subjected to the most brutal forms of violence. In this sense, shouldn't one above all reflect on the notions of shelter and aid from a social viewpoint? It is worth closely examining the figures in France in this regard. In May-June 1940, when the Wehrmacht invaded France, about 330,000 Jews lived on its territory. We know that 76,000 of them tragically fell into the claws of the Nazi occupant with the collaboration of the Vichy government, later to be exterminated in the gas chambers. But how can it be explained that two-thirds of the Jews, over 250,000 people (including 60,000 children), actually escaped deportation from France? And how can these figures be compatible with the assertion made by some that France was supposed to be largely anti-Semitic? Several factors would have to be discussed, but that goes beyond the framework of this introduction. Let us simply emphasize one essential point: it is impossible that those 250,000 Jews had their lives saved solely through the action of organized rescue networks. Certainly, such networks were very active, starting with Jewish organizations themselves, to which reference will be made several times in this volume; thanks to the devotion of their members, several thousands were rescued, perhaps a few dozen thousand (precise estimates are obviously very difficult to make). Nevertheless, the fact remains that all the Jewish or non-Jewish associations, given their lack of means and their own vulnerability to

---

[14] Jacques Semelin, *Unarmed Against Hitler. Civil Resistance in Nazi Europe (1939–1943)*, Westport (CT), Praeger, 1994.

repressive measures, could not alone prevent those 250,000 Jews from being deported from France.

Other explanations for their survival must therefore be sought, the first and most obvious being that Jews scattered throughout the various regions in the country, especially in southern France, were sheltered here and there in families in cities or in the countryside. Simone Veil's singular story is one example among others.[15] Let us add to that the benevolent complicity of those thousands of mayors who turned a blind eye to their arrival of "foreign" persons in their towns even though Vichy pressured them to report such people. This is a far cry from the restrictive figure of the "Righteous" and the notion of organized resistance with its escape channels, etc. Without ignoring cases where the presence of Jews was denounced to the authorities, the social and political phenomenon studied here is much more complex and nebulous: a civil society of nonconformity which helped and hid the man or woman banned from society on account of his or her identity or actions—not only Jews, then, but also those who refused to work in Germany (in the Compulsory Labour Service), the resistance fighter on the run, or the British airman whose plane had been shot down, as Claire Andrieu shows here.

Rescue research overlaps with another theme at the heart of research on civilian resistance: that of attitudes to the law and disobedience. Certainly, it is not true that acts of rescue always involve illegal action. As we shall see in the forthcoming pages, it is sometimes possible to be rescued legally, by asserting the applicability of this or that government regulation or procedure. But to the extent that a state increasingly institutes persecution of a group through laws, the person who helps and the person who is helped are bound one day to enter into illegality. It is appropriate to examine also the process of tipping into disobedience, whether from the standpoint of the potential rescuer or of the victim. The act of violating the taboo of unlawfulness is far from meaningless and can arouse considerable reluctance. How will these barriers be lifted, or will they remain intact? How do organizations that operate in broad daylight gradually go underground? How can they combine a legal façade and illegal practices?

---

[15] Simone Veil is a well-known Holocaust survivor, French politician and former President of the European Parliament. When the Italian zone in the south of France came under German control in 1943, Simone Veil's parents, brother and sister were each taken in by a different family (cf. Simone Veil, *Une vie*, Paris, Stock, 2007).

Such are the types of questions that will be broached in these pages through a variety of case studies.

We also wanted to give our approach a resolutely international dimension. This seemed essential to introduce the question of risk. In fact, the dangers incurred by rescuers in eastern and western Nazi Europe are not at all the same. In Poland, anyone found to be hiding a Jew was executed on the spot, whereas the risks were less in Western Europe. Furthermore, knowledge of news relating to the fate awaiting the Jews in the East, the circulation of rumours in this regard, the role of the media, including radio stations such as the BBC (listened to throughout the occupied continent), are also factors to be taken into account.

The very question of international relations itself even holds a decisive place in the success of rescue operations. Countries allied with the Reich, such as Italy, managed to be areas of relative tranquility for the Jews. States that declared their neutrality, such as Sweden or Switzerland, whereas they were in a position of compromise or even collaboration with Berlin were also lands of refuge for the Jews. Like war, understanding the act of rescue requires combining several scales of time and place.

Studying a process

Finally, a question became obvious to us as we advanced in this research: is the word "rescue" really the most suitable one to qualify our object? The use of the word seems entirely legitimate when there is a real perception of the danger. But this is not always the case, even among victims. This fact is moreover supported by psychological observation: a person can be in an objective situation of extreme danger and not be aware of it, or mentally deny the reality of this danger.

This notion of "rescue" also remains ambiguous in that it evokes lifesaving operations at sea or in the mountains, for instance. It therefore suggests that survival is played out in a very short instant, whereas very often it involves a continuous chain of acts by a series of actors more or less spread out geographically: helping a person find a hiding place, getting forged papers, escaping to a foreign country, etc. It is the sum of these various gestures of assistance that in the end will determine whether the use of the word "rescue" is appropriate or not.

Without foreseeing the fortunate or tragic outcome of these actions, should not a more neutral and indeterminate word be used, such as "aid" or "help"? In short, in a historic situation of growing persecution aimed at certain individuals, there are those who help and those who ask for help. There are those who shelter and those who agree to be hidden. Strictly speaking, the fortunate or tragic outcome of such assistance should not interfere with our analysis, if one takes the viewpoint of those who have lived through such situations.

However, falling back on the helper/helped duo is not entirely satisfactory either, in that it does not allow one to perceive potentially tragic dimensions of the experience. For instance, in ordinary language, one helps an old lady to do her shopping or a child to do his homework. That has nothing to do with what has been described here as assistance given to a man or woman who lives in the utmost exclusion. The words "aid" or "help," however simple and positive they may be, thus seem too weak or too bland with respect to the gravity of the situation. At the end of the chain, the notion of "rescue" thus maintains its full relevance, for instance when the helping party knows what will become of the victims if he does not go to their aid; or again when the smuggler is aware that those he is helping clandestinely across the border are in danger of being killed. And in general, those very people that the smuggler accompanies also are aware that the trip they are making is to save their lives. Between sheltering and helping a persecuted person as part of one's ordinary everyday life, and this extraordinary character of the act of rescue organized for people in a situation of extreme danger, we need to consider the progressive, undetermined *process* that leads from help to rescue.

A process necessarily implies taking into account a history that is social, cultural, religious, etc. preceding what we will henceforth call an act of rescue. In order to understand the sheltering of Jews in France in Protestant regions such as the Cévennes, reference is thus made to the distant past of the persecution of French Protestants, which made the latter more sensitive to the fate of the Jews, both drawing their religious spirituality from the same Bible. In the case of Chambon-sur-Lignon and neighbouring villages, we will once again emphasize that the placing of children with families of farmers or in *pensions* has been a tradition on this plateau in the upper Vivarais since the late nineteenth century, and that basically, this tradition logically continued during a time of war and Occupation to the benefit of the Jewish children whether or not they were accompanied by their families. Conceptualizing the shift from help to rescue thus involves identifying continuities and hiatuses, whether in individual conduct or social structures.

Little by little, we have thus brought to light the topics that we believe structure thinking about these practices of rescuing in genocidal situations. On this basis we have organized the book into three sections:

Between history and memory: the notion of rescue

The chapters in this section aim primarily to question the conceptual categories used, starting with the honorific title of "Righteous among the Nations." Others explore the contours of the notion of "rescue" and/or "rescuer" using very different methodologies. Finally, the conventional triad (perpetrator, victim, rescuer) inherited from work on the Jewish genocide is called into question.

The state, its borders and the conditions of aid

This section explores rescue operations as modes of circumventing national public policies oriented towards exterminating a population. It confirms the hypothesis that taking account of chronology is indispensable in considering protection of victims in reaction to measures aiming to persecute them. It also shows how members of the state apparatus can curb the destruction process at their level of authority, either regional or local. It should also be noted that the comparative approach proves a productive means of highlighting the importance of the international aspect: either transnational organizations (religious, medical, etc.) endeavor to be present to rescue victims; or, at the borders of the massacring state, the people under threat of death seek to take refuge on the neighbouring territory of a neutral state.

Networks, minorities and rescuing

This third part takes a different viewpoint: that of "micro" studies analyzing various aid and protection networks that cropped up in cities or rural areas. We will discover hitherto little-known historic examples, even unpublished field studies. The aim is to better comprehend how individuals and/or minorities mobilize at the grassroots level to attempt to come to the aid of persecuted people. Was their commitment based primarily on religious convictions? Without a doubt, for some of them. But other variables should be taken into account on an equal footing, starting with neighbourhood and friendship ties, without forgetting those formed at the workplace. Established before the time of persecution, these very diverse social ties will hold fast in a time of crisis. Along with instances of *immobile resistance* (hiding out at a neighbor's or a friend's place), other chapters show the vital nature of *itinerant resistance*, going from place to place toward the land of refuge. It thus becomes clear that chains of solidarity are formed in an informal and shifting network involving people who do not know each other but who are all working together toward a single aim, to save lives—provided, naturally, that no one is unmasked.

In this sense, diversity is a key notion. Obviously, there is not *one* but *several* forms of resistance to genocide, which take various shapes as micro-social forms of opposition to curb the process of destruction undertaken against a particular group. And so we are delighted to present to the reader this collection of articles that we believe will renew rescue research, as the book creates an echo among various approaches that sometimes diverge. The reader might also note that the degree of maturity of the research may vary from one section to the next, and from one study to another. The editors of this volume, we should point out, do not necessarily share all of the analyses defended here by all of the contributors. Each presents his or her research in total academic freedom and rigour, but also through the prism of his or her own culture and sometimes his or her own history with the object studied. We take this opportunity to thank them for having agreed to take part in our investigation. In all, this book hopes to open new paths in a field of study that has been too little explored. Let us hope that it will acquire a following and give rise to further research.

PART 1

BETWEEN HISTORY AND MEMORY
RESCUE AS A NOTION

How is it possible to constitute as an object of study for the social sciences deeds that enabled the survival of people threatened with genocide? A scholarly study of "rescues" and "rescuers" requires adopting a critical perspective to deal with facts and people the mere mention of which, like the lives of saints, generally arouses emotion and devotion. A total shift in focus from the subject admired to the objects studied is, however, unrealistic. To some extent researchers will always remain the product of their era and their social and academic positions. It is thus significant that the symposium that produced the present volume, while voluntarily setting itself apart from the commemorative context prevailing at the time, was held scarcely a month before the solemn entry of the "Righteous of France" into the Pantheon in January 2007. The contributions that follow, situated between history and memory, between desanctification and participation in the worship of the "Righteous," occupy an uncomfortable halfway mark.

The fact nevertheless remains that in investigating the categories of "Righteous," "rescuer" or even "aid," as well as "obvious facts" such as the supposed equivalence between "rescuers" and "philo-Semites"—in the case of the genocide of the Jews—the chapters in this first section renew the contours of the subject matter. A common question runs through them even if they deal with different genocides and look at them from various angles. How can we "interpret" rescue acts, the "motivations" of the "rescuers" and more fundamentally, the correspondence noted between the context of aid and the survival of people threatened by genocide? Apart from individual rescuers, it is necessary to take an interest in the practice of rescue itself—the acts that finally enabled the survival of populations doomed to be exterminated. Taking these acts into account requires investigating the contexts and timelines that made them possible.

The term "Righteous among the Nations," which has been increasingly applied over the past ten years or so by many social and institutional actors not only to the case of the Jewish genocide but also to those of the Armenians and the Tutsis, has seeped into the language of the media to talk about rescuers. The first two chapters thus take this observation as a starting point to place the notion of "Righteous" in perspective, by retracing its genesis and identifying its implications.

Sarah Gensburger's contribution thus retraces the creation of the title of "Righteous among the Nations" in Israel in the 1950s to honor these "non-Jews who saved Jews by risking their lives." The author underscores the gap that exists between the meaning currently given to this category—a vehicle for national reconciliation—and the conception of social relations between Jews and non-Jews, perceived to be antagonistic, that presided over the establishment of this award. Whereas this title was created by Israel as a foreign policy tool, today it is perceived by most governments and organizations that use it as a domestic policy tool, particularly in the management of inter-ethnic relations.

Fatma Müge Göçek's chapter also deals with the construction of "Righteous" as a notion. Recalling its Judeo-Christian heritage and drawing on a more philosophical perspective, she deconstructs the notion to suggest a redefinition that is more adapted to the aid supplied by Turks to the Armenians during the genocide in 1915. To do so, she advocates broadening of the concept of "Righteous" to the notion of "just people" that can incorporate the Muslim concept of justice.

Whereas these first two chapters emphasize the memory aspect by dealing mainly with the present, Claire Andrieu's chapter instead tries to tie in together history and memory, yesterday and today. Comparing the fate of allied airmen parachuting into France with that of French Jewry, she simultaneously takes an interest in the aid that these two groups received during World War II and the social recognition that was bestowed upon each. This comparison raises the question that runs through the entire volume: that of risk taken. Whereas this criterion is the only one that figures in the law establishing the title of "Righteous among the Nations," the question must be asked: was recognition greater for, and did it come earlier to, people who placed their own lives in danger? And if so, what risk did the French men and women who decided to come to the aid of Jews actually run under the Occupation? This paper also prepares the groundwork for a crossed history of the phenomena of resistance and rescue.

This same problematics appear in Marnix Croes' article that deals with the Dutch case. On the basis of a quantitative study, the author offers original insights into the complex and sometimes surprising correlation between the presence of resistance fighters in Dutch city governments and the arrests of hidden Jews. In his chapter, Marnix Croes makes the case for applying multivariate analysis to the study of the survival rate of Jews during World War II. He places the two questions of explanation and analysis of an event at the center of his thinking. Even if the use of quantitative methodology enables a distinction to be made between correlation and concomitancy, can it replace the researchers' interpretative task? And conversely, can the concern for understanding phenomena disregard the element of chance that seems irreducible in any event?

The question of analysis also serves as the main thread running through Renée Poznanski's contribution. She examines a dominant interpretation to gauge its relevance. On the basis of a study of the treatment of the "Jewish problem" by the French Resistance between 1940 and 1944, the author demonstrates that there is in fact no automatic correspondence between rescuing Jews and philo-Semitism. More generally, Renée Poznanski argues for shifting the interpretive framework of rescue acts from the "humanitarian" register to a more "political" one. Such redefinition would have the particular merit of restoring to the Jews the status of actors and hence studying rescue as a complex social process, whether it emanates from non-Jews or from Jews themselves.

This approach in many ways concurs with Nechama Tec's analysis, which draws on Polish examples. In her article, the author revisits her now classic research on "altruistic rescuers" to examine cases that she had previously neglected. Liberating herself a bit more from the institutional contours of the title of "Righteous among the Nations," she looks into the grey areas where rescue goes hand-in-hand with pursuing financial interests or with anti-Semitism. How, in such contexts, is it possible to understand, if not explain, the act itself? Symmetrically, she questions the need to get beyond the distinction between non-Jewish and Jewish rescuers in order to grasp the process at work and the manner in which potential victims managed to turn into actors working toward their own survival.

Florent Le Bot also deals with this last point in his chapter on the relationship between rescuing property and rescuing people. The author's view once again runs counter to the disjunction between self-interest and rescue, partly induced by the definition of the title of "Righteous." This specialist in the Aryanization process underlines the importance of financial resources in the survival of Jews under the Occupation. He attempts to take stock of the room for maneuver left open by the very process of Aryanization. Identifying several cases in which aid to people and preservation of their property were intertwined, he ends up coming back to the issue of interpretation without eliminating the element of chance.

Although the chapters dealing with France and Poland deal with a situation in which rescue was perceived as a deviant attitude with respect to that of the nation as a whole, it is a very different matter for the Italian example studied by Paola Bertilotti. She retraces the manner in which what she calls "the myth of the good Italian" has fashioned references to rescue in Italian society and permeated its historiography. She ties these references in with domestic and foreign policy issues. Since Italy as a nation is supposed to have safeguarded and helped Jews, until recently there was little mention of "rescuers," and even less of rescue as a process.

Lee Ann Fujii reaches the same conclusion, yet proceeding in reverse. Her chapter is in fact the only one in this section to deal with the Tutsi genocide in Rwanda, about which very little research has been done regarding aid to threatened people. This chapter however tackles the heart of the problem of rescuing very directly. "Acts of rescue are not always the sole province of rescuers." Starting with the observation that it was extremely difficult to hide Tutsis during neighbourhood massacres, the author urges us to go beyond the categories of "perpetrators," "victims" and "rescuers" to pay more attention to acts such as those performed by individuals in a given situation. In this regard, her article sums up one of the main contributions of this first part, as well as the perspective that guides this entire volume.

1

FROM THE MEMORY OF RESCUE TO THE INSTITUTION OF THE TITLE OF "RIGHTEOUS"

Sarah Gensburger

For the past ten years or so, a growing number of European governments have been picking up on the expression "Righteous among the Nations," which since 1963 has referred to the honor awarded by the Yad Vashem Institute to non-Jews who helped Jews during the genocide.[1] Its use has in fact spread beyond the borders of the old continent and is no longer only applied to the extermination of the Jews.[2] The "Righteous among the Nations" title is thus considered as a model to follow in the commemoration of the Tutsi genocide in Rwanda.[3] By honoring the "Righ-

---

[1] Sarah Gensburger, "Les figures du 'Juste' et du Résistant et l'évolution de la mémoire historique française de l'Occupation," *Revue Française de Science Politique*, 52 (2–3), April-June 2002, pp. 291–322, and with Agnieszka Niewiedzial-Bédu, "Figure du Juste et politique publique de la mémoire en Pologne: entre relations diplomatiques et structures sociales," *Critique Internationale*, 34, January-March 2007, pp. 127–48.

[2] Sarah Gensburger, "L'émergence de la catégorie de Juste parmi les nations comme paradigme mémoriel. Réflexions contemporaines sur le rôle socialement dévolu à la mémoire," in Carola Hähnel-Mesnard, Marie Liénard-Yeterian and Cristina Marinas (eds), *Culture et Mémoire*, Paris, Éditions de l'École Polytechnique, 2008, pp. 25–32.

[3] Aurélia Kalisky, "Mémoires croisées. Des références à la Shoah dans le travail

teous," the social actors helping to disseminate this notion intend to help Hutus and Tutsis live together again.

But, in the way it is used, the term "Righteous" is never placed in perspective with the historical and social conditions that produced it. Current trends invite us to revisit its origins and development.[4]

Commemoration of the "Righteous among the Nations" and foreign policy

The term "Righteous among the Nations" is a translation from the Hebrew *Hasidei Ummot Ha-Olam*. The expression, rabbinical in origin, refers to non-Jews who fear God and, by extension, non-Jews who have a friendly disposition toward the people of Israel. Etymologically, it represented a derogation to the principle of separation between the Jewish and non-Jewish societies and referred to a conception of these relations as being antagonistic and hostile.

This Talmudic origin reflects adherence to "the negation of exile,"[5] in other words, to the belief in the illegitimacy and risk for Jews of residing in non-Jewish states. It contrasts with the objectives of internal and "interethnic" harmony assigned to it in the various historic and national

---

de deuil et de mémoire du génocide des tutsis," *Humanitaire*, 10, Spring-Summer 2004, p. 79, and Catherine Coquio, *Rwanda. Le réel et les récits*, Paris, Belin, 2004, p. 94.

[4] The present chapter draws from a study conducted using interviews and participant observation as well as documentary analysis, particularly from the Yad Vashem archives, undertaken for a doctorate thesis in sociology, 'Essai de sociologie de la mémoire. L'expression des souvenirs à travers le titre de "Juste parmi les nations" dans le cas français: entre cadre institutionnel, politique publique et mémoire collective," under the supervision of Marie-Claire Lavabre, Paris, EHESS, July 2006.

[5] Or "*shlilat hagalout.*" This term has been preferred here to the more currently used "negation of the diaspora" (*shlilat hagola*) because although it contains the same condemnation of the existence of the diaspora now that the Yishuv, soon to become the state of Israel, existed, it does not consider the past Jewish existence in diaspora as having no value. Contrary to the second term, it unites all of the Israeli political officials in the early years. Arielle Rein, "L'historien, la mémoire et l'État. L'œuvre de Ben Zion Dinur pour la commémoration et la recherche sur la Shoah en Israël," *Revue d'Histoire de la Shoah. Le Monde Juif*, 182, January-June 2005, p. 263.

contexts in which the term "Righteous" has been reappropriated today in order to foster "reconciliation" and the ability to live together.

Dominant at the time among the ruling class and population of the Yishuv, "the negation of exile" is apparent in the first plan to honor Jewish genocide victims that finally gave rise to Yad Vashem. In 1942 its master craftsman Mordecai Shenhabi,[6] planned to include "a list of the Righteous among the Nations who rescued people or protected property of the Community" and "contributions by people who were rescued by non-Jews, and wish to express their gratitude."[7] For Shenhabi, the assumption that non-Jews were hostile toward Jews when these two groups cohabited in the same non-Jewish society did not seem to require demonstration. The only explicit motive for the initial project to create the title of "Righteous among the Nations" lay not in domestic policy but in foreign policy: Shenhabi intended the commemoration as a means of fostering diplomatic relations between the future Jewish state and other sovereign states. In April 1947, he presented his plan to pay tribute to the Hungarian "Righteous" to the Hungarian government in foreign policy terms.[8] Shortly thereafter, writing to Golda Meir to inform her of the death of the King of Denmark, he reminded her of the diplomatic advantage there would be in officially including the monarch among the "Righteous."[9]

The Eichmann trial and the creation of the Commission for the Designation of the "Righteous among the Nations"

The diplomatic conception of the title "Righteous" endured when it was effectively created. The bill for the Martyrs' and Heroes' Remembrance (Yad Vashem) Law[10] was drafted in 1953. Unlike the 1942 version of the text that inspired it, it did not pay tribute to the "Righteous."[11] The pro-

---

[6] Mordecai Shenhabi, head of the National Jewish Fund, 10 September 1942, Yad Vashem Archives (YV), AM 1/288.

[7] Shenhabi Project, 2 May version made public on 25 May 1945, YV, AM1/313. Can also be consulted at the Central Zionist Archives (CZA), S26/1326.

[8] Letter sent by M. Shenhabi to the Hungarian government representative, 2 April 1947, YV, AM1/293.

[9] Letter of 23 April 1947, YV, AM1/293.

[10] "Martyrs' and Heroes' Remembrance (Yad Vashem) Law," published in *Proposed Legislation*, 161, on 25 March 1953.

[11] The first version of the "Martyrs' and Heroes' Remembrance (Yad Vashem)

posal to include non-Jews who helped Jews among the people whose memory should be honored only came up in the parliamentary debates via an amendment.

The law of 19 August 1953 finally included a ninth and final paragraph that established the principle of commemorating the "Righteous among the Nations who risked their lives to save Jews."[12] No specific procedure was outlined, however, before Eichmann's trial was held in 1961–62. On this occasion, mention of the "Righteous among the Nations" would in turn help to heal the ties between Israel and the countries from which the Jewish state was seeking support. Thus calling the "Righteous" Heinrich Grüber to the witness stand was, according to Ben Gurion, in keeping with Israel's foreign policy toward the Federal Republic of Germany, a mechanism that was repeated throughout the entire trial and for a large range of countries. In his brief, the public prosecutor made a list of helpful non-Jews, whom he called the "Righteous among the Nations." The description was made on the basis not of their individual identities but of their countries of origin. Through collective tribute to these figures of the past, a diplomatic tie was established between "rescuer countries" and "friends of Israel." Particular care was taken not to forget any of the countries that might have been concerned.

After the trial, many requests from individuals and institutions were addressed to the state of Israel and Yad Vashem to set up an actual policy to recognize the "Righteous among the Nations." These requests argued in favour of the diplomatic advantage that Israel could derive from it.[13] In February 1962, the institute created an administrative department dedicated to this new mission.[14] Recognition was to be made by planting a tree in honor of each person named individually on the Mount of Remembrance in Jerusalem. With this symbol, the institute renewed with an ancient national insignia. In Israel, "trees carried an even greater symbolic value: they became an icon of national revival, symbolizing the

---

Law" was tabled by the government on 23 March 1953, Knesset Archives, 25/s/2.

[12] The full and exact wording of this paragraph is in the official translated version.

[13] Space does not allow further development of this point; cf. Sarah Gensburger, *Essai de sociologie de la mémoire*, op. cit.

[14] Aryeh Kubovy, assessments and proposals further to the state comptroller's report, 25 February 1962, CZA, C6/423.

Zionist success in 'striking roots' in the ancient homeland."[15] This patriotic act, the inauguration of the "Alley of the Righteous,"[16] was also a diplomatic one. In the discussions leading up to it at Yad Vashem, the Israeli government was represented by the Director-General of the Foreign Affairs Ministry, whereas selection of the "Righteous" involved various state administrations in charge of foreign policy.[17] The "Righteous" chosen planted their first tree on 1 May 1962. They were once again associated with their country of origin. The plaque placed beneath their tree specified their country of origin next to their name. Golda Meir, Minister of Foreign Affairs, represented the executive branch that day.[18]

In the wake of the discussions and controversy aroused by the case of Oskar Schindler,[19] it was decided to set up a commission of experts. The Chairman's office of Yad Vashem asked the Foreign Affairs Minister to name a representative to this commission because it was "directly involved in the Righteous among the Nations issue."[20] On 1 February 1963 the Commission for the Designation of the "Righteous among the Nations" held its first meeting.

Between 1942 and 1963, in Israel, the title of "Righteous among the Nations" thus took shape as an institutional category both gradually and sporadically. The contrast with the contemporary use of the term here is striking. Today, when European states commemorate the "Righteous among the Nations," as in the case of the Tutsi genocide in Rwanda, it is an act of domestic policy and expresses a desire to foster the peaceful coexistence of Jews and non-Jews, or Tutsis and Hutus, within one and the same state. This commemoration nevertheless takes as its reference an institutionalized reminder of the past which fits in with a foreign

---

[15] Yael Zerubavel, "The Forest as a National Icon: Literature, Politics and the Archeology of Memory," *Israel Studies*, Spring 1996, p. 60.

[16] "Report of the Yad Vashem board meeting on 15 May 1962," YV.

[17] Letters from Yad Vashem to the Investigation Department of the Foreign Affairs Ministry, 29 December 1961, and the Information Center for the Department concerning Foreign Countries, answering to the Prime Minister's office, 10 January 1962, DJYV, Charles Coward file.

[18] Memo drafted 31 December 1962 by David Alcalay, for the attention of Moshe Landau, taking stock of the initiatives taken with respect to the "Righteous," YV, AM6/946.

[19] Gabriel Nissim, *Le Jardin des Justes*, Paris, Payot, 2007 [Italian original, Milan, Mondadori, 2003].

[20] "Report of the Yad Vashem Board meeting of 3 July 1962," CZA, C6/424.

policy perspective and grew out of the belief that it was impossible for the first two groups to live together. The contemporary use of the term by many political and institutional actors thus constitutes a shift from the diplomatic to the domestic field.

The importance of social frameworks of memory

It could be assumed that the genesis of the title of "Righteous among the Nations" and the discrepancy between it and the contemporary use of the term matter little because finally we are in the domain of political "instrumentalization," of the "use" and "abuse" of memory. The expression "Righteous among the Nations," it is suggested, is what political and institutional actors make of it, here and now, in order to achieve clear objectives. This conception reduces the function of memory to the traces it leaves.

As long as this title is considered as a full-fledged object of study, it constitutes a particularly relevant case of analysis in order to get beyond this reduction. Since its inception, this honor has only been awarded by decision of a commission that deliberates on a case at the request of Jews who consider that they were "rescued," and on the basis of their testimonials. Analyzing the social and historic process of awarding the title thus enables us to determine what relations exist between the institutional framework of memory of the past and the testimonials of those who carry the memory of this same past. The institutional framework created for expressing these memories is "filled" by individuals in different ways depending on the period and the "rescuer country" involved. The table below illustrates some of these disparities.

Whereas the number of nominations in Poland reached a peak during the 1980s, an increase can be noted in the 1970s in the Netherlands and only in the early 1990s in France, where the highest number of nominations, 194, was reached in 1996. From a quantitative and chronological standpoint, the institutional framework for expressing memories offered by Yad Vashem is thus received in very different ways depending on the country where the rescue occurred. It is not enough to frame or provoke "memory." Memory seems to follow paths and beat to rhythms that obey other mechanisms. The "memory collected" in the context of the procedure established by Yad Vashem is thus neither produced entirely by the institution nor entirely spontaneous. It arises out of social frameworks, particularly national and migratory ones, that should be clarified.

Table 1: Number of "Righteous" recognized by Yad Vashem per year and per country of origin of the "Righteous" person[21]

Year	France	Poland	Netherlands
1963	0	11	4
1964	2	34	29
1965	4	60	26
1966	2	56	26
1967	9	48	39
1968	5	33	36
1969	19	24	33
1970	9	10	37
1971	24	12	48
1972	2	10	92
1973	22	13	97
1974	10	29	142
1975	13	48	82
1976	18	42	82
1977	19	43	118
1978	21	100	218
1979	39	144	225
1980	24	78	229
1981	25	150	225
1982	41	160	231
1983	21	249	377
1984	39	225	227
1985	39	221	177
1986	27	241	140
1987	33	251	106
1988	76	271	82
1989	153	359	113
1990	109	280	109

The qualitative study conducted for the case of France is a means of doing this.[22] In the early years of the title's existence, the portraits drawn up by the witnesses overwhelmingly described the "Righteous" as "friends

[21] Since the Righteous among the Nations Department claims not to have examined the trends in nominations, these have been compiled on the basis of lists of nominations from 1963 to 1989, kept in the Archives of the United States Holocaust Memorial Museum, "Righteous among the Nations—Lists, 1963–1989," then, from 1990 to 1997, on the basis of annual lists put out by Yad Vashem on its website or published in the annexes to certain books.

[22] In the framework of my doctoral research, I constructed a sample of 645

of Israel." In this regard, the memories indeed seem to be expressed in an institutional framework with diplomatic ends. However, closer examination reveals that the correspondence between the institutional perspective and witnesses' testimonials is not so much a reflection of the influence of political requirements on the public perspective as an indication of the fact that those who tend to contact Yad Vashem occupy particular social positions. And in fact, in the early years, a minority of the witnesses was Israeli, most of them secular Jews or having liberal religious beliefs, whereas among the individuals remaining in France who contacted Yad Vashem, most held conservative religious beliefs and positions of responsibility in French organizations supporting Zionism and Israel. It is thus first of all the social position of the witnesses, and especially their geographic and/or symbolic attachment to the Jewish state, that explain the initial convergence between the interpretation of the past offered by the institutional framework and expression of their memories, as well as the relative homogeneity of the interpretation of the past that the title of "Righteous among the Nations" represented for them.

In the recent period, the social characteristics of the witnesses have become considerably diversified. At the same time, typical profiles of the "Righteous" have changed. Since 1990, the discourse that is closest to that now held by Yad Vashem on the meaning of the title—a tribute to exceptional individuals in view of the assumed hostility of the rest of the world toward Israel and the Jews—emanates from individuals who live in Israel, who hold conservative or even ultra-Orthodox beliefs in Judaism and right-wing opinions on the Israeli political checkerboard. Since 1990, this category has constituted the large majority of witnesses who live in Israel. For them, the "Righteous" are "Christians," rare exceptions to the principle of general hostility among "*goyim.*" But today they form a minority of those who now contact the Righteous among the Nations Department at Yad Vashem.

At the other end of the spectrum, the share of French witnesses, most of them without any real footing in the community and sometimes no religious belief, has increased considerably to the point of constituting an overwhelming majority of those who apply to Yad Vashem today. A

"French Righteous among the Nations" nomination files, at the rate of one of two per year between 1963 and 2000. The following data (Table 2) were drawn from the analysis of the sample.

majority of them set themselves clearly apart from the institutional posture and consider the French "Righteous" as "French" or "non-Jews" who are supposed to have acted in accordance with "the values of the Republic" and "human rights."

Table 2: Distribution of witnesses by country of permanent residence, by period, calculated on the basis of a sample of 645 files.

Witnesses' present country of residence	Percentages between 1963 and 1990	Percentages between 1991 and 2000
Israel	40 %	14 %
France	55 %	80 %
Miscellaneous other	5 %	6 %

Thus it is first the change in the social characteristics of those who recount their memories that explains the transformation of the narratives offered. This quantitative observation is backed by considerable qualitative data. The reconfiguration of social frameworks of those who offer their testimony sometimes becomes apparent in one and the same case file. In 1976, the Commission for the Designation of the Righteous among the Nations awarded the title to Pauline Gaudefroy. Her nomination was mainly based on the testimony of an Israeli adult who had arrived in Jerusalem in the 1960s and practiced an Orthodox form of Judaism.[23] When he was a child in France during World War II, he had been placed in a home by this woman who was working for the Œuvre de Secours aux Enfants (OSE). In 1993, other people who as children had also been "placed" by Pauline Gaudrefoy in turn went to see Yad Vashem. Eager to bear witness, they were surprised to find out that their benefactor had already been recognized. Here, the witnesses were two French citizens, one living in Annecy, the other in Paris.[24]

In 1978, Yvonne Deltour was awarded the title of "Righteous among the Nations" after a French citizen who had been an activist in the Women's International Zionist Organization (WIZO), of which she was a local official, gave testimony. In 1994, a witness living in France, who believed he owed his life to Yvonne Deltour, addressed Yad Vashem in these terms: "I would be grateful if you would inform me on what initia-

[23] Interview of 4 June 2003, Jerusalem.
[24] Pauline Gaudefroy file, DJYV.

tive and with what proof Mme Deltour Yvonne, who hid me during the years 1942–1944, was decorated with the order of the Righteous." This time there was no mention made of any tie with the Jewish state or any particular mobilization in its favor. The word Israel appears neither in the letter making contact nor in the testimony itself. On the other hand, the expression "decorated with the order of the Righteous" apparently reveals the mental framework of the witness, evoking French Republican references such as the National Order of Merit, the Order of the Legion of Honor or the Order of Liberation.

At this stage, it would seem that rescue narratives primarily translate the witness' position in a precise social space marked out by two pillars, one being France, the other being the Jewish state. The survivors' changing attitudes toward France and Israel, as well as toward their religious beliefs and the collective non-Jewish milieu, have played a decisive role in applying for the title of "Righteous among the Nations" since its creation. This system of inter-individual relationships and relations with the various collective milieus should be taken into account in order to understand how this title has been awarded since 1963.

Testimonies and migration

The small number of requests for recognition coming from France in the years following the creation of the title and up until the mid-1970s would seem to be due primarily to the relatively low rate of immigration of French Jews to Israel in the early years of its existence. Although the figures do not provide a distribution by age for these new Israelis, they give an idea of the migration of potential witnesses, particularly for the period immediately after the war. The massive *aliyah* that took place after the creation of Israel and continued until 1951 only included 3,000 people from France. Emigration from France between 1948 and 1951 represented 25 per cent of the total French *aliyah* as of 1967.[25] In 1963, when the title was created, the number of French Jews integrated into Israeli society was therefore fairly small. This fact thus enables us to understand why in 1962, of the first twenty-six trees planted that year, only one was for a French person.[26]

---

[25] Franck Leibovici, "Esquisse d'une histoire des Français d'Israël," *Vingtième Siècle. Revue d'Histoire*, 78, April-June 2003, p. 4.
[26] It was Father Roger Braun, DJYV, Léon Platteau file. After Father Roger

Similarly, the fact that half of these plantings honored Polish rescuers can be related to immediate postwar immigration figures. Between 1948 and 1951, 106,400 Polish Jews settled in the Jewish state.[27] This mass arrival, later reinforced by the waves of 1958 and 1968, explains why in its first years of existence petitions were regularly made to Yad Vashem's Righteous among the Nations Department concerning Poles. Between 1963 and 1967, 209 Polish "Righteous" were recognized, compared with seventeen French "Righteous."

In 1968, the immigration following the Six-Day War considerably increased the number of Israelis from France. The average age of the new arrivals was about twenty-five; they were not all potential witnesses, far from it.[28] Nevertheless, "between 1968 and 1972, the influx of 18,000 French Jews more than doubled the little French community in Israel."[29] This evolution may explain why nomination requests for "Righteous" who had been active in France gradually increased in the 1970s. Although this evolution is not linear, it began precisely in 1969, the year that the number of French "Righteous" attained a two-digit figure for the first time. Changes in migration from France to Israel explain the expression of memories as manifested in nominations for the title of "Righteous." A person who decides to testify about his "rescue" thereby asserts a form of tie with the Jewish state and stresses the role of the men and women he considers as having given their implicit support for the existence of his new nation.

This explanation is insufficient, however. Indeed, in the Dutch case, the number of nominations was relatively high from the start. Between 1963 and 1967, the Yad Vashem Righteous among the Nations Department recognized 124 Dutch citizens. During the 1970s, the annual nomination figures rose constantly. For the year 1974 alone, 142 earned the title, compared with only ten French. Yet even if Dutch immigration to Israel in the immediate postwar period was proportionally higher than the French, it remained limited in absolute numbers. In 1948 and 1953, only 1,500

Braun (13 July 1962), the second Frenchman who earned the title was Eugène Van Der Meersch (26 August 1962).

[27] Official Jewish Agency for Israel data (www.jafi.org/); Amir Ben-Porat, "Proletarian Immigrants in Israel, 1948–1961," *Social Inquiry*, 60 (4), November 1990, pp. 395–404.

[28] The witnesses are supposed to have directly experienced the facts they relate.

[29] Franck Leibovici, "Esquisse d'une histoire des Français d'Israël," art. cit., p. 6.

Dutch Jews made their *aliyah*. Even after the Six-Day War, emigration to Israel did not exceed 300 departures per year.[30]

The Dutch situation differs from the French case in two main ways. First of all, adherence to Zionism appears historically broader and deeper among Dutch Jews than among those in France. Before World War II as well as through the late 1960s, Zionist activism in France was mainly carried on by Central European immigrants.[31] In contrast, in Holland there was a much older and more massive commitment among the Jewish population in favor of a Jewish state.[32]

Secondly, the Dutch political system and citizenship regime were fundamentally in tune with the "natural" distinction between Jews and non-Jews which underlies the title of "Righteous among the Nations." As it was constructed since the nineteenth century, "the Dutch model remained very different from the new French republican culture."[33] In particular, it rests on society's strong polarization around the Catholic and Calvinist pillars. Since it is common to define oneself publicly by one's religious belonging, it seems legitimate to base one's memory on a title that supposes a central and established distinction between Jews and non-Jews. As Jean-Philippe Schreiber sums it up, "beyond internal factors that partake of the construction of a collective identity or of an imagined community, there are powerful external motives […], such as the type of citizenship and the cultural or sociopolitical model that is promoted in the country where the Jews live: the nature of social relations will perme-

---

[30] Chaya Brasz, "Expectations and Realities of Dutch Immigration to Palestine/Israel After the Shoah," *Jewish History*, 1–2, 1994, pp. 323–38.

[31] Catherine Nicault, *La France et le sionisme, 1897–1948. Une rencontre manquée?* Paris, Calmann-Lévy, 1992, and Doris Bensimon, "L'immigration juive en France," *Yod*, 6, 1999, pp. 53–66.

[32] Chaya Brasz, "Dutch Jews as Zionists and Israeli Citizens," in Chaya Brasz and Yosef Kaplan (eds), *Dutch Jews as Perceived by Themselves and By Others. Proceedings of the Eighth International Symposium on the History of the Jews in the Netherlands*, Leiden, Brill, 2001, pp. 215–34, and "After the Shoah: Continuity and Change in the Postwar Jewish Community of the Netherlands," *Jewish History*, 15, 2001, pp. 149–68.

[33] Pierre Birnbaum, *Sur la corde raide. Parcours juifs entre exil et citoyenneté*, Paris, Flammarion, 2002, p. 66. Cf. also Ido De Haan, "The Postwar Jewish Community and the Memory of the Persecution in the Netherlands," in Chaya Brasz and Yosef Kaplan (eds), *Dutch Jews as Perceived By Themselves and by Others…*, op. cit., pp. 405–36.

ate the collective identity of the minority group,"[34] as in the case at hand for the expression of memories by members of this community.

By comparison, the social system induced by the "French model" based on universalism and the rejection of particularistic, especially religious, labelling, and the more recent development of support for Zionism among the French Jews, can be assumed to constitute a second factor liable to explain the belated rise and long limited number of French nominations. This interpretation allows us symmetrically to understand the rise in the number of requests for recognition in the French case at the end of the 1980s and especially during the 1990s.

This evolution can first be related to a form of naturalization of the relationship with Israel for French Jews, who since that time have formed the majority of "witnesses" appealing to the Yad Vashem Righteous among the Nations Department. Research by Doris Bensimon conducted in the mid-1980s shows that even though the Jewish state gradually constituted a pole of identification for French Jews, this relation was not shared by all at the time. "It emerges from all the surveys conducted among French Jews since the 1960s that the large majority of them state they are concerned for Israel and expressed pro-Israeli sentiments. However, the same surveys also show that there is a non-negligible fraction (of about 15 to 20 per cent) of French Jewry that is extremely critical of Israel and sometimes expresses hostility toward it."[35] This division has evolved and finally disappeared. As Martine Cohen explains, precisely since the early 1990s, "even if the existence of Israel remains an absolute imperative of the modern Jewish consciousness, the forms of expressions of solidarity with the state are less visible and less political today than they were in the 1970s […]. The relationship with Israel has become more ordinary and lost some of its ideological content."[36]

---

[34] Jean-Philippe Schreiber, "L'israélitisme belge au xixe siècle: une idéologie *romano-byzantine*," in Patrick Cabanel and Chantal Bordes-Benayoun (eds), *Un modèle d'intégration: juifs et israélites en France et en Europe, xix-xxe siècles*, Paris, Berg, 2004, p. 77.

[35] Doris Bensimon, *Les Juifs de France et leurs relations avec Israël, 1945–1988*, Paris, l'Harmattan, 1989, p. 169. Such disparities exist between all the countries where some citizens have been nominated as "Righteous." The table above adresses only the Polish, Dutch and French cases because they are the three national cases dealt with in the rest of this chapter.

[36] Martine Cohen, "Les juifs de France. Modernité et identité," *Vingtième Siècle. Revue d'Histoire*, 66, April-June 2000, p. 105.

The evolution in French Jews' relations with their country on the one hand, and with Judaism on the other, should also be placed in perspective. As Pierre Birnbaum explains, "The gradual rise in cultural pluralism considerably changes the place of Jews in French society."[37] This change is certainly not the topic of this article. It simply helps point out the complexity of the social processes that govern the expression of memories through the title of "Righteous among the Nations"—a process that makes this category not only an institutional but also a social construction—and it invites us to take into account two main types of actors: political-institutional actors who mean to draw inspiration from the Yad Vashem model to shape relationships among groups on which this very model depends, but also those who intend to raise the status of testimonies to "sources" on the basis of which history is written. At a time when more and more researchers—and the present volume attests to this—are taking an interest in the theme of the rescue of the Jews and the testimonies gathered in the context of the procedure for awarding the title of "Righteous," it appears all the more necessary to take into account the socially constructed nature of these traces of the past.

---

[37] Pierre Birnbaum, *La France imaginée: déclin des rêves unitaires?* Paris, Gallimard, 2003 [1st ed., Paris, Fayard, 1998], p. 32.

2

IN SEARCH OF "THE RIGHTEOUS PEOPLE"
THE CASE OF THE ARMENIAN MASSACRES OF 1915

Fatma Müge Göçek

The "Righteous," as the word is used here, refers to those people who value the principles of humanity over all else, including their own lives, to help the victims of systematic and intentional organized aggression. The present contribution attempts to develop a socio-historical critique of the applicability of this concept to all the genocides and massacres throughout the world, past and present. In it, I first investigate the historical emergence of the concept and critique its close connection to the Judeo-Christian experience in Europe in general and the experience of the Holocaust in particular. I then turn to the empirical case of the systematic deportations and massacres of the Armenians by the Ottoman government in 1915 and focus specifically on the case of one "Righteous" person, Hüseyin Hatemi, who helped the Armenians at the cost of his own life. I employ this empirical case to articulate the problems that might arise with the employment of the historical experience of the Holocaust as a model through which to interpret other tragedies. From my empirical analysis, I conclude the article with two proposals in relation to the concept of "the Righteous people": (i) to expand the concept of "the Righteous people" to include the Muslim experience through the introduction into the scholarly discussion of the term "the just people," based on the Islamic notion of *'adala;* and (ii) to compose the community that would decide upon who these just people ought to be, from an international body of scholars, but never representatives of states.

The emergence of the notion of "Righteous people"

Most scholars[1] have identified the European Enlightenment in the seventeenth and eighteenth centuries as the period when all the social sciences still practiced today were established. Indeed, it was first with the European Renaissance and then with the Enlightenment that the world lost its sacred roots for the first time, as humans decided that it was the individual rather than God who gave shape to the way one lived. The subsequent systematic study of the social, political, economic and psychological rules and principles of human organization formed the bases of the various social science disciplines. At the same time, the scientific method based on rationality that united them all replaced the sacred, God-given order it had been predicated upon until then. The eventual mastery over the environment through technology and the subsequent accumulation of material resources created the Industrial Revolution; the search for new markets that followed brought about wars among the European powers and led to their imperialist expansion throughout the globe.

The concomitant debates around the distribution of these resources among the peoples generated the ideological revolution of democratization symbolized by the French Revolution and its motto of "Liberty, Equality and Fraternity," whereby the relationship between the ruler and his subjects was gradually transformed into a social contract symbolically signed between the state and the citizens. The concepts of "liberty" and "equality" helped minimize the divisions that existed among subjects along religious, ethnic and racial lines; the newly emerging citizen acquired rights and responsibilities directly in relation to the state. Indeed, the rights of citizens initially expanded to overcome existing ethnic and religious divides, until the concept of "fraternity" wrought havoc, for not only did "brotherhood" remain confined to men, but the imagined community

---

[1] Ira Katznelson, *Desolation and Enlightenment: Political Knowledge after Total War. Totalitarianism and the Holocaust*, New York, Columbia University Press, 2003; Jeffery Alexander, "Modern, Anti, Post, and Neo: How Intellectuals Explain 'Our Time'," *The Meanings of Social Life: A Cultural Sociology*, Oxford, Oxford University Press, 2003.

of citizens it generated helped foster the ideology of nationalism.[2] The concept of "fraternity" quickly became exclusionist as it included certain social groups in the new political community at the expense of others.[3] Having no qualms about destroying the lives of those who were judged not to belong to this new imagined community, the concept also started to sacralize the interests of the state at the cost of human beings.

This destructive force of nationalism eventually reached such a degree that the wars of the twentieth century ended up being the bloodiest in human history. In Europe, the Jewish community suffered the most from these new social forces during World War II as 6.5 million Jews were destroyed by the Nazis. As the Jews had been mostly confined to urban centers throughout Europe as a minority community, they had initially benefited very much from the European Enlightenment and the ideas of liberty and equality to become full citizens of the newly formed republics. But whether they ever were a part of the "fraternity" was highly questionable, as was signaled by the Dreyfus Case in France before World War I and, of course, as indicated by the tragedy of the Holocaust in Germany during World War II. With the Holocaust, the idea of progress that had been the crowning glory of the Enlightenment and had motivated the Europeans to civilize the entire world after their own image suddenly became very problematic: the West lost its innocence and its unconditional belief and trust in science and technology, and in its ability to better itself and others.[4]

The lesson of the twentieth century in general and the Holocaust in particular was that even though humankind had mastered control over nature, it had not mastered control over people's capacity to destroy one another. How was it possible, the question remained, for the Western world that claimed to be the most civilized of the world during the past century to overcome this self-destructive streak? It was therefore no accident that with the advent of the twenty-first century the search for peace and reconciliation has become such a predominant aim in the West as

---

[2] Julia Adams, "The Rule of the Father: Patriarchy and Patrimonialism in Early Modern Europe," in Charles Camic *et al.* (ed.), *Max Weber's Economy and Society*, Stanford, Stanford University Press, 2005, pp. 245–6.

[3] John Dryzek, "Political Inclusion and the Dynamics of Democratization," *The American Political Science Review*, 90 (3), 1996, pp. 475–88.

[4] Ira Katznelson, *Desolation and Enlightenment*, op. cit., and Jeffery Alexander, *The Meanings of Social Life*, op. cit.

leaders seek a new world order that could somehow leave behind the twentieth-century heritage marked by nation-states, two world wars, and the bloodiest century in human history.[5] Especially after the end of the Cold War, and since the last two decades of the twentieth century that very much reduced international tensions, peace has become the primary aspiration of the twenty-first century.

The theoretical framework of the narrative outlined above was developed by the Frankfurt School, which focused exclusively on identifying the societal elements and processes that produced the Holocaust. In so doing, the School identified the elements of the authoritarian personality and the dynamics of fascism, and generated from these the methodology of aggressive criticism.[6] It was through this methodology that Jürgen Habermas was able to challenge the value-neutrality of science and technology, as well as highlighting the connection between knowledge and human interests. Habermas has further contended that the knowledge generated by the scientific method does not naturally result in human salvation but, unless guided by moral and ethical considerations, can just as easily be manipulated to lead to human destruction.

Ironically, it seems that when Enlightenment science and rationality replaced the sacred, they underestimated the significance of religious ethics and morality in bringing order to society. The moral void created by the inability of science/reason/rule of law of the Enlightenment to fulfill the ethical functions of religion/belief/divine rule led individuals to abuse science and rule of law to destroy one another. The possibility that other holocausts could occur led the Frankfurt school to raise the question as to how to formulate the elements of a new secular ethical order of the Enlightenment. As the Frankfurt School and the critical theory it gener-

---

[5] I think the vision of the European Union is particularly significant in this context, for it aspires to define and relate to human beings in a way that surpasses the narrow confines of identity instilled in them by their nation-states and those states' naturalized nationalism. The European vision aims to highlight past and present human experience with the intimate belief that humankind will ultimately persevere as it first uncovers the good, the "Righteous" and the just in its own past and present and as it then reproduces these uncovered elements for its future. The United States unfortunately lacks such a vision at the moment.

[6] Bert Adams and Rosalind A. Sydie, "Critical Theory: the Frankfurt School and Habermas," *Contemporary Sociological Theory*, Thousand Oaks, Pine Forge, 2002, pp. 59–88.

ated had already revealed how powerful interests, especially those of the state, shaped knowledge, thinkers such as Michel de Certeau[7] and James C. Scott[8] and others proceeded further to identify the sites and peoples that had managed to resist such hegemonic forces against all odds and had held on to certain ethical beliefs.

The concept of "the Righteous people" ought first to be historically contextualized within the Enlightenment narrative outlined above. Within such a context, the code of ethics of "the Righteous people" is especially significant, for it attests to resistance against the German state forces of fascism and restores hope in the future of humanity. It remains ironic, however, that the secular thinkers of the Enlightenment could not find a term other than "Righteous," because the term originates in the Judeo-Christian religious tradition, where it refers to people who abided by a set of presumably "correct" religious principles that the Enlightenment project had tried so hard to replace with secular values. So my first criticism pertains to the religious origins of a term developed in connection with acts of violence that emerge as a consequence of modernity that is predicated on secularism. Until now, studies have tended to naturalize and therefore neglect the religious origin of the notion of "Righteous," because the secular framework in which it is used, as well as the promise it holds for all of humanity, leads to an assumption that its origin is also secular. Owing to the religious origin that nevertheless underlies the notion, the Muslim ends up being excluded from it, as Muslim tradition is different.

My second criticism of the concept of "the Righteous people" is related to the boundaries of the religion upon which it has been predicated. In this case, I derive my theoretical insights from Subaltern Studies that emerged in the Indian subcontinent at the end of the twentieth century with the aim of questioning and ultimately removing the ideological hegemony of the British over Indian history.[9] Even though India had

---

[7] Michel de Certeau, "On the Oppositional Practices of Everyday Life," *Social Text*, 3, Fall 1980, pp. 3–43, and *The Practice of Everyday Life*, Berkeley, University of California Press, 1988.

[8] James C. Scott, *Domination and the Hidden Arts of Resistance: Hidden Transcripts*, New Haven, Yale University Press, 1990.

[9] Patomaki Heikki, "From East to West: Emergent Global Philosophies—Beginnings of the End of Western Dominance?" *Theory, Culture and Society*, 19 (3), 2002, pp. 89–111, and Guha Ranajit, *History at the Limit of World-History*, New York, Columbia University Press, 2002.

been decolonized, this school of thought holds, knowledge about India was still epistemologically colonized. Its scholars have argued that uncovering the power relations embedded within contemporaneous historical texts would eventually unravel this British hegemony. Dipesh Chakrabarty[10] then applied these insights to European history, stating that the history of Europe in general and the Enlightenment in particular had always narrated events by giving primacy to the role of Europe at the expense of the rest of the world, and this skewed narrative could only be corrected by "provincializing" the role of Europe as a social actor in world events.

When a Subaltern analysis is applied to the concept of "the Righteous people," the insight that emerges is that the term as it is defined at present privileges the European Judeo-Christian experience to the detriment of the experiences of the rest of the world. This is of course because the Armenian case involves, in addition to Christianity, another major monotheistic religion, that of Islam. Hence, my other argument is that the concept of "the Righteous people" has to be reformulated in a manner that also includes the Muslim experience. And such an analysis ought to commence with a discussion of what is/could/ought to be analogous to the "Righteous" person in the case of the Armenian deportations and massacres of 1915, and that is what I undertake next.

"The Righteous people" and the Armenian case

It is noteworthy that the massacres of the Armenians in 1915 were neither a part of the historical narrative of the European Enlightenment nor a part of its subsequent degeneration as witnessed by the Holocaust. The reasons for this exclusion of the Armenian case from European history were temporal, epistemological and ontological. First, temporally, what happened to the Armenians in 1915 obviously preceded the Holocaust by about two decades. Second, epistemologically, as Edward Said[11] so vividly demonstrated, the Ottoman Empire in general and the governing elite of Young Turks at the time of 1915 in particular were considered by Western Europe a part of the "uncivilized" East—as such, they could not abide, and were not thought able to abide, by the same "civilized" rules

---

[10] Dipesh Chakrabarty, *Provincializing Europe: Postcolonial Thought and Historical Difference*, Princeton, Princeton University Press, 1998.
[11] Edward Said, *Orientalism*, New York, Pantheon, 1978.

and principles of European modernity. This was assumed to be the case by all the European powers, even though all the Western European leaders of the time were at least factually aware that not only were the perpetrators of the crimes against the Armenians, namely the high-ranking members of the Committee of the Union and Progress, among the most educated people of the Ottoman Empire, but they had received Western-style education. Almost all of them had had instruction in at least one Western language and had spent some years, often in exile prior to assuming power in 1908, in Paris, Berlin or London; in addition, of these leaders, the most notorious perpetrators such as Dr Nazım, Dr Bahaeddin Şakir, and Dr Mehmet Şahingiray were, as their titles indicate, trained as physicians presumably to save lives rather than to destroy them.

The violent actions of the members of the Committee of the Union and Progress against the Armenian subjects of their own empire were actually the first public display in human and European history of the dark underbelly of the Enlightenment, of what happened when the new secular Enlightenment principle of the sacredness of the state gained priority over the primacy of human life. The debate on the French Revolution and the Terror, implemented by the Jacobin revolution, prefigured the "dark side" of reason and showed that it was not negotiated to secure liberty for everyone. *Ethnos* had replaced *demos*, the "people" were replaced by ethnicity, and the liberty project became a nationalism project.[12] Yet Western Europe was not ready to include this first massacre of modernity in its historical narrative because it had epistemologically excluded the Ottoman Empire from the boundaries of its civilized world.

This epistemological exclusion also turned into an ontological one, as what occurred in the Ottoman Empire was interpreted as a "barbarous" act that was totally inexplicable according to the premises and principles of the civilized and enlightened Western world. I believe it was this short-sightedness of Western Europe in failing to see, recognize and identify what happened in the Ottoman Empire to the Armenians as the first instance of the dark side of the Enlightenment that ultimately led to their failure to prevent the occurrence of the Holocaust two decades later.

---

[12] Eric J. Hobsbawm "The Making of a 'Bourgeois' Revolution," *Social Research*, 56 (1), 1989, p. 8; Michael Mann, *The Dark Side of Democracy: Explaining Ethnic Cleansing*, Cambridge, Cambridge University Press, 2005; Charles Tilly, *The Vendee*, Cambridge (Mass.), Harvard University Press, 1976.

When one turns from a general discussion of the concept of "the Righteous people" to the particular case of the Armenian massacres of 1915, two additional problems emerge that are not at all pertinent in the case of the Holocaust on which the concept is predicated. The first problem stems from the current political stand of the Turkish state in relation to the Armenian massacres, as opposed to that of the German state in relation to the Holocaust. Not only does the Turkish state deny that what happened to the Armenians in 1915 was a genocide, it does not even agree that they were uncalled-for massacres; the official Turkish stand on this issue constantly highlights that Turks were also massacred by the Armenians. The Turkish state attempts to marginalize what happened to the Armenians and employ everything in its power to push its viewpoint. Because of this particular stand of the Turkish state and the laws it has promulgated to support this stand, it is actually against the law in Turkey to argue that what occurred in 1915 was genocide. It therefore becomes very difficult and dangerous to collect oral histories about "Righteous people" who helped the Armenians and to identify the families of such individuals still living in Turkey today.

The second problem relates to identifying the social actors from within Turkey whose actions could be identified in ways that are analogous with those within the category of the "Righteous." There has been very little systematic research on this topic[13] except for the occasional mention of such names in the accounts by Armenian survivors or some Turkish memoirs.[14] My own analysis of the life stories of those who protected the Armenians has revealed almost all of them to be in opposition to the Committee of the Union and Progress (CUP) which was the most significant group in perpetrating the crimes against the Armenians in 1915. Even though the CUP was briefly out of power from 1918 to 1922, the

---

[13] I should note here that to date, there have only been, to my knowledge, two conference papers on "altruistic" Turks, the most recent one presented by Sarkis Seropyan at the 2005 Istanbul conference on the Armenians of the Ottoman Empire which was held at Bilgi University in September 2005, and the earlier one delivered by Richard Hovannisian at the 2003 Workshop on Armenian Turkish Scholarship at the University of Michigan, entitled "Intervention and Altruism during the Armenian Genocide."

[14] An example is the article by Hasan the Circassian, also known as "Hasan Amca," that appeared in the *Alemdar* newspaper (1919), where he mentions those Armenians he saved from the Syrian desert upon the orders of Cemal Pasha and against the machinations of Talat Pasha.

proto-nationalist ideology it advocated was ultimately sustained by the leaders of the Turkish Independence Struggle, who were predominantly former members of the CUP, as well as the Turkish Republic that these leaders subsequently founded.[15] Hence the CUP ideology that perpetrated the crimes against the Armenians—and that therefore prevented and often punished those who helped the Armenians rather than sanctioning their behavior as "Righteous"—has reproduced itself in Turkey to this day. As a consequence, not only have the actions of "the Righteous people" who opposed the CUP and protected the Armenians in 1915 remained unacknowledged and unrewarded in Turkey, but such people have actually been silenced either by death, imprisonment, exile or withdrawal from public life.

Actually, the official Turkish state instead devised its own category of "the Righteous people" in direct contrast to those who helped the Armenians: it rewarded those perpetrators of the massacres on the grounds that they had placed the interests of the state above the preservation of the lives of the Armenians. They did so by granting them significant positions within the elite cadres of the state or, if they had died, ordered the state to provide financially for their family members. This decision of the Turkish state underscores the significance of the composition of any reference group that actually determines "the Righteous": when it is the state that prioritizes its own political interests above all else in making that choice, the group of people who are identified are often not the ones defined in accordance with the humanitarian interests implied by the concept. It is for this reason that I strongly take issue with the presence on such a committee of representatives of any particular state.

I now want to further articulate how and why certain people took a stand against the CUP decision and what their subsequent fate was, through the empirical analysis of one such person, Hüseyin Nesimi, whom I came across while studying contemporaneous Turkish memoirs. Only through such an empirical endeavor can the actual search for such people, with principles that challenge loyalty to state commands, commence. I should also point out that the case also empirically articulates the two points I argue in this article: first, that the concept of "the Righteous people" has to be expanded to that of "the just" so as to include the

---

[15] Erik Zürcher, *The Unionist Factor: The Role of the Committee of Union and Progress in the Turkish National Movement, 1905–1926*, Leiden, Brill, 1984.

Muslim experience as well, and second, that the group deciding who "the just and the Righteous" are should not include any state representatives.

The case of Hüseyin Nesimi

Let me first briefly sketch the historical events of 1915. The nineteenth century witnessed the imperialist expansion of Europe at the expense of the Ottoman Empire, which was structurally unable to meet the challenges presented by the rising West. The most significant internal indication of this inability was the Empire's failure to reform in order to bring equality to all its subjects regardless of their religion. The Ottoman social structure had been based on Islamic legal principles that favored Muslims over non-Muslims, who had minority status as self-governing communities known as *millet*s. Such an arrangement had been satisfactory for both the Muslims and the minorities until the seventeenth century. After the advent of Enlightenment ideas and the emergence of the concept of citizenship, however, all the subjects of empires started to aspire for equality regardless of their religion. Of the three non-Muslim minorities of Greeks, Armenians and Jews in the Ottoman Empire, those in the Balkans were eventually able to acquire their political rights with the establishment of first the Greek state and later the Serbian, Romanian and Bulgarian states. Jews started to think of Palestine as their homeland and purchase settlements there.

As for the Armenians, their homeland was much closer to the capital of the Ottoman Empire in Constantinople and they were more scattered throughout Anatolia in the eastern regions around Van and the southeastern regions around Cilicia. Their transformation from subjecthood to citizenship followed a more checkered path as most diligently worked with the Ottoman state to bring about the social, political and economic reforms that would benefit all the Ottomans, while some joined Armenian revolutionary parties that advocated more violent means of armed rebellion for independence by forcing Western intervention in the affairs of the Ottoman Empire. Even though the Ottoman Empire did indeed undertake a series of reforms and the Armenians participated in Ottoman government in the nineteenth century and officially until 1914, ultimately the attempts to improve the conditions of rural and small town Armenian subjects, or to erase their unequal status within the Ottoman state dominated by Muslim Turks, failed.

The eve of World War I witnessed polarization of the situation with the advent of the ideology of nationalism. The reform-minded officials of the Committee of Union and Progress first intervened in 1908 to replace the autocratic rule of the Sultan predicated on religion with constitutional rule predicated on law and reason. Yet it proved extremely difficult to get both the subjects as well as the officials themselves to abide by the newly established laws. As country after country declared war against the Ottoman Empire, CUP officials had to resort more and more to violence to maintain order. This polarization through war and violence led in 1913 to a coup as a radical fraction of military minded officials within the CUP assumed direct power, thereby creating a very dangerous political context.

It was this proto-nationalist group in power that first defined the preservation of its power and of the Ottoman state, at all costs, as their top priority and sacred duty. Such a definition led them to view all activities relating to the reform of the empire as major threats and treasonous acts. Not only were the Armenian political parties and leaders that had asked for intervention of the Great Powers to bring about these reforms viewed as threatening the well-being of the Ottoman Empire, but so were all Armenian civilians regardless of age or sex living peacefully throughout Anatolia. All were now perceived as "potential threats" that had to be removed, to be replaced by "safe" populations like Turkish Muslims, who themselves had recently been forcibly and violently removed through massacres during the Balkan wars, and who would not seek Western intervention (and the West would not have been interested in them anyway).

Hence the parameters of the conflict between the Armenians and the Turks as it appears today were delineated in the years 1915–1917 during World War I, when the Ottoman Turkish government orchestrated the deportation and massacre of an estimated one million Armenians from throughout Anatolia which had been their ancestral lands for thousands of years. The government justified its actions then as the removal of a perceived threat against the Ottoman state. On the basis of victims' testimonies, eyewitness accounts of foreigners, Western consular reports and other documentation, the world community of scholars eventually identified and termed what happened to the Armenians as genocide.

It is within this larger historical framework that I introduce the case of a "Righteous" person, Hüseyin Nesimi. Information about Hüseyin

Nesimi emerges through the memoir of his son Abidin Nesimi,[16] a critic of the CUP. The memoir first carefully traces the trail of violence that the Committee of the Union of Progress engaged in prior to the Armenian massacres. Nesimi notes in particular[17] that the Salonika faction within the Committee eliminated with brute force not only the spies of Sultan Abdülhamid II, but also its own political opponents such as the journalists Hasan Fehmi, Ahmet Samim and Zeki Bey, through assassinations planned and executed by a special secret organization within the CUP named the *Teşkilat-ı Mahsusa*.

This Special Organization was very instrumental in executing the murders of especially prominent Armenian intellectuals and political leaders. The Circassian Ahmed Bey, who was the most significant member of the Salonika faction, was responsible "for the murders of the Ottoman Armenian deputies Vartkes, Zohrab and Dikran Kelekyan in the vicinity of Bilecik."[18] Later, with the onset of World War I, this Special Organization was divided into internal and external branches; while the external branch continued its activities outside the empire, the internal one "secured safety and public order, directed local resistance movements on those Ottoman lands brought under enemy occupation, and conducted guerilla warfare."

Nesimi discusses one commander in this internal branch in particular who becomes pertinent to this case, Dr Reşit Şahingiray. He notes that:

Şahingiray had taken on the responsibility of organizing Eastern Anatolia and Iraq [...] arranging as his strike force an itinerant Circassian gendarmerie. This trustworthy gendarmerie did not surpass twenty in number. The Circassians Harun, Davut (who worked during the advent of the Turkish War of Independence with Rauf Orbay who in turn was to later become the commander-in-chief of the Turkish military), and Ethem comprised Şahingiray's cadre [...]. Şahingiray had also formed a Kurdish militia organization and placed this militia under the

---

[16] Abidin Nesimî, *Yılların İçinden (From Inside the Years)*, Istanbul, Gözlem, 1977.

[17] Ibid., p. 34.

[18] Nesimî also recounts (ibid., p. 36) how the Teşkilat-ı Mahsusa was eventually prevented from committing unsolved murders within the country and charged instead with collecting information and instigating rebellions in North Africa, Iran and India and within Russia. Their name was converted into the Directorate of Eastern Affairs (*Umur-u Şarkiye Müdürlüğü*) and thus into an apparatus of the state connected to the General Chief of Staff (*Genelkurmay*).

command of the gendarmerie. This militia served in the 1915 deportation of the Armenians [...] initially worked in Iraq for the Special Organization without a title and then became the governor of Diyarbekir and carried out the Armenian deportation business. Many unsolved murders occurred when Şahingiray occupied these posts. Among those murdered was, in addition to Basra governor Ferit, Müntefek district governor Bedii Nuri, the deputy kaymakam of Besiri, journalist Ismail Mestan, also the kaimakam of Lice, and Hüseyin Nesimi [who was the author's father].[19]

So Nesimi discloses not only that Şahingiray was active in deporting the Armenians especially through the use of his Circassian and Kurdish militias during which many unsolved murders occurred, but also that he assassinated some members of the Ottoman administrative cadre who were opposed to the massacres he was undertaking.

In short, Şahingiray, who was a member of both the CUP and the Special Organization, first carried out covert operations in Iraq and was then officially appointed governor of Diyarbekir by the Ottoman state. Once he was the governor, he employed two militia forces comprising Kurds and Circassians to engage in illegal activities. It was probably through these forces that he perpetrated massacres of Armenians while deporting them, and also murdered Ottoman administrators, including Hüseyin Nesimi, who opposed his illegal actions against the Armenians.

Nesimi then recounts in more detail how his father was murdered. He first notes, "My father's murder was closely associated with the Armenian deportations," and then proceeds to discuss how "the Armenians had connections with the Western imperialist countries in accordance with their denominations… [and that] the Armenian interests were not in breaking up the empire and establishing an Armenian state, but in transforming the empire into a social federal state or, to put more clearly, into an Ottoman social state based on human rights and freedom."[20] Hence, unlike the radical fragment of the CUP that polarized and demonized the Armenians, Nesimi presents a more nuanced description of the spectrum of ideas and opinions within the Armenian community. He then discusses the destructive role of the world powers in both the Armenian rebellions and the disintegration of the Ottoman Empire, stating how neither the Ottoman Unionists nor the Dashnak Armenians (followers of the nation-

[19] Ibid., p. 37, p. 39.
[20] Ibid., pp. 40–6.

alist party Dashnaktsutiun) were aware of this reality.[21] In so doing, however, he also points out how the Dashnak Armenians were just as radicalized and destructive as the CUP, and that the inability to perceive this reality was probably due to the polarization that had already set in.

Nesimî then discusses the reasons for the Armenian deportations:

> it would have been meaningless for the Union and Progress central committee to attempt massacres under the pretense of deportations. This was also not in accordance with the *sharia*. According to the *sharia*, only the murder of those who have erred in their loyalty to a legal state (that is, under the condition of *nakz-ı ahd* and *nakz-ı vefa*) is religiously permissible. Accordingly, the Prophet Muhammed had put the Jewish Ben-i Kureysh tribe to sword, but not touched the children and the innocent. As the Ottoman state had been established in accordance with the principles of the *sharia* and therefore had to act in accordance with them, only those who had erred in their loyalty should have been murdered and others should not have been killed, but deported instead. This view was defended by those mentioned above [including his father] who were murdered themselves [by the band of Circassian Ahmed]. The Union and Progress central committee also shared the same view [...] and had considered as a precaution the murder of those who had erred in their loyalty and the deportation of the innocent Armenians. Yet the Kurdish militia organization established by Şahingiray and others who carried out the deportation turned it into a massacre. And the Union and Progress central committee partially turned a blind eye to this. There were times when they did not do so as well ... such as in the case of Vartkes, Kelekyan and others [...]. In short, while the decision of the central committee was deportation [of the Armenians], what the Kurdish militia and members of the Teşkilat-ı Mahsusa did was mass massacre.

[21] Ibid., pp. 42–4. He states specifically, "The Unionists have caused the destruction of the Ottoman Empire and the Dashnaks the annihilation of the Armenian nation. It is only very natural that neither the entire Ottoman populace was on the side of the Unionists nor the Armenian nation on the side of the Dashnaks. Actually the majority of both the Ottoman populace was against the Unionists and the Armenian nation against the Dashnaks. Yet it was impossible to perceive this reality and act according to it in practice. Most of the Ottoman populace has been the victims of the Unionists and the Armenian nation of the Dashnaks [...]. Damat Ferit Pasha had argued exactly this point, [that the Unionists and Dashnaks be penalized] when he argued against the deportation of the Armenians and the punishment of the Ottomans at the Sèvres Treaty negotiations. The Western powers instead stated that the Ottoman populace had to be penalized not for what the Union and Progress did, but for not removing them from political rule."

This discussion is interesting in that it provides a religious reason why the Armenians should not have been massacred, based on the Qur'anic example of the *hadith* of the Jewish Ben-i Quraysh tribe who had rebelled against the Prophet. This instance of a religious argument against the massacre of Armenians during deportations is very significant in a number of ways. The CUP members in general were highly secular and did not adhere to any religious principles in any of their actions. They had actually replaced their belief in the divine by total veneration of the sacredness of the Ottoman state, and they therefore justified their actions through nationalism, not religion. The other use of Islam in the case of the Armenian deportations is the one advocated by Vahakn Dadrian who argues that the ignorant Muslim populace was often incited against the Armenians by language defining the latter as "infidels," the massacre of whom would actually get the Muslims to heaven. There were also other instances, however, of Muslims who refused to engage in such behavior because they either did not think there were grounds for such action or found the killing of another human being, regardless of who they were, to be "unjust."

This necessitates a discussion of the Islamic (and Ottoman) conception of justice, *'adala* in Arabic or *adalet* in Ottoman or Turkish. This concept differs from the Judeo-Christian concept of "righteousness." Governance of the Ottoman Empire and its entire judicial system were based on the Muslim notion of *'adala*, which constitutes the framework within which Muslims judge human conduct as "just" or "unjust." This was the frame of reference within which Ottoman subjects acted benevolently toward Armenians and resisted the destructive, "unjust" orders of the CUP. A difference from the Judeo-Christian notion of "righteous conduct" is that Muslims do not act in accordance with the principle of the supreme value of humanity but in accordance with the principles of Islam. They thus acted against CUP principles that placed preservation of the state above all else. It was by acting contrary to the principles of justice (*adalet*) and by instead practicing injustice (*zulm*), that Şahingiray delegitimated his actions and caused Hüseyin Nesimi to oppose him.[22] It is evident that this conception of justice was undergoing a transformation in 1915 as it

---

[22] Indeed, as scholars have often noted (Inalcık 1973), the only legitimate grounds for removal of Muslim rulers from power could occur if they were proven to have acted "unjustly" toward their subjects.

pitted Ottoman administrators against each other. While Nesimi was still abiding by the traditional conception of justice as advocated by the *sharia* and advertised by the CUP, what the Special Organization executed and the CUP seems to have covertly practiced was another conception that defined state interests as just. In this instance, state interests defined in nationalistic terms advocated the destruction of the Armenians.

Indeed, this subversion of the Islamic concept of justice becomes more evident when one analyzes the subsequent treatment of Dr Şahingiray in Turkish history. Şahingiray wrote his own memoir later, during the Armistice period, while hiding away from the Allied forces in Istanbul to escape arrest for the crimes he perpetrated against the Armenians. His memoir ends abruptly as he committed suicide when he realized he was about to be captured. He has been lauded by the Turkish state as a "true nationalist"; for instance, Hüsamettin Ertürk, a member of the Special Organization himself, who also wrote his own memoirs, refers to Dr Reşit Şahingiray as "having achieved martyrdom" by his act of suicide.[23] Ertürk probably best captures the nationalist sentiment that still persists in Turkey today in relation to Şahingiray by this reference to perpetrators of crimes against the Armenians: "many hangings followed one another and the nation's children died at the gallows. All these were the doings of the enemies of the Turks."[24] The sentiments of these "martyrs" are captured by one such person whom Ertürk recounts as shouting "The Turkish nation will live forever and Islam will never decline. May God not harm the nation and the country; individuals die, the nation lives on. God willing, the Turkish nation will live into eternity." Hence, the sacredness of the nation and the state overwhelms the conception of justice and sacrifices all for the state; this sentiment persists in Turkey to this day. Yet, recent scholarship in Turkey conducted by those who work in accordance with standards set by the world scholarly community can critically analyze these ideological stands to decipher and deconstruct the multiplicity of layers and sites of both the "just" and the "unjust" in Turkish society at large.

Can the notion of "Righteous" be made to include all those who honor the principle of humanity to the point of sacrificing their own lives, whatever their religion? Even if the notion seems to be secular in nature, it is

---

[23] Hüsamettin Ertürk, *Iki Devrin Perde Arkası (Two Eras in the Wings)*, Istanbul, Hilmi, 1957, p. 327.
[24] Ibid., p. 306.

rooted both in the Judeo-Christian tradition and in the experience of the Holocaust during World War II. The spatial and temporal boundaries of this event present a major challenge. If this notion were applied to the violence perpetrated against the Armenians and the Turks who came to their aid during the First World War, the limits of this transposition would appear instantly. The Turkish Ottoman conception of "just behavior" toward the Armenians follows from the concept of *'adala*, what Islam considers "just." It is not a secular notion, any more than is the notion of "Righteous," which is grounded in the Judeo-Christian tradition. But the relationship between religion and the state in Islam and in Christianity is not the same. In the case of Nesimî, it is because the deeds perpetrated by the Ottoman state violated the religious conception of "justice" that he opposed the massacre of the Armenians. To differentiate from the Western experience, I suggest Nesimî be referred to as a "just" man.

All religions can be said to teach men and women to respect humanity above all else, including their own lives. But one question remains: either humanity is united around a concept that is not grounded in the experience of any particular religion or society, or we are at least aware of the limits of the concept used. The notion of "Righteous people" needs to be tested in other contexts. Another difficulty resides in the choice of deciding institutions: who is to decide who is a "Righteous person" or a "just" man or woman? At Yad Vashem, the "Alley of the Righteous" honors those who helped the Jews during the Holocaust. But if the Turkish state were to honor someone today, it would not be Nesimî, but Dr Şahingiray, the governor who killed him. Even if he would have ended up hanged for his crimes, Turkish nationalists consider him a hero, the Turkish republic honors his memory and one of the first decisions of the Turkish Grand National Assembly was to proclaim him a martyr. Rather than the state, it should be the world community of scholars and those who in Turkey wish to base their judgment on historical fact that should define who are "just persons" or "Righteous persons."

3

ASSISTANCE TO JEWS AND TO ALLIED SOLDIERS AND AIRMEN IN FRANCE
A COMPARATIVE APPROACH

Claire Andrieu

Instead of speaking of rescue, we will use the word "help." The advantage of this word is that it covers all the different kinds of help—including legal actions—and all the people who tried to extend aid to the pursued and the persecuted with no thought of the ultimate importance of their acts. The term "rescue" and "rescuer" can be deceiving in the sense that we risk focusing on one particular moment or person, instead of what was, in reality, a continuous chain of acts, carried out by a whole series of players. Moreover, "rescue" was not always viewed as such at the time. Part of those acts did not suffice in the end to save those victims who had benefited from them. The modesty of the word "help" reflects more accurately how the players themselves consciously viewed their intervention, at least in France. It is also the term that the allied armed services chose at the beginning of 1941 to designate those who assisted the fleeing soldiers and airmen on the occupied continent: "the helpers." Upon their arrival at Gibraltar or London, the escapees were greeted with an in-depth debriefing, thanks to which a "list of helpers" was created.

Two separate and not so critical corpuses of publications

Until now, the written accounts of help given to the Jews and those of help to the allied forces have rarely crossed paths. Information available in books on the subject rarely matches up. In only a few individual postwar memoirs and writings do the witnesses digress from the subject matter of their statements—away from the general direction and line of the interrogation—and reminisce about other activities that helped a quite different kind of fugitive. There exists no global history of these fugitives, who made up an exceptionally numerous population between 1940 and 1945, and of their helpers, who outnumbered them. Did these acts of assistance to the pursued and the persecuted really develop separately, in places and environments without any point of contact? Are they truly parallel and separate corridors in the history of the underground resistance to oppression?

Everything seems to conspire towards a compartmentalization of each type of help, whether at the time or later. Let us take the example of the popular image found in feature films. If we judge by French cinema blockbusters, the portrayal of help given to allied airmen in *The Longest Day* (1963), *La Vie de château* (1966), and especially *La Grande Vadrouille* which, having premiered in 1966, still held box office records in 1993 (seventeen million tickets sold, without mentioning television reruns),[1] do not include any actions of protection of Jewish families. The same goes for *Papy fait de la Résistance* (1983). On the other hand, *Le Vieil homme et l'enfant* (1966), *Les guichets du Louvre* (1973), *Un sac de billes* (1975), *Le dernier métro* (1980), *Au revoir les enfants* (1987) and *Monsieur Batignole* (2002) show us none of the support given to Allied fugitives. We can draw the same conclusions from books. Works concerning help given to Allies fleeing German Europe are basically made up of the memoirs of those who organized the escape networks. In these books, assistance given to Jews is barely mentioned. We can add to this the statements made by British soldiers held in prisoner of war camps in Italy who hid with Italian families when the German troops arrived in September 1943. Many of their stays extended until spring 1945. The large number of individuals involved, the length of time they all spent together, and the subsequent closeness of relationships that developed between them and the local population have resulted in a wealth of literature that is rarer for the rest of Western

---

[1] *Le film français*, 29 October 1993.

Europe. Western European war prisoners were transferred to Germany and were therefore unable to profit from the godsend that was the Italian armistice. Those amongst them who managed to escape from their camps sought to get out of Germany and its hostile civil population.

Regarding academic publications concerning help given to allied soldiers, the inventory is short and sweet: one sole historian has dedicated his time to the subject. Roger Absalom, currently honorary fellow at the Cultural Research Institute of Sheffield Hallam University, worked on the sheltering of British soldiers in Italy after September 1943.[2] We see nowhere in his work Italian solidarity with the Jews. Could this be due to a geographical division of work—the allied soldiers were spread out around the countryside and the mountains, whereas the Jewish population was predominantly found in the towns and cities?

On the other hand, literature regarding help given to Jews remains silent on the subject of fleeing Allied military personnel.[3] There are few direct witnesses—either helpers or those helped—to be found.[4] These published literary accounts are largely impregnated with moral discourse. Their very titles embody this; it is a question of "heroes," of "angels," of the "Righteous," of "courage" and of "Good," of "light" and of "darkness." Another difference between literature concerning help given to Allies on the run and that dealing with assistance to Jews is the substantial amount of university work dedicated to the latter. Research that began in sociology, being based on moral concepts like altruism, has evolved and now offers the possibility of deepened analysis of cases that do not conform to psycho-moral categories or a hagiographic narrative.

These two subjects, therefore, have only recently shared the common experience of critical examination. As with all new research subjects, they have faced the difficulties and hazards of the process of being recognized

---

[2] Roger Absalom, *A Strange Alliance. Aspects of Escape and Survival in Italy, 1943–1945*, Florence, Leo Olschki, 1988.

[3] We refer to the bibliographical archival verifications made by Sarah Gensburger in her thesis "Essai de sociologie de la mémoire. L'expression des souvenirs à travers le titre de "Juste parmi les Nations" dans le cas français : entre cadre institutionnel, politique publique et mémoire collective," EHESS, 2006. Published by Presses de Sciences Po as *Les Justes de France. Politiques publiques de la mémoire*, 2010.

[4] See the series "Témoignages de la Shoah," published under the auspices of the French Foundation for the Memory of the Shoah, and edited by a reading committee presided over by Serge Klarsfeld.

as a valid subject at university level. In France, integration into the history curriculum of the subject of helping the Jews was slowed down by the question of whether or not the helpers were members of the Resistance. The answer is yes. Jacques Semelin's work *Sans armes face à Hitler*[5] pushed to the forefront the idea of "civil resistance." Published in 2006, the *Dictionnaire historique de la Résistance* sanctioned this development.[6] Amitié Chrétienne (Christian Friendship), CIMADE (Comité Inter-mouvements auprès des Evacués), the Amelot committee and OSE (Œuvre de Secours aux Enfants) were all duly listed amongst the civil and military organizations of "interior resistance." Studying the birth of "Jewish Resistance in France," Renée Poznanski reaches the same integrating conclusion.[7]

Help given to Allied soldiers and airmen in France, on the other hand, has not benefited from any in-depth academic research. We only know about this form of assistance through narrative literature. The Comète, Pat O'Leary and Shelbourne escape lines all have their entries in the *Dictionnaire historique de la Résistance*. This activity is however often considered as being part of military history: "being a military organization, [the network] is in direct contact with administrative heads of the forces for which it works."[8] This is a restrictive definition and tends to exclude the help given by civil resistance to Allied servicemen on the run, despite the fact that this task, like help extended to Jews, was essentially carried out upon the initiative of the civil population. Moreover, although the escape networks did eventually work in close contact with Allied military authorities, it was only thanks to the determination of a few escapers working with officers from London's Military Intelligence to force the military hierarchy to create a service for this single purpose. The military

---

[5] Jacques Semelin, *Sans armes face à Hitler*, Paris, Payot, First edition 1989, paperback version 1996; translated into English as *Unarmed Against Hitler. Civil Resistance in Nazi Europe (1939–1943)*, Westport (CT), Praeger, 1994.

[6] François Marcot (ed.), with the collaboration of Christine Levisse-Touzé and Bruno Leroux, *Dictionnaire historique de la Résistance*, Paris, Robert Laffont, Bouquins, 2006.

[7] Renée Poznanski, "La Résistance des Juifs en France. Réflexions sur les premiers pas," paper given at the symposium « La Shoah en Europe de l'Ouest: perspectives comparatives," Centre d'Histoire de Sciences Po, Center for Holocaust and Genocide Studies, Amsterdam, Paris, 1–3 December 2005.

[8] Dominique Veillon, "Les réseaux de résistance," in Jean-Pierre Azéma and François Bédarida, *La France des années noires*, volume 1, Paris, Seuil, 1993, p. 453.

hierarchy was all the more reticent as this new service would imply working with civilians.[9]

We consider help given to Jews and help given to Allied airmen as integral parts of the Resistance. This Resistance was civilian in two ways, because arms were not used (although some leaders did have revolvers and occasionally used them), and because it was not political in the restrictive sense of the term. This resistance to oppression had no political agenda save the one shown in its actions: rejection of the Occupation and of the system of exclusion that came with it. Help extended to the pursued and the persecuted is classified as part of "network Resistance," which also included intelligence networks. It is quite distinct from the Resistance of "movements" and from the Conseil National de la Résistance (National Council of Resistance) which, alongside armed resistance activity, distributed propaganda, prepared a post-war agenda and set their sights on imposing their political legitimacy upon France and abroad. The network Resistance worked in a completely different political dimension, one without words, where acts alone expressed the commitment of the civilians against the occupier. This political project earned the civil resistance its rightful place within the ranks of the Resistance.

Separate and dissimilar processes of social acknowledgement

The witnesses, the writers and the few academics who have studied the subject have restricted their line of investigation to just one kind of help, and it appears that the processes of social acknowledgement have followed the same one-track curiosity. Similarly, after the war, the methods of identifying extenders of aid were very different according to whether they were the "helpers" of the Allied forces or the "Righteous" helping the Jews. Take France as an example; the resulting contrast is striking. The number of recognized "helpers" is greater than the number of Allied soldiers and airmen helped, which conforms to the certain facts. On the other hand, the number of "Righteous" is well below the number of Jews who escaped or who were hidden, and therefore seems unlikely.

Public recognition of helpers followed different forms and responded to specific concerns. Each time one of theirs escaped, the Allies were

---

[9] M.R.D. Foot and J.M. Langley, *M19, The British Secret Service That Fostered Escape and Evasion 1939–1945 and its American Counterpart*, London, The Bodley Head, 1979.

Table 3. Givers of assistance recognized in France[10]
("helpers" or "Righteous among the Nations")

"Helpers" acknowledged by the United Kingdom	*"Helpers" acknowledged by the United States*	*"Righteous" acknowledged by Israel*
1944–1946	1944–1946	1964–2002
About 13,500	About 10,300	2,000
For 3,600 British who escaped from France, plus those who remained sheltered, waiting for escape.	For 3,000 Americans who escaped from France, plus those who remained sheltered, waiting for escape.	For 15,000 escapees to Switzerland, about several hundreds to Spain, and an unknown number of people hidden in France.

informed of the identity and the whereabouts of the "helpers" and therefore could launch, as soon as the relevant territories were liberated, a policy of recognition of these actions of solidarity. Created especially for the task, "Awards Bureaus" were established in the liberated territories. Their job was to find the "helpers" they had been informed about and to try and find others by way of the local press. Though these departments were no longer active in the summer of 1946, the US and British civil and military authorities organized up until 1947 ceremonies in various regions of different countries, in which diplomas and decorations were accorded. The procedure for recognition combined therefore the intervention of the escaper, the country of his origin, and also the self-recognition of the "helper" or of his or her family at the end of the war. The British alone thus listed in Western Europe and in central and eastern regions more than 100,000 helpers. As it was contemporary with the events themselves or with them fresh in memory, the inquiry presents a high degree of reliability.

The way in which recognition was carried out in Israel following a law brought in by the state in 1953 was more modest and had a different sig-

---

[10] M19: "Amateur Helpers," *News-Letter* n°4, 1 June 1946, AIR20/8912, PRO; statistics based on lists from the MIS-X, NARA; Foot and Langley, *M19*, op. cit., pp. 309–15; figure given by Sarah Gensburger, "Les figures du Juste et du résistant et l'évolution de la mémoire historique française de l'occupation," *Revue Française de Science Politique*, vol. 52, n° 2–3, April-June 2002, p. 291; Ruth Fivaz-Silbermann, chapter 14 of this book; Lucien Lazare, *Organisation juive de combat. Résistance/sauvetage, France 1940–1945*, Paris, Autrement, 2002, p. 29. The estimated number of Jews in hiding in France is not known.

nificance; the Israeli law, which only came into effect in 1962 but created a still ongoing procedure, founded a group named "The Righteous," selected according to different criteria from those of acknowledged "helpers." This listing is not only affected by the passage of time and the restrictions of definition of the "Righteous" (non-Jewish people who demanded no material reward or substantial remuneration), but is also reliant purely upon the declaration of the Jew helped. Israel does not recognize self-acknowledgement and has no policy of recompense other than voluntary action on the part of Jews who lived in occupied countries or satellite states of the Third Reich. This appears to be a cautious policy in which the state intervenes only as a last resort and through the intermediary of a service of Yad Vashem, "The Holocaust Martyrs' and Heroes' Remembrance Authority," formed as a result of the law of 1953, which created the title of "Righteous among the Nations." In the case of France, where secularism and the Republic are strongly linked, the recognition of a Jewish identity was slow to develop on the public scene, as assistance to Jews correspondingly was, when the Republic was reestablished. This is one of the reasons why the number of helpers that have been recognized—3,158 in 2010—seems strangely low compared with the survival level of the Jewish population in France (around 75 per cent).[11] In 1995, the number of the "Righteous" in France was 2.8 times less than in the Netherlands (3.4 times less than in Poland) whereas the survival level in these countries was less than 20 per cent.[12] On the other hand, in Holland and in Poland, religious identity was and still is a part of social identity: the traditional and public constitution of society in religious communities has certainly contributed, amongst other factors, to a better acknowledgement of assistance given to the Jews.

After the war, public recognition of help given to fugitives thus influenced the leanings of society's memories. Inquiries and questionnaires did not ask for information about other forms of assistance activities, and it is only by accident that certain sources bear the traces of other added actions that were assisting quite different people. Is this all because of the nature of information initially given, of the passing of time, of the clouding of collective memory, or just a sign of the times? Did these two worlds of helpers really coexist without ever knowing each other?

[11] Lucien Lazare, *Le Livre des Justes*, Paris, Hachette/Pluriel, 1996, p. 263.
[12] Refer to Sarah Gensburger in her thesis, "Les Justes de France," op. cit., for evidence of this parameter.

Unequal repressive regimes

The literature available and the honors bestowed after the facts are one way to find out, but they have the inconvenience of not being contemporary to the events. Repressive policies put into place at the time give us another way of observing an underground social movement. Moreover, the nature of repression against the helpers of runaway Allied military personnel is disproportionate to that directed at helpers of Jews, and mirrors in a new way the difference between the two phenomena. In France, repression was the work of the occupier. It was ferocious towards the helpers, whether network members or simple shelterers, of members of the Allied armed forces, but although there was ruthless punishment of the assistance networks for the Jews, primary shelterers of Jews suffered less. As for the Vichy government, its interventions were rare and weak.

Repressive measures by the occupier against help to Allied soldiers and airmen were immediate and severe. Sheltering them was considered as an act of war committed by a *franc-tireur* and punished as such. So that everyone knew, the Germans regularly posted notices about this. The first we know about was on 24 August 1940.[13] Posters were displayed in the North and the Pas-de-Calais region, stipulating that "Anyone who shelters, hides or helps in whatever manner a militant [*sic*] of the English or French army risks the death penalty or forced labor." Failure to report helpers risked the same penalty. One similar poster in the Paris Metro[14] in October 1940 announced that people who "continue to shelter the English without having declared them risk being shot."[15] As from summer 1941, a capture or denunciation reward was added to posters. Then women were affected by these repressive policies. Probably the most distributed warning in France was that of 22 September 1941 which, signed by General Von Stülpnagel, head of the German military administration in France, stipulated that "women being found guilty of the same offence will be sent to concentration camps in Germany." Repressive policies took a step further in 1942, when the head of the SS in France gave out his own warning. The families of "saboteurs and trouble-makers" were henceforth targeted: "All the close male family members" will be shot, "all the women related in the same manner will be condemned to hard labor,"

---

[13] AN, 72 AJ 817, a copy is available on the Archim website.
[14] J.M. Langley, *Fight Another Day*, London, Collins, 1974, p. 85.
[15] AN, 72 AJ 790, ibid.

and all their children up to the age of seventeen will be placed in a "supervised education home."[16] Though measures by the SS stayed where they were on paper, the methods taken by the Wehrmacht were very thoroughly applied. Amongst those arrested for assisting runaway Allied servicemen, the mortality rate was high: British officers in charge of the recognition procedure were struck by how much higher the figure was in France, by comparison with the other European countries.[17] The threats against women were carried out: of all deported "helpers" 40 per cent were women, though among all the people deported from France under the repressive policies, only 10 per cent were women.[18]

What role did the Vichy government play in this repression? It does not seem to have participated. It did certainly collaborate with the Germans, delivering to them the Allied soldiers and airmen it had captured, but it did not carry out systematic searches and we are unaware of any cases of hunting down or punishment of shelterers. In the Southern Zone, police forces arrested escapers and transferred them to places of detention where there were concentrations of prisoners of war. From there, they were not handed over to the Germans, or at least not until the invasion of the Southern Zone. Until November 1942, in this zone, the risks taken by the shelterers were linked with the use of false identity papers, false ration cards, and non-declaration by a host of guests, which contravened an obligation imposed by a law of February 1943 on lodgers of any person foreign to the local community. Helping Jews ran the same risks. As far as we know, it was always the occupying power that carried out repressive measures against civilians coming to the aid of Allied fugitives.

Compared with the clampdown on the help given to Allied servicemen, which was uniformly brutal towards those who offered shelter and to the network agents who helped them to escape, repressive action against the helpers of Jews shows a strong disparity. The French state, for its part, apart from measures mentioned in the previous paragraph, intervened very rarely in the case of sheltering. Only two texts adopted by the Vichy government need be mentioned, and even for them, we do not

---

[16] Stéphane Marchetti, *Images d'une certaine France. Affiches 1939–1945*, Lausanne, Edita, 1982, p. 100

[17] M19: amateur helpers…, loc.cit.

[18] Statistics based on a list drawn up by the American army before May 1945 of 295 deported "helpers," box 1, ETO, MIS, MIS-X, 290/55/35/7, NARA.

know if and how they were carried out. A law introduced on 10 August 1942 prohibiting "the escape of inmates of the administration and the act of collusion therein" threatened those harboring an escapee from an internment camp with from three months to a year in prison.[19] In contrast to the punishment threatened by the SS at the same moment for sheltering airmen, the escapee's family was explicitly exempt from all reprimand. This law—mentioned in the collection of official texts *Les Juifs sous l'Occupation*, published by the CDJC (Center for Contemporary Jewish Documentation) in 1945, and quoted in a report in the autumn of 1942 about the situation of the Jews in France[20]—was probably aimed at curbing the escape of Jewish "foreign workers."

In the same summer of 1942, René Bousquet aimed quite explicitly at assistance to Jews: by telegram, he encouraged regional prefects in the Free Zone to entertain the possibility of "administrative imprisonment of persons of whom the attitude or actions hinder execution of my orders regarding Jewish groups."[21] We do not know of the consequences of this telegram, if there were any. Refusal to cooperate with the mass arrests during the summer of 1942 in the Southern Zone resulted in two sanctions: three months of house arrest for Father Chaillet of Amitié Chrétienne (Christian Friendship), and the dismissal of General de Saint-Vincent, who refused to place his troops at the disposal of the authorities at the time of the deportation operations at the railway station at Lyon.[22] One should also mention the arrest in February 1943, followed by several weeks' detention at St Paul d'Eyjeaux, of Pastors Theis and Trocmé, and that of the teacher Roger Darcissac from Chambon. During the "Brunner action," an SS-police campaign that ran from September 1943 to March 1944 in the Grenoble region, we note one case in which the French

---

[19] Law of 10 August 10 1942, *Journal officiel de l'Etat Français* of 5 September 1942, and its modification on the following 3 December, *Journal officiel* of 4 December.

[20] OSE archives, box XV, microfilm roll 6, report published in *La France Libre*, 27 September 1942, n° 551. My attention was kindly drawn to this report by Camille Ménager.

[21] For a reproduction of this telegram: Serge Klarsfeld, *Le calendrier*, Paris, FFDJF, 1993, p. 545.

[22] Serge Klarsfeld, *Vichy-Auschwitz*, Paris, Fayard, 1983, volume 1, pp. 283 and 481.

[23] Cf. Tal Bruttmann, "The 'Brunner Action,' a Struggle against Rescue (September 1943—March 1944)," see Chapter 17 of this book.

gendarmerie finally used the law, brought in on 2 May 1938, which made the "non-declaration of foreigners" an offence.[23] Though there was a certain will to repress on the part of the Vichy government, the rarity of these cases and their limited use show that they were not so high on the political agenda.

What is surprising is to find the same apparent indifference on the part of the German occupiers. No written texts, no posters, no execution for having sheltered Jews were announced. Moreover, calls for the public to inform upon Jews with rewards offered seem to have been rare. We hear of them in Nice, coming from the same SS officer Alois Brunner, during his presence in that town from September to December 1943.[24] As opposed to the shelterers, however, the agents working for the Jewish escape and protection networks were actively hunted down by the Gestapo from 1942 onwards and treated ruthlessly after arrest. Most often tortured, as were those who helped the Allied servicemen, they were then deported, to Auschwitz in the great majority of cases. Nearly 30 per cent of the members of these organizations perished by execution or deportation.[25]

In the *Dictionnaire des Justes de France*,[26] the rare "Righteous" who were actually punished for offering lodgings were often punished because of other resistance activities carried out alongside this act. Punishment was inflicted, however, if the person arrested with the people he or she was protecting took their side. This happened to Daniel Trocmé, who ran a children's home on the Chambon plateau and who, when arrested with his Jewish charges, refused to abandon them. He died at Majdanek in April 1944. The case of Lucien Bunel, the "Père Jacques" of the boarding school of Avon, whose story is told in Louis Malle's *Au revoir les enfants*, is no doubt similar. He was deported to Mauthausen and died soon after the liberation of the camp. Such was also the case of Adélaïde Hautval,

---

[24] Serge Klarsfeld, *Vichy-Auschwitz, 1943–1944*, Paris, Fayard, 1985, p. 125.

[25] Lucien Lazare, *Organisation juive de combat, Résistance/sauvetage, France 1940/1945*, op. cit. Out of 557 resistance members whose careers are presented in the book, 156 lost their lives because of their resistance activities.

[26] *Dictionnaire des Justes de France*, Yad Vashem, Jerusalem, Paris, Fayard, 2003, edited by Lucien Lazare; Mordecai Paldiel, *Saving the Jews, Amazing Stories of Men and Women who Defied the 'Final Solution'*," Rockville, Maryland, Schreiber Publishing, 2000; Adelaide Hautval, *Médecine et crimes contre l'humanité*, Paris, reprint Editions du Félin, 2006.

a Protestant doctor, who came out in sympathy in prison—she had been arrested for illegal crossing of the demarcation line—with badly treated Jewish prisoners. Labelled a "Friend of the Jews" and deported to Auschwitz, she refused to participate in Dr Mengele's "medical" experiments. Transferred to Ravensbrück, she survived. It was not always so dangerous to be labelled a "Friend of the Jews." The few dozen "Aryan" girls and boys thus named, and arrested in Paris for wearing the yellow star in the months following its enforcement, were liberated from the Drancy camp after three months, on 1 September 1942.[27]

Why did the Germans not punish the harboring of Jews in France as they did in Poland or in the Netherlands after 1943? Is there a link between the relatively high level of survival of Jews in France during the occupation and this absence of systematic repression? The fact remains that the mention "at the risk of his or her life," frequent in the notes related to the "Righteous of France," does not seem fully justified when speaking of primary shelterers. This, of course, is a retrospective statistical view, which tells little about the material difficulties, the insecurity and the fear caused by infringing the law and risking whatever repression might come in a context of dictatorship.

The study of a social movement—helping people on the run—with the literature available now and by methods which are external to the subject, like social acknowledgement after the fact or the laws brought in to curb these acts, does not allow us to answer all of our questions. The paths of the two types of aid meet in other sources and at other moments—during the crossing of frontiers[28] or by researchers' fine-tooth-combing of individual dossiers. An exterior approach, however, allows us to avoid the trap of a psychological discourse on motivation—always risky—and lets us understand collective mentalities and political national cultures. For example, if the frequency of help was inversely proportional to the level of oppression, then France would never have been one of the countries of western Europe where it was estimated that 90 per cent of the civil population was willing to help Allied soldiers and airmen.[29] This forces

---

[27] Serge Klarsfeld, *L'étoile des Juifs*, Paris, L'Archipel, 1992, pp. 145–53.

[28] Bartolomé Bennassar, "Le Passage des Pyrénées," *Les Cahiers de la Shoah* n°5, *Survivre à la Shoah, exemples français*, Paris, Les Belles Lettres, 2001, pp. 51–70.

[29] "Ninety-nine out of every 100 Frenchmen will be willing to aid our airmen…,"

us to introduce the parameter of a national conscience which, in the face of all the measures the Nazis took, all of its propaganda and that of Vichy, always considered the presence of the Germans as unwarrantable, and the British and Americans as the natural allies of France. It is even possible that the deportation measures, simply because they were German, be seen as illegitimate, even before they were considered inhuman.

Bulletin n°4, MIS-X, 28 May 1943, RG468, ETO, MIS-X Section 290/55/18/3, box 7.

4

RESEARCHING THE SURVIVAL AND RESCUE OF JEWS IN NAZI OCCUPIED EUROPE
A PLEA FOR THE USE OF QUANTITATIVE METHODS

Marnix Croes[1]

In this chapter it is argued that research into the Holocaust in some cases requires the use of quantitative methods. One such case concerns the explanation for differences in national loss rates. In *Accounting for Genocide: National Responses and Jewish Victimization during the Holocaust*, Helen Fein showed the results of the use of quantitative methods. Building upon her study, the dissertation by myself and Peter Tammes further advanced the analysis of loss rates and chances of survival. Historians employing traditional methods criticized both studies in the same fashion. Some of their objections are answered here. Furthermore, by briefly showing what quantitative methods have so far contributed to the understanding of the survival in hiding of Jews in Nazi occupied Europe, it is argued that more research in this direction should be undertaken.

In 1979, Helen Fein wrote that "much significant history on the extermination of the Jews was prompted by the need to evaluate responsibility for it and account for its underlying causes."[2] She thought this under-

---

[1] Thanks to Felix Croes, the editors of this volume and the participants at the international symposium "Rescue Practices Facing Genocides. Comparative Perspectives" for their comments.
[2] Helen Fein, *Accounting for Genocide. National Responses and Jewish Victimization*

standable, but stressed that it posed problems for historical research since "needs prescribe a secret agenda of assumptions that limit findings, for the evidence from which we draw our answers depends on our questions." One of the questions that thus remained unanswered was the issue of why the Holocaust was so "successful," and why the Nazis were more "successful" in some countries than in others.[3]

Although Fein is right in saying that this question had not (and so far has not) been answered satisfactorily, this does not mean it has not been posed before. In 1949 Shapiro and Sapir recognized that the extent to which Jews survived the Holocaust differed among the different countries that were controlled by Nazi Germany. The figures then known to them resulted in the table below, showing the differences in the rate of "success" of the Holocaust.[4] Building on these figures, Herzberg[5] tried to explain in 1950 what caused the remarkable differences in survival rates. Herzberg was especially interested in the question of why so few Jews in the occupied Netherlands survived. The fact that Shapiro and Sapir overestimated the number of Jews living in the Netherlands before the war, and the number that fell victim to the persecution, by 10,000 and 15,000 respectively did not alter this basic question. The loss rate of 73 per cent for the Netherlands was still very high, especially when compared to that of France (25 per cent) and Belgium (40 per cent).[6]

---

during the Holocaust, Chicago/London, University of Chicago Press, 1979, p. 32.

[3] Ibid., p. 33 ff.

[4] Leon Shapiro and Boris Sapir, "Jewish Population of the World," in Harry Schneiderman, Morris Fine and Jacob Sloan (eds), *American Jewish Year Book*, 50, 1948–1949, Philadelphia, the Jewish Publication Society of America, 1949, pp. 691–766, p. 697.

[5] Abel Herzberg, *Kroniek der Jodenvervolging, 1940–1945*, Amsterdam, Em. Querido's Uitgeverij, 1985 [5th ed.], pp. 322–4.

[6] Pim Griffioen and Ron Zeller, "A Comparative Analysis of the Persecution of the Jews in the Netherlands and Belgium during the Second World War," *The Netherlands' Journal of Social Sciences*, 34 (2), 1998, pp. 126–64. The table produced by Shapiro and Sapir has other problems too. On the basis of the numbers presented the calculated loss rate for France should be 43 per cent and not 38 per cent. Apart from that, the actual loss rate for France is 25 per cent. What the table in any case does show is that interest in differences in national loss rates existed already in 1949.

Table 4: First attempt at comparative quantification (1949)

Estimated losses in the most important communities			
Country	No. of Jews at the end of 1939	No. of Jews perished	Percentage of loss
Austria	60,000	40,000	66
Belgium	100,000	40,000	40
Czechoslovakia	360,000	300,000	83
France	300,000	130,000	38
Germany	240,000	200,000	80
Greece	75,000	60,000	80
Holland	150,000	120,000	80
Hungary	403,000	200,000	50
Latvia	95,000	85,000	90
Lithuania	155,000	135,000	90
Poland	3,250,000	2,900,000	88
Rumania	850,000	420,000	50
Soviet Union	3,020,000	1,000,000	33
Yugoslavia	75,000	65,000	86

Source: Leon Shapiro & Boris Sapir, 1949.

Herzberg postulated four reasons to explain this phenomenon. First, the Dutch Jews did not have the opportunity to escape to safety in the south like the Jews in Belgium and especially those in France. Second, the Germans ruled the Netherlands with a civil occupation administration while they chose a military one for Belgium and France, which hindered the full blooming of National Socialist institutions. Third, the Jewish community in the Netherlands consisted of a comparatively large number of workers, who, because of their social-economic position, were less able to save themselves during the occupation. And fourth, obedience to law and authority was, supposedly, higher in the Netherlands than in other countries, among both Jews and Gentiles, and this resulted in less resistance to the Holocaust.[7]

Although Herzberg did not substantiate this explanation for the high Jewish loss rate in the Netherlands, and although his four reasons have been questioned since[8]—with focus shifted to the role of the Dutch

---

[7] Abel Herzberg, op. cit., pp. 322–4.
[8] See e.g. J.C.H. Blom, "The Persecution of the Jews in the Netherlands: A Comparative Western European Perspective," *European History Quarterly*, 19, 1989, pp. 333–51, http://depot.knaw.nl/250/1/14275.pdf (accessed 14–5–2009).

bystanders, which Herzberg did not consider really important—Herzberg's account shows that historiography was not hampered by a lack of attention. Rather, it was the difficulty historians had (and have) in proving whether or not a supposed "cause" really is part of the explanation of differences in loss rates of Jews or not. This was (and is) caused not so much by a lack of data, as Fein in her 1979 study already showed, but rather by the fact that most historians lacked (and still lack) the appropriate methods and techniques to analyze them.

To explore whether supposed "causes" are actually significant, one could make use of the methods and techniques employed by social scientists. Their use of these while testing possible explanations led Fein to conclude that the variation in the national loss rates of Jews in Nazi-occupied Europe could be explained by the degree of control by the SS and the extent of anti-Semitism in the country (or territory) involved.[9] This conclusion earned her the critique of Karl Schleunes who argued that she ended up with no more "[...] than what should have been obvious from the outset,"[10] but even if that were true, which is really not as self-evident as Schleunes appears to assume,[11] at least one ought to give Fein the credit for testing her hypotheses.

Testing their possible explanations for the differences in national loss rates is, unfortunately, something that historians of the Holocaust do not often do. Frequently, their causal analysis boils down to comparing conditions under which supposedly causal mechanisms yielded their results.[12] By employing logic this method can, however, at best rule out some of the competing explanations for differences in the loss rate, but it cannot help to corroborate or rule out the remaining ones.[13] Although reduced in number, several competing explanations do live on side by side in this way, with no traditional historical method available to infer whether they were really true or not, and if true, to what extent for whom.

[9] Helen Fein, op. cit., pp. 50–84.
[10] Karl Schleunes, "Review of Helen Fein, *Accounting for Genocide*," *American Historical Review*, 85 (1), 1980, pp. 118–19, p. 118.
[11] See for instance M. Croes, "The Holocaust in the Netherlands and the Rate of Jewish survival," *Holocaust and Genocide Studies*, 20 (3), 2006, pp. 474–99.
[12] i.e. Pim Griffioen and Ron Zeller, "A Comparative Analysis," pp. 127–8.
[13] See for instance the—so far unpublished—dissertation of Pim Griffioen and Ron Zeller, "Vergelijking van Jodenvervolging in Frankrijk, België en Nederland, 1940–1945. Overeenkomsten, verschillen, oorzaken." University of Amsterdam, 2008, http://dare.uva.nl/record/284236 (accessed 14–5–2009).

In order to be able to state convincingly that a supposed factor did play a role, and another did not, one has to be able to evaluate the effects of both factors on the outcome variable at the same time. By employing multivariate statistical analysis, this is exactly what can be done. In this way, proof that supports or refutes hypotheses regarding the effects of certain factors is derived directly from the historical data. Here, the outcome variable is the national loss rate while the examined factors, or independent variables, are for instance those used by Fein: the degree of SS control and the degree of anti-Semitism among the Gentile population; but several others could be added. By making use of advanced statistical software, it is possible to find out which independent variable has an effect on the outcome variable while controlling for (or canceling out) the effects of the other independent variables in the analysis.

Black box

Although Fein made a huge contribution to Holocaust research, it is somewhat unfortunate that she was not very explicit about the methods she used and the choices she made in this regard. Mostly she used bivariate correlation, which measures the relationship between two variables and does not control the effects of other variables. However, when the independent variables that explain the loss rate are correlated amongst each other, this could produce ambiguous results.

Suppose for instance that one wants to know whether the nationality of Jews in a country like the Netherlands influenced their chance of survival. It would not be enough to calculate the percentage of Dutch Jews who survived and then compare that with how many of the German Jews who fled to the Netherlands before the war survived. If the Dutch and German Jews differed in other characteristics that were likely to have been influential regarding their chance of survival, such as age and wealth,[14] these would have to be taken into account too.

Assume for instance that the German Jews survived more often. How could this be explained? It is likely that German Jews who fled to the Netherlands before the war knew from first hand experience what to expect during a Nazi occupation. Because of this, it seems reasonable that

[14] Marnix Croes, "Jodenvervolging in Utrecht," in: Henk Flap and Marnix Croes (eds), *Wat toeval leek te zijn, maar niet was. De organisatie van de jodenvervolging in Nederland*, Amsterdam, Het Spinhuis, 2001, pp. 39–68.

they would try harder to escape deportation than the Dutch Jews did. On the other hand it could also be that the German Jews were simply more well-to-do than the Dutch Jews and were therefore better able to finance their survival in hiding or their flight to neutral countries.

One reason why Fein did not use multivariate analysis was a lack of units of analysis. Since she chose to concentrate her analysis on the national level, she had to work with no more than twenty-two units. In statistical analysis this number is small and for multivariate analysis it is too limited. Another result of this decision is that Fein had to work with aggregate numbers, the national average percentage of Jews who did not survive the war. Because of this, she ignored the variation in loss rates at lower levels of analysis than the national level (districts, municipalities). In turn, this meant that she looked for explanations of differences between countries at the national level of analysis, ignoring the possibility that the causes for a high or low loss rate could reside at lower levels within a country and could have specific regional or local origins. In essence, she treats countries like a "black box." What exactly went on within these countries remains unknown. Of course, when researching the outcome of complex multi-factor processes like the Holocaust on the national level, local variations should not be left out, since they may significantly influence national results.[15]

Peter Tammes and I showed how one could proceed.[16] To explain the variation in the loss rate within the Netherlands we tested hypotheses regarding the significance of factors, whether proposed by historians in the previous decades or derived from sociological theory, on the individual chance of survival. These factors were located at the level of the individual Jews (background characteristics), the residential municipality level (characteristics of the local Dutch government which was employed by the Germans in their persecution of the Jews; characteristics of the

---

[15] Pim Griffioen and Ron Zeller, "A Comparative Analysis," unfortunately do this. Johan C.H. Blom, "Geschiedenis, sociale wetenschappen, bezettingstijd en jodenvervolging. Een besprekingsartikel," *BMGN*, 120 (4), 2005, pp. 562–80, defends their choice but fails to convince. See M. Croes, "De zesde fase? Holocaust en geschiedschrijving," *BMGN*, 121 (2), 2006, pp. 292–301.

[16] Marnix Croes and Peter Tammes, *"Gif laten wij niet voortbestaan." Een onderzoek naar de overlevingskansen van joden in de Nederlandse gemeenten, 1940–1945*, [2nd ed.], Amsterdam, Aksant, 2006, 616 p. http://webdoc.ubn.kun.nl/mono/c/croes_m/gif_lawin.pdf (accessed 14-5-2009).

social environment of the Jews which could help or hinder their attempts to hide and survive) and the district level of the German Sicherheitspolizei (characteristics of the regional subdivision of the Sicherheitspolizei). By distinguishing between these different levels of analysis, we were able to improve upon Fein's quantitative approach. In essence, we opened her "black box." Adding the country level of analysis to this approach would be a distinct possibility, if one still had some characteristics that pertained to countries in general and did not belong to lower levels of analysis.

Among historians, this approach did not receive a warm welcome. Like Fein before, we were criticized for using quantitative methods in researching the Holocaust. At its heart this criticism has the following reservations: doubts regarding the validity and reliability of quantitative research; doubts regarding the selectivity, sensitivity and all-inclusiveness of quantitative research; and doubts regarding the value of quantitative results. Below, they will be dealt with in more detail.

Doubts

First, the doubts concerned the validity and reliability of quantitative or variable-oriented research. In the variable-oriented research of Fein and Tammes and myself, the goal is to analyze the statistical relations between variables in order to be able to make general statements regarding the direction and the extent to which one variable influenced another. Regarding the cases studied, the focus is on what they have in common. Case-oriented research, the kind usually preferred by scholars of the Holocaust, seeks to describe individual occurrences in detail. In this way, the focus of attention often slides to the differences in the characteristics of the (usually few) cases studied. This has a drawback, since differences are always to be found. But were they really meaningful, did they really have consequences? When the case-oriented method is applied to questions that are quantitative in nature, such as how to explain differences in (national) loss rates, one actually has no way to determine that, and because of this, the attention these differences get is regularly excessive. Apart from that, the application of case-oriented research to quantitative questions often results in speciously aggregating cases (of individuals, of municipalities) when their number is more than a few, in order to be able to treat them as "one" case. This is for instance done by focusing on differences in national loss rates, whereby (systematic) differences between individuals or municipalities within the countries studied are overlooked, on the unjustified assumption that they were meaningless and had no consequences.

The preference of historians for case-oriented research makes Marrus' and Paxton's[17] negative reaction to the study of relations between variables perhaps understandable, but it does not mean yet that "generalizations break apart on the stubborn particularity of each of our countries." Indeed, if it could be shown that these relations do exist, like Fein did, that statement has been proved wrong: one would have to conclude that the extent to which Jews survived was more systematic than was appreciated previously. However, showing that a relation between variables exists does not mean that this relation is or has to be apparent in every individual case, like Marrus and Paxton,[18] Weiss[19] and Hilbrink[20] appear to assume. The example that Marrus and Paxton give regarding Catholic Italy and Protestant Denmark as two outstanding but conflicting cases of consistent popular resistance to the persecution of the Jews does not yet mean that generalizations are not possible. It could for instance mean that there is a common explanation for the behavior of the Protestants in Denmark and the Catholics in Italy (and perhaps those in the Netherlands too)[21] that has, so far, been overlooked by unduly focusing on their difference in denomination.

Secondly, it can be a valid critique to say that more variables should be tested to see if they are part of the explanation of survival rates. But to state that variable-oriented research and the use of quantitative research methods equals less sensitivity to the complexity of situations than his-

---

[17] Michael R. Marrus and Robert O. Paxton, "The Nazis and the Jews in Occupied Europe, 1940–1944," *Journal of Modern History*, 54, 1982, pp. 687–714, p. 713.

[18] Ibid.

[19] Aharon Weiss, "Quantitative Measurement of Features of the Holocaust. Notes on the Book by Helen Fein," *Yad Vashem Studies* 14, 1981, pp. 319–34, p. 326.

[20] Coen Hilbrink, *De ondergrondse. Illegaliteit in Overijssel, 1940–1945*. Den Haag, Sdu uitgevers, 1998, pp. 59–64.

[21] Marnix Croes, "Gentiles and the Survival Chances of Jews in the Netherlands, 1940–1945. A Closer Look," in Beate Kosmala and Feliks Tych (eds), *Facing the Nazi Genocide: Non-Jews and Jews in Europe*, Berlin, Metropol, 2004, pp. 41–72.

torical vision,[22] and results in a too limited approach that misses essential aspects[23] of the events, overlooks two important points. Variable-oriented research is used to make generalizing statements regarding the relations between variables, not to describe individual cases in detail. Whether the details ignored in this manner are really essential depends to a large extent on the interest of the researcher, on what he tries to explain. Furthermore, the limitations of case-oriented research methods are in this context too often unappreciated. Apart from what has already been mentioned above, the application of case-oriented research methods to questions that pertain to relations between variables, like survival rates, is inherently risky because it is difficult to establish satisfactorily whether the case(s) on which the general conclusions are based is (are) representative.[24]

Presumably this fact is often recognized, since the study of the Holocaust is most often limited to those aspects that can be adequately researched with case-oriented research methods. As a consequence, many questions remain unanswered or are simply overlooked. For instance, in Dutch historiography attention in study of the Holocaust is to a large extent concentrated on the decision-making levels of the German occupation machine and its relations with the Dutch civil servants at the national level. The unstated (or sometimes stated but untested)[25] assumption in this respect is that regional and local branches of the occupation machine (as well as the Dutch civil service) worked like effective, mindless extensions of their central headquarters. As a consequence of this assumption, their role in the Holocaust—for instance in the hunt for Jews in hiding—remained unresearched. This has changed only recently.[26]

Thirdly, the doubts concerned the value of the results of quantitative research. When these results corroborate hypotheses that have been formulated by historians previously, it is sometimes argued that they tell us nothing new.[27] But is that really the case? There is a difference between

---

[22] Aharon Weiss, "Quantitative Measurement," p. 334.
[23] Johan C.H. Blom, "Geschiedenis, sociale wetenschap," pp. 579–80.
[24] See for instance Coen Hilbrink, *De ondergrondse*, op. cit., p. 58.
[25] Guus Meershoek, "Machtentfaltung und Scheitern. Sicherheitspolizei und SD in den Niederlanden," in Gerhard Paul and Klaus-Michael Mallmann (eds), *Die Gestapo im Zweiten Weltkrieg. 'Heimatfront' und besetztes Europa*, Darmstadt, Primus Verlag, 2000, pp. 383–402.
[26] Marnix Croes and Peter Tammes, op. cit., pp. 65–259.
[27] Karl Schleunes, "Review of Helen Fein," p. 118.

untested and tested hypotheses: only the latter allow for conclusions, and we should not be satisfied by merely stating hypotheses. At other times the use of quantitative results in Holocaust research is doubted because they are thought not to embody explanations.[28] The point here is also rather straightforward. The quantitative result itself does not provide an explanation, it is part of an argument that corroborates or refutes a hypothesis which does provide an explanation. Finally, some historians doubt the use of quantitative research because they think that differences in survival rates have to be attributed to coincidence.[29] They might wish for that, but when this "coincidence" shows up as clear patterns in the data, something systematic was going on.

Survival in hiding

What has quantitative research taught us so far regarding the survival of Jews in hiding? Much of this research still followed the research agenda of historians which, lamented by Fein,[30] concentrated on the motivation of Gentiles who helped Jews survive the Nazi persecution. On the basis of interviews of 309 survivors of the Holocaust in Poland who mentioned 565 rescuers, Tec[31] concluded that over 80 per cent of the rescuers offered aid while not expecting any concrete rewards. The rescuers distinguished themselves from other Poles in the sense that they were nonconformists; they were individualistic and self-reliant and shared a commitment to help the needy, the Jews in this case. To underline their value-oriented behavior, their initial engagement in Jewish rescue was unplanned and their own appraisal of their extraordinary actions was modest.

Oliner and Oliner[32] dealt in more detail with the motives of the voluntarily rescuers of Jews in Nazi-occupied Europe who received no

---

[28] Guus Meershoek, "Driedeling als dwangbuis. Over het onderzoek naar de vervolging van de joden in Nederland," in: Connie Kristel, Evelien Gans and Johannes Houwink ten Cate (eds), *Met alle geweld. Botsingen en tegenstellingen in burgerlijk Nederland*, Amsterdam, Balans, 2003, pp. 144–61, p. 154.
[29] Coen Hilbrink, "De ondergrondse," pp. 59–64.
[30] Helen Fein, op. cit., p. 32.
[31] Nechama Tec, *When Light Pierced the Darkness: Christian Rescue of Jews in Nazi-Occupied Poland*, New York/Oxford, Oxford University Press, 1986.
[32] Samuel P. Oliner and Pearl M. Oliner. *The Altruistic Personality: Rescuers of Jews in Nazi Europe*, New York, The Free Press, 1988.

reward and were motivated by humanitarian considerations. They interviewed 406 rescuers from France, Germany, Holland, Italy and Poland. Among the rescuers, they considered a distinction could be made between those whose motivations were moral (11 per cent), based on empathy (37 per cent) or based on normative considerations (52 per cent). This last group of rescuers responded to the plea for help from a respected third party who acted as an intermediary. All in all, two thirds of the rescuers were asked for aid before they gave any. Compared with the sample of 126 "matched" non-rescuers, the rescuers were oriented more "extensively": they acknowledged ties with Jews as with all people. According to Oliner and Oliner, this orientation developed for a large part during the childhood of the rescuers, as the result of the non-disciplinary child-drearing practices and instructions of their parents.

Monroe, Barton and Klingemann[33] and Monroe[34] further examined the orientation of the rescuers. On the basis of interviews with a rather limited number of rescuers of Jews in Nazi-occupied Europe, they rejected economical, socio-biological and psychological explanations for the altruism shown. Since self-interest (material or psychological rewards) and self-interested reciprocity (helping you protects my genes too) do not suffice as an explanation of the altruism shown by the rescuers, and the influence of critical role models in learning behavior, as well as the personality of the rescuer, cannot satisfactorily explain it either,[35] Monroe, Barton and Klingemann and Monroe proposed a cognitive-perceptual approach. The rescuers' perception of themselves in relation to others as

---

[33] Kristen R. Monroe, Michael C. Barton and Ute Klingmann, "Altruism and the Theory of Rational Action: Rescuers of Jews in Nazi Europe," *Ethics*, 101 (1), 1990, pp. 103–22.

[34] Kristen R. Monroe, "A Fat Lady in a Corset: Altruism and Social Theory," *American Journal of Political Science*, 38 (4), 1994, pp. 861–93; Kristen R. Monroe, "Morality and a Sense of Self: the Importance of Identity and Categorization for Moral Action," *American Journal of Political Science*, 45 (3), 2001, pp. 491–507.

[35] Regarding the role models it is not clear how behavior is learned. Regarding the personality of the rescuer as an explanation for their altruism, the core argument of Tec and Oliner and Oliner, the underlying assumption is one of stability of the personality of the individual. However, it is known that the personality of individuals is not stable and changes with experience. The personality of the rescuers could have become as it was after the war as a result of the experiences during the war. See notes 33 and 34.

being one with all humankind, as sharing a common humanity, drastically limited the number of behavioral alternatives open to them. This perception was so strong that it actually cancelled out a conscious choice about what to do: the rescuers simply had to help.[36]

Varese and Yaish[37] approached the question of the survival of Jews in Nazi Europe in a different way. While the aforementioned researchers concentrated on the motives of the rescuers, Varese and Yaish focused on situational factors. To give aid to Jews, one needed both the willingness and the opportunity to give (and receive) aid. Gentiles who were willing to give aid could have had problems with finding people in need of help. Furthermore, the more the potential rescuer thought that other people were likely to give aid, the less he was likely to give aid himself.[38] Being asked to help solves these questions to some extent,[39] so Varese and Yaish concentrated on this aspect of Holocaust history.

For their analyses, they used a sample of data gathered by the Altruistic Personality and Prosocial Behavior Institute (APPBI) whose data had also been used by Oliner and Oliner. The sample contained 346 rescuers and 164 persons who did not rescue Jews during the Nazi occupation of Europe. However, of these 164 people still claimed "to have done something out of the ordinary to help people during the war period,"[40] so the group of 164 persons was split in two: self-reported rescuers and non-rescuers. The self-reported rescuers were added to the 346 rescuers, making a total of 413.

Varese's and Yaish's analyses showed that people who were asked to help were much more likely to do so. While 66 per cent of the rescuers were asked to help, only 4 per cent of the people who were asked for help refused to do so. Taking other factors into account, being asked to help increased the likelihood that aid would be given by seventeen times. . This was especially important for strangers, since rescuers who helped of their

---

[36] Less convincingly, they also choose this way of reasoning for the self-excusing "what could I do to help, I, just one person alone against the Nazis?" line of argument.

[37] Frederico Varese and Meir Yaish, "The Importance of Being Asked. The Rescue of Jews in Nazi Europe," *Rationality and Society*, 12 (3), 2000, pp. 307–34.

[38] Jane A. Piliavin and Hong-Wen Charng, "Altruism: a Review of Recent Theory and Research," *Annual Review of Sociology*, 16, 1990, pp. 27–65.

[39] Ibid.

[40] Some were certified by Yad Vashem after 1988.

own accord offered this aid in 65 per cent of such cases to family or friends. In contrast, being asked to help, especially by authoritative mediators, in 70 per cent of the cases resulted in aid being given to strangers.

Other interesting results of Varese and Yaish were that the older people were, the more likely they were to help; that women were more likely to help than men; that a higher number of rooms in the house increased the likelihood of aid being given; and that the less religious people were, the more likely they were to help.

This last point corroborated the findings of Tec and Oliner and Oliner that faith was not a motive for rescuers to give aid. Tammes and myself[41] however found that in the Netherlands Jews living in municipalities with a relatively large Catholic community survived the war to a relatively high extent. Since Catholics were also less likely to vote for the Dutch National Socialist Movement before the war or to join the Nazi auxiliary police force during the occupation,[42] it appears likely that Catholics gave more aid to Jews than adherents of other (or no) denominations.[43] This means that more differences among European rescuers have to be taken into account when researching their motives to help.

The influence of other situational characteristics on the chances of Jews to survive the Holocaust in the Netherlands corroborates Varese's and Yaish's results. The extent to which the different religious communities in the municipalities were "closed off," measured by their intermarriage rate, correlated negatively with the survival rate of Jews. The percentage of baptized Jews in the municipalities, however, correlated positively with the survival rate. Given the extent of this correlation, this can be seen—besides the fact that most baptized Jews from the Netherlands survived the war in Theresienstadt—as an indication that baptized Jews linked the Jewish and Christian worlds and brought together the demand for and supply of help.[44]

[41] Marnix Croes and Peter Tammes, op. cit., pp. 511–34.
[42] Marnix Croes, "Gentiles and the Survival Chances of Jews in the Netherlands."
[43] The number of Catholic organisations in the municipalities explains in part this higher survival rate of Jews in municipalities with a higher percentage of Catholic inhabitants. See Peter Tammes and Anika Smits, "De invloed van christenen op de overlevingskansen van joden in Nederlandse gemeenten tijdens de Tweede Wereldoorlog: een katholieke paradox?" *Mens en Maatschappij*, 80 (4), 2005, pp. 353–75.
[44] Marnix Croes and Peter Tammes, op. cit., p. 410.

However, finding help was only the beginning of Jews' attempt to survive the Nazi persecution, and it is clear that in this attempt various situational and background characteristics were significant, such as the Nazi policy regarding the Jews;[45] the regionally varying efforts of the Sicherheitspolizei and its accomplices to apprehend the Jews in hiding;[46] and the age[47] and social position[48] of the latter. To be able to determine their significance requires that researchers continue on the way chosen by Fein and opt for use of quantitative research methods. Let us hope that they will, because many questions still remain to be answered.

Resistance

One of the most intriguing of these questions regarding the Holocaust in the Netherlands pertains to the role of the organized resistance. At least 28,000 Jews went into hiding in the Netherlands of whom approximately 16,100 survived the war. In doing so, they were dependent on Gentiles for help. Many of these were single groups of people (family, friends, neighbors etc.), but organized resistance networks also played a part. In the province of Overijssel, several of the resistance networks operating there saw it as their main task, or one of their main tasks, to care for Jews in hiding. Because of this, Tammes and I expected that in the municipalities with more resistance workers, whose numbers are known thanks to the work of the historian Hilbrink,[49] more Jews would have survived since they were more likely to receive help. However, our

---

[45] Pim Griffioen and Ron Zeller, "Anti-Jewish Policy and Organization of the Deportations in France and the Netherlands, 1940–1944: A Comparative Study," *Holocaust and Genocide Studies*, 20 (3), 2006, pp. 437–73.

[46] Marnix Croes, "The Netherlands 1942–1945: Survival in Hiding and the Hunt for Hidden Jews," *The Netherlands' Journal of Social Sciences*, 40 (2), 2004, pp. 157–75.

[47] Marnix Croes and Peter Tammes, op. cit., pp. 516–25. Generally speaking, the extent to which Jews in the Netherlands survived the war increased with their age, but the size of this effect grew smaller with their age.

[48] Marnix Croes, "Jodenvervolging in Utrecht." Regarding social status, 67 per cent of the Jews in the province of Utrecht who belonged to the highest social class survived the occupation, while on average only 50 per cent belonging to lower social classes did so in that province.

[49] Coen Hilbrink, "De ondergrondse," op. cit., Coen Hilbrink, *Illegaliteit in Twente en het aangrenzende Salland 1940–1945*, The Hague, Sdu, 1989.

analyses showed that the number of local resistance workers was *inversely* related to the extent that Jews from these municipalities survived: more resistance meant less survival.[50] Since the resistance workers aided Jews in hiding and did not persecute them, this result is remarkable.

Tammes and I suggested that this could possibly be explained by taking the behavior of the Sicherheitspolizei into account. The Sicherheitspolizei focused its investigations in response to the degree of resistance, so it appears not unlikely that, relatively speaking, more resistance meant more attention from the German police, resulting in more arrests of Jews in hiding.[51]

This higher rate of arrests could also be part of the explanation for our finding that Jews living in municipalities with a comparatively high percentage of Catholic inhabitants had a relatively high chance to survive the German occupation, while those living in municipalities with a comparatively high percentage of Calvinists had a relatively low chance. Compared with Catholics, Calvinists appear to have been more involved in the type of resistance work that would have drawn the attention of the Sicherheitspolizei, such as armed robbery of food stamps and identity papers.[52] This was on the one hand because the Roman Catholic church prohibited Catholic resistance workers from using violence, and on the other hand because the higher prevalence of Catholics meant that they were more likely to find a co-religionist in the local administration who was willing to make food stamps or identity papers "disappear."[53] This meant that the municipalities with a relatively high percentage of Calvinists were probably more often and/or more thoroughly scrutinized by the Sicherheitspolizei, resulting in relatively more arrests of Jews in hiding. Formulating this proposition is not enough, however. It would have to be tested, which would require the use of quantitative methods. It would definitely be interesting to do this, since it could shed more light on the inner workings of the processes of rescue and persecution during the Holocaust.

---

[50] Marnix Croes and Peter Tammes, op. cit., pp. 441–5.
[51] Ibid.
[52] Ibid., pp. 437–41.
[53] Alfred P.M. Cammaert, *Het verborgen front. Geschiedenis van de georganiseerde illegaliteit in de provincie Limburg tijdens de Tweede Wereldoorlog*, Leeuwarden/Mechelen, Eisma b.v., 1994.

Conclusion

In this chapter, the use of quantitative methods in research into the survival and rescue of Jews during the Holocaust is advocated. Helen Fein used these methods in 1979 to explain differences in survival rates of Jews in twenty-two countries and territories that the Germans occupied. From her analyses she concluded that the extent of SS influence and each country's degree of anti-Semitism could explain these differences. Both this conclusion and the methods she used drew much criticism, criticism which to a high degree equalled that aroused by the quantitative study of Croes and Tammes on the chances of survival of Jews in the Netherlands during the German occupation: doubts regarding the validity and reliability of quantitative research; doubts about the selectivity, sensitivity and lack of all-inclusiveness of quantitative research; and doubts regarding the value of quantitative results.

Here, it is argued that these doubts are based on a misunderstanding of the methods used. Furthermore, this brief overview has shown what we have learned so far from the use of quantitative methods regarding the survival and rescue of Jews during the Holocaust. Much of this research was focused on the motivation of rescuers. Varese and Yaish, however, stressed the role of circumstances, such as the significance of being asked to help. In this attention to the circumstances their research is comparable to the study of Croes and Tammes. In the explanation of the differences in the chance of survival for Jews in the Netherlands they distinguished between factors located at the level of the individual Jew (background characteristics), the level of the residential municipality (characteristics of the local Dutch government which was employed by the Germans in their persecution of the Jews; characteristics of the social environment of the Jews that could help or hinder them in their attempts to hide and survive), and the district level of the German Sicherheitspolizei (characteristics of the subdivision of the Sicherheitspolizei).

For the rescue process, the finding that Jews survived to a greater extent in municipalities with a relatively high number of Catholics and to a lesser extent in those with a relatively high number of Calvinists is probably the most interesting: all the more so since this finding could be related to another—counterintuitive—finding, that in municipalities with a relatively higher number of resistance workers comparatively fewer Jews survived the occupation. However, to reach more authoritative conclusions, more research employing quantitative methods would be necessary. This research does not have to remain limited to the Netherlands. The question of what kind of people aided Jews in hiding to what extent could be posed, and has already been posed, for other countries as well. For the Netherlands the results so far suggest that denomination did play a role and that the role of Catholicism was, comparatively speaking, a positive one. It still remains to be seen to what extent this was the case in other countries.

5

ANTI-SEMITISM AND THE RESCUE OF JEWS IN FRANCE
AN ODD COUPLE?

Renée Poznanski

As the noose tightened around the Jews in the Occupied Zone of France, Marthe Hoffnung's family, who had fled from Metz to seek sanctuary in Poitiers, decided to try to escape to the Free Zone. The priest of St Secondin, to whom one of Marthe's classmates had sent them, greeted them with these terms: "I'll help you because it is the right thing to do. But you should know from the outset—I'd never trust a Jew." Faced with Marthe's indignation, he answered by way of explanation, "Don't you know the story of Judas?" while repeating that he would help them because it was his duty as a Christian.[1] Is the story an unusual one? Théo Klein, in charge of a rescue network in Grenoble, came up against a similar reaction: a Catholic scout leader who headed an organization created by Vichy took "marvelous" care of two fifteen-year-old boys whom he had been asked to hide. When Théo Klein went to thank him after Grenoble was liberated, the man declared, "There's something I have to tell you... I'm anti-Semitic."[2]

[1] Marthe Cohn with Wendy Holden, *Behind Enemy Lines. The True Story of a French Jewish Spy in Nazi Germany*, New York, Harmony Books, 2002, pp. 76–7.
[2] Théo Klein and Stéphane Zagdanski, "L'antisémitisme est-il de retour?," *Le Nouvel Observateur*, 2168, 25–31 May 2006, pp. 102–3.

Recounting this anecdote over sixty years after the event, Théo Klein wondered about the meaning that this term could possibly have had for the person who used it. It does indeed seem paradoxical that an anti-Semite would agree, or even take the initiative, to rescue Jews. The terms "anti-Semitism" and "rescue" refer to phenomena of different sorts: the first, in which both the ideological and psychosocial dimensions are central, fits historically into the long term and relates to the evolution of French anti-Semitism, while the second pertains only to the period of the Occupation and describes a practice. But both are used to depict the attitude of the French population with regard to the Jews at a time when the latter were persecuted, a subject that raises considerable ethical issues. While the existence of anti-Semitism in French society, going beyond that contained in official state policies, is now well established, studies devoted to public opinion diverge as to their conclusions. Some describe the French as anti-Semitic, receptive to the dominant ideology, accessories to the enforcement of segregation and spoliation measures and at best indifferent, at worst relieved to see the Jews deported from France. For others, however, rescue operations made possible by the attitude of these same French people—civil society opposed to the state—explain how three-quarters of the Jewish population in France was able to escape the fate awaiting them at the hands of the Germans. An attempt has been made to reconcile these two perspectives by establishing a more detailed chronology that identifies a sudden change during the summer of 1942. Anti-Semitism, which was widely shared but in no way a priority in public opinion, is thought to have dissipated in view of the horror of the mass arrests of Jews, which, it is suggested, explains the development of rescue efforts.

Yet, the two examples given above prompt a more in-depth reflection on this accepted dichotomy between anti-Semitism and rescue, because the nature of relations between Jews and non-Jews in those times of Occupation was nourished by traditions that predated the defeat. They had great influence over the population's reaction to economic and social exclusion, and when roundups and deportations came to the fore, they also structured and shaped rescue procedures.

From anti-Semitism to the 'Jewish problem'

There has been much inquiry into the depth and breadth of French anti-Semitism before the outbreak of the war and its ramifications in the aftermath of defeat. In an international context where dictatorships and fascist regimes were multiplying as well as ideological and racial persecutions, while France—proportionally the largest land of asylum in the world[3]—was undergoing a serious economic crisis reflected in a growing number of unemployed, xenophobia had its hour of glory. In the drift taken by public opinion with the crises in the 1930s,[4] xenophobia and anti-Semitism underwent an unprecedented rise, often hand in hand, and as we know affected nearly all social sectors, starting with literary circles that largely contributed to legitimating them.

Yet, is the use of the term anti-Semitism, which implies a binary analysis—a person either is or is not anti-Semitic—really adequate? After Hitler had come to power in Germany, and given the centrality of anti-Semitic speech and practice in his policies, anti-Semitism, the Jews, the Jewish question or "the Jewish problem" gave rise to considerable discussion. Some aligned themselves with Hitler's anti-Semitism. Others denounced the power of the Jews in France while distancing themselves from Hitlerian practices. Some objected to his totalitarian methods but were concerned about the gravity that a "Jewish question" posed to France. Still others criticized ideological anti-Semitism but depicted the Jews with features that the most diehard anti-Semite would not have argued with.

Especially, much of the writing pertaining to the Jews outlined the characteristics of a "Jewish problem" that hinged on a certain number of key ideas: Jews formed a separate group with features that could be identified. They were naturally connected with the Jews abroad—the assimilation of one with the other thus being performed surreptitiously. They were drawn by money and power, had a tendency to group together, and did not shrink from subversive ideas. They moved with determination into certain areas—the press, political office, finance, and film—and occupied a disproportionate place in them. Without necessarily approving the idea, it was legitimate to wonder about the possible benefits of adopting a *numerus clausus*. For those who "analyzed" the "Jewish problem" that they presented as an irrefutable reality, none of this had anything to do with anti-Semitism, which was violent, hateful and irrational. It was based on

---

[3] Gérard Noiriel, *Le Creuset français*, Paris, Seuil, 1988.
[4] "*Dérives*" is the term used by Pierre Laborie in *L'Opinion française sous Vichy*, Paris, Seuil, 1990.

the idea of a Jewish conspiracy out to rule the world, viewed as absolutely harmful.[5] The violence and outrages of anti-Semitism as it was practiced on the other side of the Rhine or as expressed in the writings of the fascist or fascist-leaning far right produced antibodies. On the other hand, more serene analyses of the "Jewish problem" at the most stirred debates during which some assertions were rejected whereas others were taken up or reformulated in other terms. It was legitimate to discuss the whys and wherefores of the question. Such legitimacy meant that making anti-Semitic remarks was commonplace—sometimes even in writings that primarily set out to denounce the phenomenon. In the dominant cultural codes, the Jew was not really a French citizen like the others.

Therefore, on the eve of war, "the spirit of differentiation" denounced by Marc Bloch made any criticism of Hitler's regime expressed by a Jewish analyst suspect: Raymond Aron's testimony comes to mind. When what was soon to be described as the "Jewish" war broke out and ended in a resounding defeat for France, the ensuing trauma was hardly likely to prompt a revision of these cultural codes. Official propaganda used them precisely to justify adoption of "national recovery" measures. The Vichy French state's anti-Semitic policy with its string of exclusionary laws was officially "explained," particularly by the Commissioner-General for Jewish Questions, by making direct reference to the accepted components of the much-vaunted "Jewish problem." Although the tone was less radical in the unoccupied zone, and even if it was "less violent, the Vichy government's anti-Jewish propaganda launched in July 1940 and which was constantly heightened, was basically neither less perfidious nor less hateful than Radio-Paris," wrote Henri Sinder, a French Jewish lawyer who had just taken refuge in the United States. He added, "Its impact was much greater; it produced all the more resonance among the masses because it was 'French propaganda,' 'truths' implicitly or explicitly bearing the stamp of the 'French' government,"[6] moreover a government that at the time enjoyed considerable popularity.

---

[5] A few examples of this double talk can be found in Renée Poznanski, *Propagandes et Persécutions. La Résistance et le "problème juif," 1940–1944*, Paris, Fayard, 2008.

[6] Henri Sinder, attorney at the Paris Court of Appeal, "La situation des juifs en France depuis l'armistice de juin 1940," written in the Fall of 1942 (the study stops in early September 1942), New York, Yivo Institute for Jewish Research Archives, Territorial Collection, France during WWII, box 4, Folder 56, 16.

RENÉE POZNANSKI

The 'Jewish problem' in London and in the Resistance

During the same period, while Jews were being systematically excluded from society by new laws, while intense propaganda strove to denounce their pernicious influence, the "Jewish problem" still preoccupied certain resistance fighters in London, in the occupied capital and in Vichy France, even while they disapproved of most of the anti-Semitic policies. Lieutenant-Colonel Pierre Tissier, Chief of Staff in the early days of Free France, offered an analysis in 1942 in a book published in the United States that aroused concern among the leaders of the World Jewish Congress and alerted Jacques Maritain. In it Tissier wrote:

The Jewish problem exists, even in France. It is an undeniable fact and no realistic policy can be blind to it. It is not enough to say that the problem of the Jews is the problem of the Armenians, the Slavs or the Arabs, for this is to disregard an essential factor. The Jewish race constitutes an international community. If we exclude the Jewish State of Palestine, an artificial creation, the Jewish race has no territory of its own, and yet its members behave as if they belonged to a single nation. Among them there exists an absolute unity of language, traditions, and intellectual and moral education.

[…] As the Jew is seldom a farmer—which can be explained by the fact that for many generations and in many countries he has not been allowed to be a farmer—he is not attached to the soil; he more readily engages in industry, trade, or banking; his profession, instead of causing him to acquire stronger ties with the soil on which he lives, on the contrary helps him maintain his international ties.[7]

A year earlier, Jean Escarra, a legal scholar who had joined the Free French Forces in January 1941, wrote a note on 5 May 1941 to René Pleven who since 15 July 1940 had held the post of Foreign Affairs Minister of Free France. He specified, "It would be better if Cassin had no knowledge of this note." In this memo, he noted that "of all the domestic measures taken by Vichy, [the adoption of a statute for the Jews] was one

---

[7] Pierre Tissier, *The Government of Vichy*, London, George G. Harrap and Co, 1942, p. 155. Cf. Patrick Weill, "Racisme et discrimination dans la politique française de l'immigration, 1938–1945/1974–1995," *Vingtième Siècle. Revue d'Histoire*, 47, July-September 1995, pp. 77–102. Also the file concerning reactions in the United States as well as replies sent from London intended to be reassuring, especially those of Pierre Tissier himself (21 October 1942), Foreign Affairs Ministry (MAE) archives, Paris, 207, 235–42.

of the least criticized throughout the country." He explained the anti-Semitic sentiment in France by the hasty naturalizations of too many Jews from Central Europe—"undesirable elements"—who "have gradually invaded the public institutions and professions in France"; in it he described "the specific features of the Jewish race, considered as dangerous for the moral and political equilibrium of the country, i.e. a taste for Utopia, a love of intelligence taken as far as dilettantism, a frequent lack of character and moral courage, negative and destructive tendencies, etc." While making a distinction between "the Jews of old French stock and one of those Central European Jews who had little value for the community and of which France had become a sort of dumping ground," he reached the conclusion that these were "mere nuances for most French people." He added that "one of the dominant elements in the propaganda directed in France against the Free French Forces referred to the control the Jews had over de Gaulle's movement," pointing out that "certain outside manifestations of our movement sometimes [gave it] a semblance of justification."

These opinions led, inevitably according to Jean Escarra, to the practical conclusions of this analysis. Echoing an introductory paragraph in which he railed against a brutally anti-Semitic policy and admitted that "the Vichy statute, however moderate it may be with respect to the German status, still needed to be toned down significantly," he recommended caution, fearing that "promising the Jews, for instance, that after we win the war, we will demand that all discriminatory measures be repealed to return simply to the status quo [...] would compromise our cause, which must remain intact [...] all the more so since the Jewish mentality [was] quick to make use of any mark of sympathy in order to make ever-greater demands. The invasive, 'grabby' nature of this mentality [was] indeed a well-known feature of the race."[8]

There is no shortage of accounts confirming that such ideas were not rare in London. They also circulated in certain Resistance movements in France. "Even if everyone condemns what has been done, one should not conclude that everyone thinks nothing should be done. Many say that these measures are excessive, which implies that they are not totally unjustified," wrote Leo Hamon in April 1941 in a report on the situation of Paris Jews.[9] "In some movements [...] people claim to be both against

---

[8] Escarra to Pleven, 5 May 1941, MAE, 207.
[9] Léo Hamon, "Étude sur la situation des juifs en zone occupée, April 1941," in

anti-Semitism and against the peril represented by reverse racism, i.e. a Jewish state within a state," he added. Henri Frenay's ambiguous remarks are well known, as is the brochure published in June 1942 by the Organisation Civile et Militaire,[10] of which I will only say here that even if it raised protest among the Resistance, there was no across-the-board opposition. The "Jewish problem" sometimes provoked debate—it was picked up by other underground papers—or sometimes unease, because German policy and Vichy government policy that was deemed to be inspired by it were largely disapproved. But the idea that there was a problem and a solution had to be found was widely shared.

The point here is not to accuse the Resistance of anti-Semitism. That would be untrue and absurd. But if in the dominant cultural codes of the time the image of the Jew was tainted with prejudice, it would have been surprising not to find expressions of it within the Resistance, whatever the political tendency. This is probably one of the factors—along with the desire not to offend public opinion, which was believed to be anti-Semitic or at least won over to the idea that a solution had to be found for the "Jewish problem"—that explains the extreme discretion with which Vichy's anti-Semitic policies were handled in BBC broadcasts in French, as well as in most of the underground newspapers.[11]

Summer 1942: the tipping point

Whereas he had not made the slightest allusion to the Vichy government's anti-Semitic policies in his previous reports, Jean Moulin wrote this in a telegram sent to London on 13 September 1942:

The situation is evolving rapidly in the Unoccupied Zone as Vichy takes increasingly strong measures of repression. Arrests of foreign Jews and their handover

---

Renée Poznanski and Léo Hamon (eds), "Avant les premières grandes rafles, les juifs à Paris sous l'Occupation (June 1940–April 1941)," *Cahiers de l'IHTP*, 22, Paris, CNRS, December 1992.

[10] Organisation Civile et Militaire (OCM), *Les Cahiers. Études pour une Révolution Française*, 1 June 1942, Paris, Bibliothèque Nationale (BN), Rés. G. 1470 (48), Jerusalem, Yad Vashem (YV), Pfi-91, reel 6, "Les minorités nationales," pp. 125 85.

[11] *L'Université Libre*, *La France Continue* and of course *Les Cahiers du Témoignage Chrétien* are exceptions in this regard. See Renée Poznanski, *Propagandes et Persécutions*, op. cit.

to the Germans and even more the odious measures taken with Jewish children, at first ignored by the public at large, are starting to raise awareness among the people. The position taken by a certain number of eminent French prelates and particularly the Archbishop of Toulouse, the Bishop of Montauban and Cardinal Gerlier has done much to fuel this movement of disapproval. Numerous acts of solidarity testify to the same state of mind. From all around, Catholic and Protestant organizations have devoted themselves to protecting Jewish children.[12]

It was this change he observed in public opinion—regarding not exclusion, but the mass arrests—that prompted Jean Moulin to mention anti-Semitism in action for the first time. He reported that the religious authorities had taken the lead in this wave of indignation, thus indirectly emphasizing a kind of support that was tantamount to legitimation. It was in the name of solidarity that he placed the assistance given to the most innocent of the victims, the Jewish children.

This change in a swathe of public opinion was also taken into account in London as well as in the underground papers, which for a few weeks strongly denounced the roundups of Jews. "The Yellow Star, emblem of the persecuted, the swastika, target for patriot bullets. That is the French youths' answer to the foul anti-Semitic campaign conducted by the Krauts and traitors," wrote *L'Avant-garde*, the Federation of Young Communists of France newspaper in July 1942. It urged all French people to demonstrate their sympathy for those who wore the yellow star, by all means possible.[13] The 16 July "St Bartholomew's Night" in Paris was denounced by *Libération* (Sud),[14] the horror of the "manhunt" that had spread into the Pétain-Laval zone was described six weeks later in an issue of the newspaper that sold 70,000 copies. The article stressed the separation of mothers from their children. "Why?" the author asked. "Because that's what Nazi Germany is," he answered.[15] "We were witness to the unthinkable: two-year-old children torn from their mother; near the

---

[12] Jean Moulin, Courrier de EX.20 [Moulin], no. 14, 13 September 1942, cited in Daniel Cordier, "La Résistance et les juifs," *Annales, ESC*, 48 (3), 1993, pp. 625–6.

[13] *L'Avant-garde*, 94, July 1942, Champigny, Archives du Musée de la Résistance et de la Déportation.

[14] "La question juive. Les crimes allemands," *Libération* (Sud), 16, 1 August 1942, BN, Rés. G. 1470 (211), YV Pfi-91, reel 10.

[15] "La chasse à l'homme," *Libération* (Sud), 18, 15 September 1942, BN Rés. G. 1470 (211), YV Pfi-91, reel 10.

Lyon train station we saw a baby shivering with fever taken away in blankets to a concentration camp. Luna-Park, Louis-le-Grand, garages everywhere are being converted into jails for these dangerous terrorists, Jewish children between the ages of two and fifteen," wrote François Berteval (Christian Pineau) in *Libération* (Nord).[16] "Reveal the horrors of Paris; show solidarity with the victims, shelter them, hide them, refuse to allow France to be soiled and help resistance movements combat the Nazi killers, their traitors and their lackeys," echoed a leaflet put out by *Franc-Tireur*.[17]

This is only a very small sample. Condemnation was unanimous and omnipresent. It built on pastorals sent out by bishops who from their pulpit had condemned the summer's persecutions. These letters were often published *in extenso* in all newspapers, including the Communist press.[18] From London, voices repeated similar condemnations.

The themes contained in these protests are worth examining in detail. Consider this passage from an article published in *Combat* in October 1942 under the title "The Jews, Our Brothers," which followed the "vehement protest" against the atrocity of the round-up of Jews:

Foreign Jews, leading the way of suffering for French Jewry and the French…are subject to Hitler's persecution and are enduring terrible suffering. Such suffering and persecution make them even dearer to us. All those who suffer at the hands of the Germans, be they Jewish or not, be they communist or not, are our brothers. Their torturers, French or German, one day will have to account for their acts.

This protest, this threat of punishment, is alas the only means by which we can presently show them our fraternal feelings. But it will be an opportunity for us to spell out *Combat's* position on the "Jewish problem." There is not a denominational Jewish problem because the Jewish religion should be honored like all

---

[16] François Berteval (Christian Pineau), "Antisémitisme," *Libération* (Nord), 17 July 1942, BN Rés. G. 1470 (210), YV Pfi-91, reel 10.

[17] Centre de Documentation Juive Contemporaine (CDJC), CCXIV-46, published as Appendix 3 in Jean-Pierre Lévy, with Dominique Veillon, *Mémoires d'un franc-tireur. Itinéraire d'un résistant, 1940–1944*, Brussels, Complexe-IHTP, 1998, p. 157.

[18] *Libération* (Sud) distributed 25,000 copies of the Archbishop of Toulouse's pastoral. All the other leaflets distributed between September and November 1942 were printed in anywhere between 50,000 and 200,000 copies. *Libération* (Sud), 23 November 1942, Rapport sur l'activité de propagande, Paris, Archives Nationales (AN), 3 AG 2/378.

other religions. There is not a racial Jewish problem, there is no question of 'Jewish blood' for the simple reason that the so-called Jewish "race" is as composite [...] as the French "race" or the German "race." There is of course a Jewish community. [...] This Jewish community is a constitutive element of the French national community by the same token as the other religious, cultural or regional communities. [...] There remains the problem of foreign Jews: this is not a Jewish problem, but a specific instance of the problem of foreigners.[19]

The victims, first of all. They are presented as the *"avant-garde"* that announces persecutions bound to affect all French people. In a program broadcast from London on 8 August 1942, André Labarthe also said:

Frenchmen! You won't let this happen. Form a chain of hearts around this rising scourge in which you all might perish: Jews, Bretons, Basques, people from the Lorraine, people from Auvergne, people of France, people with round faces, dark heads, each of you with your accents and your dialects. [...] France has always been the brunt of Nazi racist attacks. Flip through their newspapers and their books and you will see how they depict us. In *Mein Kampf*, we are called bastards, a cross between Negroes and subhumans.[20]

In an August 1942 leaflet entitled *"Contre l'immonde persecution"* ("Against the Hideous Persecution"), *Franc-Tireur* warned the French:

Beware! Don't go thinking that Hitler's brutes will treat you any better than the poor foreign Jews, the suffering Poles and the Czechs! Make no mistake: for the Germans, we French are 'foreign' slaves with regard to the master people, the only one worthy of living. Hitler will take our men, our women, our children, as he has done with other peoples and with the Jews. Don't go thinking, fellow Frenchman, that we will be treated any better than the others.[21]

Besides, the Jews' torturers were the Germans, Nazis, the occupier, enemies of France. "Those who suffer at the hands of the Germans... are our brothers," wrote Henri Frenay in *Combat*. That point was underscored everywhere. "Jewish question. German crimes," was the title of an article in *Libération* (Sud) that described the mid-July roundups in the capital.

---

[19] "Les juifs, nos frères...," *Combat*, 35, October 1942, BN Rés. G. 1470 (68), YV Pfi-91, reel 7.

[20] André Labarthe, 8 August 1942, BBC: French Transcripts, Institut d'Histoire du Temps Présent (IHTP), Microfilm B-76, August 1942.

[21] "Contre l'immonde persécution," published by *Le Franc-Tireur*, August 1942, reproduced in Jean-Pierre Lévy, with Dominique Veillon, *Mémoires d'un franc-tireur*, op. cit., p. 157.

Furthermore, the measures enacted against Jews were pure barbarism, "Hitlerian bestiality"; the particularly cruel fate of children torn from their parents was mentioned in all leaflets and articles. Appeal was thus made to the population's moral conscience. The occupying force and its accomplices were tarnishing France's conscience. They had already soiled the face of Paris and it was for moral reasons that it was essential to stand up to them. "Catholics, Protestants, freethinkers, a great hour of humanity has just rung," André Labarthe declared. It was a question of human solidarity. The support of certain religious leaders was therefore crucial. The issue was thus often shifted from the political register (persecution of Jews) to the humanitarian regime (Jewish children were brutally torn from their mothers' arms).

Lastly, to avoid any confusion and to indicate clearly that certain political sensibilities were kept in mind, reference was made to the "problem of the foreigners" (or sometimes the Jewish problem). Attempts were made to reformulate it, denying its existence or relevance at least for the time being. Such clarification took up two-thirds of the article in *Combat*. In the fall of 1942, the persecution of the Jews vanished from the columns of the underground press, never to return.

The indignation was real and the point here is not to diminish the scale of it. The fact nevertheless remains that for all resistance movements, it was part of a political struggle in which the French population constituted one of the main actors. All the reports on public opinion received in London—which were usually put out by internal resistance movements—played the same tune.

Beware of philo-Semitism!

This brief anthology is representative. One author of such reports wrote in February 1943:

> The persecution of the Jews has deeply wounded the human principles of the French. It has even at certain times made the Jews almost sympathetic. There is no denying, however, that there is a Jewish question: the present circumstances have even contributed to establishing it. Blum's ministry, bursting with Jewish elements, the entry into France of dozens of thousands of exotic Jews, has provoked a defensive reaction. There is no wish to see another such invasion recurring at any cost…[22]

---

[22] "Note sur l'état de l'opinion en France," February 1943, AN, 3 AG 2/334.

Another author wrote in March 1943:

> Persecutions targeting the Jews have caused ceaseless emotion and indignation among the population. Public opinion nevertheless harbors reservations about them. It is afraid that after the war, certain dominant professions (banking, radio broadcasting, journalism, film) will once again be invaded and to some extent controlled by Jews [...]. Certainly we don't want to see the Jews bullied or manhandled. We sincerely wish to see their rights and property restored to the greatest extent possible. But we don't want them to have supremacy in any field.[23]

And another of these reports, dated October 1943, declared:

> The French are revolted by the exceptional measures taken with regard to individuals. But they are sometimes pleased to unload part of their responsibility on the Jews and these bear the weight of Léon Blum's boisterous entourage, the excessive naturalizations, their rapid success, their intellectual value even. They are feared and envied, and many French don't want to see them reoccupy many of their former jobs.[24]

The same story in December 1943:

> The Frenchman is not an anti-Semite: he finds racial persecution distasteful. He is not cowardly exclaiming that the death of the Jews is necessary for us to find our place in life. But he curses the banks of Israel (while doing his best to copy them!) and would like to get rid of those ghetto escapees run out of everywhere and invading our country with no hope of assimilation.[25]

Not a single discordant note in these reports addressed to General de Gaulle. Everywhere reluctance was expressed at the idea of returning to the previous status quo; the abolition of anti-Semitic laws should not be either automatic or complete, it was argued; everywhere, the BBC was advised not to lament too much over the fate of the Jews; everywhere, there was concern about the detrimental effects of the philo-Semitism that Nazi cruelty to the Jews was bound to provoke. "Don't go thinking

---

Another version in May 1943: 3 May 1943, 5 811, source: Fouquet, Champigny, Archives du Musée de la Résistance et de la Déportation.
[23] "Rapport de Lavergne," on the basis of a report on Paris, 2 March 1943, AN, 3 AG 2/34.
[24] "Note sur l'opinion française en matière de politique intérieure au début de l'été 1943," drafted on 5 October 1943, AN, 3 AG 2/34.
[25] Information 8 December 1943, référence 13 426, Champigny, Archives du Musée de la Résistance et de la Déportation.

that the French population is prepared to erect Arcs de Triomphe for the return of the Jews,"[26] wrote one of these reporters in December 1943.

Rescue, a humanitarian cause?

It is thus easier to understand the difference between the reactions to the Vichy government's anti-Semitic laws that were supposed to solve the "Jewish problem" and to the cruelty of the brutal persecutions that struck imaginations and aroused compassion. Before the summer of 1942 (actually before the yellow star was instituted) and in the eyes of some, anti-Semitic legislation was to be judged in light of the answers it provided to a "problem." As long as Germany's victory seemed a sure thing and the French government seemed to enjoy a certain degree of autonomy, anti-Semitic policy was part of an overall policy of "national recovery" that people had faith in and a reality that was undisputed. That summer's roundups produced a radical change: anti-Semitic policy had turned into appalling persecution. The moral compromises to which the government had stooped shed new light on the price of collaboration. The Vichy government's legitimacy suffered the consequences; it diminished even further when an Allied victory was no longer doubted. All the measures it enacted and particularly those that bore a German stamp became tainted with illegitimacy.[27] After the roundups of summer 1942, the policy of hounding Jews was clearly linked to the occupier. Its concrete manifestations could no longer be disguised as a solution to the "Jewish problem."

As an alternative society gradually took shape in France, the Jews could more easily find in that society allies who would help them escape persecution. Individual compassion was not a new thing and it has always and everywhere been compatible with deep-seated anti-Semitism. But

---

[26] Source Paris, information 1 December 1943, received 9 February 1944, AN, F1a 3756.

[27] This relation between the passage of anti-Semitic laws and French attitudes to the Vichy regime is again confirmed in this gendarmerie report: "The stamping of the word "Jew" on Jewish ID cards took place without a hitch, but the population agrees that it is a persecutory measure and proof once again of German interference in government decisions. The public increasingly feels that the government only exists and can be maintained by subordination to German demands." (Summary of monthly reports of gendarmerie legion commanders, January 1943, AN, 3 AG 2/330.)

the indignation aroused that summer, as well as religious authority support, encouraged the multiplication of individual gestures of solidarity, which as a result took a collective turn. The change was palpable at all levels. Starting with the summer of 1942, the Jews, deserting the cities where they traditionally grouped, increasingly scattered into small villages. Certainly, there were particular places where they enjoyed the genuine and active complicity of the local population, particularly in regions with a Huguenot majority. But elsewhere, in many cases, they were able to live discreetly without being denounced as Jews by their neighbors. And as the gap widened between the population and the state, certain arms of the state lost their effectiveness, civil servants being obliged to take into account the population among which they operated. The same gendarmes who had gone without qualms to arrest Jews in 1942 thus managed a year later to give advance warning to those who were on their lists of potential victims, so that they would not appear to be doing the occupiers' dirty work. Jewish organization members involved in rescue operations were then able to find the complicity they needed among social organizations or religious institutions, or in the French administration to help them falsify identification papers or hide threatened Jewish adults and children.

Several factors thus converged to organize rescue of the Jews: moral rejection of proven horrors, mobilization of social and/or Jewish organizations, increasing delegitimation of the government, and adoption of these themes by religious authorities who dispensed legitimacy, particularly in the eyes of resistance groups. And so, in most cases, it was the humanitarian chord that was struck.

Indeed, when the religious authorities came out against the Jewish roundups, it was "in the name of humanity and Christian principles";[28] when voices of the Resistance roared their indignation, they often mentioned the police officers' horror at the atrocity of what was demanded of them. The fate that awaited children occupied the foreground. When Jewish and non-Jewish organizations asked individuals to help in the rescue efforts, they appealed to their compassion: by using "a discourse without adversaries,"[29] they increased their chances of being heard; by

---

[28] Title under which some of these protests were reported in *Combat*, 34, September 1942, BN Rés. G. 1470 (68), YV Pfi-91, reel 7.

[29] Philippe Juhem, "La légitimation de la cause humanitaire: un discours sans

focusing attention on the "individualized beneficiaries with attributes likely to stir emotion," particularly on the Jewish children, they neutralized ideological or political criticism that would have compromised the action itself. That helped to avert the controversy that any reference to the "Jewish problem," however indirect, might arouse.

The motives of many rescuers were thus indeed humanitarian. Yet, the rescue of the Jews had an eminently political meaning. At a time when official propaganda was striving to dehumanize them, the assertion that Jews were people, and that treating them as anything less was unacceptable, had political significance. At a time when the Jews were persecuted, any gesture of solidarity towards them, by foiling the aims pursued by the authorities, was in defiance of them. Furthermore, among rescue organizers, there were many social activists who from the start were involved in underground action against the Vichy government and occupiers. Historically, the rescue of Jews was in continuity with the assistance that had been given from the start of the occupation by minority groups and organizations to the various groups persecuted by the regime. "The spineless apathy everywhere evident during my first weeks in France was depressing. Apparently the only real effort to thwart the Nazis was being made by foreign organizations that were able to operate in very limited fields: emigration, restricted feeding, and amelioration of various kinds. Most of this work was done for refugees who had been driven into France from other countries."[30] Howard Brooks, a pastor for the Unitarian Service Committee, had crossed the Atlantic in spring 1941 and, in the course of a few months, shared the life and activity of these social activists to which he refers in a few lines written on his return to the United States in January 1942. Observing the early signs of resistance that "came out of limbo," Jean Rabaut also explained that one of "its early forms [had consisted in] assistance to foreigners persecuted on political or 'racial' grounds, rather often both at once."[31]

In September 1942, describing the rescue of ninety Jewish children by the Amitié Chrétienne ("Christian Friendship") organization in Vénissieux

---

adversaires," *Mots. Les Langages du Politique*, 65, March 2001, pp. 9–26. I would like to thank Claire Andrieu for having drawn my attention to this article.

[30] Howard L Brooks, *Prisoners of Hope. Report on a Mission*, New York, B.L. Fischer, 1942, p. 59.

[31] Jean Rabaut, *Tout est possible! Les "gauchistes français," 1929–1944*, Paris, Denoël-Gonthier, 1974, p. 345.

as well as the aid given to the Jews by the inhabitants of Chambon-sur-Lignon, Donald Lowrie (YMCA) wrote in one of his reports:

As the handbills indicate, this public emotion may take political form. It is too early to predict results in this direction, but it must be noted that for the first time since the Armistice, deep public feeling has united all the decent elements in France on a question of a moral rather than a political nature. At the same time, this feeling gives each one something he can do, and the doing, i.e. aid to hunted Jews involves resistance to the authorities at Vichy.[32]

The political significance of rescuing Jews was thus well perceived. At least one of its political dimensions was clear: the form of resistance to Vichy or the occupying force involved in helping the Jews.

The implication of these "humanitarian" motives to escape the shadow of the "Jewish problem" for the nature of rescue operations remains to be explored. They determined a chronological framework: not until visible persecutions exceeded a certain degree of horror did action and reaction come about. Before that, only specialized social organizations such as Amitié Chrétienne and CIMADE or Jewish organizations such as the Amelot Committee expressed indignation about the fate of the Jews. They put on hold political prejudices, which lost their priority without entirely disappearing, because nothing was done by the political elites to make them disappear. They designated potential rescuers. Indeed, even after the shock of summer 1942, political organizations—underground parties and movements—deliberately avoided getting actively involved. The "Fight against Deportation" of French workers deported into forced labor under the STO was a political combat; the secret support for solidarity actions toward the persecuted Jewish population was a humanitarian issue. On the eve of Liberation, the French administration in Algiers, approached about six Jewish children rescued from France by the World Jewish Congress, expressed its gratitude to this organization for "[its] humanitarian action."[33]

Lastly, focus on humanitarian motivations weighed heavily on the historiographic developments. First of all on the historiography of the Resis-

---

[32] Geneva, 17 September 1942, Donald Lowrie to Tracy Strong, cited in Jack Sutters (ed.), *American Friends Service Committee, Philadelphia*, volume 2: *1940–1945*, Archives of the Holocaust, New York and London, Garland Publishing, 1990, pp. 337–9, document no. 357.

[33] MAE, Guerre 1939–1945, 1 037, 212, Algiers, 22 August 1944, Diplofrance in Lisbon.

tance, which long disregarded the activity of rescuing Jews, but not only on that. In a typological essay on the Resistance drawn up in 1986, François Bédarida[34] describes the aid given to victims of oppression and persecution as humanitarian resistance. The rescue of the Jews naturally fell into this category. That amounted to making historiographic use of a term from the war period without the slightest critical attention to its implications and connotations, particularly as regards the contours of rescue. Moreover, by focusing attention on the rescuers' motives[35] and the results of persecution, this "humanitarian" perspective transforms the victim into a passive object of a history that was no longer his own, while sidelining cooperation between Jews and non-Jews in organizing rescues. Indeed, a dichotomy between rescuers and victims leads to minimizing the role of Jews involved in organizing rescues. Or else it relegates to a separate chapter the rescue efforts organized by activists from certain Jewish organizations whose acts were surely not motivated only by empathy for anonymous victims. For some of them, it had been preceded by social welfare action in Jewish circles, whereas for others, it flowed from a political commitment, either Bundist (Jewish Socialists) or Zionist. The history of the rescue of the Jews must bring into the same analysis the history of the Jews—as victims and as resistance fighters—and the history of French society on the whole. It constitutes a chapter in the history of relations between Jews and non-Jews in France, a complex chapter of cultural and social history that blends together often contradictory elements.

---

[34] François Bédarida, "L'histoire de la Résistance, lectures d'hier, chantiers de demain," *Vingtième Siècle. Revue d'Histoire*, 11, July-September 1986, pp. 75–89.

[35] To such an extent that "humanitarian resistance," and "particularly the rescue of hunted Jews," has been ranked as a "spiritual experience" by certain Christians, on a par with the "apostolic mission to the STO labor conscripts working in Germany by secret priests and young laymen" or the spiritual experience some went through in prison—"between interrogations and torture." Bernard Comte, *L'Honneur et la Conscience. Catholiques français en résistance, 1940–1944*, Paris, Les Éditions de l'Atelier, 1998, p. 15.

6

WHO DARED TO RESCUE JEWS, AND WHY?

Nechama Tec

During World War II, under the German occupation of Europe, the appearance of rescuers of Jews signaled opposition to the German policies of Jewish annihilation. Since the German occupiers targeted all Jews for murder, the rescuing of Jews was a humane response to German assaults. Protection of Jews automatically endangered the lives of rescuers and often their families as well. Nevertheless, with time, each European country had some people who ignored these threats and assumed the role of rescuers of Jews.

Concentrating on various kinds of rescuers of Jews, this paper explores several interrelated issues: What kinds of rescuers of Jews are most frequently examined in the Holocaust literature? What characteristics do the various types of rescuers share? Considering how small the number of rescuers of Jews was, why does interest in them continue to grow?

Most of the Holocaust publications on rescuing Jews refer to Gentiles who selflessly and altruistically risked their lives to save Jews. A substantial part of this research is more specifically based on those Gentile rescuers who were officially recognized by Yad Vashem as "the Righteous Among the Nations of the World."[1] To qualify for such a Yad Vashem

---

[1] Examples of such titles are Gay Block and Malka Drucker, *Rescuers*, New York: Holmes & Meier Publishers, Inc., 1992; Eva Fogelman, *Conscience and Courage*, New York, Doubleday, 1994; Martin Gilbert, *The Righteous: The Unsung Heroes*

award the actions performed by these Gentiles had to involve "extending help in saving a life; endangering one's life; absence of reward, monetary and otherwise; and similar considerations which make the rescuers' deeds stand out above and beyond what can be termed ordinary help." These criteria, to some extent ambiguous, leave little doubt that those who saved Jews solely because of payment do not fit into the definition of "Righteous Gentiles."[2]

It is generally agreed that many more of the altruistic Gentile rescuers deserve a Yad Vashem award than have obtained it. A wide range of factors, some known and some unknown, interfere in the issuing of this award. My research on altruistic Gentile rescuers of Jews does not distinguish between those who did and did not receive the Yad Vashem title of "Righteous." What characteristics did the altruistic Gentile rescuers of Jews share? What prompted these rescuers to risk their lives for Jews who were frequently defined as "Christ killers"?[3]

When altruistic Polish rescuers were systematically examined, in terms of social class, level of education, type of political involvement, degree of anti-Semitism, extent of religious commitment and friendship with Jews, they proved to be a socially heterogeneous group. None of the comparisons in terms of those attributes had predicted altruistic rescue. Only

---

of the Holocaust, Basingstoke, Macmillan, 2003; Phillip Hallie, *Lest Innocent Blood Be Shed*, New York, Harper and Row, 1979; Peter Hellman, *Avenue of the Righteous*, New York, Atheneum, 1980; Samuel P. Oliner and Pearl M. Oliner, *The Altruistic Personality*, New York, The Free Press, 1988; Kazimierz Iranek-Osmecki, *He Who Saves One Life*, New York, Crown Publishers, 1971; Mordechai Paldiel, *The Path of the Righteous: Gentile Rescuers of Jews During the Holocaust*, Hoboken, NJ, KTAV,/JFCR/ADL, 1993; Michael Phayer and Eva Fleischner, *Cries in the Night, Women who Challenged the Holocaust*, Kansas City, Sheed & Ward, 1997; Alexander Ramati, *The Assisi Underground: The Priests Who Rescued Jews*, New York, Stein & Day, 1978; Nechama Tec, *When Light Pierced the Darkness: Christian Rescue of Jews in Nazi Occupied Poland*, New York, Oxford University Press, 1986.

[2] Nechama Tec, op. cit., pp. 3–4.

[3] To be consistent, I nevertheless used only fictitious names in this book. The evidence for this discussion is based on 189 Gentile Poles who selflessly rescued Jews and 309 Jewish survivors who survived by passing through or hiding in the forbidden Christian world. Part of this comes from various archival collections. Another part of this information comes my personal in-depth interviews with Gentile rescuers and Jewish survivors.

when these rescuers were reexamined at a closer range, in terms of their life styles and special characteristics, did the pieces of the puzzle fall into place, yielding a cluster of six interrelated characteristics and conditions, suggesting a set of interrelated hypotheses.

I identify one of these basic shared characteristics as individuality or separateness. That is, these rescuers did not quite fit into their social environments—a condition they were often unaware of. Their individuality appears under a variety of guises, in turn related to other shared conditions and motivations. Outsiders are, by definition, on the periphery of their communities. Whether they are or are not aware of it, they experience fewer social constraints. With fewer social controls comes greater independence. Freedom from social constraints and independence promote opportunities to act in accordance with personal values and moral precepts, even when these are in opposition to societal expectations.

The Gentile rescuers in my research spoke rarely about their individuality or separateness. But they had no trouble talking about their self-reliance and their need to follow personal inclinations and values. Nearly all of them saw themselves as independent (98 per cent). Jewish survivors also described their protectors as independent and as being motivated by special personal values. Besides, a quality often mentioned in the testimonies and memoirs of survivors, one that comes close to independence, was the rescuers' courage. The overwhelming majority (85 per cent) of Jewish survivors described their protectors as courageous.

With the rescuers' view of themselves as independent came the idea that they were propelled by moral values that did not depend on the support and approval by others. Rather they relied on their own self-approval. Again and again, they repeated that they had to be at peace with themselves and with their own ideas of what was right or wrong.

Closely related to the rescuers' moral convictions and values was their enduring commitment to protect the needy. This commitment was expressed in a wide range of charitable acts that extended over long periods of time. Much of the evidence about the rescuers' selfless acts came from survivors who described their protectors as good-natured and as people whose efforts on behalf of the needy were long-lasting. Risking their lives for Jews fitted into a system of values and behavior that involved helping the weak and the dependent.

This analogy, however, has built-in limitations. Most disinterested actions on behalf of others may involve inconvenience, even extreme inconvenience, but only rarely do such acts require the ultimate sacrifice, of one's life. Yet, for these rescuers, during the war, there was a convergence between historical events demanding the ultimate self-sacrifice and their already established habits of helping others. We tend to take our repetitive actions for granted. What we take for granted we accept and rarely analyze or wonder about. In fact, the more firmly established patterns of behavior are, the less likely we are to think about them. In a real sense, constant pressure of and familiarity with ideas and actions does not mean that we know or understand them. On the contrary, when customary patterns are accepted and taken for granted, this often impedes rather than promotes understanding.

In addition, what we are accustomed to repeat we do not see as extraordinary, no matter how exceptional it may seem to others. And so, the rescuers' past history of helping the needy might have been in part responsible for their modest appraisal of their life threatening actions. This modest appraisal was expressed in a variety of ways. Two-thirds of the rescuers saw their protection of Jews as a natural reaction to human suffering and almost a third insisted that saving lives was nothing exceptional. In contrast barely 3 per cent felt that their saving of Jews was extraordinary.

Given these matter-of-fact perceptions of rescue, it is not surprising that help often began in a spontaneous, unpremeditated way, either gradually or suddenly. More than three-quarters of the Jewish survivors reported that their rescue happened without prior preparation. When asked why they had saved Jews, the rescuers overwhelmingly emphasized that they responded to the persecution and the suffering of victims and not to their Jewishness. What compelled them to act was the persecution, the unjust treatment, and not who the victims were.

This ability to disregard all attributes of the needy, except their helplessness and dependence, I refer to as universalistic perceptions. Evidence for the presence of these perceptions comes from a variety of sources. The majority of these rescuers (95 per cent) felt that they were prompted to help by Jewish neediness. This is in sharp contrast to the 26 per cent who claimed to rescue because it was a Christian duty, or the 52 per cent who described rescue as an act of political opposition.

The compelling moral force behind the rescuing of Jews, the universal insistence that what mattered was the victims' position of dependence and their unjust persecution, combined to make such actions universalistic. In a sense it was a moral force that motivated the rescuers, independently of personal likes and dislikes. Some were aware that to help the needy Jews, one did not have to like them.

Embedded in the preceding discussion of altruistic rescue and rescuers are six interrelated, shared characteristics and conditions. Together they provide a theoretical explanation of altruistic rescue, suggesting also a profile of these rescuers. A look at rescuers from other countries shows that these theoretical explanations apply to them as well. Briefly these shared characteristics and motivations are: (1) individuality or separateness, which means that they did not quite fit into their respective social environments; (2) independence or self-reliance to act in accordance with personal convictions, regardless of how these were viewed by others; (3) broad commitments to stand up for the needy and an enduring history of performing charitable acts; (4) a tendency to perceive aid to Jews in a matter-of-fact, unassuming way, with consistent denials of heroic or extraordinary qualities of rescue; (5) unpremeditated, unplanned start of rescue, that is, rescue which was extended gradually or suddenly, even impulsively; and (6) universalistic perceptions about the Jews. Rather than seeing Jews in those they were about to protect, they saw them as people totally dependent on aid from others. Such perceptions come with an ability to disregard all attributes except those expressing extreme suffering and need.[4]

These altruistic Gentile rescuers of Jews do not exhaust all categories of rescuers. The qualitative Holocaust evidence suggests other kinds of rescuers. During one of my interviews with a survivor, I asked whether she was grateful to the man who had saved her. She answered with a question: "Why should I be grateful? ...He loved money...He did it only for money, besides every week he kept raising the price...and threatened that if the war would drag on, he would not keep me."[5]

This exchange alerted me to a different kind of rescuer. I realized that most Jewish survivors whose protection had depended on payment shared negative attitudes about their Gentile rescuers. Moreover, views about rescue for profit spilled over into other situations. Some who had altruistically protected Jews were insulted when others suspected that their

---

[4] Nechama Tec, op. cit., pp. 150–83. These discussions rely on Chapter 10.

[5] Ibid., p. 87. My personal experiences show what it meant to live with paid helpers. See: Nechama Tec, *Dry Tears: The Story of a Lost Childhood*, New York, Oxford University Press, 2004.

protection of Jews was motivated by a desire for profit. One rescuer, who was recognized as a "Righteous among the Nations," complained: "For many years, I was accused of having saved Jews for money. These ideas were like a curse hanging over me. There was no way in which I could have made them (the accusers) change their minds…"

These consistently negative attitudes about rescuers whose basic motivation for saving Jews was profit explain why the Holocaust literature includes no direct evidence from these "profit" rescuers. Nor did such rescuers write any wartime memoirs about their aid to Jews. Perhaps they were embarrassed to admit that they made a business out of saving lives. Information about their wartime protection of Jews comes only indirectly, from Jews who were protected for profit.

How should this kind of Gentile rescuer be defined? All these profit-seeking individuals risked their lives when saving Jews, just as the altruistic rescuers did. Nevertheless, in significant ways, they do not fit into the category of those who selflessly protected Jews. I refer to them as "paid helpers" rather than rescuers. Paid helpers are individuals whose aid to Jews was motivated *mainly* by financial gain. Excluded from this category are those who might have accepted payment but for whom payment was neither the only nor the main reason for rescuing Jews. What do we know about the paid helpers?

In a sample of over 300 Jews who benefited from the protection of Gentiles, only a minority of 16 per cent was protected by Gentiles whose main reason for helping was profit. Jews who describe their experiences with paid helpers report practices involving a range of mistreatment: demands for higher payment, deliberate starvation, threats to throw them out, even murder.[6]

Why did the paid helpers behave so differently from the altruistic rescuers? Answers are at once speculative and tempting. Unlike human life, money as a means to an end is rational and quantitative, leaving hardly room for passionate emotions.[7] Free of feelings, monetary transactions are impersonal arrangements. Life, on the other hand, is an emotional,

[6] Nechama Tec, *When Light…*, op. cit., pp. 87–98. A vivid example of abuse and murder by a paid helper is provided by Thomas (Toivi) Blatt, *From the Ashes of Sobibor*, Evanston, Northwestern University Press, 1997, pp. 181–7.

[7] S.P. Altmann, "Simmel's Philosophy of Money," *American Journal of Sociology* 9, 1903, pp. 46–68; Georg Simmel, *The Philosophy of Money*, Boston, Routledge & Kegan Paul, 1978.

most highly valued entity. Risking and sacrificing one's life calls for a readiness to give up what is deeply cherished. Because we tend to separate passion from rationality, we object when rational and emotional forces intrude upon each other. Given the rational nature of money, to use it as a basis for emotionally valuable parts of life is a travesty, denying the essential quality of life. In as much as life-threatening actions involve a high level of emotionality, to use money as a reason for life threatening actions undermines the very value and essence of life.

In some ways paid helpers were caught in a vicious circle. With the economic improvement that came with the Jewish presence, reasons for sheltering them disappeared. Yet it was difficult and dangerous for paid helpers to disengage themselves from this relationship. Such a disengagement was life-threatening. Had the Jew revealed that the paid helper offered him protection, then both the Jew and the helper were equally guilty of a crime. In the absence of moral commitments to rescue, there was hardly anything that could prevent these paid helpers from feeling anxious and trapped. Some reacted by asking the Jews to leave, some denounced them, some murdered them, and some continued to mistreat them. Ill-treatment might have served as an outlet, a way of venting their pent-up frustrations and disappointments.

The reactions of these paid helpers were not necessarily homogenous. Moreover, information about them is based only on the survivors' accounts, with built-in limitations. How many Jews were protected mainly for commercial reasons and how many were betrayed or murdered by those whom they paid remains a mystery. On the other hand, in the few cases where a warm relationship developed, it might have served as a buffer against negative reactions on the part of these paid helpers. Still, we know that the small proportion of Jews who were saved exclusively for money suffered because both they and those willing to risk their lives for payment were soon caught in their own cycle of dangers, frustrations, and helplessness. In this life-threatening and unstable situation, money could serve only as a transient, inadequate incentive—an incentive that soon denied its own significance.[8]

Yet another kind of rescuer was suggested to me by my research into Gentile Polish rescuers. It was unexpected and intriguing to find rescuing of Jews by avid Polish anti Semites. This theme had occasionally surfaced

---

[8] Nechama Tec, *When Light…*, op. cit., p. 97.

in the course of my research without directing me to a careful study on the subject.⁹ Who were these anti-Semitic rescuers of Jews and what does the rescuing of Jews by anti-Semites mean? I define anti-Semitic rescuers of Jews as individuals who through their actions and/or ideology had the reputation of anti-Semites, and who were aware of this image. They were overt anti-Semites. One of them, Jan Mosdorf, had caught the imagination of many who had touched on the subject; some survivors were interested in Jan Mosdorf's help to Jews.

Mosdorf came from a socially prominent family. He was a devout Catholic, a national leader of the extreme right (ONR), and a distinguished lawyer. Mosdorf's reputation as an anti-Semite was well known. He was also politically active, both before and during the war. His patriotism and nationalism precluded cooperation with the Germans. Threatened by Mosdorf's political influence and independence, the Germans sent him to Auschwitz. He participated in the camp's underground and became known for his help not only to Gentile Poles, but also to Jews. Unexpected as his aid to Jews was, it led to many exaggerated claims. In the end, a Polish inmate denounced Mosdorf as a Communist and a Jewish sympathizer. Mosdorf was promptly executed.

Among the anti-Semitic Poles who stood up for Jews, the name of Leon Nowodworski is also frequently mentioned. Before the war, as the dean of the Council of Lawyers, he supported the exclusion of Jews from the legal profession. Like Mosdorf, Nowodworski came from an upper-class family. He was also an influential and active member of the highly anti-Semitic National Democratic Party. Yet, during the war, despite his overt anti-Semitism, he openly disobeyed a Nazi order and refused to dismiss Jews from the bar, arguing that Poles would deal with the Jewish question later on in a free Poland. For his disobedience, he was sent to prison.

I have interviewed Jan Dobraszynski, a well-known writer, who made his anti-Jewish views known through his publications. A conservative and a devout Catholic, he looked with disfavor on the Jewish presence in Poland. Nevertheless, as a director of the Warsaw's Municipality's social welfare division, he had illegally placed 300 Jewish children in orphanages and convents by signing orders for their acceptance.[10]

---

[9] Ibid., p. 99.
[10] Ibid., pp. 100–2. Bender and Krakowski (eds), *The Encyclopedia of the Righteous Among the Nations, Poland*, Yad Vashem, Jerusalem, 2004, p. 176.

While other prominent anti-Semitic Poles have also been identified as rescuers of Jews, together they constitute a small and select group. The same few names appear again and again.

Resemblances among these few anti-Semitic rescuers suggest some tentative conclusions. Most of them were devout Catholics; all were highly nationalistic, intellectual, and socially prominent. It is probably no coincidence that most of them were socially prominent and highly intellectual. Nor is it an accident that most were devout Catholics. The Catholic Church asks of its followers a reassessment of their values. This option, however, is more likely open to intellectual Catholics. Rather than follow the religious precepts in a narrow, concrete way, these anti-Semitic, intellectual rescuers had reflected on the meanings and implications of their anti-Semitism. As devout Catholics and intellectuals some of them saw the connection between their anti-Semitism and the devastating persecution of the Jewish people. Some felt responsible for the Jewish suffering, concluding that their personal anti-Semitism was partly responsible for the injustices that were committed against the Jewish people. As devout Catholics they had to repent for their sins. For a few, the redemption led to protection of Jews. In view of the many forces that had to be overcome in the process of saving Jews, it is not surprising that the Polish rescuers who were overt anti-Semites were a rare and small group. Anti-Semitic rescuers remain an intriguing, hardly noticed kind of rescuers.

In addition to the kinds of rescuers of Jews mentioned, the Holocaust literature contains scattered references to Jews who took on the role of selfless rescuers. I became aware of Jewish rescuers by chance, when I examined Oswald Rufeisen's testimony. In 1939, Oswald was a Jewish youth of seventeen. He survived by pretending to be half Polish and half German. Through an unusual set of circumstances, he became an interpreter and secretary to the head of a German gendarmerie, in Mir, a small town in Western Belorussia. With the acceptance of this position came a determination to help all prospective victims of the Nazis. Eventually, Oswald took advantage of opportunities offered by his official position and saved an entire Belorussian village, a large but unknown number of Russian POWs, partisans, and hundreds of Jews. He armed Jews in the Mir ghetto and arranged a ghetto breakout. As a result 305 ghetto inmates escaped into the surrounding forests; most of them survived the war.[11] Rufeisen's war-

---

[11] Nechama Tec, *Oswald Rufeisen: The Life of Oswald Rufeisen*, New York, Oxford University Press, 1990.

time history shows that he was at once a survivor and a rescuer. My subsequent study of Rufeisen alerted me to the existence of Jewish rescuers. This research led to my additional research on Jewish rescue of Jews.[12] Examining partisan groups in forested areas like those of Western Belorussia I came upon a Jewish detachment, the Bielski partisans. The history of the Bielski group began in these inaccessible forests in 1942, with forty Jews who formally organized a partisan detachment. The charismatic Tuvia Bielski, a former Jewish peasant, became the group's commander. Tuvia introduced an open door policy that admitted all Jews regardless of who they were. Influenced in part by a war ideology of the forest, the Bielski unit focused on mutual cooperation, on rescue and survival. With time this group became obsessed with the idea of rescuing Jews, particularly those who had no way to find shelter. This unit participated in military ventures because it had to, as this was the accepted way, not because it wanted to. In 1944 when the Soviets recaptured the area, the Bielski detachment numbered more than 1,200 Jews. Most of them were women, older people, and children, precisely those whom no one in the forest wanted. Gradually, I realized that many more Jews whose lives I had studied previously had participated in different kinds of rescue. Earlier, I had had no idea of Jewish rescuers.

Why this oversight? Was my conceptual blindness caused by the idea that self-preservation is the most basic human drive—even though I knew that altruistic Gentile rescuers were risking their lives to save Jews and that through these actions they were defying the principle of self-preservation? Only when I directly came upon Jewish rescuers did my awareness about them emerge. I saw clearly that some survivors I had already studied engaged in rescue. Voices pointing to research into Jewish rescuers had been heard,[13] but as yet, they did not lead to systematic research into Jewish rescuers.

Why this inattention? Exploration of this subject must begin with an understanding of the reasons for the initial inattention to it. Under the

---

[12] Nechama Tec, *Defiance: The Bielski Partisans*, New York, Oxford University Press, 1993.

[13] Marion Pritchard, "Circles of Caring: An Insider's View," *Dimensions: A Journal of Holocaust Studies*, Vol. 5, No. 3, 1990; Marion Pritchard, "Rescue and Resistance in the Netherlands," in John Michalczyk, *Resisters, Rescuers and Refugees. Historical and Ethical Issues*, Lanham, MD, Rowman & Littlefield Publ., pp. 193–8.

German occupation, among the different categories of persecuted groups, the Jews were targeted for total annihilation. Deprived of all rights, pushed into most dependent and humiliating positions, Jews were easily seen as victims even before their death. And because we believe in the supremacy of self-preservation, we assume that when faced with a cruel death, people concentrate on their own survival rather than on the survival of others. Closely connected to this expectation is the reality that under the occupation Jews' helplessness and humiliation overshadowed all of their other attributes. Some altruistic Gentile rescuers whom I studied argued that in the Jews they helped they saw only haunted and persecuted human beings, and it was their suffering that motivated them to engage in rescue. Often, Gentile rescuers would add that because the Jews were in the worst predicament they could not even help themselves.[14] I must have tacitly accepted the implied assertion that those who face overpowering threats are incapable of helping themselves and, by extension, of offering aid to others.

Common sense and some available facts seem to justify such conclusions. Exposed to extreme dangers people may be paralyzed into inaction. Whether this occurs depends in part on the extent to which people define a situation as hopeless. Fighting for oneself and for others requires hope. Hope wanes with grave dangers. Danger and no hope often add up to no struggle. And so, it is not uncommon for individuals who have been sentenced to death to give up hope. Most heroic revolutionaries when captured have been known to go to their execution without a struggle.[15]

Perhaps my initial insensitivity to Jewish rescuers was based on the idea that one could not be a victim and a rescuer at the same time. Was I agreeing with the Gentile rescuers I studied, who felt that, as victims, the Jews could not even help themselves?

In view of the Jews' plight, this assumption makes sense; they were made powerless, and were deprived of all options. The expectation that the Jews could not act on anyone's behalf makes sense. Still, theoretically, and under special circumstances, a victim may also be a rescuer. Extreme

---

[14] Nechama Tec, *When Light…*, op. cit, One of the rescuers, Dr Estowski, insisted that, "After all, a Pole could somehow help himself, but the Jew was in a more horrible situation and could in no way help himself." p. 177.

[15] A vivid example of this is found in Hersh Smolar, *The Minsk Ghetto*, New York, Holocaust Library, 1989. Smolar describes a planned revolt by Russian prisoners of war and how its leaders were slaughtered by the Germans, pp. 61–3.

situations lead to extreme reactions. At this point I can only suggest the need to further study Jews who assumed the roles of rescuers.

Finally, why, when faced with many unanswered questions about rescue and rescuers, does interest this area continue to grow?

It is comforting to know that there were some people, no matter how few, who were willing to sacrifice their lives and interfered with the murderous assaults against a people whose only sin was having been born Jewish. Thus, the mere presence of altruistic rescuers suggests that a criminal and murderous political system could not extinguish all expressions of mutual caring and basic goodness.

Jan Karski, a "Righteous among the Nations," a World War II hero, an emissary for the Polish underground and the Polish Government in Exile, justified our continuous interest in rescue. Karski was convinced that even though in wartime Europe those who murdered Jews by far outnumbered those who saved them, it is counterproductive to concentrate only on the murderers of Jews and ignore the minority that saved them. Karski felt that at least for two reasons we cannot ignore the few who rescued Jews. First, it would be incorrect to forget the rescuers who were a morally significant part of history. This history shows that thousands of Gentiles tried to save Jews and were ready to die for them: some did. Second, to deny altruistic rescuing of Jews, we perpetuate the idea that "everybody hates the Jews." Not everyone hates the Jews. Noble, Gentile rescuers felt that Jews were valuable enough to risk their lives for them. To ignore these bright glimmers of light would be historically incorrect and psychologically unhealthy.[16] The very presence, and the study, of such rescuers undermines anti-Semitism.

---

[16] Jan Karski, Personal Interview, by phone, December 1999. Nechama Tec, "A Glimmer of Light," in C. Rittner, S. Smith and I. Steinfeldt (eds), *The Holocaust and the Christian World*, Beth Shalom Holocaust Memorial Centre and Yad Vashem, 2000, pp. 150–5.

7

RESCUE AND SELF-INTEREST
PROTECTING PROPERTY TO SAVE PEOPLE?

Florent Le Bot

What situations are conducive to rescuing people? By asking the question, the author does not at all doubt that human qualities specific to rescuers play an unknown but very real part in carrying out rescue operations. However, the circumstances are also worthy of attention. The context of economic Aryanization in France between 1940 and 1944, that is, confiscation of Jewish property—would appear to be an acceptable vantage point in this regard. About 50,000 buildings and companies were among the property seized, either entirely—essentially via liquidation or sale—or incompletely, having been managed by an *administrateur provisoire* (AP), a government-appointed trustee. Thousands of people, trustees, civil servants, actors in economic circles (employer organization members or others), tenderers, buyers, solicitors, bankers, insurance agents, etc., took part in the process. This installed a lasting relationship between actors and victims. The former wound up being potentially among the best informed about the fate of the latter—if not of the full extremity of its horror, at least of some of its aspects. They found themselves placed in a situation that was conducive to raising awareness, which could lead to rescue, even if, depending on the case, obedience to authority, the routine of the task, covetousness and, for some of them—though in what proportion and to what extent will never be known—anti-Semitism usually got the better of them.

Anti-Semitic measures: genocide and spoliation

It must be remembered that economic Aryanization, on the one hand, and the arrests and deportations on the other did not form a political unity; the two processes were not organized in the same way by the German and French authorities and did not follow the same timetable. Yet, the common dimension of anti-Semitism proves not to be the sole point of intersection between the two phenomena.

Those involved in implementing Aryanization were forced to be aware of and take into consideration the arrest, internment and even deportation of their victims. Many trustee reports after 16 and 17 July 1942 (the Vélodrome d'Hiver Roundup) therefore mentioned such facts. Some well-informed or attentive trustees knew what actually happened. Others spoke merely of "disappearance(s)" or even "escape(s)." The arrests in fact had begun well before summer 1942, and the trustee of a little leather goods workshop reported that "since 20 August 1941, [the owner] has been interned in the Drancy camp."[1]

To what extent did the trustees understand at the time that their activity was part of a more overall anti-Semitic policy that would have tragic consequences? Those who clung to the fiction of trusteeship as a strictly economic function seem not to have wanted to admit any of this. The archives at any event let no glimmer of awareness shine through. For others, the combination of these measures did not seem to weigh on their conscience. For instance, one trustee complained to his regulatory authority about the shortcomings in the spoliation system:

"[…] In the Prado Passage, at n° 25 there is a shop, D. Leather Goods, administered by Mr. M. […]. Appointed last June, Mr M. has come to the shop only twice, according to D.'s employee. It is still Mrs. D. who has free disposal of the merchandise and the cash register. Since news of the arrest of a certain number of Jews has appeared in the papers, since still in relation with the customers, Mrs. D. comes a little more infrequently, but remains the boss, which angers Jews [sic] for whom government trustees have faithfully fulfilled their mission."[2]

---

[1] French National Archives (Archives Nationales—AN hereafter), AJ^{38}2114 (6778), trustee report, 15 May 1942. 20 August 1941 was the date of the second wave of mass arrests of Jews, the first having taken place on 14 May 1941.

[2] AN, AJ^{38}2233 (10627), Letter from Eugène B. to the Trustee Control Service, 6 October 1941.

A certain number of trustees brandished the threat of internment, considering that the person for whom they were administering was not being cooperative:

"Sir,
Please note that in fulfillment of the instructions that I have received from the Service de Contrôle des Administrateurs Provisoires [SCAP] and by virtue of the powers vested in me, I have decided to close your business until such time as business can be reopened, limiting it to the repair of shoes. Consequently, you should make all of the following arrangements [...]. If you do not comply with these instructions, I shall be forced to give your name to the authorities, requesting sanctions which may go as far as internment."[3]

Trustees, whoever they were and whatever their attitude or relationship to the person whose affairs they managed, were in a position of strength by virtue of the economic Aryanization policy as well as the context of the "manhunt." A shoemaker, Israël Z., was incarcerated in the Santé prison in 1941. He seems to have been denounced by his trustee for concealing goods. Acquitted of this charge, he was not, however, released, and ended up being interned successively in the Voves and Châteaubriant (Loire-Inférieure) camps, before being transferred to Drancy. On 11 November 1942, Israël Z. was deported by convoy number 45 to Auschwitz, never to return.

The two courses of action, against property and against people, converged to identify and fragilize both, especially small businesses in the most working-class circles: people who could no longer work to meet their most basic needs ended up being dependent on charity organizations, easy prey for the roundups. Businesses whose main capital was an owner's skills were therefore instantly liquidated, with no solution being envisaged to maintain the activity by transforming the owner into a manufacturer or by selling it. Thus the trustee of a small glove manufacturer reported that it was impossible to recategorize the person whose business he managed as a craftsmen, owing to his internment.[4]

It should be pointed out that source documents on the spoliations prove to be very laconic as regards internments and deportations. The victims were to a large extent erased from them. However, the chronologies of the conflict (from 1943, purchase offers were increasingly rare)

[3] AN, AJ^{38}2113 (6748), Letter from André J. to Mr. D., 7 April 1941.
[4] AN, AJ^{38}2233 (9796), report of 24 August 1943.

and anti-Semitic policy (measures relating to the "final solution" starting in 1942) converge to make a large number of pieces of property and people disappear. In 164 of the some 400 files that this author consulted regarding the leather and pelt industry in the Department of the Seine, there are reports of owners who were interned, deported or disappeared in conditions such that it seems likely that arrest was made with a view to deportation. We thus reach a total of 178 people deported which, compared to the 583 victims of spoliation identified (still pertaining to the present sample), gives a ratio of 30 per cent deported. André Kaspi mentions that 23 per cent of the Jews in France were deported and that among them 68 per cent were foreigners.[5] The large proportion of deported in the sample study compared with the total of Jews in France can probably be explained by an over-representation of foreigners in this sample.[6]

During the restitution era, the forms returned to Professor Émile Terroine, head of the French Department for Restitution of Property of Victims of the Legislation and Spoliation Measures, with the phrase "no forwarding address," "unknown at this address," also serve as indications of deportation. Some are more precise, marked "deported." The following note is rather unusual: "M. and Mme P., during the year 1941, being Jewish, were sent back to their country in Russia by the Germans. Since that time, no news."[7] The end of the Occupation obviously did not mean the end of ignorance or prejudice.

Historical research reveals that the Commissariat-General for Jewish Questions (CGQJ), despite its ambition to control the full range of anti-Semitic policies over the entire French territory, was gradually divested of arrest, internment and deportation measures. The Police for Jewish Questions (PQJ) was formed independently of it; negotiations with the

---

[5] André Kaspi, *Les Juifs pendant l'Occupation*, Paris, Seuil, "Points" series, 1997, p. 283.

[6] For more detail, see the author's PhD thesis in history, "La Réaction industrielle. Mouvements antitrust et spoliations antisémites dans la branche du cuir en France, 1930–1950," supervised by Professor Michel Margairaz (Université Paris-8–Vincennes-Saint-Denis), 2004; as well as the book drawn from it, *La Fabrique réactionnaire. Antisémitisme, spoliations et corporatisme dans le cuir, 1930–1950*, Paris, Presses de Sciences Po, 2007.

[7] AN, AJ^{38}2208/4011, the notes were written on the back of an envelope sent by the Department for Restitution to the address of a shoemaker.

Occupation authorities escaped it, particularly to the advantage of police chief René Bousquet; and so on.[8] In the field of Aryanization, those implementing the process were generally informed of a possible incarceration by peripheral sources and indications: the closing of a business, testimony from customers, neighbors, friends, etc.

Lastly, the result of an act of spoliation itself depends much more on the nature of the businesses affected: the smallest of them (actually the majority) were usually liquidated; the larger ones were usually maintained under administration or sold off. That being the case, the aim is to investigate the role of individuals, actors, social groups in the population as a whole at the juncture of two courses of action: against property and against people.

In what situations was it possible to protect property?

It is possible to identify a certain number of situations in which the property targeted for expropriation could be preserved by transfers or arrangements to safeguard the future. One possibility was the official transfer of property to a friend or relative considered a non-Jew, in a camouflaged manner, via a fictitious sale or sale with the right of redemption. For instance, one could attempt to secure the right to transfer one's company to a family member defined as "Aryan." German officials established the regulatory framework in February 1941 stipulating that in the event of "mixed marriages," transfer to an "Aryan" spouse was not sufficient Aryanization. On the other hand, if in the same circumstances the transfer was made to adult offspring with professional experience, the business could according to the officials be considered as having been extricated from any "Jewish influence."[9] In this way, André M., who placed his shoe shop in the hands of his daughter in October 1940, managed to protect his property, the donation having been approved by the authorities in June 1941.[10] However, such possibilities proved limited, the cases encountered being few and far between.

Arrangements were also sometimes made between seller and buyer. In November 1940, the limited liability British Shoe Thread and Leather

---

[8] Cf. Laurent Joly, *Vichy dans la "Solution finale." Histoire du Commissariat général aux questions juives, 1941–1944*, Paris, Grasset, 2006.
[9] AN, AJ^{38}2056 (497), p. 170, Note Abt Wi IAZ 5634/4, 8 February 1941.
[10] AN, AJ^{38}3319 (1267).

Manufacturing Co. was converted into a public limited company while the share capital changed hands and the "Jewish" managers, in particular André B., resigned, to be replaced by new trustees. On 19 March 1941, the chairman of this wholesale leather thread company requested of its own accord that the SCAP appoint "a trustee [...] to verify the full Aryanization of the business."[11] To this end, he suggested the name of an engineer who was approved by the control service on 4 April 1941. In November 1941, the trustee concluded that the "Aryanization" operations had been completed. On 4 February 1946, André B. confirmed the authenticity of the arrangements in a letter to the Department of Restitutions: "Our shareholders were not despoiled. The trustee appointed by the former CGQJ was given full discharge."[12]

The Aryanization process had other favorable outcomes. Two types of situation can be mentioned: the fairly common one in which economic "Aryanization" cases were delayed (depending on the sector of activity, between 20 and 80 per cent of the cases were not settled at the end of the Occupation, the two extremes being real estate property and textiles and leather goods respectively); and another that resulted in the formal liquidation of the property (being struck from the roll of craftsmen or trade register, or patent register), which enabled the entrepreneur to easily repair what had been administratively undone.

However, to escape anti-Semitic measures the safest way was to be officially recognized as non-Jewish so as to protect oneself while protecting one's activity. This was handled by the Personal Status Department of the CGQJ, run by Jacques Ditte until October 1943 in Paris, with the occasional help of George Montandon, the regime's "ethnoraciologist" and director of the Institut d'Étude des Questions Juives et Ethnoraciales. For instance, Henri B. wanted to have his status as Eastern Orthodox recognized and supplied the SCAP with various certificates in 1941. These documents seem to have met with the department's approval, as it relieved the trustee of his duties in June 1942. However, in January 1943, it turns out that Ditte's department finally considered that these papers were insufficient and a new trustee was appointed. On 2 July 1943, Henri B. was obliged to undergo an examination at the hands of Montandon to verify his "racial origin."[13] We do not know what the conclusions were. However,

---

[11] AN, AJ^{38}2210 (6115).
[12] Ibid.
[13] AN, AJ^{38}3320 (1478), Memo of 3 July 1943.

in March 1945, Henri B. was in a position to inform the Department of Restitutions that his company was never sold or liquidated.[14]

One could also request a waiver of the prohibitions contained in the anti-Semitic "legislation" in accordance with article 8 of the "law" of 2 June 1941, known as the second Jewish status law, which offered this opportunity to Jews 1) who have rendered exceptional services to the French State; 2) whose family has been established in France for at least five generations and has rendered exceptional services to the French State."[15] The expression "exceptional services" left the CGQJ room for interpretation that did not really work in favor of the applicants. Lucien D., owner of a wholesale shoe business, argued that his family had been established in France for at least five generations, that seven of his ancestors going back five generations had died for France, that he took part in the fighting in 1940, that he had no criminal record and that he had never gone bankrupt. The Economic Aryanization Office in Vichy considered that these facts were not enough to exempt him.[16] Roger L., one of the two owners of Chaussures André, also stressed his status as a veteran and the number of years his family had been established in France to have the prohibitions waived. He did not have any better luck.[17] The files examined in fact showed no cases of exemption. The CGQJ obviously had a very narrow interpretation of the idea of "exceptional services."

Even if it were not possible to avoid anti-Semitic stigmatization, people could try to protect their property by disguising or closing their businesses, while fleeing with the money, equipment and merchandise, especially to the Southern Zone where it seemed easier to escape arrest.[18] In such cases, protection of property and persons went hand-in-hand.

---

[14] Ibid., Letter to Professor Terroine, 30 March 1945.
[15] "Law of 2 June 1941 replacing the law of 3 October 1940 regarding the status of the Jews," article 8, and "Law of October 3, 1940 regarding the status of the Jews," article 8 of which mentioned exceptional services rendered in the literary, scientific and artistic fields. See Mission d'Etude sur la Spoliation des Juifs de France, *La Persécution des juifs de France, 1940–1944, et le rétablissement de la légalité républicaine. Recueil des textes officiels, 1940–1999*, Paris, La Documentation Française, 2000, pp. 89 and 103.
[16] AN, AJ^{38}3665 (1961), Decision of 4 August 1942.
[17] AN, AJ^{38}2045 (Chaussures André file), Letter from Roger L. to the trustee for transmittal to the CGQJ, 9 October 1941.
[18] See for instance AN, AJ^{38}2185 (37391).

Lastly, spoliation could paradoxically lead to safety for people. When it occurred very early (this was particularly the case for many businesses in the Paris area for some people in the spring of 1941), the victims no longer had any economic attachment to their place of residence and could seek shelter in safer regions. Thus the G. family, despoiled of their parents' business, took refuge in the Southern Zone where they found aid and assistance.[19]

Protection of property depending on the spoliator and the victims

The circumstances must also be approached from the angle of individuals who took part in them. Two categories should be considered: the victims, their family and entourage; and the actors of the process—those who were involved in implementing it. As regards the victims, setting up a front, a fictitious sale, organizing the preservation of one's property, one's person, one's family first of all required awareness of the risk involved in doing nothing and secondly, strong family and/or social integration within French society. This could for example have involved obtaining a certificate of "Aryanity" from a sufficiently trustworthy and understanding priest, thereby preserving both person and property. Lawyers were also called on, and some proved to be staunch defenders of their clients' interests. Jean Guiolet for instance chose to attack the CGQJ on the legitimacy of the appointment of certain trustees. In the case file of the Maison Pierre business, he rejected the appointment of a trustee in March 1941 after sales of "Aryan" shares in the business had begun as early as December 1940. The CGQJ only disputed them in March 1942, well after the six-month grace period beginning with the nomination of a trustee, after which such disputes became impossible.[20] Jean Guiolet's correspondence is abundant and stretches at least from June 1941 to May 1942. In it he takes a very bossy and even threatening tone toward the trustees, which disconcerted some of them. He also criticized the CGQJ virulently, no doubt considering that the best defense was attack:

"Dear Sir,
It was with great amusement that I received your letter of 29 April 1942 given to the threats it contained [...] and I exercise the most rightful reservations

---

[19] Israel Gutman (ed.), *Dictionnaire des Justes de France*, edition compiled by Lucien Lazare, Jérusalem, Yad Vashem, Paris, Fayard, 2003, p. 157.
[20] AN, AJ[38] 2107 (5868).

regarding the threats contained in said letter, which will be qualified as need be, and if they should be pursued in any way whatsoever I will not neglect to summon you before the competent court for the new offense contained in the body of your letter of 29 April 1942, very unfortunately written, and it is highly probable that at the time you will not be able to assume the right to refuse any summons that might occur, which is absolutely against the law and which prompted a memo to His Honor the Public Prosecutor on this particular point. I therefore request that you refrain from writing such letters and urge you, before making any threats, to please reread the legislation which you claim to refer to and in this case you shall receive no further reply, feeling as I do that I have no time to waste in reminding you of the law."[21]

These proceedings did not produce all the expected results, but at least they had the virtue of being undertaken. My study on the leather and pelt sector serves to point out that professional contacts (suppliers, competitors, customers or even employees) could be conducive to rescuing property through fictitious sale or a change of status to craftsman (a colleague would supply a fake custom tailoring certificate). Take the case of Tréfousse, a major glove manufacturer at the time. This business was "self-Aryanized" between October 1940 and June 1941 by the resignation of the "Jewish" administrators and its chairman, Paul M., and, at the same time, the sale of all capital held by "Jewish" owners to non-Jews. Those who purchased capital were members of the staff, outside industrialists, and a deputy, Jean Desbons, who had family ties with one of the main despoiled shareholders. "Aryanization" was ratified by the authorities, in particular thanks to the personal contacts that Desbons had with the occupier. Upon Liberation, most of the shares reverted to their legitimate owners and Paul M. recovered his job. Throughout the entire Occupation, the factory workers took turns helping him to hide in the Saône-et-Loire Department. The significance of this story will be placed in perspective further on. Reading the *Dictionnaire des Justes de France* (Dictionary of the Righteous of France), which outlines the circumstances in which people were rescued, is instructive in that it stresses the importance of relations of proximity and sociability of the people who were stigmatized, excluded and hunted.

More unexpectedly, some involved in the plunder were either unwittingly or consciously and voluntarily agents of preservation and protec

---

[21] Ibid. Letter from Jean Guiolet to the director general of the SCAP, 5 May 1942.

tion. Cases have been noted of administrative officials involved in spoliation stepping in to preserve property: mayors wanting businesses to remain open because of the jobs they provided and/or the consumer goods they offered the population; Marshal Pétain's staff or CGQJ officials (in particular Xavier Vallat) sometimes intervening in favor of a person on the grounds of his recognized merits (particularly veterans of the First World War). The prefect of Indre-et-Loire, Jean Chaigneau, for example played a beneficial role concerning at least one "Aryanization" procedure that in fact led to a fictitious sale. When he was appointed prefect of Alpes-Maritimes in July 1943, he proved to be particularly protective, telling the local representatives of Jewish organizations: "I will henceforth no longer allow any arbitrary act toward Jews, even in a dubious or illegal situation. I will not allow the Italians the noble privilege of being the only champions of the tradition of tolerance and humanity that is nonetheless that of France."[22]

The CGQJ staff as well as the trustees could also, through incompetence (in this case entirely welcome from the victims' standpoint), neglect to complete cases; a number of such instances were observed in this study. But there is another, more particular situation: that in which the administration allowed the victim to appoint his own trustee himself. Such cases were found in the provinces, and I was able to study the phenomenon more closely in Seine-et-Oise, where for a certain number of businesses the victim was consulted in the appointment of his trustee. The result in many cases turned out to be favorable to the victims, as these few accounts suggest:

"Henri Gaudin was my accountant until 1940. I'm the one who requested that he act as my trustee, which was granted. Full discharge for his management. Was able to recover my business."[23]

"I inform you that Monsieur Niedhammer [...] has agreed to be the trustee for my business upon my request [sic] and as a favor to me. It was following an order from the Prefecture of Versailles asking me to choose my trustee myself that I informed him of it. Monsieur Niedhammer was paid no honorarium and did so much to stall the case to gain time that he was eventually replaced. By doing so he did me a great service and I have absolutely no demands to make on him."[24]

---

[22] André Kaspi, *Les Juifs pendant l'Occupation*, op. cit., pp. 289–90.
[23] AN, AJ^{38}3317 (1033), Statement by Jacques Sapira, shoe salesman, 18 December 1944.
[24] AN, AJ^{38}3311 (798), Letter from M. Chayet, shoemaker in Sannois, 5 April 1945, to the director of the Department of Restitution, Paris.

"After I had appointed my friend M. Jamet myself as trustee of my company, he helped me to conceal all my property, and so thanks to his good deeds I lost absolutely nothing and even better I recovered all of my property and thus I have no demands to make on him in this regard."[25]

Circumstances can moreover be complicated. Thus the following example shows the combined effects of a case that dragged on, the action of an "Aryan" spouse and the help of a complicit trustee. On 24 July 1941, the civil court of the Seine department in Corbeil issued a court order legally separating the spouses F. The shoe store was awarded to Mme F. The SCAP, considering that the "Jewish influence" had not been eliminated, retained the trustee in his position and considered selling the business. The steps taken by Mme F. to assert her rights resulted in no confiscation taking place and upon Liberation her husband wrote to Professor Terroine: "Thanks to the efforts of M. Cotel, my trustee and friend, as well as my Aryan wife, we were able to avoid having to sell the business."[26]

Along the same lines, the most moving document encountered in this study is worth quoting in full:

"Béthune, 24 August 1945

Jacobson Zélick, furrier, 33, rue des Treilles in Béthune to the Minister of Finance,

Department for Restitution of Property of Victims of the Legislation and Spoliation Measures, Paris

Dear Sir,

Miss Odette Renault, Grand Place in Béthune, trustee for my property during the Occupation, forwarded me your letter of this 13 August concerning the management of property entrusted to her. To follow up on it, I am pleased to inform you that I have nothing but praise for Miss Renault's administration. With the help of friends she managed to safeguard the interests better than I could have ever thought; my personal assets are intact, my wife had no trouble reopening our business upon her return, for Miss Renault, using subterfuge, managed to prevent the liquidation of my business as well as of proceeds from the sale of merchandise that existed at the time of my wife's deportation, I was supplied with accounts that I acknowledged as exact and recovered the amount of the liquidation; there too, Miss Renault managed not to pay anything to the receiving authorities.

---

[25] AN, AJ^{38}3316 (952), Reply from M. Bialowas to the "Terroine" form, 22 April 1946.
[26] AN, AJ^{38}3322 (2051).

I should add that Miss Renault and her family took in my three-year-old daughter in December 1940, who should have been deported with her mother, and took care of her like their own child up to now.

From all that precedes, Your Honor, there is no reason to ask Miss Renault for any further account. We owe her all our gratitude.

Signed: Jacobson, former prisoner of war."

At the very heart of the criminal undertaking there were real opportunities to rescue property and persons.

Levels of awareness

The aim here is to take stock of the situations described and draw conclusions regarding both the question of rescue and the notion of "Righteous." An overall assessment regarding the active preservation of property, or a more detailed one concerning the number of people rescued in the same momentum, proves difficult. The cases examined nevertheless indicate that the proportion of rescues was only minimal.

Early spoliation sometimes enabled victims to foresee the worst and make arrangements to avoid it. Moreover, since the procedure strove to be "legalistic" (a very peculiar sort of "legality" that had no parliamentary oversight and brought anti-Semitic brutality down to the level of routine), it could also leave victims escape routes. However, the possibilities were extremely limited. The procedures themselves could lead to a positive outcome for the people involved: delays in the handling of cases, trustees proposed by the victims themselves, benevolent attitudes on the part of some of actors in the process.

Lastly, an essential aspect is the degree of the victims' social integration, which sheds light on situations in which property was preserved and/or victims were rescued. The relationship between the two aspects, preservation and rescue, seems all the stronger in cases of entrepreneurs when the business could be defined, in addition to its economic aspect, as an entity at the core of various networks of sociability.

To conclude with these observations, it may appear that preservation and rescue are the result only of specific circumstances: specific provisions of anti-Semitic measures, administrative delays in the settling of cases, chance meetings of benevolent or understanding spoliators, victims benefiting from opportunities. It seems moreover that the preservation of property by third parties involved in fictitious purchases was not always the result of a humanitarian ambition: Jean Desbons, who bought Tréfousse, was strongly pro-collaboration and was a guest of Chancellor Hitler before the war and several times during it. Did he sincerely believe in 1941 that Germany would lose the war and that the rightful owners of Tréfousse might recover their business? Some despoiled persons reinstated after the war doubted this, and took the case to court.

It would appear however that even if these aspects must be taken into account, awareness of the issues should also be considered for both the actors and the victims. On 22 June 1942, Plik M. wrote to the "Officer for Jewish Affairs" (*sic*):

"Sir,

Plying the trade of shoemaker [...] in the 17th arrondissement in Paris, I appeal to your benevolence to appoint a trustee to enable me simply to pursue my trade. In anticipation of prompt satisfaction. Yours sincerely."[27]

The author of the letter clearly did not perceive the risk he was taking. After a PQJ inquiry and on noting that the property had not been previously declared, a trustee was appointed on 15 September 1942. As for Plik M., he was arrested in the Vélodrome d'Hiver roundup.

A minority, who could be called "fanatics," was involved in the process at the CGQJ, in other administrative structures or in economic branches, as trustees, as property buyers, because they subscribed to the ideology and policy of the authorities. On the contrary, a large majority seemed clearly less motivated by these concerns than by finding a means of subsistence or profit. Were the latter fully aware of the consequences of their acts? In the case of Odette Renault, hired as a trustee, the answer would appear to be affirmative, because she preserved property and rescued people; the same is true, moreover, of the "fanatics" who acted in accordance with ideological convictions. But for the others, all the others who were cogs in this anti-Semitic machine designed to steal, destroy and exterminate, what was their degree of awareness? The fact that the two processes ("Aryanization" and internment with a view to deportation) were disconnected thickened the smokescreen. However, in conducting this research it became clear that involvement in spoliation precluded any possible ignorance of the ongoing roundups.

Those who carried out spoliation, often involved in the process in the long term and without in most cases being vassals of the Vichy French

[27] AN, AJ^{38}2259 (35837).

state or the Nazi regime, had considerable opportunities to preserve property while at the same time possibly rescuing people. More than a question of individual courage, it was a matter of awareness. The author subscribes to this statement by Albert Camus in *The Plague*:

> [...] by attributing overimportance to praiseworthy actions one may, by implication, be paying indirect but potent homage to the worst side of human nature. This attitude implies that such actions shine out as rare exceptions, while callousness and apathy are the general rule. The narrator does not share that view. *The evil that is in the world always comes of ignorance*, and good intentions may do as much harm as malevolence, if they lack understanding. On the whole, men are more good than bad; that, however, isn't the real point. But they are more or less ignorant, and it is this that we call vice or virtue; the most incorrigible vice being that of an ignorance that fancies it knows everything and therefore claims for itself the right to kill. The soul of the murderer is blind; and there can be no true goodness nor true love without the utmost clear-sightedness.[28]

---

[28] Albert Camus, *The Plague*, New York, Random House, The Modern Library, trans. Stuart Gilbert, 1948, p. 129, author's emphasis.

8

ITALIAN JEWS AND THE MEMORY OF RESCUE (1944–1961)

Paola Bertilotti

In Italy, the Jews had to face two different types of persecution between 1938 and 1945: persecution by the fascists between 1938 and 1943, and then Nazi persecution between 1943 and 1945, conducted in collaboration with the Salò Republic. Over 46,500 Jews were living in Italy in 1938. Between 1938 and 1945, some 12,300 of them emigrated, nearly 5,000 escaped from the country and about 6,800 were deported. Some 5,971 died in the camps and 322 were murdered in Italy. Moreover, an estimated 1,000 victims were never identified. In 1945 only 27,000 Jews remained in Italy.[1]

Contrary to a common idea, the Jews of Italy were not spared persecution and the Italian Social Republic took considerable part in their arrest.[2] Nevertheless, they did not suffer the same losses as the Jews of Poland or—along different lines—those of Holland, particularly because they did not have to contend with the same Nazi German occupation policy

---

[1] These figures were given by Liliana Picciotto Fargion, *Il libro della memoria*, Milan, Mursia, 2002, p. 27.
[2] It has been possible to establish with certainty that out of a total of 7,013 arrests, 2,444 were made by the Germans and 1,951 by the Italians, and 332 were due to collaboration (cf. Liliana Picciotto Fargion, *Il libro della memoria*, op. cit., p. 29).

and the fascist regime, even if anti-Semitic, did not undertake deportation of Italian Jews until 1943; but also because Italian Jewry was highly assimilated and the Jews were helped by part of the Italian population and certain religious institutions.

The rescue of the Jews by non-Jews was thus a reality, but it represented only one of several factors contributing to the survival of Italian Jews.[3] A recent survey[4] of the "survival paths" of a sample of 149 individuals in the Roman Jewish community showed that only forty-two of them owed their survival to the intervention of a non-Jewish rescuer.[5]

However, the reality of rescues was extensively mystified in the immediate post-war period, particularly on the basis of the memory of the Italian occupation in southeastern France. Italy enjoyed the image of a country favorable to Jews, especially abroad, which was supposed to be an exception with respect to other European countries.[6] In Italy, memory of rescue served as one of the bases for what has been called "the myth of the good Italian"—the tendency to consider the Italians as kind by nature and human, contrary to their cruel and ruthless German allies.[7]

---

[3] Cf. Anna Bravo, "Giusti tra le nazioni in Italia," in Walter Laqueur (ed.), *Dizionario dell'olocausto*, Italian edition put together by Alberto Cavaglion, Turin, Einaudi, 2007, p. 348–51. The list of Italian "Righteous" recognized by Yad Vashem is published in Israel Gutman, Bracha Rivlin and Liliana Picciotto Fargion (eds), *I Giusti d'Italia. I non ebrei che salvarono gli ebrei 1943–1945*, Milan, Mondadori, 2006 (1st ed. Jerusalem, Yad Vashem, 2004).

[4] Federica Barozzi, "I percorsi della sopravvivenza: salvatori e salvati durante l'occupazione nazista di Roma (8 settembre 1943–4 giugno 1944)," *La Rassegna Mensile di Israel*, 64 (1), 1998, pp. 95–144.

[5] This finding corroborates the work currently conducted by Raffaella Di Castro on testimonials collected in 1999–2000 for the Fondo Svizzero per Vittime della Shoah in Stato di Bisogno (Swiss Fund for Shoah Victims in Need). Entitlement to aid depended largely on the victim's social position and relations, and many of the poorest among them were reduced to vagrancy and begging (the author thanks Raffaella Di Castro for this information).

[6] See for instance Hannah Arendt, *Eichmann in Jerusalem. A Report on the Banality of Evil*, New York, the Viking Press, 1964, pp. 176–80. Some of the papers in the recent book on the "Righteous" of Italy published under the aegis of Yad Vashem take up this common theme (Israel Gutman, Bracha Rivlin and Liliana Picciotto Fargion (eds), *I Giusti d'Italia…*, op. cit., in particular pp. xvii-xx).

[7] Cf. Filippo Focardi, "La memoria della guerra e il mito del "bravo italiano." Origine e affermazione di un autoritratto collettivo," *Italia Contemporanea*, 220–1, 2000, pp. 393–9; David Bidussa, *Il mito del bravo italiano*, Milan, Il Sag-

This myth, recently taken to task by historical study,[8] was nevertheless the basis for the founding mythology of the Italian Republic—that of an entirely anti-fascist Italy that resisted the Nazis[9]—and also weighed in the evaluation of the Vatican's attitude toward Nazism and Fascism.

What memory did the Jews in Italy develop of the help they occasionally received between 1943 and 1945? The question has not yet been the topic of a specific study.[10] Yet the memory of rescue—and more generally the aid received between 1938 and 1945—have since 1944 constituted one of the essential aspects of the memory of anti-Semitic persecutions. Examining this memory does not only involve seeking "any conflict between memory and history,"[11] it also means examining the reconstruction of an Italian Jewish identity in the post-war period and the nature of relations between Jews and the Italian nation after more than seven

---

giatore, 1993. The expression "*bravo italiano*" ("good Italian") refers to the title of the film by Giuseppe De Santis, *Italiani brava gente* (1964), which retraces the odyssey of an Italian regiment on the Russian front in 1941 and helped to set the image of an inoffensive and debonair Italian soldier (cf. Mario Isnenghi, *Le guerre degli italiani*, Milan, Mondadori, 1989, pp. 153–4).

[8] Regarding anti-Semitic persecution in Italy, see (among others) Enzo Collotti, *Il fascismo e gli ebrei. Le leggi razziali in Italia*, Rome-Bari, Laterza, 2003; Marie-Anne Matard-Bonucci, *L'Italie fasciste et la persécution des juifs*, Paris, Perrin, 2007; Michele Sarfatti, *Gli ebrei nell'Italia fascista. Vicende, identità, persecuzione*, Turin, Einaudi, 2000. Regarding the occupation policy of Fascist Italy, see Davide Rodogno, *Il nuovo ordine mediterraneo. Le politiche di occupazione dell'Italia fascista in Europa, 1940–1943*, Turin, Bollati Boringhieri, 2003.

[9] See in particular Filippo Focardi, *La guerra della memoria. La Resistenza nel dibattito politico italiano dal 1945 a oggi*, Rome-Bari, Laterza, 2005; Claudio Pavone, "La Resistenza in Italia: memoria e rimozione," *Rivista di Storia Contemporanea*, 23–24 (4), 1994–1995, pp. 484–92.

[10] Guri Schwarz, in his book *Ritrovare se stessi. Gli ebrei nell'Italia postfascista* (Rome-Bari, Laterza, 2004), suggested some initial avenues for analysis that this author intends to pursue in the present work.

[11] The expression is borrowed from Marie-Anne Matard-Bonucci, "L'antisémitisme en Italie: les discordances entre la mémoire et l'histoire," *Hérodote*, 89, 1998, pp. 217–38. See the definition of memory forged by Pierre Nora, which is based on the difference between history—as a scientific reconstruction of the past leaning toward truth—and memory, a subjective reconstitution of the past that is potentially false and mythologized (Pierre Nora, "La mémoire collective," in Jacques Le Goff (ed.), *La Nouvelle Histoire*, Paris, CEPL, 1978, p. 398).

years of persecution. It means raising the question of establishing a shared identity and memory by the Italian Jews after 1944.[12]

The present study begins in June 1944 with the liberation of Rome, marking the end of the war for one of the largest Jewish Italian communities but also the beginning of the discovery of the genocide. It ends in 1961 with Eichmann's trial at the time when judicial current events contributed to raising consciousness of what the Shoah was but also fixed a lasting representation of events. In the first phase, from 1944 to 1947, the memory of rescue, even if it was present in individual recollections, was also buoyed up by Italian Jewish institutions and by the Italian state for which it represented a political issue. In these immediate post-war years, such memory contributed to the emergence of the "myth of the good Italian." After 1947, when the peace treaty between Italy and the Allies came into effect, the memory of rescue ceased to be a political issue, without however falling into oblivion. Beginning in 1953, concomitantly with the establishment of the title of "Righteous" in Israel, memory of rescue, celebrated by the Union of Jewish Communities with the support of the Italian government, became institutionalized and official, and fostered the dissemination of the "myth of the good Italian" which, as we shall see, received international recognition due partly to the Eichmann trial.

1944–1947: memory of rescue, individual memories or a political issue?

For the Jews of Italy, the years 1944 to 1947 were a time of gradual awareness of the genocide, abrogation of the anti-Semitic legislation and their reintegration into Italian society.[13] It was in this context that they published the first accounts of rescue and the first essays devoted to fascist and Nazi anti-Semitic persecution; from 1944 to 1947 seven books were

---

[12] See the definition of memory elaborated by Marie-Claire Lavabre (*Le Fil rouge*, Paris, Presses de Sciences Po, 1994) who, drawing her inspiration from the research of Maurice Halbwachs and Roger Bastide, views collective memory as a result of the passage from several individual memories to a shared memory.

[13] Most of the regime's anti-Semitic measures were abrogated between 1944 and 1947. Cf. Mario Toscano (ed.), *L'abrogazione delle leggi razziali in Italia (1943–1987). Reintegrazione dei diritti dei cittadini e ritorno ai valori del Risorgimento*, Rome, Senato della Repubblica, 1988.

published on persecutions in Italian territory[14] and eight accounts by former deportees.[15] The Search Committee for Deported Jews (CRDE), created by the Italian Union of Israelite Communities (UCII) in September 1944, also took charge of gathering survivor accounts on their return to Italy starting in June 1945.[16]

Individual recollections in the immediate post-war period offer a contrasting representation of the persecution; recollections of aid received from non-Jewish Italians can be found alongside accounts of denunciation, widespread indifference among the Italian population, and collaboration of the Salò *repubblichini* with the Nazis. Out of sixty-six deportees whose unpublished depositions can be consulted in the CRDE archives, only two give accounts of aid received from non-Jews. Memoirs from former deportees published between 1945 and 1947 follow the same lines: only Alba Valech Capozzi mentions attempts to help, especially by her own husband, who was a non-Jew.

The assessment is logically not so dismal if one considers the viewpoint of Italian Jews who escaped deportation. Among them, all praised the rescue efforts made by the Catholic Church. But while some of them, such as Luciano Morpurgo, emphasized solidarity manifested by the majority of the Italian population and heroic rescue attempts,[17] others,

---

[14] Giacomo Debenedetti, "16 ottobre 1943," *Mercurio*, December 1944 (then Rome, OET, 1945); Giacomo Debenedetti, *Otto ebrei*, Rome, Atlantica, 1944; Rinaldo Debenedetti, "La tragedia degli ebrei d'Europa," in Anna Errera (ed.), *Vita del popolo ebraico*, Milan, Garzanti, 1947; Silvia Lombroso, *Diario di una madre (si può stampare). Pagine vissute*, Rome, Dalmatia, 1945; Eucardio Momigliano, *40 000 fuori legge*, Rome, Carboni, 1944; Eucardio Momigliano, *Storia tragica e grottesca del razzismo fascista*, Milan, Mondadori, 1946; Luciano Morpurgo, *Caccia all'uomo! Vita sofferenze e beffe. Pagine di diario 1938–1944*, Rome, Dalmatia, 1946.

[15] Alberto Cavaliere, *I campi della morte in Germania: nel racconto di una sopravvissuta*, Milan, Sonzogno, 1945; Luigi Fiorentino, *Cavalli 8 uomini…: pagine di un internato*, Milan, La Lucerna, 1946; Primo Levi, *Se questo è un uomo*, Turin, De Silva, 1947; Liana Millu, *Il fumo di Birkenau*, Milan, La Prora, 1947; Frida Misul, *Fra gli artigli del mostro nazista*, Livorno, Stabilimento Poligrafico Belforte, 1946; Luciana Nissim, *Ricordi della casa dei morti*, in Luciana Nissim and Pelagia Lewinska, *Donne contro il mostro*, Turin, Ramella, 1946; Giuliana Tedeschi, *Questo povero corpo*, Milan, Editrice Italiana, 1946; Alba Valech Capozzi, *A 24029*, Siena, Soc. An. Poligrafica, 1946.

[16] UCII Archives (AUCII), CRDE collection, boxes 1 and 2.

[17] Luciano Morpurgo, *Caccia all'uomo!…*, op. cit., pp. 138–42.

the foremost being Silvia Lombroso, denounced the indifference of their fellow citizens.[18] All however tend to consider that ardent pro-fascists were only a minority among the Italian population.

The diversity of viewpoints reflects the diversity of individual experiences and appraisals. Some scenes remained etched in people's minds, such as the rescue of Jewish children by non-Jewish neighbors during the 16 October 1943 roundup. Other rescue attempts, however, have been forgotten, such as that of the Jewish relief organization Delasem, which only Silvia Lombroso, one of its former members, seems to remember. The memory of rescue is a selective memory: above all, a memory of rescue efforts performed by non-Jews, and particularly the Church.

Even if individual recollections provide a contrasting portrait of events, within Jewish institutions, particularly the Zionist organizations, memory of rescues is a hypertrophied memory. The Italian Zionists' convention that met in Rome in January 1945 expressed "its gratitude for the silent but often heroic displays of solidarity that a large portion of the oppressed Italian people—following the admirable example of the Catholic Church—gave the persecuted and refugees of other parts of Europe, who were thus able to find shelter despite the barbaric laws of Nazism."[19] Statements by foreign Jewish institutions (Joint[20] and the World Jewish Congress) go even farther. During the 22nd Zionist Congress held in Basel between 12 and 22 December 1946, a motion to express the Jews' "gratitude" for rescue efforts and the "humanism" of the Italian people was adopted.[21]

On the collective level, the stance taken by community institutions and Zionist organizations prompted no reaction among the Italian Jews, all the more so since they only amplified the accounts of a portion of them—those who escaped deportation. Even more, since Jewish organizations restricted their statements to general considerations—rescuers are never mentioned by name, nothing is done to pay tribute to them on an individual basis—certain Italian Jews obtained recognition for their rescuers'

---

[18] Silvia Lombroso, *Diario di una madre...*, op. cit., pp. 195–8.
[19] *Israel*, 18 January 1945.
[20] Letter of 6 January 1946 from the Italian ambassador to the United States, Tarchiani, to the office of political affairs in the Foreign Affairs Ministry, Foreign Affairs Ministry archives (ASMAE), "Political affairs 1946–1950," series, Italy 1946, box 20, file "Zionism."
[21] *Israel*, 2 January 1947.

action outside the community framework. Some notified Vatican officials of these acts of solidarity, others worked to have their rescuers officially decorated with the Order of Merit or the Resistance Medal.[22]

All things considered, it is not the memory "for the prosecution" that prevails. Of all the essays written by Italian Jews devoted to anti-Semitic persecutions, it is those of Giacomo Debenedetti and Eucardio Momigliano, renowned intellectuals and anti-fascists, that would have the greatest resonance and the largest dissemination not only among Jewish communities but throughout the whole of Italian public opinion. Their works were reviewed and republished several times.[23] Both of them tend to present the Italian people as impotent and passive in the face of events and consider that only the anti-fascists were the "real" Italians (the Fascists, on the other hand, had betrayed their Italian-ness by striking an alliance with the Germans). This point of view had however been expressed in the Jewish community press in December 1944, prior to the success of those books,[24] which shows that the idea was in the air at the time.

The origins of the 'myth of the good Italian'

There are several explanations for these memory "overflows." Among Italian Jews, former deportees were a minority. Memories of rescue were vivid among all those who escaped deportation. Furthermore, as Carla Forti's study on Pisa demonstrated, previously persecuted Jews were generally reluctant to openly express criticism of their fellow citizens right after the war; they still feared hostile reactions and above all wanted to blend back into Italian society.[25] The memory of rescue was very likely

---

[22] Archives of the Centro di Documentazione Ebraica Contemporanea (ACDEC), box 9.1 "Riconoscimento ai benemeriti per l'opera di soccorso," file "Comunità di Firenze," Letter from Guido Calderoni to the UCII dated 18 April 1955; file "Comunità di Modena," letter of 15 April 1955 from Carla Valabrega to UCII; file "Comunità di Trieste," Correspondance concernant Feliciano Riccardelli. Cf. ACDEC, box 9.1, file "Comunità di Firenze," Letter from Anita Urso to the Milan community, 17 April 1955.

[23] *16 ottobre 1943* published in 1944 and republished in 1945. La *Storia tragica e grottesca del razzismo fascista* is a revised and corrected edition of *40 000 fuori legge* published two years earlier.

[24] *Israel*, editorial of 7 December 1944.

[25] Cf. Carla Forti, *Il caso Pardo Roques, un eccidio del 1944 tra memoria e oblio*, Turin, Einaudi, 1998. Regarding the Italian Jews' hope to go unnoticed after seven years of persecution, see also Giacomo Debenedetti, *Otto ebrei*, op. cit.

put forward by Italian Jewish institutions for its pacifying potential. Beyond that, emphasis on this memory was probably the expression of a desire of the Italian Jews to salvage their prewar identity foundations, in other words their attachment to the Italian homeland, their support for the liberal society that grew out of the *Risorgimento*, and their belief in the existence of anti-Semitism in Italy.[26]

Furthermore, in their reconstruction of events, Italian Jews were bound to be influenced by the dominant analyses and thought patterns right after the war. Giacomo Debenedetti and Eucardio Momigliano helped to spread viewpoints that were widely shared in Italy during the years 1944–47. At that time, political and cultural circles mostly went along with the idea that fascism was an interlude in Italian history.[27] The parties that grew out of anti-fascism and the Resistance, especially the Communist Party, the Socialist Party and the Christian Democratic Party, all participating in government in the spring of 1944, tended to popularize the image of an entirely anti-fascist Italy to boost their legitimacy.[28] The regime and its anti-Semitic policy were supposed to have enjoyed no sort of consensus. As early as 1945–46, in fact, the Italian authorities themselves maintained the memory of the rescue of Jews. In 1946, for instance, the Foreign Affairs Ministry published a report on its action "to assist Jewish communities (1938–1943),"[29] aimed at demonstrating that as an administration it resisted Mussolini's anti-Semitic policy. Successive Italian governments intended to use this documentation—as well as that concerning the Resistance and the massacres perpetrated by the Nazis in the peninsula—to lighten the anticipated punitive measures against Italy

---

[26] See in particular Mario Toscano, *Ebraismo e antisemitismo in Italia. Dal 1848 alla guerra dei sei giorni*, Milan, Angeli, 2003.

[27] Cf. Pier Giorgio Zunino, *La Repubblica e il suo passato*, Bologna, Il Mulino, 2003. The use of the word "*nazifascist*," common after the war to refer to the Fascists and Nazis in a single word, also helped to reinforce the idea that fascism was foreign to Italian tradition.

[28] Cf. Giovanni Miccoli, "Cattolici e comunisti nel secondo dopoguerra: memoria storica, ideologia e lotta politica," *Studi Storici*, 38 (4), 1997, pp. 951–91; Giovanni Miccoli, "Tra memoria, rimozioni e manipolazioni: aspetti dell'atteggiamento cattolico verso la Shoah," *Qualestoria*, 19 (2–3), 1991, pp. 161–88.

[29] Ministero degli Affari Esteri, *Relazione sull'opera svolta dal Ministero degli Affari esteri per la tutela delle comunità ebraiche (1938–1943)*, Rome, 1946. Cf. Guri Schwarz, *Ritrovare se stessi…*, op. cit., pp. 124–40.

under the peace treaties.³⁰ As for the Vatican, it only mentioned the question of anti-Semitic persecution in 1945 to emphasize its role in the rescue of the Jews.³¹

However, even if the Italian context weighed in the development of Jewish memory of rescue, Jewish institutions themselves directly and willingly contributed to validating these dominant representations. The memory of persecutions was the object of political negotiations between the Italian state and Jewish organizations.³² In the first quarter of 1945, in order to facilitate the reintegration of formerly persecuted Jews into Italian society, UCII chairman Giuseppe Nathan offered to intervene with the Allies in Italy's favor in exchange for the Italian government adopting compensation measures. He argued that Italy would reap benefits in terms of international image from his intervention.³³ This proposal came just at the right time. In 1944, the Foreign Affairs Ministry was in fact arguing there needed to be a change in Italian policy toward the Jews in general, and the Zionist movement in particular, from which it hoped to obtain support during the peace conference.³⁴ The steps Nathan took came to naught. On the other hand, through negotiations with UCII officials, in exchange for its tacit support for illegal immigration to Palestine (known as *aliya bet*) between November 1945 and the creation of

---

[30] ASMAE, Secretariat-general, 1943–1951, box 42, file "1945, reserved affairs," file 3 "Israelite questions (miscellaneous)" and box 28–2, "Documentary exhibit organized by the occupied Italian ministry on the war for liberation and the damage to Italy" and "Italian contribution to the war effort" files. On this point, see also the remarks made by Davide Rodogno (*Il nuovo ordine mediterraneo…*, op. cit., pp. 432–3).

[31] See for example *La Civiltà Cattolica*, 96 (1), 3 March 1945, p. 327.

[32] On this point, see also Guri Schwarz, *Ritrovare se stessi…*, op. cit., pp. 124–40.

[33] See his correspondence with the president of the Council of Ministers, Ivanoe Bonomi, and the Foreign Affairs Ministry in ASMAE, Cabinet 1943–1958, box 107, file "Jews, Italian Israelite community."

[34] See the 8 November 1944 memo to the Italian embassies in Washington, London and Moscow, where the Foreign Affairs ministry undersecretary, Visconti Venosta, repeated the anti-Semitic stereotypes about Jewish power, the "appealing perspective of support from a very powerful organization for the future peace conferences" (in ASMAE, "Political affairs," Great Britain, box 63, file 3 "Zionism," author's translation). The document is cited by Mario Toscano in *La "porta di Sion." L'Italia e l'immigrazione clandestina ebraica in Palestina (1945–1948)*, Bologna, Il Mulino, 1990, pp. 17–18.

the state of Israel in 1948, Italy obtained the support of the World Jewish Congress (WJC) during the peace treaty negotiations.[35] This obviously explains the wording of the statements made at the Congress of Italian Zionists and the motion in the Zionist Congress in Basel regarding the rescue of Jews in Italy.

The stands taken by the Zionist movement and the WTC had only a limited effect on the development of the memory of persecutions by Italian Jews and the outcome of peace treaty negotiations. On the other hand, they probably had an effect on the perception of Italy abroad, all the more so since the Foreign Affairs Ministry did its best to publicize them widely.[36]

The stands taken by non-Italian Jewish organizations, beyond political considerations, were probably influenced by the fact that the human toll of persecutions in Italy was one of the lowest in all of Europe in absolute figures. Furthermore, the memory of the Italian occupation in southeastern France was an impediment to analysis of anti-Semitic policy under fascism and the persecutions in Italy, particularly because of the 1946 publication in France of Léon Poliakov's book *La Condition des Juifs en France sous l'occupation italienne*.[37] The French historian in fact asserted on the basis of documentation that Italy was an exception with regard to other European countries during World War II, in that it rescued Jews. Referring mainly to documentation proving that the Italian occupying force in France between 1940 and 1942 was opposed to the Nazi deportation policy, Poliakov tended to underestimate the reach of Italian anti-

---

[35] See the promise to intervene made by the president of the UCII, Raffaele Cantoni (ASMAE, Cabinet 1943–1958, box 107, file "Jews Italian Israelite community," Unsigned memo of 27 August 1945 to the Office of Political Affairs) and copy of the letter sent 13 February 1946 by WJC Secretary-General, Riegner, to Cantoni outlining WJC action in favor of Italy (ASMAE, Secretariat-general 1943–1951, box 42, file 1946–3).

[36] See letter of 26 January 1945 by which Secretariat-General of the Foreign Affairs Ministry informs the embassies in London, Moscow, Madrid, Ankara, Buenos Aires, Berne, Sofia, Dublin, Lisbon, Bucharest and Stockholm, and the consulate in Tangier, of the motions passed by the Congress of Italian Zionist Organizations, requesting that it be given "the circulation they deserved in the press and political circles" (ASMAE, Secretariat-general 1943–1951, box 42, file 1946, "General and confidential affairs," 3).

[37] Published in Paris, Editions du Centre, 1946; co-authored with Jacques Sabille, Howard Fertig; 1st American edition, December 1983.

Semitic legislation, the effects of the Italian occupation policy in the Balkans and the extent of the Salò Republic's collaboration with Nazi Germany after 8 September 1943. In the immediate post-war period, the "myth of the good Italian" was thus validated by historical writing. In return, this positive image of Italy abroad necessarily had consequences on Italian recollections and particularly those of the Italian Jews.

From 1944 to 1947, the memory of rescue was thus at once a matter of individual recollections, collective memory and institutional memory. It was also a hypertrophied memory for reasons related to the situation of the Jews in Italy after the war, the Italian political and cultural context, the international political context and a distorted perception abroad of how the persecutions in Italy were carried out.

1948–1952: rescue 'between memory and oblivion'[38]

After the peace treaty was signed in February 1947 and came into effect in the following September, and with the end of the *aliya bet* and the creation of the State of Israel in 1948, the memory of rescue ceased to be a political issue for the Italian government as well as for Zionist organizations. It now became merely a silent memory, to which the community press devoted very few articles.[39]

That does not mean that the memory of rescue fell into oblivion. It was especially present implicitly in the Italian Jews' refusal to cooperate with the CRDE charged by the UCII to collect evidence against collaborators and informers,[40] as well as in the lack of interest generated by Massimo Adolfo Vitale's historical research, which probed the issue of the Vatican's silence[41] and, in an essay entitled *The Persecution of Italian Jews, 1938–*

---

[38] We borrow the expression from Annette Wieviorka, *Déportation et génocide: entre la mémoire et l'oubli*, Paris, Plon, 1992.
[39] Between 1948 and 1953, *Israel* devoted only one article, published on 9 June 1949, to the question of rescue (the obituary of a rescuer).
[40] See ACDEC, Private document collections, 1.3.1. Massimo Adolfo Vitale, box 1.
[41] See his paper "Pellegrinaggio tra l'orrore" (1947) in AUCII, CRDE, box 2, file "Al processo contro Bosshammer abbiamo mandato fotocopie" "Campi di concentramento nazisti," and his unpublished article (not dated but prior to 1956) on the Church's attitude during the persecutions entituled "Per la verità e per la storia" in AUCII, CRDE collection, miscellaneous documents, white fascicle, grey folder.

1945, published in 1949, paints a very different picture of the Italians' reaction to the persecutions, where indifference prevailed over displays of solidarity.[42] Whereas Italian Jewish institutions, community press and publishers in the lead, did nothing to promote Vitale's research, Poliakov's work on the other hand was reviewed upon publication in the Italian Jewish cultural monthly, *La Rassegna Mensile di Israel*.[43]

Between 1948 and 1952, the memory of rescue, although no official commemorations or statements were made, continued to influence the overall assessment that Italian Jews made of the Italian responsibilities in the extermination of European Jews.

1953–1961: the memory of rescue made official

The memory of rescue developed by the Italian Jews took a new turn starting in 1953, when Israel passed the Yad Vashem (Remembrance of Martyrs and Heroes) law, which among other provisions instituted the title of "Righteous among the Nations."[44]

Earlier, in 1953, the UCII organized a series of remembrance ceremonies designed to commemorate the memory of rescue. In 1953, ceremonies were organized in Milan for the "10th anniversary of Swiss hospitality."[45] In the framework of the 10th anniversary of Liberation, the UCII initiated celebrations that aimed to commemorate not only Jewish resistance but also the help received by Italian Jews from their fellow citizens during the persecutions. Without making explicit reference to the Israeli law, even in the terminology,[46] the UCII invited its members

---

[42] Massimo Adolfo Vitale gave this report at a European conference organized by the Paris Centre de Documentation Juive Contemporaine in 1947. His text would be published in *Les Juifs en Europe, 1939–1945. Rapports présentés à la première conférence européenne des commissions historiques et des centres de documentation juifs*, Paris, Éditions du Centre, 1949, pp. 43–6.

[43] See the lengthy review of Léon Poliakov's article, "Mussolini and the Extermination of the Jews," *Jewish Social Studies*, 11 (3), 1949, published in *Rassegna Mensile di Israel* in October 1949.

[44] Cf. Mooli Brog, "Yad Vashem" and Nechama Tec, "Giusti tra le Nazioni," in Walter Laqueur (ed.), *Dizionario dell'olocausto...*, op. cit., respectively pp. 829–34 and pp. 342–8.

[45] *Israel*, 8 October 1953.

[46] In Italy, during the 1950s, the "Righteous" were known as "*Benemeriti*" (citizens "decorated with merit").

to identify "non-Jews who, during the time of persecution, exposing themselves to great dangers, and sometimes sacrificing their lives, worked to help their [Jewish] brothers by all possible means, whether through ordinary or exceptional gestures."[47] A committee for the celebration of the 10th anniversary of Liberation was put in charge of collecting testimonials and selecting the people who would be decorated by the UCII.

Although Israel may have inspired these celebrations, it must be noted that the distinctions awarded by the UCII had specifically Italian referents.[48] On 17 April 1955, a national ceremony was held in Milan during which twenty-three "golden medals of merit"[49] were handed out.[50] Other award ceremonies to deliver "certificates of merit"[51] were organized with great pomp at the local level, attended by the authorities and a large audience.[52]

As in the preceding period, the UCII extolled the memory of rescue to the point of exaggerating the truth. Thus the president of the UCII, Sergio Piperno, during a ceremony held at the Capitol in Rome on 14 December 1956, stated: "All [Italians] spared no effort; whoever in one way or another was in a position to monitor the movements of the occupier or its henchmen benevolently warned those who were destined to become innocent victims; all friends, all acquaintances, all neighbors were quick to welcome, to hide and to help them; all worked to secure false papers for the Jews and frustrate searches."[53]

The UCII initiatives most likely stemmed from a desire to proclaim renewed confidence in the Italian nation and strengthen the ties between Jews and non-Jews in Italy, even to improve relations between Jewish

---

[47] Announcement published in *Israel*, 31 March 1955. Certain communities had also sent out a circular making a call for testimonies (cf. ACDEC, box 9.1, file "Comunità di Firenze").

[48] It was, moreover, not until 1963 that a special Yad Vashem commission was instituted to award the title of "Righteous among the Nations."

[49] "*Medaglia di benemerenza*" in Italian.

[50] Cf. *Israel*, 31 March 1955, 21 April 1955. Cf. ACDEC, boxes 9.2 and 9.3.

[51] "*Attestati di benemerenza*" in Italian.

[52] A ceremony was organized in Rome, at the Capitol, on 14 December 1956 (Cf. *Israel*, 20 December 1956; *Rassegna Mensile di Israel*, January 1957, pp. 11–22; *La Voce della comunità di Roma*, January 1957). Regarding other local ceremonies, see *Israel*, 17 January 1957, 15 December 1955, 19 February 1959 and ACDEC, box 9.1.

[53] Cited in Renzo De Felice, *Storia degli ebrei italiani sotto il fascismo*, Turin, Einaudi, 1993 edition, p. 472.

institutions and the Catholics, voluntary organizations and the government. Suggestions from the Catholic hierarchy or associations of former resistance fighters and deportees sometimes weighed in the awarding of rewards for merit.[54] More broadly speaking, the twenty-three gold medal recipients in the 17 April 1955 ceremony were explicitly chosen by the UCII in such a way as to represent Italian society on the whole: from simple soldiers to generals, from priests to magistrates, from peasants to prefects.[55] On 15 April 1955, the day of commemoration of the tenth anniversary of the general insurrection in northern Italy, the UCII distributed a poster addressed to "the Italian people" which, while mentioning the memory "of martyrs who died for freedom" and the "innocent victims" deported and murdered by the Nazis, also "praised" the "courageous undertakings, sometimes even involving sacrifice, of all the Italians—partisans, soldiers and military personnel, religious and lay figures, simple people from all walks of life and all religious persuasions—who, thereby making up for the sins of a minority, strove *Italianly* [*sic*] to rescue defenseless victims of persecution."[56]

The UCII managed to achieve the aim it had set for itself: the ceremonies paying tribute to the rescuers were extremely well received throughout the Italian press.[57] The Socialist and Communist dailies saw the rescue of the Italian Jews as a sign that the Italian population was anti-fascist in its majority.[58] The Catholic press interpreted the ceremonies as a tribute

[54] ACDEC, box 9.1, file "Comunità di Genova," express on 25 January 1956 from the Genoa community to the Committee for the 10th Anniversary of Liberation; file "Comunità di Milano," Letter of 12 May 1955 from Ermete Sordo of the National Association of Political Ex-Deportees (ANED to the Milan community.

[55] Cf. ACDEC, box 9.2, Letter from Lelio Valobra on 14 February 1955 to Giuseppe Ottolenghi. Also see *Israel*, 28 April 1955, and the article published by a Milan community official, Raoul Elia, in *Nuova Repubblica*, 8 May 1955.

[56] Cf. *Israel*, 21 April 1955. Guri Schwarz cites and comments on this text in "Gli ebrei italiani e la memoria della persecuzione fascista (1945–1955)," *Passato e Presente*, 17 (47), 1999, p. 120.

[57] See the impressive press digest in ACDEC, box 9.3.

[58] See, for instance, the evocative titles in the Milan editions of *Avanti!* and *Unità* on the occasion of the 17 April 1955 ceremony ("Rendono omaggio agli antifascisti le comunità israelitiche italiane," *Avanti!*, 16 April 1955; "Contro le persecuzioni e le deportazioni. 25 mila ebrei salvati dal coraggio degli antifascisti," *Unità*, April 15, 1955).

to the rescue work carried out by the Church in the name of Catholic faith and values.[59]

UCII initiatives also met with the approval of the highest state authorities.[60] Whereas the successive governments throughout this period[61] usually attempted to oppose the staging of commemorations scheduled by associations of former partisans and former deportees,[62] they dispatched representatives to rescue remembrance ceremonies organized in Milan in 1955 and in Rome in 1956. In the context of internal tensions, against the backdrop of the Cold War, that Italy was experiencing, the Christian Democrats in power viewed with a very critical eye ceremonies organized by associations having any relation whatsoever to do with the left and the Communist Party. Eager to wrest from the Italian Communist Party its monopoly over liberation celebrations, the governments at the time could only be delighted to see the Italian Jews organize apolitical ceremonies and promote the image of popular, unarmed and often Catholic resistance to fascism.

The UCII thus also probably pursued a political aim. As an advocate of strict political neutrality after the war, it probably wanted to participate in the 10th anniversary of Liberation avoiding allegiance to the left-wing parties, and maintaining good relations with government bodies. These political choices were not, however, unanimously approved. Italian Jewish youth organizations, and particularly the Federation of Young Italian Jews (FGEI), did not actively take part. More sympathetic to left-wing parties and anti-fascist organizations and opposed to the UCII's neutral line, its members had already organized highly political ceremonies to commemorate the persecutions, in 1952. If the UCII was banking on the memory of rescue to foster the Jews' reintegration into Italian society, the FGEI

---

[59] See especially the article entitled "Salvarono in nome di Cristo migliaia di ebrei," *L'Osservatore Romano della Domenica*, 8 May 1955.
[60] Cf. Central State Archives (ACS), Prime Minister's office (PCM), 1955–1958, file 14.2 /19036, "Rome."
[61] These were two DC-PSDI-PLI coalition governments. Both were led by Christian Democrats: Scelba from February 1954 to July 1955 and Segni from July 1955 to May 1957.
[62] ACS, PCM, 1955–1958, file 14.2/22851, "National commemoration of the Italian concentration camps" and PCM, 1951–1954, fascicle 3.3.3/8859.7, "Celebrations for the tenth anniversary of the Resistance and fight for liberation."

on the other hand was counting on the memory of anti-fascism and resistance to enable Jews to find their place among their fellow citizens.

In broader terms, the aims pursued by the UCII were at odds with those of its members. It is true that the Italian Jews had enthusiastically responded to calls for testimonials. Overwhelmed by the initiative's success, the UCII moreover decided in 1957 to dissolve the committee in charge of examining the cases, for the reason that the ceremonies organized up to then had served to express symbolically the gratitude of Italian Jews to all of the rescuers.[63] But none of the letters of testimony sent to the committee expressed the idea that Italy as a whole had "spared no effort" to rescue the Jews.[64] On the contrary, many emphasized the exceptional and heroic nature of the rescuers' actions. A letter of protest against the soothing rhetoric of the UCII in fact finally reached the community weekly *Israel* in 1961.[65]

But such reactions remained isolated. Probably because, as can be noted on reading the letters that reached the committee, for many of the former victims of persecution the displays of solidarity they were shown from 1938 were what enabled them to keep faith in man and in their country.[66] Beyond that, publication of the Italian translation of Poliakov's *Bréviaire de la haine. Le IIIe Reich et les Juifs* and then of his *Jews under the Italian Occupation* in 1955–56 lent historiographic support to the arguments defended by the UCII.[67]

---

[63] See *Israel*, 17 January 1957.
[64] This committee's archives are incomplete. There is abundant documentation concerning the communities in Milan and Florence, but there is only limited documentation for the communities in Alessandria, Bologna, Casale Monferrato, Ferrara, Genoa, Livorno, Modena, Naples, Padua, Pisa, Rome, Trieste, Turin, Venice, Vercelli and Verona. All the letters that were kept can be viewed at the ACDEC, box 9.1.
[65] Letter from Raffaello Sacerdoti published in letters from readers of *Israel*, 26 October 1961.
[66] ACDEC, box 9.1, file "Comunità di Firenze," Letter of 20 February 1955 from the D'Urbino family; file "Comunità di Milano," Letter from Ugo Sciaky of 31 May 1955; file "Comunità di Trieste," Letter from Esla Vig nee Straus 4 December 1954.
[67] Léon Poliakov, *Il nazismo e lo sterminio degli ebrei*, Turin, Einaudi, 1955; Léon Poliakov and Jacques Sabille, *Gli ebrei sotto l'occupazione italiana*, Milan, Edizioni di Comunità, 1956. Léon Poliakov's works, particularly *Bréviaire de la haine (Harvest of Hate)*, were widely distributed in Italy and were the topic of

In any event, the ceremonies organized by the UCII in 1955–56 were to have a lasting effect on the development of an Italian memory of anti-Semitic persecution. The viewpoints expressed on this occasion by Jewish community leaders were repeated verbatim first of all by the whole of the Italian press, and then by historiography. Entrusted by the UCII with drafting of "history of the Italian Jews under fascism,"[68] the historian Renzo De Felice adopted the judgment made by Sergio Piperno during the ceremony organized at the Capitol on 14 December 1956 without questioning it.[69]

The Eichmann trial did not alter these representations, and on the contrary had particular repercussions on the theme of the rescue of Italian Jews. During the trial, the prosecution, drawing on Poliakov's work,[70] in fact used the example of Italy to defeat Eichmann's system of defense. If the entire Italian society was able to resist anti-Semitic policy under fascism, that meant it was possible to resist the orders of a totalitarian power: Eichmann should thus be held responsible for his acts. The media coverage of this trial would influence the memory of anti-Semitic persecutions in Italy for a long time to come.

In Italy, exceptionally among West European countries, the memory of rescue occupied an essential place in the national memory in the immediate post-war years. In contrast, in France, as Sarah Gensburger has shown,[71] it was at the time when the memory of the Resistance was weakening that the memory of the "Righteous" and the rescue of the Jews was affirmed. In Italy, this memory existed as early as 1944 and contributed to the emergence of the "myth of the good Italian."

As regards Jewish memories from an individual standpoint, the memory of rescue contributed to reintegrating Italian Jews in Italian society.[72]

---

numerous reviews in all the press—especially the Jewish press (see Einaudi Archives, Reviews, box 277, file 3776).

[68] On this point, see Pasquale Chessa and Francesco Villari (eds), *Interpretazioni su Renzo De Felice*, Milan, Baldini e Castoldi, 2002, pp. 8–27.

[69] See note 52.

[70] Annette Wieviorka, *Le Procès Eichmann*, Brussels, Complexe, 1989, p. 31.

[71] Sarah Gensburger, "Les figures du "Juste" et du résistant et l'évolution de la mémoire historique française de l'Occupation" in *Revue Française de Science Politique*, 52 (2–3), April-June 2002, pp. 291–322.

[72] This is an aspect of what can be called, to use Roger Bastide's term, their "identity bricolage." Cf. Roger Bastide, "Mémoire collective et sociologie du bricolage," in *L'Année Sociologique*, 21, 1970, pp. 65–108.

From an institutional standpoint, it fostered the establishment of good relations between Jewish communities and Italian community organizations and politics. Contrary to what Peter Novick asserts in *The Holocaust in American Life* on the basis of interviews conducted in the 1990s among a few American and Israeli Jewish organization officials, it does not appear that in Italy's case "the intention of most commemoration of the 'righteous minority' has been to damn the vast 'unrighteous majority' and foster a 'fortress-like mentality'."[73] The present study reaches similar conclusions in this regard to those made by Sarah Gensburger in her contribution.

---

[73] Peter Novick, *The Holocaust in American Life*, New York, Houghton Mifflin Company, 2000 [1st ed. 1999], p. 180.

9

RESCUERS AND KILLER-RESCUERS DURING THE RWANDA GENOCIDE
RETHINKING STANDARD CATEGORIES OF ANALYSIS

Lee Ann Fujii

Analyses of genocide generally classify people into "perpetrators," "victims," "bystanders," and "rescuers."[1] Sorting people into these categories enables identification and explanation of specific groups of actors, such as "rescuers" or "victims." But the problem with these categories is that they can obscure as much as they reveal. As classification schemes, they help us to make sense of complex events, but they also structure what we expect to see in the first place. We expect "perpetrators" to perpetrate and rescuers to rescue. We also expect perpetrators not to rescue and rescuers not to perpetrate. Viewing actors through this lens, however, leads us to overlook acts of killing and acts of rescue that do not originate with those we would normally classify as "perpetrators" and "rescuers." This paper thus calls on analysts to think in terms of "acts," not just actors. Instead of thinking only of "perpetrators" and "rescuers," I propose that analysts also take into account "acts of killing" and "acts of rescue." This alternative approach leaves open the question of who is doing what and in what con-

---

[1] The title of Raul Hilberg's classic study, *Perpetrators, Victims and Bystanders*, New York, Aaron Asher Books, 1992, is but one prime example. Needless to say, scholars' adherence to or reliance on these categories varies with the type of questions they ask.

text, and by doing so, forces scholars to confront the grey zones of activity during genocide, where people often elide, straddle, and violate standard categories of analysis.

I illustrate this argument by focusing on "acts of rescue" committed by various people during the Rwandan genocide. By "acts of rescue," I mean deliberate actions that people took to keep another person from being killed. I focus on "acts of rescue" because scholars who study rescuing during genocide often restrict their line of view to those who risked their lives to save others and did not participate in or profit from the genocide in any way.[2] Utilizing data collected in two Rwandan communities and central prisons, I show that during the Rwandan genocide, perpetrators and bystanders also engaged in acts of rescue. Taking into account acts of rescue performed by these actors provides a more comprehensive view of the extent and form that rescue took during the genocide.

Rescuing during the Rwandan genocide and the limits of categories

It is impossible to estimate the number of people who tried to rescue Tutsis or Hutus targeted for elimination.[3] Many rescuers were killed alongside those they were trying to save; others do not consider themselves rescuers; still others have reason to stay quiet about their activities, fearing retribution from one side or another. What we might safely assume, however, is that the number of rescuers and prevalence of rescuing varied by region and local community, as did the number and prevalence of killers and killing. The reasons for this variation are multiple. In some areas, local officials actively spoke out against the killing of Tutsis and punished those who engaged in related violence, such as the burning of Tutsi homes or theft of Tutsi property. In these communities, local leaders were able to forestall the mass killing of Tutsis. The progress of the civil war between Rwandan government forces and the Rwandan

---

[2] See, e.g., Kristen Renwick Monroe, *The Hand of Compassion*, Princeton University Press, 2004. In this book, Monroe investigates rescuers of Jews during World War II. Her sample includes only people vetted and certified by Yad Vashem.

[3] Hutus who were targeted for killing during the genocide included people who refused to join the dominant political party of their region and/or joined a different party; local elite people or leaders who came out publicly against the genocide; and people who rescued or tried to save Tutsis.

Patriotic Front (RPF), a rebel group made up of mostly Tutsi refugees that had invaded Rwanda on 1 October 1990, also shaped the dynamics of the genocide, and thus the dynamics of rescue. The RPF's quick advance through the northern *préfecture* of Byumba, for example, enabled one *commune* (Giti) to escape genocidal violence altogether.[4] In areas like these, where violence was contained or prevented, rescue activities were much less critical to survival than in communities that suffered a lot of violence. In these areas, rescue activities would have been crucial to survival, but the extent to which such activities took place is an open question. In some communities, attempts at rescuing or helping Tutsis appear to have been non-existent. In the region of Bugesera, for example, both survivors and confessed killers interviewed by journalist Jean Hatzfeld report that they never once saw a person try to help a Tutsi after the killings began.[5] One reason that rescue activities may have seemed minimal or non-existent is that in some places, killers may have succeeded in killing all the rescuers, leaving little or no trace of their efforts.

What does seem clear, given the ferocity of the genocide itself—the fact that killers succeeded in slaughtering over half a million people in less than 100 days—is that acts of killing clearly outnumbered acts of rescue. Regardless of their small numbers, those who tried to save Tutsis still made a difference. Indeed, given the intimate nature of the violence—the fact that killer and victim often came from the same community—acts of rescue may have been even more crucial to people's survival than in other 20th century genocides. In the rural hills outside the capital of Kigali, where the majority of victims met their fate, killers and their intended victims lived together, knew one another, and knew of one another. In rural communities across the country, social proximity made detection likely and escape virtually impossible. Topography, too, added to the difficulty. The landscape of rolling hills provided multiple vantage points for surveillance, and the network of roads provided endless opportunities for killers to catch people trying to flee. In many localities there simply was no place to hide (other than in someone's house), and few ways to flee without drawing attention. This level of physical and social intimacy meant that Tutsis often had no choice but to rely on others for their survival.

[4] Scott Straus, "Local dynamics," in Scott Straus, *The Order of Genocide*, Ithaca, Cornell University Press, 2006.
[5] Jean Hatzfeld, *Une Saison des Machettes*, Paris, Seuil, 2003, pp. 127–37.

Acts of rescue took many forms. They came in different guises, as single acts of assistance or sustained gestures of aid.[6] They also come from all quarters: young and old, rich and poor, men and women, Catholics and Muslims.

Those in the best position, materially and socially, to help others were of the elites.[7] Church officials, for example, feature prominently in the African Rights' book *Tribute to Courage*,[8] one of the few studies of rescuers during the Rwandan genocide. Of the seventeen rescuers profiled in *Tribute to Courage*, the majority are clergy, one being a nun. Only five were ordinary people in the sense that they held no position of authority through the government or an established church at the time of the genocide. As African Rights point out, church officials were in positions that facilitated both killing and rescue. Church clergy held positions of social prominence and respect in their communities; their words carried great weight among parishioners. Church clergy also had access to church buildings and other places of potential refuge (and, conversely, potential mass slaughter). Using their resources and influence enabled many church authorities, including nuns, to save many Tutsis and Hutus targeted for killing.

In my research community of "Kimanzi"[9] located in the northern *préfecture* of Ruhengeri, for example, a local Seventh Day Adventist pastor was able to save countless Tutsis from his own and surrounding communities. He and his fellow pastors were able to protect fleeing Tutsis by harboring them in their church and, literally, placing themselves between the mass murderers and their targeted victims, warning the killers that they would have to kill the pastors first to get to their intended victims. The pastor was able to save the Tutsis assembled in his church by handing them over to RPF soldiers who then escorted the refugees to RPF-controlled territory or across the border into Uganda.

---

[6] Alison Des Forges, *Leave None to Tell the Story*, New York, Human Rights Watch and Fédération Internationale des Ligues des Droits de l'Homme, 1999, p. 13.

[7] See also Jefremovas (1995) who chronicles four stories of Tutsi who survived with the help of prominent persons, including a high ranking (Hutu) military officer.

[8] African Rights, *Tribute to*, Kigali and London, African Rights, 2002; also published in French, *Hommage au Courage*, Kigali, 2002.

[9] I use pseudonyms for people and place names to protect the identity of those who participated in my study.

Other local elite people found creative ways to use their social standing. In the research site of "Ngali," located in the central *préfecture* of Gitarama, a former local councilor was able to save a man by hinting at the man's possible family connections to the president. A group of local killers had arrived at the man's house, accusing him of being Tutsis and threatening to kill him. The former councilor stepped in and warned the killers that the man was an *umukiga* or person from the northern region of Kiga, and thus possibly related to President Habyarimana, who also hailed from the north. The ruse worked. The killers left, threatening to gather more information on the man's background. They did not return, however, and the man survived.

Low social status, however, could also work in a rescuer's favor, as was the case of one woman profiled in *Tribute to Courage* named Sula. As part of my own fieldwork, I interviewed Sula extensively. She was a poor, elderly widow at the time of the genocide with only a small plot of land and a tiny house, so no one suspected her of being able to hide anyone. Yet, despite her modest resources, she managed to hide twenty people in her home and feed them with what she could grow on her small field.

In one of my many interviews with Sula, she pointed out that her social marginalization actually helped her in her rescue efforts. Sula had told us that from childhood, she had decided it was not good to have too many friends because she saw how people often revealed their friends' secrets, especially after they had been drinking. She thus made it a policy to maintain only a small circle of close friends. Having few friends helped Sula to keep her "secret," she explained. If she had had lots of friends, she would not have been able to hide so many people in her house.

It was not just her marginalization that enabled Sula's success. Sula also showed a remarkable ingenuity for dealing with the killers roaming throughout Ngali and neighboring *secteurs*. She worked out a system whereby she signaled to those fleeing whether it was safe to come to her house. If the *interahamwe*[10] were not in the vicinity, she would post a sign by the road with the name of the *secteur* or similarly innocuous information, to indicate that it was safe to come to her house. When the *interahamwe* were in the area, she would remove the sign and hide it in her house. When the *interahamwe* finally became suspicious, she played the part of a witch,

[10] *Interahamwe* is the term that people in my study used to refer to the bands of local killers and not the militia specially recruited and trained in Kigali who were officially so designated. I follow local usage here.

shaking an empty gourd with pebbles inside as she pretended to summon the spirits of Nyabingi, a powerful woman in the Ndorwa court in the past, whose followers and self-appointed mediums remained active long after her death.[11] At one point, when the *interahamwe* threatened to enter her house to search for Tutsis hiding inside, Sula warned them that evil spirits would harm them if they dared to violate the sanctity of her "chapel."[12] In another daring move, she refused 50,000 Rwanda francs ($125US at the time, an enormous sum by local standards) that the *interahamwe* offered her if she revealed the hiding places of Tutsis.

Not all those who rescued were as ingenious and determined as Sula. Many people simply found themselves in positions where a fleeing neighbor, friend, or family member came to them for help. In the community of Ngali, for example, an elderly man agreed to take in two children who had shown up at his door one evening looking for a place to hide. The two were the children of a Tutsi friend who had died years before the genocide. In the same community, several Tutsis married to Hutus escaped the genocide by hiding in the homes of their Hutu in-laws.

The danger for those hiding or helping Tutsis was the possibility that neighbors and even family members would denounce them to the authorities. Denouncing someone for hiding or helping a Tutsi was tantamount to a death sentence, since the killers threatened to kill anyone helping a Tutsi. Denouncing was thus an easy way to get rid of unwanted family members or rivals.

The man who agreed to hide the children of his deceased friend, for example, was denounced by his son. Another man who was married to a Tutsi woman was denounced by his brother. In both cases, the motive was personal. The son wanted his father killed so he could "inherit" his father's property. The brother wanted to get rid of his brother and the brother's wife so that he could take over their house and belongings.

Despite the risk of being denounced, people did try to help Tutsis in whatever way they could. Gestures of aid even came from the most unlikely source—active *génocidaires*. One man in Kimanzi, for example, told us that he survived the January 1991 massacres of Tutsi[13] because of

---

[11] Alison Des Forges, "The Drum is Greater than the Shout: The 1912 Rebellion in Northern Rwanda," in Donald Crummey (ed.), *Banditry, Rebellion and Social Protest in Africa*, London, James Currey, 1986, p. 312.

[12] Cf. African Rights, *Hommage au Courage*, p. 39.

[13] These massacres of local Tutsis followed an RPF attack on the town of

the help of friends who had joined in the killings. These friends-turned-killers, the man explained, spared him because they had been long-time friends. A man in Ngali told a similar story. He had sought refuge in a neighbor's house when the killings began. A friend who had been forced to join the *interahamwe* came to the man's hiding place to alert him that a group of killers was on its way to kill him. The man fled and survived the genocide.

Faced with these acts of rescue during the Rwandan genocide, the "rescuer" category proves inadequate. While some people, like Sula and the Seventh Day Adventist pastor, do seem to fit the category, many others do not; yet their acts of rescue were no less critical to the survival of the Tutsis they helped than the heroic actions of Sula and the pastor.

Acts of rescue by non-rescuers

To understand how changing contexts produced possibilities for rescuing or helping Tutsi, let us look at the actions of three men, one from the northern community of Kimanzi and two from the centre-south community of Ngali. What these profiles help to illustrate is that even those whom we would normally categorize as bystanders (that is, people who stood by and did nothing) or perpetrators (that is, active killers) were capable of acts of rescue given the right circumstances.

Gérard (former *responsable* (leader) from Kimanzi)

Gérard had been *responsable* for his *cellule* for ten years by the time the RPF invaded Rwanda in October 1990. Gérard had moved to Kimanzi in 1966 as a young man, when his father bought a parcel of land and gave it to him.

Gérard did not have much formal schooling, despite the support and wishes of his grandfather who helped to raise him. "I wasn't able to go to school very often because I was difficult. After a while, I left school," he explained. Gérard did eventually learn how to read and write as an adult. As *responsable*, he used these skills to keep neat and copious written records that he showed my interpreter and me at our first interview.

Ruhengeri on 23 January 1991. The RPF held the town for a day and released all the prisoners from the main prison.

When talking about the period of the war and genocide (1990–94), Gérard talked mostly about having to flee the fighting between Rwandan army troops and the RPF. When he and the other Hutus fled, they followed the government troops because, he explained, "We didn't know where the RPF came from." In February 1993, after another attack by the RPF, everyone from his community fled, including two Tutsi families from an adjacent *secteur*. There had been one Tutsi family in Gérard's *cellule* but that family had fled in January 1991, during the first wave of massacres that had targeted local Tutsis.

I interviewed Gérard because I had heard from another resident that Gérard had helped the single Tutsi family living in his *cellule* by alerting them that the killers were on their way to kill them. As this resident explained:

The threatening of Tutsis and certain Hutus started before the downing of President Habyarimana's plane. When Habyarimana died, there were Hutus who were killed accused of being *ibyitso* [accomplices] of the *Inkotanyi* [RPF]. In our *secteur* of K—, there was one Tutsi household. When the *responsable* found out that they were going to kill them, he told the family to flee. For now, the members of this family are still alive.

Gérard never mentioned this incident himself, yet if the account is true, alerting the family was clearly an act of rescue, for most Tutsis in the vicinity survived by fleeing, not hiding.

Gérard, however, did not seem to see himself as a rescuer but as a bystander, and at times a victim (albeit of war, not genocide). As a Hutu, he had reason to fear the RPF, which had forced several local residents to carry supplies for the army; many of these forced conscripts were never seen alive again. Fear of the RPF is the reason why he and other Hutus in Kimanzi fled many times throughout the period of the war (1990–94). As Gérard explained: "We believed that the RPF was capable of killing us and we fled but we noticed that the people were surrounded by the RPF were not killed and that's why we came back [from the Congo] in a few days." Viewing Gérard as a bystander or victim of war, however, should not take away from his actions toward the single Tutsi family living in his *cellule*, particularly if those actions meant the difference between life and death for the family. In other words, while he may have fitted the category of "bystander," Gérard may have also been responsible for an act of rescue.

Michel (confessed killer from Ngali)

In addition to ordinary Hutus, there were also active killers who helped Tutsis during the genocide. Michel is one such man. He had been in prison since 15 March 1995 and had confessed to participating in the murder of a Tutsi man at a roadblock near his house. At our second interview, Michel told us not about his crimes, but how he and his siblings tried to save four Tutsi neighbors by hiding them in their homes.

Q. The last time you told us that you saved four people. Tell us how you decided to hide these four people.
I saw that the killing was terrible and I saw especially that our neighbors were suffering, that I had to do some good. I give you the example of the lady PT. Between her house and mine, there is a sister house. As we had shared everything before, I decided to save her.

Q. Did PT ask you to save her?
She did not ask me to save her. She just came to our house and we agreed to hide her and to share with her what we had at the time until the end of the war.

Q. Who were you with at your house?
My sister [name deleted], my little brothers [names deleted]. Except that [one of my brothers] had his own house and we hid them together.

Q. Did you hesitate to hide this woman at first?
We did not hesitate to hide her except each time the killers would come to search for people to kill. But we did everything possible to protect her.

Michel's rescue activities did not keep him from participating in the murder of another man. This victim was a stranger to Ngali and had stopped at Michel's house to ask for directions to a neighbor's house. Michel describes his involvement in this man's murder in extremely ambiguous terms.

Q. What happened next at your house? after this man's arrival?
Once he got there, he asked me to show him the path that leads toward [a neighbor woman's] house. I kept him at my house a while and after a few minutes, a man named MG came to my house and asked him [the stranger] to follow him. This man followed MG to the roadblock where they were working.

Q. Who was this man named MG?
He was the leader of the roadblock.

Q. What did he want with this man?
He wanted to have him killed and he was killed at the roadblock.

Q. Were you able to see the killing of the man from your house?
No, because between the roadblock and my house, there is a forest.

Q. How did you know this man was killed at the roadblock?
The killers passed by near my house saying they had killed him.

Q. How did MG know that this man was at your house?
I don't know.

Q. Why did MG and the others want to kill the man who was at your house?
When MG arrived at my house, he started to ask him lots of questions and maybe he figured out that this man was among those people whom they were supposed to bring to the roadblock.

Q. Did you know that MG was going to kill this man when he took him to the roadblock?
Yes, I thought about him being killed because there were some others who were killed like that but there was nothing I could do for him.

Q. Did you try to keep MG from taking this man from your house?
Yes, I tried to stop him but he didn't listen to me. Afterwards, I ran into [the neighbor woman] who had me imprisoned and I told her that MG did not want to let this man go.

Q. What did you say to MG in trying to keep him from taking this man to the roadblock?
After talking to this man, MG asked me what this man was doing at my house. I told him that he came to ask me the path that leads to [the neighbor woman's] house. He told me he was going to take him to the roadblock and I asked him to let him go to [the neighbor woman's] house before taking him to the roadblock. MG refused and asked the man to follow him.

Q. Was MG alone or was he with some others?
Yes, he was alone.

Q. Was he armed?
I don't remember if he was armed.

As these two contrasting stories illustrate, rescue activities on the part of *génocidaires* were highly context-dependent and based, in part, on the existence of prior ties to the Tutsi person in question. That is, *génocidaires* like Michel were not inclined to rescue anyone and everyone; rather, they helped those they knew when circumstances permitted. When the leader of the roadblock was present in his house, for example, Michel made only a half-hearted effort at helping the stranger. Indeed, Michel's suggestion that they take the man to the neighbor's house first before going to the roadblock was hardly a sincere effort to help the man since, once at the roadblock, the man would have been killed anyway. Whatever the extent of Michel's actual involvement in the man's death, the difference between this stranger and the four Tutsis whom Michel and his siblings were hiding was that Michel had a prior relationship to the latter. They were, as Michel explained, among those Michel saw "suffering" when the killings began. Michel had no such ties to the stranger. This lack of ties may have meant the difference between Michel trying harder to save the man and his going along, however reluctantly, with the man's murder.

As Michel's case illustrates, *génocidaires* were also capable of acts of rescue. Killing, in other words, did not keep killers from trying to save others.

Olivier (confessed killer from Ngali)

Like Michel, Olivier had been in prison for nearly ten years by the time of my interviews in 2004. He, too, had taken part in a government program that offered the possibility of a reduced sentence to those who confessed to participating in the genocide. In his formal letter of confession to the prosecutor, Olivier admitted to participating in the murders of seven people. In his interviews with me, however, he admitted matter-of-factly that he and his group were responsible for nearly every killing in Ngali, a community that had close to 300 Tutsis when the genocide began.[14]

What was most startling, however, was not Olivier's admission that he had been so active in the genocide, but his remarks about the possibility of trying to save or rescue someone.

Q. Did you ever try to save someone during the genocide?
No, it was impossible.

Q. Why was it impossible?
Because when you would say something about saving someone, they would tell you to kill him yourself. There was a boy who was fleeing. When I ran into him, I told him to take another path because he was headed toward the *interahamwe*. He's alive.

Q. Did you know this boy?
Yes, I knew him. He lived in our *cellule*.

---

[14] République Rwandaise, *Recensement général de la population et de l'habitat au 15 août 1991, Résultats provisoires*, Kigali: Service National de Recensement, 1991.

Q. Why did you help this boy?
He was my neighbor, but not close, we weren't close friends. But I ran into him when I was alone and that's why I saved him. But when you ran into someone when you were in a big group, it was hard to save someone.

Olivier's remarks support the hypothesis that rescuing was highly dependent on immediate context—on who else was physically around or present. Olivier's case also suggests that immediate context was more important than prior ties in leading killers to help Tutsis, instead of hurting them. When asked whether he knew the boy, for example, Olivier says that he knew who the boy was, but adds that he had no special relationship to the boy. In other words, prior ties did not prompt Olivier to do what he did. Instead, Olivier explains his actions by pointing to the fact that he was alone when he ran into the boy, and not with his group of fellow *génocidaires*. Being alone presented Olivier with an option he did not believe he had when he was with the group; alone, he could help the boy escape, rather than help to kill him.

Olivier's explanation also indicates that like Gérard, Olivier did not consider what he did an act of rescue. Yet, insofar as his actions were intended to help the boy avoid the *Interahamwe* and thus avoid being killed, they clearly constitute an act of rescue. Olivier does not consider what he did an act of rescue because, according to his own definition, an act of rescue required acting in defiance (and in the presence) of the group, a risk that Olivier seems to indicate he was never willing to take.

As Olivier's case demonstrates, even the most active killers—those who clearly fall under the category of "perpetrator"—were capable of acts of rescue when the circumstances allowed them to do so. Acts of rescue, to be sure, did not absolve or make up for their participation in mass murder. Yet, to overlook these acts of rescue would be to overlook the extent and form of rescue activities during the Rwandan genocide.

Conclusion

Categories form a necessary part of any analysis, but analysts should use them with caution when examining the complexities of behavior during genocide. Even the category of rescuer, seemingly self-evident, can lead analysts astray. The problem with looking only at "rescuers" when explaining patterns of rescue during genocide, particularly one as intimate as the Rwandan genocide, is that acts of rescue are not always the sole province of rescuers. To arrive at a complete picture of rescue activities during genocide—their numbers, form, and context—scholars need to include all acts of rescue in their analyses. By doing so, scholars can begin to theorize the conditions and circumstances that make rescue possible for any person, rescuer and non-rescuer alike.

PART II

THE STATE, ITS BORDERS AND THE CONDITIONS FOR AID

The second section brings together contributions which, while broaching all dimensions of rescue, well illustrate the way in which public policies influence the scope and nature of rescue actions. The 20th-century genocides, a series of planned, large-scale massacres, were the work of state powers. The chronology and modalities of survival strategies and rescue actions in response to these state undertakings and designed to circumvent them were partly conditioned on the action of these same state powers. The same remark applies to the way in which rescue techniques adapted to policies of assistance—or non-assistance—to victims conducted by bordering states.

As illustrated by the three genocides examined in this book, the chronology of mass murder policies generates a chronology of rescue. Hasmik Tevosyan shows that the rescue of Armenians differed profoundly depending on whether one was in the phase prior to deportation or in the middle of it. After deportation, families had to be hidden in Muslim homes. During the death marches, the situation was different; most of the men had already been killed, acts of rescue concerned mainly women and children. The modalities raise the problem of the definition of rescue because they also involved at the time kidnapping, enslavement, conversion and forced marriages with eradication of the victims' Armenian identity. As Ugur Ümit Üngor points out, "the survivors literally escaped with only their lives, leaving behind cultural ties and religious practices." In the case of the genocide of the Jews, as regards its implementation in France, the Vélodrome d'Hiver roundup in July 1942 and the occupation of the southern zone in November triggered active rescue mobilization.

Katy Hazan and Georges Weill show that the OSE, a Jewish charity to rescue children represented in France since 1935, formed its own underground networks to place children and families in the southern zone in early 1943. However, in the northern zone, it was as early as September 1941, therefore well before the first families were rounded up, that the OSE created its placement networks. Here is a case of remarkable anticipation that warrants closer study.

The longer extermination goes on for, the more likely it is to achieve its ends. But the opposite is also true. It is the extreme rapidity with which the genocide was carried out that facilitated the extermination of Tutsis. During the three months it lasted, this genocide exceeded the average pace of the genocidal murders organized by the Nazis in the course of four years. In Rwanda, as Scott Straus shows, open resistance to genocide, when it occurred, did not last any more than ten days. The very fact that it could occur, even in this short time span, is also a unique characteristic unknown in the two previous genocides. It partly has to do with decentralized massacre modalities involving the participation of local populations; local authorities sometimes resisted impetus coming from the capital before they were finally swept up in the wave of murderous violence.

After chronology, it is in fact the territorial level of administration that plays a decisive role in the organizing rescue. Raymond Kévorkian gives several examples of Ottoman civil servants in the provinces who played for time in carrying out deportation orders or even refused to enforce them. He also cites the case of the prefect in Der el-Zor who strived to protect the Armenians interned in concentration camps in his constituency, nicknamed the "Armenian patriarch" by the Turks. Irene Herrmann and Daniel Palmieri mention a similar dichotomy that can be noticed between the leadership level of the International Committee of the Red Cross (ICRC), basically passive during the genocide of the Jews, and the lower level of the organization chart where some ICRC officials worked tirelessly, "the idea of witnessing these tragic events impotent and disarmed [being] almost unsupportable." Laura Hobson-Faure introduces a comparable debate within Joint, an American philanthropic organization for Jewry abroad, whose the executive board in the United States wanted to remain within the confines of legality, whereas at the grassroots level, especially in the person of Jules Jefroykin in France, its agents determinedly used Joint funds to hide Jewish children and finance the Jewish resistance.

THE STATE, ITS BORDERS AND THE CONDITIONS FOR AID

Aside from the effects of proximity, the forms of punishment for rescue efforts also had a direct influence on such activities. One can imagine that the fiercer the repression—it was barbaric in Poland during World War II—the more seldom rescue occurred. Yet this cause-and-effect link should be qualified. In the Netherlands, the deportation rate of Jews was very high, but as Bob Moore indicates, punishment for aiding Jews only began in the second half of 1943, a year after the deportations began. Punishment for acts of solidarity does not completely explain the sheer numbers of people deported. Moreover, during the war period, assistance to Jews was not punished as such in Belgium, or in France as Claire Andrieu shows in the first part of this book. And yet the proportion of Jews deported was much higher in Belgium than in France. There were cases of punishment for aid to Jews in France, however. Tal Bruttmann mentions a few of them, inflicted by the Vichy authorities or the SS, in the specific context of hunting down Jews conducted in the area of Grenoble by the SS officer Alois Brunner in early 1944. Another fact that nuances the link between punishment of help and refusing to help is that assistance was given practically across the board to allied airmen coming down on Western European soil, even though the severe punishment for this was well known and had begun in early summer 1940.

But the territory of the genocidal state, however extensive it may be, as was the Ottoman Empire or the Third Reich, reaches its limits. At its borders or beyond, neutral states or those with no hostility toward the victims serve as potential shelters and contribute by their mere presence to developing a form of assistance to people in danger. Besides, religious or civil organizations that depend on neutral states can serve to thwart genocidal policies. As Hans-Lukas Kieser shows in the third section of this book, American consulates—the United States did not enter the First World War until April 1917—and foreign Christian missions in Turkey were able to offer help to the Armenians. During the next world war, the OSE used the prolonged neutrality of the United States particularly to engage in an administrative struggle to obtain visas for children. In this case, rescue was legal and took root in an administrative task that was all the more considerable since similar efforts were required to obtain two additional visas for each refugee, one from Spain and the other from Portugal.

Alongside these legal rescue activities, escape was also organized in the form of secret border crossings. The neutrality of Switzerland, a democratic island in the middle of a subjugated Europe, gave rise to the creation of smuggling networks and increased the activities of traditional smugglers. Ruth Fivaz-Silberman shows that the total closure of Switzerland's borders, announced in August 1942, was followed in the month of October by a restrictive refugee policy to which the rescue networks had to adapt. By falsifying the identities of refugees to meet the criteria of authorized family immigration, by composing fictitious families and changing children's ages, the networks were able to continue to smuggle a few thousand Jews. In the course of the war, nearly 15,000 Jews were able to enter Switzerland, but about 3,000 of them were rejected. During the Rwandan genocide, Burundi's attitude was less restrictive. It opened its borders to the Tutsi refugees; Charles Kabwete Mulinda points out that the Burundi Army benevolently greeted the few survivors who manage to cross the border. In this case, they reached the country of refuge in much smaller numbers, because of the particular way in which this genocide was perpetrated on site by a civilian population mobilized in the manhunt. It was not arrest that the fugitives feared, but the likelihood of being slaughtered en route by the countless killers. Among the numerous techniques of aid from abroad, Frank Chalk points out one significant absentee, the BBC Hungarian service, which only warned Hungarian Jews of the fate that awaited them once the deportations had begun. This silence of the radio waves once again raises the question of the discretion of Allied propaganda in denouncing the worst Nazi crimes.

The practical aspect of external constraints—the timeline of genocidal policies, the effects of proximity on territorial administration or organization leadership, differences in forms of punishment for providing help and the opportunity offered by the existence of neutral states—form the central theme of this second section.

10

RESCUE PRACTICES DURING THE ARMENIAN GENOCIDE

Hasmik Tevosyan

This paper analyzes the broad range of rescue practices employed during the Armenian genocide. It focuses on conditions and motives for rescue in the light of contextual variables before, during and after the deportation of the Armenians. It devotes special attention to analysis of the concept of the "Righteous among the Nations" in the framework of the Armenian Genocide and the significance of this designation for future reconciliation between the victim and perpetrator. Materials and sources include recorded testimonies of survivors and witnesses (audio and visual), historical novels, autobiographies and memoirs as well as academic publications on the subject matter.

The concept of the "Righteous" in the comparative perspective of genocide studies

Under the Yad Vashem definition, a non-Jewish person who risked his/her life, freedom, and safety in order to rescue one or several Jews from the threat of death or deportation to death camps without exacting monetary or any other material compensation can qualify for consideration for the title of "the Righteous Among the Nations."[1] If we apply the defi-

---

[1] See the official website of Yad Vashem: www1.yadvashem.org/about_yad/index_about_yad.html

nition of the "Righteous" used by the Yad Vashem commission to the Armenian genocide, very few historical figures qualify for that title. Moshe Bejski, who was the president of the Yad Vashem commission for over thirty years, insisted that "the bestowal of the title of "Righteous" should never be based on an abstract definition, a heroic or dogmatic formula."[2] In this light, a question arises: who should be considered and defined as the "Righteous" in the case of the Armenian genocide?

The "Righteous" figures in the Armenian consciousness are often identified with the active witnesses of the Metz Yeghern (the Great Evil, as Armenians refer to the first genocide of the twentieth century), who documented and raised their voices against the genocide, in a vain attempt to prevent the deportation and annihilation of the Armenians from their homeland. Boghos Levon Zekiyan has remarked with insight on such "Righteous" figures in the Armenian consciousness as the American Ambassador Henry Morgenthau, the German evangelical pastor Johannes Lepsius, and the German army officer Armin Wegner[3] (who symbolizes the common ground between the Armenian and Jewish genocides); "It would be hard to find anyone who had so persuasively, zealously, consistently and passionately endeavored to help the Armenians… though their actions had no immediate practical effects that saved a single life!"[4]

How do we explain this difference in the perception of "righteousness" in the case of the Armenian genocide? For the most part, it is due to the fact that the perpetrator country continues to deny the genocide and blames the victims themselves. Under these circumstances, it is not surprising that a witness of the genocide who puts the truth and justice above all other considerations and, despite threats and blackmails, is not

---

[2] Gabriele Nissim, "The Universal Value of the Concept of 'the Righteous' in Connection with the Genocides of our Century," in Ulianova Radice and Anna Maria Samuelli (eds), *There is Always an Option to Say 'Yes' or 'No.' The Righteous against the Genocides of Armenians and Jews*, Padua, Cooperativa Libraria Editrice Università di Padova, 2000, p. 13.

[3] Armin Wegner was awarded the title of "Righteous" by the Yad Vashem Committee in 1967 for the letter he sent Hitler in 1933 denouncing the regime's anti-Semitic behavior. He was consequently arrested and imprisoned by the Nazi government.

[4] Boghos Levon Zekiyan, "Reflections on the Semantic Transposition of the Concept of 'the Righteous' to the Context of the Armenian 'Metz Yeghern'," in Ulianova Radice and Anna Maria Samuelli (eds), *There is Always an Option to say 'Yes' or 'No.'*, op. cit., p. 239.

afraid to speak up becomes the Just—the "Righteous"—whether or not his efforts are successful in saving lives or in persuading others about the crimes committed. Hrant Dink, a Turkish journalist of Armenian descent, who was recently murdered by Turkish nationalists for his courage in speaking publicly about the Armenian genocide in Turkey, is considered by many Armenians as "Righteous." Likewise, Taner Akçam, a Turkish historian in exile and the first Turkish scholar who used the word "genocide" describing the systematic destruction of the Armenians in the Ottoman Empire, is often referred to as the "Righteous" of our time.

Hence, the concept of the "Righteous among the Nations" should not be limited to a dogmatic and universal formula. Its definition is shaped to a large extent by a) the historical context of the genocide; b) available historiographical data; c) the current state of affairs between the perpetrator state and the victims, or the victimized nation; and d) the individual memory and collective perception of the "Righteous" figures by the survivors and their subsequent generations. Despite its universal value, the concept of the "Righteous" can have a different definition and implication when viewed from the comparative perspective of genocide studies. As social scientists we should avoid making any generalized statements or conceptualizations that fail to incorporate this comparative dimension.

Historical context of the "Metz Yeghern"

In order to understand the rescue practices in the Armenian genocide, it is important to examine the genocidal plan, pattern, and method of extermination carried out by the Young Turk rulers of the Ottoman Empire. Three strategic actions of the government precluded the possibility of Armenian collective resistance and self-defense. As during the Hamidian massacres of 1894–96, when 250,000 Armenians were slaughtered, the Young Turks first targeted the able-bodied Armenian men, most capable of defending their towns and villages.[5] Thousands of Armenian men who had been conscripted into the Ottoman Army were the first to be eliminated; they were disarmed and placed into labor battalions. Those who did not die from starvation, disease, or attrition were taken in groups of 50 to 100 and were executed.[6]

---

[5] Vahakn Dadrian, *The History of the Armenian Genocide: Ethnic Conflict from the Balkans to Anatolia to the Caucasus*, Providence, Berghahn Books, 1995, pp. 124–55.

[6] Donald Miller and Lorna Touryan Miller, *Survivors: An Oral History of the*

A second measure was to requisition all guns owned by Armenians. According to many eyewitness accounts, Armenians were given quotas of weapons to hand in.[7] If they did not collect enough, they had to buy guns from their Turkish or Kurdish neighbors. The confiscated weapons were photographed and presented as official proof that the Armenians were armed and were planning a rebellion. Government officials used this "evidence" as justification for mass arrests of the male population. The government also used propaganda about Armenian insurgency to incite the local Muslims against Armenians.

A third action that facilitated the genocidal plan was the extermination of the Armenian community leaders, government officials, and the intellectual elite. They were instructed to report to the local government and subsequently imprisoned without trial.[8] Hundreds of Armenian intellectuals, religious and political leaders, writers, lawyers, educators, and musicians were arrested in Constantinople and brutally murdered.

These government actions set the stage for the deportation of the entire Armenian population, who were forced to march through mountain passes, on circuitous and remote routes. The destination of these caravans of exhausted, starving and dehydrated people was the deserts of Syria. Needless to say, most of the people in these caravans died of attrition, dehydration, or starvation on the death march. Those who survived were butchered in the death camps of Der el-Zor and in the deserts of Mesopotamia.[9]

As Leslie Davis, American consul at Harpoot (Kharpert) from 1914 to 1917, wrote, "Another method has been found to destroy the Armenian race. This is no less than the deportation of the entire Armenian population... from all six (Armenian) *vilayets*. A massacre would be humane in comparison with it. In a massacre many escape, but a wholesale deportation of this kind in this country means a lingering and perhaps more dreadful death for nearly everyone."[10]

Armenian Genocide, Berkeley and Los Angeles, University of California Press, 1993, pp. 40–1.

[7] Ibid., p. 41.

[8] Merrill Peterson, *Starving Armenians: America and the Armenian Genocide, 1915–1930 and After*, Charlottesville and London, University of Virginia Press, 2004, p. 32.

[9] Ibid., pp. 33–45.

[10] Ibid., p. 7.

Local Kurds, Arabs, and Turks were not permitted to assist the Armenian deportees and were threatened with imprisonment by the Turkish government if they tried to hide any Armenians in their households. According to many survivors' accounts, Kurdish and Cherkess (Circassian) tribal groups were encouraged by Turkish officers to raid Armenian deportee caravans. These caravans were consequently pillaged; women and girls were abducted and many of the remaining deportees were assaulted and killed. Those who survived the deportation marches were butchered by members of the "Special Organization," which was created by the Ministries of Justice and Interior and was composed of criminals and murderers recently released from Turkish prisons. These death brigades, led by officers from the Ottoman War Academy, committed unspeakable atrocities.[11] More than half of the Armenian population of the Ottoman Empire was annihilated during the genocide. The estimated number of the genocide victims within the narrow time frame of 1915–23 reached 1.5 million.[12]

Venues for rescue

Armenian survivors typically fell into one of the following groups: a) Armenians living in Constantinople and Smyrna (Izmir), who escaped deportation because of the many foreign officials present in these cities of the Ottoman Empire; b) children who were taken in and adopted by Arabic, Turkish, and Kurdish families; c) Armenians who, under the protection of the Russian army, escaped across the border into Russian Armenia; d) Armenians who had valuable and rare skills or were professionals irreplaceable for Turkish society; e) women who were married, in most cases against their will, to Turks and Kurds, f) remnants, typically orphans, that miraculously survived months of deportations and were rescued by foreign missionary and relief organizations, g) and finally, a small number of Armenians who escaped deportations and massacres because Turks, Greeks, Arabs, and Kurds, at considerable personal risk to themselves, hid Armenian children, and sometimes even an entire family, in their households or helped them to escape to a safer place.

---

[11] Donald Miller, Lorna Touryan Miller, *Survivors: An Oral History of the Armenian Genocide*, op. cit., p. 43.
[12] Ibid., p. 44.

Some Armenians escaped the deportations by resistance and self-defense. In the famous case of Musa Dagh, Armenians of nearby villages fled to the mountains and resisted the Turks for fifty-three days and were eventually rescued by French and British cruisers. This heroic resistance of Armenian villagers later served as the historical basis for Franz Werfel's acclaimed novel, *The Forty Days of Musa Dagh*.

In other instances, small Armenian partisan groups, referred to by many survivors as defenders of the homeland, came to the rescue. A real-life story of an orphaned Armenian girl who was rescued by the Armenian resistance hero, General Andranik, was depicted in an American movie entitled *Ravished Armenia* or *Auction of Saints*. The movie was produced for the American Committee for Armenian and Syrian Relief (later Near East Relief) and proved to be an effective public relations campaign for this organization, which was among the first that responded to the Armenian genocide and financed Armenian relief efforts. This and many other accounts testify to the existence of organized efforts by survivor Armenians to come to the rescue of their suffering compatriots. Hilmar Kaiser writes in his article on Beatrice Rohner and the Protestant relief effort at Aleppo:

The active resistance of the local Armenian communities and that of the deportees made Rohner's efforts possible. While Armenians were victims, generally earmarked for death, they did not give up. At each stage on their deportation routes, Armenians organized some communal structure and provided thereby a base for the relief workers. The orphanage work at Aleppo was a spontaneous creation of the local Armenian communities. Certainly, the available funds were insufficient in every respect but the communities had managed to demonstrate that something could be done. Their positive example was in part instrumental in motivating Rossler and Jackson to appeal for more help from abroad.[13]

Annman Arakelian's (born 1903 in Dspni village, Kars) testimony is a typical example of how in extreme situations a victim can also be a selfless and courageous rescuer:

The people were compelled to migrate towards Aragads and come to Eastern Armenia. At that time the Turks opened fire from the Mount Yaghloudja. The Arpachay waters had risen, and when the Armenians tried to cross the river, the

---

[13] Hilmar Kaiser, "Beatrice Rohner and the Protestant Relief Effort at Aleppo in 1916" in Ulianova Radice and Anna Maria Samuelli (eds), *There is Always an Option to Say 'Yes' or 'No.'*, op. cit., p. 210.

strong water current drifted them away. Seeing that the people were perishing, they (Armenian villagers) put six oxen on one side and six on the other, they carried the people across. And the Turks were firing from the Yaghloudja slopes giving no rest to the poor people… My uncle Khachatour, who was a very brave man, gathered forty young men and began to fight against the Turks, so that the people might cross the Arpachay River. During the fight, eighteen Armenians were taken prisoner and my uncle, who was the commander, among them. The Turks made a fire and began torturing him… and at the end they roast him to death. They killed the rest (of the prisoners). Meanwhile the people had crossed the river.[14]

These and many other Armenian rescuers who sacrificed their lives to save their fellow villagers became national heroes for the survivors and subsequent generations. Their stories of heroic rescue and self-sacrifice are still being passed down from one generation to another through beautiful folk songs and ballads. These key historic figures, however, are often overlooked by the scholarship of rescue. Should we classify them as heroes and consequently exclude them from our scholarship because of a narrow definition of the "Righteous," which excludes the Armenian or Jewish survivors and victims who were at the same time selfless rescuers of their countrymen and neighbors? Should the nationality or ethnicity of an altruistic rescuer play such a defining role in our research? As Nechama Tec suggested in her reflections on rescuers, there is a need for systematic study of this category of victim-rescuers and conceptualization of the notion that under certain circumstances a victim may also be an altruistic rescuer.

Rescue before deportation

Muslims and Christian minorities of the Ottoman Empire were prohibited from hiding or rescuing Armenian families when the deportations started. On 19 April 1915, Djevdet Bey, Vali of Van and brother-in-law of Enver Pasha (Minister of War), issued an order: "The Armenians must be exterminated. If any Muslim protects a Christian, first, his house shall be burnt; then the Christian killed before his eyes, then his family and

---

[14] Verjine Svazlian, *The Armenian Genocide: Testimonies of the Eyewitness Survivors*, Yerevan, Gitutiun, 2000, online book (http://www.cilicia.com/armo_book_testimony–testimony.html).

himself."[15] However, there were compassionate Turks, Greeks, Arabs, and Kurds who, despite these threats by the government, tried to rescue Armenians and saved them from the horrors of the death marches.

Survivors' accounts and memoirs vary widely when examined in terms of motivation for rescue and characteristics of the rescuers. Rescuers, including those who were not motivated solely by humanitarian or purely altruistic considerations, came from different ethnic, socio-economic, educational, and religious backgrounds. It should be noted, however, that purely altruistic rescue (which did not involve economic or any other selfish interests and considerations) was more typical for the rescuers with relatively high socio-economic status. This seems plausible when we consider that wealthier rescuers would be less tempted by monetary or any other material rewards. Likewise, rescuers with higher social status would be less inclined to exploit the rescued as cheap labor, compared with poor peasants.

Unfortunately, we do not possess sufficient information about the rescuers' true motives, their individual characteristics, the history of their deeds and their lifestyle that would enable us to establish correlations and make any representative generalizations. The rescuers of the victims of the Armenian genocide are no longer living, obviously, while the ongoing politics of genocide denial and political repercussions in Turkey hinder any efforts by researchers to identify and interview the subsequent generations of these "Righteous" figures in the Ottoman period. Our analysis is thus limited to the recorded testimonies of survivors and witnesses of the Armenian genocide, their autobiographies and memoirs. Another limitation to the quality of the collected information is that most of the survivors were children at the time of the genocide.

The rescue practices during the Armenian genocide can be divided into two categories: rescue practices before deportation and rescue practices after it. This classification helps to shed some light on motives for rescue in view of different situational factors and contextual variables.

Rescue before the deportation typically falls into one of the following categories: a) contract rescue, including "paid help," as Nechama Tec calls it; and b) rescue by family friends or neighbors. In the latter case, even a good friend or a neighbor often accepted some financial or other form of

---

[15] Christopher Walker, *Armenia: The Survival of a Nation*, London and New York, Croom Helm and St. Martin's Press, 1990, p. 207 [2nd ed.].

material compensation for the risk and "inconvenience." This does not imply, though, that their main and only motivation for rescue was financial or material reward.

Contract rescue

Accounts of contract rescue vary and often involve Turkish gendarmes, officials, and notables. According to Serop Chiloyan (born in 1903 in Kharpert), his father paid a Turkish notable to save his family from the death marches. Despite his efforts, several family members were deported, while the rest were forced to work for the Turkish *agha* (master). Baghdasar Bourjikian (born 1903), Vahe Churukian (born 1906), and Beatrice Ashkharian (born 1902), all from Kessab, managed to avoid death marches through the bribes paid by their families.[16]

Bribery of Turkish officials, gendarmes, and soldiers demonstrates the strong role of the economic factor in rescue practices before deportation. The Ottoman bureaucracy was traditionally corrupt. As Antonia Arslan explains, "precisely because they were sensitive to the allure of money, Ottoman officials were not fanatics: and as long as they were able to keep their behavior hidden from the Ittihadists and from the powerful Special Organization, they often tried to attenuate the orders and protect the Armenians."[17] In some cases, however, these rescuers did not keep their word, and Armenian families who paid them hefty bribes were betrayed by their protectors, and consequently deported and killed. This can be explained in the light of escalating threats of severe sentence and public execution of those who tried to hide or rescue the Armenian families. As Taron Khachatryan (born 1911, province of Sasoun) testifies, Selim Agha, a Kurdish leader in a small village of Sasoun province, bribed a Turkish officer so that he could save several Armenian families from slaughter; he declared that the Armenians worked for him. A few days later, Selim Agha was beheaded for his assistance to Armenians, and his head was

---

[16] Richard Hovhannisian, "Intervention and Shades of Altruism during the Armenian Genocide," in Richard Hovhannisian (ed.), *The Armenian Genocide: History, Politics, Ethics*, New York, St. Martin's Press, 1992, pp. 181–2.

[17] Antonia Arslan, "Righteous Figures in the Armenian Consciousness," in Ulianova Radice and Anna Maria Samuelli (eds), *There is Always an Option to say 'Yes' or 'No.'*, op. cit., p. 36.

sent to the town of Mush as a warning to other Kurds who might think of hiding Armenian children and families in their homes.[18]

In examining how far the local Muslim population was ready or willing to risk security and life in order to save their Armenian neighbors, we should take into consideration that Armenians and Greeks, as Christian minorities of the Ottoman Empire, were historically discriminated against on religious grounds. The Young Turks elite effectively used this religious divide to pursue their secular geopolitical goals and well-calculated genocidal plan. The Young Turk leaders themselves were atheistic and "progressive" in their personal beliefs, but they appealed to religious differences to rationalize their criminal actions against the Armenians and arouse the Muslim populace against the Christian victims. Hundreds of accounts and testimonies of the survivors demonstrate that Armenians were dehumanized and compared to livestock. The local Muslim population and tribes routinely referred to them as *gyavours* (religious infidels, nonbelievers).

In view of this collective dehumanization, it is not surprising that there were few among local Turks and Kurds who were willing to sacrifice their lives in order to rescue the life of an "infidel." This should not, however, undermine the urgent need for collection, documentation, and further study of the accounts of altruistic Muslim rescuers who acted courageously and selflessly. These "Righteous" figures were able to think independently and act in accordance with their personal moral values despite the official propaganda and collective rationalization of the mistreatment and slaughter of the Armenians.

Humanitarian rescue

As Nechama Tec remarks with insight in her description of six interrelated characteristics of the Gentile altruistic rescuers, "freedom from societal constraints and independence promote opportunities to act in accordance with personal values and moral precepts, even when these are in opposition to societal expectations."[19] In opposition to the Young Turk government's incitement of religious and ethnic hatred and dehumaniza-

---

[18] Interview conducted by the author with the late genocide survivor Taron Khachatryan (b. 1911, Sasoun).

[19] Nechama Tec, "Who Dared to Rescue Jews, and Why?". Chapter 6 of this volume.

tion of the Armenians, these faithful Muslims recognized a neighbor, a friend, a fellow human being in the suffering victims and felt compelled to help, whether following their sense of religious duty or their personal moral convictions of what was right or wrong.

Gevorg Burnazyan, whose parents fled from their home town of Bayazed, relates a story about Bagh Effendi, the governor of Bayazed, who rescued the Armenian population of the city. A CUP (Committee of Union and Progress) meeting was held in the city of Erznka, where it was decided to send officers to each town and village in the province with the order to slaughter the Armenian population. The CUP members delivered the news of this order to Bagh Effendi as well, and informed him of their intention to start the massacre the next morning. The governor, however, did not permit the officers to enter the city and sent them back, saying that he would make the decision on that matter himself. In the meantime, he held a meeting with the Armenian notables of Bayazed (Gevorg's father, Soghomon Burnazyan was among them) and informed them about the danger, urging them to flee to the Russian border. The Armenians of Bayazed would have been slaughtered by the CUP members if Bagh Effendi had not interfered that night on their behalf.[20]

Interviewees from the Sasoun province of historic Armenia repeatedly refer to Kurds who tried to save Armenian families and children. According to Taron Khachatryan, a Kurdish woman promised her Armenian neighbors that she would save their seven-year-old boy from deportation.[21] After the Armenians were deported from the town, local Kurds and Turks searched for any remaining and hidden Armenians. They came to the Kurdish woman, looking for the boy, demanding: "Give us that boy; our bayonets are bloody and warm." The woman deceptively responded that she would have killed that Armenian *gyavour* (infidel) by her own hands had she found him. Instead, she secretly hosted the boy in her home for about a year. Kurdish rescue stories such as this are prevalent in regions like Sasoun, where Kurds outnumbered Turks. This story is also a typical example of the rescue accounts, where Kurdish and Turkish women played a crucial role in rescuing Armenian children, compelled by their maternal instinct.

---

[20] Personal Interview conducted by the author with Gevorg Burnazyan, son of Soghomon Burnazyan, genocide survivor (b. 1883, Bayazed).

[21] Personal interview conducted by the author with late genocide survivor, Taron Khachatryan (b. 1911, Sasoun).

In most pre-deportation rescue cases that involved humanitarian motivation, the rescuers were either neighbors or family friends. Many of these humanitarians endangered their own lives by rescuing Armenians. As Henry Riggs remarks:

> One fact, however, gave some hope to the poor Armenians. Their Moslem neighbors were inclined to side with them rather than with the government. In spite of all the efforts of the government to inflame the minds of the Turk, the more intelligent Turks for the most part remained either indifferent or positively friendly to the Armenians. Some were very outspoken in their condemnation of the government and expressed their sympathy with the Armenians. There were plenty of Turks, of course, who gladly took advantage of this opportunity to clear up old scores with their Armenian rivals, or of enriching themselves at their expense. But there was no outbreak of popular fanaticism on the part of the Turks... So it happened that the Turks individually did much to help their friends (and neighbors) and rescue them from their fate. Some did it from real neighborly kindness, some from motives of cupidity or worse. At first a large number of Armenians took refuge in the homes of their Turkish neighbors hoping thus to be overlooked in the general search. Soon however, it became apparent that the government officials would not tolerate this. Threats of severe punishment and the systematic searching of suspected Moslem houses by the police soon brought most of the Turks to terms, and all but a few of the Armenians so sheltered fell into the hands of the police. Some were directly betrayed by their protectors, but more were secretly turned out to shift for themselves, which was little better. There were some Turks, however, who were either fearless enough or influential enough to defy the threat of the government. In spite of repeated commands and threats, they kept the Armenians whom they were sheltering out of sight of the police and refused to reveal their hiding places.[22]

Riggs further remarks that it is best not to dig too deeply into the reasons why some Turks defended their Armenian friends and neighbors. Very often humanitarian motives were combined with some other considerations for rescue. As Richard Hovhannisian points out in his study of intervention and altruism during the Armenian genocide, it is hard to classify motives for intervention and rescue as purely humanitarian or strictly economic in many of the intervention and rescue accounts, since multiple motivations were often present at the same time. Nonetheless, Hovhannisian concludes that, using the definition of altruism adopted in

---

[22] Henry Riggs, *Days of Tragedy in Armenia. Personal Experiences in Harpoot, 1915–1917*, Ann Arbor, Gomidas Institute, 1997, pp. 96–7.

studies of the Holocaust, a significant number of cases that he originally termed as humanitarian in his study of the Armenian genocide would have to be disqualified as such.[23]

Considering the difficulties associated with constructing the socio-psychological profiles of the rescuers of the first genocide of the 20th century, researchers often encounter a gray area in their analysis of the underlying motivations for rescue. For example, Hovhannisian raises the question whether we should classify a particular case as altruistic rescue despite the fact that the rescued person had to labor for his rescuer.[24] In situations like this when a researcher encounters the "gray zone" predicament, contextual and situational variables can play a crucial role. We could categorize the case above as altruistic or humanitarian if the rescuer was a peasant, and it was expected that everyone in the family (including the rescuer's own children) must work or in some way contribute to the housework. The survivor's personal attitudes and depiction of his/her rescuer may also serve as criteria for classification when we are faced with the gray area in our retrospective study of motives for rescue.

Conversion to Islam

The story of Mabel Morookian (born 1908 in Marsovan, province of Sivas) shows that even an influential officer like a *kaimakan* (district governor) could not protect Armenians for long if they preserved their national identity. Marsovan's *kaimakan* was a good friend of Mabel's grandfather, and housed his family for a couple of months before confessing that he could not keep them any longer unless they converted to Islam and became Turkified. When questioned, he needed to be able to say that the people living with him were Turks.[25]

Some Armenian families, like Morookian's, were offered the choice of conversion to Islam as the only way to escape the deportations. Muslim rescuers often insisted on conversion to Islam for their new wards, as according to religious tradition the rescue and conversion of Christians were good deeds essential to the physical and spiritual wellbeing (for

---

[23] Richard Hovhannisian, "Intervention and Shades of Altruism during the Armenian Genocide," in Richard Hovhannisian (ed.), *The Armenian Genocide: History, Politics, Ethics*, New York, St. Martin's Press, 1992, pp. 179–80.

[24] Ibid., p. 179.

[25] Ibid., p. 192.

example, receiving great rewards in heaven) of both the rescuer and the rescued.

Conversion to Islam was, however, only a temporary solution for the Armenian male population before the deportation marches. While Muslim rescuers of the persecuted were encouraging, even forcing the Armenians to convert to Islam, motivated by piety and religious beliefs, the Young Turk leadership did not welcome the apostasy of the Armenian men and their willingness to convert in order to survive. The government's goal was to wipe away the Armenian *ethnos* from its historic homeland, while these "voluntary" converts could later be mobilized against their persecutors. Only children under age of 10–12 who were fortunate enough to survive the first waves of mass deportations and consequent massacres were targeted for Islamization and assimilation by the government. As Antonia Arslan writes, "the chance to convert was often a false opportunity, since the religious war was only apparent, dust thrown in the eyes of simple people by atheistic members of the Young Turks *elite*."[26]

Lucky exemptions from the death marches

Some Armenians who possessed professional or special skills, regarded as irreplaceable by local elites, were spared and exempted from deportation. A majority of them were required to convert to Islam, change their Armenian names, and abandon their national identity. As Vartanoush Zakarian, born in 1898 in Sebastia (Sivas), recalls:

> A Turkish official, who was a close friend of my father, in confidence said to him before the deportation, "This is not a picnic they are going to go to, this is not like a trip to the church Saint Nshan, don't say to anybody, but we are going to keep certain people that we need, and you're one of them."[27]

Zakarian's father was an engineer and stove-maker. The few other Armenians who were allowed to remain in Sebastia and escape the death-march included two barbers, three doctors and the Encababian photo-

---

[26] Antonia Arslan, "Righteous Figures in the Armenian Consciousness," in Ulianova Radice and Anna Maria Samuelli (eds), *There is Always an Option to say 'Yes' or 'No.'*, Padoue: Cooperativa Libraria Editrice Università di Padova, 2000, pp. 36–7.

[27] David Boyajian and Rafael Guroian, *Our Story. Oral History of the Zakarian Family*, Family publication, Boston, 2004 (interviews conducted by Vigen Guroian), pp. 38–9.

graphers. These spared Armenian families were forced to convert to Islam and change their Armenian names to Turkish names. Vartanoush Zakarian testifies that they were scared to speak Armenian and to call each other by their Armenian names for fear that Turkish women might overhear them.

Rescue during and after deportation

The majority of the Armenian male population was killed either before the deportation or relatively early in the deportation process, whereas women and children were left to endure endless death marches. Most cases of survival during the deportation marches (such as the abduction of young women for marriage and the kidnapping of children for labor) cannot be classified as acts of rescue. We should take into consideration that at this stage of the persecution of the Armenians, the victims (mostly women and children) were deprived of all means of survival. Under these circumstances and given the inevitable end of this journey to nowhere, even those survivors who were forcibly kidnapped from their families or who were sold for labor often refer to their kidnappers and "masters" as life-saving rescuers. As Hambardzoum Karapet Sahakian, born in 1898 in Sebastia, recalls:

> They drove us like sheep; they expelled us from our houses and our orchards. They drove us to the desert. We were walking in the open air for 110 days almost without rest… The old and the sick people couldn't walk, they remained on the road or the gendarmes killed them. They were driving us forward hungry; they didn't even allow us to drink water. The Kurds and the Chechens attacked us, plundered and kidnapped the girls and young women. Many women and girls threw themselves into the water. The Tigris and Euphrates rivers were filled with corpses… I remained alone. One day I was lying on the sand to die, hungry and naked. An Arab came close, approached the gendarme, gave him some money and said: "Let me take this one to work for me." He took me with him as a servant. I became a shepherd. That Arab saved my life. I always bless him. It is true that I lived in the cowshed; I slept with the animals, but my life was saved.[28]

---

[28] Verjine Svazlian, *The Armenian Genocide: Testimonies of the Eyewitness Survivors*, Yerevan, Gitutiun, 2000, (http://www.cilicia.com/armo_book_testimony-testimony.html).

Some parents gave away their children to passing Kurds and Turks in order to save them from starvation and inevitable death. As a child-survivor recalls:

> About this time, Turkish or Kurdish women would come and take children away. They approached my mother, too. Realizing that there was nothing but death facing us at that point, she gave me to them... So these two women held my hand and took me away... I kept walking—with my eyes and heart behind me.[29]

After the death marches, when the majority of the Armenian population was already annihilated, Turkish families could take in Armenian orphans on the condition of conversion to Islam and Turkification. Many survivors refer to their host families as their rescuers as many of them were, indeed, treated well in their new homes. We should note, however, that this category of rescuers was not faced with life-threatening risks, unlike the earlier discussed "pre-deportation rescuers." As Richard Hovhannisian remarks on the rescue after the deportations, "while many Muslims who took in Armenian women and children must be regarded as performing humanitarian deeds, on the whole they had little to fear in case of exposure."[30]

Unlike pre-deportation rescue, which was generally premeditated and often well thought out in advance in terms of risks versus awards associated, post-deportation rescue stories, as a rule, feature spontaneous, last minute intervention by a complete stranger to rescue a suffering victim who is a step away from the inevitable end. It indicates that the rescuer was compelled to intervene when faced with inhuman suffering and agony of the victim, irrespective of who the victim was. Taking into consideration the contextual variables and factors contributing to these spontaneous acts of rescue, discussed above, we face the dilemma whether to classify the recorded post-deportation humanitarian interventions by complete strangers as acts of "Righteous" rescue even though many of those who intervened on behalf of the victims had little to fear from sheltering the persecuted after the first waves of mass deportations and massacres.

Many post-deportation rescue accounts concern Arabs taking in Armenians who miraculously survived the death camps of Der el-Zor and the

---

[29] Donald Miller, Lorna Touryan Miller, *Survivors: An Oral History of the Armenian Genocide*, op. cit., p. 108.
[30] Richard Hovhannisian, "Intervention and Shades of Altruism during the Armenian Genocide," op. cit., p. 180.

deserts of Mesopotamia. Arab sympathy for suffering Armenians was due in part to their own oppression and struggle in liberating Syria from the Ottoman rule. The account of Gyurdji Harutyun Keshishian, born 1900 in Zeytoun, is a typical story of rescue by Arabs of those few remnants who miraculously survived the death camps of Der el-Zor:

They (Turkish soldiers) drove us like sheep; they took us to the deserts: women, children, there was no male among us; they had already taken away the men and killed them… Misery, hunger; we had no clothes: we were naked and barefoot. They kidnapped my three sisters… They stabbed me, too, and threw me in the pit, but I was alive. Under the corpses, drenched in blood, the smell of blood had spread all about. When the gendarmes finished their work, they poured petrol in the pit to burn the corpses. The dead didn't feel, but the voices of those alive would tear your heart into pieces. I was under the dead and I felt someone holding my hand tightly. I remained there in the pit a whole day… Finally, there was a brave woman. She somehow put her head out, saw that the gendarmes had gone and began shouting, "Whoever is alive, come out, let's run away."… We were about twenty women and children. One was wounded, all in blood, the other's hair was burnt and her face blackened. All were hungry and thirsty… But worst of all was that we feared the Turks would see us and slaughter us. We were going this was, that way, where were we going? We didn't know. That was the reason why we hid in the caves at daytime and walked by night… We reached the tents of the Arabs. The Arabs were very kind, good people… They took us in and kept. They asked me: "What's your name?" I said, "Gyurdji." "After this, let it be Farida," they said… We remained there for two years. Then the Americans came, gathered the Armenians and took them to Aleppo in carriages. They put the children in orphanages.[31]

International relief efforts

After Turkey signed the armistice in 1918, Allied forces were instructed to find remaining Armenian survivors and place the children in orphanages. International relief organizations—in particular, the American Committee for Armenian and Syrian Relief, which evolved into Near East Relief upon its incorporation by act of Congress in 1919—raised over $40 million by the end of 1920 for Armenian relief work.[32] Its

---

[31] Verjine Svazlian, *The Armenian Genocide: Testimonies of the Eyewitness Survivors*, Yerevan, Gitutiun, 2000, (http://www.cilicia.com/armo_book_testimony-testimony.html).

[32] Donald Miller and Lorna Touryan Miller, *Survivors: An Oral History of the Armenian Genocide*, op. cit., p. 121.

devoted field workers, along with Armenian resistance heroes such as General Andranik, played a crucial role in rescuing Armenian orphans and women from Turkish and Kurdish homes and saving thousands of Armenian refugees from starvation and inevitable death. As Rehan Manouk Manoukian (born 1910 in Taron) recalls:

In 1918 we were taken to Kars. Amercom (American Committee for Armenian and Syrian Relief) protected the orphans, brought them to Kars. We were at dinner when the fighting of Kars began. The Turks knocked at the door. The Americans stood before the door and didn't let them rush in. They hoisted their flag, so that the Turks might not harm us. Our American principal said to the Turks, "We don't have Armenian orphans only; we have Turk orphans as well."... Me, and many others like me, are very thankful to the Americans, since they saved our lives. Besides, in the American orphanage I learned needlework, which helped me to support my family in the future. Then, at school I learned well also. The Turks wanted to kill me, too, as they did with all my relatives, but I not only survived, I lived with my strong willpower and created three generations.[33]

Considering that the vast majority of the Armenian orphans had been Turkified while living in Turkish and Kurdish homes, this undertaking was crucial in returning thousands of Armenian orphans to their ethnic roots and saving them from assimilation. Thanks to American and European orphanages, children learned about their own history and religion, and re-learned their native language, which many had forgotten while living in Muslim households. The orphanages did not just provide the children with a safe haven, but also educated them and prepared them for adult life. This was an act of both physical and cultural rescue.

The "Righteous" as agents of change

As Pietro Kuciukian, one of the founders of the Committee for the Gardens of the Righteous Worldwide, writes:

There are some important symbolic figures who have played and continue to play decisive roles: they are the saints, the heroes, the righteous. While saints place the quality of death before the quality of life, sacrificing themselves in anticipation of another infinite life, heroes sacrifice themselves for their countrymen and for their nation, sustained by an earthly ideal. But righteous people and active

---

[33] Verjine Svazlian, *The Armenian Genocide: Testimonies of the Eyewitness Survivors*, Yerevan, Gitutiun, 2000.

witnesses sacrifice themselves for their fellows, they are motivated from within, they side with the victims of abuse from whoever is in power and, in saving their own dignity, they save the dignity of the victim as well… Their actions and active testimony do affect reality, they do have the power to bring about change and to rebuild the shattered web of human society.[34]

"Righteous" people do not need to be saints or heroes. They are often ordinary people and neighbors, who recognize a fellow human being in the victim and who value a single human life to the extent that they are willing to opt for risk, make a greater or lesser sacrifice to protect that life, and by doing so preserve their own dignity, their own self-esteem as a human being worthy of the gift of life. The "Righteous" are those who are capable of independent thought despite the ruling regime's effort to rationalize the committed crime, deny it, blame it on the victims, and dehumanize humanity.

The Jewish journalist and resistance scholar Gabriele Nissim writes of the Armenian genocide, "The worst thing that could happen to a victim was for the crime he had undergone to be removed."[35] Turkey still applies a policy of denial by claiming that Ottoman Armenians perished as a result of civil war, fighting for their independence. We live in a world where people still try to rationalize and even legitimize the genocide against Armenians by projecting the blame onto the victims themselves. Under these circumstances, when the victims of the genocide are denied due respect or memorialization, the notion of the "Righteous Among the Nations" can play an important role of "moral purification," perhaps even move a country responsible for a crime against humanity to embrace the truth. Thus the memory of the "Righteous" may indeed point a way toward the reconciliation between the victim and the perpetrator.

As Etty Hillesum, a Jewish writer and a victim of the Holocaust, wrote in her diary, "if there were only one decent German, then he should be cherished despite that whole barbaric gang, and because of that one decent German it is wrong to pour hatred over an entire people."[36] The notion of the "Righteous" is extremely important in the Armenian con-

---

[34] Pietro Kuciukian, "The 'Righteous for the Armenians. Memory is the Future.' Plan for an International Committee," in Ulianova Radice and Anna Maria Samuelli (eds), *There is Always an Option to say 'Yes' or 'No.'*, op. cit., p. 246.
[35] Gabriele Nissim, "The Universal Value of the Concept of 'the Righteous' in Connection with the Genocides of our Century," op. cit., p. 16.
[36] Ibid., p. 9.

text, given that generations of the Armenians were and are still faced with the Turkish denialism and the world's indifference. In order to overcome the collective trauma of the forgotten and unrecognized genocide and renew their hope in humanity, the Armenians need to believe that not all of the Turks hated them, that not all of the Turks supported the government's genocidal plan, and that not all of the Western world was compliant with or indifferent to their inhuman treatment.

11

OTTOMAN OFFICIALS AGAINST THE ARMENIAN GENOCIDE
A COMPARATIVE APPROACH TO TURKISH TOWNS

Raymond Kévorkian

Surviving the programmed extermination of a group apparently depends on good fortune, or pure luck. However, age, sex, religious confession, location of residence, social status, intellectual qualities, physical aptitude, "beauty" are all objective elements that help us understand with more clarity, in the case of the Ottoman empire, why one particular individual or group was able to escape death and get away rather than another. The central project of the Committee of Union and Progress (CUP) (or Young Turk party) state, the foundation of a Turkish nation, was the expression of an ideology which was inspired by social Darwinism, by the expulsion of "foreign bodies," of "microbes" which were polluting the body of Turkish society, because they did not adhere to its national project. Destroying the other to create oneself became, at its most radical phase, the unique obsession of the CUP, to which the whole "Turkish nation" was supposed to adhere. This ideology of exclusion did however allow for integration into the nation under construction of certain categories of victim groups showing signs of potential for assimilation, which would reinforce its plan of ethnic homogenization in Asia Minor. This led to rejection of the Armenian group, yet had no "biological" repugnance for its members provided they were integrated into Turkism. Thus, this part of the project has permitted us to create several categories of "saved" people.

Specific 'rescues' for young women and children

Young women and girls who were educated, preferably French or English speaking, who played the piano or the violin, were particularly coveted by Young Turk officers who hoped, with them, to lay the foundations of the "modern" Turkish family. This category of Armenian women, made up of several thousand individuals, forms a first category of survivors, married against their will to their "saviours." A second category of those who escaped death, again observed within this group of young women and in this case time amounting to tens of thousands, were captured by local notables, by simple soldiers, by civil servants, by tribal chiefs of all origins, Turkish, Kurdish, Arab, Bedouin, even peasants, and even more frequently by a neighbor: kidnapped or bought along deportation routes, with no ideological reason, they were destined to enrich harems, to be sexual objects, to supply the official brothels of the Ottoman army. They were, nonetheless, saved. Several of them even raised families with their persecutors, after conversion. A percentage of them were found at the end of World War I, in refuges created for their rehabilitation. Many, impregnated with a strong sense of guilt, preferred to remain with their "saviours."

Children of both sexes under the age of five in 1915 form the largest category amongst survivors. Their deliverance however reveals extremely contrasting situations. Those who were considered the "healthiest" were used by baby traffickers to supply childless urban couples, in Constantinople or Aleppo for example, mainly "Turkish" and of upper social categories—superior officers, provincial notables, magistrates, top civil servants, members of the Young Turk movement—sometimes becoming the darling of the family.[1] The great majority of these children, however,

---

[1] As well as its political intelligence work, the Deuxième Bureau of the French Navy assembled information concerning "Armenian orphans who are currently living in Turkish homes in and around Constantinople." The report contains a census of 47 Turkish families in the capital who had taken in Armenian children. And what does the census show? That the people who have taken them in are doctors, officers, upper-level civil servants, pashas, magistrates, lawyers, the military commander of the General Security Service, Ali Bey, the commandant of the Sivas gendarmerie, members of parliament like Faraci (member for Salonika), the commandant of the VI army, Hashid Pacha, etc. This means that these children were taken in by the elite of the Ottoman Empire—young girls aged between 7 and 14 years old for the most part—care being taken to convert

found themselves in the countryside, in modest Bedouin, other Arab or Kurdish environments, frequently treated as slaves and often sexually abused. A small minority was even taken into orphanages, especially those founded by the state with an aim of creating "new Turks." Even so, they were saved. Investigation groups organized by Armenian institutions following the Armistice of Mudros took many of them in.

Young women and very young children form the two principal categories of Armenians who survived, if one can call it surviving, because of an ideological aspect of the genocide plan: capturing a percentage of the victim group and integrating it into the project to build a Turkish nation. Other rescues reveal the intervention not of the dominant group but of representatives of neutral countries, notably missionaries or American diplomats, who used their own networks to hide a few Armenians in their institutions—those sharing the same religion were preferable—or brought financial aid for the deportees in concentration camps in Syria and Mesopotamia.[2] Hans-Lukas Kieser explores these operations at length. We also note successful intervention by neighbor states like Bulgaria, in the frontier zones, notably in the issuing of false passports to Armenians.[3]

The most elaborate rescue operations were carried out in secret by the Armenian Patriarchate of Constantinople—until its suppression in July 1916—supported by a network made up of Armenian executives of the Asian Turkish railroad company and American and German diplomats.[4] These particular rescues were mainly of young intellectuals, extracted

---

them (the first names listed in the eyewitness report are proof of this): Archives de la Marine (Vincennes), 1BB7–231, Service de renseignement de la Marine, Constantinople, letter of 6 February 1919 and report dated 30 December 1918, signed by Colonel Foulon, n° 256.

[2] See Hans-Lukas Kieser's contribution to this volume, Chapter 22.

[3] According to an Armenian source, several thousand of the more than thirty thousand Armenians of the *vilayet* of Edirne escaped the deportations thanks to the energetic intervention of the Bulgarian authorities: R. Kévorkian, *Le Génocide des Armeniens*, Paris, Odile Jacob, 2006, p. 864.

[4] The company's Armenian white-collar workers were momentarily reprieved from deportation through a request by its German superiors, for the time it took to train their "Turkish" replacements. R. Kévorkian, op. cit., pp. 718–19. The German and American Consuls in Aleppo, Walter Rosler and Jesse Jackson, played a capital role in the transfer of money from Constantinople; the director of "Bible House," Dr Peet, was one of the principal providers of funds.

from convoys and then hidden thanks to an urban network, notably in Constantinople or Aleppo.

Ottoman officials' attempts to oppose genocide

The success of a genocide project, however methodical it may be, depends upon numerous parameters. It is especially conditional upon the cooperation of civil servants. The Armenian extermination program shows clearly the respective roles played by the civil service and the army on the one hand, and the political and paramilitary groups linked to the CUP on the other. One observes a repeated situation where the "legal" part of the process is assigned to the state services (lists of people to be arrested, organizing convoys, confiscation of property) and the "somber" part to the Teshkilât-i Mahsusa (Special Organization), directly controlled by the Central Young Turk Committee via the "secretary-official" that it delegated for the provinces to coordinate operations and, if need be, denounce inaction or remove reluctant civil servants. Concerning the latter, we must remember that following its coming to power in 1908, the CUP worked to eliminate in the heart of its civil service and army those who disagreed with its policies, replacing them with men who were in whole-hearted agreement. In the first few months of the war, this policy was extended with the expulsion of Armenian civil servants, their replacement with Young Turks, and the appointment of Party executives as governors (*vali*) of Armenian "*vilayet*s," the administrative districts into which Turkey was divided.

The six eastern *vilayet*s, the Armenian provinces, make up of course the most interesting field of observation, even more so as the Young Turkey plan reserved a particular treatment for them: the total liquidation of Armenian territory, the systematic destruction of its population (between 15 and 20 per cent of deportees reached their "place of banishment" in the deserts of Syria and Mesopotamia).

The confiscation of Armenian goods, notably the transfer of business to Turkish businessmen, supervised by the Commissions for "abandoned goods," permitted abuses from which civil servants and local notables were able to profit. But it also engendered conflicts of interest, especially when a non-Armenian was in business with an Armenian deportee and thus found himself the injured party. There was also sometimes anger amongst the local population, which suddenly found itself deprived of its doctors, its chemists, its artisans etc., and saw the collapse of the economic activity of its region. Amongst the notables of the provinces, several were apparently aware that the eradication of the Armenians was going to provoke a severe economic crisis and protested. Others sought either to protect the goods of their Armenian neighbors and associates or even to save at least certain members of their families: children especially were hidden more easily from officials. Others suggested to their Armenian friends that they convert to escape deportation. Others again tried to save their neighbors by hiding them in their own homes. This phenomenon could not have been rare since a coded telegram circular from the commandant of the III Army, Mahmud Kâmil, sent from his headquarters at Tortum on 10 July 1915 to the chiefs of the *vilayets* of Sivas, Trabzon, Van, Mamuret ul-Aziz, Diyarbekir and Bitlis, concerned families sheltering Armenians:

> We learn that in certain places where the population is relatively confined, certain [elements] of the Muslim population are sheltering Armenians in their homes. This being contrary to the decisions of the government, heads of families keeping or protecting Armenians must be put to death in front of their homes and it is indispensable that their homes be burned. This present order must be transmitted and communicated to all those it may concern. Watch that no non-deported Armenians be able to remain, and inform us of your action. Converted Armenians must also be expelled. If those who attempt to protect them or maintain friendly relationships with them are people of the military, you must, having informed their commanders, immediately sever all their links with the army and bring them before the courts. Civilians, on the other hand, must be dismissed from their job and court-martialled.[5]

In the *vilayet* of Erzerum, one of the most exposed to the effects of the war, and of mixed population, the new *vali*, Hasan Tahsin Bey, was appointed in February 1915 after a brief period spent in Van, where Cevdet Bey took over his post. He had however to deal with the headquarters of the III Army, which had jurisdiction over the six eastern *vilayet*s, based

---

[5] Transcription of the decoded telegram (dated 10 July 1915) from Mahmud Kâmil published in the Takvim-i Vakayi, n° 3540, a certified copy dated 23 February 1919, Sublime Porte, ministère de l'Intérieur, Direction de la Sûreté générale, according to the document sent by the Sivas authorities on the same day, 23 February 1919, at the request of the Interior ministry, then transmitted to the court martial sitting in Istanbul after the war to try the crimes of the Young Turks.

to the north of Erzerum, at Tortum, and with the headquarters of the Teshkilât-i Mahsusa, set up in the town under the supervision of its president, Dr Bahaeddin Shakir, a member of the CUP Central Committee, seconded by Ahmed Hilmi Filibeli. According to an Armenian eyewitness, a secret meeting took place at the *vali* Hasan Tahsin's home, from 18 to 21 April 1915, in the presence of local Young Turk chiefs and town notables, 120 in total. It split into three groups: a first group of forty local notables suggested limiting the measures to just moving Armenians well away from the frontier zones; a second group of twenty people recommended leaving the Armenians alone; a third, including the *vali*, the deputy Seyfullah and the main Young Turk leaders of the town, insisted upon "the destruction of the Armenians and their expulsion from their homes, then their massacre, leaving no survivors."[6] It seems therefore that a majority of the Turkish local elite were hostile to the "measures" demanded by Constantinople and that under these circumstances, the CUP was trying in vain to involve the local elite in its project (this experiment was not to be repeated elsewhere).

Under pressure from the Commander in Chief of the III Army, Mahmud Kâmil, a classmate of both the War Minister and Dr Shakir, the *vali* probably had to give public support to the CUP project. He did however attempt to convince the Interior Minister—Talât Pasha, the real coordinator of the extermination of the Armenians—of all the inconveniences that this deportation could bring to the local economy, to army supplies, and more generally to civil peace in the *vilayet*. The *vali* Tahsin was also worried about the allegation of rebellion, which seemed too unlikely to him, and suggested keeping the civil population in its homes.[7] "Instead of deporting the Armenians in the middle of war to save our country and our army, [he wrote to the Minister] I suggest, for my part, on the contrary, that we keep them in their current positions awaiting further orders, and not push them towards revolt by undue force."[8] He reminds him that "with their cereals and their transport methods, they

[6] Bibl. Nubar/Fonds Andonian, P.J.1/3, liasse 59, Erzerum, f° 62, eyewitness account of Boghos Vartanian, from Erzerum, 5 August 1916.
[7] Coded telegram from the *vali* of Erzerum, Tahsin Bey, to the Interior Ministry, dated 13 May 1915: Archives of the Patriarchate of Constantinople/Armenian Patriarchate of Jerusalem, dossier XLIX, T 285, original Ottoman, transcription in Armenian characters and French translation. Our translation into English.
[8] Ibid.

[the Armenians] ensure the provision of our troops. This is a point that should be taken into account for, today, we only just manage, with a thousand difficulties, to ensure this provision," not to mention the fact that "90 per cent of the building industry tradesmen indispensable to the population and to the army are made up of Armenians. Over and above one or two grocers and butchers, there is not one single artisan amongst the Turks. That has its importance as well."[9] The Interior Minister's reply, dated 23 May, recommends all the same to the civil servants of the eastern *vilayet*s to implement the orders coming from the military authorities,[10] meaning the commandant of the III Army, who had jurisdiction over the six eastern *vilayet*s.

In the same *vilayet*, at Bayburt, the Turkish population also showed hostility to the deportation of the Armenians, to the extent that the deputy prefect (*kaimakam*), Mehmed Nusret Bey, a Young Turk leader, had three Turks executed in order to calm the locals.[11]

In the *vilayet* of Van, also on the border, densely populated with Armenians and with a large Kurdish tribal element, the appointment of Cevdet Bey, brother-in-law of the War Minister Enver, in February 1915, marked the beginning of tension. We find no opposition to the Young Turk policy voiced by the civil servants. Only the forty-five villages of the Kaza of Moks and its 4,459 Armenians escaped being massacred thanks to the protection of a Kurdish chief, Murtula Beg, who refused to carry out the orders of the *vali* Cevdet and held out until the Russian army arrived in the region.[12]

The *vilayet* of Diyarbekir gives us a different picture of Ottoman civil service action concerning the program to eradicate the Armenians. Dr Cerkez Mehmed Reshid, one of the founding fathers in the history of the CUP, with a diploma from the Academy of Military Medicine of

---

[9] Ibid.
[10] BOA, DH. Snf n° 53/93 telegram from Talât to the *vilayet*s of Van, Erzerum, and Bitlis, dated 23 May 1915: Osmanli Belgelerinde Ermeniler (1915–1920), T.C. Basbakanlik Devlet Arsivleri Genel Müdürlügü, Osmanli Arsivi Daire Baskanligi, Armenians in Ottoman Documents (1915–1920), n° 25, Ankara 1995, pp. 36–7.
[11] Nubar Library/ Andonian Funds, P.J.1/3, liasse 11, Bayburt, f° 1, eyewitness account of Mgrditch Mouradian.
[12] Clarence D. Ussher, *An American Physician in Turkey*, London 2002 (2nd ed.), p. 143; A-To [Hovhannès Ter Martirossian], *Les grands événements au Vasbouragan*, 1914–1915, Erevan 1917, p. 427.

Istanbul, was appointed *vali* of Diyarbekir on 25 March 1915,[13] that is, at the very moment when the CUP Central Committee decided to set in motion its extermination plan. In a few weeks, this intimate of the Interior Minister carried out to the letter the orders from the Centre. But to do this he had to overcome the reluctance of several prefects and deputy prefects of his province. The prefect of Mardin, Hilmi Bey, who refused to carry out his orders, was dismissed on 25 May[14]—he had been working there since 30 November 1914—and replaced by Shefik Bey, who was to be dismissed a month later for the same reason.[15] This prefect came to no harm, which was not the case for some deputy prefects. The deputy at Derik, Rashid Bey (who held this post from 12 October 1913 to 2 May 1915), was not only dismissed for having demanded a written order from the Centre, but executed by the personal guard of Dr Reshid, made up of Circassians, on the road from Diyarbekir.[16] Hüseyin Nesimî Bey, the deputy prefect of Lice, and Nadji Bey, deputy prefect of Beshiri, originally from Baghdad, were also murdered by order of the *vali* of Diyarbekir, for having refused to organize the liquidation of the Armenians of their areas.[17] A few years later, when Dr Reshid was summoned

---

[13] Hans-Lukas Kieser, "Dr Mehmed Reshid (1973–1919): A Political Doctor," in Hans-Lukas Kieser and D.J. Schaller (ed.), *Der Völkermord an den Armeniern und die Shoah*, Zurich, Chronos, 2002, p. 261.

[14] Ishaq Armalto, *Al-Gosara fi nakabat annasara* [The Calamities of the Christians], Beirut, Kaslik, 1970 (reprint of the anonymous edition of 1919), p. 145; Ara Sarafian, "The Disasters of Mardin during the Persecutions of the Christians, Especially the Armenians, 1915," *Haigazian Armenological Review* XVIII (1998), quotes a Chaldean eyewitness who clearly states that Dr Reshid asked one of his colleagues to have Hilmi murdered en route to Mosul.

[15] Jacques Rhétoré, "Les chrétiens aux bêtes! Souvenirs de la guerre sainte proclamée par les Turcs contre les chrétiens en 1915," ms. conserved at the library at Saulchoir, in Paris, pp. 200–1.

[16] Ishaq Armalto, *Les Calamités des chrétiens*, op. cit., p. 149. The replacement, Hamid Bey, installed on 30 June 1915, stayed in his post until 2 May 1916, the same day that the liquidation of the Christians in Derik was completed.

[17] The murder of the two *kaimakam*s was mentioned during the first session of the trial of the Unionists on 27 April 1919: Takvim-t Vakayi, n° 3540, dated 5 May 1919, p. 8, col. 1, lines 15–20; we also possess on this subject the report of an inquiry mission headed by Mazhar Bey into the crimes of Dr Reshid: Archives of the Patriarchate of Constantinople/Armenian Patriarchate of Jerusalem, bureau d'information du Patriarcat, L 119 (original Ottoman) and H 465 (transcript).

to answer magistrates' questions during an inquiry commission set up after the Armistice, he denied having had his colleagues executed, until the son of Hüseyin Nesimî, Abidin, told how his father was called to Diyarbekir and murdered en route by a group from the Special Organization, whose local chief was Dr Reshid.

But resistance to orders shown by certain senior civil servants in the region did not stop there. Apart from the three executed deputy prefects, others were dismissed: Mehmed Hamdi Bey, replaced by Ferik Bey on 1 July 1915 at the head of the *kaza* of Cermik; Mehmed Ali Bey, *kaimakam* of Sevur, who occupied this post from 2 May to 1 October 1915; Ibrahim Hakki Bey, in charge at Silvan, who "resigned" on 31 August 1915.[18] In other words, almost half of the deputy prefects of the *vilayet* of Diyarbekir were removed for having refused to follow orders, but this was not enough to save the Armenians and Syriac-speaking inhabitants of this region. The latter, found in large numbers in this *vilayet*, suffered a similar fate to that of their Armenian neighbors.

In the *vilayet* of Bitlis, it was Mustafa Abdülhalik—brother-in-law of Mehmed Talât, the Interior Minister—who was appointed *vali* in order to eradicate the dense local Armenian population. He was helped in this by Lieutenant Colonel Halil, uncle of the War Minister, who had at his command a hastily summoned division of the Special Organization. We know of only one case of rescue here, carried out by a military doctor who was posted at Bitlis. It concerned young Armenian girls at the local American school, well brought up, multi-lingual, having escaped deportation thanks to their American protectors, but now coveted as potential spouses by Young Turk officers stationed at Bitlis.[19] The chief doctor of the town's military hospital, Mustapha Bey, an Arab who had studied in France and Germany, realizing that "the presence of these girls in the school was a constant thorn in the government's side," opposed these demands, claiming that the girls were absolutely indispensable to the smooth running of his hospital.[20]

In the *vilayet* of Mamuret ul-Aziz/Harput, the *vali*, Sabit Cemal Sagiroglu,[21] installed at the beginning of September 1914, was certainly

---

[18] Mehmed Resid, *HayatH ve Hât ralari*, op. cit., pp. 87–9.
[19] Grace H. Knapp, *The Tragedy of Bitlis*, Princeton, NJ, Gomidas Institute, 2002 (2nd ed.), pp. 45–7.
[20] Ibid., pp. 89–91.
[21] Known also under the name of Safi irzâde, Sabit, he was born at Kemah (sankat

more frustrated than his colleagues in neighboring *vilayet*s, but very aware of the local population's ways and reputedly clear-sighted. In his region, he organized the deportation of the Armenian population, but according to the American Consul Leslie Davis, showing no particular zeal: "He was always explaining to me [he wrote] that he was obliged to carry out his orders [and] it is highly possible that his personal wish was not to cause people to suffer and that he was only carrying out orders against his wishes. [...] In any case, I feel that he was more human than many others."[22] In his *vilayet*, the mountainous zone of the north, the Dersim, was still under the control of the Kizilbashs (or Zazas) and because of this, in the course of events in 1915, was a refuge for 10–15,000 Armenians from the Harput plain and the zones west of Erzincan.[23] Eyewitness accounts from Pastor H. Riggs and from N. Piranian speak of rescue at high financial cost: the first runaways paid up to 100 lira for their passage; later, Kurdish price demands fell to 10 lira. We observe, however, cases of people without means who were also welcomed.

Toward the southern extremity of the *vilayet*, the region of Malatia saw the transit of thousands of deportees, and notably was the site of the abattoir at Firincilar, run by the Special Organization. One man, Mustafa Aga Azaizoglu, the president of the Malatia municipality (*belediye reisi*), unavailingly attempted to denounce these mass murders. Originally from a family from Baghdad living for several generations in the region, Mustafa Aga Azaizoglu immediately took measure of the situation and worked to palliate the effects of the measures to be carried out by the deputy prefect (*mutessaref*) appointed by Constantinople. The German pastor Hans Bauernfeind, who was the interim manager of the German establishment for the blind of Malatia, known as "Bethesda," first thought he was mad when he described in his presence the local killings, and noted that he

---

of Erzincan), in 1881. Under the Kemalist regime, he was *vali* of Erzerum, director-founder of the Ziraat Bankasi and member of parliament for Erzincan, then for Elmazig. He died in 1960 in Istanbul: Adnan Isik, *Malatiai, Adlyaman, Akçadafii, Arabkir, Besni, Darende …, 1830–1919*, Istanbul, Kurtiş Matbaacılık, 1998, p. 761, note.

[22] Leslie A. Davis, *La province de la mort: archives américaines concernant le génocide des Arméniens*, Brussels, Complexe, 1994, pp. 107–10.

[23] Henry Riggs, *Days of Tragedy in Armenia*, op. cit., pp. 108–17; Nazareth Piranian, *The Kharpert Holocaust*, Boston, Mass., Baykar, 1937, pp. 516 and 522 (in Armenian).

"was sometimes sheltering to up to forty Armenians" at his home.[24] The pastor himself housed in the garden of his mission, in tents lent by Mustafa Aga, up to 240 people.[25]

Further to the west, in Anatolia, where Armenian colonies had for centuries been flourishing amidst the Turks, the situation was far less tense than in the east. The *vilayet* of Angora (Ankara) had the particularity of being the home of an Armenian population whose majority was of the Catholic faith, spoke Turkish (though writing with Armenian letters), and had the reputation of being unconcerned with political matters and perfectly inoffensive. The *vali*, Hasan Mahzar Bey, appointed on 18 June 1914, was so convinced of this that he resisted deportation orders addressed to him by the Interior Minister. Constantinople's response was telling. At the beginning of July 1915, the CUP Central Committee sent one of its most eminent members to Angora, Atif Bey (Kamçill), whose role as delegate at the heart of the political department of the Teshkilât-il Mahsusa is known.[26] Through his direct intervention, the Interior Minister terminated the employment of the *vali* Mahzar on 8 July 1915, and appointed as acting *vali* the Party delegate Atif Bey,[27] who was to set in motion the liquidation of the Armenians in the region.

---

[24] Tessa Hofmann and Méliné Pehlivanian, "Malatia 1915: carrefour des convois de déportés d'après le Journal du missionnaire allemand Hans Bauernfeind," *Revue d'Histoire Arménienne Contemporaine* II (1998), p. 255.

[25] Ibid., pp. 260–1. Mustafa Aga was murdered in 1921 by one of his sons, a Young Turk militant, for his activity in favour of the Armenians during the war (ibid., p. 303).

[26] Atif bey, officer, militant of the CUP, was from Makriköy, a town to the west of Istanbul, and would later be member of parliament for Ankara and for Biga. He became, through his membership of the Central Committee of the CUP, one of the heads of the Teshkilat in the autumn of 1914. After his interim appointment at Angora, he was named *vali* of Kastamonu. His role at the centre of the Special Organization was established during the second hearing of the trial of the Young Turk chiefs on 4 May 1919: Takvim-rl Vakayi, n° 3543, of 12 May 1919, pp. 29–31, during the examination of Atif Bey regarding the figures used by the Teshkila-fl Mahsusa and during the examination of Cevad Bey, in the course of the fourth hearing on 8 May 1919: Takvim-Vakayi, n° 3549, p. 63. Cevad named the heads of the Special Organization: the Director of General Security, Aziz Bey, Dr Nâzum, Atmf Bey, etc.

[27] Examination of Midhat Chürkrü, general secretary of the CUP, during the fifth hearing in the trial of the Unionists on 12 May 1919: Takvim-r Vakayi,

In another canton of the same *vilayet*, at Stanoz, many of the women and the children of this Armenian township—the men had already been liquidated or were conscripted—owed their survival to the *müdir*, Ibrahim Chah. He managed to keep the families of the conscripts in their homes and to spread the rest of the population out amongst the Turkish villages.[28]

There is also the case of Celal Bey, who first worked at Aleppo (from 11 August 1914 to 4 June 1915) and was then appointed to Konya, from where he refused to deport the Armenians. It was during his absence that the local Young Turks set about deporting nearly 3,000 Konya Armenians to the south. On the *vali* Celal's return from Constantinople, towards 23 August he managed to stop the departure of a second convoy. As long as he remained at his post, that is to say up to the beginning of October, these people lived and survived in Konya and gave, with American missionaries, eminent assistance to the tens of thousands of Armenians from the western provinces in transit at Konya railway station. They were all finally deported by order of the secretary head of the CUP at Konya, Ferid Bey, as soon as the *vali* was transferred.[29] We observe, however, that lists of wanted people were regularly made and men deported, and Celal was unable to intervene.[30] Dr Dodd noted, "The *vali* is a brave man, but utterly powerless. The Ittihad Committee and the Salonic clique make all decisions. The Police chief seems to be the real boss."[31]

---

n° 3554, 21 May 1919, p. 85. The direct intervention of the CUP in local affairs was clearly established. Mazhar was nominated head of the inquiry commission instigated on 23 November 1918, after the signing of the armistice and the flight of the principal Young Turk criminals, to bring charges against those implicated in the destruction of the Armenians. Endowed with extensive power, the "Mazhar" Commission—as it was customarily named—accomplished remarkable work, with the hearing of numerous witnesses from all levels of the state hierarchy, the assembling of secret orders and instructions connected with the massacres, retained by certain high functionaries as proof that they were only obeying orders.

[28] Garabèd Terzian, *In Memory of Armenian Stanoz*, Beirut, 1969, p. 71 (in Armenian).
[29] APC/PAJ, Bureau of Information of the Patriarchate, pp. 388–89, n° 85, Deportation from Konya.
[30] Gaydzag [=Mgrditch Barsamian]; "Le drame des Arméniens de Konya (d'après le cahier de souveniors d'un témoin)," *Joghovourt*, 20 December 1918.
[31] Letter from Dr W. Dodd to H. Morgenthau, dated 8 September 1915, in Ara

In the *sancak* of Ismit, close to Constantinople, all the Armenians were deported in August 1915, with the exception of those at Geyve, whose deputy prefect, Said Bey (in this job from 19 September 1913 to 21 August 1915) refused to carry out orders and was consequently dismissed and replaced by Tahsin Bey (in the post until 5 September 1916), a Young Turk militant.[32]

Successful rescues by Ottoman civil servants

While all these facts reveal acts of courage, they never really permitted the rescue of Armenians. But in Kûtahya, a prefecture to the west of Angora, the Armenian population was never deported. The *mutesarif* Faik Ali Bey did not carry out deportation orders, nor was he dismissed because of this. According to the journalist Sebuh Aguni, who asked him personally after the war how he managed to keep the Armenians of this region in their homes, it seems that the local Turkish population, led by two important families, the Kermiyanzâdes and the Hocazâde Rasik, was firmly opposed to the deportation of the Armenians. This was not without effect upon the local powers that were. Whilst threatening the *mutesarif* and these notables with reprisals, Mehmed Talât showed a certain leniency in this particular case, a sort of exception that proved the rule. Although initially, this leniency only applied to less than 5,000 people, several thousand deportees originally from Bandirma, Bursa and Tekirdag took advantage of the benevolence of the *mutesarif* and the local population in order to escape the fate awaiting them on the Konya-Bozanti-Aleppo axis.[33]

A similar destiny awaited the Armenians of the city of Smyrna and part of the *vilayet* of Aydin. With the appointment as *vali* there of a member

---

Sarafian (ed.), *United States Official Records on the Armenian Genocide, 1915–1917*, Princeton, NJ. Armenian Genocide Documentation, 2004, p. 254; Archives du ministère des affaires étrangères (Nantes), Marine, Syrie-Liban, Cilicie, Administration, Service de renseignement de la Marine, dossier 159, rapport secret du lieutenant de vaisseau Goybet, dated Constantinople, 19 December 1919, n° 1451–B-29.

[32] R. Kévorkian, *Le Génocide des Arméniens*, op. cit.
[33] Sébouh Agouni, *Histoire du massacre d'un million d'Arméniens*, Constantinople, Assadourian et Fils, 1920, pp. 251–3; APC/PAJ, Bureau of Information of the Patriarchate, H 920.

of the CUP as influential as Mustafa Rahmi, probably linked to the Young Turk project for the "homogenization" of the Ottoman shores of the Aegean Sea to eradicate the Greek population of the coastal zones,[34] the worst could have been feared. However, the *vali*, deeply involved in these operations, as well as being the commander in chief of the IV corps of the army, General Pertev Pasha (Demirhan), limited himself to the extermination of the local Armenian elite. The town's Armenian population was for the most part saved. Certain observers affirm, though, that it was the German General Liman von Sanders who ensured that the Armenians could remain in Smyrna. Given the context of the time—Turkey was working to maintain Greece's neutrality in the world conflict—we can also surmise that the elimination of the Armenians in Smyrna would have probably created tension with Greece, who in turn would have considered their own position threatened.[35] In the rest of the *vilayet*, in the *sancak* of Manisa, other Armenians were saved thanks to the *mutesarif*, Tevfik Bey, who managed to save the Armenian population by only superficially following orders: 400 people were, somewhat belatedly, evicted from their homes on 15 October 1916, but this action was initiated by the commandant of the local gendarmerie, Fehmi Bey.[36]

The Armenians of Aydin and Denizly benefited from the actions of a local civil servant, the commandant of the gendarmerie of Aydin, Nuri Bey, who stopped the *mutesarif*, Reshid Bey, former head of the political section of the Constantinople police force, from executing deportation orders. At Denizly, a few dozen men were arrested during searches at the beginning of May 1915, one of whom was executed on 16 September 1916; otherwise, the community was spared.[37]

In the south, at Adana, the *vali*, Ismail Hakki Bey, an Albanian with a reputation for moderation, seems to have resisted all pressure from the local Unionist (CUP) club, which demanded that he carry out deporta-

---

[34] Taner Akçam, *From Empire to Republic: Turkish Nationalism & the Armenian Genocide*, London, Zed Books, 2004, pp. 144–6; the American Consul George Horton, *The Blight of Asia*, London, Taderon Press, 2003, pp. 23–33, shares his impressions of these events.

[35] Raymond Kévorkian, *Le Génocide des Armeniens*, op. cit., p. 707.

[36] SHAT Service Historique de la Marine, Service de renseignement de la Marine, Turkey, 1BB7 245, doc. N° 109, Smyrne, 29 April 1919, "Rapport sur les actes injustes…," pp. 19–21.

[37] Ibid., p. 21.

tion orders. Without openly opposing his orders, he sometimes managed to delay the departure of the convoys, if not have them returned.[38] Another sign of the *vali*'s benevolent attitude was seen when he received an order from Constantinople at the end of February 1915, demanding that the Patriarch of Adana, Khachadur Arslanian, should be immediately transferred to the capital. He saw that the Inspector of Sanitary Affairs took care to make out a certificate that the prelate was unable to make such a journey.[39] The appointment on 19 March 1916 of Cevdet Bey, ex-*vali* of Van, to head the *vilayet* of Adana marked the end of such measures to spare Armenians, and heralded the installation of the necessary framework for the second phase of the genocide.

To the north of the *vilayet* of Adana, in the *sancak* of Hacin, the American missionary Edith Cold informs us that the mufti of the town refused to support the deportations and even kept the goods of one of his Armenian friends to guard them from looting.[40] According to the same source, the Muslims in the neighboring communities of Feke and of Yerebakan were hostile to the deportations, the Turks of Feke behaving in a "particularly honorable" manner.[41]

In the deserts of Syria, in the regions of Ras ul-Ayn and Der el-Zor, we observe the benevolent attitudes of some civil servants. The deputy prefect of Ras ul-Ayn, Yusuf Ziya Bey, who remained at his post until February 1916, tried to save some of the Armenians held in the concentration camp near the town (he was later dismissed during the initiation of the second phase of the genocide).[42]

---

[38] Report by William N. Chambers, British missionary working for the American Board of Turkey, at Adana, for 37 years, dated 3 December 1915: James Bryce and Arnold Toynbee, *The Treatment of Armenians in the Ottoman Empire*, uncensored edition, edited with an introduction by Ara Sarafian, Princeton, NJ, Gomidas Institute, 2000, doc 128; Sébouh Agouni, *Histoire du massacre d'un million d'Arméniens*, op. cit., p. 305; Diary of Miss Wallis: Bryce and Toynbee, *The Treatment of Armenians in the Ottoman Empire*, op. cit., doc 129; Letter from the consul at Mersin, Edward I. Nathan, to H. Morgenthau, dated from 18 to 25 May 1915: Sarafian (ed.), *United States Official Records on the Armenian Genocide, 1915–1917*, op. cit., pp. 43 and 46.

[39] Puzant Yeghiayan (ed.), *History of the Armenians of Adana*, Antelias, Armenian Catholicosate, 1970, p. 321 (in Armenian).

[40] Report by Edith M. Cold, dated 16 December 1915: Bryce and Toynbee, *The Treatment of Armenians in the Ottoman Empire*, op. cit., doc 126.

[41] Ibid.

[42] Raymond Kévorkian, *Le Génocide des Arméniens*, op. cit., p. 802.

The prefect of Der el-Zor, Ali Suad Bey, was in charge of the Euphrates region which housed the biggest of the concentration camps, at Meskene (it housed up to 100,000 people until the autumn of 1916, and 80,000 deaths were counted), at Dipsi (operating from November 1915 until April 1916 and counting 30,000 dead) and that of Der el-Zor/Marat (opened in November 1915: 192,750 victims). Among the administrative and military staff who were present at Der el-Zor during Ali Suad's tenure of office, we must point out the benevolent actions of Nureddin Bey, delegate inspector (*menzil mufettis*) and Naki Bey, navy commander, both of whom fought alongside Ali Suad so that a large number of deportees could stay at Der el-Zor, and Haci Faroz and his relative Ayial, notables of Der el-Zor, who had great influence over the Bedouin tribes of the region. An Armenian escapee reports that "The protection proffered by Ali Suad to the Armenians of the area was legendary even as far away as Aleppo, and the Turks gave him the ironic nickname of 'the Armenian Patriarch'."[43]

We should add, in order to complete our study of the behavior of local senior officials, that certain prefects or deputy prefects, notably in the regions where the concentration camps were located, saved Armenians or helped them avoid deportation in exchange for enormous sums of money, whilst others extracted a ransom whilst sending the "donors" to their deaths. This was of course a vital difference. With experience, certain families with the wherewithal to pay, in order to stay alive, devised a sort of riposte to this cynical behaviour by using exchange letters which were only signed by the interested parties once a month. This system of monthly payment allowed some people to survive for a year or more, or at least until their money ran out.

By way of conclusion, I would say that recent research related to establishing facts locally has allowed different types of rescue to be identified. However, this aspect of research remains too little explored. What do we really know about how young women and children were "adopted" by Turkish, Kurdish or even Bedouin families, thus sometimes saved by the very people who killed their husbands or parents, whether civil servants,

---

[43] R. Kévorkian, *L'Extermination des déportés arméniens ottomans dans les camps de concentration de Syrie-Mésopotamie, la deuxième phase du génocide (1915–1916)*, RHAC II (1998), p. 174; T.C. Basbakanlik Artsivi, 2R1334, 3R1334, 6R1334, 7R1334, 7, 8, 11 and 12 Subat [February] 1916, DN, telegrams from Ali Suad [DH. EUM, 2.S.69/6, 7, 8, 9], doc. N° 158, 159, 161, 160.

military personnel or members of the civil society? What do we know about rescues that occurred thanks to Masonic solidarity? (We have only one testimony of such an event in Cilicia, but there must have been others). The same can be asked about Turkish religious brotherhoods—the leader of one of the main brotherhoods in Konya was deported to Beirut for condemning violence against the Armenian people, violence that he believed violated the precepts of Islam.

No doubt a systematic examination of such intervention by civil servants or secular or religious civil society would reveal that, in 1915, a segment of Turkish society was hostile to the extermination policy designed by the Young Turks. Such case studies, of obvious educational value, could contribute to offering far more worthy models than the Young Turk perpetrators whose deeds have been officially immortalized by having mausoleums and boulevards named in their honor.

12

CONVERSION AND RESCUE
SURVIVAL STRATEGIES IN THE ARMENIAN GENOCIDE

Ugur Ümit Üngör

In the opening scene of Lars von Trier's critically-acclaimed movie *Dogville* (2003), a woman named Grace (played by Nicole Kidman) walks into a 1930s village called Dogville. She claims she is pursued by men who are out to kill her and desperately asks the locals for help. The villagers, a conservative group of peasants, hesitate at first but then decide to shelter her. It is sufficient for the mob to be misled and continue their search for Grace elsewhere. Grace decides to stay in Dogville and initially does various small chores for the villagers, trying to blend into the local culture, seeming quite content with her situation. But then, it doesn't take long for the villagers to gradually maltreat her with a stereotypical rural cruelty. Her situation deteriorates as she is cheated, bullied, raped, beaten, stoned, chained, and finally incarcerated in a stable like an animal. By the end of the movie, when the mob unexpectedly shows up at Dogville and requests Grace to be delivered, she has effectively become the village slave and her spirit is broken. The storyline discloses that she is the daughter of an influential Mafia boss who wants his runaway child back. Grace, by then understandably vindictive, gives in to her violent impulses and requests her father to destroy the village. The mobsters raze Dogville and brutally massacre all of its inhabitants, bringing a shocking end to a remarkable movie.

What is the relevance of *Dogville*? During the movie one realizes that the scorned Grace's fate is a metaphor for the experiences of many Armenian women during World War I: rescue from death was often the harbinger of a life of misery. Using this angle, this chapter will address notions of rescue and conversion during the 1915 Armenian genocide.

Genocide and identity

"The twentieth century," Anthony Giddens solemnly reminds us, "is a bloody and frightening one."[1] The Ottoman Empire and its successors, including the Turkish Republic, have not been exceptions to this rule. Turkish nation formation consisted of a broad scope of minority policies, ranging from marginalization, isolation, incarceration, border alteration, deportation, forced assimilation, population exchange to outright indiscriminate massacre, and in the most extreme case fully fledged genocidal destruction. The fate of the victims depended on their perceived ethnic and political distance from the newly proclaimed and Islamized ethnic-Turkish national identity, as well as on the contingency of international politics. In this process, ethnicity was equated with loyalty, so that for example loyal Christian Armenian government employees were doomed to be excluded from this new identity whereas tax-evading Turkish Alevi peasants were categorized into it. Because of non-eugenic definitions of the nation, peoples such as Muslim Kurds, Sephardic Jews, or sometimes even Christian Armenians were considered more "Turkifiable" than others, albeit ambiguously.[2] Much of this was carried out with little regard for proclaimed and real loyalties. Once these processes of persecution escalated, points of no return were reached fast enough to cleanse millions from their ancestral lands in just years.

How do persecuted people react to assaults on their identities? According to Donald Horowitz, in processes of persecution and mass violence, "members of a victim-group often attempt to pass as members of an

---

[1] Anthony Giddens, *The Nation-State and Violence*, Cambridge, Polity Press, 1985, p. 3.
[2] The Nazi term *Eindeutschung*, which denoted the envisioned forced assimilation of non-Germans eligible for Germanization during World War II, is a useful analogy. Nazi intellectuals devised the concept of *eindeutschfähig*, which can be literally translated as "Germanizable," the degree to which non-Germans were suited for assimilation under racial criteria.

attacker-group or bystander-group. They do this by miscuing... Their degree of success is a function of their ability to miscue."[3] In such a process, the persecuted may attempt to change their identity in various ways: changing their personal names, wearing different dress, adopting a different religion, ultimately blending in with other ethnic groups, until the persecution abates. The success of such a process of deception depends not only on their own ability to maintain the smokescreen, but also, possibly, on two other factors. First, if there are any appreciable physical differences between them and other ethnic groups, hiding their own identity might be impossible, while if these differences are negligible, the possibilities for behavioral escape can be considerable. A second factor is the attitude of bystander communities to the identity change of the persecuted person or group. A hostile bystander community that believes in the purity and sanctity of its own group identity may reject the victim's assumption of it. A more open (either welcoming or colonizing) attitude may be to the advantage of the persecuted group for it allows them an avenue for dodging the persecution.

During the Armenian genocide, an unknown number of persecuted people were rescued by people who were not persecuted. CUP (Committee of Union and Progress) definitions of "internal enemies" created sharp dividing lines within the complex and socially stratified Ottoman society. In some cases families were torn apart—one half of a family was subjected to deportation, and the other half was not. In other cases, one half of a village was subjected to persecution, whereas the other half was not. In either case, this created situations in which the persecuted group could only escape their violent fate if the non-persecuted (or less persecuted) were ready to secretly intervene and resist the persecutions. This response usually turned into what is now called "rescue": any "behavior, clandestine or not, to physically or juridically hide the identity of wanted people and/ or to help them escape to secure places."[4] The crucial concept in this useful definition is the notion of hiding one's identity. The destruction of the Ottoman Armenians was as much an attack on the abstract category of Armenian identity as on the concrete physical existence of large numbers of Armenians, especially in the eastern provinces.

---

[3] Donald L. Horowitz, *Ethnic Groups in Conflict*, Berkeley, CA, University of California Press, 2000, pp. 18–9.

[4] Jacques Semelin, "Rescue, Rescuer, Rescued: 'Righteous among the Nations' and the Holocaust: European and Comparative Perspectives," Call for Papers, 14 October 2004.

The research conducted on the rescue of Christians during the wartime persecutions is only in its incipient phase. Richard Hovannisian points out that had it not been for numerous Ottoman Muslims, many Armenians could not have survived the genocide. Relying on survivor testimony, he argues that the rescuers were generally motivated by humanitarian and economic concerns. He also identifies most rescuers as Turkish peasant men who sheltered the persecuted Armenians for several years. Hovannisian concludes his essay by pointing out that new avenues of research should address risk assessments of harboring Armenians, and the moral ambivalence of rescue.[5] A shorter but equally insightful analysis was articulated by Raymond Kévorkian. In an article about the "Righteous" in the Armenian genocide, he distinguishes Western actors from Ottoman citizens. Kévorkian emphasizes the need to connect the rescuer's social position with the decisions emanating from that position and function. He also points out that the various rescuers' motivations for acts of rescue were very diverse. Having drawn these general demarcation lines, he then proceeds to identify several Ottoman officials who resisted the genocide. Finally, Kévorkian also raises the issue of the ambiguities of rescue and indicates that a closer look needs to be taken at Ottoman archival documents and survivor testimony.[6] Recently, Boghos Levon Zekiyan presented a paper at a conference in Istanbul reiterating that in the post-genocide era, many rescued Armenians used to recall their rescuers with great admiration and respect.[7]

Despite this developing body of research on the Armenian genocide, two contradictory popular myths haunt its historiography. On the one hand, Armenians are said to have bravely resisted cultural and religious

---

[5] See Richard G. Hovannisian's chapter entitled "Intervention and Shades of Altruism during the Armenian Genocide," in his edited volume *The Armenian Genocide: History, Politics, Ethics*, New York, St Martin's Press, 1992, pp. 173–207.

[6] Raymond H. Kévorkian, "Pour une typologie des 'Justes' dans l'Empire ottoman face au génocide des Arméniens," paper presented at the conference *Si può sempre dire un sì o un no: I Giusti contro i genocidi degli Armeni e degli Ebrei*, University of Padua, 30 November 2000.

[7] Boghos Levon Zekiyan, "The Conceptual Relationship Between 'Tehcir' and 'Genocide', with a special Reference to the Armenian Case, both from an Anthropological and a Legal Philosophical Viewpoint," paper (work in progress) presented at the conference *New Approaches to Turkish-Armenian Relations*, Istanbul University, 17 March 2006.

colonization by the Young Turk authorities. In this myth, Ottoman Armenians are presented as vigilant defenders and gatekeepers of Armenian ethnic and religious identity who resisted any form of cultural "Turkification." They are portrayed as possessing an unbending will to cling to their ethnic identity and rather die as Christians than survive as Muslims. On the other hand, a complementary but contradictory myth holds that many hundreds of thousands of crypto-Armenians currently live in Turkey as descendants of those who converted during the genocide. The realities and relationships of conversion and resistance were arguably subtler and much less clear-cut than in these dichotomous myths.

The history of the Armenian deportations is replete with references to rescue and conversion. Conversion to Islam was *both* a concomitant effect *and* a precondition of rescue. In order to sidestep the clutches of the CUP dictatorship, many Armenians saw themselves obliged to convert. Studies of rescue and conversion during the Armenian genocide should consider both objectivist and subjectivist interpretations. On the one hand, it is possible to describe and explain the events: how were different people rescued in different regions under different circumstances? How did they convert and what happened after their conversions? But one should also take into consideration the meanings that the rescued and rescuers themselves attributed to the rescuing process. For converts it is crucial to gauge how their conversion affected their self-image, and how they were viewed by their surroundings after their conversions. These are different (but not necessarily conflicting) interpretations that can greatly enrich our understanding of crucial aspects of the Armenian genocide.

Slavery is another question that has not been explored fully in the scholarship. After all, the dull fact remains that for a long time, the practice was quite common in the Ottoman Empire.[8] Well until the 1970s one could find individual pariahs (generally orphans and women), as well as entire Christian families, within large Kurdish households holding social positions close to slavery. This was an accepted and socially institutionalized form of feudalism. Efforts of states attempting to intervene in this constellation were met with adamant resistance by both Kurdish

---

[8] Ehud R. Toledano, *Slavery and Abolition in the Ottoman Middle East*, Seattle, University of Washington Press, 1998; Y. Hakan Erdem, *Slavery in the Ottoman Empire and its Demise, 1800–1909*, Basingstoke, Macmillan, 1996.

patrons and Christian clients. For them, it represented the established routine and securities of the *ancien régime*'s ranked ethnic system. Therefore, it was common for Kurdish chieftains to invest great efforts in locating and finding Armenians after the genocide, in the hope they could find spouses among each other and continue their custom of endogamy. Before turning to an overview of behavioral escape, a discussion of conversion is in order.

Conversion in the Armenian genocide

The phenomenon of conversion has a long history in the Ottoman Empire. Ever since the Ottoman army conquered large territories inhabited by non-Muslims, conversion was a highly complex issue involving at least as many economic, status-related, political, and personal considerations as purely religious ones.[9] For many converts it was more a means to attain status than a conscious decision based on religious conviction, in other words, more a means than an end. Especially when compared with contemporary Russian and Spanish policies of forced conversion, the Ottoman case seems negligible, but dependent on local and temporal conditions.[10] Obviously, there was not one single unchanging Ottoman policy on conversion. Speros Vryonis' words on the Ottoman Empire are valid for the identity politics of states in general: "With the collapse or weakening of [...] centralized states or at times when they felt threatened by the real or potential power of Christians (either internally or externally) then the legal status and protection of the non-Muslims lapsed in some form or another."[11]

Judging from this historical backdrop, the 1915 deportation and persecution of the entire category of Ottoman Armenians was a remarkable

[9] Speros Vryonis, *The Decline of Medieval Hellenism in Asia Minor and the Process of Islamization from the Eleventh through the Fifteenth Century*, Berkeley, University of California Press, 1971.

[10] Selim Deringil, "'There Is No Compulsion in Religion': On Conversion and Apostasy in the Late Ottoman Empire, 1839–1856," *Comparative Studies in Society and History*, vol. 42, no. 3, 2000, pp. 547–75.

[11] Speros Vryonis, "The Experience of Christians under Seljuk and Ottoman Domination, Eleventh to Sixteenth Century," in Michael Gervers and Jibran Bikhazi (eds), *Conversion and Continuity: Indigenous Christian Communities in Islamic Lands*, Toronto, Pontifical Institute of Medieval Studies, 1990, pp. 185–216.

breach of pre-existing forms of Ottoman minority policies when Mehmed Talaat Bey (1874–1921) issued orders for the integral deportation of all Armenians to Deyr-ul Zor, starting with the northeastern provinces.[12] Deyr-ul Zor (or Der Zor) was situated on the southern border of the Ottoman Empire, right at the entrance of desert. That same day Mehmed Talaat urged the Fourth Army Command to court-martial any Muslim who collaborated with Christians.[13] The Third Army was instructed that "any Muslim who protected an Armenian [be] hanged in front of his house, the burning of his house, his removal from office, and his appearance before a court-martial."[14] From then on, the persecution process was official policy and major steps were taken to seal its net around the targets.

The forced conversions were also a very un-Ottoman thing to do. In an article addressing this problem, Ara Sarafian characterizes four main trends in conversions:[15] "voluntary"[16] conversions of individuals in the initial stages of the 1915 persecutions; selection of individual Armenians by individual Muslim hosts for absorption into Muslim households; distribution of Armenians to Muslim families by government agencies; and the use of government-sponsored orphanages as a direct means of assimilating Armenian children. Consequently, many Armenian children were more or less forcibly converted to Islam.[17] The categorical nature of the persecution process notwithstanding, these strategies denote the absence

---

[12] *Başbakanlık Osmanlı Arşivi* (Ottoman Archives, Istanbul), DH.ŞFR 53/91, 53/92, and 53/93, Talaat to provinces, 23 May 1915. This is the single instance in which the empire-wide nature of the deportations is reflected in one order at the most central level.

[13] *BOA*, DH.ŞFR 53/85, Talaat to Cemal Pasha, 23 May 1915.

[14] *Takvim-i Vekâyi*, no. 3540, p. 7.

[15] Ara Sarafian, "The Absorption of Armenian Women and Children into Muslim Households as a Structural Component of the Armenian Genocide," in Omer Bartov and Phyllis Mack (eds), *In God's Name; Genocide and Religion in the Twentieth Century*, Oxford, Oxford University Press, 2001, pp. 209–21.

[16] "Voluntariness" is a highly disputed concept in the history of conversion, as it seems that most converts that converted "voluntarily" were always under a certain degree of pressure, although much more often socially than administratively. Maria Todorova, "The Ottoman Legacy in the Balkans," in Carl Brown (ed.), *Imperial Legacy: The Ottoman Imprint on the Balkans and the Middle East*, New York, Columbia University Press, 1996, pp. 45–77, and p. 49.

[17] See also: Yavuz Selim Karakışla, "Savaş Yetimleri ve Kimsesiz Çocuklar: 'Ermeni' mi, 'Türk' mü?," *Toplumsal Tarih*, vol.XII, no. 69, 1999, pp. 46–55.

of biologistic-racialist definitions of the target group. The conduct of the deportations, too, showed that the indelibility of Ottoman Armenian group identity could be tampered with and forged into another identity. As Matthias Bjørnlund has written: "What had to be formally changed as well as violently and systematically suppressed was not only religion, but also expressions of Armenian language, culture, even the personal names of the survivors, whether in private homes, government-run orphanages, or the public sphere, leaving only the biological 'raw material' to be systematically Turkified."[18] These twin processes, the tearing down of the old selves and the building of new ones, were to be carried out simultaneously.

Contemporary Western observers, whether neutral, allied with, or hostile to the Ottoman Empire, quickly realized that this policy of forced conversion was one of the methods used to secure the disappearance of the Ottoman Armenians as a community. As with most other aspects of the genocide, the Germans in particular were very well informed about the nature of the forced conversions and assimilation campaign. In the summer of 1916, when the campaign was in full effect, the German Ambassador Paul Wolff Metternich (1853–1934) wrote to Chancellor Theobald von Bethmann-Hollweg (1856–1921):

> One should not see in the forced Islamization of Armenians a measure prompted by religious fanaticism. Such feelings are unknown to the Young Turk power holders... they hold true inasmuch as the leading motive is not religious fanaticism, for example like the forced conversion of Jews and Moors in Spain in the fifteenth and sixteenth century, but the purpose is to amalgamate the Armenians with the Mohammedan inhabitants of the empire.[19]

---

[18] Matthias Bjørnlund, "'A Fate Worse Than Dying': Sexual Violence During the Armenian Genocide," in Dagmar Herzog (ed.), *Brutality and Desire: War and Sexuality in Europe's Twentieth Century*, London, Palgrave Mcmillan, 2008, pp. 16–59, and p. 37.

[19] *PAAA*, R14092, Wolff-Metternich to Bethmann Hollweg, 10 July 1916: "[Ebenso] darf man in der zwangsweisen Islamisierung der Armenier zunächst keine von religiösem Fanatismus eingegebene Maßregel erblicken. Den jungtürkischen Gewalthabern dürften solche Gefühle fremd sein... sie treffen aber insofern zu, als das leitende Motiv nicht religiöser Fanatismus ist, wie z.B. bei der zwangsweisen Bekehrung der Juden und Mauren in Spanien im 15. und 16. Jahrhundert, sondern die Absicht, die Armenier mit den mohammedanischen Bewohnern des Reiches zu amalgamieren."

The ambassador made what seems an accurate assessment of the motives underlying the conversion policies: the dilution of Armenian demography. Through this particular historical lens, the CUP's forced conversion campaign was a breach of traditional Ottoman population policies, despite continuities in patriarchal structures. The levels of coercion and threat of mass violence towards Ottoman Christians were unprecedented, and symbolized the shift from Ottoman imperial rule over a religious minority to Young Turk nationalist rule.

The government agency to oversee the conversions was the Interior Ministry, most notably the Interior Minister himself, Talaat Pasha. Talaat Pasha's secretary, Falih Rıfkı Atay (1894–1971), noted in his memoirs that the CUP had established a committee on enforcing the mass conversion of Armenians. The committee convened in his house several times and discussed that Armenians could even be given farmland if they would convert, but that idea was quickly abandoned.[20] Talaat's telegrams, stored in the Ottoman archives in Istanbul, open an interesting window onto the everyday history of this process, during which he authorized the forced conversion of Armenians. Besides specific instructions guiding governors' behavior, Talaat released several national decrees defining the categorical scope of those to be persecuted and deported. In June 1915, he excluded the Armenian converts to Islam from deportation to the south.[21] Most converts were not persecuted any more and, provided they kept their silence, were allowed to continue living in their homes. Two weeks later he reincorporated the converts into the deportation program. Talaat's order read that "some Armenians are converting collectively or individually just to remain in their hometowns," and that "this type of conversions should never be lent credence to." Talaat contended that "whenever these types of people perceive threats to their interests they will convert as a means of deception."[22] In other words, at times, the CUP dictatorship found conversion to Islam not satisfactory and trustworthy enough. Therefore, to follow up on the previous persecutions, on 22 February 1916 Talaat issued an empire-wide decree to the Ottoman police to keep close control over converted Armenians with new identity cards.[23]

---

[20] Falih Rıfkı Atay, *Zeytindağı*, Istanbul, Bateş, 1981, p. 66.
[21] *BOA*, DH.ŞFR 54/100, Talaat to provinces, 22 June 1915.
[22] *BOA*, DH.ŞFR 54/254, Talaat to provinces, 1 July 1915.
[23] *BOA*, DH.ŞFR 61/71, Talaat to provinces, 22 February 1916.

Even later, he maintained his grip on converted Armenians and Syriac-rite Christians by having their names, manners of conversion, and post-conversion actions registered.[24]

The response of Armenians to the government's conversion policies was ambivalent. It ranged from fearful acquiescence to adamant resistance. Some Armenians were flexible at the prospect of changing their identity. Danish missionaries witnessed how desperate women deportees shouted to them in the street, "We want to become Muslims. We want to become Germans, whatever you want, just save us, they are about to take us to Kemagh and slit our throats."[25] A young Armenian boy, Henry Vartanian, whose father had been murdered, was offered shelter by a Turkish acquaintance, who demanded he renounce Christianity and convert to Islam in a ceremony attended by an imam. The young Henry testified the Islamic statement of faith "There is no God but Allah and Mohammed is his prophet," was ritually circumcised, and from then on went through life as Esad, son of Abdurrahman.[26]

But having to abandon one's identity was unacceptable and humiliating to many others. During the deportations, Aurora Mardiganian was kidnapped by a Kurdish tribesman. The fact that she bore him two children was too embarrassing for her to narrate in detail in her memoirs, and she glossed over this period with great shame.[27] The forced changing of names was humiliating and confusing as well. Khachadoor Pilibosian, a child survivor of the Armenian genocide, was also kidnapped by a Kurd during the deportations, and taken to live with him as a slave. In his memoirs he writes how he was absorbed into a Kurdish household and the Kurds renamed him "Mustafa." After the war he managed to escape to Aleppo and contact his father in America. Reaching America in 1920, he opened his own business in Massachusetts.[28]

---

[24] *BOA*, DH.ŞFR 86/45, Talaat to provinces, 3 April 1918; *BOA*, DH.ŞFR 87/259, Directorate for General Security to Elaziz province, 23 May 1918.

[25] *PAAA*, R14087, Schuchardt to Auswärtiges Amt, 21 August 1915, appendix 1.

[26] Donald E. Miller and Lorne Touryan-Miller, *Survivors: An Oral History of the Armenian Genocide*, Berkeley: University of California Press, 1993, p. 146.

[27] Aurora Mardiganian, *The Auction of Souls*, London, Phoenix Press, 1934, p. 185.

[28] Khachadoor Pilibosian, *They Called Me Mustafa: Memoir of an Immigrant*, Watertown, NY, Ohan Press, 1992.

Other Armenians persevered in their faith even in the face of drawn guns and swords. Kerop Bedoukian was a young deportee who noted in his memoirs:

> My mother was saying that we had an offer from the Mayor via my aunt, a teacher who had established six Turkish kindergartens, the first in the city. The offer was that my aunt and forty-two of her relatives could be saved from deportation if they turned Mohammedan. My father's answer still rings in my ear as he said, while he fixed my belt: "You will go and die on one mountain and I will go and die on another but we shall not deny our Christ." I still feel his goodbye kiss on both my cheeks. We parted. No-one shed any tears.[29]

This conservative resistance to conversion and absorption into the despised Other's religion may seem typical and characteristic of the era and the region. No matter how fluid, hybrid, and entwined identities were in the peasant society that Eastern Turkey was (and is), certain ethnic boundaries persisted, especially among nationalists and the more pious people. Having to abandon one's identity was unacceptable and humiliating to many of them.

This is where subjective experiences clash with objective observations: even though many deportees experienced conversion as a (gross) breach of moral and social norms, the fact remained that their chances of survival were at their highest if they converted to Islam and lived inconspicuously, under Muslim domination or not. But Talaat's post-1915 attitude toward the converts demonstrates that conversion did not lull his suspicion. Rightly not, perhaps, as one may suggest that it did not always warrant loyalty to the regime. Paradoxically, even though the CUP imposed forced conversion upon many Christians (Armenians and Syriac-rite Christians), it did not have the perceptiveness to take into consideration that, as Arenal argued, "forced conversion usually entails a stronger rejection and distrust of the convert group by the dominant society."[30] Consequently, one can witness traumatic experiences of identity in the afterlife of the converts. For example, a Kurdish politician recalled how he grew

---

[29] Kerop Bedoukian, *The Urchin: An Armenian's Escape*, London, John Murray, 1978, p. 8.
[30] Mercedes Garcia Arenal, "Conversion to Islam in the Mediterranean-Muslim World," in Randi Deguilhem (ed.), *Individual and Society in the Mediterranean-Muslim World: Issues and Sources*, Paris, European Science Foundation, 1998, p. 15.

up in Van with an Armenian grandmother and never understood why the grumpy and depressed woman used to curse her own family as "Kurdish scum."[31] There was often "compensatory piety" to mask the obvious lack of "Islamic pedigree." Understanding these complex events requires a detailed look at them on the provincial level.

'Behavioral escape' in Diyarbekir province

Interethnic and inter-faith relations in Diyarbekir in the years before 1914 were not as idyllic as some observers have portrayed. In fact, they were frail on account of the prolonged crisis that afflicted the Ottoman Empire. The gradual crumbling of Ottoman rule in the Balkans occurred alongside massacres of Ottoman Muslims in places like Crete and Macedonia,[32] and raised questions about the loyalty of Christian citizens to the Ottoman state. During the Abdulhamid-era massacres that struck Diyarbekir on 1 November 1895, the destruction of human lives and property was massive and profound.[33] According to one detailed account, approximately 25,000 Armenians converted to Islam under compulsion in all of Diyarbekir province, 1,100 Armenians were killed in Diyarbekir city and 800 or 900 Armenians in the outlying villages, while 155 women and girls were carried off by Kurdish tribesmen. In Silvan county 7,000 Armenians converted and 500 women were carried off. In Palu 3,000 and in Siverek 2,500 converted to escape being massacred. In Silvan, along with Palu (where 3,000 Armenians converted), "7,500 are reduced to destitution and 4,000 disappeared: killed, died of cold, etc., or escaped elsewhere."[34] According to Kévorkian and Paboudjian, 2,000 houses and 2,500 shops and ateliers were burnt down in the province during the 1895 massacres.[35] An unknown percentage of these converts reconverted to their faiths, returned to their villages, reclaimed their possessions, and rebuilt their homes and businesses once the persecution was halted.

Taking this prehistory of violence into consideration, to many Armenians the genocide must have come as yet another Ottoman massacre.

---

[31] Interview conducted with B.Y., 12 July 2004, Istanbul.

[32] Justin McCarthy, *Death and Exile: The Ethnic Cleansing of Ottoman Muslims, 1821–1922*, Princeton, NJ, The Darwin Press, 1995.

[33] Gustave Meyrier, *Les Massacres de Diarbekir: Correspondance diplomatique du Vice-Consul de France 1894–1896*, Paris, L'Inventaire, 2000.

[34] *Blue Book Turkey*, No. 8 (1896), enclosure in document no. 140, p. 127.

[35] Kévorkian and Paboudjian, *Les Arméniens*, op. cit., p. 398.

Little did they know about the true nature of the genocidal deportations once they were launched. But a difference from the ultra-ethnic Nazi or Rwandan genocides was that there were limited but real possibilities of "behavioral escape" in the Armenian genocide. Escaping or being rescued was closely related to conversion, even though without help (which could come from nobody else but Muslims) these chances were very slim. An elderly Kurd from Ergani recalled that his father told him the story of an Armenian man who converted to Islam and was then sheltered and hidden in a stable of friendly villagers; when the bloodiest momentum of the summer of 1915 passed, he reconverted to Christianity, was tracked down, and was killed.[36] The case of Fethiye Çetin, a lawyer from a Muslim family in North-Diyarbekir, is instructive as well. The memoir she wrote disclosed her Armenian grandmother's roots and offered a textbook example of conversion, rescue, and survival during the genocide. Çetin notes that her grandmother was saved because she accepted conversion. Muslim villagers were only interested in sheltering Armenian children who either already converted or were willing to convert.[37]

The fate of the converts became a bone of contention after World War I. The liberal government led by Grand Vizier Ahmet İzzet Pasha (1864–1937) had to reverse the damage done by CUP persecution. On 8 February 1919 he sent out the empire-wide order that "because of the fact that conversions of all Armenian men and women under twenty years of age are not acknowledged, their identity certificates have to be corrected as Armenians immediately." Those converts over twenty years of age were ordered to be left free "to return to their true religion" (*din-i aslilerine rücu*).[38] All state officials were ordered to obey closely and follow these directives, but it seems that in practice the local genocide perpetrators, especially in Diyarbekir, were visibly too powerful for the terrified con-

---

[36] Interview conducted with M.Ş. in Kurdish in Diyarbekir city, August 2004.

[37] Fethiye Çetin, *Anneannem*, Istanbul, Metis, 2004. In a later interview Çetin noted she was living in the twilight zone between Turkishness, Kurdishness, and Armenianness, in the margins of ethnicity and nationality. She also remembered that after finding out about her roots, she now understood why her grandmother used to bake a special sweet bread during spring with other women, unknown to the family: they were female genocide survivors, celebrating Easter. <http://www.frederike.nl/cgi-bin/scripts/db.cgi?&ID=403&ww=1&view_records=1>

[38] *BOA*, DH.ŞFR 96/100, Interior Ministry to provinces, 8 February 1919.

verts to step out from the anonymity of their hiding places in public and disclose themselves as Armenians. A British agent passed through Diyarbekir in 1919 and wrote:

On the following day a number of Armenians called upon me, mostly in the Muslim garb, which they have adopted as a protective measure. Three hundred of them, survivors of the massacres and deportations of 1915, wished to return to their homes at Kharput, Sivas, and Erzerum. I advised them to wait until the spring, when the journey would be less arduous and the British government might be able to arrange for their protection, both en route and at their destinations. This hope was, unfortunately, never to be realized... More urgent than repatriation was the release of the thousands of Armenian women and children living with Kurds, Turks, and Arabs. There was scarcely a girl over twelve who had not been a wife to some Moslem. A decree that Christians were free to leave Moslem houses had been received from Constantinople, but the officials were inactive, and the men with whom the refugees were living were not inclined to surrender them... Many children were separated from their mothers, and wives from their husbands, simply through ignorance of their whereabouts. Some of the children in Moslem hands were, indeed, unaware that they were of Christian parentage.[39]

After Mustafa Kemal's Nationalist movement defeated the Armenian state in the east and the Greek invasion in the west, the converts kept a low profile, living either as so-called "crypto-Christians" or fully silencing their Armenian identities and living as Muslims.[40]

The afterlife of these Christian families that converted to Islam to survive the genocidal persecution, and indeed managed to live in Diyarbekir for several decades before migrating to Diyarbekir city, Istanbul, or Western Europe, merits attention not only for the study of the genocide itself.[41] The existence of these people has also been important for the post-war history and economy of Eastern Turkey: some converts stayed in their villages and ignored their Armenian past, whereas others lived as crypto-Christians. As a Kurdo-Armenian convert from Diyarbekir noted:

---

[39] E.H. Keeling, *Adventures in Turkey and Russia*, London, John Murray, 1924, pp. 213, 225.

[40] Maurus Reinkowski, "Hidden Believers, Hidden Apostates: the Phenomenon of Crypto-Jews and Crypto-Christians in the Middle East," in Dennis Washburn *et al.* (eds), *Converting Cultures: Religion, Ideology of Transformations of Modernity*, Leiden, Brill, 2007, pp. 409–33.

[41] Interview conducted with an anonymous Armenian family (Lice district) in Dutch, Amsterdam, February 2003.

I always knew that my father's father was Armenian. We all knew, but we didn't talk about it. Everyone knew, and a lot of people used to say to my grandfather that he was Armenian by origin, but we didn't talk about it in our family. My uncles are fanatic Muslims, there are religious officials—imams—among them, who don't want to talk about it.[42]

The notable Armenian family of Merjanian (now Mercan) is an interesting example of these "doubling" strategies. During the genocide, the Merjanians were saved upon conversion. When they migrated from Diyarbekir to Amsterdam in the 1970s, upon arrival they reconverted to Christianity. Now, whenever they visit their remaining family members in Diyarbekir, their flights back and forth between Europe and Turkey also represent switching between Christianity and Islam. The women put on their headscarves during the flight, the Muslim names are used instead of their Armenian ones, and they behave like Muslims in Turkey.[43] These few people escaped the Armenian genocide through a mostly coincidental combination of conversion and rescue.

Discussion

In this chapter I have suggested that many cases of rescue were contingent upon conversion to Islam as a *sine qua non* of acceptance into the community, more than the altruism of individuals. The identity-based (as opposed to race-based) persecution created a porous persecution process from which a number of Armenians escaped. What was rescued and escaped destruction in this perspective was the physical existence of that particular Armenian person. The self was stripped of anything Armenian, including one's name, which was buried deep into private memory and banned from public memory, never to be exhumed from the shadows of oblivion. The survivors literally escaped with only their lives, leaving behind cultural ties and religious practices. Much more work is needed in this field: What did conversion mean for the converts themselves? What kind of pressure was put on them to convert by their rescuers, and why? How was slavery during the Armenian genocide different from

---

[42] Liana Sayadyan, "A Wound That Wouldn't Heal," *Hetq Online: Investigative Journalists of Armenia*, available at: <http://hetq.am/eng/society/0603-gender.html>.

[43] Interview with D.E. (from Piran/Dicle district) conducted in Turkish in Amsterdam, May 2005.

"regular" Ottoman slavery? Were there any noticeable continuities? A major reason why regional slave markets (more or less legally functioning until 1915), saw a devaluation of their "product," was namely the possession of human beings for use in household slavery and the abundance of supply in relation to demand. That they were mostly Armenians who were forced into that predicament seemingly did not bother many Muslims, who eagerly profited from the "bargains."

Another issue is the existence of crypto-Armenians in Turkey at the present time. Both Armenian and Turkish nationalists compete for the loyalty of this population, which finds itself besieged by identity politics. Whereas the former wish to "wake them up" from Islam and urge them to reclaim their dormant Armenian identity, the latter have intransigently declared that if they wish to "return" to their Armenian roots, they are no longer welcome in Turkey.[44] After the publication of Çetin's book in 2004, the fate of converts or so-called "crypto-Armenians" in Turkey became politicized even further.[45] Ostensibly, 30,000 to 40,000 crypto-Armenians currently live in Turkey (around a thousand families in Diyarbekir province), with varying degrees of awareness of and interest in their past.[46]

Although most of them fear that exposure to society would make them vulnerable to nationalist pressures and threats, the Internet has provided a convenient and anonymous platform for assembling information and reaching out to family members abroad. On the website www.hyetert.com for example, aimed at the Armenian community of Istanbul, one can frequently observe messages like the following:

First of all I would like to convey you my greetings and respect. I have a request for you. Nigar Metin, born 1894, mother's name Hilito, father's name Casper,

---

[44] The crypto-Armenians have even been openly threatened by the Turkish Historical Society, the official organ founded under the patronage of Mustafa Kemal and still producing strongly nationalist historical narratives. The director of the Turkish Historical Society, Yusuf Halaçoğlu, went as far as implicitly threatening that he had in his possession a "list" of names, "house by house," of crypto-Armenians living in Turkey, and claiming he would not hesitate to "make it public." *Radikal*, 22 August 2007; *Zaman*, 25 August 2007.

[45] Dorian Jones, "Armenian Quest for Lost Orphans," *BBC World Service*, 1 August 2005; "Ma grand-mère turque était arménienne," *Le Monde*, 26 February 2007.

[46] *Milli Gazete*, 28 December 2005.

and registered to Hizan district in Bitlis province is my grandmother. I just found these records. With your help I would like to reach my family members.

Haydar Y., 1 November 2005
I live in Mut district in Mersin province. My grandmother is also here. Her mother is an Armenian from Kayseri. Her name is Sofia and it is known she moved to Istanbul. Where can I find information about her?

Ulaş Ş., 3 October 2005
I am descended from our fellow Armenian citizens who used to live in the Niksar Cedid neighborhood in Tokat between 1900 and 1915 and have migrated elsewhere. My grandmother's name was Oski, her father's Mevzik, and her mother's Anna. My grandmother had four siblings. We don't know her sister's name. Her brothers were named Karapet and Murat. Unfortunately we don't know their last name. We know they were involved in trade and they owned a store with a depot. I would like to request anyone who is related to the above persons, or knows them, or has information to please write me an e-mail and contact me.

Nihat S.E., 15 February 2005[47]
Although generations have passed since the genocide, traumatic family memories seem to persist and apparently many of these people feel the need for filling in the gaps in their self-narrative.[48]

The most common interpretations of the forced assimilation of Armenian orphans, forced marriages of Armenian women, and forced conversion of Armenians in general have been Armenian-nationalist ones. The conversions and assimilations are seen as loss of identity and absorption into the "other's" identity. But sociologically, they were constituent aspects of the genocide, aimed at the destruction of the most basic social ties of the victim group: family ties. They were also survival mechanisms: if one had to pretend to be a Muslim in exchange for one's life, the choice may not always have been unanimous, but was definitely made by many.

[47] Erhan Başyurt, *Ermeni Evlatlıklar: Saklı Kalmış Hayatlar*, Istanbul, KaraKutu, 2006, pp. 30–1.
[48] Habermas argued that people "can develop personal identities only if they recognize that the sequences of their actions form narratively presentable life histories; they can develop social identities only if they recognize that they maintain their membership in social groups by way of participating in interactions, and thus that they are caught up in the narratively presentable histories of collectivities." Jürgen Habermas, *The Theory of Communicative Action*, Boston, Beacon Press, 1987, vol. 2, *Lifeworld and System: A Critique of Functionalist Reason*, p. 136.

13

HUMANITARIANISM AND MASSACRES
THE EXAMPLE OF THE INTERNATIONAL COMMITTEE OF THE RED CROSS

Irène Herrmann and Daniel Palmieri

"The International Red Cross should not show indecisiveness when a general calamity plunged a part of humanity into distress."[1] From this declaration, formulated in 1909 after the massacre of the Armenians at Adana, one would be led to believe that the International Committee of the Red Cross (ICRC) got immediately involved in helping the victims of the genocides that drenched the twentieth century in blood.

In reality, the extent of actions brought about by the Geneva-based institution varied considerably in timing and intensity. In appearance, the curve showing the involvement and intervention of the ICRC has an ever-increasing upward trajectory. No mention was made, however, of the annihilation of the Hereros in South-West Africa (Namibia) between 1904 and 1908; it railed "against the systematic extermination of the Armenians"[2] in 1915, whose instigators it explicitly denounced,[3] but

---

[1] *Bulletin International des Sociétés de la Croix-Rouge* (henceforth *Bulletin*), 159, July 1909, p. 191.
[2] Archives of the International Committee of the Red Cross (henceforth ACI-CR), A PV, Agence Internationale des Prisonniers de Guerre, meeting of the 14 September 1915.
[3] "An Armenian committee having sent us a vibrant call regarding Armenian

without making any attempt at concrete action; and it contented itself with a prudent pusillanimity during the Shoah.

This evolution is undoubtedly a reflection of the ICRC's mandate. The International Committee, founded in 1863 to come to the aid of servicemen wounded in international wars, has progressively extended its activities to include civilians[4] as well as the victims of civil conflicts.[5] Until 1949, however, the institution had no *ad hoc* legal tool available to it to protect civil populations from the effects of conflicts, and was unable to give a legal foundation to its interventions on behalf of these people. The argument most frequently put forward about the ICRC is based on this deficiency when one attempts to understand its (in)action during the majority of massacres perpetrated in the twentieth century.[6]

Though not exactly wrong, this explanation, with its tone of justification, will never be entirely satisfactory. It only partially answers a historical reality: that of an ICRC fighting in one instance for the cause of the Armenians during one World War and, in another, showing a lack of initiative in the face of the Holocaust, even though both of the victim populations were deprived of any conventional protection. Furthermore, and most profoundly, this interpretation appears to favor an ontological conception of the legal framework in which humanitarian action is inscribed and thus conceals the behavior of the Red Cross from analysis.

In order to decipher the attitude of the ICRC and its ambivalence regarding the extermination of the Hereros, of the Armenians and of the Jews, it is important to reconsider the relationships woven between the principal protagonists of these "general calamities" and those who claim to have remained neither indifferent nor passive when faced with them.

---

populations massacred by the Turks with a non-secretive aim of extermination …" *Bulletin*, 184, October 1915, p. 438.

[4] This protection came into practise at the beginning of the 1914 War, but the 4th Geneva Convention regarding the protection of civilians in times of war was not adopted until 1949.

[5] "14th resolution," Dixième conférence internationale de la Croix-Rouge tenue à Genève du 30 mars au 7 avril 1921. Compte-rendu, Geneva, Imprimerie Albert Renaud, 1921, pp. 217–18.

[6] L'activité du CICR en faveur des civils détenus dans les camps de concentration en Allemagne (1939–1945), Geneva, CICR, February 1946; Rapport du Comité international de la Croix-Rouge sur son activité pendant la Seconde Guerre mondiale (1er septembre 1939—30 juin 1947), 3 volumes, Geneva, CICR, May 1948.

The victims

The victim of the violence of war is at the heart of the ICRC's mandate and constitutes, in a way, its raison d'être. However, the history of the institution shows that not all of the victims of conflicts are treated in the same way. The distinction between civilians and the military has for a long time remained the normative criterion, deciding whether or not humanitarian intervention is justified. In the context of massacre, however, this classification has proved to be permeable, as the Armenian example proves. It is necessary, from now on, to use a reading grid tabulating the distance, or, on the contrary, the proximity of identity between the victim (and therefore his suffering) and those who are going to help.

In these conditions, it is not surprising that the Armenian victim found a special echo within the ICRC. First and foremost, this concerned a Christian people persecuted by non-Christians, which evoked the compassion of European citizens, if not their identification with the oppressed. This attitude is still reinforced by the fate of the Armenians, which has preoccupied Europe since the second half of the nineteenth century. The ICRC has not escaped from this tendency.[7] By analogy, other populations subjugated to the Ottoman authorities also interested the ICRC. Thus, during the War of 1875–78 it did not hesitate to send delegates to Montenegro, inaugurating in this manner the era of missions.[8] In the same way, it remained attentive to the Macedonian uprising of 1903,[9] and, quite exceptionally, launched a call to the societies of the Red Cross to come to help the *civilian* victims of the insurrection.[10]

These surges of charity were lacking when the victims were black. In ICRC documentation, there is no mention made of the massacre of the Hereros. The ICRC did, however, regularly highlighted events in German South-West Africa in its *Bulletin*. Between July 1905 and July 1908, there were no less than six reports (extracts from the German Red Cross, *Das Rothe Kreuz*) giving information about the activities of German aid work-

---

[7] Cf. *Bulletin*, 107, July 1896, pp. 194–196; 113 January 1898, pp. 11–12.
[8] ACICR, AF, box 21, dossier 13, Monténégro and Herzégovine, 1875–1876, "Mission au Monténégro. Rapport présenté au Comité international de la Croix-Rouge par ses délégués, MM. Aloïs Humbert, Dr Frédéric Ferrière et M. Goetz, 6 avril 1876."
[9] *Bulletin*, 136, October 1903, p. 206.
[10] Ibid., 137, January 1904, pp. 7–9.

ers regarding their own nationals. When *Das Rothe Kreuz* published a photograph showing skeletal Hereros escapees,[11] the ICRC made no mention of this photograph, shocking as it must have been.

It seems as though the black victims suffered from a plural handicap in gaining recognition of their situation. Over and above the difference of skin color and geographical distance, it was also a disparity of "civilization" which appears to have hindered all possibility of closeness with the black victims: "No Negro State ...," as the president of the ICRC Gustave Moynier explained, "has yet to adhere to the Geneva Convention; it is not even desirable that they do, for the black peoples of Africa are, for the most part, still too wild to be capable of joining forces with the humanitarian thought which inspired this treaty, and to put it into practice."[12]

This last element appears to be crucial in the (non) consideration of the victim's status if one believes in the ICRC's pusillanimity regarding the European Jews persecuted by the Nazi system. The ambiguous attitude of the International Red Cross regarding the Shoah[13] can thus be largely explained by the cultural and racial prejudices circulating in Switzerland. The ICRC, made up of Swiss citizens who were for the most part members of the upper bourgeoisie, could not avoid "anti-Semitic impregnation"[14] that affected the country. From the beginning of the twentieth century, in the name of the "defense of the Fatherland" and because of the fear of an over-population of foreigners, the elite of the

---

[11] *Das Rothe Kreuz*, 2 January 1908, p. 36.

[12] *Bulletin*, 41, January 1880, p. 5. Unfortunately, this negative view of Africa was held for decades in the heart of an institution deeply marked by a Eurocentricity interbred with racism which still retained belief in the Western ideology of the civilization of Africa. In this way, during the events in Rwanda from 1959 to 1960, the ICRC labelled the African situation as being like the "pre-middle-ages" (ACICR, A PV, Conseil de Présidence, meeting of 15 December 1960 at 14.30) and Rwandan troubles as "feudal wars" (Ibid., meeting of Thursday 11 November 1965 at 14.30 or A PV, Comité, plenary meeting on Thursday 13 February 1964).

[13] Jean-Claude Favez, *Une Mission Impossible ? Le CICR, les déportations et les camps de concentration nazis*, in collaboration with Geneviève Billeter, Lausanne, Editions Payot, 1988; Arieh Ben-Tov, *Facing the Holocaust in Budapest. The International Committee of the Red Cross and the Jews in Hungary, 1943–1945*, Geneva, Henry Dunant Institute; Dordrecht, Boston, London, Martinus Nijhoff Publishers, 1988.

[14] Daniel Bourgeois, "La Suisse, les Suisses et la Shoah," *Revue d'Histoire de la Shoah*, 163, 1998, p. 150.

Right wing bourgeoisie had developed an anti-Semitic xenophobia which was echoed by several ICRC members, so that it was not rare to find allusions reflecting this state of mind in the Institution's documentation.[15] That this "impregnation" had a harmful effect on help for the Jewish victims of Nazism is not improbable. Similarly, one cannot exclude that it contributed to relegation of "the Jew" to a category of second class victim; that is, a victim who was to be neither rejected outright nor saved as a matter of priority.

The persecutors

Indeed, to speak of the victims of massacres implies speaking of those who are responsible for them. The capacity to imagine social players as persecutors often depends upon the possibility of considering their targets as victims. The ICRC is not an exception to this mirror-image rule, and documentation—or its absence—permits us to see how the institution created an image of perpetrators. From the outset, one can show that the persecutor is more often than not presented as the absolute opposite of the victim. In this manner, in the case of the Armenians and other populations persecuted by the Ottoman government at the beginning of the 20th century, the innocence of the former responds as an echo of the barbarity of the latter.[16]

The reasoning was naturally quite different in the case of the Hereros. Here, the absence of victims recognized by the ICRC resulted in an absence of the guilty. Moreover, those upon whom disgrace should have fallen were, in their turn, considered as victims, for whom the German Red Cross led their "charitable acts."[17] In reports that it published about the campaign in German South-West Africa, the ICRC cheerfully endorsed the position of this national organization. Meanwhile, German officers returning from Africa went to regain their health in Alpine convalescent homes in Switzerland![18]

---

[15] ACICR, A PV, Commission P.I.C, meeting on Friday 13 April 1945 at 10am.
[16] *Bulletin*, 28, October 1876, p. 164; ACICR, AF, 19,2/218, "Note confidentielle pour les membres du Comité international," s.d. [Gustave Moynier].
[17] *Bulletin*, 147, July 1906, p. 199.
[18] ACICR, AF, 14, 3, Mail received from Prussia, 1897–1977, items 1542–1548.

The First World War saw a notorious change of opinion. If the Turks continued to occupy a privileged rank amongst persecutors, they were joined by the Germans who had become their accomplices in the extermination of the Armenians, about which the ICRC did not fail to remind them. Thus, when the Reich denounced the atrocities perpetrated by colored Allied troops and demanded that "in the interests of humanity and civilization" they be removed from the theatre of war in Europe, the response of the ICRC was biting: "One can only sincerely deplore atrocities of this type. However, one cannot help but regret … that the German government did not 'in the interests of humanity and civilization' impose another type of conduct upon its troops in Belgium, upon the Austro-German armies in Serbia, and upon its allies the Turks in Armenia."[19]

For the rest, during World War II, the ICRC seems to have returned to more "moderate" sentiments. Aligning its policies with those of the Swiss Confederation, the ICRC adopted a conciliating attitude regarding its omnipresent German neighbor. Furthermore, the fear of putting in jeopardy its traditional activities in Germany, notably visiting prisoners of war, by responding to requests from the civilian detainees in concentration camps, could explain the wait and see policy of the Red Cross. Finally, it is not to be excluded that personal affinities of certain members of the ICRC[20] with German personalities of the highest rank could have had weight upon this desire for accommodation, and, as an indirect consequence, upon the efforts deployed to help the victims. This ideological affinity with a totalitarian regime, if not tacit agreement of the highest echelons of the institution with certain aspects of the ideology that it was preaching, was part of a continuing trend, the examples of fascist Italy[21] and Franco's Spain[22] acting as precedents. More than anything else, perhaps, this affinity makes it easier to understand how it must have been

---

[19] *Bulletin*, 185, January 1916, p. 88.

[20] Paul Staffer, *Zwischen Hofmannsthal und Hitler, Carl J. Burckhardt. Facetten einer aussergewöhnlichen Existenz*, Zurich, Verlag Nueue Zürcher Zeitung, 1991.

[21] Rainer Baudendistel, *Between Bombs and Good Intentions. The International Committee of the Red Cross (ICRC) and the Italo-Ethiopian War, 1935–1936*, Oxford, New York, Berghahn Books, 2006.

[22] Daniel Palmieri, "Un Comité sous influence? Le CICR, Franco et les victimes," Communication for the international symposium "War without Limits: Spain 1936–1939 and Beyond," University of Bristol, 17–19 July 2006, forthcoming.

difficult to class the Germans in the category of persecutors and hence to treat the Jews as "real" victims.

The blindness towards persecutors is not always a direct result of an ideological *a priori*. On the contrary, it can arise from an immediate confrontation with the conflict and the impossibility to make decisions when one is directly seized by the complexity of the event; in other words, humanitarian deeds are largely dependant upon the human.

The weight of men

From here on, everything moves us to wider questioning of the role of the social actors in the mechanisms of a humanitarian organization faced with mass murder. In the case of the ICRC, it is necessary to introduce from the outset a distinction between the members of the committee, its executive organ in Geneva, and its delegates present on the terrain of war.

For a long time, the ICRC identified itself with its sole committee, composed uniquely of Swiss citizens. Until the end of the 1930s, the committee was, in effect, in itself the institution, as it employed so few subsidiary collaborators.[23] Traditionally, the successive presidents at the head of the ICRC carried a determining weight in the orientations taken by the organization. Thus it was with Gustave Moynier, its second president, in office from 1864 to 1910, and his successors, Gustave Ador (1910–28) and Max Huber (1928–45). Each of them had to face at least one massacre during his presidency. In fact, the management or mismanagement of responses to these killings seems, amongst other elements, intimately linked with the personalities of these three leaders.

Although Moynier was passionately interested in African studies, the ICRC under his presidency showed no interest in the annihilation of the Hereros. The fact that he was designated by King Leopold II as consul general of the Congo Free State in Switzerland (a post that he would actively occupy until 1904, and then as honorary consul later) was perhaps not unconnected with this collusive silence, as the German crimes in Africa were exceeded by those of the Belgian King. Moreover, who, in

---

[23] Diego Fiscalini, "Des élites au service d'une cause humanitaire: le Comité international de la Croix-Rouge," degree dissertation, Faculté de Lettres, Université de Genève, 1985, 2 volumes.

Switzerland, was worrying about the disappearance of the indigenous peoples of South-West Africa? In the same order of ideas, the ICRC's vehement protests in 1915 during the Armenian massacres could be linked to the personal attitude of Gustave Ador during the Great War and with his notorious Francomania.[24] In denouncing the Turks, the president of the ICRC was implicitly aiming at their German allies. He was aided in this by Swiss public opinion, greatly moved by the events in Armenia,[25] and by certain colleagues in the ICRC who were active in pro-Armenian movements.[26]

As for the trials and errors of the institution in the face of the extermination of the Jews, they can be explained in part by the direction that Max Huber had inspired the institution to take. He was certainly a renowned lawyer but was rarely inclined to action and acted with extreme prudence. More, Huber's economic connections as president of the board of the Aluminium-Industrie Company, and the close collaboration of this firm with the Third Reich during the war,[27] together with the very conservative political orientations of the president of the ICRC and his closest advisers,[28] give additional explanations for the institution's disengagement.

The ICRC, which was physically absent on the battlefield during the massacres in South-West Africa, had its baptism of fire during World War II. Though access to Nazi concentration and extermination camps was forbidden to it until the last days of the war, in late April 1945 (with the exception of an orchestrated visit under high surveillance to the Theresienstadt ghetto in June 1944), the institution delegated several of its collaborators in countries where massive deportations of Jews had taken place. Moreover, contrary to the ruling authorities in Geneva, the ICRC delegates on the ground seem to have largely disregarded ideologi-

---

[24] Irène Herrmann and Daniel Palmieri, "Genève ou la neutralité, 1914–1945" in Philippe Chassaigne and Jean-Marc Largeaud (eds), *Villes en guerre, 1914–1945*, Paris, Armand Colin, 2004, pp. 219–28.

[25] In 1896, more than 450,000 signatures were collected in a petition demanding the intervention of the Swiss government, despite the country's neutrality, See Karl Meyer, *l'Arménie et la Suisse*, Berne, Oeuvre de la Croix-Bleue, 1974 (Villeurbane, s.l., 1974 for the French translation), pp. 56–7.

[26] Diego Fiscalini, op. cit., volume 2, p. 219.

[27] Sophie Pavillon, "Aluminium Industrie AG (Alusuisse) et le Troisième Reich," http://www.alencontre.org/EdPage2/p2_2GM_alu.html

[28] Daniel Palmieri, "Un Comité sous influence?…," op. cit.

cal questions in order to dedicate themselves solely to humanitarian acts.[29] The inaction, the passivity of the Swiss government, much like the inadequacy of the instructions received from Geneva regarding real needs, seemed to them to be irreconcilable with the very mission of the ICRC, to help those who suffer. Frédéric Born, a delegate in Budapest who was confronted with the anti-Semitic policies of the Hungarian government in 1944, summed it up perfectly: "I understand the extraordinary difficulties facing the committee regarding this, but the idea of witnessing these tragic events impotent and disarmed is almost unsupportable."[30] Some delegates, going over and above the orders that came from their hierarchy, at their risk and peril, did all that was possible to help the populations threatened by Nazi fanaticism. We owe to them, regardless of the failure or the success of their undertakings, the fact that the victims and, more widely, the phenomenon of the massacres, were taken into account.

Conclusions

Thus, with all due respect to the elite of the ICRC, despite its affirmations, the International Red Cross remained for a long time indifferent or inactive when a general calamity plunged a part of humanity into distress; or rather, what it considered to be a general calamity largely depended upon which part of humanity this misfortune affected. In other words, the institution's sensitivity to the massacres of the twentieth century was mainly a function of the mental categories into which the protagonists of these genocides fell, and in consequence, of the circumstances and the men who encouraged the creation of such classifications.

Consequently, one notes the ever-moving contours of the ICRC's notion of the victim. Over and above the purely legal distinction between those protected or not by the Geneva Convention, one can see that the ICRC carried out a veritable selection amongst massacre victims outside humanitarian law. The Armenians are a reflection of this in that some of them were judged to be worthy of interest, and the ICRC came out from behind its habitual reserve, if not its official attributions, to carry out

---

[29] Irène Herrmann and Daniel Palmieri, "Le geste contre la parole: le Comité international de la Croix Rouge et le Goulag (1921 1950)," *Goulag: le peuple des zeks*, Genève, Infolio, Musée d'Ethnographie, 2004, pp. 137–41; Daniel Palmieri, "Un Comité sous influence?...," op. cit.

[30] Jean-Clause Favez, op. cit., p. 320.

actions in their favor. For other victims, on the other hand, the institution sought refuge in a policy of silence.

The major factor determining the degree of preoccupation for the victim can be expressed in terms of geographical, "ethnic," cultural or ideological proximity. An uncomplicated and pluridimensional identification resulted in a greater tendency to consider the victims as such; however, if differentiation was easier, then the suffering was less recognized. This causal relationship was however, counterbalanced—either qualified or more often reinforced—by the "media" impact that the tragic events had on the Swiss, if not the international, community.[31] The more massacres incited public indignation, the more the ICRC seemed moved[32] to go beyond its legal competence. Thus, in consideration of World War II and then decolonization, one sees a widening of the range of victims who could potentially be assisted. Along the same lines, there was also a relaxation of the hierarchization of assistance so respected by the ICRC until that point. It was only with the Biafran war, its huge impact on the media, and the arrival of a new generation of delegates that the victims of the black continent were truly taken into consideration by the institution. Finally, the increase in categories of victims goes hand in hand with the rise in numbers of their persecutors. Though logical, this phenomenon also encouraged the ICRC to be always wary of the notion of "civilization," and hence, to extend its attention and relief to new suffering.

It remains that the most decisive proximity is human proximity, one which the institution's collaborators maintained with the theatre of the atrocities, and therefore with the victims' pain. The presence of the ICRC's staff at the scene of the drama was prerequisite to any real—and not theoretical[33]—taking account of the phenomenon of massacres by the institution. Regularly, it was only by being personally confronted with the suffering that the delegates were able to understand it; that they decided to fight it; that they made an uproar about the doctrinal conception of

---

[31] The massacre of the Hereros provoked strong protests in Germany, which, however, were hardly seen across the border. On the contrary, the events in Rwanda during the 1960s were followed by the Swiss press.

[32] ACICR, A PV, Agence internationale des prisonniers de guerre, meeting of 9 May 1916.

[33] The usage of terms such as "systematic extermination" during events in Armenia shows that the ICRC had however become aware of the special nature of these acts.

the neutrality of the Red Cross; that they denounced the institutional sclerosis of the organization, and eventually forced the ICRC to shake itself out of its lack of will power. It was, therefore, through their individual closeness to the adversity of others that the delegates were able to construct other proximities, and in this way arouse the interest of the ICRC. Even better, they demonstrated that one could not remain indifferent to the massacres without finding oneself sullied, and without becoming in some way an accomplice.

This development, which was instigated at the beginning of the twentieth century, has not yet been completed, since, as late as 1994, the delegate Philippe Gaillard, a witness of the massacres of Rwanda, had no hesitation in breaking the law of silence:

> I had to speak, to be outspoken, in such a context. When you're seeing it every day in the streets, in your hospital, on the roads… In such circumstances, if you don't at least speak out clearly, you are participating in the genocide… It's a responsibility to speak out […]. The International Committee of the Red Cross … was not active during the Armenian genocide, and shut up during the Holocaust—everybody knew what was happening with the Jews… but nobody spoke out, and as a humanitarian organization it was our moral obligation to tell publicly what everybody knew and what nobody had the courage to say…[34]

In this manner, in the course of one of the last genocides of the twentieth century, the International Red Cross only recognized the amplitude of the genocide thanks to private initiatives which, though coming from within of the institution, had to do battle with it in order to perfect the mission which the ICRC had given itself. Currently, this situation reminds us that to explain the attitude of the ICRC by referring exclusively to its mandate is to inverse the problem and its causes. Certainly the ICRC was founded in order to "humanize" war, but it is men who conferred upon this role a humanitarian character.

---

[34] http://www.pbs.org/wgbh/pages/frontline/shows/ghosts/interviews/gaillard.html. (accessed 17/05/2010)

14

THE SWISS REACTION TO THE NAZI GENOCIDE
ACTIVE REFUSAL, PASSIVE HELP

Ruth Fivaz-Silbermann

Faced with the genocide of the Jews, I argue in this chapter, Switzerland clearly took the stance of bystander—he who stands on the pavement and watches as the caravan of history passes by—and not that of eyewitness, as the French version of Hilberg's work incorrectly states.[1] An eyewitness, for example, even if he is prevented from helping for various reasons, can at least raise the alarm, perhaps by getting into contact with other eyewitnesses—communication with other neutral states could have been envisaged—or officially denouncing the atrocities brought to light, or at least not opposing the broadcasting of information about them in the country. The Swiss government, however, did none of this, aligning itself with an interpretation of its neutrality that was rapidly found insufficient after the war. It only reacted in any significant way in spring 1944, when Hungarian Jews found themselves threatened. Jewish refugees were not considered political refugees and were only allowed into Switzerland unconditionally after 12 July 1944.

---

[1] Raul Hilberg, *Exécuteurs, victimes, témoins. La catastrophe juive, 1933–1945*, Paris, Gallimard, 1994. Original version: *Perpetrators, Victims, Bystanders: Jewish Catastrophe, 1933–1945*, New York, HarperCollins, 1992.

A policy of restricted asylum

Neutrality and adaptation. The key tendencies of Swiss policy at the time of the genocide can be summed up in two words; neutrality and adaptation.

The first key word clamoured if not trumpeted from the roofs was "neutrality." The Swiss, in 1938, had returned to a doctrine of integral neutrality, and had, of course, pulled out of the League of Nations, not wishing to participate in economic sanctions. Neutrality as state policy implied most precisely that one was not to get mixed up with any of the belligerents. It goes without saying that economic interests played a predominant role, notably economic ties with Germany, which had been in a privileged partnership with Switzerland since the end of the nineteenth century. Neutrality was an element of prime importance in calculating the interests of the country and was, because of this, invoked by both its economic and its political elite. Taken this way, neutrality allowed, in principle, the maintaining of good relations with both the victorious and the defeated, victims and persecutors. Add to this a natural aversion to politics, and neutrality provided the perfect shield against sentimentality.

What might be said of the majority of the political classes and of the elite was not necessarily true of the rest of the population, whose feelings at the time are difficult to reconstruct; it is certain that they were not indifferent to the personal fate of the persecuted.

The second key word, less frequently voiced but always in mind, was "adaptation": that is, adaptation to the prevailing political circumstances when they moved toward conservative stability and (curiously, since Switzerland is profoundly federal, in the direction of a strong, centralized regime); the revolutionary component of European fascism seems to have been hardly noticed. As Hans-Ulrich Jost says, "One can say that 'adaptation'—combined with occasional bursts of patriotism and accompanied by a permanent mistrust by the majority of all foreign influences—characterized fairly well [Swiss] external relations between 1914 and 1945."[2]

So who were the decision-makers of this policy of neutrality and adaptation? The Swiss government (a federal council), elected by parliament, was all-powerful for the duration of the war and could manage without the backing of parliament. Moreover, as noted in the report made by the

---

[2] Hans-Ulrich Jost, "Menace et repliement," in *Nouvelle Histoire de la Suisse et des Suisses*, Lausanne, Payot, 1998, (2nd edition), p. 689.

International Commission of Swiss experts on World War II, this government proved to be weak in economic and banking fields, letting its main officials act freely after choosing them to head the institutions of the war economy. Power was thus delegated. Similarly, as far as asylum was concerned, one senior civil servant governed the country's entire policy: Heinrich Rothmund, chief of the police division of the federal department of Justice and Police, who elaborated upon, negotiated with, then carried out each directive, in complete agreement with his minister-supervisor Eduard von Steiger. Generally, the elite in power was perfectly happy with the way in which its elitist delegates governed the economy, and vice versa; the Left had no seat in government until 1943, and this same Left signed a workers' peace treaty and accepted the national defense program. The Swiss state then had a corporatist structure, or at least ran along those lines.[3]

The Confederation managed to delegate its humanitarian action to an extra-governmental body: the International Red Cross (ICRC), run by the very same elite, which seems to show Switzerland's humanitarian side through the action of the Swiss Red Cross, which welcomed cohorts of foreign children for health reasons. Switzerland's reputation as the "land of sanctuary," forged in the nineteenth century for political reasons, was sustained through the twentieth century taking on medical orientation, at around the same time as political asylum was being refused to those being pursued by the Nazis.

Political ignorance and unawareness of the genocide

A third trail we can follow to try to understand Switzerland at that time was its aversion to political ideologies, of whatever sort. Anti-communism was then virulent, as was anti-Nazism; Fascist fronts existed, but had little influence. In their great majority, the Swiss were and wanted to remain Swiss, that is, to live according to the bourgeois and patriarchal model that was proposed to them by their elites, where the authority of the head of the family, the company, and the army reigned supreme. While it might seem, to all levels of the hierarchy, to work well as an ideology of identity,

---

[3] We use the term "corporatist" within the context of this synthetic presentation. The reality is obviously more complex and qualified, and Swiss historical documentation still suffers from a certain theoretical deficit. Cf. Hans-Ulrich Jost's bibliographic overview in "Menace et repliement," op. cit., pp. 766–70.

as an ultimate policy reference, this "Swiss" national character, its acts, its promises, a Helvetian myth, could only be a fiction in such a multilingual, multi-confessional, strongly federal country such as this—and could become a convenient shield protecting Swiss interests. This notion of identity, with the exception of the left wing, did not draw upon any transcending values such as the equal rights of men or universal justice. It is significant that the majority of protests were made in the name not of universal values, but of the Christian notion of brotherly love.

Along with this political obscurantism and for reasons that are probably linked with it—we could bring up the "lack of the sense of tragedy on the part of the Swiss and its tragic lack of sense of excessiveness" lamented by Philippe Burrin[4]—we see a Switzerland gripped with a sort of general incapacity to admit, to understand or to believe that somewhere within the war between the Axis and the allies, there might be a war of extermination of the Jews. This, despite the fact that since 1942 at least, the Swiss government had been in possession of reliable information on the extermination through diplomatic circles and from German deserters (it would only be informed about the gas chambers of Auschwitz at the end of June 1944 by the Vrba-Wetzler report)[5]. This incredulity even affected the official in charge of help given to Jews in the ICRC, Prince Jean-Etienne de Schwarzenberg, who upon receiving in 1944 a postcard from Birkenau, concluded that the Jews were not having so bad a time of it.[6] Even the leaders of the Swiss Jewish community feared that too much alarmism would further close frontiers to Jews. Thus, in May

---

[4] Interview with the historian Philippe Burrin in the *Tribune de Genève*, 20 October 2004.
[5] Two Slovakian Jews, Rudolf Vrba [Walter Rosenberg] and Alfred Wetzler, escaped from Auschwitz in April 1944 and drew up a precise and detailed double report on the camps of Auschwitz, Birkenau and Majdanek, which made its way to the World Jewish Congress in Geneva via Bratislava and Budapest. The Swiss authorities (and the Allies) were informed and the Swiss press, from the end of July 1944, let freely flow a sentiment of compassion and indignation. The genocide of the Jews of Hungary was, however, in no way halted. Cf. Rudolf Vrba (with Alan Bestic), *I Cannot Forgive*, London, Sidgwick and Jackson, 1963); Léonard Mach, "Les milieux officiels et la presse Suisse face à la "solution finale," avant et après la campagne de protestation de l'été 1944 contre l'extermination des Juifs de Hongrie," unpublished paper from the Department of History at the University of Geneva, 2006.
[6] Archives of the International Committee of the Red Cross, Geneva, G 59.

1943, when Rothmund and von Steiger asked them to prepare a memo about French deportations, they gave forth only the following information: the men were going to work camps and the women to brothels![7] It was only with great difficulty that progress toward acknowledgment that the extermination was planned and programmed was made. This was even the case for those in direct contact with Gerhart Riegner, secretary to the Geneva Office of the World Jewish Congress and a true centre of information about the genocide—information concerning all relief agencies, be they Swiss, Jewish or Christian, governmental or not, Jewish communities and all sorts of Jewish organizations. Certain confidential information—held by the likes of Carl J. Burckhardt, former diplomat, member and future president of the ICRC, as well informed as Riegner—did not, it seems, manage to filter through to the government, secrecy remaining part of Swiss political tradition.[8] The rest of the work was done by the official censorship, forbidding all items considered defamatory—which included mention of all Nazi crimes—and strengthening the tendency to pay no attention to the relationship between the politics of Nazi persecution and the politics of Swiss asylum.

Xenophobia and anti-Semitism

The fourth important element was hostility toward the foreigner and in particular the foreign Jew. Not only were foreign influences frowned upon

---

[7] Cf. notes taken by George Brunschvig, secretary of the Swiss Federation of Jewish Communities, on the interview accorded by the Federal Councillor von Steiger on the 31 May 1943 to the President of the Federation, Saly Braunschweig and Brunschvig himself, Archiv für Zeitgeschichte [Centre of documentation of contemporary history of the Federal Polytechnic School], Zurich, IB SIG 9.1.1.1. The memorandum sent contains no concrete mention of torture, murder or extermination, but refers to a recent article in the New York German Jewish review, *Der Aufbau*, enclosed with the consignment. For more information about this interview, see also Stefan Mächler, *Hilfe und Ohnmacht*, Zurich, Chronos, 2005, p. 373 and note 89.

[8] Recent studies on World War II in Switzerland reveal, in general, a great opacity in the channels of information before, during and after the war. Cf. final report by the Independent Commission of Swiss Experts—"Second World War [the Bergier report], La Suisse, le national-socialisme et la Seconde Guerre mondiale," Zurich, Pendo, 2002, Introduction, 1.1 and passim; Luc Van Dongen, *La Suisse face à la Seconde Guerre mondiale, 1945–1948: Emergence et construction d'une mémoire publique*. Geneva, Société d'Histoire et d'Archéologie, 2000.

in Switzerland, foreigners themselves were rarely welcomed unless they were tourists. Switzerland suffered until 1936 from the serious world economic crisis; it was still reeling from the general strike of 1918 and feared all potential social troublemakers. This "Swissness" varnished over xenophobia that was omnipresent except amongst the Left and the more socially engaged churches. A Swiss form of anti-Semitism—latent, restrained—raged at all levels. Foreign Jews—Jews in Switzerland were only emancipated in 1874—were considered impossible to assimilate and their requests for naturalization were put to the side.

What of Rothmund the decision-maker? Historians have examined the question of his personal anti-Semitism. From the evidence, he was troubled by the religion of the Jews, by their national and social culture. He considered Swiss Jews equals provided that they were predominantly Helvetian—that is to say, integrated. He did not consider himself an anti-Semite, but, in a reaction summing up his entire political action, struggled to avoid the intrusion of too large a number of Jews for fear that their foreign habits—which from an economic point of view had negative connotations—might bring about a "Semitization" (*Verjudung*) of the country. And yet he was repulsed by Nazi anti-Semitism on the lines of Julius Streicher[9] and considered it unworthy of his country; in February 1941, he even forbade a National Propaganda conference on the supposed Jewish peril in Switzerland.

Instead of anti-Semitism, in Rothmund's case, it is better to speak of an anti-Jewish xenophobia; he would have probably behaved in the same way faced with any community with a strongly profiled social culture, at a time when the country was defending itself against a wave of immigration that was considered economically untenable. He is a good example of "Helvitude" as a mental limit: the "otherness" of foreigners was irredeemable, and only reinforced the understandable reasons for barricading oneself against their arrival: it was in this manner that they convinced themselves that "the boat was full," as the expression went, coined by federal councilor Eduard von Steiger and earmarked for posterity.[10]

---

[9] Julius Streicher, close to Hitler from the beginning of the NSDAP, and executed in 1946 at Nuremberg, called continually for the murder and the extermination of the Jews in his weekly *Der Stürmer*, whose tone was filthy and violent.

[10] Eduard von Steiger, a lawyer from Berne, was an influential character in the Parti des Paysans, Artisans et Bourgeois (now the right-wing Union Démocra-

Swiss asylum policy was therefore the product of diverse factors: an absence of any reference to Justice, which meant that those responsible could not see the German crimes for what they were; a lack of clear humanitarian standards; an irrational fear of immigration, propped up by understandable reasons such as shortages, fear of spies and the defense of the labor market.

Breaches of humanity

It was not, however, without mature reflection and an authentic moral debate that Rothmund resorted to dire measures in the summer of 1942, measures which we can now judge as nonsensical, since Nazi Germany had never pressured Switzerland over the question of refuge. One thing set him apart from his collaborators and subordinates; he took the risks run by the persecuted seriously and was never indifferent to their misery.

The closing of Switzerland's border on 4 August 1942 took place according to Rothmund's recommendations; he justified himself using a thirty-page report prepared for him by his colleague Robert Jezler.[11] Only one sentence in this report refers to the "overwhelming information" about "[the] manner in which the deportations were carried out and the living conditions in the 'Jewish regions' to the east," the rest of the report purely and simply recommending the turning back of fugitives, even if their lives were in danger. As well as the usual understandable reasons, Jezler confined himself to misinformation: at the moment when Vichy began to empty its camps, he judged the danger for "undesirable

---

tique du Centre), and was elected to the Federal Council in December 1940. He ran the Department of Justice and Police until 1951. On 30 August 1942 he gave a speech, which has passed into posterity, to an assembly of the Young Church, a Protestant Youth movement, in which he affirmed that he who finds himself, in the course of a catastrophic shipwreck, in charge of a small lifeboat which is already full and has limited provisions must concern himself with the saving of at least those who are already aboard, regardless of the calls for help from thousands of others and at the risk of appearing harsh. Cf. Hermann Kocher, *Rationierte Menschlichkeit*, Zurich, Chronos, 1996, p. 21.

[11] Robert Jezler was the principal collaborator of Heinrich Rothmund during the war, and temporarily replaced him in the Police Division. His long report of 30 July 1942 is conserved in the Swiss Federal Archives, AF E 4001 (C) in volume 14 of the *Documents Diplomatiques Suisses*, Berne, Benteli, 1997.

foreigners" as non-existent in unoccupied France, "except for De Gaulle's supporters." He foresaw pressure from the Germans in an odd manner: Germany could easily demand the return of the interned refugees and Switzerland would not be able to give them up because of its sovereignty... a situation to be avoided if one did not wish to offend the Germans!

Rothmund did not, however, opt for an indefinite closure of frontiers, but rather for dissuasion tactics. One could not just turn back all the Jews, in as much as the Belgians and the Dutch had their legations. One could not just totally abandon the tradition of asylum. The plan was instead to reinforce the frontiers with mobile units that would intercept all arrivals and turn them back for a certain period only; the Jews would, logically, stop trying to flee to Switzerland and the escape networks would abandon their activities. This directive was planned as a temporary measure.

It provoked a general outcry from Swiss public opinion, informed by courageous journalists, themselves lobbied by the bravest of Swiss Jewish notables. The Left and the Churches intervened in favor of the duty to offer refuge, as opposed to the government's right to grant or refuse. The wave of protest—which Riegner called "magnificent" in a telegram in English to the American president of the World Jewish Congress—influenced the closure policy at least for a while. While the frontier remained officially closed, the district police received on 31 August the order to "halt and turn back the fewest possible," and in particular, to turn no one over to the Germans.[12] Rothmund, speaking with the directors of the district police forces, underlined the dangers that people threatened with deportation faced—and the pressure of public opinion.[13] In September and October, apart from a certain number of people considered "undesirable"—a group of escapees among the Vichy foreign workers were deported because of absurd suspicions of spying—all Jews were admitted into Switzerland. Several thousand of them, harassed by the

---

[12] Private note of 1 September 1942 passed on to the Arrondissement territorial de Genève, Genevan State Archives, Justice and Police, Eb. A7.17.1.67, quoted in Catherine Santschi (ed.), *Les réfugiés civils et la frontière genevoise durant la Seconde Guerre mondiale*, Geneva, 2000, p. 78.

[13] Carl Ludwig, *La politique pratiquée par la Suisse à l'égard des réfugiés de 1933 à nos jours*, Berne, report given to the Federal Council [Federal Chancellery], 1957, p. 198.

Vichy Police, crossed the Franco-Swiss border at Geneva, via the lake and the Valais mountains. Hundreds were arrested en route.

Rothmund would never refer to this resolutely humane behavior. With his "supervising minister" von Steiger, as with the representatives of the constituency corps and civil society, he would continually justify the harshness of his policies. It was only logical that, as sole inventor and principal executor of these policies, he would come to embody them in the eyes of the public and would have to carry alone the responsibility for what would very quickly after the war seem to be one of his worst errors: the introduction in 1938 of the "J" which would appear in the passports of German Jews, and the turning away of people at the frontier. There is, however, a certain injustice in treating him as the scapegoat for the elite in power. Moreover, as the personal dossiers of refugees show, Rothmund would always judge in their favor in response to requests by military authorities in the frontier zones. In this way (but, ultimately, without a good result) he ruled in favor of two Jewish furriers from Amsterdam, Benediktus Wijnman and Siegfried Wijnschenk, who entered Switzerland on 22 May 1942. They were considered suspect in the eyes of both the Swiss authorities and the Dutch vice-consul (representative of the government in exile in London): they had fled without their wives and one of them was being followed by his mistress; neither of them made it clear that they faced death, saying only that the Gestapo had demanded of them the delivery of leather jackets and rabbit skins that they were unable to deliver. They were probably unaware, at the time, that they were selected victims; their fear and their youth, however, pushed them into flight. They were provisionally interned. Geneva's military authority wanted to expel them, declaring that their flight was merely due to "commercial irregularities." Rothmund retaliated on 4 June: "It is very relative. They are in great danger in Occupied France. Advise the Dutch legation and intern them at the penitentiary in the quarters reserved for internees."[14] Being unable to expel them without Rothmund's permission, the military chiefs made them sign—probably by force, since their passports stayed in the Swiss dossier—a voluntary promise to return to the Netherlands. Expelled from Switzerland on 30 August almost certainly into the Occupied Zone of France, they were arrested almost immediately in France and sent to Drancy, from whence

---

[14] Swiss Federal Archives, AF E 4264 (-), dossier 3321.

they were immediately sent to Auschwitz on 18 September 1942 in a one-way convoy, number 34.[15]

Even when he learned of the wiles and lies used by a Belgian escape networks in order to manipulate and exploit Swiss tolerance, Rothmund, who was certainly morally outraged, did not decide upon a general expulsion of the "guilty" parties as was laid down by the law; the "guilty" were to spend a long and depressing spell in prison, but their lives would be saved.

Switzerland as a passive tool of the resistance

The image of Switzerland's response to genocide would not be complete, however, without the other side of the coin: not only did it react and/or refuse to act, it was also exploited.

From October 1942, passage into Switzerland without a visa (rarely given but not totally unobtainable) became much more difficult since the authorities only decreed as admissible the elderly, pregnant women, the sick, children on their own, families with a child under sixteen years old, and those having close family in Switzerland; the age of the youngest child was lowered to six years at the end of the year in an general effort to tighten up admission instructions. In fact, this policy divided the fugitives into two groups: those who corresponded—or who were made to correspond—to the criteria, and those, whose numbers became less and less, who tried their luck all the same, at the mercy of local passage networks, and who were turned away. Fortunately, all those turned away were not arrested or deported: at Geneva, where figures have been established, around 9 per cent of fugitives were turned away, and of these, 14 per cent were deported.[16]

Jewish assistance groups soon began to profit from these possibilities. They were well informed about tolerance regarding, for example, age lim-

---

[15] Serge Klarsfeld, *Le Mémorial de la déportation des Juifs de France*, Paris, by the author, 1982, p. 296.

[16] Ruth Fivaz-Silbermann, *Le refoulement des réfugiés civils juifs à la frontière franco-genevoise durant la Seconde Guerre mondiale*, followed by *Mémorial de ceux parmi eux qui ont été déportés ou fusillés*, Paris, Fondation Beate Klarsfeld, 2000. This study is based upon the archives of the Arrondissement Territorial de Genève (the military authority whose mission was to either admit or expel), which are conserved almost in their entirety and are complemented by the Departmental Archives of the Haute-Savoie.

its for children who were either traveling alone or accompanied—which were not the same thing! The road to Swiss asylum increasingly led to the Jewish resistance and the falsification of identity. All "seniors" would from now on be 65 years old, all adolescents would be less than sixteen (eighteen for girls); and since each family needed a child under the age of 6, each was given a young child, an orphan or one "borrowed" from a large group of siblings. Fake couples were created through the marriage of perfect strangers; a certain number of adults and children were saved by this method.[17] When, in August and September 1943, the protection of the Italian occupation troops in France collapsed, the Megève office of the Oeuvre de Secours aux Enfants (OSE) organized by Jacques and Nicole Salon managed to get through to Switzerland seven convoys of families and children, 148 people in all, many of whom had fake identities; one quarter of Megève's "Jewish colony" was saved in Switzerland, thanks to a maximum exploitation of Swiss tolerance, stretched beyond measure.

The OSE's activity was much wider than this. With the Zionist Youth Movement and the EIF (Eclaireurs Israélites de France), it got 106 convoys of children through, around 1,100 children and adolescents. All of those over 16 years of age were given false dates of birth. None of them were turned away because of this, and Berne made no effort to seek out and punish the network agents. Everything indicates that when it came to children, the central authority—which had accepted a contingency figure of 1,500 admissions—tacitly tolerated this discreet form of salvation, whereas local authorities, on the borders, multiplied their enquiries but with little success.[18]

At the end of 1943, the Czech Jewish resistance fighter Motke Weinberger, of Antwerp, organized twenty convoys to Switzerland, with more than 200 fugitives hidden in Brussels and Antwerp, some of whom had already escaped from the trains from the Malines camp to Auschwitz. They would do anything to escape Nazi hounding, as we learn from

---

[17] Cf. Ruth Fivaz-Silbermann, "Par la porte de secours. La fuite des Juifs en Suisse dans l'après-8 septembre 1943," in *Le refuge et le piège. Les Juifs dans les Alpes 1938–1945*. Paris, L'Harmattan, 2008, pp. 223–37; Jacques Salon, *Trois mois dura notre bonheur. Mémoires 1943–1944*, Paris, FMS—manuscrit.com 2005, chap. 5.

[18] Cf. Ruth Fivaz-Silbermann, "Le sauvetage clandestin des enfants juifs à travers la frontière genevoise, 1942–1944," in *Espaces Savoyards: frontières et découpages*, Archamps, La Salévienne, 2004, pp. 171–81.

Fanny S., thirty-two years old, from Brussels, who, with her husband, presented a child at the frontier who was not their own: "We were doing everything we could to save our lives, we would have sworn on anything we were asked to, even on our children's heads." When the network was exposed in March 1944, the Geneva military authority turned back Fanny, her husband and all the false parents who were still arriving. (On the other hand, they still accepted all of the children). Some of these desperate people were immediately arrested by the German police and deported. Berne remained silent: local authorities retained the right to turn people back.[19]

Conclusion

There coexisted therefore, in the Swiss practice of asylum, a passive tolerance, which was, up to a certain point, closely monitored, and a refusal of assistance. Neutral, and devoid of any guiding political direction, Switzerland was neither humane nor inhumane. Saly Mayer, president of the Swiss Federation of Jewish communities until the end of 1942 and Joint's representative in Europe, observed after the war: "We could have done more but we could also have done less." On the side of tolerance, considering the numbers of Jewish deportees from France (76,000), more than 15,000 Jews crossed the Franco-Swiss border (a figure which includes, it is true, people who were turned back), of whom perhaps 10 per cent had made-to-measure identity papers; this was much more than a drop in the ocean. Those turned back (research on this subject is not yet complete) probably did not number more then 3,000 at this frontier; arrests made on French territory, before the frontier, must have claimed at least as many victims as border controls. On the side of refusal: how to accept that Berne was allowing the local military authorities, until June 1944, to turn away Jews in danger, carefully selecting who, out of a group of people, had the right to live, and who did not?

After the war, nobody was entirely satisfied with the role that Switzerland played, except those who had been able to benefit from its welcome.

[19] Cf. Ruth Fivaz-Silbermann, "La fuite en Suisse. Migrations, stratégies, fuite, accueil, refoulement et destin des réfugiés juifs venus de France durant la Seconde Guerre mondiale." Doctorate thesis at the University of Geneva, currently being completed. About Fanny S., Genevan State Archives, Justice and Police Ef/2—6946.

Successive generations resurrect the debate. The final report from the Independent (and international) Commission of Swiss Experts-World War II was still asking in 2002 why, despite the information it possessed, the Swiss government did not opt, in 1938 or at latest 1942, for a real policy of protection and assistance in the face of genocide.

15

THE OSE AND THE RESCUE OF JEWISH CHILDREN, FROM THE POST-WAR TO THE PRE-WAR PERIOD

Katy Hazan and Georges Weill

The *Œuvre de Secours aux Enfants* (OSE)—Children's Welfare Organization—is well known for its considerable role in rescuing Jewish children in France: all the books on the fate of the Jews under the Occupation contain descriptions of its fight against Nazism and the Vichy government. An exhibition, "The OSE, 90 Years of History," and an illustrated volume honored the memory of its leaders and retraced its history from its founding in Russia in 1912 under the name OZE through to the present day, since the association continues its work for children's welfare in France. Several symposia have detailed everyday life in its children's homes and collected personal accounts retracing the itineraries of many children who were hidden. Publication of the memoirs of several OSE officials has started to shed new light on their role during the Occupation. Although these studies are still in their infancy, there is fortunately no longer reason to lament, as Jean Laloum did fifteen years ago, that "the fate of the Jewish child under the Occupation occupies an extremely minor place in the historiography."[1]

---

[1] Regarding the origins of OZE (Obschestvo Zdravookhranenya Yevreyev), a Russian Jewish Welfare Association, see *Une mémoire pour le futur, 90 ans de*

This new methodological approach has been allied with the growing awareness within the OSE itself of its own history. The organization has undertaken to reconstitute its archives and conducted methodical research in several countries. This has enabled us, for instance, to better understand the functioning of the World Union OSE, founded in Berlin in 1923, of which Albert Einstein was the honorary president until he died in 1955. The goal of this international federation was to coordinate the social welfare efforts of Jewish communities in several Central European countries. The French branch, the best known today, was founded in 1934, one year after World Union OSE headquarters were transferred to Paris and Geneva.

This chapter could have begun with the year 1912, since OZE was created in order to help underprivileged Jewish populations, promote a healthier lifestyle in their communities and prevent epidemics. Its best-known achievements were in care for infants and young children, particularly through milk stations for mothers, as well as the distribution of brochures and the opening of dispensaries and soup kitchens. This effort grew during the fighting of 1914–17 and then the ensuing civil war. These periods do not, however, qualify as genocidal, despite the terrible pogroms in Ukraine and White-controlled areas of Russia and their dramatic consequences.[2]

---

l'OSE, A Legacy for the Future, Paris, OSE, 2003. For a provisional bibliography, see Georges Weill, "Le sauvetage des enfants juifs en France," *Revue des Études Juives*, 163, July-December 2004, file 3–4, pp. 507–16; Pierre Bolle (ed.), *Le Plateau Vivarais-Lignon, accueil et résistance, 1939–1944. Actes du colloque de Chambon-sur-Lignon, octobre 1990*, Le Chambon-sur-Lignon, Société d'Histoire de la Montagne, 1992; Bernard Reviriego, *Les Juifs en Dordogne, 1939–1944. De l'accueil à la persécution*, Périgueux, Édition Fanlac, 2003; Pascal Plas and Michel Christophe Kiener (eds.), *Enfances juives: Limousin-Dordogne-Berry, Terres de refuge, 1939–1945*, Saint-Paul, Souny, 2006; Jacques Fijalkow (ed.), *Les Enfants de la Shoah*, proceedings of the Lacaune colloquium, September 2005, Paris, 2006.

[2] The Russian attorney and politician Maxime Vinaver informed the central committee of the Universal Israelite Alliance, of which he was a member, of the massacres of Jewish populations and the OZE's rescue efforts using ambulances and dietary cooking to stem epidemics and famine (Archives AIU, France, VIII A 65). Collection RU 1122 at the Central Archives for the History of the Jewish People in Jerusalem (CAHJP) holds a file on rescue efforts made by OZE during the 1920–1922 pogroms. The American Jewish Joint

OZE put an end to its activities in Russia in 1922 but pursued them in Lithuania, Latvia, Poland and Bessarabia in Romania. Unfortunately, destruction of all the health centers by the Nazis and the killing of 90 per cent, or even 100 per cent, of OZE members makes it difficult to pursue historical research into the organization in these countries. New research into the subject would usefully supplement the collection of articles and biographies published in their memory in the United States in 1968. The Berlin archives of the World Union have vanished. All that remain are the recently rediscovered archives of its Geneva headquarters. Also of note are the still unmined public and private archives in St Petersburg, Minsk, Vilnius and Kaunas, as well as in Poland, Romania, Hungary, Switzerland, Israel and the United States.[3]

In keeping with the precise topic of this book, the present chapter will begin only with Hitler's rise to power in 1933, but will extend a few years beyond the fall of Nazism. In fact, while OSE's role, with the help of some twenty other international charities, was decisive during this period in sheltering, hiding and rescuing over 6,000 Jewish children in France, its activity did not end with Liberation. It continued well after the war, because hidden children still had to be found, new children's homes opened and shelter, healthcare, education and social integration reorganized for about 1,500 surviving children. That number could be raised to 2,000 if we include the adolescents known as the "children of Buchenwald" who were placed in the organization's care in 1946. The consequences of the genocide seem at least as important as the circumstances of the rescue of the children, and we now know that the post-war decades were painful for many orphans.

The first part of this study will provide an overview of the various responsibilities taken on by Union OSE in Europe according to World Union OSE documents found in Geneva, now kept in Paris. In the second part, we will retrace the stages of the rescue of children in France

---

Distribution Committee (Joint) archives in New York hold correspondence and reports on the dramatic fate of Jews who were victims of pogroms in the 1920s.

[3] *Mélanges dédiés au D^r B[oris] A[rkadievitch] Tschlenoff à l'occasion de son 80e anniversaire*, Geneva, Union OSE, 1946; Dr. L. Wulman (ed.), *In Fight for the Health of the Jewish People (50 years of OSE)*, New York, 1968; Katy Hazan and Georges Weill, *Inventaire du fonds Tschlenoff*, Union OSE Archives and OSE Switzerland Archives in Geneva, typescript., Paris, OSE, 2004.

from the late 1930s until the end of the war, as well as successful or aborted attempts to send children to the United States, certain Latin American countries and the Palestine Mandated Territory. The third part will study the essential role of Dr Joseph Weill and OSE officials in organizing the rescue of several thousand children. The last part will be devoted to the reconstruction of Jewish youth, a vital extension of rescue work.

The successive responsibilities of OSE Union

OSE's Role in Central Europe. After independence, Poland founded its own society, called TOZ (Towarzystwo Ochrony Zdrowia), which remained faithful to OZE ideas, whereas the former provinces of the Russian Empire organized international or local branches. To handle the financial and medical coordination of its initiatives, a Congress held in Berlin in 1923 created a federation called World Union OSE for the Protection of the Health of the Jews. In addition, a joint committee with the World ORT (*Organisation, Reconstruction, Travail*) Union was to help centralize donations and subsidies while allowing each federation the right to pursue its own health and training policies. Actually, in the field, Union OSE and ORT Union work was often complementary, especially in the opening of ORT workshops in OSE children's homes in France.

But very little first-hand information is available on Union OSE activities in Central Europe in the years 1920–30, except through testimonials and articles.[4] Union OSE files kept in the Tschlenoff collection only start in 1939. They contain extensive correspondence in Russian and Yiddish, undergoing translation, reports on the situation of the Jews, and activity reports. Appeals for medical relief from colleagues in countries invaded by the Nazis are all the more heartrending when one knows what became of the extensive and costly aid supplied by Union OSE in Geneva via the International Committee of the Red Cross: hundreds of pounds of food and medicine for children, for which complete lists remain, were sent by Swiss factories at OSE's expense and were entirely misappropriated by the Germans, never to reach the Jewish doctors in those countries, except in rare cases.

---

[4] A complete collection of *Revue OSE* from 1934 to 1940 is held in the private OSE archives.

The death toll suffered by World Union OSE, established in 1968, showed that a staff of over 1,000 was employed by the Polish society TOZ in 1939, including thirty-two doctors; there were only about fifty survivors. The list of real estate property owned by the organization included a dozen health centers and hospitals, and sixteen establishments for children, mainly summer camps and dispensaries throughout the country, for which Union OSE received no compensation.

Information concerning Lithuania, Latvia and Romania is at present too sparse to be usefully analyzed.[5] There remain, however, handwritten and printed documents as well as iconographic sources that have yet to be examined, for instance in New York in the archives of the Joint and the YIVO Institute, which organized a fine exhibition on OSE's accomplishments in Europe.[6]

The Geneva Union OSE. From 1933 to 1939, the Union OSE delegation in Switzerland was run by Dr Laserson, who migrated to Australia in 1939, then by Dr Boris Arkadievitch Tschlenoff, a phthisiologist of Russian descent. Actually, it was the secretary general, Lazare Gurvic, who ran the federation from Paris, simply informing Geneva of its main operations in Europe. However, when the war began, Dr Tschlenoff became an essential intermediary between OSE and the American organizations that funded the society and the Swiss authorities. He established regular contact with Swiss humanitarian organizations. He also received, via OSE branches, increasingly alarming reports on the situation of the Jews in invaded countries, indicating the tragic stages of the OSE's destruction in Central Europe. Several attempts were apparently made in 1940 to smuggle groups of children from Poland into the Baltic countries, but to no avail.

The daily correspondence in 1940–41 shows the scale of OSE France's financial needs as well as attempts to smuggle children to the United States. All the expenses were assumed, not without difficulty, by the American Joint Distribution Committee, known as the Joint, whose European representative was a Swiss jeweler, Saly Mayer, also president of the Swiss Federation of Jewish Communities (Schweizerische Israel-

---

[5] The camp for 2,000 children of Kreslavka (in Latvian Latgalie) owed its existence to a generous gift from the sculptor Aronson in 1921.
[6] *The Society for the Protection of Jewish Health. Fighting for a Healthy New Generation*, New York, Yivo, 2005.

itische Gemeinschaft, SIG) until 1942. The Joint Office in Lisbon, run by Dr Schwartz, liaised with the New York office.

In addition to his many administrative duties, Dr Boris Tschlenoff represented Union OSE in meetings of the Committee for Refugee Children in unoccupied France, held in Geneva in 1942 and 1943. Made up of representatives from a dozen Swiss secular and religious (Catholic and Protestant) organizations, it was presided by Donald Lowrie, a representative of the Young Men's Christian Association (YMCA), and president of the so-called Comité de Nîmes, which brought together some thirty humanitarian organizations in this city whose mission was to help the foreign Jewish internees—including over 2,000 children later taken in by OSE—and French camps in the Southern Zone. Starting in summer 1942, committee members working in France were perfectly well aware of the situation of Jewish children taken in the roundups and of the internment and deportation of many of them. They envisaged a dozen solutions to try to rescue at least 5,000 children among an estimated 22,000 in France (an estimate for the most threatened), placing their hopes in certain North and South American countries as well as South Africa to welcome them, while knowing that Portugal would accept none, although it might grant transit visas. The Quakers and Unitarians took steps to obtain visas in Vichy and in Washington. During the last meetings of 1943, OSE representatives were able to give precise figures for the number of children already deported, over 5,500, but the committee only obtained from the Swiss government a vague promise of temporary admission, with no other specification regarding the age or the number of admissions that would be granted.[7]

The stages of rescue of children in France

OSE before the June 1940 Armistice. OSE activity in France began in 1935 as an association under French law and presided by Senator Justin Godard. Dr Alexandre Besredka, a biologist who studied under Metchnikoff, took over the central management of Union OSE, replacing Albert Einstein who had left for the United States in 1933 but who agreed to

---

[7] The first meeting took place on 29 August 1942, followed by five other until 30 October 1942. The committee then ceased to meet for a year, until 23 September 1943 and held its last meeting on 30 November 1943 (Archives OSE, Tschlenoff collection, box 15, file 11).

be honorary president. Dr Eugène Minkowski was president of the Union OSE executive committee in Paris.

Living conditions in pre-war France, although they were far from ideal, were obviously different from those in Central Europe. The needy Jewish population was much smaller, at least before the arrival of refugees from Germany and occupied countries.

OSE France concentrated its efforts on the immigrant Jewish population in the poor neighborhoods of Paris and the suburbs. It created a day camp for children in Montmorency and a dispensary in Paris, as well as a psychological care center to treat the traumas of immigrant children. This initiative can be considered as the first OSE response to the consequences of Nazi persecutions.

Most of the initiatives taken by OSE France are owed to Dr Alexandre Besredka (and his team of Russian doctors), who ran the organization from his laboratory at the Institut Pasteur until his death in 1940, in conjunction with the Lithuanian lawyer Lazare Gurvic, secretary general of Union OSE, and Doctors Julius Brutzkus, Eugène Minkowski, Valentina Cremer and H. Pollnow.

Jewish charity organizations naturally appealed to OSE when it came time to take in their first young German Jews who had taken refuge in Alsace and later in a Parisian area, after *Kristallnacht* in November 1938. Through the Russian doctors' experience, it had become the only French Jewish organization with a competent staff that specialized in the medical and social fields. Already in the month of January 1939, 300 German, Austrian and Czech children refugees without their parents were entrusted to OSE, which placed them in four homes located near Montmorency. The Viennese pedagogue and politician Ernst Papanek was put in charge of them, and he worked to heal the children's traumas using cooperation and active participation that he had tried out during the educational reform in the Austrian Republic in 1918.

Other groups of children were taken in by Baroness Germaine de Rothschild in the Château de la Guette and by Count Hubert de Monbrison in the Seine-et-Marne department, and then some were entrusted to the OSE at the start of the Occupation. In the spring of 1940, OSE gradually organized the evacuation of homes in the Paris region toward new children's homes, sometimes a bit pompously called "castles," located in the Allier, Creuse, Haute-Vienne and Var departments. With the Armistice, the division of France into two zones caused OSE to split into two committees, one in the Northern Zone, the other in the Free Zone, but both were integrated the following year into the UGIF (Union Générale des Israélites de France), whereas the Bureau of Union OSE remained independent, though under close surveillance by the German and French authorities.[8]

The OSE Committee in the Northern Zone. The OSE committee continued to function in the Northern (Occupied) Zone under the leadership of Dr. Eugène Minkowski, under German army surveillance, to provide relief for the Paris Jewish population in the form of medical care, distribution of clothing, legal aid and especially homes for children who could no longer play outdoors.[9]

Starting in September 1941, thus well before the Vélodrome d'Hiver Roundup in July 1942, OSE undertook to place children individually in non-Jewish families, using the same network of contacts as the Rue Amelot Committee of which Dr Minkowski, who had a hospital appointment, was a personal member. He continued to practice at Henri-Rousselle and Sainte-Anne hospitals, thanks to the connivance of the head doctors who enabled him to find hiding places for the hunted Jews or children requiring sanctuary. This underground children's network was able to shelter nearly 600 children out of a total 3,650 children that the Jewish and non-Jewish charities managed to save in the Northern Zone. A team led by Enéa Averbouh worked mainly in the dispensary placed at OSE's disposal by the "For Our Children" Association (Pour nos Enfants) located at 35 rue des Francs-Bourgeois, which was to become service 27 of the UGIF. Dr Valentine Cremer, who had gone into hiding in the Southern Zone, was replaced by Doctors Saly Goldberg and Irène Opollon.[10]

---

[8] In March 1942, the Union des Sociétés OSE was dissolved and integrated into the various departments in the UGIF-Northern Zone. See Michel Laffitte, *Un engrenage fatal, l'UGIF face aux réalités de la Shoah*, Paris, Liana Levi, 2003. By the same author, *Juifs dans la France allemande*, Paris, Tallandier, 2006.

[9] See the memoirs of Eugène Minkowski, Enéa Averbouh's notebooks and the Rue Amelot Committee archives held at the YIVO Institute in New York.

[10] Supplied with forged identification papers and not wearing the yellow star, the psychiatrist Irène Opollon hid children in the Paris area whom she visited and paid room and board for. She continued working with OSE after the war.

Attempted evacuation to the Americas

In 1940, with the help of several international Jewish and non-Jewish organizations, particularly the Quakers (American Friends Service Committee), the Comité Inter-mouvements auprès des Evacués (CIMADE) and the Young Men's Christian Association (YMCA) and the American Jewish Joint Distribution Committee, the OSE organized the departure of children to the United States as those interned in the Southern Zone camps were gradually released. OSE received 1,408 immigration requests, but only one child in ten had any hope being able to leave France. It was necessary to obtain three successive visas to leave France, for transit through Spain or Portugal and then for landing in New York. The United States had planned to receive between 1,000 and 5,000 of them. Finally, only a very small number managed to emigrate before November 1942.[11]

Indeed, little was known about the situation in France on the other side of the Atlantic. The famous affidavits so coveted by the Jews caught in Hitler's Europe's net were issued only in dribs and drabs, and on an individual basis as long as the children had family at the place of destination or someone who would assume responsibility for them. The Jewish committee for children coming from Germany and Central Europe, presided by Guy de Rothschild, completed considerable paperwork for the children hosted by his family.[12] At the start of the war, however, the emigration of many Union OSE officials, including Ernst Papanek, helped to accelerate the procedures and obtaining the preferential visas for groups of children under sixteen.[13]

The OSE committee in the United States (Amerose), run by Dr Wulmann, was no more effective than the Swiss committee described above. In January 1940, it examined the problem of children, but offered no solution. American Jewish associations did not realize the scale of the

---

[11] Jenny Masour-Ratner, *Mes vingt ans à l'OSE, 1941–1961*, edited by Katy Hazan, Paris, Le Manuscrit, "Témoignages de la Shoah" series, 2006. Regarding departures of children to America, see Sabine Zeitoun, *L'Œuvre de secours aux enfants sous l'Occupation en France*, Paris, L'Harmattan, 1990, pp. 137–44. CIMADE later added to its logo "Ecumenical Mutual Aid Service."

[12] AJDC Archives, New York, Child Care, 611.

[13] See Ernst Papanek, *Out of the Fire*, New York, William Morrow, 1975, pp. 217–28. He tried in vain to bring over all the children from Montmorency, but the Americans refused categorically to accommodate the children in a home.

problem and very few understood the urgency of the situation. Community leaders themselves considered that children were safer in Vichy France and the options suggested—the Philippines, the Dominican Republic, Kenya or the Belgian Congo for Polish children—seemed completely unrealistic. They attest to the powerlessness of American Jewish charities and even a certain wariness about the arrival of a large number of Jewish children from Europe.

The quota system for entering the USA was also difficult to overcome. In 1941, Congress decided to relax the legislation by instituting exceptional quotas of 5,000 entry visas for children from France. Negotiations dragged out; only three convoys left with children, not all of whom were Jewish. The lists were drawn up jointly by the OSE and the Quakers, thanks to subsidies from the Joint based in Lisbon. A first convoy of 100 children left Lisbon on 10 June 1941 on the SS *Mouzinho*; a second convoy of two groups left in August and September, with about 100 children from OSE homes. A third convoy left Casablanca on 14 May 1942. Estimates today put the total number of OSE children who migrated to the United States at about 350 by that date.

The children who remained in France became an issue in the negotiations between Vichy and the Germans after the Vélodrome d'Hiver Roundup.[14] Laval and Bousquet decided to hand over the foreign Jews, including children of under sixteen years of age, for reasons of family reunification. With the beginning of roundups in the Southern Zone in July and August 1942, exit visas were suspended and those for children had to be renegotiated. The Comité de Nîmes and OSE haggled with René Bousquet over 5,000 departures of foreign Jewish children whose parents were interned.[15] Bousquet finally only accepted 500 orphans on the pretense that "we do not want children to cross the Atlantic and leave their parents in Poland."

---

[14] 12,700 arrests instead of the expected 22,000.
[15] Comité de Coordination des Œuvres Intervenant dans les Camps d'internement de la Zone Sud, known as the Comité de Nîmes. Cf. Anne Grynberg, *Les Camps de la honte. Les internés juifs des camps français, 1939–1944*, Paris, La Découverte, 1991 [new ed. 1999]; Denis Peschanski, *La France des camps*, Paris, Gallimard, 2002.
[16] AJDC Archives, Child Care, 611, 21 September 1942 report. The aim of the committee was to bring over 5,000 children, at an estimated cost of $4,500,000, whereas it only had $800,000.

Frantic telegrams came from the United States. The Committee for the Care of European Children sponsored by Eleanor Roosevelt had to guarantee that the children would not be a tax burden.[16] It worked actively to raise funds, whereas the Jewish Labor Committee released funds for the rescue of 500 Cercle Amical Bundiste (Workman's Circle) children. The State Department finally granted 1,000 visas for foreign Jewish children under the age of sixteen at risk of being deported; Canada took 1,000 of them, as did the Dominican Republic. These were only temporary visas for the duration of the war because all of these children were supposed to return to their families afterwards.

OSE France tried to favor the most endangered children. A departure was planned for mid-November from Lisbon on the SS *Nyassa*, aboard which were American women to escort them. But on 9 November the French authorities only granted exit visas to children who were entirely orphaned or whose parents were abroad.[17] In late November 1942, the landing of American troops in northern Africa and the occupation of the Southern Zone by the German troops put an end to authorizations definitively. OSE in Geneva tried to get the most exposed children to Argentina via Switzerland, but it placed drastic conditions on them, demanding Argentine government guarantees.[18] Thus Vichy France was a real trap for non-French children, whom the OSE had to protect and rescue by other means.

From protection to rescue

OSE's role in the Southern Zone. With 230 employees, doctors, teachers and social workers, the OSE created health and social welfare centres in provincial towns as well as children's homes, nurseries, sanatoria and day care centers to ensure the protection of several hundred orphaned children or needy refugee families. It offered medical assistance for the children cared for by several Jewish organizations such as the Jewish Scouts of France and the Œuvres Sociales Israélites d'Alsace et de Lorraine.

---

[17] The authorities held for deportation children whose parents were still interned. Others were blocked after the Allied landing in North Africa. The *Nyassa* left with many fewer children than originally planned. 200 children who were prepared to leave from Marseilles were taken back to their respective institutions.

[18] AJDC Archives, Child Care, 611, note from Lisbon to New York dated 14 January 1943.

Beginning in autumn 1940, OSE obtained the support of several Alsatian and Lorraine figures, particularly Andrée Salomon, whose crucial role is described in all books about Jewish resistance, and Dr Joseph Weill, whose work we will emphasize. We will not describe in detail the stages of rescue of children by OSE in the Southern Zone, as these operations are now fairly well known: they involved the opening of fourteen children's homes to accommodate youngsters from internment camps, and then in the early months of 1943 the creation of underground placement networks, including the famous "Garel circuit" in the Southwest. About 2,000 children managed to get into hiding and some thousand of them were evacuated by small convoys into Switzerland thanks to the clearsightedness of Joseph Weill, who set up the program before being forced to seek shelter in Switzerland with his family in March 1943.

Dr Joseph Weill, an extremely active organizer

A renowned endocrinologist, speaking perfect German, with contacts in the French secret service, Dr Joseph Weill was regularly kept abreast of the Nazis' criminal plans; he had been one of the rare analysts before the war to take the threat seriously. In 1940, he asserted that assistance to internees should not help legitimate the illegal existence of the Vichy camps.[19] He was the one who imparted to the crippled and isolated Jewish charities an overall vision of social welfare action. In the month of January 1941, he took part in the creation of the Commission des Camps des Œuvres Israélites d'Assistance aux Réfugiés, where he first undertook to make immediate improvements in the atrocious internment conditions in close conjunction with the OSE.

Within the Comité de Nîmes he presided a Commission d'Hygiène et d'Aide à l'Enfance et aux Vieillards, a pivotal part of this council of

---

[19] In addition to his pioneer work, *Contribution à l'histoire des camps d'internement dans l'Anti-France*, Paris, Édition du Centre, 1946, which still serves as a reference, other writings include his posthumous memoirs, *Le Combat d'un Juste*, n.p., Saumur, Éditions Cheminements, 2002, as well as his as yet unpublished reports to the Comité de Nîmes and his correspondence with the Jewish community in Switzerland. See entry on him by Georges Weill, Katy Hazan and Ruth Fivaz-Silbermann in the *Nouveau Dictionnaire de Biographie Alsacienne*, vol. 48, Strasbourg, Fédération des Sociétés Savantes d'Alsace, 2007, pp. 5011–16.

voluntary organizations working to feed, care for, and ensure the ongoing education of refugees. But the main goal of the charity was to get the internees out of the camps, at least some categories of adults and especially the children, for whom the commission obliged the prefects to issue "certificates of accommodation."[20] Thanks to his work as head of the OSE France medical service, and that of the OSE "volunteer internees" run by Andrée Salomon, there were no more children under sixteen in the internment camps on the eve of the July-August 1942 roundups. Maintaining regular correspondence with Union OSE in Geneva and the leaders of the Swiss Federation of Jewish Communities which managed the Joint's funds, he was one of the most active links between France and Switzerland, where he made several clandestine journeys in 1941–42 before being obliged to seek sanctuary there with his family in the spring of 1943. In autumn 1942, he had recommended that the Jewish charities of the UGIF go underground while maintaining an official front. Despite protests from certain leaders, he secured the gradual closing of children's homes and the dispersal of the children. A small number of people refused, or delayed complying, setting the stage for certain tragedies as in Voiron and Izieux. Before his departure, he had created a smuggling channel to Switzerland, entrusted to Georges Loinger, and two concealment circuits, entrusted to Andrée Salomon and Georges Garel.

Placed under house arrest in Geneva, Joseph Weill had to settle for an advisory role within Union OSE in Geneva and one of liaison agent with Jewish and philanthropic associations. In the alarming reports on the situation of the Jews in France sent to the president of the Federation of Jewish Communities and to Saly Mayer, a Joint representative, it is clear that he had no illusions about the fate awaiting the Jews if they were not rescued.[21] Thanks to him, Saly Mayer was certainly one of the best-informed people in Switzerland about the deportations of children from France. He kept a journal in code where he kept a record in a mixture of English, Yiddish and Hebrew of his daily telephone conversations with OSE and the Lisbon office.

---

[20] The remarkable attitude of Hérault prefect Jean-Baptiste Benedetti and his deputy Jean Fridriciis is well known.
[21] Report to Joseph Brunswick, president of the SIG, dated June 1943, in attempt to alert the Swiss press, banned by the censors; see *Archiv für Zeitgeschichte*, Zurich, SIG collection, 1943, and Saly Mayer collection, microfilm, ibid.

Joseph Weill negotiated the possibility for underground convoys of children from France to Switzerland.[22] He wanted to secure authorization for the entry of 2,000 children. In November 1943, the Geneva action committee managed to extract from Rothmund, chief of the police division of the Swiss federal department of Justice and Police, the promise of 1,500 visas as long as responsibility for the children was entirely taken by the Jewish organizations and that smuggling was not encouraged. Joseph Weill also took part in the Comité de Secours aux Enfants (children's relief committee) created by the Union OSE in Geneva, which had devised a professional training program for after the war by creating children's homes and schools in Switzerland and then in liberated France. He was aware that the rescue of children also involved rebuilding their future.

Reconstruction, the natural extension of rescuing

An example of advance planning: Ruth Lambert's survey of Swiss camps. On 1 June 1944, the Comité d'Action pour le Sauvetage des Enfants (children's rescue committee) in Geneva was issued with 6,900 visas including 4,000 for the United States, 500 for Canada and 1,000 for the Palestine Mandated Territory, which were certified to be valid after the war. Jewish organizations that funded maintenance for these children decided to take a general census. They entrusted this task to an OSE social worker from Lorraine, Ruth Lambert, a refugee in Switzerland who had a work permit. She surveyed eleven Swiss refugee camps out of some hundred that harbored adolescents and drew up questionnaires with a view to their emigration.[23] Out of the 12,477 internees, there were nearly 2,000 children from the ages of one to nineteen for which Union OSE was partly responsible.[24]

Ruth Lambert's report provides us with information about the state of these work camps, their everyday life and their organization under leader-

---

[22] Georges Loinger and Katy Hazan, *Aux frontières de l'espoir*, Paris, Le Manuscrit, 2006.

[23] OSE Archives, Tschlenoff collection, box V, file 13. The camps were La Chasselotte (Fribourg), Tivoli (Lucerne), Davesco, Mezzovico, Magliaso, Brissago, Cordola, Mont-Bré (Tessin), Herberg and Hilfikon (Aargau).

[24] Including 279 infants, 565 children up to the age of eight, 1,194 between eight and nineteen (Tschlenoff collection, box V, file 13).

ship teams. It supports and supplements the book of interviews with Jewish refugees in Switzerland compiled by Fabienne Regard.[25] The toughest camp seems to have been La Chasselotte, in a disused convent near Fribourg, which accommodated some hundred Jewish and non-Jewish girls. The woman directing it ruled with an iron hand and restricted food. The two other girls' camps, Tivoli and Hilfikon, seem to have enjoyed a better reputation. Tivoli, located in a disused palace on Lake Lucerne, was a center for ailing women, including some thirty adolescents.[26] It was in charge of mending and washing linen for the other camps, a thousand sheets or 3,000 towels per day. The Brissago camp in Tessin was also located in a large hotel with a private beach where the women sewed and mended linen from other camps in very severe working conditions. Lastly, the Messovico camp, also in Tessin, assembled a group of some hundred internees, half of them youths, in sheds by the side of the railroad. They worked in the mornings in the fields.

The "model" camp, considered by some as "paradise on earth" in comparison to the others, remained Davesco, a large manor near Lugano with eighty-seven young boys (including twenty non-Jews). Farm work was organized in rotation with schoolwork, in French or in German, inside the camp. Two communist counselors approved by the management organized cultural activities.

The Lambert report contains the inventory of the exit possibilities for these youths depending on their wishes, job offers or academic possibilities, and suggesting solutions. Many of these young people were eager to learn and wanted to continue their interrupted studies in the camps under Berne's orders. Others wanted to earn a living as radio mechanics, electricians, tailors, cooks, dental technicians, etc. so as no longer to depend on charity. One last category of youths felt they had been abandoned and had no future plans.

Children's Homes in Switzerland. OSE had smuggled about a thousand children under the age of sixteen into Switzerland in separate convoys, half of them between January and June 1944.[27] They were scattered in

---

[25] Fabienne Regard, *La Suisse, paradis de l'enfer? Mémoires de réfugiés suisses*, Yens-sur Morges, Cabédita, 2002.

[26] The report mentions 300 internees, Fabienne Regard about 100.

[27] See the statistics in the central file in Genève, Tschlenoff collection. We thank Ruth Fivaz-Silbermann for the statistical information she kindly gave us.

private families, refugee camps and children's homes. Coming under the Geneva section of the Comité d'Aide aux Enfants d'Emigrés, some of these homes were directly managed by OSE. This was the case of Les Murailles in Vésenaz, already run by the pedagogue Isaac Pougatch, and the La Forêt home (or pension Diana) opened in 1943.[28] The home in Versoix was run by the Zionist Hehalutz movement, part of Youth Aliyah.

The Les Murailles home, which was originally a multi-denominational institution, became entirely Jewish, with kosher food and religious instruction. The La Forêt home took up to ninety children from ages twelve to twenty from OSE homes in France; it had a carpentry school and mechanical workshops managed by the ORT.[29] The young men from camps such as Les Charmilles were readapted to schoolwork in order to follow the curriculum in Geneva schools. Language classes were organized in the home to round out their education.[30] The people interviewed later had good memories of their time in these homes, which had enabled them to come out of the war with certain qualifications.[31]

Custody of children in France. After the war, an entirely arbitrary estimate puts the number of Jewish children that were scattered throughout France at 3,000.[32] How many were they really? The impossibility of achieving a definitive count and the reserved, if not closed attitude of Catholic institutions accused of proselytism fueled considerable suspicion. Finding hidden children nevertheless became a priority as people gradually

---

[28] Joseph Weill was part of the commission that organized the La Forêt home (Pension Diana).

[29] A good forty or so young people took practical or theoretical ORT courses. The teaching staff included Isaac Pougatch, his wife Juliette Pary, Ruth Lambert, Isidore Bernstein and his wife femme Miriam who were already instructors at Masgelier (Creuse). It was managed by a Swiss couple, Camille and Marcelle Dreyfuss.

[30] These were taught by Lotte Schwartz, former director of the Château de Chaumont (Creuse), by Professor Jacques Bloch, president of OSE Switzerland, and by his wife Hélène.

[31] Some of these youths later accepted responsibilities in the children's homes. We could mention Paul Niederman at OSE and Maurice Wulfmann at the Commission Centrale de l'Enfance (Communist).

[32] See Katy Hazan, *Les orphelins de la Shoah, les maisons de l'espoir, 1944–1960*, Paris, Les Belles Lettres, 2000. About 10,000 children are believed to have been saved from deportation via Jewish and non-Jewish organizations: 6,000 in the Southern Zone and 4,000 in the Northern Zone.

became aware of the catastrophe and it seemed obvious that their parents would not return from deportation. Retrieving the children became not only a vital necessity, but a sort of issue fueled by various motivations: as soon as the country was freed, the Jewish charities literally began a race to find the children.

In fact, the issue of returning children back to the lap of Judaism posed a political problem in this immediate post-war period. It was not understood by the regulatory bodies and public opinion, which were quick to accuse the Jews of practicing reverse racism, given the extent to which their attitude ran counter to republican secular practices.

The religious aspect of the question was no less complex. Recovery of all the children in danger of being converted was probably a unanimous demand among all Jewish charities, but to whom should they be entrusted? Judaism was at the very least multifaceted, if not deeply divided, and its religious dimension was far from being defended by all French Jews. On the other hand, Catholic influence was still very strong in the years 1945–50, and figures who favored Judeo-Christian relations were few and far between.

And then there was the social aspect: what should be done with the orphans? Place them in the care of foster families or keep them in orphanages? The Joint, which agreed to contribute 60 per cent of the funding of children's homes, and other private charities could not bear all the costs. But if the state agreed to participate, it would have a right of oversight, which it would assume via legislation. Furthermore, the state administration wanted a single representative to deal with the issue, which, despite attempts at unity, was never provided.

Even if throughout the year 1945 mobilization in favor of Jewish children reflected the political balance of power within the community, it was nevertheless a secondary issue. The real issues had to do with the Conseil Représentatif des Israélites de France (CRIF) and its relationship with the Consistory and its position on Zionism. The remarkable accomplishments of Jewish charities such as OSE concretely posed the question of Jewish identity after the Shoah. OSE alone opened twenty-five children's homes in 1945. A 1946 statistic drawn from the central records of Union OSE in Geneva reported 5,263 children under the protection of OSE France.[33]

---

[33] To which must be added 2,152 children still in Switzerland, 1,300 children under the protection of OSE Belgium, 474 under the protection of OSE

To that must be added the accommodation of the "children of Buchenwald"—youngsters from the Central European work camps and ghettos in Poland, Slovakia and Hungary, most of whom had gone on "death marches," and had been gathered in late 1944 in the Buchenwald camp. OSE was authorized by the French government to host 426 of them temporarily. They were housed in June 1945 in the Écouis Preventorium (Eure). After a traumatic start in life, they came to lead often brilliant careers in the four corners of the world, particularly in the United States, Australia, Canada and especially Israel, considered by all as their second home. Only about twenty chose to remain in France.[34] Lastly, in the name of family reunification, OSE facilitated the emigration of children to the United States or the Mandated Territory of Palestine, later Israel, starting in 1945. Much has yet to be learned about this story, although the source material is abundant.[35]

Created under the Russian Empire as a preventive healthcare organization, OSE managed to adapt to the needs of the various countries in which it worked as well as the most dramatic circumstances. Its action extended to infant protection, civilian and military war victims, victims of pogroms and famines, destitute refugees and camp internees. At the time of the genocide, its effectiveness in the rescue of French Jewish children benefited from these tragic experiences. It managed to organize accommodation for them by finding homes, and it went underground early enough to be able to protect all of the hidden children that had been placed in its care. The social and medical work it continued after the war should be considered as the indispensable extension of the rescue that it agreed to assume.

Although it is not customary for a historical study to end on an emotional note, it seems right to quote a tribute Albert Einstein paid to OSE during the celebration of its 40th anniversary of its founding: "Let us never forget the remarkable rescue work undertaken by the OSE when

---

Romania and 800 children still in Germany, i.e. 10,726 records identified. Tschlenoff collection, box V, central file department on 31 December 1946.

[34] Katy Hazan and Eric Ghozlan, *À la vie! Les enfants de Buchenwald du Shtetl à l'OSE*, Paris, Le Manuscrit, "Témoignages de la Shoah," series 2005.

[35] Similar operations were undertaken in Poland and Romania. See the archives of Amerose, the US branch of OSE, held at the YIVO Institute in New York. There are also records of sponsorships of children and homes.

it saved thousands of children from Nazi barbarity and helped them return to normal life. Let us remember with gratitude these men and women who devised and implemented our international relief efforts."[36]

---

[36] Message sent in June 1953 to Israël Weksler, president of Amerose, kept in its German manuscript version in the *Albert Einstein Archives*, microfilm, series 28, no. 958 and 1046.

16

THE CONTEXT OF RESCUE IN NAZI-OCCUPIED EUROPE

Bob Moore

The rescue of the Jews hunted by the Nazis during the German occupation of Western Europe has formed part of the debate on the role of "Righteous Gentiles" during the Holocaust period, and has also been used as a counterweight to the widespread view that the indigenous peoples of France and the Low Countries did not do enough to save their Jewish neighbors.[1] As with the wider issues of comparative history of the Holocaust, attempts at generalization often break apart when confronted with the "stubborn peculiarities"[2] of each of the countries surveyed, and this phrase does highlight the problems involved in such studies—namely the vast array of changing circumstances and situations that existed within

---

[1] This is most apparent in the Netherlands where Jewish mortality (70+ per cent) was much higher than for Belgium (c. 40 per cent) or France (c. 25 per cent). Cornelis J. Lammers, "Persecution in the Netherlands during World War Two. An Introduction," *The Netherlands' Journal of Social Sciences* XXXIV/2 (1998) pp. 111–25, here p. 111. This "discovery" is often attributed to the work of Helen Fein, *Accounting for Genocide. National Responses and Jewish Victimisation during the Holocaust*, New York, Free Press, 1979, but the raw statistics were known, if not well publicized, long before then.

[2] M.R. Marrus and R.O. Paxton, "The Nazis and the Jews in Occupied Western Europe 1940–1944," *Journal of Modern History* LIV (1982) pp. 687–714, here p. 713.

each national case study, and how difficult it is to define a national picture, let alone draw parallels across national frontiers. More recent studies in the Netherlands and in Belgium have also suggested that the national model is much too broad to be meaningful, and that regional and even local models may be more instructive in understanding both the limitations on rescue and its role in the survival of Jews in hiding.[3]

Perhaps because the Netherlands had by far the highest Jewish mortality of the Western European states, it has also had the most extensive public and scholarly debates on how this national disaster occurred. One simple, but nevertheless insightful observation was that, unlike its neighbors, the Netherlands had no "favorable factor" that served to prevent arrests and deportations or favored hiding and rescue.[4] Further comparative analysis of the Holocaust in general, while providing no definitive answers to the central question of why so many more Jews fell victim to Nazi persecution than in other states, did at least identify a series of issues for investigation under the three umbrella headings of persecutors, victims and "circumstances."[5] In the Dutch case the key variables were perceived to be the relative cohesion of German rule in the Netherlands compared with the situation elsewhere, and the influence of the SS; the relative compliance of both the Dutch public and the bureaucracy with German measures against the Jews; and the relatively high level of integration of the Jewish community. More recent analyses of Belgium and the Netherlands have also identified specifics within the German system of rounding up and deporting the Jews, and differences in the Jewish organizations created or adapted to represent the community. One final factor identified in this context and directly relevant to the question of

---

[3] See for example, Marnix Croes and Peter Tammes, *"Gif laten wij niet voortbestaan" Een onderzoek naar de overlevingskansen van joden in de Nederlandse gemeenten, 1940–1945*, Amsterdam, Aksant, 2004; J.C.H. Blom, "Gescheidenis, sociale wetenschappen, bezettingstijd en jodenvervolging. Een besprekingsartikel," *Bijdragen en Mededelingen betreffende de Geschiedenis der Nederlanden, BMGN* CXX (2005) pp. 562–580; Marnix Croes, "De zesde fase? Holocaust en geschiedschriving," *BMGN* CXXI (2006) pp. 292–301.

[4] A.J. van der Leeuw, "Meer slachtoffers dan elders in West-Europa," *Nieuw Israëlitisch Weekblad*, 15 November 1985.

[5] J.C.H. Blom, *Crisis, Bezetting en Herstel. Tien Studies over Nederland 1930–1950*, Rotterdam: Universitaire, 1989," pp. 134–50. Pim Griffioen and Ron Zeller, "The Persecution of the Jews: Comparing Belgium and the Netherlands," *The Netherlands' Journal of Social Sciences* XXXIV/2 (1998), pp. 126–64.

rescue was that Belgium (and by implication France as well) offered more opportunities to go into hiding than the Netherlands.[6]

The comparative approach to the general questions of Jewish victimhood also provides a basis for analyzing the incidence and likelihood of rescue. This begs the important question of what actually constitutes rescue. For the purposes of this chapter, it will be defined as either effecting the escape of Jews to neutral countries, or hiding them inside occupied territory. Much of this activity began with individuals but was often later taken up by existing or specially created organizations, but we are concerned here not with the motivations or objectives of the people involved, but the factors that affected their ability to operate—the circumstances and context. What follows is by no means a comprehensive survey, but one intended to prompt future research on the subject as a whole, based exclusively on material from France, Belgium and the Netherlands.

The first salient contextual factor relates not to the specifics of the German occupation of World War II at all, but to the popular memory of earlier events and their impact on behavior between 1940 and 1945. Communities across Belgium and large swathes of Northern France had first hand experience of German occupation during the First World War, and all sections within society had developed behavior strategies ranging from collaboration through compliance and indifference to opposition and resistance. State and local governments charged with continuing their roles under foreign control thus had models on which to draw. These continuities can be seen in bureaucratic behavior, but also among the population at large. From May 1940 onwards, the first forms of organized resistance activity often came from people and groups who had been active in 1914–18.[7] Networks were re-formed to carry out intelligence-gathering and sabotage work, while others were resurrected to help Allied soldiers and airmen, or prisoners of war on the run from German captivity. Neither resistance nor "rescue" work should therefore be seen as something devel-

---

[6] Lammers, "Persecution in the Netherlands during World War Two," p. 112; Griffioen and Ron Zeller, "The Persecution of the Jews," pp. 152–3. In the French case, this can be partly explained by the existence of the unoccupied zone until November 1942 and the zone of Italian occupation until September 1943, rather than purely by topographical features.

[7] Bob Moore, "The Rescue of Jews in Nazi-Occupied Belgium, France and the Netherlands," *Australian Journal of Politics and History* L/3 (2004), pp. 385–95, here p. 395.

oped exclusively in response to the events of 1940. In contrast, neither the Netherlands nor most of France had undergone these experiences directly, but they had nonetheless seen the effects second-hand—through the floods of refugees and the privations wrought by four years of warfare. This inevitably created a diversity of experiences and attitudes within individual national contexts and was to have a noticeable, but unquantifiable impact on the incidence of rescue activities in different areas.[8]

A further contextual element that has its roots in the pre-1940 period is the position of the Jewish communities in these Western European states. It is important to talk of communities in the plural here as one can point to major class, religious and national differences among the Jewish populations within these countries and even within municipalities. Some studies have highlighted the more established position of the Jews in the Netherlands when compared with their Belgian and many French counterparts, yet this apparent integration was into a vertically organized social (and political) system that gave Jews full civil rights but effectively separated them from other confessional or ideological groups.[9] Their emancipated and undifferentiated political position may have masked a more isolated social position in which many Jews had few non-Jewish friends or even contacts outside their own *milieu*. Assimilation was essentially impossible. Paradoxically, it has been suggested that political equality tempered only by a degree of cultural anti-Semitism in the Netherlands lulled its Jews into a false sense of security by comparison with their Belgian and French counterparts.

In Belgium, the overwhelming majority of Jews were recent immigrants whose citizenship was often in doubt and whose attitude to state bureaucracy was tempered by earlier experiences in Eastern Europe. Levels of integration were also affected by local factors. Most Jews were to be found in either Brussels or Antwerp, but indigenous anti-Semitism was much more virulent and obvious in the latter.[10] France likewise had

---

[8] See, for example, Maxime Steinberg, "The Judenpolitik in Belgium" in, Dan Michman (ed.), *Belgium and the Holocaust*, Jerusalem, Yad Vashem, 1998, p. 208. Lieven Saerens, *Vreemdelingen in een Wereldstad*, Tielt, Lannoo, 2000, pp. 686 ff.

[9] Ido de Haan, "Routines and Traditions: The Reactions of Non-Jews and Jews in the Netherlands to War and Persecution" in David Bankier and Israel Gutman (eds), *Nazi Europe and the Final Solution*, Jerusalem, Yad Vashem, 2003, pp. 449–53.

[10] Dan Michman, "Problematic National Identity, Outsiders and Persecution:

high proportions of recent Jewish immigrants, including many refugees, and they were heavily concentrated in Paris. In both Belgium and France many of the resident Jews had had only a limited time to become either integrated or assimilated and were still dependent on social and organizational structures that prevented their assimilation into mainstream society—even if they wished to do so. Thus in all three countries, albeit for different reasons, Jews found difficulties in calling on non-Jewish help after 1940. However, one further important factor was the ability of Jewish organizations to mobilize in opposition to Nazi rule. While the Germans attempted to create collaborationist Jewish institutions in all three countries, in both Belgium and France immigrant working-class Jewish organizations were able to mobilize, either in their own right, for example as the Comité de Défense des Juifs (CDJ) in Belgium and the Comité de la Rue Amelot in France, or ultimately by forming links with the wider resistance.[11] By contrast, the relatively small number of immigrant Jews in the Netherlands had no such organization save the Committee for Jewish Refugees that became a central component of the compliant Amsterdam Jewish Council.[12]

Moving to the political context of occupation during World War II, as we know, the structures of German rule in occupied Western Europe were by no means uniform. A relevant comparative element can be seen in the German policies adopted toward various national and linguistic groups that became apparent after May 1940, when the supposedly more "Aryan" Flemish and Dutch peoples were singled out as a means of winning them over to Nazi pan-Germanism, although it should be noted that even in France, *les Boches* did not live up to their expected barbarian

---

Impact of the Gentile Population's Attitude in Belgium on the fate of the Jews in 1940–1944" and Jean Philippe Schreiber, "Belgium and the Jews Under Nazi Rule: Beyond the Myths," both in Bankier and Gutman (eds), *Nazi Europe and the Final Solution*, pp. 455–88.

[11] Lucien Lazare, *Rescue as Resistance. How Jewish Organisations Fought the Holocaust in France*, New York, Columbia University Press, 1996, p. 39.

[12] These were the Amsterdam Jewish Council, the Association des Juifs de Belgique (AJB) and the Union Générale des Israélites de France (UGIF). Immigrant Jews in Belgium and France had pre-existing organisations such as the Main d'Oeuvre Immigrée (MOI). Lazare, *Rescue as Resistance*, p. 17. Maxime Steinberg, *L'Etoile et le Fusil: 1942 Les Cent Jours de la Déportation*, Brussels, Vie Ouvrière, 1984, pp. 60–1.

stereotypes.[13] One example of this was the more generous attitude toward the armies interned after the surrender in the spring of 1940. Almost all the Dutch armed forces were released within weeks, as were most Flemish elements within the Belgian military. The major difference between the Netherlands, on the one hand, and Belgium and France on the other was that in the former, the competition between the Nazi Party/SS and the military was largely resolved in favor of the former under the civilian leadership of Reichskommissar Arthur Seyss-Inquart, whereas in the latter, the military authorities maintained a large element of control and saw the anti-Jewish policies desired by the RSHA and Party in Berlin as counterproductive to the interests of a stable and uncomplicated occupation regime. Thus, while they were happy to allow the Vichy authorities to comply with Himmler's demands for deportations if Pétain's government was prepared to organize and carry them out, they were unwilling to use too many coercive measures when the supply of non-French Jews for deportation had been exhausted, for fear of compromising existing working relationships. This is equally evident in the Belgian case where the military governor Alexander von Falkenhausen valued the co-operation of the Belgian Secretaries-General too much to force their compliance in the face of objections and a potential withdrawal of bureaucratic collaboration in other aspects of governance.

The success of rescue activities depended to some extent on the degree of direct control the Germans managed to exert on the executive apparatus they needed to carry out their program against the Jews. This involved the relationships between the German leadership structures, whether military or civilian, and the indigenous local bureaucracies. Over time, both direct and indirect pressures were brought to bear to ensure compliance among the lower echelons of government service. Mayors in major cities and even small communes were gradually replaced if their attitudes were perceived to be unsympathetic. Lack of zeal for Nazi measures was one thing, but civil servants' attitudes to their everyday work were also of importance. For those in hiding or those engaged in some form of illegal work, identity and ration cards were crucial, and officials charged with their issue and control who were prepared to conspire with

---

[13] Although this had some ideological underpinnings, it was also based on the military imperative of limiting the numbers of troops devoted to internal security when they were needed for active campaigns elsewhere.

frauds or turn a blind eye to thefts and deceptions were of enormous value.[14]

Likewise, the existence of a positively inclined mayor or village policeman could be a positive benefit. As an example, one might cite Vincent Azéma, the socialist mayor of Banyuls-sur-Mer, a French commune on the border with Spain. Adopting a friendly attitude to foreign refugees fleeing toward the Spanish frontier, he was also prepared to volunteer information on how and where to cross the frontier in order to avoid both French and Spanish border controls. Needless to say, the Vichy authorities soon replaced him with someone more "reliable."[15] Likewise, research has highlighted the major role of the mayor of Hengelo in the eastern Netherlands in limiting the number of Jews deported from his municipality.[16] To judge from these admittedly limited examples, perhaps there may be some correlation between examples of bureaucratic disobedience and physical distance from the organs of central government. Across occupied Western Europe, even where government servants were naturally disposed to resist what they perceived as unreasonable or illegal German actions, their behavior was inevitably tempered by the closeness of central control, the degree of oversight of their work and the attitudes of their superiors. Even positive guidance from above was inevitably nuanced and open to interpretation. Willingness to bend or contravene normal working practices was unpredictable and dependent not only on individual decisions but also on the leadership, culture and operations of critical (local) government offices and departments. Moreover, a propensity towards assisting those on the run was affected by changing circumstances, both positively and negatively. Thus, while those involved in resistance received more co-operation as the war turned against the Germans, this was to some extent offset by the increased penalties (both real and

---

[14] For example, Peter Romijn, *Burgemeesters in Oorlogstijd. Besturen onder Duitse bezetting*, Amsterdam, Balans, 2006. Nico Wouters. "Municipal Government during the Occupation (1940–1945): A Comparative Model of Belgium, the Netherlands and France," *European History Quarterly*, XXXVI/2 (2006), pp. 221–46.

[15] Lisa Fittko, *Escape Through the Pyrenees* (Evanston, IL, Northwestern University Press, 1991), p. 133.

[16] M.J. Schenkel, *De Twentse Paradox. De lotgevallen van de joodse bevolking van Hengelo en Enschede tijdens de Tweede Wereldoorlog*, Zutphen, Walburg, 2003, p. 88.

imagined) for acts prohibited by the occupiers. Conversely, diligent and conformist civil servants and policemen could make life extremely difficult, and rescuers might also have had to contend with adverse local feelings or might have found themselves hamstrung by a single committed National Socialist in a position where he or she could inform the Germans about an uncooperative attitude or breaches of regulations and ordinances.

One manifestation of how bureaucratic practice had a direct impact on rescue can be seen in the role of the police agencies. As others have argued, the level of Nazi "coordination" of the indigenous police could have had a major effect on the efficiency with which Jews were rounded up for deportation and later hunted down in their hiding places. In Amsterdam, the co-operation of Sybren Tulp as Chief of Police was a major factor in organizing roundups in the city, although his motivation may have had more to do with maintaining the position of the Dutch police than any commitment to anti-Semitism.[17] Likewise, René Bousquet as Secretary-General of the Police Nationale in France was a willing collaborator in rounding up foreign Jews, but less keen on persecuting French citizens, arguing that his men would become "uncooperative" if asked to perform such tasks.[18] In Belgium, with few exceptions, the SS was unable to use the indigenous police for anti-Jewish measures and had to rely on German police and various collaborationists to carry out its work.[19] The subsequent work of hunting down Jews in hiding was often devolved to private or semi-private agencies that worked for the bounties that the Germans placed on Jewish heads. Thus the infamous Henneicke Collonne in the Netherlands was made up of men who worked for the Germans in securing sequestrated Jewish property but then spent their spare time using information gathered from their daytime work to track down fugitives. In Belgium, there were similar groups such as those

---

[17] Guus Meershoek, *Dienaren van het Gezag. De Amsterdamse Politie tijdens de Bezetting*, Amsterdam: van Gennep, 1999. Guus Meershoek, "De Amsterdamse hoofdcommissaris en de deportatie van de joden," *Oorlogsdocumentatie '40–'45 Derde Jaarboek van het Rijksinstituut voor Oorlogsdocumentatie*, Zutphen, Walburg Pers, 1992, pp. 9–43. Walter de Maesschalk, *Gardes in de oorlog. De Antwerpse politie in WO II*, Antwerp/Rotterdam, C.de Vries-Brouwers, 2004, pp. 295–300.

[18] Michael R. Marrus and Robert O.Paxton, *Vichy France and the Jews*, Stanford University Press, 1995, p. 306.

[19] Steinberg, *Les cent jours de la déportation*, pp. 210–13.

headed by Prosper de Zitter or Felix Lauterborn, again working directly or indirectly for the Gestapo/SD.[20] These men had no real interest in the rescuers as capturing them would not earn the bounties paid for Jews, and they were thus frequently left alone on the flimsiest of excuses, for example that the hosts were unaware that their guests had been Jews.[21] These groups began their operations in the cities, where the pickings were thought to be richest, and only traveled further afield if they had specific information. Thus rescuers and their guests in the larger cities ran potentially greater risks of discovery than their counterparts in rural areas—at least until the later stages of the occupation.

Yet to understand how the structures of occupation affected rescue activities, we have to look beyond these national examples to the regional and communal level. Rescue was in origin essentially a local activity, predicated on local circumstances.[22] Thus the propensity to help those in need would have been determined in part by the attitudes of local occupation authorities and their indigenous counterparts. Research has shown that some areas had German agencies that were far more committed to rounding up the Jews than others. Areas where the Gestapo or SS-Aussenstelle were less assiduous in carrying out the ideological aims of the regime may have given the Jews a better chance of avoiding deportation, but at the same time may also have reduced the imperative for local populations to engage in rescue activity because the threat involved was not seen to be so great. If the perceived threat to the victims was one important determinant, then the perception of the penalties involved in helping Jews was another. Perhaps surprisingly, the precise punishments for people caught helping Jews were not always widely known. This was partly because they were often not promulgated in the ordinances that forbade helping Jews, or because the German authorities were inconsistent in punishing such crimes. For example, it was only in the second half of 1943 that it became common knowledge in the Netherlands that people caught helping Jews were likely receive six months in a concentra-

---

[20] Ad van Liempt, *Kopgeld. Nederlandse premiejagers op zoek naar joden 1943*, Amsterdam, Balans, 2002. Belgium, Ministerie van Justitie-CPG Dossier Lauterborn I. Rechtpleging tegen Lauterborn en anderen.

[21] Bob Moore, *Victims and Survivors. The Nazi Persecution of the Jews in the Netherlands, 1940–1945*, London, Arnold, 1997, pp. 207–10.

[22] On France, see Limore Yagil, *Chrétiens et Juifs sous Vichy (1940–1944). Sauvetage et désobéissance civile*, Paris, Éditions du Cerf, 2005.

tion camp for their "crime." The increasing German propensity for punishing entire families for individual crimes also played a role here. Rescue network organizers frequently noted that refusals of help were often based on the need to protect wives and children from the probable consequences of discovery and arrest.[23]

Another potentially important factor is the degree to which the Germans tried and succeeded in "coordinating" all forms of social structures in the occupied countries. Crucially, they made few attempts to control the Christian Churches directly, although they nevertheless used knowledge of what had happened in Poland as a threat. At the secular level, German control and coordination were much greater—which meant that the scope for existing organizational forms becoming the basis for opposition and resistance was lessened. The most successful networks—both for resistance in general and for rescue in particular—tended to come from informal structures, for example within families, among workmates or fellow students, or between professional colleagues such as army officers or doctors, priests or pastors. The personal nature of the linkages based on prior experience, friendship and trust made them difficult to infiltrate and break. Such networks seldom had a prior history as a form of resistance, but were brought together through the agency of one of more committed individuals who mobilized a particular circle into action. The one exception to this rule was the political groupings that continued to function underground and protected their members, both Jewish and non-Jewish. The prime example here is the various national communist parties that had a history of opposition to the state often predating the occupation, and were thus in a better position to adapt to the clandestinity required after May 1940.

Local cultures may have also played a crucial role in the incidence of rescue. Much has been made of the Christian *milieux*, both Catholic and Protestant, in many areas closely associated with collective rescue activities. Claims have been made about minority religious groups having a greater empathy with the plight of the Jews, seeing it as an enhanced version of their own situation. In this regard, one can point to the Calvinists in the Netherlands and the Protestants in France, although the larger Catholic population in the Netherlands also shared this sense of inferior-

---

[23] This may well have been the result of German punishments being published in the increasingly circulated and read clandestine newspapers.

ity. The line taken by religious leaders of all denominations on the question of persecuted and hunted Jewry had the potential to exercise a substantial influence on the behavior of church subordinates and congregations at large. This was of course more evident in the hierarchical Catholic Church than in the federal or autonomous nonconformist religions. In the Netherlands, religious leaders generally seem to have been more guarded and conservative than in Belgium and France. While there were statements critical of the treatment of the Jews, there was no hint at or call for practical action.[24] In the latter countries, one can point to the statements and actions of Cardinal Archbishops Gerlier (Lyon) and van Roey (Malines) that, while guarded, showed at some points actual criticism.

The precise lead given from the top had the potential to mobilize (or immobilize) help across an entire diocese. In areas dominated by Catholicism there were also many more spiritual and temporal institutions, from monasteries and convents to orphanages and old people's homes, that were under the influence if not the control of leading churchmen. While not a definitive guide, a word or a hint from a religious superior could do much to influence abbots and abbesses as well as directors and managers of secular charitable foundations into providing hiding places for Jews. Assessing the precise impact of this is complicated. Belgium seems to have had proportionately more of such Catholic institutions than either the Netherlands or neighboring France, and was therefore able to provide a greater number of hiding places, especially for children. While there were condemnations of the persecution from church leaders, it was often the guarded comments in priests' and pastors' sermons that had a greater impact at a communal level in hinting at what individuals might be able to do to provide a measure of practical help. However, it should not be assumed that all churchmen were equally supportive. While Jews on the run were probably right in thinking that most clerics, even if they were not prepared to help in any way, would not betray them to the Gestapo, there were some who remained indifferent and others who were thoroughly hostile on political or religious grounds.[25]

---

[24] J.M. Snoek, *De Nederlandse Kerken en de Joden*, Kampen, Kok, 1990, pp. 67–8.

[25] See, for example, the marked disparity between rescues in Flemish and French speaking areas of Belgium. Saerens, "Die Hilfe für Juden in Belgien" in Wolfgang Benz and Juliane Wetzel (eds), *Solidarität und Hilfe für Juden während der NS-Zeit, Vol. 2*, Berlin: Metropol, 1998, pp. 231–2.

However, there are other features of local cultures that played a role in motivating help, both for Jews and for others on the run from the occupying power. The first of these is peculiar to isolated rural areas and involves longstanding traditions of helping neighbors and travelers in need on the basis that there was no other help available. In more isolated parts of the eastern Netherlands, this was called the "*noaberplicht*," but is manifest in other places under different names.[26] Its application to those on the run from the Germans was a natural extension of an existing cultural norm, especially where the ideological/racial imperatives of the occupier were seen to go beyond any acceptable demands that properly constituted state authority could make. This was also widely apparent when the Germans began conscripting labor from indigenous populations for work in Germany. This measure brought home the realities of occupation to a wider cross-section of the population and produced a response that included the creation of networks to assist those in hiding. Evading labor service became a major facet of life for many families under occupation after the summer of 1942. While this did create structures to help those on the run and increased the supply of hiding places, these structures often emerged after most of the deportations to the East had taken place. In any case, Jews were often excluded since they were regarded as too much of a risk.

This in turn raises a wider question, namely the degree to which state authority during the occupation was seen as legitimate and therefore to be obeyed, or conversely as illegitimate and to be resisted. Perspectives on this undoubtedly changed over time as German economic and ideological demands increased, but it is important to remember that the relationships between individuals, communities and the state were not forged when the occupation began, but stretched back decades if not centuries, and undoubtedly varied between one country and another and between different localities. This suggests that the propensity to resist (in all ways) was dependent both on the severity of the occupation and on potentially longstanding traditions of resistance to state authority. In general, this seems to have been greater in France than in the Netherlands where respect for constituted authority (*gezagsgetrouwheid*) was more ingrained. Whether these generalizations would stand close empirical scrutiny is

---

[26] C. Hilbrink, *De Illegalen. Illegaliteit in Twente en de aangrenzende Salland, 1940–1945* (The Hague, SDU, 1989), p. 73.

another matter. One specific possible exception, of direct relevance to the history of rescue, can be found in border regions where longstanding traditions of smuggling and avoidance of state regulation of trade and the payment of duties and taxes were often endemic. This can be seen in the Pyrenees, where both Spanish and French mountain guides were able to make money by guiding people over the frontier in secret. However, similar traditions—albeit across less challenging terrain—can also be found further north in the border regions of more conformist Belgium, Germany and the Netherlands. The adaptation of these traditions to exceptional circumstances had in many cases precedents in the First World War, and there are examples of individuals whose careers as professional smugglers (*passeurs*) spanned both periods. In these areas, the notion of what was legal and acceptable behavior may have been somewhat different from that in other parts of the country.

In conclusion, it is important that the rescue of Jews during the Holocaust period is not analyzed in isolation, lest it ignores the wider social context and local traditions that framed the nature of rescues and the behavior patterns of rescuers. It is also important to find a balance between the national generalizations about rescue, which fall apart when exposed to detailed empirical scrutiny, and too much attention to the "stubborn particularities" identified by Marrus and Paxton, a course that ultimately reduces us to describing and comparing individual instances of rescue and destroying any possibility of a meaningful comparison. As yet, we have only a limited understanding of why some communities became hotbeds of rescue activity while other places that seem socially similar had no involvement whatsoever. Local leadership and network contacts probably provide most of the answers, but there is much more to learn from such studies. As has become apparent from work carried out in the Netherlands, a mixture of empirical, quantitative, and sociological-historical perspectives may well provide the key to a more in-depth understanding of the processes involved. Local studies across occupied Western Europe may then allow for new forms of comparison that have not been attempted thus far, for example between rural communities in different countries. Their points of similarity may prove to be much better starting points for analysis than the use of national case studies with their broad mixture of social, geographical and political variables.

17

THE "BRUNNER AKTION"
A STRUGGLE AGAINST RESCUE
(SEPTEMBER 1943–MARCH 1944)

Tal Bruttmann

After the massive round-ups of 1942 and the deportation of more than forty thousand Jews, the application of the "final solution of the Jewish problem" in France in 1943 encountered numerous difficulties. Nearly two-thirds of the Jewish population were to be found henceforth, according to the Germans, in the former Free Zone.[1] However, after two big round-ups carried out in this zone in the beginning of 1943,[2] Vichy opted for a more prudent attitude and, in contrast to the active collaboration which was prevalent in the Occupied Zone, was more reticent regarding its participation in the deportations in the Southern Zone. This side-stepping left few available means to the occupation forces without the assistance of French policemen or gendarmes, since, in the former Free Zone, they had few men to carry out the task. Moreover, the hunt for Jews was further complicated by the civil resistance movement[3] and the activity of the rescue networks, which were established following the massive raids in the summer of 1942. From then on, the arresting of Jews

---

[1] See Röthke's report "L'Etat actuel du problème juif en France," 21 July 1943, in Serge Klarsfeld, *La Shoah en France*, volume III, *Le calendrier de la persécution des Juifs de France, septembre 1942—août 1944*, Paris, Fayard, 2001, p. 1583.

[2] In January 1943, the French police, together with German troups, participated in the imposition of their order on the Vieux-Port in Marseilles, during which nearly 800 Jews, mainly French, were arrested. Later, in mid-February, following a request from the Germans, Vichy organized the second big roundup of foreign Jews in the former "Free Zone," which resulted in the deportation of 2,000 people.

[3] Jacques Semelin, *Sans armes face à Hitler, la résistance civile en Europe (1939–1943)*, Paris, Payot, 1989.

would drag its feet remarkably, producing results far below the objectives fixed by the Nazi services.

As a response to repeated requests by Heinz Röthke, chief of the Jewish Affairs Service (IVB4) in France, and by Helmut Knochen, chief of the SIPO-SD (Sicherheitspolizei, security police) in France, demanding more staff to deal with the "Jewish question," Adolf Eichmann dispatched the person he considered his best deputy, Hauptsturmführer Aloïs Brunner. Brunner came to France to accelerate the deportations and, to do this, reinforced all initiatives, notably taking over the Drancy camp. Most important, he prepared, in collaboration with Heinz Röthke, an extensive search operation aimed at the Italian occupation zone,[4] which had become a zone of refuge for the Jews and, indirectly, the rescue networks. The announcement of the Armistice between the Italians and the Allies in September 1943 provoked the invasion of the Italian occupation zone in France and allowed Brunner to initiate his operation. Areas of obscurity still cloud our understanding of this action, which began in Nice in September 1943 and definitively ended on 16 March 1944, when Brunner's Kommando left Grenoble. However, despite many gaps, attributable primarily in the first place to the absence of German documents—principally about the part of the operation that took place in Grenoble—much of what happened is known today.[5]

If the main objective was to capture as many Jews as possible, it had one consequence, which would be omnipresent during the rescue organizations that hindered the carrying out of the "final solution" in France. Throughout the operations, Brunner was to make a dogged attempt to elimination systematically all rescue structures, Jewish or not, as well as to limit help given by the "French"[6] population.

---

[4] Centre de Documentation Juive Contemporaine (CDJC), XXVa-338, notes Röthke, 4 September 1943, reproduced in Serge Klarsfeld, op. cit., pp. 1650–2.

[5] Many works mention what took place in Nice (September to December 1943) but no real analysis of the details of the operation exists. See, for example, Serge Klarsfeld, *La Shoah en France*, volume I, *Vichy-Auschwitz. La "solution finale" de la question juive en France*, Fayard, Paris, 2001, pp. 302–12; Didier Epelbaum, *Aloïs Brunner*, Calmann-Lévy, Paris, 1990, pp. 187–97; Mary Felstiner, "Commandant de Drancy: Aloïs Brunner et les Juifs de France," *Le Monde Juif*, 128, 1987, pp. 143–72. On the way in which the operation in Grenoble took place, see Tal Bruttmann, "L'Action Brunner' à Grenoble (février-mars 1944)," *Revue d'Histoire de la Shoah*, 174, January-April 2002, pp. 18–43.

[6] For this, read the opposite of "Jewish."

TAL BRUTTMANN

Action against Jewish resistance (Nice, September to December 1943)

The occupying forces were kept perfectly aware of the underground activities carried out by the different Jewish networks,[7] for some time, thanks to information collected by their own services and by other departments such as the Commissariat Général aux Questions Juives. In 1943, Darquier de Pellepoix, the second Commissaire aux Questions Juives, warned Röthke that "the former OSE was continuing its activity which was specifically limited to Jewish children and youths, preferably of foreign origin, by ensuring avoidance of possible discovery by sheltering them with people considered safe."[8] The organizations operating throughout France under the umbrella of the Union Générale des Israélites de France (UGIF)[9] and their leaders were placed under careful surveillance, and even before the arrival of Brunner in France, arrests were made.

Faced with this danger, those in charge of the organizations present in the former Free Zone retreated on a massive scale to the Italian zone—essentially to Nice and Grenoble—where they hoped to escape from the Germans. This retreat did not, however, stop the occupiers from being informed of their activities, which often took place in broad daylight thanks to the connivance and support of certain Italian officials. One man in particular attracted the attention of both the Sipo-SD in France and the IVB4 in Berlin: Angelo Donati, an Italian Jewish banker who played a preponderant role in the rescuing of clandestine Jews. Donati took many initiatives,[10] notably trying to help Jews leave Nice with the help of Italian authorities.[11]

---

[7] Concerning the Jewish Resistance, see Lucien Lazare, *La Résistance juive en France*, Paris, Stock, 1987.

[8] Archives Nationales (AN), AJ38 111, Commissaire général aux Questions juives to Röthke, "elements of information concerning certain intrigues attributed the UGIF."

[9] On the same subject, see Michel Laffitte, *Juif dans la France allemande. Institutions, dirigeants et communautés au temps de la Shoah*, Paris, Tallandier, 2006, notably Chapter 9.

[10] Röthke sent Adolf Eichmann a detailed report on Donati at the end of September 1943 (see documentation in Serge Klarsfeld, *Le calendrier de la persécution des Juifs de France, septembre 1942—août 1944*, op. cit., pp. 1667–8).

[11] Regarding the Italians' attitude in their occupation zone in France, see Marie-Anna Matard-Bonucci, *L'Italie fasciste et la persécution des juifs*, Paris, Perrin, 2007, pp. 392–401.

His capture was one of the priorities of the SS, as Röthke clearly announced to Eichmann when the Nice "Aktion" began: "the arrest of Donati is of the highest importance" because he was "the leader" of the Jews in the Italian zone of influence.[12] In addition to the massive arrests of Jews in Nice and in the region,[13] Brunner and his Kommando were systematically tracking the militants of the Jewish Resistance movement.

While Brunner's Kommando did not succeed in capturing Donati, despite intensive searching, it managed on the other hand, in the first weeks of the operation, to arrest several leaders of the Jewish Resistance: on 23 September Jacques Weintrob, in charge of the *Education Physique* (Physical education) network was taken; on 26 September, it was Germaine Meyer, Donati's secretary; on 28 September, Claude Gutmann, head of the *Sixième* (Sixth) division in Nice was captured. Numerous other members of rescue networks were captured in Nice during the following weeks. The action by the SS against Jewish networks was on such a scale that a report about it appeared in a brochure published in 1944, during the occupation, by the Union des Juifs pour la Résistance et l'Entraide (UJRE), devoted to the situation in Nice. In a paragraph entitled "The Gestapo against the Jewish Resistance Movement," the organization reported that:

with a most particular savagery, the Gestapo executioners fought passionately against those of the Jews that they suspected were members of resistance organizations or Jewish anti-Hitler groups. Known militants like Grégoire Spolianski (30 years old) and the lawyer Joseph Roos were tortured savagely for several days at the Hôtel Excelsior [...].[14] The young patriot Raymond Fresco, who was attempting to escape Gestapo agents who had come to arrest him, was brought down by machine gun fire. As he fell to the ground, the assassins fired another 10 bullets into him.[15]

Amongst the rare German police documents on the Brunner Action that have come to our attention are a series of reports linked to the arrests

---

[12] Ibid.

[13] In total, 1,417 people were to be arrested in Nice and its surroundings by the Brunner Kommando, and sent to Drancy between September and December 1943 (Serge Klarsfeld, *La Shoah en France*, volume I, op. cit., p. 310).

[14] Grégoire Spolianski died under torture on 18 November. Joseph Roos died on 1 April, 1944.

[15] *Cinq mois de persécutions anti-juives à Nice*, Union des Juifs pour la Résistance et l'Entraide (UJRE), no date or place of publication given.

of Jacques Weintrob, Claude Gutmann and Germaine Meyer.[16] These reports show how important the fight against rescue organizations was in the eyes of the German police. As one of these reports indicates, the arrests took place "in the course of action taken against major Jews in Nice,"[17] which clearly confirms that dismantling the Jewish resistance movement was one of the objectives of the "Aktion," that was pursued from the beginning.

The way in which those arrested were treated was identical to the treatment reserved by the German police for any member of the resistance. They were detained for varied lengths of time (Germaine Meyer was held for a month in Nice) before being sent as Jews,[18] to Drancy to be interrogated about the organization to which they belonged and the role they played. Thus, Jacques Weintrob was identified as the "head of the Jewish youth and organizer of children's convoys" (*Kindertransporte*) to Switzerland.[19] The rescue networks' activities were systematically unraveled and their ramifications updated:

> the under mentioned Jews [Meyer, Weintrob, Gutmann] hugely supported by the population and by the French authorities: the woman, Meyer, was hidden at the home of a Frenchman aged seventy […]; Gutmann was arrested in the house of the Jesuits at 8, rue Mirabeau in Nice where he was discussing the question of help that the Catholic Church could bring to young Jews. According to papers we found upon him, it appears that Les Compagnons de France, Le Comité National des Unions Chrétiennes des Jeunes de France as well as Le Mouvement des Eclaireurs Unionistes de France had given him their full support. Weintrob had already organized three convoys of twenty-five Jewish children to Switzerland and was arrested half an hour before the departure of the convoy.[20]

This report also shows the limits of German police action. Although the help given by the French population was clearly followed and, above all, numerous organizations were identified, the Germans were unable to

---

[16] Interrogation and report concerning Germaine Meyer by the Nice SD sent to Brunner, 21 October 1943 (CDJC, 1–59), report sent by the Marseilles EK to Section IV at Paris, 18 November 1943 (CDJC, 1–60), and its transmission by Röthke to the IVB4 in Berlin on the following 27 December (CDJC, 1–61).
[17] CDJC, 1–60.
[18] Then deported to Auschwitz.
[19] CDJC, 1–60.
[20] Ibid.

strike. For the men who were charged with carrying out the "Final Solution," this was probably one of the principal difficulties that they encountered in France. Whether in the Occupied Zone or the Free Zone, no measure either prohibited or punished the sheltering of Jews nor any other form of "legal" aid given to them, whereas in the East, in the territories under Nazi domination, the death penalty was imposed.[21] Nothing in the legislative framework put into place by Vichy, however imposing it might have been, brought restrictions upon this subject. Certainly, there were some policemen or gendarmes of a particularly zealous nature who, with justification from legislation concerning foreigners, reported hosts for the "non-declaration of foreigners" and "failure to register tenants" in application of the law of 2 May 1938.[22] These were isolated cases, however, and, according to the facts seem to have been fairly rare.[23] According to Vichy laws, the only acts that really went too far were forms of help such as the furnishing of false papers, for example, an act covered by a law, or articles of a penal code, which were not motivated by anti-Semitic policies. So, in the absence of any particular French policy of repression in this domain, and in the equal absence of any German prohibitions in France, the Sipo-SD was unable to arrest, at least in any official manner, a person because he or she was sheltering a Jew, and only activities that were "illegal" could bring about sanctions.[24]

---

[21] On the Eastern territories and the German efforts against rescue, see for example Leonid Smilovitsky, "Righteous Gentiles, the Partisans and Jewish Survival in Belorussia, 1941–1944," *Holocaust and Genocide Studies*, 11, 1997, pp. 301–29 and Wladyslaw Bartoszewski, Zegota, *Juifs et Polonais dans la résistance. 1939–1945*, Paris, Critérion, 1992.

[22] Two articles of this law permitted the punishment of those who gave assistance to foreigners: Article 4, which punished "ail individuals who, by direct or indirect help, offer assistance or attempt to offer assistance regarding the entry, circulation and illegal residence of a foreigner" by a fine of between 100 and 1,000 francs and from one month to a year in prison; article 6, which obliged "all persons housing a foreigner in whatever manner, whether by free lodging or by renting a property without furniture" to make out a declaration either for the commissioner, the police station or the town hall of the relevant commune, or to risk the sanctions set out in article 4 (*Journal Officiel de la République Française*, 3 May 1938, pp. 4967–9).

[23] For one example, see the Archives départementales de L'Isère (ADI), 57M 9, minutes of the brigade of the gendarmerie of Moirans, n° 124, 17 March 1944.

[24] Even if the Sipo-SD acted as it pleased, it had, however, certain limits; the

However, the blows dealt by Brunner's team greatly affected the majority of Jewish organizations active in Nice, either by dismantling them or by forcing them once again to retreat towards less exposed areas, in particular Grenoble.[25]

Liquidating the Jewish resistance movement (Grenoble, February–March 1944)

It was during the second phase of the operation in Grenoble from the beginning of February 1944 that the dismantelement of rescue organizations was seen most clearly. Its execution was planned from the conception, in September 1943, of the search operation in the ex-Italian-zone, the Isère department being identified as the other main Jewish centre in the Italian zone.

Beginning on 8 February 1944, the Kommando carried out operations in Chambéry against the Chambéry-Grenoble dismantlement of the UGIF, where the staff of the OSE worked. The speed with which this operation was performed, scarcely a few days after the Kommando's installation in Grenoble, shows that once again this was one of the priority objectives pursued by Brunner. Everybody in the building was arrested, eight of whom were members of the OSE, one being one of the principal leaders of the organization, Alain Mossé. They were transferred to Grenoble and detained in the Suisse et Bordeaux hotel, the Kommando headquarters, where they were interrogated. In the following days, more operations against the OSE took place in Grenoble. Around 9 February the Kommando raided the home of Madeleine Khan, a UGIF social worker. She wasn't there but the SS was able to arrest her sister. On 16 February another member of the OSE, Herta Hauben, was arrested at her home after several fruitless attempts during the preceding days.[26] The OSE was not the only organization targeted. On 18 February Marc Haguenau, director of the Service Social des Jeunes (SSJ) and above all General Secretary of the underground movement of the Eclaireurs Israélites de France (EIF), and his secretary Edith Pulver were arrested in the

---

arrest of French people who weren't guilty of any crime would only add tension to the relationship between Vichy and the German authorities.

[25] See Lucien Lazare, op. cit. pp. 252–4.
[26] ADI 7291 W 394, dossier 106 032 (Herta Hauben).

street in Grenoble as they were going to the post office to collect the mail in the SSJ post box.[27]

Here again, the circumstances surrounding this arrest show that Marc Haguenau was being actively sought by the IVB4. Whilst the arrest was taking place, the SS was unaware of the whereabouts of Haguenau and his secretary. So it was probably through use of information received, and no doubt shadowing by agents, that the arrests were made. Edith Pulver managed to get a letter out from the Suisse et Bordeaux hotel describing the conditions under which they were captured and what followed:

Last Friday, as I was going from my home to Marc's, we were arrested, taken away in a car and lead to the Gestapo Hotel Suisse et Bordeaux. I had a briefcase full of official UGIF papers. After the usual interview, Marc gave his address and they found all his identities. Marc was in a sorry state, his face was all puffy, etc. He tried to escape on the Saturday night but didn't manage to, and fell; he is in the hospital. I don't really know how he is, leg broken etc.[28]

[…] To the great displeasure of my mentors, I withstood several examinations, which brought me a great deal of personal satisfaction. They usually take place at night after an evening bout of drinking. What is done is physically supportable. One's nerves, however, are little by little unable to stand it but they give me a sedative, Gardenal, whose effects I feel.

[…] Advise family and friends Grenoble is very dangerous like all the county.

[…] The cousins are unaware of the family's address. It is not worth letting them know since their visit is not really desirable. As for me, I won't let on; I don't think that I had my family papers on me. I was completely searched. 50 bills unfortunately lost […].[29]

The operations carried out by the men of the IVB4 were aimed at dismantling not only the Jewish resistance movement, but all the underground organizations offering to help Jews. Thus, in Grenoble, the Polish network Monika was targeted. Acting under the cover of the Groupement d'Assistance des Polonais en France (Assistance Group of Poles in France, GAPF), which permitted the partial financing of underground

---

[27] A Red Cross intervention shows that Edith Pulver was "arrested in the street" (ADI, 13R 907, DU 458). See also Alain Michel, *Les éclaireurs israélites de France pendant la Seconde Guerre mondiale*, Paris, Editions des EIF, 1984, pp. 166–7.

[28] Haguenau died following this fall.

[29] A document published in *Le Monde Juif*, 161, September-December 1997, pp. 61–2. Edith Pulver was deported to Auschwitz on 7 March 1944.

activities—as with the Jewish organizations using the UGIF as a legal façade—this network helped Polish Jews who were in hiding by giving them: an allowance, as well as concealment in GAPF shelter centers in the Isère. Informed about these activities, the Kommando set out to attack the Monika network. On 2 March a trap was set at the office of the headquarters of Polish students, a place where Jewish students came to collect their allowances. In addition, on that day, an underground meeting attended by all those in charge of the Polish resistance movement in the Isère was taking place, and all of them were arrested. The treatment that the men of the IVB4 reserved for them clarifies the manner in which the German police operated: the first preoccupation of the SS, once those arrested had been detained at the hotel Suisse et Bordeaux, was a "physical verification";[30] once it was established that prisoners were not Jews, but "only" Polish resistance members, the case was transmitted to the Grenoble section of the Sipo-SD.

This raid, however, gave the German police the possibility of mounting an operation which would satisfy both services: for the Grenoble SD, the liquidation of the Polish resistance structures, and for the IV-B4, the capture of hidden Jews. On 9 March a joint operation of the SD police, Kommando men and troops from the Wehrmacht began. Polish reception centers at Sappey in Chartreuse and Saint Nizier in Vercors were raided. At the same time, the office of the Contrôle Social des Etrangers (Social Control of Foreigners) in Grenoble was served with a warrant. The operation finished with the arrest of several dozen people of whom many were Jewish, as well as many high level representatives of the Polish resistance movement. The Monika network, set up in 1940 in Grenoble, was, because of the action of the Brunner group, totally annihilated.[31]

Harsh actions against the population

While the Kommando enjoyed a certain success against the rescue networks, its actions did not reduce the assistance given to the Jews. On the contrary, this manhunt provoked strong hostility in the heart of the popu-

---

[30] "One began by examining their bodies in order to declare their race" (ADI, 13R 1043, eyewitness account of Mr Godlewski, 28 February 1947).

[31] It seems that operations against Polish centers were extended during the month of March 1944 and the Grenoble Kommando's departure in no way ended the action.

lation who, in reaction, offered protection and assistance. Eyewitness accounts on this subject are abundant. The brochure from the UJRE which has already been quoted (with its political aims and typical rhetoric) offers us a tableau of what this assistance was:

> From the very first day, the attitude of the French population in Nice (in its almost totality) in the face of these persecutions was admirable. Everywhere, help was given to Jews being hunted; warnings were given regarding round ups and the arrival of agents; they were hidden and fed when they could not go out. During the bigger raids, thousands [printed in bold in the text] of Jews were hidden spontaneously by French inhabitants. The clergy and Catholic groups in the city also largely contributed to the saving of the Jews, especially the children whom they spent much effort in placing in safe houses [...]. The help given by the entire Nice population largely contributed to the saving of the Jews of Nice. How many French people still shelter Jewish families, often without even accepting remuneration? How many households are still bearing the burden of feeding hidden families? [...][32]

This attitude is one constant factor found as often in Nice as in Grenoble. Even the prefect of Isère was forced, in a report for Vichy, to communicate the "anti-German fanaticism of the people of Grenoble"[33] provoked by the manhunt led by Brunner. The behavior of the Kommando only served to increase the support for the Jews in the heart of the population. At the beginning of 1944, however, the German attitude shift regarding the population giving assistance became perceptible. In Grenoble, the Kommando took various measures to dissuade the population from helping the Jews. Anyone suspected of sheltering or protecting Jews was to be henceforth arrested, to which the French police would regularly attest during the Grenoble part of the "Aktion." Seeking to terrorize the "French" population, Brunner and his men wanted to isolate the Jewish population, depriving it of support and protection. His Kommando implemented arrests, tortures, executions and deportations of protectors, in order to drain the civil resistance movement of its strength and remove this one hindrance to the manhunt.

---

[32] Union des Juifs pour la Résistance et l'Entraide, op. cit., p. 13. Numerous eyewitness accounts regarding assistance offered by the population are found amongst the archives of the CDJC (some are reproduced in Serge Klarsfeld, *La Shoah en France*, volume I, *Vichy-Auschwitz. La "solution finale" de la question juive en France*, op. cit., pp. 306–8).

[33] AN, F1cIII, 1158, monthly report, this for the month of Feb 1944 (special chapter: relationship with the German authorities).

Everything was done to drain the civil resistance movement of its strength and remove this one hindrance to the manhunt. It seems that the hardening of repression against the civil resistance movement did not just involve the Kommando, but was widespread. During the preparations for the roundup of 4 February 1944 in Paris, Heinz Röthke let it be known to the French police that, from then on, if any persons "hide Jews or give false information to prevent them from being arrested," they would be held "personally responsible."[34]

Brunner applied this method in Grenoble, more or less at the same time. The prefect of Isère made it known in a report that the arrests made by the SS were specifically of the "Jews and their friends."[35] Traces can be found of arrests of these "friends of the Jews" from 9 February onward, just a few days after the beginning of the "Aktion" in Grenoble, with the arrest of two members of the Menthonnex family in La Tronche during a raid.[36] While, as in most cases, the "Aryan" people arrested were eventually released after a long period of detention at the Suisse et Bordeaux Hotel, their fates were sometimes far more tragic. Those helping the Jews or obstructing anti-Jewish services would be henceforth faced with the risk of deportation, and this threat was made in no uncertain terms. During the arrest of the members of a Jewish family in Domène in the Isère, the person who had been sheltering them, Cyprien Soulier, helped two children escape.[37] He was arrested by the SS and taken to the Kommando headquarters. A week later, the mayor of Domène was summoned to the hotel Suisse et Bordeaux where he was informed by the Germans that Cyprien Soulier "had placed himself in a grave situation" by helping the Jews escape, and that "if by any means he was unable to have the two Jewish fugitives arrested within ten days, on 3 March the aforementioned Mr. Soulier would be taken to Compiègne."[38] Although the children were never found, it seems that these threats were never carried out.[39]

---

[34] Serge Klarsfeld, *Le calendrier de la persécution des Juifs de France, 1940–1944*, Paris, les Fils et Filles des Déportés Juifs de France, 1993, pp. 954–5.

[35] AN, F1cIII, 1158.

[36] ADI, 13R 971.

[37] Interview with Eliezer Lev Zion, from a recording made on 8 June 1998 for the Musée de la Résistance et de la Déportation de L'Isère.

[38] ADI, 13R 971, a letter from the mayor of Domène to the prefect, 24 February 1944.

[39] There exists no other information concerning this matter in the archives.

At least one case has been discovered where a person sheltering a Jew paid for it with his life. In the course of an operation carried out on 12 February 1944 in the commune of Corenc near Grenoble, the Germans arrested Major Paul Croux "for having hidden a Jew."[40] He was then sent to Compiègne from whence he was deported to Mauthausen, where he died on 25 August 1944. However, if the reason for the arrest was helping Jews, it would appear that the deportation—if the finding of a post-war police investigation can be believed—was for another reason: it would seem that during the arrest of Major Croux's lodger, the Germans had discovered compromising documents, since he was in contact with the Resistance.[41]

On 16 March, "Aktion" in the former Italian zone was brought to a halt and Brunner and his men returned to Drancy. In the end, the results after five months of operations could only be disappointing from Brunner's point of view. "Only" some 2,000 Jews had been arrested, whilst the SS had been counting on capturing several tens of thousands. It is certain that several resistance organizations were severely affected by this operation.[42] For the anti-Jewish service of the Gestapo, the fight against rescue was an integral part of their mission and anything that got in the way of the "final solution" was to be destroyed.

Within this operation, it was essentially structures using the cover of a "legal façade" which were hit, as opposed to organizations operating completely underground such as the Mouvement de la Jeunesse Sioniste or the communist groups like the UJRE. Above all, despite their dogged zeal, the SS found itself confronted with a major difficulty: civil resistance. According to one witness's account, Eichmann's deputy

---

Cyprien Soulier was not deported (his name is not amongst the lists published by La Foundation pour la Mémoire de la Déportation, *Livre mémorial des déportés de France arrêtés par mesure de répression et dans certains cas par mesure de persécution, 1940–1945*, 4 vol, Editions Tirésias, 2004). There remains the possibility that he may have been sent to Compiègne.

[40] ADI, 13R 971.

[41] ADI, 7291 W 285, dossier 84 498 (Paul Croux).

[42] During the Grenoble phase of the operation, Aloïs Brunner was twice mentioned in the dispatches of the Gestapo in Berlin, on 26 February and 18 March 1944 (Didier Epelbaum, *Aloïs Brunner*, op. cit., p. 204). The reasons for this praise are unknown to us but it could have been made following his dismantling of various networks.

ended the operation "because the environment in Grenoble scarcely favored it."[43]

This statement allows one to measure the crucial importance of the civil resistance movement in view of this manhunt. It was this "environment"—attributable to thousands of unknown people who had helped, individually or collectively, in all different ways, the thousands of Jews on the run from the manhunt—that thwarted the Kommando of the IVB4, forcing it to halt its search operations in the refuge zone without attaining its preestablished objectives.

---

[43] CDJC, CCXVI-53a, account given by Sala Hirth (a member of the "Jewish team" brought from Drancy to Grenoble to take charge of captured Jews at the Hôtel Suisse et Bordeaux).

18

"GUIDE AND MOTIVATOR" OR "CENTRAL TREASURY"? THE "JOINT" IN FRANCE, 1942–1944[1]

Laura Hobson Faure[2]

The American Jewish Joint Distribution Committee (JDC, also known as the "Joint") has served as the major overseas philanthropic organization of the American Jewish community since it was established in 1914. Throughout World War I and the interwar period, the JDC sought to improve the welfare of Jews outside the United States by providing food, medical care and economic aid. In order to operate freely, the JDC maintained a policy of political neutrality, preferring to remain uninvolved in politics both overseas and in the United States. As the need to help European Jewry grew increasingly urgent in the 1930s, American Jews

---

[1] The first phrase quoted, cited by Yehuda Bauer, *American Jewry and the Holocaust: The American Jewish Joint Distribution Committee, 1939–1945*, Detroit, Wayne State University Press, 1981, p. 177, is from a memo from Joseph Schwartz to the JDC administration. The second comes from a report by Jules Jefroykin to the JDC administration. Archives of the American Jewish Joint Distribution Committee, New York (hereafter as JDC-NY) file 596 general, file 2 of 2, France 1942–1944. *Report on the General Situation in France, November 1942–June 1944* (translated from French), August 1944.

[2] The author would like to thank Nancy L. Green, Diane Afoumado and Veerle Vanden Daelen for their helpful comments on this paper. She would also like to thank the French Ministry of Education, the Fondation du Judaïsme Français and the American Jewish Archive for their support.

established a national fundraising structure called the United Jewish Appeal, providing the JDC with a broad base of financial support to aid as many Jews as possible.[3] The important role assumed by the JDC during the Shoah has been extensively documented in Yehuda Bauer's three-volume history of this organization and elsewhere.[4] However, other historians have criticized the JDC for obeying American government regulations while European Jewry perished.[5] Primary sources from this period also paint a bifurcated image of both a law-abiding organization and a resistance organization:

> [...]"Reports are continually coming into us [...] telling of deportation and death. [...] I want to assure you, however, that our every activity is known to our government and to its State and Treasury Departments."
>
> – *Paul Baerwald, JDC Chairman, at the 29th Annual Meeting, 5 December 1943*[6]

---

[3] On the United Jewish Appeal, cf. Abraham J. Karp, *To Give Life. The UJA in the Shaping of the American Jewish Community*, New York, Schocken Books, 1981; Marc Lee Raphael, *A History of the United Jewish Appeal*, Chico, Scholars Press, 1982. The JDC would receive approximately 57 per cent of funds generated from the UJA, but this varied from year to year, according to changing needs, see Abraham Karp, op. cit., pp. 84–7.

[4] Cf. Yehuda Bauer, *My Brother's Keeper: A History of the American Jewish Joint Distribution Committee 1929–1939*, Philadelphia, The Jewish Publication Society, 1974; *American Jewry and the Holocaust*, op. cit.; *Out of the Ashes: the Impact of American Jews on Post-Holocaust Jewry*, Oxford, Pergamon Press, 1989. On the extensive role of the JDC in France, see Lucien Lazare, *La résistance juive en France*, Paris, Stock, 1987, among others.

[5] In his article "Jewish Organizations and the Creation of the U.S. War Refugee Board," *The Annals*, 450, 1980, p. 136, Monty Penkower states: "As for the more established JDC, it insisted on complying with all American regulations and refused throughout the war to contemplate some modus vivendi with the WJC while Jews abroad underwent mass annihilation." Sarah Peck, while focusing on Zionist organizations, also blames American Jewish organizations for inaction in her article "The Campaign for an American Response to the Nazi Holocaust, 1943–1945," *Journal of Contemporary History*, 15 (2), 1980, pp. 367–400. Henry Feingold presents a more nuanced approach, asking why American Jews and their organizations were assumed powerful enough to save European Jewry in his article, "'Courage First and Intelligence Second': The American Jewish Secular Elite, Roosevelt and the Failure to Rescue," *American Jewish History*, 72 (4), 1983, pp. 424–60.

[6] Address by Paul Baerwald, Chairman, JDC, 29th Annual Meeting, 5 December

"Until the German occupation of Southern France, the Joint was a legal organization with headquarters in Marseilles. After America entered the war, JDC declared to the Vichy Government that it had been dissolved. But this was merely camouflage. We did not go out of existence. We, just like other Jewish organizations, continued to work illegally. […] JDC encouraged the Jewish resistance movement morally and financially. Thus in 1943, we passed on to another form of activity, we encouraged active and passive resistance. First of all the Jews had to be saved physically, to be hidden, given non-Jewish names, and new identification papers. Our resistance organizations distributed thousands of false identification papers, ration books, birth certificates, etc.. All this work was supported by the Joint. It would be erroneous to believe, however that the Joint limited its activities to financial aid."

– *Joseph Fisher, French Zionist leader, at a meeting held on 19 December 1944 in New York*[7]

The case of France during World War II provides an excellent opportunity to explore how the JDC responded to the challenges of saving lives while maintaining political neutrality during the Shoah. On one hand, France had a considerable pre-war Jewish population and developed strong networks of Jewish resistance during the war. On the other hand, the United States and the Vichy government cut off diplomatic relations in November of 1942.[8] The JDC thus found itself in an area with great need and potential for saving lives, yet with an organizational policy of political neutrality, and, as an American organization, under the additional constraint of compliance with American governmental regulations dictating relations with enemy nations. We can thus question if the JDC played an active role in resistance and rescue in France during the Shoah or if it preferred a more conservative role.

Jewish resistance: terminology and theoretical considerations

The role played by the JDC in France from 1942 to 1944 demonstrates tensions related to the shifting notions of legality as conditions changed.

1943. Report included in letter from Baerwald to Sir Herbert Emerson of the Intergovernmental Refugee Committee, 23 December 1943. Archives Nationales, AJ/43/13.

[7] Minutes of meeting held on 5 December 1944 at the office of the JDC, JDC NY, file 596 general, file 2 of 2, France 1942–44.

[8] The American ambassador to Vichy, Admiral Leahy, was recalled in May 1942

This is especially evident in the study of the intersection points that linked the JDC to the Jewish resistance. Before highlighting the machinery that the JDC mobilized for this activity, it is important to define the terms that will be used to describe the role of the JDC in the Jewish resistance in France, which should be seen not as a monolith but as a nebulous structure of organizations and networks from diverse factions of Jewish life. Indeed, while individual Jews fought in the general (or national) resistance, other individuals and organizations mobilized to form a specifically Jewish resistance. The objectives of the general and the Jewish resistance in France were not identical. For the first, the rescue of Jews was considered only within the larger framework of ending the German occupation of France, whereas the Jewish resistance specifically responded to the war against Jews, waged by the Nazi occupiers and the Vichy French State.[9] These objectives were not contradictory—there was cooperation and overlap, especially toward the end of the war.[10] Without attempting to rewrite this history, we will focus on aspects of the Jewish resistance because it was with this faction that the JDC worked with in France.[11]

---

after the establishment of the Laval government (26 April 1942). However, diplomatic relations between the US and Vichy were tense but still officially intact: the US maintained a Chargé d'Affaires in Vichy, H. Pinkney Tuck. It was not until the Allied invasion of North Africa (8 November 1942) that diplomatic relations were broken. See Robert O. Paxton, *Vichy France: Old Guard and New Order 1940–1944*. New York, Columbia University Press, 2001, pp. 134, 312–13.

[9] See Lucien Lazare, "Introduction: les combatants de la résistance juive à vocation communautaire," in Les Anciens de la Résistance Juive en France (ed.), *Organisation Juive de Combat. Résistance/Sauvetage. France 1940–1945*, Paris, les Editions Autrement, 2002, pp. 19–27; Asher Cohen, *Pérsécutions et sauvetages. Juifs et Français sous l'occupation et sous Vichy*, Paris, Editions du Cerf, 1993, pp. 359–97; Renée Poznanski, "A Methodological Approach to the Study of Jewish Resistance in France," *Yad Vashem Studies*, XVIII, 1987, pp. 1–39.

[10] See Renée Poznanski, op. cit., p. 33.

[11] Cf. David Knout, *Contribution à l'histoire de la résistance juive en France, 1940–1944*. Paris, Centre de Documentation Juive Contemporaine, 1947; Anny Latour, *La Résistance juive en France*, Paris, Stock, 1970; David Diamant, *Les Juifs dans la résistance française, 1940–1944 (Avec armes ou sans armes)*, Paris, Le Pavillon, 1971; Lucien Lazare, *La Résistance juive*, op. cit.; Asher Cohen, op. cit.; Renée Poznanski, op. cit.; among others.

Secondly, there is a need to distinguish between relief, rescue and resistance. Relief implies providing for the general welfare of a population, including food, medical care, and financial aid. This was especially important due to the discriminatory laws that greatly hindered the access of Jews to employment, education and general resources.[12] Historian Asher Cohen distinguishes between rescue and resistance, defining rescue as the actions to protect the lives of the Jewish population, including forging of papers, hiding of individuals (especially children) and illegal crossing of borders, whereas in his view resistance implies military action.[13] Despite variations in terminology, historians agree that the Jewish resistance in France consisted of both rescue work and military activity, with a stronger emphasis on the former.[14]

Finally, it is crucial to examine the notions of legality and illegality, noting that these notions shifted depending on the period in the war, the place where an action took place, and the nationality of the actor.[15] Americans and American organizations, even outside the United States, were bound by the changing regulations of their government. Therefore, the same action—for example, transferring money into Nazi-occupied territories—could be "legal" if performed by a Swiss national, yet would be illegal for an American. These shifting notions of legality led to a general lack of clarity and acted as both a hindrance and a help to rescue and resistance: a hindrance because conservative leaders of the JDC preferred to "draw a fence" around American laws and demonstrate their strict adherence to them;[16] a help, because those who preferred to challenge

---

[12] The first of a series of discriminatory legislation began in September 1940, forcing the Jews in the Occupied Zone to register with authorities, followed by the *Statuts des Juifs*, which removed Jews from public office, press, and radio, among others. Yehuda Bauer, *American Jewry*, op. cit., p. 160.

[13] See Asher Cohen, op. cit., p. 365.

[14] See Asher Cohen, ibid.; Renée Poznanski, op. cit., p. 14.

[15] The author would like to thank historian Diane Afoumado for her insights on this topic.

[16] Letter from Chairman National Council of the JDC, Vice Chairman JDC, James Rosenberg to Joseph Hyman, Secretary and Executive Director, 21 September 1939, file AR3344/193, reproduced in Sybil Milton and Frederick D. Bogin (eds), *Volume 10. American Jewish Joint Distribution Committee, New York, Parts One and Two., Archives of the Holocaust. An International Collection of Selected Documents*, New York and London, Garland Publishing, Inc., 1995, p. 227.

these laws were able to use the ambiguities and gray areas to their advantage, all while claiming that the JDC acted according to the law.[17]

The JDC in France

The JDC began funding small projects in France in 1916.[18] With the arrival of German Jewish refugees in 1933, this organization transferred its European headquarters from Berlin to Paris and began to play an important role in the coordination of Jewish welfare in France (see Table 5 for the JDC allocations by year, 1933–1944).[19] On the defeat of France in June 1940, the JDC closed its Paris office and, like other American organizations, re-established itself in the Southern Zone, in Marseilles. Among other important activities, the JDC helped organize the Comité de Nîmes, a group of twenty-five non-governmental organizations, to provide food and medical care to those interned in French camps.[20] While the JDC was wary of the Vichy-Nazi-imposed Union Générale des Israélites de France (UGIF), its funds supported this organization.[21] After the break in diplomatic ties between Washington and Vichy in November 1942, American employees of the JDC were required to leave France.

---

[17] Joseph Schwartz interview, Oral History Division, Avram Harmon Institute of Contemporary Jewry, Hebrew University of Jerusalem (hereafter OHD), (47)19, p. 15.

[18] See American Jewish Joint Distribution Committee, *JDC Primer*, New York, 1945, p. France-4.

[19] See Yehuda Bauer, *My Brother's Keeper*, op. cit., pp. 138–79.

[20] The Comité de Nîmes was established in November 1940. Of the twenty-five organizations, seven were of Jewish affiliation, see Yehuda Bauer, *American Jewry*, op. cit., p. 160.

[21] Historians and contemporaries remain divided on the role the UGIF. JDC aid to this body is harshly judged by those who consider the UGIF as form of French Jewish collaboration, such as Jacques Adler, *The Jews of Paris and the Final Solution: Communal Response and Internal Conflicts, 1940–1944*, New York and Oxford, Oxford University Press, 1987, pp. 142–5. However, Richard I. Cohen, *The Burden of Conscience: French Jewish Leadership During the Holocaust*, Bloomington and Indianapolis, Indiana University Press, 1987; Yehuda Bauer, *American Jewry*, op. cit., p. 168; and a contemporary of the events, Jules (Dika) Jefroykin (interview, OHD (1)61, p. 4), hold a more moderate view of the JDC funding of the UGIF.

Table 5: JDC Allocations to France by Year 1933–1944 (in US dollars)

Year	Amount
1933	95,657
1934	285,070
1935	70,106
1936	115,910
1937	147,629
1938	112,486
1939	698,761
1940	620,662
1941	793,384
1942	872,683
1943	1,748,500
1944	1,657,223

Source: JDC Catalogue, France (JDC, NY).

Preparing for war

As the outbreak of war became inevitable, JDC representatives began to prepare for the possible departure of their organization from Europe. Chief overseas representative Morris Troper and his deputy, Dr Joseph Schwartz, quickly toured Europe in May 1940. During this journey they met with Jewish leaders in several countries, and appointed Saly Mayer, head of the Federation of Jewish Communities of Switzerland, to act as a JDC representative should the JDC be forced to withdraw from Europe.[22] The JDC also established an office in Lisbon to serve as its European headquarters. In France, Dr Schwartz hired Jules (Dika) Jefroykin, a naturalized French citizen of Russian origin, as the assistant to the director for France in December of 1940.[23] In spring of 1942, Jefroykin was named JDC representative for France and, on a June trip to Lisbon, was given *carte blanche* to borrow funds in the name of the JDC, which would be reimbursed after the war.[24] However, he was told that no armed resistance could be funded by the JDC.[25]

[22] See Yehuda Bauer, *American Jewry*, op. cit., p. 42.
[23] Jefroykin dates his employment with the JDC to December 1940, in Jules Jefroykin, OHD (1)61, p. 1, whereas Bauer places it one month later, see Yehuda Bauer, *American Jewry*, op. cit., p. 163.
[24] Anny Latour places Jefroykin's appointment as director for France in the spring of 1942, yet Bauer places it in June 1942; Anny Latour, op. cit., p. 120; Yehuda Bauer, *American Jewry*, op. cit., p. 241.
[25] See Anny Latour, op. cit., p. 120.

While the JDC held a legalistic stance from 1940 to 1942, its policies began to change in the summer of 1942, before the departure of its American employees. After the massive Vel d'Hiv round up in Paris in July of 1942, during which 12,884 Jews were arrested for deportation to Auschwitz, Dr Schwartz went to France.[26] Breaking with the non-interventionist JDC policy, Schwartz met with American governmental officials in France to try to prevent future deportations, and with French Jewish leaders to emphasize the need for Jewish unification and a limited role for the UGIF, directing relief programs outside official channels. Schwartz's actions during this trip indicated a willingness to depart from official, legal methods.

As the JDC prepared for the war, local Jewish organizations and individuals did the same. The stirrings of Jewish resistance were felt from 1940 onwards, yet the deportations of the summer of 1942 acted as an important catalyst for recruitment. As Jacques Adler and Renée Poznanski have pointed out, Jews from Eastern Europe were particularly likely to resist. In contrast to French Jews, Eastern European Jews tended to see the state as a hostile force. In addition, the first arrests made by the Nazis in France were among Communists, among them left-wing Zionists. This "political persecution" led to a political response, and to new needs, such as false papers.[27] Thus, in 1940, two Zionist-Revisionist couples of Eastern European origin established an organization that became known in 1942 as the Armée Juive (AJ; until then this organization had multiple names, including La Main Forte, B'nei David and, after 1944, the Organization Juive de Combat).[28]

In an important step, Jules (Dika) Jefroykin, president of the Mouvement de Jeunesse Sioniste (MJS) and member of the Fédération des Sociétés Juives de France (FSJF), became a member of the top leadership

---

[26] See Yehuda Bauer, *American Jewry*, op. cit., pp. 174–7.

[27] See Renée Poznanski, op. cit., pp. 4–6.

[28] As Zionist Revisionists, these followers of Jabotinsky believed in military struggle for the creation of a Jewish state. This faction of Zionism was seen as marginal and extreme by the socialist-Zionists, the dominant group among the Zionist leadership of France, strongly represented in the FSJF. However, this network was able to broaden its membership to include socialist-Zionists. On the establishment of the AJ, see Asher Cohen, op. cit., pp. 378–84; Lucien Lazare, *La résistance juive*, op. cit., pp. 111–18; and Les Anciens de la Résistance Juive en France, op. cit.

of the AJ in 1941, all while working for the JDC.[29] Jefroykin's distinct political profile indicates that Dr Schwartz, who became the chief of JDC overseas operations in February 1942, did not select him arbitrarily: Jefroykin represented the more radical, Zionist, immigrant faction of French Jewish life.[30] He was the son of a Zionist leader, Israël Jefroykin, who had been the president of the FSJF, the federation that organized the many immigrant mutual aid societies (*Landsmanshaftn*) to form a counterweight to the native French Jewish establishment, organized around the Consistoire Central and its philanthropic organizations.[31] Jefroykin's multiple organizational affiliations determined the JDC's connection points to the Jewish resistance. They also led to the financing of the AJ by the JDC, and may have influenced the unification of different factions of the Jewish resistance through the collaboration between the AJ and youth organizations (MJS, Eclaireurs Israélites) and the unofficial branches of welfare organizations (Œuvre de Secours aux Enfants [OSE], FSJF, among others).

The JDC under French leadership

With the landing of Allied forces in North Africa and the German occupation of the Southern Zone, JDC offices in Marseilles were closed and subsequently stormed by Nazis.[32] Jefroykin and his assistant, Maurice Brener, found themselves the sole representatives of the JDC in France,

---

[29] See Jules Jefroykin, OHD (1)61, p. 7.

[30] Strangely, Raymond-Raoul Lambert, head of the UGIF in the Southern Zone, notes that he was asked to represent the JDC in France in November 1942: Raymond-Raoul Lambert, *Carnet d'un témoin 1940–1943. Présenté et annoté par Richard Cohen*, Paris, Librairie Arthème Fayard, 1985, p. 198. Perhaps the JDC discovered Jefroykin's affiliation with the Armée Juive and attempted to reorient its initial choice? Oral history interviews with JDC leadership and Jefroykin do not mention Lambert in this context, nor any tensions between the JDC and Jefroykin before the JDC's departure.

[31] For an analysis of the divisions in French Jewish life preceding World War II, cf. David H. Weinberg, *A Community on Trial. The Jews of Paris in the 1930s*, Chicago and London, University of Chicago Press, 1977; Paula Hyman, *From Dreyfus to Vichy. The Remaking of French Jewry, 1906–1939*, New York, Columbia University Press, 1979; and Vicki Caron, *Uneasy Asylum: France and the Jewish Refugee Crisis, 1933–1942*, Stanford University Press, 1999.

[32] See Jules Jefroykin, OHD (1)61, p. 10.

with limited possibilities for communication with Schwartz.³³ The US Trading with the Enemy Act, now applicable to France, severely limited the funds the JDC could legally send.³⁴ Jefroykin fled to Nice and met with the heads of the major Jewish organizations to determine how JDC funding should be spent:

> I was excluded (*sic*) the direction of the Joint and (…) I didn't think I could take on all the responsibility. I thus asked several members of the Jewish community to help me with their advice and experience. I was still pretty young at the time and had constituted on my own a sort of advisory board for the Joint (…). I wasn't prepared to allocate all the budget to official organizations and I asked their moral approval to decide on an amount of money I would allocate to underground activities but also to armed struggle. (…) With the support of my friend and collaborator Maurice Brenner (sic) (…) we got the principle approved. And this Nice meeting changed the organization of the work I was doing for the Joint. This is when I started being able to give money to the MJS network. (…and) that we could allocate a large part of the budget to underground activities.³⁵

In the spring of 1943,³⁶ a JDC council was formed to distribute JDC funds, comprising Jefroykin and representatives from the Consistoire Central, OSE, FSJF, the Comité d'assistance aux réfugiés, MJS, and the Zionist organizations.³⁷ According to Jefroykin, the JDC was not aware of his decision to divert the JDC funding for clandestine purposes and armed resistance, although he eventually cleared this unofficial activity with Dr Schwartz.³⁸ But how did he obtain this funding if American regulations strictly limited the transfer of dollars into Nazi occupied territory?

---

[33] Brener, cousin and secretary of Raymond-Raoul Lambert, began working with Jefroykin in the summer of 1942; Yehuda Bauer, *American Jewry*, op. cit., p. 241.

[34] See Monty Penkower, op. cit., pp. 122–39, on the efforts of American Jewish organizations to work within these regulations. The JDC obtained a special license from the Treasury department in December of 1942, allowing it to transfer limited sums of money into Nazi-occupied territories. Penkower does not specify where this money was used.

[35] See Jules Jefroykin, OHD (1)61, pp. 10–11.

[36] "American Joint Distribution Committee," Centre de Documentation Juive Contemporaine (hereafter CDJC), file CCCLXVI-14.

[37] Minutes of meeting held on 5 December 1944 at the office of the JDC, JDC NY, file 596 general, file 2 of 2, France 1942–44.

[38] Jefroykin specifies that he cleared his unofficial activities with Schwartz, but

Resources for rescue

Through their French representatives, the JDC was able to fund relief, rescue and resistance through four sources. The first and most important was by reestablishing a "loan après" system that the JDC had used during World War I, by which individuals desiring to loan their money would lend it to the JDC in exchange for repayment after the war.[39] Along with Jefroykin, two seasoned Zionist fundraisers led this operation—Joseph Fisher, who represented the Jewish National Fund (KKL), and Nahum Hermann, who headed the National Association for Reconstruction (Karen Hayessod).[40] In addition to these loans, donations to Zionist organizations were reallocated to the JDC and then repaid in Palestine after the war. Once established, the JDC Council distributed this money to the Armée Juive, the youth organizations, the clandestine branches of major welfare organizations, and other resistance networks.[41]

A second means of funding from the JDC became operational for France in the summer of 1943, via Switzerland. In February 1942, in light of American restrictions, Saly Mayer suggested that the JDC double its subsidy for Switzerland, which would free Swiss Jews to transfer their resources into Nazi-occupied territories. This plan received authorization from the US Treasury Department in March 1942.[42] While initially told not to interfere with France, Mayer was eventually authorized to provide funding to France for legal activities. Mayer was in contact with the

---

not at what point in the war he did so; Jules Jefroykin, OHD (1)61, p. 15. Bauer cites the dissertation of Modechai Kefir, who indicates that Schwartz learned of this only in 1943; Yehuda Bauer, *American Jewry*, op. cit., p. 475 (note 33).

[39] On this system, see Lucien Lazare, Ibid., pp. 279, 284–6; Anny Latour, op. cit., pp. 119–24; Dana Adams Schmitt, "Six Millions [sic] Lent Jews by French," *New York Times*, 11 January 1945, p. 8; and Yehuda Bauer, *American Jewry*, op. cit., p. 159. This system was stopped by Mayer and Schwartz when they learned of the poor exchange rates practiced in France in spring of 1944, but had stopped functioning well from the middle of 1943, see Yehuda Bauer, op. cit., p. 243; JDC-NY, Saly Mayer Archive, 1939–50, file 33, "SM-Lisbon Conversation 22 March 1944."

[40] See Lucien Lazare, *La résistance juive*, op. cit., p. 280.

[41] CDJC, file CCCLXVI-14, "American Joint Distribution Committee." This document provides some indication of the organizations funded by the JDC.

[42] See Yehuda Bauer, *American Jewry*, op. cit., p. 222.

French Jewish leadership, however, only after the arrivals of the Zionist Marc Jarblum, in March 1943, and Joseph Weill of the French OSE in May 1943.[43] Jarblum, as the president of the FSJF, had been "appointed" to be one of the members of the UGIF. He fought this appointment, convincing several others of the danger of this body. Jarblum was a personal friend of Léon Blum, active in the French Socialist party (SFIO), and the French representative for the World Jewish Congress (WJC).[44] In 1943 he became affiliated with the AJ.[45] This individual, a seasoned negotiator in both Jewish and national politics, began a vigorous letter writing campaign from Switzerland to raise funds for clandestine activities, especially those of the FSJF and the AJ, communicating with representatives of the Vaad Hatzalah of the Jewish Agency in Istanbul, the WJC, and the JDC.[46]

While Mayer viewed Jarblum with suspicion and showed a preference for the work of OSE, he supplied funds to both men, which entered France via different secret routes. Weill was able to smuggle the funds across the border to JDC representative Maurice Brener with the help of a resistance group led by a pro-Gaullist pharmacist from Geneva and a priest, who, thanks to creative use of his wooden leg, was able to perform this task with efficiency.[47] Jarblum used the services of a professional cyclist and a mechanic, who received a 1.5 per cent commission on the

---

[43] See Marc Jarblum interview, OHD (27)86, p. 20; Lucien Lazare, *La résistance juive*, op. cit., p. 286. Jefroykin claims that he knew Mayer from before the war, but had absolutely no contact with him during this period: OHD (1)61, p. 15.

[44] On Jarblum's political affiliations, see Philippe Boukara, "L'ami parisien: Les relations politiques et personnelles entre David Ben Gourion et Marc Jarblum," in Doris Bensimon and Benjamin Pinkus (eds), *Les Juifs de France, Le Sionisme et L'Etat d'Israël, Actes Du Colloque International 1987*, Langues Orientales, Paris, Publications LanguesO, 1987, pp. 153–70.

[45] See Asher Cohen, op. cit., p. 381.

[46] See Haïm Avni, "The Zionist Underground in Holland and France and the Escape to Spain," in Yisrael Gutman and Efraim Zuroff (eds), *Rescue Attempts During the Holocaust. Proceedings of the Second Yad Vashem International Historical Conference. Jerusalem, April 8–11, 1974*, Jerusalem, Yad Vashem, 1977, p. 575.

[47] See Lucien Lazare, *La résistance juive*, op. cit., p. 287. While Lazare specifies that Mayer's allocations to Weill were provided to Brener (and hence distributed through the JDC Council), Bauer notes that Weill received some direct funding from Mayer for OSE, which was a source of conflict among the Jewish organizations according to Yehuda Bauer, *American Jewry*, op. cit., p. 244.

smuggled funds they delivered. This funding, procured from the JDC, the Jewish Agency and the WJC, went directly to the AJ and was deposited at an AJ-operated newsagent's shop in Lyon, which sold collaborationist newspapers while doubling as an arsenal and meeting point for this organization.[48]

A third source of JDC funding came indirectly for specific activities, through international organizations that had received JDC funding. For example, the Quakers in Marseilles received $100,000 from the JDC to "help children out of France to Spain and possibly Switzerland," which they provided to the AJ for this purpose.[49]

Finally, it appears that the JDC was able to send some funds directly to France during the 1942–44 period. According to Schwartz, this was quietly facilitated by the American Treasury department.[50] After Roosevelt created the War Refugee Board in January of 1944, a government body that was in fact largely subsidized by the JDC, past restrictions were eased.[51]

The JDC allocations in France appear exceptionally high when compared with those of other occupied countries. For example in 1944, official JDC allocations for France were $1,657,223, while those for Belgium were $540,000, for Yugoslavia $1,745, and for Italy $347,534, while Holland received nothing at all.[52] According to one estimate, the JDC provided 60 per cent of the funds of the Jewish resistance in France.[53] Other international Jewish organizations contributed to work in France as well, such as the World Jewish Congress and the Vaad Hatzalah of the Jewish Agency for Palestine; however, historians have been unable to determine the extent of their aid.[54] The history of how these funds were used—from

---

[48] See Lucien Lazare, *La résistance juive*, op. cit., p. 287.

[49] Bauer does not specify the dates of this request, nor how the JDC transferred the money, see Yehuda Bauer, *American Jewry*, op. cit., p. 258.

[50] See Joseph Schwartz, OHD (47)19, pp. 2–3. Lazare also states that the JDC received a license from the Treasury department at the end of 1943, allowing it to contract loans in France with a $600,000 limit, noting that Schwartz authorized the loan system one year before this; Lucien Lazare, *La résistance juive*, op. cit., pp. 280–1.

[51] On the creation of the WRB, see Monty Penkower, op. cit., pp. 122–39 and David S. Wyman, *The Abandonment of the Jews: America and the Holocaust, 1941–1945*, New York, Pantheon Books, 1984, pp. 209–307.

[52] See Yehuda Bauer, *American Jewry*, op. cit., p. 292.

[53] Lucien Lazare, *La résistance juive*, op. cit., p. 282.

[54] The Vaad Hatzalah of the Jewish Agency should not be confused with the

border crossings to armed resistance—has been explored in numerous works on Jewish resistance in France.⁵⁵

Here, we highlight the role of local initiative in the distribution of these funds, and the largely unanswered question: how much did the JDC know about the rescue and resistance activities it was funding in France?

Table 6: JDC Funding for France, by Source and Year (in US Dollars)[56]

Year	Official JDC Allocation for France ($)	JDC allocation from Switzerland to France ($)	Total Global JDC expenditure ($)	France Allocations as % of Total Global JDC Budget
1941	793,384	–	5,716,908	13.8%
1942	872,682	–	6,318,205	14%
1943	1,748,500	149,935	8,470,538	31.7%
1944	1,657,223	1,056,930	15,216,643	10.9%
Total	5,071,789	1,206,865	35,722,295	14.2% to 19.8%[57]

Source: Yehuda Bauer, *American Jewry and the Holocaust*, p. 244

Orthodox organization of the same name. According to Renée Poznanski, op. cit., p. 32, this group allocated $8,800 per month to Jarblum, but it is not known how much was received. The WJC fought to prove it played a larger role in rescue work than the JDC, especially over the Spanish border crossings, cf. Haim Avni, op. cit., pp. 555–90. According to one internal memo, the WJC provided a total of $90,000 for rescue in France. American Jewish Archives, WJC (coll. 361) file D49/19, France (children). Riegner, Gerhard "Note sur l'action de sauvetage d'enfants en France" 4/12/1945. Bauer and Lazare refrain from determining the official amounts provided by these two organizations, for lack of documentation.

⁵⁵ Cf footnote 11 of this Chapter.

⁵⁶ This is a reproduction of Bauer's table (see Yehuda Bauer, *American Jewry*, op. cit., p 244), which unfortunately appears to contain an error: for the year 1943 he reaches the figure of 31.7 per cent by adding the official sum ($1,748,500) to an exceptional unofficial sum ($789,599) and the figure for payments from Switzerland ($149,935). Yet for 1944, he seems to consider the money from Switzerland as included in the official figure for France ($1,657,223). It is therefore not possible to know if the money from Switzerland was in addition to or included in the official allocations.

⁵⁷ This range was reached by the author to account for the ambiguity in Bauer's original table. The low end of the range was determined by dividing the official allocations by the total JDC global budget (14.2 per cent) and the high end by

Discourses on the role of the American Joint Distribution Committee

If the JDC provided the majority of the funds for rescue and resistance in France, how can we characterize its role during World War II? Did it "guide and motivate," as Schwartz reported in 1942, or was it merely a "central treasury," as Jefroykin suggested in 1944?[58] Furthermore, do accusations of the passivity of the JDC during the war hold up when compared with the actions that occurred in the name of this organization in France? An underlying theme here is "ownership": if rescue and resistance were paid for by an outside organization yet performed by another body, which group can take credit? This theme proves particularly important to understanding the postwar reconstruction of French Jewish life after the Shoah, a period during which the cooperation between the JDC and the French Jewish leadership intensified greatly.

Primary sources on the role of the JDC provide a glimpse into the complexity of these questions, as strikingly different conclusions can be drawn according to the date and the nature of the source. As seen above, Jefroykin was given *carte blanche* but with the limitation of "no armed resistance." Transcriptions of telephone conversations between Saly Mayer and the Lisbon office confirm the desire of the JDC to remain legal.[59] This supports the theory of a legalistic-minded JDC, as reflected in the JDC chairman Paul Baerwald's words (cf page 1), a theory advanced by political opponents of the JDC[60] and criticized by historian Monty Penkower and others.

---

dividing the sum of the official, unofficial and Swiss allocations by the total budget (19.8 per cent).

[58] Cf note 1.

[59] JDC-NY, Saly Mayer (SM) Archive, File 33: SM Lisbon conversation with Robert (most likely Robert Pilpel), 11 July 1944 and SM Lisbon Conversation, to Joe (most likely Joseph Schwartz), 1 August 1944: "SM: He [Marc Jarblum] has to tell me if money is also being used for Resistance, otherwise I cannot account for all the money allotted for relief. I do understand that Joint is not paying any money towards Resistance Joe: quite right." This is most likely a conversation between Mayer and Schwartz (no other persons by the name of Joe worked in Lisbon) and thus counters Bauer's observation that Schwartz never made such discouraging statements to Mayer; see Yehuda Bauer, *American Jewry*, op. cit., p. 256.

[60] Supporters of the World Jewish Congress, among others, have criticized the JDC for inaction. For an example, see the oral history interview with Joseph

Yet oral history sources—the actors' recall—reveal a different version of the facts, shedding light on what could not be written down during the war. For example, Joseph Schwartz, interviewed in 1967, indicated that all communication was censored, including telephone lines.[61] When faced with Saly Mayer's direct questions, it may have been difficult to advance a more nuanced position than the one in strict accordance with American regulations. Schwartz also emphasizes informal verbal agreements with the US Treasury department, and an overall priority of saving lives over saving records. Furthermore, Schwartz states that he knew about and supported rescue and resistance in France, which is confirmed in oral history interviews with Jules (Dika) Jefroykin.[62] Finally, a recent oral history interview conducted with a former employee of the JDC highlights new evidence to support the active role of Schwartz during World War II. This individual referred to a series of cables that have remained in obscurity, which reflect a high level of conflict between Joseph Schwartz and the leadership of the organization in New York. According to this source, Joseph Schwartz threatened to resign from his position as director of overseas operations if the organization did not support his attempts to save lives.[63] This information, in addition to the overwhelming financial contribution of the JDC, establishes a more active portrayal of this organization.

How does one reconcile these two different images? Historian Yehuda Bauer provides several helpful observations. Firstly, he acknowledges that the JDC pursued a "double policy" on France: one set of directions was given to Jefroykin and Brener in France, while European headquarters in Lisbon maintained a legalistic stance with Mayer in Switzerland.[64]

Kruh, "Croustillon," member of the AJ, in the Latour Collection of the CDJC (DLXI-54). Croustillon was sent to Spain to seek JDC support for illegal border crossings, yet he failed to gain the trust of the JDC. He did manage to obtain funds from the WJC, which then attempted to claim a larger role than the JDC in rescue work in France; see Yehuda Bauer, *American Jewry*, op. cit., pp. 184–5, 212–15. Haim Avni, op. cit., pp. 555–90, bases his analysis of the crossings into Spain on the Central Zionist Archives, leading to a more positive portrayal of the WJC and critical view of the JDC.

[61] Joseph Schwartz, OHD (47)19, pp. 1–17.
[62] Jules Jefroykin, OHD (1)61, pp. 1–33.
[63] Interview conducted by author with former JDC employee, Paris, 3 July 2006. This person has asked to remain anonymous in this context.
[64] Yehuda Bauer, *American Jewry*, op. cit., p. 256.

Secondly, Bauer's study of the overall activity of the JDC during World War II enables him to discern the establishment of three separate "branches" of the JDC—New York, Lisbon and the local committees in individual countries—which were "experiencing conditions so utterly different that the emergence of different philosophies as well as of widely diverging views on practical matters was quite natural."[65] Our own research concurs with Bauer's observations by emphasizing the need for a broad reading of the sources, both oral and written. The oral sources, even if they may be exaggerated through memory, point out the need to accept a certain level of ambiguity and uncertainty, as lives were clearly more important than records to the director of JDC's European operations.

In closing, let us return to the issue of ownership—who can receive credit for the Jewish resistance?—in order to understand how the post-war period was influenced by the war, but also how that period conditioned our vision of the JDC and the Jewish resistance. The 1942–44 period is crucial for understanding how the JDC was able to return to France with American management and speak with credibility. In contrast to the inter-war period, we see that the JDC selected new contact points within the French Jewish population: the immigration Zionist faction moved to a new prominence in Jewish life and became close interlocutors of the JDC, forming the leadership of post-war Jewish institutions. This shift began long before the liberation, as seen in the selection of Jefroykin as representative for France in 1942. On a personal but symbolic note, one cannot help being reminded of the marriage between Laura Margolis, JDC director for France from 1946 to 1953, and the Zionist Marc Jarblum.[66] Secondly, the JDC's support for both Jewish resistance and post-war Jewish organizations, by enabling and organizing their existence, indirectly encouraged overlap between these two forms of aid to the Jewish population.[67] The Jewish resistance repre-

---

[65] Yehuda Bauer, op. cit., p. 178.
[66] This marriage shocked many, especially the highest realms of the native French Jewish establishment. Interview with Tito and Gaby Cohen, conducted by author, Paris, 2 August 2005.
[67] Les Anciens de la Résistance Juive, op. cit., dedicated to the members of the Organisation Juive de Combat, can be read as a postwar roster of Jewish social services. Examples, followed by postwar affiliations, include Maurice Brener and Ignace Fink (COJASOR), Gaby Wolff Cohen (OSE, JDC, FSJU), and Vivette Samuel (OSE), just to cite a few.

sented a body of young individuals with a strong sense of duty, who had largely been deprived of educational and professional opportunities during key formative years. Because of this ideological commitment, social work was seen as a form of peacetime resistance. It also lay at the heart of misunderstandings between the American JDC social workers, who emphasized distance, professionalism, and accountability, and the French Jewish communal workers, who saw the need to provide the education and love of missing parents to ensure the future of French Judaism.[68]

If the JDC support for the Jewish resistance in France influenced the post-war reconstruction of Jewish life, we must also note the role of post-war reconstruction in shaping the discourse on the JDC's wartime activities. Indeed, the JDC remained the largest source of funding for Jewish welfare in France until the 1960s. Financial dependence on American funds influenced the way French Jewish leaders publicly discussed the JDC. Toward the end of the war, these leaders feared the JDC would not recognize the debt that had been contracted in its name.[69] Once the JDC did so, it appears that it was "rewarded" with the small means French Jewry had at its disposal. Notably, in the battlefield of international Jewish organizational life, credit for rescue and resistance was given to the JDC over its competitors, such as the WJC. For example, the Armée Juive signed an accord with the JDC, turning over children who crossed the Spanish border under their aegis to this organization, instead of to the WJC, which had prepared a children's home in Lisbon. Jefroykin explains the factors, both ideological and pragmatic, that motivated this accord:

I had pushed a lot for the agreement [between the AJ and the JDC] that was established after the infamous story of the World Jewish Congress home in Lisbon, since I was the Joint's representative and God, I knew that if we eventually had managed to do anything in France it was thanks to the JDC's money, and it was after Dr. Schwartz had declared that the JDC considered itself responsible for all the money I had spent in France, and as a consequence, it was normal for

---

[68] Gaby Wolff Cohen, Interview, Paris, 38 May 2004.
[69] Letter from Joseph Fisher to Joseph Schwartz, 17 April 1944, JDC-NY, Saly Mayer Archive, 1939–50, file 33, indicates the JDC did not initially recognize part of the loans obtained in its name. In the meantime, JDC officials in New York tried to find a way to lessen their costs, suggesting that those who would be reimbursed should be required to donate for post-war reconstruction; Memorandum (no author, internal JDC), 6 December 1944, JDC-NY, file 596 general, file 2 of 2, France 1942–44.

the JDC to get what it deserved. As much as I was opposed to a political agreement with the JDC given the circumstances at the time, I was in favor of a social agreement with the JDC (...). The JDC had the merit of having provided the necessary funds throughout the Occupation to rescue thousands and thousands of Jews, not the World Jewish Congress."[70]

Our inquiry into the role of the JDC in France from 1942 to 1944 has allowed us to revisit the sources that buttress the historical accounts of this period. These accounts inform our analysis, allowing us to discern the key individuals and means the JDC employed in order to remain active after the break in diplomatic relations between the United States and Vichy. We establish that the JDC supported rescue and resistance among Jews in France both through financial contributions and through the leadership of Dr Joseph Schwartz. Our analysis of primary sources points to contradictory discourses on the JDC support for resistance in France. Furthermore, we highlight that the nature and the period of the sources influence the conclusions that can be drawn. In addition, we show that the second half of the war influenced the way the JDC was to reinsert itself into post-war Jewish life. Finally, we demonstrate that post-war concerns of the French Jewish leadership and the JDC emphasized the JDC's role in resistance and rescue, presenting the JDC as an equal partner, allowing Jefroykin to conclude in a JDC publication that in its decision to fund clandestine activities, the JDC "left its position at headquarters to enter onto the battlefield."[71] We are still left to wonder who made this decision.

---

[70] Jules Jefroykin, OHD (1)61, pp. 31–2.
[71] "Il quittait son poste à l'Etat-major pour pénétrer sur le champ de bataille." Jules (Dika) Jefroykin, "Témoignage de Jules Jefroykin," *Echanges: périodique consacré aux Oeuvres juives de santé, d'assistance sociale et d'éducation*, 20, 1964, p. 24.

19

THE BBC HUNGARIAN SERVICE AND RESCUE OF JEWS OF HUNGARY, 1940–1945

Frank Chalk

From the 1970s, archival research revealed that at certain crucial moments during World War II American and British government officials played down evidence of coordinated German efforts to annihilate the Jewish people in Europe, and sidestepped requests to receive large numbers of Jews as refugees when it seemed that the fate from which they might be rescued was certain death. Historian William D. Rubinstein argues that the possibility of the Allies saving Jews from Nazi genocide once World War II was underway is little but a myth.[1] According to Rubinstein, the main thing the Allies could do when faced with Hitler's determination to kill all Jews was exactly what they did do—try to win the war as swiftly as possible and then liberate the surviving inmates of the ghettos and camps. Rubinstein takes issue with critical scholarship blaming the Allies for doing too little to aid the victims. But it is the first major argument of the present chapter that he fails to identify the Allies' late, limited and unimaginative use of radio broadcasting. This paper argues that BBC broadcasts to Hungary were a weapon capable of providing early warning to even the most isolated Jews and of alerting them to the Nazis mass murders while it was still possible for some to flee, and for others to seek

[1] *The Myth of Rescue*, London, Routledge, 1997.

sanctuary with the aid of neighbors similarly alerted and mobilized by the power of radio.

The second major argument of this chapter—truncated because of length constraints—is that lessons learned from studying the failure of the BBC Hungarian Service to assist in the rescue of Jews during the Holocaust also apply to the Rwanda genocide of 1994 and can still be applied profitably in new cases of apprehended genocide and crimes against humanity. But before those lessons can be applied, we must first understand the reasons for the Allied failure to use radio to broadcast early warnings to the victims and mobilize local rescuers in Hungary.

To London

When did the news of the mass murder of Jews first reach the Allies? By November 1941, the German *Einsatzgruppen* had killed about half a million Jews and reports of the massacres were beginning to reach the Jewish Telegraphic Agency, which published them in the *Jewish Chronicle*. In June 1942, the BBC broadcast evidence from various reports originating in Eastern Europe, including some from the Jewish Labor Bund, that by spring 1942 700,000 Jews had already been murdered. The London *Daily Telegraph* summarized these reports in two articles published that June: "More than 700,000 Polish Jews have been slaughtered by the Germans in the greatest massacres in the world's history," the first dispatch began. There followed details, supplied by Shmuel Zygielbojm of the Polish Bund, recounting the use of mobile gas vans. The second article published by the *Telegraph* a few days later announced that more than 1,000,000 Jews had been killed in cold blood and that the Nazis planned "to wipe the [Jewish] race from the European continent," including Jews living in Western Europe. By September 1942, at least a million and a half Jews had been killed and the Warsaw Ghetto had been practically emptied of Jews. That the Nazis might be systematically planning to kill all the Jews of Europe using poison gas received further confirmation in a cable, based on information from a well-placed German industrialist, which Dr Gerhardt Riegner, the representative of the World Jewish Congress, sent to the British and American governments in July 1942.[2]

---

[2] Walter Laqueur, *The Terrible Secret: An Investigation into the Suppression of Information about Hitler's 'Final Solution'*, London: Weidenfeld and Nicolson, 1980, pp. 73–90.

For its own reasons, the British Foreign Office took a decidedly cool view of reports recognizing and advertising a coordinated plan to end the lives of all European Jews, choosing to believe, at least publicly, that able-bodied Jews were cruelly treated, but kept alive because they still were needed by the Germans as laborers. The Foreign Office's public statements persisted in this vein throughout most of 1942, despite what must have been a treasure trove of contrary information gleaned from neutrals living in Germany and the decoding of intercepted German wireless reports on the mass killing of Jews by the staff of Project Ultra at Bletchley Park.[3]

On 16 and 17 December 1942, the British Government, in concert with ten other Allied governments and the Free France Committee, issued a major joint declaration announcing to the world that the German authorities were carrying out a mass deportation of Jews:

> From all the occupied countries Jews are being transported in conditions of appalling horror and brutality to Eastern Europe... The above-mentioned Governments and the French National Committee condemn in the strongest possible terms this bestial policy of cold-blooded extermination.... They re-affirm their solemn resolution to ensure that those responsible for these crimes shall not escape retribution ....

Breakthrough though it was, the Allied announcement contained a number of oddities. It made no mention of death camps where poison gas was used, although that fact was by now well known to senior Allied officials. While it used the phrase "cold-blooded extermination," the only substance given to the term was in the reference to the transportation of Jews to Eastern Europe under inhuman conditions. Nothing in the statement spoke of the fate of the Jews once they arrived in Eastern Europe. And were those Jews already living in Eastern Europe being spared the experience of "horror and brutality" because they were already in the East?

It would not have been surprising if many who heard the Allied announcement in Axis Europe, Britain and America had thought that the crime referred to in the statement was the brutality of the deportations of Jews under horrible conditions rather than their deliberate mur-

---

[3] Laqueur, *Terrible Secret*, pp. 82–90; Richard Breitman, *Official Secrets: What the Nazis Planned, What the British and Americans Knew*, New York, Hill & Wang, 1998, especially Chapter 6.

der. In context, "cold-blooded extermination" seemed to refer to the breaking of the age old bonds of community created over centuries by Jewish residents of cities, villages, and towns throughout Central and Western Europe. The authors of the Allied announcement omitted the key "get it"—that millions of Jews were being *systematically murdered in cold blood* because the Nazi perpetrators assigned them to membership in a racial group whose significance, identity and boundaries were constructs of the perpetrator's ideology.[4]

The fuzziness of British statements denouncing the treatment of Jews reflects the ambivalence of the majority of Allied officials who were still unwilling to identify the treatment of Jews as something systematic, intentionally lethal and nearly unparalleled among Nazi atrocities. About two weeks before the joint Allied statement was issued, on 27 November 1942, Derek Law of the British Foreign Office had written: "It is of course undeniable that large scale persecutions are taking place, but whether they are the result of a plan is more questionable." Earlier in November, the Foreign and Home News Board of the BBC reported: "we are considering the question as to whether there is a 'plan' of murder …In the meantime it seems desirable to soft pedal the whole thing."[5] Lack of clarity about the scope and intent of the Nazis' crime suggests that the Foreign Office still wanted to avoid the policy consequences for Britain and the United States of pinpointing what the Nazis were actually doing.

The British were especially afraid that a tidal wave of public opinion would form in the West, putting them under overwhelming pressure to admit hundreds of thousands of European Jewish refugees to Palestine. After the Allied invasion of North Africa in November 1942, senior American commanders and Secretary of War Henry L. Stimson feared a similar build up of pressure around them to admit large numbers of European Jewish refugees to liberated North Africa. Stimson noted in his diary on 27 December 1942 that in French North Africa there were

[4] State Department Press Release, 16 December 1942, quoted in Richard Breitman and Alan M. Kraut, *American Refugee Policy and European Jewry: 1933–1945*, Bloomington, Indiana University Press, 1987, p. 160.
[5] See BBC Written Archives, R34/178, Foreign Adviser News, 2 November 1942, cited in Jean Seaton, "Reporting Atrocities: The BBC and the Holocaust," in Jean Seaton and Ben Pimlott (eds), *The Media in British Politics*, Aldershot, Avebury, 1987, p. 167 and note 53, p. 181.

25 million Arabs and only 350,000 Jews. German propaganda in North Africa already claimed that the Allies intended to turn North Africa over to the Jews. The United States, Stimson told President Roosevelt, was vulnerable to such claims and would be playing into Germany's hands if it resettled thousands of Jewish refugees in the region.[6]

Jean Seaton, who has studied the relevant documents in the British archives, argues that three major factors explain the refusal of the British Political Warfare Executive (PWE)[7] and its main media instrument, the BBC World Service, to widely broadcast to the home audience that the Nazis were pursuing concerted actions all over Europe to annihilate enormous numbers of Jews supposedly unfit for labor and to work the remainder to death as slave laborers:

1. Rather than making the British public more sympathetic to the plight of the Jewish victims of the Nazis, BBC administrators believed that the Allies' December 1942 announcement had brought latent British anti-Semitism to the surface.[8]
2. Officials at the BBC believed that to broadcast domestic programs specifically intended to arouse sympathy for the plight of European Jews would be to fall into the Nazi trap of emphasizing racialism.[9]
3. BBC officials regarded anti-Semitism as "an historical anachronism" and refused to take it seriously.[10]

Social anti-Semitism among BBC staff and government officials played a much smaller role in deciding how the Corporation would report on the Holocaust than any one of these three major factors, Jean Seaton found.[11]

---

[6] See Richard Breitman and Alan M. Kraut, *American Refugee Policy and European Jewry: 1933–1945*, Bloomington, Indiana University Press, 1987, p. 170.

[7] The Political Warfare Executive integrated in August 1941 parts of the Ministry of Information, the Special Operations Executive, and the British Broadcasting Corporation. It was responsible for all British propaganda in all enemy and enemy-occupied lands. The Foreign Office retained the right to participate in regard to propaganda on foreign policy issues addressed to enemy territory. The PWE held the authority to issue instructions and guidelines to the BBC. See Richard Breitman, *Official Secrets: What the Nazis Planned, What the British and Americans Knew*, New York, Hill and Wang, 1998, p. 102.

[8] Seaton, "Reporting Atrocities," p. 170.

[9] Seaton, "Reporting Atrocities," p. 175.

[10] Seaton, "Reporting Atrocities," p. 172.

[11] Seaton's view that social anti-Semitism was a less important factor may have

In Hungary

By March 1944, the Jews of Hungary were the largest surviving group of Jews within Germany's sphere of influence. Following the Munich Agreement of 1938, Hungarian Jews numbered some 500,000 persons or about 5 per cent of Hungary's population of 10 million. An additional 100,000 Jews in Hungary had converted to Christianity; many of these converts also came to be constructed as members of the "Jewish race" under Hungary's third anti-Jewish law when it was adopted by the Government of Hungary in 1941.[12]

Hungarian Jewry was divided into two distinct parts. The first consisted of the orthodox Jews of rural Hungary, who "led a miserable existence" as destitute small shopkeepers, artisans and farmers, and who suffered from "an extremely high birth and death rate." The much more prosperous Jews of Budapest and the suburbs included "merchants, some tradesmen and to a very high percentage physicians, lawyers, engineers, employees, clerks, journalists, actors, etc." In Budapest, some 200,000 out of one million inhabitants were Jews.[13] The economic indispensability of the urban Jews of Hungary and the fact that they survived until the middle of 1944 when the Germans had already annihilated some five million Jews in other parts of Europe lulled the Jews of Hungary into a false sense of security, as Raul Hilberg points out.[14]

Even while they were being officially separated from their livelihoods by a series of Hungarian government decrees introduced from 1938 to

---

to be revised in light of the claim by Marista Leishman, the daughter of Lord Reith, founder of the BBC, that her father "abhorred Jews." *My Father–Reith of the BBC* was published by St Andrew Press in September 2006. See Marc Horne, "Lord Reith Revered Hitler, says Daughter," *The Sunday Times*, 24 September 2006.

[12] Tim Cole, "Constructing the 'Jew', Writing the Holocaust: Hungary 1920–45," *Patterns of Prejudice*, 33, 3 (1999), 21–25; Document, "The Position of Hungarian Jewry, c. February 1939," in Nathaniel Katzburg, *Hungary and the Jews: Policy and Legislation 1920–1943*, Ramat-Gan, Bar-Ilan University Press, 1981, 269–71.

[13] Document, "The Position of Hungarian Jewry, c. February 1939," in Nathaniel Katzburg, *Hungary and the Jews*, pp. 270–1.

[14] Raul Hilberg, *The Destruction of the European Jews*, Chicago: Quadrangle Books, 1961, pp. 510 and 514.

1944, the Jews of Hungary had every reason to think that their remaining economic value to Hungary at least granted them a measure of protection from mass annihilation. Their fatal blind spot, as historian Christian Gerlach has recently pointed out, was their failure to anticipate that opportunistic initiatives by right-wing Hungarian extremists and a strategically-motivated German invasion of Hungary would converge to vaporize their protection. The very wealth and status of some Hungarian Jews, Gerlach shows, encouraged the Hungarian political extremists to view the elimination of the Hungarian Jews and the seizure and redistribution of their property as the keys to stabilizing the Far Right's political victory and building its path to eventual freedom from German control.[15]

Many Hungarian survivors of the Holocaust say they knew very little about the mass killings of Jews elsewhere and did not believe the rumors they heard. They use words similar to Andrew Salamon's when they speak today of listening to BBC's Hungarian Service during the Holocaust. For Salamon, the BBC was "like a ray of light piercing the darkness surrounding us" and served as "our lifeline to the outside world." Salamon recalls Jewish refugees in Hungary speaking about the "mass evacuation of Jewish communities and the disappearance of those deported to some unknown destination," as well as Nazi atrocities committed in Austria and Poland. But he and his family, he writes, "could not fathom the full meaning of what the anti-Semitic press described as the 'final solution' of the Jewish question. We imagined to ourselves some mass, forced exodus of all of us to some far away, inhospitable land–Uganda, perhaps, or Mauritius."[16] Salamon's family, like many resourceful Jewish families, refused to surrender all their radios. "We handed in an old crystal radio set, which had ceased to work years before… We also handed in the large furniture-sized radio which would have been impossible to conceal… We kept for ourselves a smaller radio apparatus," he remembers.[17]

Scholars often argue that the Hungarian Jews had every reason to know that a German invasion of Hungary followed by "transportation to

---

[15] Christian Gerlach, "The Decision-Making Process for the Deportation of Hungarian Jews," an overview of Dr Gerlach's research on German decision-making for Hungary in 1944 provided by courtesy of the author, 2006.
[16] Andrew Salamon, *Childhood in Time of War*, Montreal, Concordia University Chair in Canadian Jewish Studies, 2001. Available on the Web at: http://migs.concordia.ca/memoirs/salamon/salamon_whole.html
[17] Ibid.

the east" would mean death for them. Sociologist Helen Fein concludes that provincial Jews, isolated from news and undervalued by *Judenrate* leaders in Budapest, either ignored or denied the early warning signs around them, as did Jews in many other parts of Europe.[18] Historian Asher Cohen points out that Zionist youth *halutzim* (pioneers or messengers) carried news to Hungarian Jewish communities between 1942 and 1944 telling them about the destruction of Polish and Slovak Jewry.[19] From the evidence he collected, Cohen found:

> First, that there was extensive information available in Hungary about the Final Solution prior to March 1944; and, second, that the information on the mass extermination of vast numbers of Jews appeared to have no practical implications for the future of local Jewry.[20]

Historian Yehuda Bauer emphasizes more strongly than Cohen Hungarian Jewry's doubts that the information it possessed constituted accurate knowledge on which it had to act if it hoped to survive. Bauer lists many human sources who could have provided Hungarian Jews with crucial knowledge of the fate that awaited them if they registered to join the "transports to the East," but, he argues, people "did not want to believe that what they did not want to hear was the truth."[21] He does not blame them since most had no place to hide, no one to help them, and nowhere to run. Their situation made them vulnerable to German tactics, according to Bauer:

> When the Germans told them that they were being sent to labour camps, they believed it, in many cases one can say that they believed it eagerly, because it saved them from facing a life-endangering truth… They behaved, as a group… not unlike a patient with a terminal illness who refuses to admit his or her condition.[22]

---

[18] Helen Fein, *Accounting for Genocide: National Responses and Jewish Victimization during the Holocaust*, New York, The Free Press, 1979, pp. 324–5.

[19] Asher Cohen, "Resistance and Rescue in Hungary," in David Cesarani, *Genocide and Rescue: The Holocaust in Hungary*, 1944, Oxford: Berg, 1997, pp. 124–6.

[20] Cohen, "Resistance and Rescue in Hungary," p. 126.

[21] Yehuda Bauer, "Conclusion: The Holocaust in Hungary–Was Rescue Possible?" in David Cesarani, *Genocide and Rescue: The Holocaust in Hungary*, 1944, Oxford, Berg, 1997, p. 196.

[22] Ibid.

FRANK CHALK

The BBC Hungarian Service in action

As abundant survivor testimony shows, Hungarian Jews revered the BBC Hungarian Service. They risked their lives to listen to it. In periods of uncertainty they relied on "Auntie,"[23] as the BBC was known at home, to follow the progress of the war and as an authoritative Allied antidote to Nazi propaganda saturating Hungary's airwaves. In light of BBC's influence, we need to ask: 1) What did the Political Warfare Executive want the BBC Hungarian Service to tell listeners about the Holocaust in Europe in the years before Germany's invasion of Hungary on 19 March 1944?, 2) Did the BBC urge Jews to flee Hungary or go into hiding in 1942 when Germany for the first time strongly pressured Hungary to hand over its Jews?, 3) What efforts did the BBC make from 1939 to 1944 to interest Hungarian Christians in assisting Jews while they suffered under Hungary's anti-Semitic regime?, 4) Did the PWE understand what a German invasion would mean for the fate of hundreds of thousands of Hungarian Jews?, 5) What contingency plans did the BBC make to react if Germany invaded Hungary?, 6) When the Hungarian gendarmes and their German advisers demanded in March and April 1944 that Jews should be concentrated in ghettos and camps served by nearby rail lines for transportation to labor in the East, what advice did BBC broadcast to them?, 7) How did the BBC react to firm intelligence while the process was underway that hundreds of thousands of Hungarian Jews were being gassed to death at Auschwitz from May to July 1944?

Answers to these questions can be found by examining the manuscript records of the Hungarian Service of the BBC at the BBC Written Archives in Caversham Park and the records of the Political Warfare Executive at the National Archives in Kew. BBC Hungarian Service broadcasts were guided by the PWE's "Plan of Political Warfare for Hungary." The plan was the result of consultations and negotiations in February and March 1942 between Ralph Murray of the PWE and Britain's leading academic expert on inter-war Hungary, Professor Carlisle Aylmer Macartney of the University of Oxford.[24] The plan set out four basic objectives for British radio broadcasts to Hungary:

---

[23] The phrase "Auntie knows best" is commonly understood to be the origin of this nickname.

[24] See Political Warfare Executive, "Plan of Political Warfare for Hungary," Draft

1. To reduce the Hungarian military effort on behalf of Germany;
2. To reduce Hungarian food and general supplies to Germany;
3. To impede German communications through Hungary; [and]
4. Eventually to compel Germany to divert a certain number of troops to Hungary, either as a safeguard against disorders and sabotage, or as an occupying force.

Objectives one and two could be achieved in the short-term, Murray argued, through political and social propaganda. Objective three would be the work of "individual exploits," but British propaganda could "create an atmosphere favorable to them." Objective four could only be achieved at the conclusion of a lengthy "plan of political and social propaganda." It took for granted the desirability of forcing the Germans to station troops in Hungary, away from the Western Front.

Constraining the BBC's broadcasts to Hungary was Professor Macartney's warning that Britain must tread carefully through the minefield of Hungarian politics and must never identify its cause in Hungary with a host of taboo groups and -isms including:

Legitimism.
High Toryism and positive support for the "feudal" idea, large landed interests, etc.
Big business and capitalist interests.
The names of liberalism and democracy. Each of these has been so twisted in Hungary as to bear today an unfortunate connotation: "liberalism," that of unrestricted Jewish exploitation of the peasant and worker; "democracy," a mask for Czech hegemony in the Danube basin.
Jews in general.
Anything containing more than a cautious and qualified mention of the word "international."
"Octoberism," i.e. the Karolyi regime of 1918–19.
Communism or Bolshevism.[25]

Macartney introduced the BBC to the idea of the "floating vote" to characterize the political situation in Hungary:

---

of 3 February 1942, FO371/30965, 1942 Hungary, File No. 116, UK, National Archives (PRO), Kew.

[25] Carlisle A. Macartney, Foreign Research and Press Service, Balliol College, Oxford, Memorandum, 17 February 1942, FO371/30965, 1942 Hungary, File No. 116, PRO.

...it is important to remember that the great majority of opinion in Hungary is really a sort of floating vote. The irreconcilables on either side are really very few, and include few Magyars indeed: the irreconcilable pro-German group is mostly Swabian, the pro-British [group], Jewish. It is more important to gain the floating vote than to please the faithful supporters.[26]

Pro-Germans in Hungary argued, according to Macartney, that if Britain won the war:

We shall once again bring about the dismemberment of Hungary; alternatively, or in addition, that we shall Bolshevize Central Europe, including Hungary; and thirdly, that we represent a form of anti-social Judeo-capitalism, an antiquated social system which contrasts dismally with the blessings of the [German] New Order. The latter will bring Hungary an assured market, with elimination of Jewish exploitation.[27]

Macartney sympathized with the charge of "Jewish exploitation." He revealed his attitude first in his discussion of those who would "regard the things of which we are accused as desirable *per se*": there were Communists; there were Jewish financial interests; and there were supporters of antiquated social systems in various forms. Authentic Magyarism, Macartney continued, incorporated the idea of Christianity, "But both German and Swabian influence and international Judaism are rejected." The Hungarian Church was "fairly strongly anti-Semitic," he noted, "and the whole trend of thought is clearly permeated by the feeling—not unjustified—that in the past Jews made a much better thing out of Hungary than the poorer Magyars did themselves."[28]

Macartney recommended that BBC make no mention of Jewish Hungarians in its Hungarian broadcasts: "We should not mention the Jews at all except to say that on the one hand we want a national Hungary, on the other hand, a tolerant Hungary—appeal to Hungary's traditions real or imagined."[29]

The Political Warfare Executive rejected a counterview propounded by Major Peter Broughey of the Special Operations Executive that BBC broadcasters should concentrate on winning over Leftist Hungarian groups who were most likely to become active in sabotage and to take

[26] Ibid.
[27] Ibid.
[28] Ibid.
[29] Ibid.

part in a revolutionary post-war government of Hungary. Arguing that Hungary stood to lose if Britain and Russia won the war and that the BBC could never convince the present rulers of Hungary—"the landowners and the bourgeoisie"—Broughey advocated winning over Leftist groups "who are more concerned with civil liberties than territorial gains [for Hungary]."[30] Broughey's analysis rolled off the Foreign Office like water off a duck's back. "There is a long standing difference of opinion between S.O.E. and the F.O. on the question of our Hungarian propaganda," M.J.A. Spears minuted for the Foreign Office. "Since Hungarian propaganda policy is not the business of the S.O.E. there seems to be no point in embarking on a controversy with Major Boughey."[31]

Under the guidelines of February and March 1942, Jews were barely mentioned in BBC broadcasts to Hungary from 1942 until Germany invaded Hungary in March 1944. The Germans, on the other hand, kept their eyes on the Jews of Hungary like a pack of hungry wolves trailing an injured sheep. In September and October 1942, they increased their pressure on the Hungarian government to surrender Hungary's Jews to the Final Solution. Döme Sztójay, the Hungarian Minister to Berlin, reported that the Germans had elevated the Jewish question to the major issue between Hungary and Germany. Sztójay recommended that the Kallay government speed up the resettlement of Hungarian Jews in occupied Russia and admitted that "resettlement" really meant annihilation. But Prime Minister Miklos Kállay refused.[32]

In January 1943, 850,000 Axis troops, including at least 120,000 Hungarian soldiers, were killed, wounded, or captured by the Russians in the Battle of Stalingrad. Leaders in Hungary and Romania took note and began to search for ways to distance themselves from the German alliance and join the Allies. The Germans detected their new body language, and noted Kallay's continuing refusal to send Hungarian Jews to ghettos and concentration camps.[33]

---

[30] Major Peter Broughey, SOE, to Frank Roberts, FO, 27 September 1942, FO371/30965/Hungary, PRO.
[31] Political Warfare Executive Weekly Directive for B.B.C. Hungarian Service, 1–8 September 1944, FO371/39272, PRO.
[32] Summarized in Nathaniel Katzburg, *Hungary and the Jews*, pp. 221–2, note 20.
[33] Political Warfare Executive, Weekly Directive for B.B.C. Hungarian Service, 19–25 December 1942, FO371/39272, PRO.

The Jewish Agency's office in Britain contemplated Admiral Horthy's possibly premature defection from Hungary's alliance with Germany with some trepidation about its consequences for Hungarian Jewry. While forcing Germany to divert some of its troops to Hungary was one of the four long-term goals elaborated in Britain's propaganda plan of February 1942, the consequences of a German military occupation for Hungary's 800,000 Jews could be catastrophic. Lewis B. Namier, representing the Political Department of the Jewish Agency in London, visited the Foreign Office on 13 October 1943 to discuss the matter. He stated:

The Jews here [in Britain]... feel that Germany could not possibly tolerate Hungarian defection, and as long as the German army was in position to do so would answer such a move by the Hungarian government by a German occupation of the country, the result of which would be extermination of the last important body of Jewry left in Europe.[34]

Alec Walter George Randall of the Foreign Office replied that Britain had listed this consideration "as a reason for Hungary not making any premature move to the Allied side."[35] In fact, I have found no archival evidence that the British asked Hungary to delay its withdrawal from the alliance with Germany or that they took seriously into account saving the lives of Hungarian Jews. British policy and the BBC's Hungarian service worked toward only one goal: to advance the cause of an Allied victory in the War. In January 1944, three months before the German invasion, the BBC used every means at its disposal to rally Hungarians to rise up against the Germans and their Hungarian collaborators. It exhorted them to derive their inspiration from the Yugoslav Partisans, who were tying down fifteen German divisions, according to the BBC broadcasts. It urged Hungarians to demand the return to Hungary of its troops fighting the Russians on the Eastern front. A Mr Petrovic and other BBC Hungarian Service broadcasters underscored the importance of acts of resistance to dissolve Hungary's reputation as a fascist collaborator state.[36]

---

[34] FO 371/34498 C12035 quoted in Katzburg, *Hungary and the Jews*, p. 223.
[35] Ibid.
[36] Mr Petrovic, Yugoslavia's Fight, Hungarian News Talk, 21 January 1944, FB, Folder Hungarian News Talks, 1/1/44–31/3/44 in B.B.C. Written Archives Centre, Hungarian Talks Scripts (in Hungarian), January–December 1944, Karolyi Statements Scripts, 1944–1945; also see N. Szusz, Questions for the Workers, Hungarian News Talk, 28 January 1944, ibid.

Fears in the British and American governments that calling attention to the mass murder of Jews would heighten anti-Semitism at home and produce a political backlash against the party in power persisted throughout the war. On 8 March 1944, less than two weeks before the Germans marched into Hungary, John W. Pehle, director of the War Refugee Board, met with Judge Samuel Rosenman, one of President Roosevelt's closest political advisers. Rosenman declared that the President "wanted the statement rewritten so as to be aimed less directly at the atrocities against the Jews." Pehle pointed out that the Moscow Statement of Atrocities issued in November 1943 by the Big Three

> had made no reference to the atrocities against the Jews as such, and that while that might not be important in the United States it was singularly important in Germany where the people were led to believe that this country was not concerned at all about the atrocities against the Jews who were not particularly human beings.

To Pehle's rejoinder, Rosenman, who was Jewish, replied: "I don't agree with you. Do you want me to say I agree with you when I don't?" According to Pehle's confidential memorandum detailing the meeting, "Rosenman then went on to say that he had advised the President not to sign the declaration because of its pointed reference to Jews because he felt any such statement would intensify anti-Semitism in the United States."[37]

Aware of Hungarian peace overtures to the Allies through intercepts of Hungarian diplomatic messages and from sympathizers in the Horthy regime, the Germans occupied Hungary on 19 March 1944.[38] A government of German-approved Hungarians was put in place on 22 March. Adolf Eichmann arrived soon afterwards in command of a Special Task Group (*Sondereinsatzkommando*) of Gestapo and SS men. A *Judenrat* was soon created.[39] On 7 April Hungarian provincial Jews were ordered into ghettos. Implementation of the order began on 15 April 1944. The Germans and their Hungarian allies deported and killed 450,000 Hungarian

---

[37] J.W. Pehle, Memorandum for the Files, 8 March 1944, in David Wyman (ed.), *War Refugee Board: Special Problems*, Vol. 9 of *America and the Holocaust*, 13 vols., New York, Garland Publishing, 1990, pp. 4–5.

[38] Robert Hanyok, *Eavesdropping on Hell: Historical Guide to Western Communications Intelligence and the Holocaust, 1939–1945*, Washington, National Security Agency, 2004, p. 97 and note 116.

[39] Hilberg, pp. 526–30.

Jews, about 70 per cent of the Jews of Greater Hungary.[40] In February 1945 the Russians liberated Budapest from the Germans and Hungarian fascist forces led by Szalasi. 119,000 Jews had survived in the city; 11,000 returned from forced labor on fortifications at the border. By August 1945, 72,000 others returned, including those who had been deported to Austria rather than Auschwitz in June 1944 (some 15,000) and those who had survived slave labor in Auschwitz and other camps.[41]

It is quite true that the German invasion of Hungary and the installation of Sztójay as Prime Minister galvanized the BBC into action. In addition to calling on Hungarians to resist the Germans and sabotage the German war effort, BBC pulled out the stops and devoted portions of many broadcasts to the importance of Hungarian Christians helping Jewish Hungarians and to warnings against collaborating with the Nazi persecution of Jews. These are the BBC broadcasts to which William Rubinstein and Yehuda Bauer point. But these broadcasts came too late. When they were delivered, Hungarian gendarmes were already rounding up Jews and escape had become far more difficult.

The lessons of history

Therein resides a key lesson. As with preparations to cope with hurricanes, floods and other natural disasters, early warnings are vital precisely because they allow potential victims and rescuers time to plan and to mobilize resources well in advance of disasters. The Allied broadcasts urging help for Hungarian Jews after the German invasion were next to useless, tantamount to informing the residents of New Orleans that they were in the middle of Hurricane Katrina the day after it struck.

My research in the BBC archives proves that from 1939 until March 1944, in keeping with Macartney's recommendations of 1942, the BBC broadcasts to Hungary ignored Hungary's anti-Semitic policies and German demands that Hungary surrender Jews for "transportation east," passing up valuable opportunities to rally the small number of Hungarian pro-Allied resisters to organize an effective Hungarian underground capable of forging documents, locating sympathizers and safe houses in the countryside, and developing effective communication networks.

---

[40] Lucy Dawidowicz, *The War Against the Jews*, p. 517.
[41] Ibid.

When the Germans invaded, the only resisters possessing these skills were a few dozen youthful members of the Zionist underground in Budapest who had honed their clandestine tradecraft through hiding Polish and Slovakian Jewish refugees. In Budapest, working together with diplomats from neutral countries, they accomplished miraculous rescues, but aid to hundreds of thousands of rural Jews was far beyond their resources.

Once the German invaders had overthrown and imprisoned the more moderate Hungarian leadership, the BBC also missed a crucial opportunity to warn Hungarian Jews against reporting for "transportation to labor in the East." Knowing the significance of Auschwitz as the destination of Hungarian trains heading north from Carpatho-Ruthenia through Slovakia in the spring and summer of 1944, the Allies had a duty to raise the alarm using every means possible. The odds are strong, given the authority of the BBC in the minds of Hungarian Jews, that explicit warnings specifically addressed to them would have broken down the psychological barriers immobilizing their defense mechanisms. Not only did the BBC not warn Hungarian Jews against reporting, it had no previously prepared contingency plan on the shelf ready for implementation when the expected German invasion took place. Even after Allied intelligence knew for a fact that hundreds of thousands of Hungarian Jews had already been gassed to death at Auschwitz, the BBC failed to inform surviving Jews that it knew the gassings were verified facts.

In *Accounting for Genocide*, Helen Fein points out that people facing imminent disasters are capable of mobilizing themselves to act when feasible actions to save themselves and their loved ones are available to them. The application of disaster theory to the Holocaust teaches us that "the recognition of collective threat did not depend primarily on the extent or directness of the reports ... but on how one could anticipate coping with the threat."[42] Here "coping" is used in the sense of the availability of practical means to resist the perpetrator or feasible routes for escape, and not in the sense of finding the psychological means to relieve stress. "The more isolated, the more likely Jews were to deny the existence of a collective threat against all Jews and to fail to acknowledge the Germans as a collective enemy, persisting instead in defining them as exploiters or oppressors," Fein observes. Isolated, vulnerable Jews disbelieved eye-

---

[42] Helen Fein, *Accounting for Genocide*, p. 314.

witness reports of mass killings, she notes, "in order to disassociate themselves from the category of the most vulnerable …"[43]

Fein expands these observations into two important conclusions:

> When the source of the danger is clear, and people can anticipate what to do to avoid it, their perception is sharpened and their energy released: they are not immobilized by anxiety but mobilized to avoid danger. But if the costs of accepting a new definition of the situation call for discarding one's social identity and disrupting one's way of life while the nature of the threat cannot be determined with certainty, people are more likely to perceive the threat as overwhelming and either to react with terror or to defend themselves against the threat by denial.[44]

In light of what we have learned about BBC broadcasts to Hungary, would different strategies of radio broadcasting have improved the outcome for the victims of genocide? While we cannot give a definitive answer to this hypothetical question, the simple answer is "Yes." Thousands of Jewish lives might have been saved, especially after the beginnings of the German retreat from Russia in February 1943. Attempts at flight and evasion would have been more numerous if the British Government had:

1. Publicly announced in 1941–42 that prevention of the physical extermination of the Jews was a part of Allied war strategy;
2. Informed Hungarian Jews in 1943 that the destruction of Polish Jewry was a fact and they eventually faced the same fate unless they escaped from Hungary or went into hiding;
3. Called on the whole Hungarian nation in 1943 to help Jews escape to neighboring countries, to provide hiding places, false papers and food, and, in 1944, to do everything possible to stop the deportations;
4. Told Hungarians via radio and air-dropped leaflets in 1944 about the crimes of their leaders against the Jews, and named the top officials directing and implementing the program of annihilating Jews;
5. Appealed to Hungarian Christians to put pressure on their leaders to stop the deportation and killing of Jews.[45]

---

[43] Helen Fein, *Accounting for Genocide*, pp. 314–15.

[44] Fein, *Accounting for Genocide*, p. 316.

[45] These recommendations are modeled on the measures requested by Polish Jewish leaders in the Warsaw Ghetto in the message carried to London by Jan Karski in November 1942. See Jan Karski, "Jan Karski's Account" in Zofia Lewin and Wladyslaw Bartoszewski (eds), *Righteous Among the Nations*, Zofia

Had the Allies launched a full-scale propaganda campaign mentioning explicitly the German strategy of annihilation, it would have sparked greater resistance and more uprisings among the victims. In other cases, it would have vastly expanded the attempts at escape. The overall effect would have been to force the Germans and their collaborators to devote a far greater proportion of their resources to the business of killing Jews. And that reallocation of resources, in turn, would have sabotaged the German and the Hungarian war effort, further encouraging resistance in the German and Hungarian military and the civil service. Very many Jews would have died in any case, but their deaths while resisting and seeking to escape would have had more meaning and the war would have ended sooner.

With Bernard Wasserstein, we can say:

> The essence of this story is a clash of priorities. For the Jews of Europe the essential goal was survival, for which victory over the common enemy was an indispensable, but not a sufficient, condition. For the British Government the first priority and chief preoccupation was, of necessity, victory in the war.... The clash in priorities was the natural result of discrepant interests. Yet the question arises, and it is the fundamental question ...: was Britain's wartime policy towards the Jewish problem the *only* possible one compatible with the overriding end of victory?[46]

This chapter argues that the answer is "No."

Lewin and Wladyslaw Bartoszewski (eds), London, Earlscourt 42 Publications, 1969.

[46] Bernard Wasserstein, *Britain and the Jews of Europe: 1939–1945*, Second edition, London and New York, Leicester University Press, 1979 and 1999, Preface, p. xii.

20

FROM "RESCUE" TO VIOLENCE
OVERCOMING LOCAL OPPOSITION TO GENOCIDE IN RWANDA

Scott Straus

This chapter[1] makes a simple claim: if we employ a broad conception of "rescue," then rescuing activities in Rwanda during the early stages of the genocide were more widespread than is often acknowledged. In many parts of Rwanda, within days and sometimes within weeks after the genocide began, local officials, local elites, and ordinary citizens sought to prevent violence from breaking out in their communities. Local officials did so by organizing joint civilian patrols of Hutus and Tutsis; local officials and policemen moved around through their home areas seeking to calm tensions; and in some locations Hutu officials arrested other Hutus who sought to promulgate violence. At the individual level, some Hutus sought to protect Tutsi family members and friends, sometimes at great risk to themselves. Over time, most of these efforts failed, genocidal violence swept the country, and a significant number of people who initially

---

[1] The author would like to thank Lee Ann Fujii for tremendously helpful comments on an earlier draft, as well as Claire Andrieu, Sarah Gensburger, and Jacques Sémelin for their pioneering role in organizing the conference. The chapter is developed from the arguments and materials in Scott Straus, *The Order of Genocide: Race, Power, and War*, Ithaca, Cornell University Press, 2006.

opposed violence subsequently stood by to allow killings to occur or directly participated in the genocide. The result is what we know: the 20th century's most rapid genocide and the murder of at least 500,000 civilians. But although the situation should not be romanticized, activities that might be construed as "rescue" occurred in some magnitude, at least in the first ten days of the genocide and in certain parts of the country.

The idea that rescuing activities were more common than usually acknowledged runs contrary to much common wisdom about the Rwandan genocide. The standard image of the genocide is that of mass-participation violence in which many Hutus acted quickly and without great compunction to murder their Tutsi neighbors. Much commentary on the genocide, including the standard explanations offered by the current government in Rwanda, supports that view. The most common views are that Rwandan citizens were hostage to an "ideology of genocide," ethnic "divisionism," racist and hateful media, a culture of obedience, and manipulative leaders. Such paradigms present a fairly undifferentiated picture of how the genocide happened, which in turn elides the actual micro-level dynamics that led to rapid and widespread participation in the killing. If we examine those dynamics, this paper intends to shed light on substantial evidence that authorities and citizens acted to prevent violence and in some cases protect Tutsis within the first ten days of the genocide.

At the outset, it is important to be clear about what "rescuing" activities signify in this chapter. The dynamics described here concern for the most part local opposition to efforts to start the genocide in particular communities. Most commonly local actors sought to protect their communities from the onset of violence, not necessarily to protect those who were specifically endangered. Local actors did so usually in ways that put themselves and at times their families at risk. Thus, by "rescue" I mean not so much selfless attempts to save lives of those who were targeted for genocide than a risky behavior that was in opposition to genocidal violence and thereby saved lives.

Widespread rescue as conceptualized here was short-lived in Rwanda. For the most part, open opposition to genocidal violence ended fairly quickly. Broadly speaking, this finding indicates that the line between rescue and violence was in many cases fluid during the Rwandan genocide. This point is consistent with Lee Ann Fujii's chapter in this volume and the broader findings of her field research in Rwanda. Neat categories of "rescuer" and "perpetrator" do not often fit well with the empirics of the Rwandan genocide. That being the case, for Rwanda—and arguably for other cases—any analysis of rescuing broadly construed should consider the dynamics of violence. More specifically, a key thread of analysis is why opposition to violence failed, and hence, what might have sustained it?

In the first part of this chapter, to demonstrate the fluid line between rescue and violence, I focus on the dynamics of genocide in three communes during the genocide. The first is Giti, which is widely credited as the one commune under government control where genocidal violence did not occur in April 1994. Of all the possible symbols of opposition to genocide in Rwanda, Giti stands out as an exemplary candidate. The second is Musambira, where a Hutu burgomaster resisted the killers for about two weeks in April. He ultimately fled the commune for his life, and shortly thereafter genocidal violence started. For the discussion of these communes, I rely principally on interviews I conducted in Rwanda in 2002. The third commune of note is Taba. The commune is now infamous because its burgomaster during the genocide, Jean-Paul Akayesu, was the subject of the first decision handed down by the International Criminal Tribunal for Rwanda.[2] That decision was the first since the promulgation of the Genocide Convention to find an individual guilty of genocide. Despite the three different trajectories that the communes represent, I will show that in the early stages of the genocide local officials acted somewhat similarly and in ways that we might recognize as "rescuing." The critical question then becomes, how and why rescuing activities and opposition to violence ended—why violence started where it was initially opposed; and this is the question taken up in the second part of the chapter.

Three communes: Giti, Musambira, and Taba

There are no *a priori* sociological or political reasons why Giti was an exception in Rwanda. Giti was in Byumba Prefecture, where the then President, Juvénal Habyarimana, and the ruling party in 1994, the MRNDD, had strong support. The burgomaster and other key local offi-

---

[2] International Criminal Tribunal for Rwanda, "The Prosecutor vs. Jean-Paul Akayesu," Case No. ICTR-96-4-T, Judgment and Sentence.

cials were in the MRNDD, and the party was dominant in the commune. Prior to the genocide, the burgomaster had distributed firearms as part of the civil defense program, and night patrols had been instituted as part of that program. The commune had internally displaced persons from previous civil war fighting in the country. All radio stations could be heard in the commune, according to former residents. Socio-economically, according to former officials, the commune had normal levels of education and population growth rates. If anything, the commune was marginally poorer than most and entirely rural. These are among the most notable factors—MRNDD strength, civil defense, internally displaced persons, radio propaganda, and poverty—that observers often claim were drivers of genocidal violence in Rwanda.[3]

However, genocidal violence did not happen in Giti. In interviews in Giti and elsewhere in Rwanda, many accorded a decisive influence to the burgomaster (or head of the commune) at the time, Edouard Sebushumba. He is often credited with being what we might recognize as a "rescuer," as someone who acted to stop violence from starting in his community and to protect Tutsis in the first days after the genocide began. Sebushumba and Giti are thus good places to start to consider the dynamics of rescuing in Rwanda. Below is an excerpt of an interview I conducted with Sebushumba. The excerpt starts at the point Sebushumba learned that President Habyarimana had been killed the night of 6 April 1994. The president's death was the triggering event that started the genocide throughout the country.

I learned of it [the assassination] in the morning. I was at my place. I had signed a check. But I saw that people had not left with this check, and I asked why. They told me.

What was your reaction? Fear took hold of me. I said that the consequences would be bad. A president who died! One expected something terrible...One saw in Kibungo [a neighboring area] houses burning...There was a tension in the population. In Giti, some wanted this to break out. I multiplied the patrols. I remember that in the sectors near Murambi [a neighboring commune], people began to eat Tutsis' cows. I put those people in prison. If you do not put people in prison

---

[3] For example, see the main arguments found in Alison Des Forges, *Leave None to Tell the Story: Genocide in Rwanda*, New York, Human Rights Watch, 1999; Linda Melvern, *Conspiracy to Murder: The Rwandan Genocide*, London, Verso, 2004; and Peter Uvin, *Aiding Violence: The Development Enterprise in Rwanda*, Hartford, CT, Kumarian Press, 1998.

and they take cows, the next day they would kill.... The *conseillers* [local administrative officials] and I all spoke the same language....

Did you hold a meeting? It was difficult to organize meetings. Sometimes I found people near a cabaret [a local bar], or in front of a church, and there we held meetings.

Did you move around the whole commune? Yes. There were gendarmes and communal police.

However, having initially succeeded in stemming the violence, Sebushumba and others interviewed claimed that they saw the tide was turning. But rather than the dynamics of genocidal violence starting as they did elsewhere in the country, rebel soldiers from the RPF, who were winning against government forces in this period, arrived in the general area. Their arrival changed the dynamics, as Sebushumba and others acknowledge:

If things had continued, one could have lost control. If things had lasted for a long time, the killings could have started.

When [RPF soldiers] arrived, were you close to losing control? It was nearly finished....

But [throughout this period] were you not afraid? You did not want to go out and fight for your country [as other had claimed they were doing]? One cannot fight for one's country by killing people, especially the innocent.

But others did. Why not you? Some wanted to keep their positions. I told myself that if I was not a burgomaster, I could be a teacher, but I did not want to shed blood.

There is much to note in these excerpts. In terms of rescuing activities, the account shows that Sebushumba acted to prevent violence from breaking out. He arrested agitators, he organized patrols to keep out attackers from other communes, and he generally sought to calm the situation. He succeeded for a while, and ultimately Giti became the one commune in Rwanda under government control where local officials acted to stave off genocidal violence. Giti is thus often held up as the figure for resistance and rescue during the genocide, as the Rwandan government Memorial Commission argued.[4]

But even by Sebushumba's own admission, he was already losing control of the situation by 9 and 10 April which is about two to three days after the genocide began. Other interviews I conducted with local Hutu

---

[4] Commission pour le Mémorial du Génocide et des Massacres au Rwanda, "Rapport préliminaire d'identification des sites du génocide et des massacres d'avril-juillet 1994 au Rwanda," Kigali, Rwanda.

and Tutsi elites in Giti corroborated the point: violence was imminent. The key difference—the major reason why Giti avoided genocide—is that the commune and a neighboring one were occupied by the RPF around that time. Giti is located north of Kigali, and the commune is along the route that the RPF took as it advanced from their northern positions to attack the capital.

Even though Giti stands out as a commune that resisted genocide, the early dynamics there in fact strongly resemble what happened elsewhere in the country. Particularly throughout southern, south-central, and parts of western Rwanda, burgomasters and other officials acted to protect Tutsis and prevent violence in the first two weeks of the genocide. The difference between these communes and Giti is that, in the former, RPF soldiers did not arrive until *after* those who acted initially to oppose the violence had either lost control of the situation or decided to join the attackers. That is, the dynamics that stopped violence in Giti—the arrival of the RPF and the turning of the tide away from genocidal violence—did not happen in southern areas until well after opposition to genocide had ended and genocidal violence had begun.

The communes of Musambira and Taba are good examples of the point. Musambira is in Gitarama Prefecture, just south of Kigali. Throughout Gitarama and Butare Prefectures during the first two weeks of the genocide, local authorities acted to prevent violence.[5] And in large measure, they succeeded—at least initially. The dynamic changed for a number of reasons but especially after the interim president and prime minister toured the areas, threatening those who resisted and removing the prefect of Butare, who was subsequently killed, and after militias and soldiers were deployed to the regions. Hardliners and those advocating violence also killed several burgomasters in other communes. In Musambira, the resisting burgomaster was not killed, but driven from his post. Here is an excerpt from an interview I conducted with that burgomaster, Charles Nyandwi:

> We knew there were killings in Kigali. With our prefect, we took the decision to thwart this, to repulse this, and each commune organized to struggle against this. *There was a meeting?* Yes. After we heard testimony that killings had started in some regions, we organized with the goal to prevent what was happening elsewhere.

[5] On Butare, see Des Forges, *Leave None To Tell the Story*, pp. 432–594.

What could be done? In my commune, I gave the order to the communal police to be ready on the borders of our commune...We took the police and placed them anywhere there was a problem and we contacted the population to help the police if necessary.

Was the commune threatened? There were many threats for us because the people from Kigali had begun to penetrate.

In short, Nyandwi acted as Sebushumba had. He posted police to prevent incursions from attackers, he rallied citizens in the community, and he generally sought to prevent an outbreak of violence. He went even further, as we shall see.

For a while, the strategy worked. Nyandwi secured the peace. But after about a week, he started to lose control, as Sebushumba had started to lose it in Giti. The first key incident was when civilians acting to protect the commune from incursion killed an Interahamwe militiaman who had attacked from Kigali. That was followed by Nyandwi being denounced on RTLM, the extremist radio station that broadcast inflammatory messages before and during the genocide. Nyandwi describes what happened:

The week of the 11th, there were incursions of Interahamwe. There was also a very serious incident for me. The population killed an Interahamwe, and that was very expensive for me. It was said directly on RTLM that I was killing Interahamwe and helping the Tutsis. It was said many times. It was the 14th. The population began to be afraid, calling a burgomaster an enemy!

They called you an "enemy"? Of course.... It was serious for me. The population helped me, but the police began to be afraid. People started asking themselves, what will we do? I tried to calm them. We continued all the same, up until the 20th. Then they came to my place to kill me. I was not there. I was in another sector trying to assure security. My wife told me there were people in military uniform that came and went around asking where I was.

Hearing this, Nyandwi decided to flee the commune. First he spent the night in the bush, he said, and then he fled south toward Burundi. He escaped alive.

After Nyandwi fled, a group advocating violence and siding with the hardliners then in control in Kigali took control in Musambira. The new authorities included a Musambira native who before the genocide had been on a national committee of the ruling MRNDD party. He collaborated with soldiers from the Army and Presidential Guard as well as with a number of local Hutu elites, including an assistant to the burgomaster, according to a number of witnesses in the commune. Soon after Nyandwi's departure, the new authorities rapidly made killing the order of the day. They organized bands of men to search the community for Tutsis, and they issued instructions to kill whomever they found and whoever resisted.

As it did throughout southern Rwanda, the violence intensified quickly once the resisters were overpowered. At one point, the new authorities in Musambira warned that anyone who sheltered a Tutsi would also be killed. Below is a quotation from a Hutu businessman who is not implicated in the genocide. He describes how Presidential Guard soldiers were the first to kill in the commune and how the violence intensified thereafter.

The Presidential Guard soldiers, after having killed these people, said, "We have given you the example, go kill people and for compensation take their goods." There were people who did not have a good heart, who started to circulate. Other soldiers were at a center, and they said to them, "go burn! and then eat their cows and take all their things and anyone who tries to stop you, kill him, even if he is Hutu."

And then? That is when the war began. People began to hide everywhere. Some were killed on the road. Others were killed in their homes. Others were killed in hiding. Others were killed where they fled. There was no place to hide. That is how the war became very bad. Even if you had hidden someone and they found him at your place, they told you to kill him yourself. That is what caused a lot of deaths because everyone was afraid of hiding someone because it was said that if they found you with him they would ask you to kill him.

The narrative here is one that many repeated not only in Musambira, but also in other parts of Rwanda: once the hardliners pushing for genocide succeeded in starting violence in a particular community, then hiding people in that community carried a high risk. Some Tutsi civilians still managed to hide—most often in the bush but sometimes in pit latrines and attics—but as the interviewee above suggests, many Hutus living in neighborhoods chose not to conceal their neighbors.

The broader point about Musambira is that even by a certain point violence carried the day, there were acts of rescuing in the early stages of the genocide. Moreover, what happened in Musambira strongly resembles what happened in Giti. The difference in the former is that the resistance to genocide was overcome, while in the latter the RPF rebel soldiers arrived in time. Had the dynamics continued over time in Giti, genocide might well have occurred; by contrast, had the Hutu resisters been supported in Musambira, genocide might have been avoided. In short, the dynamics that led to the onset of genocide were more fluid than is often acknowledged. They involved a contestation for control between those who sought to prevent violence and those who sought to start it. However, once the latter consolidated their control, they dominated communities and quickly mobilized large numbers of civilians to join the genocide—for reasons that I sketch in the next section of the paper.

The final example comes from the commune of Taba. As noted above, Akayesu was the first person in the world to be found guilty of genocide by an international court. The decision was handed down in 1998, and was well deserved: the court demonstrated that Akayesu gave a green light to the killers and actively participated in the violence. But a close examination of the court's decision shows that in the first ten days of the genocide, Akayesu acted as Sebushumba and Nyandwi had: he sought to prevent violence and to protect Tutsis. In the court's words:

There is a substantial amount of evidence establishing that before 18 April 1994 the Accused did attempt to prevent violence from taking place in the commune of Taba. Many witnesses testified to the efforts of the Accused to maintain peace in the commune and that he opposed by force the Interahamwe's attempted incursions into the commune to ensure that the killings which had started in Kigali on 7 April 1994 did not spread to Taba. Witness W testified that on the order of the Accused to the population that they must resist these incursions, members of the Interahamwe were killed. Witness K testified that Taba commune was calm during the period when Akayesu wanted that there be calm. She said he would gather the population in a meeting and tell them that they had to be against the acts of violence in the commune. Witness A testified that when the Interahamwe tried to enter the commune of Taba, the burgomaster did everything to fight against them, and called on the residents to go to the borders of the commune to chase them away. The Accused testified that he intervened when refugees from Kigali were being shot at by the Interahamwe. The police returned fire and three *Interahamwe* were killed. The Accused testified that he confiscated their weapons and their vehicle.[6]

In short, Akayesu acted in such a way that might be labeled as "rescuing" during the first ten days of the genocide. He actively sought to prevent violence.

However, at a certain point, Akayesu changed dramatically. The switch came after Akayesu held a meeting with the interim prime minister and

---

[6] International Criminal Tribunal for Rwanda, "The Prosecutor vs. Jean-Paul Akayesu," Case No. ICTR-96–4–T, Judgment and Sentence, paragraph 184.

after the interim president traveled in neighboring Butare, encouraging residents and authorities to take part in the genocide. The president's speeches were broadcast nationally, signaling a clear directive to start the violence. Here is how the court puts it:

> The Chamber finds beyond a reasonable doubt that the conduct of the Accused changed after 18 April 1994 and that after this date the Accused did not attempt to prevent the killing of Tutsi in the commune of Taba. In fact, there is evidence that he not only knew of and witnessed killings, but that he participated in and even ordered killings. The fact that on one occasion he helped one Hutu woman protect her Tutsi children does not alter the Chamber's assessment that the Accused did not generally attempt to prevent the killings at all after 18 April.... [The Chamber] finds beyond a reasonable doubt that he did not attempt to prevent killings of Tutsi after this date. Whether he had the power to do so is not at issue, as he never even tried and as there is evidence establishing beyond a reasonable doubt that he consciously chose the course of collaboration with violence against Tutsi rather than shielding them from it.[7]

In short, Akayesu decided to advocate violence. He publicly "chose the course of collaboration," even after seeking to prevent violence and even while acting privately to protect a Tutsi family. He decided—like many other authorities and citizens in Rwanda—that the better path was to join the killers rather than to fight them. The result is what we know: massive, intensive, and participatory genocidal violence.

From rescue to violence

The previous section shows that rescuing activities were more common in the early stages of the genocide than is usually acknowledged. In fact, the difference between Giti (a figure of rescue and resistance in Rwanda) and Taba (a figure of genocidal violence) lied largely in time and location. In the former, the burgomaster held out until the RPF arrived; in the latter, the burgomaster seems to have decided at a certain point that he no longer had the power to resist and that he should collaborate with the hardliners. In Musambira, the burgomaster fled. The evidence thus suggests that the line separating rescue from violence in Rwanda was fluid, the product of contests for control at the local level. Whether rescuers succeeded was the function of a dynamic *among Hutus* over who con-

---

[7] International Criminal Tribunal for Rwanda, "The Prosecutor vs. Jean-Paul Akayesu," Case No. ICTR-96-4-T, Judgment and Sentence, paragraph 193.

trolled the balance of power. In most places, the hardliners and those advocating violence won before the RPF arrived.

In this section, I elaborate briefly on these points and in particular I address three related questions: why were some areas more prone to early rescuing activities than others, why did the dynamics change, and what might have prolonged rescuing activities?

The answer to the first question is that in my research in Rwanda, I found that generally speaking political alliance was the most important trigger to the violence that started in the different regions. In northern and northwestern Rwanda, and areas in and around Kigali, the MRNDD had the strongest support and the most firepower. Generally speaking—Giti is an exception and there were others—in those areas violence started almost immediately after the president's assassination and the resumption of civil war between the government and RPF forces. By contrast, areas where resistance initially succeeded are those locations where the political opposition had the strongest support, in the southern and south-central areas.

The answer to the second question is more complex. In each location, there appears to have been a tipping point when the balance of power shifted from fluid or anti-violence to pro-violence. By "balance of power," I mean that a plurality of force existed locally, and it depended on two main dimensions, one internal to the commune and one external. The internal dimensions consisted of administrative officials, armed elements within the commune, local elites, and non-elite citizens. The second consisted of national officials, prefecture officials, the military, and activity in neighboring communes. To tip the balance—to consolidate a pro-violence position—some combination of intra- and extra-communal elements were needed. In Giti, for example, the burgomaster lacked a strong challenge from within the commune—he and his subordinates "spoke the same language," as Sebushumba said—and was able to maintain an anti-violence position. But conditions were changing around him and especially in a neighboring commune; as they did, the balance began to shift; he was losing control—only to be saved by the RPF's arrival. In Musambira, with prefectural support backing, the burgomaster maintained an anti-violence position for two weeks. The tip came from a military incursion, national pressure, and a change in a neighboring commune. In Taba, the change mirrored that in Musambira, though in Taba Akayesu decided to join the attacks rather then flee as Nyandwi did.

What we are witnessing here is a dynamic of power and politics. In the end, the hardliners who advocated genocide in the aftermath of the president's death controlled most force in the country in April 1994. They had the loyalty of the best armed units in the military, of the militia, of the media, and a significant number of citizens in certain parts of the country. The moderates and initial opponents of violence could not match their power. Moreover, two other factors contributed to the success of the hardliners. First, the genocide was committed in a war and throughout that war the RPF steadily advanced against government forces. The war and the president's assassination (which was widely blamed on the RPF at the time) heightened fear and washed out the middle ground in the country. That is, war helped force a choice between "us" and "them," shunting aside calls for moderation and deliberation. Second, the international forces that were stationed in Rwanda pulled out, which similarly undermined the moderates' position.

The net result is that the hardliners consolidated control within the first two weeks of the genocide; they overwhelmed the resisters and rescuers. Once the hardliners succeeded, they exploited Rwanda's pre-existing institutions of mobilization, the dense networks of authority, and the country's hilly topography and dense demography to organize large numbers to participate in the genocide. Rescuing existed from that point forward, but usually it was private and somewhat exceptional. The force of genocidal violence and the pressure to comply publicly were high, as the Musambira testimony demonstrates, and open disobedience to the genocidal program was costly. Genocide became the order of the day. In short, the hardliners' balance of power, the civil war, and international flight were key factors in the way the hardliners defeated the moderates and the "rescuers." The war, the country's institutions, and the country's geography were critical to the way in which those who advocated genocide succeeded in quickly mobilizing so many to take part in the genocide.

With regard to the third question—what might have prolonged rescuing activities—the answer stems from the analysis above. An effective ceasefire, however difficult to achieve, would have calmed the situation. So would a decision by the international community to, at the very least, stay the course and, at best, reinforce its positions. Both actions would have opened a space for maneuver for moderates and "rescuers" to prevent violence and to protect Tutsis.

Conclusion

In conclusion, the Rwandan case indicates that public "rescue" as conceptualized here is not determined so much by individual will or even by pre-existing inter-communal ties. Rather, the example of Rwanda suggests that decisions for peace or violence are a function of balance of power and the facilitator for maneuver in a particular community. When those committed to genocide control the balance of power, when the space for maneuver and moderation evaporates, and when the costs of public disobedience are high, open rescuing will be rare. There will be exceptions to the rule. Certain brave individuals will risk health and home to save friends and family. But at the public level, rescuing of the type examined here—open opposition to violence—will be unlikely once hardliners advocating violence control the balance of power.

This chapter cannot illustrate every dimension of the genocide's dynamics. More space is needed to show how and why the hardliners won control and succeeded in enforcing their positions. Rather, the main purpose has been to demonstrate that "rescuing" was more common in the early stages of the genocide than the death toll, the speed of violence, and common wisdom would suggest. In highlighting those moments when public "rescuing" did happen, the chapter seeks to show that the line between rescue and violence was fluid and often the function of contests for power at the local level. There is a point here that matters not just for comparative research on rescuing, but also for social relations in post-genocide Rwanda. Recognizing early acts of bravery and resistance to genocide as well as the dynamics of violence that snuffed out much public rescue—rather than seeing the genocide as a product of unmitigated volition to commit violence—could be a valuable step toward peaceful reconstruction in Rwanda.

21

CROSSING A BORDER TO ESCAPE
EXAMPLES FROM THE GISHAMVU AND KIGEMBE COMMUNITIES OF RWANDA

Charles Kabwete Mulinda

This contribution analyses the circumstances surrounding the rescue of victims in the Gishamvu and Kigembe communities during the 1994 genocide in Rwanda.[1] As the genocide of the Tutsi ethnic group spread over almost all of Rwandan territory, it was carried out in multiple and varied ways.[2] Consequently, the means by which the survivors avoided being killed were equally varied according to the situations in which they found themselves. This chapter focuses its attention on how time, space and the participants played a role in these two communities, located in

[1] The author thanks the Research Commission of the National University of Rwanda for its financial help, which made this research possible. He also thanks the Programme on the Study of the Humanities in Africa (PSHA), and the Centre for Humanities Research (CHR), University of the Western Cape, for their outstanding contribution in the improvement of this chapter during the CHR Seminar on 13 November 2007 and at the PHSA Symposium from 13 to 15 November 2007. Finally, the author is grateful to Professor Leslie Witz for editing corrections made on an earlier version.

[2] Cf. Alison Des Forges, *Leave None to Tell the Story: Genocide in Rwanda*, London, Brussels, Human Rights Watch, Paris, Fédération Internationales des Ligues des Droits de l'Homme, 1999; African Rights, *Rwanda. Death, Despair and Defiance*, Revised 1995 Edition, London, African Rights, August 1995.

the far South of the country on the Burundi Frontier. The genocide began there two weeks later than in other regions of the country.

This work will thus try to answer the following question: How did the majority of survivors escape extermination in the communities of Gishamvu and Kigembe? For this purpose, I will use the eyewitness accounts of twenty-two genocide survivors, the majority hailing from the communal bureau of Kigembe, the Nkomero market, and the parish of Nyumba in Gishamvu.[3] These oral accounts form the principal source of this work.[4] The written documentation available has also been most useful, especially for helping place the case of Gishamvu and Kigembe in its correct context, both theoretically and empirically, in the wider sphere of genocide. Indeed, I have noted that eyewitnesses speak in the plural and sometimes speak of events which took place far from where they lived and events in which they did not participate. Their statements are therefore more than just individual accounts. These reports are adorned with an indubitable social character. After a brief overview of the genocide, this chapter explores the circumstances of the rescue of escapees in Gishamvu and Kigembe.

Genocide

Between 1990 and 1994, political life in Rwanda was rich in tumultuous events, notably the rebellion of the RPF (Rwandan Patriotic Front), multiparty-ism and the economic crisis that began at the end of the 1980s. It was also in 1990 that the ideology of hate began to appear in the press. In the political and military struggle for power between the regime and the political and military opposition parties, the Habyarimana regime chose to define the conflict in ethnic terms.[5] Violence against the Tutsis in Gishamvu and Kigembe began, for the most part, after 1993.[6] This violence was both verbal and physical, vertical and horizontal.

---

[3] See the list of eyewitness at the end of this chapter.

[4] Human Rights Watch, "The Rwandan Genocide: How it was Prepared. A Human Rights Watch Briefing Paper," n°1, April 2006.

[5] Eyewitness accounts from Rurangwa and Rwandema, Nsengimana and Mutwarasibo. According to Mutwarasibo, it was at this moment that newspapers backing ethnic division began to proliferate in Kigembe: "The parties selectively targeted articles and distributed them in the clubs and members came there to read them."

[6] Cf. Linda Melvern, *Conspiracy to Murder: The Rwandan Genocide*, London, Verso, 2004.

The prefect of the Butare Prefecture, Jean-Baptiste Habyarimana, resisted the carrying out of genocide in Butare from 6 April 1994 until his dismissal on 18 April 1994.[7] The protective attitude of the Butare authorities attracted the vulnerable populations of Gikongoro towards Butare[8] because, in Gikongoro, the genocide had started just after the death of President Juvénal Habyarimana.[9] This pacification by the Butare Prefecture inspired the victims' confidence in those in power, which was apparent in the flight of several Tutsis in the direction of official establishments—local council offices, schools—but also churches, notably because of their reputation for inviolability during the violence that occurred from 1959 to 1964.

In these two communes there were several sites of mass murder, but also massacres of individuals or families. The list of sites mentioned here is surely not exhaustive; more detailed research is necessary.[10]

When the murders began in Kigembe, certain Kigembe Tutsis began to run away from their murderers who were attacking them in their own homes, and made their way to government offices. It was there that they met the displaced people from Gikongoro.[11]

---

[7] African Rights, Rwanda. *Death, Despair and Defiance*, op. cit., p. 338, 348.

[8] Ibid., 290; Linda Melvern, op. cit., pp. 168–9. The account given by Kandanga, from Gikongoro, corroborates this. She tells how the genocide began in her commune, Mubuga, in the Kibeho sector of Gikongoro, on 7 April 1994. She and her family, as well as several Tutsi neighbours, left their homes around 10 April after being attacked by some of their neighbours, by other people coming from Rwamiko, and by the Interahamwe, all clad in red hats. She and her husband, with two of her sisters-in-law, crossed the frontier into Burundi on 14 April 1994.

[9] For the Kigembe commune, the carrying out of the genocide is amply described in Jean Paul Kimonyo's PhD thesis, op. cit., Chapter 7. This thesis has developed into a book that was published in 2008 (Jean-Paul Kimonyo, *Rwanda: Un génocide populaire*, Paris, Karthala, 2008). My doctorate research includes the commune of Gishamvu (Charles Kabwete Mulinda, "A Space for genocide: Local Authorities, Local Population and Local Histories in Gishamvu and Kibayi (Rwanda)," forthcoming thesis, University of the Western Cape).

[10] Eyewitness account from Mutsinzi.

[11] Several informers indicate that the majority of these people on the move were Tutsi, since they were targeted. However, a small number of Hutus who felt in danger were found amongst them, such as Hutu women and other Hutus who were related to Tutsis through marriage.

Until 18 April the refugees[12] thought that the calm was there to stay. It was on this day that they saw the arrival of a man who played a key role as organizer and inciter.

The accounts of several other eyewitnesses show us that the massacres that began on around 18 April seem to have continued until 22 April. During the day, the murderers (certain policemen, a great number of the local population, several Hutu Burundi refugees, Interahamwe militia and the military) killed the Tutsis on the move, and at night, they went looting or rested.[13] This meant that surveillance was slackened at night. It was for this reason that the vast majority of escapees got away at this time.

Besides the genocide at council offices, another place was the Centre of Rural and Artisan Integrated Education (CERAI) and the market in Nkomero. In Nkomero, around 5,000 people perished.[14]

Reports of the murders at the parish center of Nyumba (Gishamvu) begin with a description of the arrival of refugees from Gikongoro, Runyinya and Nyakizu and how the populations of Gishamvu joined them there. This somewhat resembles the situation in Kigembe. The local authorities of the commune of Ngoma sent around 500 people to the Nyumba parish center and to the Nyakibanda Grand Seminary.[15] It must be noted, however, that certain Tutsis from Gishamvu (Nyumba) were in turn forced to flee to other nearby communes.[16]

Seeing that the situation was becoming serious, several Gishamvu Tutsis fled to Nyakibanda and Nyumba. In the countryside, only a few Tutsis remained who were able to seek refuge and hide with the Hutus.[17]

The decisive implementation of the murders took place between 18 and 24 April 1994.[18] The local authorities were implicated in the organi-

---

[12] See, for example, eyewitness accounts given by Célestin Rwandema and by Ernest Mutwarasibo.

[13] Eyewitness accounts given by Musabyemariya and Rurangwa. Also see African Rights, *Rwanda. Death, Despair and Defiance*, op. cit., pp. 335–6 and René Abandi, "Dieudonné (témoignage de)," in *La Source*, "Spécial: Génocide de 1994 à l'UNR et au Rwanda," n°72, May 1997, pp. 13–15, p. 13.

[14] Alison Des Forges, op. cit., pp. 445–6.

[15] African Rights, *Rwanda, Death, Despair and Defiance*, op. cit., p. 338.

[16] Eyewitness account given by Mukantabana.

[17] Eyewitness accounts given by Théoneste Hakizimana, Nsengimana, Musabyemariya and Murindwa.

[18] Eyewitness account given by Nsengimana.

zation and the enactment of the genocide in Nyumba. Supervisors of the *cellules* were also associated with this genocide campaign. "Those in charge made it clear to the population that anyone hiding anyone would die with them."[19] Indeed, the central government took measures so that civil servants participated in the genocide. A large number of them in fact did, mainly to keep their jobs.[20]

The massacres seem to have started after the visit of President Théodore Sindikubwabo on 18 April 1994.[21] As the majority of Tutsis in the Gishamvu sector fled, their houses were looted and often burnt down. Then began the initiation and perfection of the genocide process.

It is estimated that several thousand people died at Kigembe and Gishamvu.[22] The solitude of the escapees suggests that the genocide was in fact a quasi-extermination in Kigembe and in Gishamvu; amongst our eyewitnesses, very few of them managed to escape with other family members, the majority were alone.

Rescue

This section shows how it was possible for a certain number of survivors from Gishamvu and Kigembe to be saved.

As is shown in a certain number of written documents concerned with rescue, and in eyewitness accounts given by those who survived the genocide, the ways in which help was given were multiple and varied. They included offering shelter to someone in danger in one's home so that they could remain hidden, giving food, giving drink, giving clothes, offering medicine, fighting for someone's protection, negotiating their release, organizing their transportation, accompanying them in their flight as a scout or shield, passing on information regarding the state of the road ahead of them and how they could escape the massacres, dying for them, etc.[23]

---

[19] African Rights, Rwanda. *Death, Despair and Defiance*, op. cit., pp. 51–2.
[20] African Rights, *The History of the Genocide in Sector Gishamvu. A Collective Account*, June 2003; Alison Des Forges, op. cit., p. 459; PRI (Penal Reform International), "Rapport de la recherche sur la Gacaca," Rapport V, September 2003, p. 45.
[21] Eyewitness account given by Nsengimana.
[22] Cf. Minaloc, *Dénombrement des victimes du génocide*, Rapport Final, Rwanda, Kigali, November 2002.
[23] African Rights, *Tribute to Courage*, London, African Rights, 2002; Jean-Marie

On the road to the frontier, and the difficulties on the way. In Gishamvu and Kigembe, the majority of survivors chose the road to Burundi as their road to salvation. It was possible and feasible because of the proximity of these two communes with the Burundi frontier. Any difficulties encountered on route were due to varied factors.

The first factor was the time it took to cross the border. According to the statements of the witnesses Mutwarasibo and Kandanga, those who chose to take the road to Burundi immediately, instead of first grouping together in towns, escaped the genocide.[24] Initially, there were very few attacks on the roads. It was later that the roads became difficult to travel on.[25]

Another factor was one's distance from the Burundi border. Those who escaped from the commune office and the CERAI in Kigembe met few difficulties compared with the people from Gishamvu, since these people came from far away and were faced with many more roadblocks. For example, a large number of escapees from Gishamvu were killed at roadblocks along the routes and especially in the Nkomero town centre.[26]

Moreover, the younger and more physically resistant one was, the better one managed to struggle and continue on one's route. The elderly, small children, and women were amongst those who perished in great numbers at these barriers.[27] One example is Muhire from Kigembe who was able, thanks to his young age, to travel on foot to Kansi, Nyaru-

---

Quemener and Eric Bouvet, *Femmes du Rwanda*, Paris, Catleya Editions, 1999; Abbé Hildebrand Karangwa, *Le Génocide au centre du Rwanda. Quelques témoignages des rescapés de Kabgayi* (2 June 1994), no place of publication, 2000; Esther Mujawayo and Souâd Belhaddad, *SurVivantes, Rwanda, dix ans après le genocide, suivi de entretien croisé entre Simone Veil et Esther Mujawayo*, La Tour d'Aigues, Editions de l'Aube, 2004; Maria Augusta Angelucci *et al.*, *C'est ma taille qui m'a sauvée. Rwanda: De la tragédie à la reconstruction*, Johannesburg, Colorpress, 1997; Johan Pottier, "Escape from Genocide. The Politics of Identity in Rwanda's Massacres," in Vigdis Broche-Due (ed.), *Violence and Belonging. The Quest for Identity in Post-colonial Africa*, London and New York, Routledge, 2005, pp. 195–213.

[24] Eyewitness accounts given by Kandanga and Mutwarasibo.
[25] Eyewitness account given by Rwandema. See also Murindwa.
[26] Eyewitness accounts given by Vincent Hakizimana, Théoneste Hakizimana and Musabyemariya.
[27] Eyewitness accounts given by Kamuyumbo, Nsengimana and Hakizimana Théoneste.

hengeri, to Ngoma, to Nyumba and to the Grand Seminary of Nyakibanda (Gishamvu), and finally to Burundi.

Certain victims encountered far less difficulties than others because they were escorted by friends or family members who were Hutu. For example, Félix Nzabirinda was protected by his brothers-in-law Pascal Ntahiganayo and Alexis Sindahuga and accompanied by his future father-in-law Augustin Bajyanama. He escaped, despite crossing the border very late, on 13 May 1994.

Others managed to reach the frontier, but only by fighting their way through. This was the case of several inhabitants of Sheke and Bitare (Gishamvu) who managed to defend themselves against killers they met en route and escaped in great numbers.[28]

The accounts of Musabyemariya and Mutsinzi also show that the Burundi military forces helped the victims to cross over the border from the Rwandan territory.[29]

However, of all these explanations, good luck seems to be the most convincing, since for the most part, only providence saved all these survivors: they were simply at the right place at the right time, or met the man they needed at the opportune moment.

Arrival at the border and help from Burundi soldiers. Arriving at the frontier did not guarantee survival. As the experiences of many escapees indicate, one could easily be killed at the border since roadblocks maintained by Kigembe killers had become legion. Even once across the border into Burundi, one could still fall victim to killers in that country, since there were still armed conflicts occurring there. Several escapees were attacked in Burundi, and had to be protected by Burundian soldiers.[30]

But, generally speaking, the Burundi army helped the escapees to cross over the border, gave them emergency help and found transport for these escapees to refugee camps in Burundian territory. There are survivors who were fished out of the waters of the Kanyaru river and then brought to the customs post.[31] There are survivors who were helped by the Burundi army immediately upon their arrival at the customs post, with food and shelter.[32] Some were driven in Burundi military vehicles to Mparami-

---

[28] Eyewitness account given by Musabyemariya.
[29] Eyewitness accounts given by Musabyemariya and Mutsinzi.
[30] Eyewitness accounts given by Twagirumukiza, Nzabirinda, etc.
[31] Eyewitness accounts given by Théoneste Hakizimana and Rurangwa.
[32] Eyewitness account given by Mwumvaneza.

rundi, which was a primary transit base.[33] Others were directed towards temporary camps in Mihigo[34] and Busiga.[35] There were those who were provisionally placed in the Burundi military camp of Mihigo and then moved to the temporary camp in Mparamirundi.[36] The military gave food and drink to all. Many say that they received clothes. It seems that relief services existed in Mparamirundi since, for example, Théoneste Hakizimana says that a Red Cross worker regularly brought milk to him there. Twagirumukiza insists that he was cared for there since his entire body was wracked with pain. Vincent Hakizimana was also treated by Red Cross doctors at the Kayanza Hospital.

Transfer to camps in Burundi and elsewhere by Burundi soldiers, the UNHCR and NGOs. After being helped by the Burundi military forces, many refugees were guided towards refugee camps that were situated in Burundi territories in Mureke and Muduga. The majority of survivors interviewed survived in Mureke thanks to humanitarian aid from the UNHCR or from relief organizations.[37] Some of them remained there until their return to Rwanda in July 1994 after the victory of the RPF.

Other survivors did not wait for the RPF victory to return to Rwanda, and went to Bugesera in June 1994 after that area had been taken over by the RPF. They were impatient to leave the camp in Mukere, since life there was precarious; there was not enough food, they lacked medical supplies and safe lodgings, etc. In Bugesera, conditions were more satisfactory: the fields were filled with soya beans and sweet potatoes, and there were houses belonging to the Hutus who had fled after the RPF occupation.[38] Other survivors, mostly men, went and joined the RPF campaign; Murindwa, Théoneste Hakizimana and Mutsinzi did this.[39]

Not all escapees went to refugee camps. A small number of survivors made their way towards other parts of Burundi because they knew people

---

[33] For example, Twagirumukiza, Rurangwa, and Kamuyumbo.
[34] For example, Rwandema.
[35] In the case of Bunyenzi.
[36] In the case of Théoneste Hakizimana, who spent four days there.
[37] This was the case of Mutwarasibo, Musabyemariya, Ndayisaba, Nsengimana, Muhire and some of their close relatives.
[38] This is the case of Bunyenzi, Kayumba, Mutsinzi and some people close to them.
[39] Eyewitness accounts given by Murindwa, Théoneste Hakizimana and Mutsinzi.

there, or more simply because they had been able to find transportation in that direction.[40]

Other rescuers. It was not only Burundi soldiers who helped victims cross the frontier to Burundi or toward the neighboring Congo to seek refuge in refugee camps or in people's homes. There were also civilians who hid and accompanied victims, welcomed them into their homes and sheltered them, and later helped them to return to Rwanda and rebuild their lives there. Three people hid Innocent Ndayisaba and went with her to the Kanyaru River so that she could cross over to Burundi: Evariste, Thomas and another.[41]

Amongst the survivors who did not cross the Burundi border was Brigitte Mukantabana, originally from the Gishamvu commune, who had been living between 1990 and 1994 in Kigali, the capital, in the Kanombe camp. She was the wife of a Hutu soldier named Callixte Mugemangango. She left Kigali around 15 April 1994 and arrived in Gishamvu two days later. She witnessed the genocide in Gishamvu, watched as members of her family and close friends were murdered, hid in the sorghum fields, and was protected by her father-in-law Augustin Sebashongore, who was a Hutu. They paid attackers several times. On 13 May 1994 she fled to Cyangugu, helped by Rwagasore, a soldier sent to her by her husband.[42]

Bernadette Urayeneza did not cross Rwandan frontiers at all. She moved from place to place and hid with neighbors and Hutu relations in the communes of Gishamvu and Runyinya. After leaving the Grand Seminary of Nyakibanda, she went and hid in the sorghum fields and then in the homes of friends and neighbors, notably with Misigaro, Sekimondo, André Gatera and Candide Nyiramatama, spending only a few days there and being obliged to move on again in order to keep those who hid her out of danger. In May 1994, she decided to leave Gishamvu, having realized that this was extermination. She arrived in the commune of Runyinya in May and lived there in June and July 1994 in the home of old Barigira to whom she was related on her mother's side. In July 1994, as the RPF rebels approached, the Barigiras fled and Bernadette

---

[40] In the case of Kamuyumbo, Twagirumukiza, Mwumvaneza and Rurangwa, alone or with those close to them.
[41] Eyewitness account given by Ndayisaba.
[42] Eyewitness account given by Mukantabana.

Urayeneza left with them. Barigira, however, asked his sister Madamu to take Urayeneza with her to Gikongoro, to the place called Mu Wururembo.[43]

Emérite Musabyimana was helped across the border by her brother-in-law Isaïe Sindikubwabo, who lived in the Ruhororo sector of Kigembe. He took her to Burundi, to the home in Murama of a Burundi woman named Angela who gave her lodgings until July 1994, when she went back to Rwanda. Before the genocide, Musabyimana lived in the Mugusa commune of the prefecture of Butare. She only returned to Kigembe in April 1994, her husband and child having just been murdered, around 13 April 1994. On her way from Mugusa to Kigembe, she escaped death thanks to the intervention of three unknown rescuers who, each time, asked the killers to let her go saying she was a Hutu in order to save her.[44]

Murindwa's wife, Belthilde Kamanzi, was saved because she was amongst the people of Bitare who fled in large numbers and successfully fought off their killers. Kamanzi was originally from the Nyakizu commune. All of her family survived except for those who died of illness en route.[45] Floride Ntibaziyandemye, the wife of the informant Nsengimana, was also from the Nyakizu commune. Neighbors in Gishamvu—Simon, Sebasoni and several others—hid her since nobody was aware of her ethnic identity. "In fact, she went from hiding place to hiding place and travelled over many hills, hiding anywhere and everywhere until the end of the genocide and of the war."[46] She therefore never left Gishamvu.

Another case concerns the experience of Christine Vuguziga, a Hutu woman who had married a Tutsi by the name of Mujyakera. After losing her husband, she struggled to hide her two children, a girl (Rose Mukantabana) and a boy (Célestin Mbazumutima). The neighbors killed the boy but the girl was saved by a group of young Hutus, Alexis and Eugene. She was able to flee with her mother Vuguziga to Burundi. They took the forest route toward Nshiri and arrived in Burundi in the Rugombo commune in the province of Cibitoke. A Muslim named Jyuma gave them shelter and a small field. Another man helped them, named Maurice. They lived there until 2002 or 2003 and then returned to Rwanda.[47]

---

[43] Eyewitness account given by Urayeneza.
[44] Eyewitness account given by Musabyimana.
[45] Eyewitness account given by Murindwa.
[46] Eyewitness account given by Nsengimana.
[47] Eyewitness account given by Vuguziga.

The return to Rwanda. A large number of escapees from Gishamvu and Kigembe returned home on dates varying according to where they had fled from. The majority, however, got back to their respective communes in July, August and September 1994, returning from Burundi, Bugesera or the GSOB (the Butare Official Secondary School).

Most of them came to live in the small semi-urban centers of Kigembe or Gishamvu, and then went back to their homes after the total pacification of these communes. Soldiers of the RPF, who had just claimed victory, assisted those who went to the centers. Other escapees got back home a little later for various reasons.[48]

Some survivors did not return to their communes of origin, and went to live in the cities or in rural areas.[49]

Finally, concerning rescue aid, there were benefactors who gave material and financial assistance to escapees to assist them in their return to Rwanda. A fine example is Twagirumukiza who speaks of a Burundian named Tharcisse Surwanone, whom he had never met before, who gave him 4,000 Burundi francs to pay for the transport costs of returning to Rwanda.[50]

Motivations behind assistance. One of the reasons for helping others was simple kindness. It is clear that the Burundi soldiers and the RPF were following the orders that they were given. So concerned and courageous were they, however, in the accomplishment of their task that many of them are given credit by the escapees individually. Even if the majority of the survivors cannot remember the names of the soldiers who helped them, they have kept intact the memory of infallible protectors during the most serious moments. Almost invariably these soldiers did not know the people they were protecting. So we can affirm that the main characteristic of their assistance was kindness. Félix Nzabirinda recalls two Burundi soldiers who helped him during his stay in Burundi, Sylvestre and Ndikumana.[51] Rwandema mentions the name of another Burundi officer, Lieutenant Cyiza.[52]

---

[48] Eyewitness accounts given by Kamuyumbo, Mukantabana and Muhire.
[49] In the case the Kandanga and Musabyemariya families.
[50] Eyewitness account given by Twagirumukiza.
[51] Eyewitness account given by Nzabirinda.
[52] Eyewitness account given by Rwandema.

Other Hutu rescuers acted out of kindness. Since they had lived happily with the Tutsis, they felt obliged to save them, even if they were risking their own lives. Here is the eyewitness account of Vincent Nsengimana who gives us more information about such cases:

"There was a Hutu who was caught with a lot of Tutsis who were all in hiding and to whom he had been regularly bringing food. He was killed by other Hutus, he and his wife, who was Tutsi. He was called Protais—I do not know his other name, because he was not from our neighborhood. He must have come from the Nyakizu commune. They were caught just before the end of the war. [...] Protais acted out of kindness. There are other Hutus who were married to Tutsi women but they did not behave like Protais."[53]

Mutwarasibo speaks of other Hutus who took risks with personal disregard in order to save the Tutsis: "Amongst rescuers, there was an old man called Sibose. I know him well because he even helped us. I also know Emmanuel who hid five girls. Old Sibose would say, 'I'd rather die with the victims than be a coward.' Nobody would ever besmirch him with acts of genocide."[54]

Other Hutu helpers saved Tutsis because of intermarriage with them. Others were motivated by money or material goods. A Burundian Bosco, even though he was a killer, helped Mutwarasibo and his companions to cross the border in exchange for drink. This phenomenon was called *Kwigura* (literally, redeeming oneself).[55]

Another reason for Hutu men to help Tutsi girls and women was a desire to marry them. This took place notably in the Kivuru and Karama sectors of Kigembe.[56] Under these conditions, it is clear that these so-called marriages were not the result of mutual consent. The girls and women found themselves obliged to accept these unions simply in order to save their lives. This is what Florence Mukamugema called sexual slavery.[57] In

---

[53] Eyewitness account given by Nsengimana.
[54] Eyewitness account given by Mutwarasibo.
[55] Eyewitness account given by Mutwarasibo. Mahmood Mamdani (*When Victims Become Killers, Colonialism, Nativism, and the Genocide in Rwanda*, Princeton University Press, 2001, p. 221) also mentions the case of Hutus who saved certain Tutsis and killed others. See also Johan Pottier, op. cit., pp. 205–10 where the escaper Chika survives thanks to money.
[56] Mutwarasibo notes given by him to the author.
[57] Florence Mukamugema, "La Femme rwandaise et les événements de 1994," in Jacques Fierens (ed.), *Femmes et génocide: le cas rwandais*, Brussels, La Charte, 2003, pp. 75–112, p. 90.

another eyewitness book, there is mention of Francine, thirty years old, who was saved because of her forced marriage to a Hutu.[58]

Reasons for limited numbers being saved. The saving of Tutsis was limited mainly because of the meticulousness with which the genocide was prepared. Secondly, those who were caught hiding Tutsis were also killed or had their property looted.[59] Moreover, the border was extremely well guarded by the killers, who included the Interahamwe and civilians, which reduced the chances for many fugitives to cross the border.[60]

Survivors' thoughts about their rescuers. Several survivors reply categorically, when asked who rescued them, that they survived the genocide thanks to God.[61] It was not due to their own efforts, they say, nor to those of Hutu or Burundi helpers or anyone else for that matter. Others consider that it is God who saved them, but add other situations which in practice facilitated their escape, like being close to the frontier of Burundi, or being able to run, etc.[62] Finally, many escapers affirm that they owe their lives to the people who hid them. Here is, for example, Dieudonné's statement: "I would like to take this occasion to say thank you; thank you to you, Zachary Rony, to Marie Paul, to Doctor Bernard Manony, to Bruno Bataille, Marcel Bovy and to the others. I owe my life to you and that is a lot."[63]

Generally, all of the survivors are grateful to the people who helped them. Their statements depict the gravity of the situations in which these well-doers had to make the decision to help them, to protect them and to contribute to their salvation. "To have survived is due to such an exceptional series of circumstances that it leaves one staggered."[64]

[58] Jean-Marie Quéméner and Eric Bouvet, op. cit., p. 26; Cf. Alison Des Forges, op. cit.
[59] Eyewitness accounts given by Mutwarasibo and Nsengimana.
[60] Michele D. Wagner, "All the Bourgmestre's Men: Making Sense of Genocide in Rwanda," *Africa Today*, Volume 45, Issue 1, January-March 1998, pp. 331–45,
[61] I have translated *Imana* (a Kinyarwanda word) as God, but *Imana* also signifies providence, luck and blessings (Cf. Danielle de Lame, op. cit., p. 224 and 232).
[62] Eyewitness accounts given by Murindwa, Théoneste Hakizimana and Vincent Hakizimana.
[63] René Abandi, art. quoted, p. 15. Dr Zachariah Rony of MSF is also mentioned in Alison Des Forges, op. cit., pp. 463, 471, 482, 503–4 and in Linda Melvern, op. cit., pp. 211, 219.
[64] Michele D. Wagner, "All the Bourgmestre's Men," op. cit., p. 342.

Conclusion

In this chapter, I have shown the circumstances in which several escapees from Gishamvu and Kigembe managed to escape the genocide: their experiences, their attackers, and their rescuers. This work demonstrates that the majority of victims survived by crossing the border and that very few of them survived only because they were saved or protected by their Hutu neighbors. The Burundi military seems to be the most important actors in the rescuing of those who fled Gishamvu and Kigembe as they crossed the frontier. Only a few Hutu individuals, both known and unknown to the escapees, provided indispensable help in their flight. Humanitarian organizations helped the escapers in refugee camps. RPF soldiers intervened, especially when the escapers returned to Rwanda.

Those who assisted people escape have shown that it is possible to fight against a strong killing machine with few means but with a firm desire to do good. These heroines and heroes[65] were, for the most part, effective. Very few of them have been thanked or even recognized by name.[66] On the other hand, those who were saved know who their rescuers are and are grateful. Research done on rescue has the merit of celebrating this bravery and perpetuating the memory of these benefactors.

Speaking methodologically, I have noted—both during this research and in the other books of eyewitness accounts that I have consulted—that every genocide survivor's story is a historical account of the acting out of genocide and the escape from it. This will help us in transcribing as widely as possible the history of rescue in the future. Work concerning rescue should also highlight places where there was an unexpected absence of escape.[67]

---

[65] David Newbury, "Understanding Genocide," *Africa Studies Review*, Vol. 41, n° 1, April 1998, pp. 73–97, p. 81.

[66] Cf. African Rights, *Tribute to Courage*, op. cit.; Jean-Marie Quéméner and Eric Bouvet, op. cit.

[67] Cf. Larry Minear and Philippe Guillot, *Soldats à la rescousse: Les leçons humanitaires des événements du Rwanda*, Paris, Organization for Economic Cooperation and Development, 1996; Elizabeth Neuffer, *The Key to my Neighbour's House: Seeking Justice in Bosnia and Rwanda*, New York, Picador, 2001; Vénuste Kayimahe, *France-Rwanda: Les coulisses du génocide. Témoignage d'un rescapé*, Paris, Dagorno, 2002; Esther Mujawayo and Souâd Belhaddad, op. cit.

The escapers survived the genocide but for many, life after this disaster is far from rosy. Fifteen years after the genocide, many who escaped from Gishamvu and Kigembe have not yet been able to return to the social stability they so greatly desire. Solitude, ill health and poverty still haunt them. Government aid and assistance from private national and international help groups offer them social assistance. Through their accounts, it is clear that this help has not yet reached everybody and that this aid does not resolve all their problems. The struggle for survival continues.

Table 7: Eyewitnesses interviewed

N°	Full name	Sex	Year of birth	Town of birth	Sector of birth	Place and date of interview	Occupation
1	Isaië Bunyenzi	male	1947	Kigembe	Murama	Kigembe 72 March 2006	farmer/invalid
2	Théoneste Hakizimana	male	1971	Gishamvu	Gishamvu	Gishamvu 24 March 2006	farmer
3	Vincent Hakizimana	male	1982	Gishamvu	Gishamvu	Gishamvu 24 March 2006	farmer
4	Consesa Kamuyumbo	female	1937	Gishamvu	Mukuge	Gishamvu 24 March 2006	farmer
5	Dative Kandanga	female	1965	Muguba	Kibeho	Butare 9 Sep. 2005	domestic
6	Charles Kayumba	male	1942	Kigembe	Nyanza	Kigembe 27 March 2006	farmer and small businessman
7	Martin Muhire	male	1973	Kigembe	Murama	Kigembe 27 March 2006	farmer
8	Mukantabana Brigitte	female	1964	Gishamvu	Muboni	Gishamvu 24 March 2006	farmer
9	Evariste Murindwa	male	1954	Gishamvu	Gishamvu	Gishamvu 24 March 2006	farmer
10	Claire Musabyemariya	female	1981	Runyinya	Gikombe	Butare 22 Sep. 2005	student
11	Emérite Musabyimana	female	1971	Kigembe	Nyanza	Kigembe 27 March 2006	farmer

12	Sylvestre Mutsinzi	male	1980	Kigembe	Karama	Kigembe 27 March 2006	administration
13	Ernest Mutwarasibo	male	1979	Kigembe	Karama	Butare 8 Sep. 2005	student
14	Vincent Mwumvaneza	male	1965	Kigembe	Kivuru	Kigembe 27 March 2006	farmer
15	Innocent Ndayisaba	female	1968	Kigembe	Nyaruteja	Kigembe 27 March 2006	farmer
16	Vincent Nsengimana	male	1969	Gishamvu	Gishamvu	Gishamvu 24 March 2006	farmer
17	Félix Nzabirinda	male	1972	Kigembe	Rubona	Kigembe 27 March 2006	farmer, craftsman and small businessman
18	Vincent Rurangwa	male	1971	Kigembe	Ngoma	Kigembe 27 March 2006	Farmer and carpenter
19	Célestin Rwandema	male	1968	Kigembe	Kigembe	Kigembe 27 March 2006	administration
20	Alphonse Twagirumukiza	male	1965	Kigembe	Kigali	Kigembe 27 March 2006	farmer
21	Bernadette Urayeneza	female	1959	Gishamvu	Gishamvu	Gishamvu 24 March 2006	farmer
22	Christine Vuguziga	female	1955	Gishamvu	Gishamvu	Gishamvu 24 March 2006	farmer

PART III

NETWORKS, MINORITIES AND RESCUE

One of the most productive approaches for studying a genocidal process involves observing how hatred and violence are propagated (or not) at the regional or even the town or village level. This "micro" perspective is adopted in most of the articles assembled in this section, so as to attempt to understand the rescue efforts on the part of this or that individual or group. For instance, Yves Ternon compares the fate of Armenians in 1915–16 in two very different provinces of the Ottoman Empire: Mardin, where they were almost all exterminated, and Sinjar, where they received protection, a little known fact. We will also see how an outside actor (who today would be called "humanitarian") necessarily relies on a network of local complicity to be effective: such is the case recounted by Hans-Lukas Keiser of the Swiss Beatrice Rohner, whose actions during the Armenian genocide protected over a thousand children sheltered in an orphanage in Aleppo in Syria. In the heart of Nazi Germany, Mark Roseman analyzes the long overshadowed history of the Bund, a socialist reform group established in the city of Essen that saved several Jews from death. Michel Fabréguet offers another study on the same period, on Nieuwlande, in the Netherlands, a "land of rescue," a scene of action that can be compared with the village of Chambon-sur-Lignon in France, although their stories are very different. As regards Rwanda, Emmanuel Viret gives us results of new fieldwork on the role of the inhabitants of the town of Mabare, who in April 1994 attempted to put up violent resistance to the militias that came to kill Tutsis. All those authors demonstrate the weight and the specific combination of factors that explain how in one place but not in another certain acts of aid and rescue came to be undertaken. Aside from the personality of this or that individual, singular factors must always be taken into account: the history of the region, its ethnic or religious mix, the attitude of local elites, force of circumstance, without neglecting geography.

Can certain common features nevertheless be identified that might explain their actions? The weight of the religious factor immediately comes to mind, as various forms of it can easily be identified in most of the cases. For instance, how can Beatrice Rohner's commitment be understood without taking into account the fact that she belonged to German Protestant philanthropic organization working in the East (Hülfsbund für christliches Liebeswerk im Orient)? For this very devout woman, her dedication to the Armenian children was simply a matter of God's calling. In Rwanda, the inhabitants of Mabare mostly belonged to the Muslim religion, very much a minority in Rwanda. Some analysts note that in many cases Muslims were involved in rescuing Tutsis in 1994, an observation that precisely warrants further investigation. In Germany, the Bund certainly did not describe itself as a religious organization but, as Mark Roseman points out, functioned a bit like a religious sect with its own codes and rituals in the service of social change. In Nieuwlande's land of rescue, Michel Fabréguet grants particular importance to the sermons of Pastor Frits Slomp who encouraged his coreligionists to protect the Jews, backed by a strict Calvinist farmer, Johannes Post. Patrick Cabanel suggests that the commitment of French Protestants in acts of rescue had much to do with to their spiritual affinities with the Jews, given their common reference to scripture.

But then, is there not the risk of essentializing the religious factor, whereas it would be much more appropriate to contextualize it? Even if the Protestants were indeed on the side of rescue in Denmark, they offered strong support for the Nazi regime in Germany (aside from the Confessing Church), whereas in the Netherlands their stance was more divided. Another hypothesis thus warrants attention: it is perhaps not so much the fact of being Protestant or Muslim in itself that matters, but more the fact of having a past or present minority experience in a given country? As Patrick Cabanel himself suggests, that would spontaneously act as a source of particular empathy toward someone who in turn is undergoing persecution. In short, those who rescue in a time of crisis can already be described as dissidents in peacetime. These actors, already in effect at odds with the social norms, prove more reactive in times of crisis, coming to the rescue precisely of those who are banished from society.

NETWORKS, MINORITIES AND RESCUE

We should not for all that conclude that the person who rescues necessarily lives on the fringe of society. In France and in Belgium, where the Catholic Church boasted a large majority in 1940, some of its members also became involved in helping the Jews (a bit later than the Protestants, admittedly) such as Father Chaillet's Amitiés Chrétiennes network in Lyon.

It is in fact extremely difficult to put forward any theory of the decision to perform an act of rescue, all the more so since, in addition, these minority actors sometimes had paradoxical relations with the authorities. For instance, the pietistic Beatrice Rohner enjoyed relative protection from Jamaal Pasha, one of the leaders of the Young Turks' regime. She cleverly took advantage of this official protection to administer her orphanage, while at the same time conducting illegal rescue operations in camps in the region. Thus we see instances of rescue networks being created that combine both a legal façade and underground activities. In the very different context of Vichy France, Michel Laffitte looks into the controversial and ambiguous role of the Union Générale des Israélites de France (UGIF). He shows that this organization imposed by the German occupying force was also used as the legal façade for underground rescue activities. This legality/illegality relationship is indeed at the crux of our investigation, since one aim is to find out to what extent victims themselves also agreed to cross the line into underground activity.

Acts of rescue should also be considered from the "bottom up" perspective of society, that is, through the texture of social and friendship ties that victims can potentially benefit from. Camille Ménager's study on the rescue of Paris Jews shows that the nature of encounters between Jews and non-Jews mainly had to do with relationships formed at various levels before the war. Research on that topic had yet to be undertaken. The most common link is generally through the workplace, she notes, slightly ahead of friendship and neighborhood ties. Other studies underway seem to confirm this hypothesis; for instance, that of Rafiki Ubaldo who narrates the case of a Hutu family who agreed to hide the children of their Tutsi neighbors, remembering that they had once given them a cow, an inestimable gift in Rwanda.[1] Once again, the protective gesture cannot

---

[1] The author was unfortunately unable to finalize his research for this publication. We should also mention Sergey A. Kizima's ongoing research on the rescue of Byelorussian Jews by Tatar families.

be understood without making reference to the history of a relationship. What remains to be seen is whether this relationship will hold fast in a time of crisis. Nothing is ever certain in this regard; neighbors sometimes turn into informers, if not killers.

Whatever the case, social ties and friendship ties always remains fragile. Protection may only be momentary when danger approaches. In that case one must run away, flee to another place that one hopes is safer. Thus, in occupied France it was better to leave Paris and seek shelter in the countryside, preferably in the Southern Zone, or even cross the border into Switzerland. In Rwanda, safety involved escaping into neighboring Burundi. Moving of victims (adults or children) thus required setting up chains of solidarity from place to place. With time and experience, escape channels were set up and became better organized, which sometimes ended up incurring a charge for the service.

For it must not be forgotten: saving lives costs money. This fact is often underestimated in the hagiographic literature devoted to the "Righteous," which is more concerned with commemorating selfless acts. For instance, farmers in Chambon-sur-Lignon who hosted a Jewish child received a stipend to feed them. Does that mean that their shelter should be depreciated? It is true that the act of rescue can provide an extra source of income in times of shortage. On a farm, an extra "mouth to feed" sometimes also meant an extra hand in farm labor. But how can one define the threshold beyond which the hosting party ends up exploiting the hosted party? Abuse, blending self-interest and altruism, probably always occurs. Beyond this moral question, a simple fact should be admitted: like any other resistance activity, those that involve rescuing victims require means, including financial means. Theorizing about acts of protection and rescue thus requires us to consider both their moral dimension and their material contingencies, which condition their always-uncertain success.

22

BEATRICE ROHNER'S WORK IN
THE DEATH CAMPS OF ARMENIANS IN 1916

Hans-Lukas Kieser

At the end of 1915, an important encounter took place. Let us imagine a bareheaded youngish woman, smiling but determined, and a slightly older, bearded man who wears a uniform with decorations and an Ottoman headgear. They discuss with each other. We are in Aleppo, capital of an Ottoman province where the second phase of the Armenians' genocide, their death by starvation in large camps and the violent suppression of these camps, was taking place.[2] The man is Jemal Pasha (1872–1922), one of the so-called triumvirate heading the Young Turk regime in 1913–18, Minister of Naval Affairs and Commander of the Fourth Army in Syria. The woman is Beatrice Rohner (1876–1947), a Swiss lady who has grown up in Basel, been a teacher in Paris and Istanbul and then, in 1900, settled in Marash (today Kahramanmaraş) where she has worked for the German Protestant Hülfsbund für christliches Liebeswerk im Orient (Aid Association for Christian Charity in the East). From December 1915 to April 1917 she stayed in Aleppo and led the modest inter-

---

[2] Cf. Kévorkian, Raymond H., *L'extermination des déportés arméniens ottomans dans les camps de concentration de Syrie et de Mésopotamie (1915–1916): la deuxième phase du génocide*, Paris, Centre d'Histoire Arménienne Contemporaine, 1998 (= *Revue d'Histoire Arménienne Contemporaine*, vol. II).

national efforts to help the hundreds of thousands Armenians who had survived the "removal" from Anatolia to the desert camps of Northern Syria. Rohner met Jemal for the first time in the second half of December 1915. There was no pleasant friendship between them. Enjoying nevertheless, at least partly, Jemal's protection, Rohner began to care for about a thousand Armenian orphans. She managed moreover to undertake rescue actions in the camps illegally, spending large sums of money that she received from American, Swiss and German philanthropic circles. Not less important, she established correspondence with people condemned to be starved to death or massacred.

Hilmar Kaiser has published on those rescue efforts in Aleppo and has the merit of having recalled the names of Beatrice Rohner and Hovhannes Eskijian, the pioneer of that "humanitarian resistance to genocide," to a scholarly public.[3] This article follows a biographical perspective and goes beyond the context of 1915–16. It outlines Rohner's life, including her experience in Aleppo. It draws particular attention to the impact of those efforts upon her life, on her attempts to come to terms with her experience, and the role of her pietistic spirituality in rescue work and beyond. Her spiritual biography is accessible through her writings, which we must contextualize within time, space and personal networks.[4]

A beautiful sunny childhood' and a commitment in Marash

Like her compatriot Jakob Künzler (1871–1949), the non-Armenian rescuer later best known to Armenians,[5] Rohner, born in Basel on 24

---

[3] Kaiser, Hilmar, *At the Crossroads of Der Zor. Death, Survival, and Humanitarian Resistance*, Princeton, NJ, Taderon, 2001.

[4] Sincere thanks to Hannelore Graf, Mutterhausarchiv der Evangelischen Diakonissenanstalt Stuttgart (MEDS), to Bruno Blaser, Christlicher Hilfsbund e.V., and to Daniel Kress, Staatsarchiv des Kantons Basel-Stadt.

[5] "The non-Armenian mentioned most frequently in our interviews was Papa Kuenzler, a Swiss missionary," write Donald E. Miller and Lorna Touryan Miller in their book *Survivors. An Oral History of the Armenian Genocide*, Berkeley, University of California Press, 1999 (1993), p. 130. Rohner is not mentioned in this book, but is now honored on the web pages of the "Gardens of the Righteous Worldwide Committee" (www.forestadeigiusti.it, visited on 13 April 2009). On Künzler see the introduction to Jakob Künzler, *Im Landes des Blutes und der Tränen. Erlebnisse in Mesopotamien während des Weltkriegs (1914–18)*, Zürich, Chronos, 2004. English edition: *In the Land of the Blood and Tears. Ex-*

April 1876, grew up as a half-orphan. Her father died when she was three years old and her sister Anni one year old. It seems that her mother, Maria Magdalena Rohner-Thoma, provided for the family after the death of her husband, a shopkeeper, while little Beatrice stayed with her grandmother. In her house she "lived a beautiful sunny childhood," as she wrote around 1901. After four years of primary school, she spent six years at a high school for girls and then two years at a teacher training college. For five years she worked as a private teacher mostly in Paris; then she joined the Hülfsbund für christliches Liebeswerk im Orient, a relief organization founded in Frankfurt in 1896. Pastor Otto Stockmayer, a leader of the Pietistic Revival (*Gemeinschaftsbewegung*) of the late 19th century, had invited her to do so.[6] The Hülfsbund had a more pietistic character than the more liberal Deutsche Orient-Mission of Dr Johannes Lepsius, but both originated in the common relief movement of 1896 after the anti-Armenian massacres of 1895.[7]

Beatrice Rohner taught in the Hülfsbund orphanage school in Bebek in Istanbul in 1899. In fall 1900 she moved to Marash in Central Anatolia where she was a housemother and teacher in the Hülfsbund orphanage "Beth-Ullah" or "Bethel." She was the first of her all-female family: her mother followed her in 1908, her sister in 1913. Full of praise for her, an Armenian author who had lived in Marash writes that her "work was not merely to adopt children into her heart and superintend an orphanage. [...] In the midst of her important and exacting responsibilities in the orphanage, she found time and created opportunities to conduct revival meetings [...]. Beatrice Rohner's testimony was one much to be coveted and emulated. She was a woman of gentleness and humility, full of compassion and tender solicitude toward the needy and weak, and generous with things entrusted to her care."[8] Thus, on the eve of the First

---

periences in Mesopotamia during the World War (1914–1918), Arlington, MA, Armenian Cultural Foundation, 2007.

[6] Handwritten Curriculum of Beatrice Rohner, c. 1901, in the archives of the Christliche Hilfsbund, Bad Homburg (ACH), and *Gedenkschrift für Schwester Beatrice Rohner*, Wüstenrot: Kurt Reith Verlag, 1947, p. 5; Civilstand L 1 1876 Nr. 475, Staatsarchiv des Kantons Basel-Stadt.

[7] On the particular context of the humanitarian protest and relief movement in Switzerland after 1896 see Hans-Lukas Kieser (ed.), *Die armenische Frage und die Schweiz / La question arménienne et la Suisse (1896–1923)*, Zürich, Chronos, 1999.

[8] Bilezikian, Vartan, *Apraham Hoja of Aintab*, Winona Lake: Light and Life Press,

World War, Rohner lived in her "own Jerusalem" in Ottoman Marash, surrounded by her students and together with her family from Basel.

On 6 April 1915 Karl Blank, Rohner's colleague in Marash, reported to the Hülfsbund director Friedrich Schuchardt how difficult the times had become since the general mobilization in August 1914, and that since March 1915 massacres had been imminent, partly because of the upheavals in Zeytun, near Marash. Therefore Beatrice Rohner went to Aleppo and called on the German Consul Rössler, who then made a trip to Marash.[9] But the low-profile intervention of lesser diplomats was not to stop the general anti-Armenian policy. The people of Zeytun were deported first to Konya, then, by order of the minister of the Interior Talat on 24 April to Deir ez-Zor.[10] The Armenians from the villages around Marash were also sent to the desert, and in mid-August the Armenians from the town of Marash itself.[11] Rohner was one of the informants of Andreas Vischer of the Swiss Relief Committee in Basel, a doctor on furlough from the joint Germano-Swiss hospital in Urfa which their common friend Jakob Künzler managed during the War.[12] One of her reports was also included the famous collection of documents by Bryce and Toynbee.[13]

Aleppo 1915–17

Protestant missionary networks sought ways to help the hundreds of thousands of survivors of the deportations who were suffering in the

---

  1951, pp. 98–9. Many thanks to Mehmet Ali Dogan who sent me copies of these pages.
[9] Blank's letter enclosed in Schuchardt to German Foreign Office (GFO), 20 August 1915. Cf. German Ambassador Wangenheim to GFO, 27 March 1915; long report of Rössler to GFO, 12 April 1915; documents of the GFO, edited by Wolfgang and Sigrid Gust, on www.armenocide.de.
[10] The Turkish Republic Prime Ministry, General Directorate of the State Archives, Directorate of Ottoman Archives (ed.), *Armenians in Ottoman Documents (1915–1920)*, Ankara 1995, p. 26.
[11] Rössler to Embassy, Istanbul, 16 August 1915 (GFO, www.armenocide.de).
[12] Article "An die Armenierfreunde" in the *Basler Nachrichten* of 16 August 1915 (also among the diplomatic documents on www.armenocide.de, because the German Consul Wunderlich had sent the article to the Chancellor on 22 September 1915).
[13] James Bryce, and Arnold Toynbee (eds), *The Treatment of Armenians in the Ottoman Empire. Documents Presented to Viscount Grey of Fallodon by Viscount*

camps around Aleppo. On 11 October Schuchardt openly asked the German Foreign Office for a travel permit in order to "visit our stations in the centre of Asia Minor and, together with our brothers and sisters of the mission, to find a way of bringing practical and spiritual help to the Armenians in the so-called concentration camps in the region of Aleppo and Urfa."[14] The German Embassy opposed this idea, saying it would be understood politically and "resources would be wasted without us gaining anything."[15] Nevertheless Schuchardt obtained a travel permit, but only as far as Constantinople. German diplomacy understood that German help for starving Armenians was important for publicity in the West, but should not be revealed to the Turks.[16] Schuchardt visited William Peet, the informal chief of the Protestant American Board of Commissioners of Foreign Missions (ABCFM) in Ottoman Turkey and, on 12 November, the US Ambassador Henry Morgenthau.[17]

The right person for Aleppo, though, was not Director Schuchardt, but Rohner. She was fluent in Turkish, French, German, English and Armenian (and possibly Arabic) and, as a woman and a citizen of a neutral country, enjoyed a low profile. She too had obtained a travel permit and come to Istanbul. There was also a friend of hers, the old ABCFM doctor Fred Shepard from Ainteb (today Gaziantep, some 60 km southeast of Marash). They all met and discussed plans for rescue in November. "During the negotiations in Constantinople an old friend, a doctor of the American mission [Shepard], visited me. He had seen much of the deportation, but his efforts to do something for the deportees had failed. The Americans possessed important sums of money from the USA, but the real area of deportation—Aleppo and its surroundings—where thousands fell victim to hunger and illness daily, was completely closed to them because of the Turkish military authorities' ban. During the discussion

---

Bryce, London, 1916; new, uncensored edition: Princeton, NJ: Gomidas Institute, 2000, p. 470.

[14] Enclosed in GFO to Ambassador Wangenheim, 15 October 1915 (GFO, www.armenocide.de).

[15] Wangenheim, 21 October, and Neurath, five days later (GFO, www.armenocide.de).

[16] Metternich, German Embassy, to Chancellor Bethmann Hollweg, 17 February 1916 (GFO, www.armenocide.de). Cf. Kaiser, *Crossroads*, p. 35.

[17] Schuchardt to GFO on 12 November 1915 (GFO, www.armenocide.de); Kaiser, *Crossroads*, p. 34.

my friend suddenly said: 'You are Swiss and belong to a German missionary society. Could you not enter that area? Be assured that we would give you all the money we have.' This was a ray of hope! I understood God wanted to do something! Aleppo closed, infected, that centre of need and misery, should be opened!" From then on, the "call to Aleppo stood urgently and imperatively before my soul," Rohner wrote in 1934, when for the first time she was able to look back and compose a retrospective account of 1915–16.[18]

Once she was back in Marash, this "call" prevented her from staying and celebrating Christmas there, as she had intended to do, but impelled her to travel quickly to Aleppo together with her "mission sister" Paula Schäfer. During the journey the two investigated the situation in several camps.[19] In a letter of 29 December to Schuchardt from Aleppo, Rohner writes that on that day she obtained Jemal Pasha's permission by telegraph to run the big Armenian orphanage in Aleppo. Shortly before, she had met Jemal and Abdülhalik Mustafa (Renda), the governor (*vali*) of Aleppo, a hardliner who had replaced the generally respected and moderate Jelal Bey. Around 22 December she had met Jemal for a first time, the following day for a second time. A meeting, on the urgent issue of orphans, of Jemal with Germans in Aleppo, among them General von Kressenstein and the director of the Baghdad Railway construction at Aleppo, on 21 December[20] may have prepared her finally successful encounter with Jemal. Jemal insisted however that he did not agree to her traveling outside Aleppo. "I think we must do as much as we can in this matter, albeit collaboration with the officials may be unpleasant," Rohner concluded.[21]

Rohner enjoyed freedom of movement in the town, hired employees, among them Armenian fugitives who thus acquired protection, and organized care for the orphans. She made Sisag Manughian, a pastor she knew from Marash who was living in hiding in Aleppo, a co-worker, saving him and his family from death. Another permanent collaborator was

---

[18] "Pfade in grossen Wassern," *Sonnenaufgang* 36 (1934), pp. 14–15, 21, 30–1, 38–9, 45–6, 54–6, here p. 21.
[19] Three reports enclosed in Schuchardt to GFO, 26 January 1916 (GFO, www.armenocide.de).
[20] Kaiser, *Crossroads*, p. 54.
[21] Enclosed in Schuchardt to GFO, 14 February 1916 (GFO, www.armenocide.de).

Anna Jensen from Mamuretülaziz, like Rohner a member of the Hülfsbund.[22] Harassed by officials, Rohner had to change the orphanage buildings three times within a few days, but nonetheless the government gave her some food for the orphans. "Though [...] the *vali* was not at all sympathetic to us, he was obliged to allow us the absolute necessities. [...] We depended on our enemies, and nonetheless lived from what the heavenly Father gave us," she commented, looking back on the difficult start of the orphanage where she finally cared with her team for about a thousand Armenians.[23] Early on she knew that her children were threatened, and that the government intended to take them into government orphanages and to assimilate them to Muslim Turks, attempting to thoroughly change their identity.[24]

"I was confronted with my new duty. It far exceeded my physical and mental forces. But I knew one thing. There comes a gift from the God who has called, a gift that perfectly fits the duty."[25] The orphanage was only a part of Rohner's work. From January she is fully engaged in organizing help for the camps outside Aleppo.[26] The official work in Aleppo "gave the opportunity to do relief work in all silence" in the camps, as she wrote to Andreas Vischer.[27] Freedom of action in the town, the backing of the German Consul Walter Rössler and the American Consul Jesse Jackson (in them "I found two men who had their hearts in the right place"),[28] an international network of friends in Aleppo (among them the Swiss merchants Emil Zollinger and Conrad Schüepp) and in Europe, much money from the ABCFM or from Near East Relief which was just beginning, and, above all, an underground network of courageous, intelligent young men, mostly Armenians, who smuggled letters and money

---

[22] "Pfade," p. 45.

[23] "Pfade," p. 39. Cf. Letters of Rohner of 13 February and of 3 May 1916 in *Sonnenaufgang* 18 (1916), pp. 61 and 78–9.

[24] Cf. her letter to Peet on 17 January 1916, enclosed in Peet to German Embassy, 10 February 1916 (GFO, www.armenocide.de).

[25] "Pfade," p. 31.

[26] Rohner's letter to Peet of 17 January 1915, enclosed in Peet to German Embassy, 10 February 1916 (GFO, www.armenocide.de).

[27] Copies of this document (an answer to a questionnaire of the Swiss Relief Committee) and of a letter of Rössler to Vischer were enclosed in Metternich, Geman Embassy, to the Chancellor, 28 April 1916 (GFO, www.armenocide.de).

[28] "Pfade," p. 38.

in the camps: all this made possible this perilous commitment that helped thousands of people to survive for a time, and some of them also to escape final destruction.

Rohner cooperated with the Armenian Protestant pastor Hovhannes Eskidjian, who had built up a large network of help for the deportees of all denominations since summer 1915. According to John Minassian, who worked for Eskidjian and later for Rohner, she once succeeded in stopping a dangerous investigation directed against Eskidjian. But this pillar of humanitarian and consciously Christian resistance died of typhus on 25 March 1916, leaving 250 orphans to the care of Rohner's team. She used spiritual humor in the difficult moment when inspectors came. "She invited the officials in and showed them the children in their classrooms, saying 'Come in and see my garden of flowers'. Their skeleton-like bodies, sheeted in their shabby clothes, were living proof of hunger nearing the starvation point," Minassian writes.[29]

Men from Marash, travelers, businessmen and other courageous young men enabled Rohner to contact the camps. A young trader from Izmir, who had first been a teacher in the orphanage, voluntarily began to act as a messenger to the deportees outside Aleppo;[30] in May 1916 he worked together with a young Armenian from Marash named Garabed in Deir ez-Zor.[31] Under Ali Fuad, the administrator (*mutasarrıf*) of that district and a man much esteemed by Rohner,[32] many Armenians had managed to begin a modest new life in the town. In the camp on the left bank of the Euphrates, however, the situation was horrible. Fuad was replaced in July 1916 by the Circassian Salih Zeki, who massacred the remnants of the Armenians sent to Deir ez-Zor in groups of a few thousands.[33] "Those

---

[29] John Minassian, *Many Hills yet to Climb*, Santa Barbara, CA, Jim Cook, 1986, pp. 104 and 121 (quotation). Cf. M.H. Shnorhokian, *A Pioneer during the Armenian Genocide: Rev. Hovhannes Eskijian*, 1989. Many thanks to Nancy Eskijian, the granddaughter of Hovhannes Eskijian, who sent me this unpublished paper that incorporates first-hand accounts.

[30] See Rohner's detailed report on relief between 1 January and 1 June 1916, enclosed in Rössler to Chancellor of Germany, 17 June 1916 (GFO, www.armenocide.de).

[31] Letter of Rohner, 3 May 1916, in *Sonnenuntergang* 18 (1916), pp. 78–9. Rohner's biographical homage to Garabed in Beatrice Rohner, *Die Stunde ist gekommen. Märtyrerbilder aus der Jetztzeit*, Frankfurt am Main, Verlag Orient, n.d. (c. 1920), pp. 7–14.

[32] Rohner, *Stunde*, p. 30.

[33] Kévorkian, *Extermination*, pp. 37–44.

in Deir ez-Zor and its surroundings, about 80,000, who had scarcely enjoyed a little rest, were gathered into camps in order to be brought in groups to the other side of the Euphrates. Again a hopeless wandering took place, and then, far from the eyes of any European, gangs of irregulars were waiting on orders from their government, and made a bloody end to them all," Rohner summarized what wounded fugitives of that massacres had reported her.[34]

The messengers normally came to Rohner after nightfall, after the daily work in the orphanage.

[One of them] told us about the different camps. [...] The *fellahs* [peasants] would always give us some grain or bread for money. We quickly took our cashbox [...] and while the messenger rested for a few hours, we sewed into his clothes as many of pieces of gold as could be put in. During this time I read the mail that he had brought with him. What mail! Letters, sheets of papers from friends to whom we felt close [...]. What enormous amounts of need and wretchedness these letters contained! Quickly I had to answer a few lines, to tell them that God had not forgotten them, that his love was the same even if all that could be shaken was shaken. After a few hours, long before daybreak, our friend had to set off, [...] our hearts with him. How we longed for a message that he had come through.[35]

The translated texts of a few of these shattering letters to Rohner from Deir ez-Zor and elsewhere have been preserved in the German diplomatic archives,[36] other parts in later quotations by Rohner,[37] but we don't have any of Rohner's letters of consolation. About another messenger Rohner wrote: "In this way he managed to bring help many times until the henchmen seized him at last and he sealed his service with his life. 'No man has greater love than to give his life for his friends' [John 15,13]."[38]

Sad good-bye to Aleppo

Rohner's network of rescue worked relatively well from January to September 1916, even though the help reached only a small fraction of the

---

[34] Rohner, *Stunde*, pp. 13–14.
[35] "Pfade," pp. 54–5.
[36] Enclosed in Rössler, Aleppo, to Chancellor Bethmann Hollweg, 29 July 1916 (GFO, www.armenocide.de).
[37] Rohner, *Stunde*, several quotations.
[38] "Pfade," p. 55.

hundreds of thousands of Armenians in northern Syria. Not only the material help was important, but also the communication, the show of sympathy and the empowerment. In a letter from Rössler to the German Chancellor Bethmann-Hollweg on 20 September 1916, we read that the "distribution of American back-up funds by Sister Beatrice Rohner through Armenian intermediaries has faced obstacles in the Euphrates area," because one of her messengers had been seized by the authorities and under torture revealed information about the relief organization. In order not to endanger the whole work, Rohner withdrew provisionally and concentrated her effort upon the orphanage. She kept informing Consul Rössler and others about what she knew.[39]

"The greatest difficulties arise from the double fact that I am scarcely tolerated in my work for the orphans [in Aleppo], while officially the relief work [in the camps] is not allowed at all. It must be done secretly and where it becomes public, it is forbidden and suppressed. This time the Armenians will not expect any help from outside," Rohner wrote on 24 November 1916 to Emanuel Riggenbach, a representative of the Relief Committee in Basel. "Until now the officials could not get rid of little me, because they themselves gave me the work [for the orphans], but they do everything to put me off." Very discreet publicity in Europe, in order to collect funds, and a low profile on the ground were preconditions for—relatively—successful relief work. She exhorted her correspondent not to publish letters with her name and said that, if ever possible, Riggenbach should write the "poor" (*Arme*) not "Armenians" (*Armenier*).[40] "Little would be gained for the remnants of the Armenian people if I report everywhere, but for the emergency itself I could no longer do anything." In the same letter she writes that it had been possible to open workplaces for thousands of Armenian women in Aleppo where they spun and sewed for the military but were safe. Colonel Kemal Bey, responsible for this work, was cooperative.[41]

---

[39] Rössler to Reichskanzler, 20 September and 5 November 1916; Rohner's statistics about the origin and fate of the parents of 720 orphans enclosed in Radowith, German Embassy, to Chancellor of Germany, 4 October 1916 (GFO, www.armenocide.de).

[40] Rohner to Riggenbach, 24 November 1916, enclosed in Rössler to Reichskanzler, 25 November 1916 (GFO, www.armenocide.de).

[41] Rössler to Chancellor of Germany, 16 March 1917 (GFO, www.armenocide.de).

When Rohner withdrew provisionally from the distribution of help in the camps in September, the murderous suppression of the camps had already begun, as mentioned above with regard to Deir ez-Zor. Furthermore it was not rashness, but the harsh politics of Turkification that finally caused Rohner to lose the most intimate part of her commitment, the orphans. "In Aleppo the government has taken seventy boys from the orphanages directed by Sister Beatrice Rohner to bring them to a government orphanage in the Lebanon where they shall be raised with children of Muslim refugees from Eastern Anatolia. Similar transfers of this kind to government orphanages are planned," Rössler reported on 14 February 1917 to the Chancellor of Germany. Some of Rohner's orphans had gone to a government orphanage in Aintoura in Lebanon, which Jemal entrusted to Halide Edib, a well-known writer and Turkish patriot who, however, had not condoned the CUP policy of extermination.[42]

On 16 March Rössler confirmed that Rohner's work had been completely wound up, adding that she had been asked by the American Consul to reorganize relief in Aleppo, which she did for about 20,000 people in need in the town, including 1,200 children. Shortly afterwards, on 17 March she broke down and withdrew for good, entrusting her "work to a commission of Armenians supervised by Zollinger."[43] Rohner was exhausted and had been deeply affected since her orphans had been taken away. Karl Meyer, the chronicler of the Swiss relief to the Armenians, who himself had worked among Armenian refugees in Lebanon, writes that Rohner "suffered a nervous breakdown on 17 March. Jakob Künzler was called from Urfa, came to Aleppo and accompanied her to Constantinople from where she returned later to Germany."[44] Künzler probably accompanied her to Marash, not to Istanbul, for a first period of rest.[45] Toward the end of 1917 she traveled to Germany via Istanbul after she had obtained the Ottoman travel permit on 5 October.[46] On 28 August

---

[42] Cf. Atay, Falih Rıfkı, *Zeytindağ*, Istanbul, Bateş, 1981 (1938), pp. 63–5.

[43] Rössler to German Embassy, 14 and 17 May 1917 (GFO, www.armenocide.de).

[44] Meyer, Karl, *Armenien und die Schweiz*, Berne, Blaukreuz-Verlag, 1974, p. 249.

[45] Rohner to German Embassy, 14 May 1917 (GFO, www.armenocide.de).

[46] "Maraş'da Muessese-i Muavenet Reisesi İsviçre tebeasından Beatrice Rohner'in hemşire olarak yaptığı güzel hizmetlere binaen Almanya'ya seyahatine müsaade olunduğu" (19/S/1336, Ottoman State Archives, Istanbul, DH.EUM.5.Şb 50:15). Many thanks to Nazan Maksudyan for sending me this document.

1918 Schuchardt reported to Rössler that Rohner was his, or the Hülfsbund's, guest in Frankfurt, and that her departure to return to Aleppo was planned only for Fall 1919.[47]

According to Minassian, Rohner was already back in Aleppo in March 1919 when she "invited me to visit the grave of Reverend Eskijian, to commemorate the third anniversary of his death. 'Only a few will come to remember the great man who died without fear,' she said, 'because he did all he could to serve his people.'"[48] But it took many years before Rohner recovered. Meyer says that she lived for a while on the Hasliberg in the Swiss mountains where, in Fall 1926, Hewig Büll from Aleppo, her former co-worker in Marash, visited her and told her that all her orphans were still alive.[49] According to Meyer and to Rohner herself, this brought her depression to an end. She worked as a "free missionary" to Germans in Württemberg and in 1928–29 made a trip to Marash, Aintab and Syria. In 1932 she began to run a Christian guesthouse in Wüstenroth, near Stuttgart. Again she had a team and young people around her, held prayers and explained the Bible. In addition she wrote or translated books of spirituality. Although she used a non-political pietistic language, she made it clear that one must not join the Nazis. She and her team had a difficult time when a part of her house was occupied by Nazi nurses in July 1944. They "coldly declined our best," i.e. the spiritual message, she wrote in a circular letter.[50] She died in her house in Wüstenroth on 9 February 1947.

---

[47] *Deportation der Armenier Dezember 1914 bis August 1918. Schriftverkehr von Hilfsbundmitarbeitern mit offiziellen Stellen in Deutschland*, ACH.

[48] Minassian, *Many Hills*, p. 199.

[49] In Lebanon Büll had met Pastor Sisag Manughian, Rohner's right hand man in Aleppo in 1916; he told her that he had investigated the fate of Rohner's former orphans (Meyer, *Armenien*, p. 267). Rohner confirms this and adds that all her children finally survived Turkish rule ("Pfade," p. 14).

[50] Abschrift eines Rundbriefes von Beatrice Rohner vom Jahr 1945, MEDS. Cf. "Vita für Beatrice Rohner" in Beatrice Rohner, *Jünger Jesu aus der Kirche der Armen. Abraham Levonian*, Wüstenrot, Kurt Reith Verlag, p. 30 (p. 27 on her trip to Marash); Beatrice Rohner, *Worte für Wanderer zur Herrlichkeit. Gedanken über den Hebräerbrief*, Giessen and Basel, Brunnen-Verlag, 1938; she translated from English Amy Carmichael, *Die goldene Schnur. Das Werden einer Gemeinschaft*, Giessen and Basel, Brunnen-Verlag, 1934.

Coming to terms

Shortly after the Nazis came to power in the beginning of 1933, Rohner began to write the memoir from which we have already quoted some passages.

Again and again I was asked in this time [after 1917] to write [on my experience in Aleppo]; but I had too heavy a heart. Again and again there appeared before my soul the conclusion of my service in Aleppo, when with a short dry order the Turkish government took the nearly 1000 children from me to settle them in their own homes and institutions. I fell ill and had to return to Europe [...]. The last thing that I saw of them was that special train which carried them off, and thus the curtain of darkness was drawn on them, on me, on all I had lived through in Syria. In that situation what could I write?[51]

Nevertheless she made a first attempt when, around 1920, she published a booklet entitled *Die Stunde ist gekommen. Märtyrerbilder aus der Jetztzeit* (The Hour has Come: Portraits of Present-day Martyrs).[52] Over thirty-two pages Rohner paid homage and a last farewell to eight Armenian friends from Marash, lost in 1915/16. It is a text of painful memory and mourning, mobilizing all the spiritual resources Rohner had, to give meaning to the lives and deaths of these dear human beings. There was for example Minas, a young man and gifted singer from Bunduk (a mountain village that had been destroyed in 1895 and lost nearly all its men) whom Rohner had taught to read on the eve of the First World War; he then became an informal pastor in the village. In 1915 Rohner saw him passing through Marash, with the whole village. She was able to save one girl. "Now he can sing [his song] before the throne of the lamb. The little village of Bunduk is desolate and deserted [...]. Will there ever be a new beginning?"[53]

The longest homage is that to Garabed, called "a devoted messenger," whom we have already mentioned in relation to Deir ez-Zor. Garabed, a silversmith in the town, had been seized by the spiritual revival Rohner worked for, and became active in it. In 1915 he survived the deportation, went from his camp to Aleppo (which was forbidden on pain of death)

---

[51] "Pfade," p. 14.
[52] Beatrice Rohner, *Die Stunde ist gekommen. Märtyrerbilder aus der Jetztzeit*, Frankfurt am Main, Verlag Orient, n.d. (c. 1920).
[53] p. 7.

in order to get help to relatives, and finally became one of Rohner's messengers to Deir ez-Zor. "He felt it was now time not only to speak about, but to live God's love […]." At least three times he came and went. "Everywhere he had found compatriots from Marash […], he gave them a little help which eked out their lives for a while, and comforted them in their courage and faith, like greetings from eternal love." Then his trail was lost. "[…] Garabed had become an old man, his full black hair turned very grey […]. But he had a deep earnestness, a saintly determination, and peace that is not of this earth." In Deir ez-Zor there was daily prayer in inter-confessional assemblies. The informal group of *Christossa-Siroz* (Lovers of Christ), mostly Gregorian Armenians (Armenian Orthodox), who had had their center in Anteb, played a leading role. "Each evening they met […] and during the day they went as messengers of his [God's] love into the huts of misery and to all the desperate people around them. […] According to a letter which another messenger brought me, they planned to penetrate further into the desert in order to bring consolation and help to the Christians scattered there."[54] It was too late; the murderous elimination of the remnants was beginning.

Another chapter is on Haig, a shoemaker from Zeytun near Marash, and at the same time a free evangelist on his own account. As a "political suspect," he was arrested early on in spring 1915, brought to the prison in Marash and executed in public in one of Marash's squares.[55] The only chapter Rohner devoted to one of her cherished orphans is the short one on Setrag, whose deported mother married a Muslim in Aleppo; she had to convert, but her little son refused to do so and was brought to the orphanage.

The fact that Rohner refused to think that lost life was lost for good becomes clearer in her chapter on Araxia, an exceptionally gifted girl, one of those who had emancipated themselves from tradition, including early marriage, through their education in missionary or other institutions in late Ottoman times. Back from two years in England she joined the *Christossa-Siroz* and settled down in Anteb before the war. She too had to leave in 1915. "I cannot say what grief struck me when I learnt about this. Araxia on the road!" After several months of silence, Araxia was found in Deir ez-Zor. Thanks to Rohner's messengers, they could cor-

[54] pp. 11–14.
[55] pp. 16–17.

respond. "I have no words to describe the misery to you [...]. We live God's presence in our midst as never before; the prayers are fervent and all separations have disappeared," Araxia wrote. Rohner received a last message from her as she was being taken away for the final massacre. "The life from which we expected so much was shattered so early. Was it for nothing?"[56]

Rohner's memoir of 1933–34 differs from that of 1920, as it is a complete narrative. After seventeen years, Rohner was able to articulate the whole story. More than in 1920, she argued that despite everything the God of love had not been completely absent. Even if she does not make an explicit link, it is difficult not to think that her readiness to write was also a reaction to the Nazis' coming to power. There is no doubt that she wanted to empower her readers against the "demons" she herself had faced in the First World War. "Yes, our house [in Aleppo] would perhaps have become an oasis in the desert, but never let us forget that the Pharaoh of Turkish hatred and the will to destruction [*Vernichtungswillen*] was after us and wanted at all costs to prevent a little people escaping his power."[57] Unfortunately, there are no sources available on how she perceived the rise of the Nazis on a more concrete level.

Rohner wanted to show that a feeble being like herself was able to organize efficient humanitarian resistance:

How much we were disliked in Aleppo! Our simple presence was a permanent thorn in the flesh of those who were determined to destroy the remnants of the Armenian people. Every opportunity to scatter these children, the hope of the future, again, to ban me from Aleppo, to hunt my co-workers into the desert, would have been warmly welcomed. But something hindered the enemies, something paralyzed all the spies and stooges who were with us every day, something held back the Turkish authorities from destroying everything with a single order, although we were completely exposed to them.

Rohner gives several examples of critical situations, concluding: "What held the enemies back? They, at least, did not know it themselves, but we knew it and knew it every day again, when in prayer together we spoke of our utter helplessness and our impossible situation to the Lord [...]."[58]

---

[56] pp. 28–32.
[57] "Pfade," p. 38.
[58] "Pfade," p. 54

Conclusion

Pietists were often mocked as unrealistic, sanctimonious people. It was nevertheless Beatrice Rohner, member of a pietistic organization, who organized the most important rescue effort during the second phase of the Armenian genocide. Unlike some German colleagues, she never had illusions about the perpetrators' will to exterminate. She used her potential, her connections, her symbolic capital and the sympathy Jemal probably felt for her to organize efficient relief. Backed by Near East Relief, German and American diplomacy (weak where the Armenians were concerned), and international philanthropic circles and Swiss connections, she built up an efficient network of trusting friends, mostly people who shared her faith in Jesus, whom she knew already from Marash. She used them in the orphanages and for the most difficult task of illegal intervention in the camps. Despite the pietists' well-known loyalty to authority, she did not refrain from illegal humanitarian action. A strong spiritual life existed in her team, in her mind and during difficult moments—including her long depression after 1917. She was aware early on that she would probably lose the children, but when she so did, it was too much for her. Spirituality was not the superstructure but a vital motor in this rescuer's case. Whether there is generally something like a "spirituality of rescue" remains an open question, but this study makes it clear that this was the case with Beatrice Rohner. To a large extent her thinking, behavior and relations were conditioned by a spiritual life.

Rohner carried her experience back to Germany, where she built up a little center of spiritual resistance to Nazi power in Wüstenroth. Her late Ottoman experiences remained omnipresent in her books and talks. Another transfer of analogous experiences was that from Rohner's friend Jakob Künzler to his compatriot of Walzenhausen, Carl Lutz, the Swiss Consul in Budapest, who helped save tens of thousands of Jews in 1944 by issuing illegal visas.[59] Like Franz Werfel, but without any literary ambition, in 1933/34 Beatrice Rohner clearly articulated her encounter with massive evil in the past in 1915–17 in order to be ready to face evil in the present, that is, under the Nazis. Faithful to her own spiritual biography, she did so however with elaborate references to the Gospel. She paid particular attention to the Letter to the Hebrews, addressed to a small group of early Jewish Christians whom she explicitly compared with the Armenians.[60]

---

[59] Cf. Künzler, *Im Lande*, p. 128.
[60] Cf. "Pfade," p. 14–15, and *Worte für Wanderer*, p. 111.

23

THE IMPOSSIBLE RESCUE OF THE ARMENIANS OF MARDIN
THE SINJAR SAFE HAVEN

Yves Ternon

During the First World War, in 1915 and 1916, Armenians in the Ottoman Empire were victims of a genocide perpetrated by order of the Committee of Union and Progress (CUP), in power since 1908. Turkish nationalism was at the root of this genocide: the Young Turks wanted a homogenous Turkish nation and took advantage of the war to resolve the Armenian issue, the main obstruction standing in the way of their political plan. In order to achieve their plan to destroy the Armenian people, the Young Turks of the CUP, themselves secular-minded, appealed to Islamic solidarity, as the Turkish people were for the most part Muslim. The *jihad* declared in November 1914 allowed them to mobilize all of the Empire's Muslims against the Armenians. The first phase of the genocide took place from May to July 1915 in the six provinces (*vilayet*) of Eastern Anatolia, where Armenians had resided since high antiquity and where in some districts (*sanjak*) or cantons (*kaza*) they were the majority community. Two of these provinces—Van and Erzerum—shared borders with Russia, and therefore were in the theatre of war. Another, Bitlis, also became the stage of military operations in 1915. Two others—Mamuret ul-Aziz (Kharput) and Sivas—were more central and therefore removed from the front. Likewise, the *vilayet* of

Diyarbekir, further south, remained at a distance from the conflict between the Russian and Ottoman armies.

The result of these massacres and deportations was the same for all seven *vilayet*s: the definitive uprooting of the Armenians. But the conditions in which this genocide was perpetrated varied, as did the conditions of any possible rescue. The evacuation of Armenians from the *vilayet*s of Van or Erzurum to Transcaucasia during the Russian army's retreat in July, which saved them in April and May, cannot be considered rescue. In the same way, help supplied by foreign missionaries—Catholic or Protestant—to the Armenians of the *vilayet*s of Sivas and Kharput followed a different logic: the help was conditioned by the presence of these missions and the preservation of a dialogue between them and the Ottoman authorities. The situation in the Diyarbekir *vilayet* was unusual for two reasons: the majority of Muslims were Kurds, and the Christians were not all Armenians. The *sanjak* of Mardin, in the south of the *vilayet*, presented two more particularities: all the Armenians were Catholics, and there was a patchwork of different Christian denominations. Before outlining the issues surrounding the rescue of the Mardin Armenians, it is essential to define the warp and woof of the dual-layered social fabric of Kurdistan (*vilayet* of Diarbekir) and the Mardin plateau, which borders it to the south.

The social fabric: Kurds and Christians

The Kurdish people are of Iranian origin, converted to Islam in the tenth century. In the fifteenth century their area of settlement had spread to the region of Diyarbekir. Until the nineteenth century, they provided military cover for the Ottoman Empire against Persia. Kurdish society is tribal; some of the tribes are nomadic, others semi-nomadic or, since the beginning of the nineteenth century, sedentary. The repression of Kurdish rebellions by the Ottomans in the mid-nineteenth century shattered the feudal structure which united these tribes and provoked a fragmentation of Kurdish society and a return to the original tribal system. In this system, each tribal chief—sheikh, bey or agha—has absolute authority since he holds temporal and religious powers. But sedentarization created other ties. For centuries Kurds had shared their mountains with Christians, and Kurdish society is in fact dimorphic: sedentary Kurds who were craftsmen rather than traders, their products being sold by Armenians, other Christians, and Turks; and nomadic Kurds—each tribal chief had his own Christian village (or villages) from which he exacted tribute. The villages—nearly one thousand in the *sanjak* of Mardin alone—were rarely mixed: some were Kurdish, others Christian. Each winter, in southern Mardin, the nomadic herders went down to the Mesopotamian steppes of the Djezireh, where they came into conflict with the Bedouin. Thus, between Kurds and Christians a shared memory developed, fraught with massacres, but also rich with loyalty, debts of honor and sworn oaths.

At the end of the nineteenth century the Porte took advantage of the antagonism between these two groups and gave the Kurds impunity for their abuses, which upset the balance that had allowed the two communities to live side-by-side in relative peace. The administration's utter negligence worsened this climate of insecurity. Lastly, Sultan Abdulhamid, by creating the Kurdish Hamidie regiments, a light cavalry that he used as a political tool in the repression of the Armenians, completed destruction of the ties between Kurds and Christians.

The *vilayet* of Diyarbekir is a patchwork of eastern Christian denominations. These communities were the result of dual divisions. The first occurred through the fifth century heresies, after which there were Nestorians, Jacobites—or Orthodox Syrians—and Apostolic Armenians. The second resulted from the work of the Catholic missions, which divided each entity in two: Chaldeans, Syriac-rite Catholics and Catholic Armenians. The union with Rome brought these three groups of converts closer together while at the same time placing each one in opposition to the rest of its community which had remained schismatic. Tensions were particularly rife between Syriac Catholics and Jacobites and between Catholic and Apostolic Armenians.[1] In the *sanjak* of Mardin, influenced by the missions of Mosul, all the Armenians were Catholic. And to the east of Mardin, the plateau of Tur Abdin was the hub of the Jacobite community whose patriarchate headquarters were at the monastery of Deir al-Zaafaran. In the town of Mardin, the Armenian and Syriac Catholic middle classes held positions as traders and professionals. Mixed marriages were frequent between families of the same social standing.

---

[1] There were no Nestorians in the *vilayet* of Diarbekir. They gathered in the Hakkâri mountains in the south of the *vilayet* of Van, which they shared with the Kurdish tribes. In the nineteenth century, the Protestant missions recruited Apostolic Armenian and Jacobite followers.

We cannot rely on statistics to estimate the numerical ratio of Christians and Muslims in the *sanjak* of Mardin. The Christians represented over two-fifths of the population of about 200,000 inhabitants, and in the town of Mardin (about 25,000 inhabitants), nearly half. On the plateau of Tur Abdin, half of the 45,000 inhabitants were Kurds, the other half Jacobites. At the end of the nineteenth century, the Kurds raged against the Christians. In 1895 and 1896, during the Armenian massacres, Kurdish tribes ravaged the villages and market towns in the *sanjak*. Abductions and forced conversion to Islam were the common counterparts to these massacres. For a Christian, apostasy was the only way to save his life and that of his family. On the other hand, in Mardin, Kurds and Christians were united and allied against the attacks by Kurdish tribes.[2]

The genocide of the Armenians of Mardin and the rare rescue opportunities

In November 1914, the call to *jihad* enabled the Kurdish tribes to direct their warrior instincts against the Christians. In the *vilayet* of Diyarbekir, the order to destroy the Armenians came from the capital and was carried out with a rare efficiency by the *vali* (governor) appointed for this purpose, Dr. Mehmed Reshid, a Circassian who had been a member of the CUP since its origin. Not only did he annihilate the whole Armenian community of his province, but he also exterminated all the convoys of deportees who had come from the neighboring provinces and were bound for Mesopotamia. In this *vilayet*, the genocide spread to the other Christian communities, and oddly, to the Chaldeans.[3] On the plateau of Tur Abdin, the Jacobite villages were also destroyed, as were all the Christian villages in the rest of the *sanjak* of Mardin. Who took the initiative for spreading this violence and what was their reason for doing so?

No document or testimony makes it possible to accuse Reshid, though he was one of the worst perpetrators of the Armenian genocide, of

---

[2] For an in-depth study on the history of Mardin and its inhabitants, see Yves Ternon, *Mardin 1915. Anatomie pathologique d'une destruction*, Paris, Geuthner, 2007. The main source of this work is the documents of the process for beatification of Monsignor Maloyan, Armenian bishop of Mardin, killed in June 1915, file drawn up in French and Latin by the Vatican.

[3] The same thing occurred in the *vilayet* of Bitlis where the Chaldeans of Seert were massacred.

ordering the murder of all the Christians. There is even evidence of a countermand from Constantinople asking for the non-Armenians in a convoy of deportees to be saved, as execution orders were only meant for the Armenians.[4] In any case, the initiative seems to have been taken locally. Thus, the elimination of the Armenians of Mardin Reshid entrusted to an execution committee made up of three men: Bedreddin, his right hand man, Shakir, his aide-de-camp, and Memduh, the police commissioner.

Arrests, tortures, ransoms, pillaging, confiscation of property, executions, deportations and killings were controlled and carried out by this "committee" and the police officers and armed men under their command. Some convoys of deportees were slaughtered by the Kurdish tribes called in to participate in the pillaging. In the Christian villages, the killings were immediate, without the artifice of deportation, and the main perpetrators of these massacres were the neighboring villages—police officers and armed men helped them or remained passive. The Kurdish tribes believed they had the right to kill all Christians, with no distinction. In Mardin, on the other hand, the Syriac Catholic bishop, Monsignor Gabriel Tappouni, had much local support and solid help from high places: his community was spared.

Even if precise figures are not available, it is estimated that 95 per cent of Armenians of the *vilayet* of Diyarbekir were murdered—3,000 survivors out of 72,500. Ninety per cent of Chaldeans, two-thirds of Jacobites and nearly two-thirds of Syriac Catholics were killed in this *vilayet*. Nearly all of the surviving Chaldeans and Syriac Catholics found themselves in the *sanjak* of Mardin.[5] The Armenians in this area could not be rescued. The number of disappeared given by Father Rhétoré is however implausible: 10,200 out of 10,500 in the *sanjak*, which brings the number of Armenian survivors down to 300.[6] In fact, the various tales of Armenian rescues lead us to estimate a higher number of survivors, even if it is difficult to know where each of them came from. Without statistical

---

[4] Yves Ternon, *Mardin 1915...*, op. cit., pp. 135–6.

[5] The manuscript by the Dominican Father Jacques Rhétoré, *Les Chrétiens aux bêtes! Souvenirs de la guerre sainte proclamée par les Turcs contre les chrétiens en 1915*, can be found at the Saulchoir library in Paris. It was published in a comentated edition (Paris, Éditions du Cerf, 2005). The references—here, pp. 241–243—refer to the manuscript.

[6] Jacques Rhétoré, quoted manuscript, p. 243.

data, we can reckon that no Armenian present in Mardin when the arrests began was able to escape the raids. In fact, as everywhere in the Ottoman Empire, citizens were identified by the administration as well as by their neighbors as Muslim or Christian, Kurdish or Armenian, etc.

On a basic level, friendship between prominent figures rarely held firm. An analysis of the complex relationships between the Kurds and Christians of Mardin show that someone who was ready to help a neighbor in trouble was capable, if put under pressure or threatened, or even for no reason, of killing the very person he was protecting. The efficient intervention of leading figures of the Kurdish family of Chelebi is, however, noteworthy. The mayor of Mardin, Hildir Chelebi, defended the Christian employees of his town hall and protected Monsignor Tappouni.[7] Abdelkader Chelebi protected the Armenian family of Hancho and allowed several of its members to escape to Aleppo.[8] Likewise, Said Effendi, director of the bank, warned his Christian friends of the imminence of the arrests and helped them get to Aleppo. In May 1915, the *mutasarrif* (administrator of the *sanjak*), Hilmi Bey, stood against Reshid's orders to imprison the leading Armenian figures of Mardin. He was dismissed at once and Reshid sent the execution committee to arrange for their elimination. The extra time allowed some Armenians to leave the town.

However, when the arrests began on 4 June the noose tightened around the Armenians. Chaldeans were also arrested. The Syriac Catholics had no way of helping them and watched helplessly as the convoys were sent off to their death. The Jacobites did not even consider saving other Christians. The convoys of men were exterminated near Mardin. The convoys of women and children often made it further but they were, for the most part, slaughtered by Kurdish tribes once the women and young girls had been raped, then killed or abducted with the children. It was at this point, after the massacres and abductions, that selfless aid was occasionally given to some Armenians, thereby ensuring their survival. The cases were rare, the actors varied, and the accounts, gathered in particular by three missionaries who took refuge in the Syriac Catholic bishop's palace in Mardin or by a priest from that diocese, Father Armalé, are credible but defy

---

[7] Monsignor Tappouni was also protected in Mardin by the head of the gendarmes, Hassan Tahsin Bey, and his three brothers.

[8] Later he would help the Chaldean priest Joseph Tfinkdji get to Sinjar.

belief.⁹ One example is the story of the "survivors of the tanks." The killers threw their victims' corpses into empty tanks, which were plentiful in the region. Some people had not been mortally wounded or had thrown themselves into a well before they were struck. But they could not get out of them alone. Sometimes a passing Muslim or Christian would hear their cries and throw down a rope, enabling survivors to extract themselves from the pile of corpses, and would help them return to Mardin, to take shelter with a Syriac Catholic family. Likewise, some Armenians—children especially—managed to escape the Kurdish villages where they were being held and hide in Mardin.

There was one particular instance where Mardin's Syriac Catholic community was able to organize the rescue of Christians. A number of Armenians abducted by the Kurds were sold in the main markets of the *vilayet*. In Mardin, the public sales began on 15 August 1915—when the deportation of Armenians had ended—and continued into 1916. It was possible to buy a child between the age of five and seven for the sum of five to twenty piasters, an adolescent for two or three *medjidie*, a woman for one Turkish lira, but the auctions sometimes went up to over thirty liras if it was a member of a well-known family.¹⁰ The Christians of Mardin saved from deportation, for the most part Syriac Catholics, endeavored to buy back the "slaves" to save them and, when necessary, made the prices rise. Monsignor Tappouni undertook the purchases using funds he had collected. He was reported to have distributed hundreds of Christians—some of whom were Armenians from Mardin, but that was not specified—among Christian families. When the police carried out searches to check whether anyone was hiding Armenians, they would say they had only bought Syriac Catholics. Some Muslims treated the "slaves" they had bought as members of their family. A prominent figure in Savour took in about twenty young girls to rescue them, without forcing them to convert.¹¹

---

⁹ These individual accounts were given by the three Dominicans taking refuge in the Syriac Catholic diocese: Jacques Rhétoré (quoted manuscript), Marie-Dominique Berré (archives of the Ministry of Foreign Affairs, Levant 1918–1919, Armenia, volumes 1 and 2) and Hyacinthe Simon (*Mardine, la ville héroïque*, Jounieh, Maison Naaman, 1991).

¹⁰ 1.1 Turkish lira was worth £1 sterling in 1914.

¹¹ Father Rhétoré (quoted manuscript, pp. 325–30) speaks of 2,000 Christians, but that is almost certainly an exaggerated figure, as it does not correspond with the numbers of survivors he gives in his statistics.

The Kurdish tribes participated to a great extent in the genocide. However, some village chiefs took in refugees, most of whom were Jacobites or Syriac Catholics. Thus, thirty inhabitants of Gulia were received as guests by Khalil Agha, who refused to hand them over to the Kurds who had razed the village, and protected them until the end of the war. The imam of the Hafir tribe, Ali Batti, friend of the Jacobite chief of the village of Bâsabrina, housed the survivors of his friend's family until the end of the war. In several Jacobite villages around Nisibe, the Sheikhs refused to participate in the massacre and even helped the Christians to flee to the Sinjar region. Thus, Sheikh Mohamed forbade his men to touch the Christians and he refused all gifts.[12] These rescues, which involved tragic odysseys, were an exception. The deportees knew this: to escape death, one had to leave the province of Diyarbekir, flee to the south, reach the railway at Ras ul-Ain and get to Aleppo; or from Nisibe, in the East, reach Mosul, but most important, make it to the Sinjar.

Aleppo was a large Arab town. Armenians who had been there for over ten years were exempt from deportation. Thousands of others who had taken flight poured into the town. By bribing policemen, those who had money left were able to find a secret place to stay. But these hiding places were not safe and the police relentlessly hunted down the Armenians hidden in Aleppo. Only those who had family in Aleppo and managed to get to them were relatively safe. Thus, when their convoy reached Ras ul-Ain, some Armenians from Mardin bought train tickets and reached Aleppo.

During the war the small Chechen village of Ras ul-Ain gained in importance with the construction of the Baghdad railway. The rare survivors of the convoys from the *vilayet* of Diyarbekir who made it there were protected until March 1916 by two Ottoman officials, who incorporated them into the work crews supervised by German engineers. The two officials were denounced and replaced. From March to November 1916, all of the deportees were slaughtered.

The *vali* of Mosul, Ali Haidar, refused to obey orders from the capital concerning the Armenians. The rare survivors of the convoys that left Mardin, Djezireh or Nisibe reached Mosul in a state of extreme distress; the Chaldeans and Syriac Catholics were authorized to take them under their wing. A witness to these events, the headmaster of the Universal

---

[12] Yves Ternon, *Mardin 1915*, op. cit., pp. 162, 178 and 322.

Israelite Alliance School, David Sasson, recounted the miserable conditions of these refugees who died en masse of cholera, typhus fever, malaria and also hunger.[13] In Mosul, Armenian women who survived the convoys worked as maids in rich households. Others concealed their identity using Arabic names, passed themselves off as Muslims and helped their compatriots—all the Armenians in Mardin spoke Arabic. The bakers, servants of Turkish high-ranking civil servants, Armenians married to Syriac Catholics or Chaldeans, and employees of oil prospectors constantly helped these refugees. This primarily Christian and Jewish solidarity enabled many refugees to survive.[14]

The Sinjar safe haven

The last hills of Kurdistan, the Sinjar mountain range rises up above the Mesopotamian desert. It was the only place in the entire Ottoman Empire where Armenians were taken in and protected. Administratively, Sinjar was a *kaza* in the *vilayet* of Mosul. Over half of its 18,000 inhabitants (according to the 1884 census) were Yezidis. The Kurdish Yezidi sect is one of many esoteric sects that attest to the survival of pre-Islamic Paganism and Iranian Zoroastrianism in Kurdish culture. Like the Nestorians of Hakkâri and the Jacobites of Tur Abdin, they found refuge in the mountains. Their religion was syncretic, influenced by the Ismailian sect derived from Shi'ism. The Sunnis, like the Shias, detest the Yezidis, whom they accuse of having assassinated the son of Ali and of respecting Christian beliefs. This is why the Yezidis willingly welcomed the Christians, while they kept their distance from the Muslims. Farmers and herders, the Yezidis of the Sinjar were organized into around fifty tribes, all Kurdish-speaking, distributed according to a precise hierarchy. At the head, Sheik Hamo Shero, the chief of Sinjar Yezidis,[15] engineered the rescue of several thousand Christians, most of them Armenians. Despite the risks he was taking, he offered them shelter and food. From August 1914, Christian defectors took refuge in the Sinjar to avoid conscription—

[13] Élisabeth Antébi, *Les Missionnaires juifs de la France, 1860–1939*, Paris, Calmann-Lévy, 1999, pp. 230–8.
[14] *Les Mémoires de Mgr Jean Naslian, évêque de Trébizonde, sur les événements politico-religieux en Proche-Orient de 1914 à 1928*, vol. 1, Vienna, Imprimerie Mekhitariste, 1951, 2 volumes, pp. 346–7.
[15] Basile Nikitine, *Les Kurdes*, Paris, Éditions d'Aujourd'hui, 1956, pp. 226–54.

effective from this date, although the Empire only entered the conflict in November. The stream of refugees who managed to reach the Sinjar was endless. From July 1915, escape networks to the Sinjar were organized from Nisibe and Ras ul-Aïn. The smugglers were Arabs or Circassians—in fact it is more likely they were Chechens, as the witnesses readily confused Circassians and Chechens. They charged fees, but, with just a few exceptions, honored their contracts. Circassians, as one Chaldean witness declared, went from Ras ul-Aïn to Mardin with their beasts of burden. During the night, in collusion with the police officers, they sent 400 to 500 Armenians to the Sinjar, averaging a payment of ten to twenty Turkish lira. Arabs from Jabour also took part in this rescue.[16]

Hamo Shero set aside houses and tents for these refugees, and he provided them with work and sustenance. He gave them land opposite his village where they built huts and later brick houses. They even had a place of worship. As soon as summer came, they worked in the orchards and vineyards. Some of them sent letters to Mardin so that Christians who remained there would send them needles, sugar and money, which they exchanged from one village to the next for wheat, barley or lentils. When a typhus epidemic broke out in October 1915, several Sheikhs, including the one from Marussa, forbade the refugees to leave their houses. Hamo Shero proposed isolating part of the village and keeping the sick there until they recovered. When the Sinjar was threatened with famine, the Armenians went to the Arabs of the Tai tribe for grain. In the spring of 1917, when Baghdad fell to the British, some Arabs went to the Sinjar to offer to take the Christians to Baghdad, earning on average £3 per person. Thirty Armenians from Mardin followed them. They sent messages to those who had stayed behind in the Sinjar to urge them to join them, but most were reluctant to leave their place of refuge. During the summer of 1917, some of them were employed by the Baghdad railway—whose construction continued beyond Ras ul-Ain—to earn money and send it to their family who were taking refuge in the mountains. In March 1918, an Ottoman army corps tried to destroy this small rebel group. The commander ordered Hamo Shero to give up his arms and the Christians he was protecting. He summoned the Sheikhs from the mountain, told

---

[16] Ara Sarafian, "The Disasters of Mardin during the Persecutions of the Christians, Especially the Armenians, 1915," *Haigazian Armenological Review*, vol. 18, Beirut, 1998.

them of the commander's order and suggested a refusal. The group was divided. Hamo Shero demanded a unanimous decision. The Sheikhs went away to discuss the matter. Shero didn't wait for them and, with a small group of men, massacred a group of Ottoman soldiers. The army then invaded the mountain and, despite the ambushes carried out by the Yezidis, Ottoman soldiers reached Shero's village, looted it and set it on fire. The Christians had already left and taken refuge in the mountains or made it to the south. As soon as the bulk of the army had withdrawn, the Yezidis attacked the remaining soldiers and disarmed them. The Turks then abandoned the Sinjar. The Christians returned to the villages where they remained until the end of the war. Those who left the mountain went to the houses of Tai Arabs who welcomed them and guided them as long as they could pay.

After the war, the rare Armenian survivors from the *sanjak* of Mardin were subjected to the rigours of the Turkish administration. Following the Proclamation of the Turkish Republic in 1923, they gathered in Mardin. The authorities took away the last of their property, demanding tax arrears from them and forcing them to buy high-priced passports. Between 1928 and 1930, they were expelled to Syria. On their passports was stamped: "No re-entry."[17]

---

[17] Vahé Tachjian, *La France en Cilicie et en Haute-Mésopotamie*, Paris, Karthala, 2004.

24

WAS THE UGIF AN OBSTACLE TO THE RESCUE OF JEWS?

Michel Laffitte

It seems paradoxical at first to refer to the Union Générale des Israélites de France (UGIF) in terms of rescue. This body was founded by order of the Germans, through a law brought in by the Vichy government in November 1941. Its mission was to preside over the fusion of Jewish assistance organizations and to serve as an instrument in the policy of location and persecution. Through its origin and by the ultimate purposes that were assigned to it, this compulsory organization looks at first like an obstacle to rescue activities. The presumed compromise of principle by its leaders, whose political shortsightedness and intellectual isolation must have been derived from class prejudice, was repeatedly faced with the opposition of the leaders of the Consistoire, which remained the institutional conservatory of republican values, or the foreign Jews in the Resistance army. This rigid polarization of views dominates a good part of the historical documentation regarding the subject.

The UGIF was however, above all a fusion of Jewish assistance organs and, since it had its equivalents in Belgium and in the Netherlands, its story merits consideration in the European dimension of the Shoah, but also with constant reference to an institutional, political, cultural and social history unique to France.[1] In 1947, Zosa Szaj-

---

[1] On the subject of a European comparative approach emphasizing the distinc-

kowski,[2] whose point of view would later be developed notably by Serge Klarsfeld, made an early analysis of the dispersal of the Jewish communities, together with individual or local administrative aid given by non-Jews as a vital asset. He contrasted this situation with the impossibility of dispersal in Central Europe where the Jews were rapidly concentrated in ghettos and were to suffer even more hostility from the non-Jewish civil society. However, since the 1980s, following the first cautious and reasoned approaches of the pioneers in this research, such as Léon Poliakov and Joseph Billig, a series of works were published that dwelt less upon the personalities of the Jewish leaders, their complex relationships with non-Jewish society, and the continuity of their engagement from the 1930s, and more upon institutional or social adherence that was judged to be decisive.

However, new sources make it possible to delimit the margins of negotiation that the Jewish leaders had with Vichy and the Germans, their involvement in underground rescue operations, and the places where contact was made between the Jewish organization that was set to become an "isolate" and other civilians. The aim here is not to describe the organization's internal rescue activities, notably the role of households sheltering Jewish children as part of the underground network, which have already been described elsewhere,[3] but to determine the relationships between Jewish leaders and civilians.

France was cut in two by the movement of the refugees who fled the persecutions and attempted to find refuge in the Southern Zone, notably after the great roundups of summer 1942. What were, on a France-wide scale, the capacities for action of a Jewish body that was more and more under the Germans' control?

---

tions between *Judenrat* and national union, I direct the reader towards the twenty previously unpublished contributions united under the title "Les conseils juifs dans l'Europe allemande," *Revue d'Histoire de la Shoah*, 185, July–December 2006.

[2] Zosa Szajkowski, "L'organisation de l'UGIF en France pendant l'Occupation," *Jewish Social Studies*, volume IX number 3, July 1947/"Analytical Franco-Jewish Gazetteer, 1939–1945," 1966.

[3] I refer notably to my contribution to the Lacaune Symposium of September 2005, the proceedings of which were published as Jacques Fijalkow (ed.), *Les enfants de la Shoah*, Paris: Les Editions de Paris, 2006.

MICHEL LAFFITTE

Neither Judenrat *nor class collaboration*

Did the UGIF function in isolation regarding the rest of the non-Jewish civilian society, as the Germans wished? Were its leaders, nominated by Vichy in January 1942 and French Jews "of old stock" for the most part, simply the Germans' "creatures," or, on the contrary, were they men and women who knew how to preserve and consolidate the multiple social and institutional contacts formed before the war in the heart of French society—and for whose benefit?

The terms of the debate were settled in the 1980s, both by controversial attacks[4] and by academic works carried out in the wake of the institutional approach privileged by Raul Hilberg, who tended to see the institution as having spoken with one voice. In this manner, Cynthia J. Haft,[5] who could only see in the UGIF an institutional trap, destroying any and every free judgment, concluded that its leaders never took part in rescue activities. That author presents a picture of a "French *Judenrat*," suggesting that it was a reproduction of the model tested from 1939 onwards by the Nazis in Poland, notably of leaders placed in charge of ghettos for the correct execution of Nazi orders. This perception of a machinery as efficient as it was implacable, transposable in all countries with its irrefutable efficiency, left the men who composed it, as well as the story itself, out of consideration.

At the same time, this strictly institutional approach was coupled with a new model offering explanations relating to the presumed class and nationality reflexes of the Jewish leaders. Jacques Adler[6] does not see in the UGIF the initial coercive mechanism of the *Judenrat*. He emphasizes the alliance of objective interests among the "French Jewish notables," both those of the Consistory—the body founded in 1808 to represent the Jews in relations with the authorities—and those of the UGIF, which, he suggested, delayed the awakening of a unified Jewish resistance and abandoned the foreign Jews in the Northern Zone to their fate. The "class politics" of the leaders of the "Jewish councils," with a background confined to the traditional practice of "philanthropy," would never have been

[4] Maurice Rajsfus, *Des juifs dans la collaboration*, Paris: EDI, 1980.
[5] Cynthia Haft, *The Bargain and the Bridle, the General Union of the Israelites of France, 1941–1944*, Chicago, Dialog Press, 1983.
[6] Jacques Adler, *Face à la persécution-Les organisations juives à Paris de 1940 à 1944*, collection Diaspora, Paris, Calmann-Lévy, 1985.

capable of establishing the "solidarity" necessary for a policy of resistance—whether an organized one, or one born from a latent rejection of the occupiers' orders, if we refer to Martin Broszat's distinctions between "*Widerstand*" and "*Resistenz*." It is this last nuance that Vicki Caron[7] develops, emphasizing, on the contrary, that the UGIF was instrumental to the resistance through different underground connections benefiting refugees in the non-Jewish civil society. It would be therefore more relevant to study the UGIF as a specific institution, never monolithic, in constant interaction with the history of the country. Such an approach must take into account the doubly elusive character of a community affected by profound divisions, linked with the partial success of assimilation, and also by the new geography of Jewry due to the defeat of France.

The pluralism of Jewish communities arose from their social immersion. Membership of associations of veterans of the Great War, but also contacts through work and neighborhood, were reasons for steps being taken both individually or collectively toward Vichy or the Germans in favor of Jews who had been arrested. The compulsory Jewish organization was not, however, the ideal channel to respond to calls by neighbors or friends of arrested Jews. Everything was done so that non-Jews should be unaware of such actions. In the Northern Zone, the UGIF's "Service n°14," led by Leo Israelowicz and then, from summer 1943, by Kurt Schendel, filtered every procedure directed at the Germans. The UGIF bulletin, to which Jews were obliged to subscribe in the Occupied Zone, was not to be accessible to non-Jews. Its distribution was only by subscription through databases from the 1940 census, and its presence in libraries and public reading rooms was strictly forbidden. In the UGIF's archives there are very few eyewitness accounts revealing the informal neighborhood and business solidarities that signaled spontaneous reaction by civilians faced with the drama of the arrests and deportations.

The Jewish leaders, still confident of the support of the French administrative institutions as late as the summer of 1942, were furthermore victims of a veritable fool's bargain, as shown by the notebooks of Raymond-Raoul Lambert, director general of the UGIF in the Southern Zone. Between August and November 1942, the Vichy authorities kept him under the illusion that he was negotiating and saving categories of

---

[7] Vicki Caron, *The UGIF: the Failure of the Nazis to Establish a Judenrat on the Eastern European Model*, New York, Columbia University Press, 1997.

the population from deportation when, in fact, their fate had already been sealed.[8] In the same way, the negotiations initiated by Georges Edinger, who was administrator and then the last president of the UGIF from October 1943 until the Liberation, through veterans' associations achieved nothing better than delaying the persecution.[9] Official steps taken through administrative channels were in vain, with no echo in public opinion, because the Church's afforts in the Occupied Zone were so discreet, as seen in the confidential support given by Cardinal Suhard to André Baur at the end of July 1942, regarding attempts by the UGIF to exempt "spouses of Aryans" from wearing the star, as it was happening in Germany itself and in Belgium.[10] Spontaneous reactions of civilians were transmitted by the Jewish apparatus to its supervising department, the Commissariat Général aux Questions Juives, with the same discretion, as even contact with non-Jews could be a motive for accusation. André Baur found this out the hard way in July 1943, when his request for an audience with Laval in order to protest the brutalities of the SS at the camp at Drancy led to his own arrest. *A priori*, any legal proceedings were destined for failure. This was due to the restrained margin for maneuver promised to the Jewish leaders and the fact that the terms of negotiation, suggesting a veritable partnership, were not adapted to their situation. But were legalistic discourses and posturing the marks of an absolute opposition to rescue activities?

Links preserved with non-Jewish civilians

Traditional historical writing suggests a clear opposition between the leaders who kept legal positions and others whose rejection of new legal activities established by Vichy and by the Germans was to be the foundation stone of resistance activity. However, in spite of their links with the escape networks for thousands of Jewish children, Juliette Stern, in charge of the UGIF social benefits department in the Northern Zone, and Ben-

---

[8] Michel Laffitte, *Un engrenage fatal. L'Union générale des Israélites de France face aux réalités de la Shoah*, foreword by Pierre Vidal-Naquet, Paris, Liana Levi, 2003, pp. 85–133.

[9] Michel Laffitte, *Juif dans la France allemande. Institutions, dirigeants et communautés au temps de la Shoah*, foreword by Annette Wieviorka, Paris, Tallandier, 2006, pp. 175–201.

[10] Michel Laffitte, op. cit., pp. 126–74.

jamin Weill-Hallé, chief of its medical commission, remained members of its board until July 1944; this illustrates the complexity of the choices made by the "notables" who were in charge of vital charitable organizations. In the Southern Zone Robert Gamzon, founder of the Eclaireurs Israélites de France (EIF) and a supporter of the Zionist movement, set up an underground organization, "la Sixième" ("the Sixth"), in cooperation with Joseph Millner, leader at the Œuvre de Secours aux Enfants (OSE), who was to become a member of the third management of the UGIF. Robert Gamzon, who was also a member of the central Consistory, remained on the UGIF administrative council until he joined the Maquis in spring 1944. Prolonged presence at the helm of an organization backed by the Germans did not, *a priori*, signify acceptance of the occupiers' views or the ideology of Vichy's national Revolution. If one attempts to define the individual motivations, choices and opportunities that do not seem to have been motivated '*a priori*' by any ideological convictions, the reality was even more complex.

This is shown by the example of the lawyer Lucienne Scheid-Haas, solidly conservative and hostile to all messianic, Zionist or communist adventures. She was head of the UGIF's legal service in the Occupied Zone, and her articles written for the UGIF bulletin offered this woman—born in Strasbourg in 1911, and who would convert to Catholicism in 1949—the opportunity to renew a profound attachment to her French homeland despite the anti-Semitic laws. Her last articles seem to express resignation and a real warning against all illegal activities. In issue 101 of 7 January 1944, in interpreting the principles of collective responsibility imposed on the Jewish leaders by the SS, Lucienne Scheid-Haas wrote in an article entitled "The communion of faults": "He who commits an offense [must] weigh up his choice taking into account all those of his brothers and his equals that he drags behind him." To the delegates of Southern Zone UGIF on a mission in Paris in May 1943, including Robert Gamzon, Lucienne Scheid-Haas was part of a clan, "that of the leaders who were more or less xenophobic, more or less anti-Semitic, and opposed to Zionism." This clan contrasted, according to them, with "that of the leaders who were more or less xenophiles, pro-Semitic and Zionists," as symbolized by Juliette Stern, in charge of the social benefits service at the UGIF.[11] Lucienne Scheid-Haas, alongside André Baur,

---

[11] CDJC CDX3.

was anxious to centralize the Jewish assistance apparatus in order to receive, via the Joint in Geneva, funding from the Southern Zone for those seeking assistance in the Parisian region, and she was against the dispersal of activities. This latter principle, defended by Gamzon and by Maurice Brener,[12] was, in their eyes, inseparable from the protection of foreign Jews and the establishment of escape routes in the direction of Switzerland.

However, it was outwardly law-abiding positions of appearance that led Lucienne Scheid-Haas toward illegal rescue activities. In January 1942, having been the first woman to pass the required examination in 1936, she was one of the five Jewish lawyers the Council of the Order proposed to retain in addition to the quota of 2 per cent authorized by the decree of 16 July 1941, in consideration "of the eminent character of their professional merit." Accepted by Xavier Vallat, the measure was finally cancelled by Laval in September, following Darquier de Pellepoix's unfavorable decision. Lucienne Scheid-Haas took this occasion to plunge into genealogical research to establish that her family had been French for more than five generations. This worry about her legal position, and her distrust of armed activism revealed in her articles for the UGIF bulletin, were combined with involvement in an organization forging false papers. From this moment on it would appear that whenever she was anxious to prove how French she was, Lucienne Scheid-Haas had talks with the engineer Alfred Valabrègue, who had become a forger, and with the genealogist Georges Andry. They then decided to take advantage of the loopholes in the French registration system, where deaths were rarely transcribed onto birth certificates. This way, real birth certificates of deceased people were used for the production of false papers, and the solicitor René de Sariac made inquiries at the services of the Commissariat Général aux Questions Juives (CGQJ) in order to obtain certificates of "non-adherence to the Jewish race." Father Ménard, brother of the comedian Dranem,[13] drew up false baptism certificates. Ginette Martenot, the fiancée of Didier Lazard who was Lucienne Scheid-Haas's cousin, furnished temporary hiding places.

---

[12] Maurice Brener was former personal secretary to Raymond-Raoul Lambert, who became social inspector at the UGIF in contact with the children's rescue networks.

[13] Dranem is an anagram of Armand Ménard's (1869–1935) surname.

In compiling her memoirs in 1963, Lucienne Scheid-Haas alluded to her brief internment at the camp at Mérignac in May 1942, and noted: "Through prudence, and in spite of the offer from Colonel Brull, at whose house we met up almost every Sunday to bring false papers, I did not agree that our group should be registered in London, and I believe that I did well, because, except for me (and that is not important) none of us has been arrested or bothered."[14] These resistance activities were confirmed by eyewitness accounts collected after the war. Paul Levy, Lucienne Scheid-Haas' former classmate at the faculty of Law at Strasbourg, and then magistrate at Sarreguemines from 1937, was mobilized in 1939 and imprisoned the following year in a Stalag near Leipzig. Later, when he was a prisoner of war on the run, he was sheltered by Lucienne Scheid-Haas in Paris and after two days, and with the help of her non-Jewish friends, she was able to give him false papers in the name of Lefebvre. Paul Levy was thus able to find refuge in the Limoges region, and continue his career after the war at the court at Mulhouse before retiring as assistant public prosecutor at the Court of Appeal in Paris.[15] The Parisian home of Lucienne Scheid-Haas, at 11 rue de Verneuil, was a centre for trafficking false papers, with blank baptism certificates hidden in the library amongst the pages of volumes of Racine, whilst an old woodburning stove in the dining room was where Valabrègue hid the false identity cards he brought. Lucienne Scheid-Haas's account is equally informative about the multiple forms of protection she benefited from, from even the very heart of the administrative apparatus of the French state. One example is that of the Commissioner Charles Permilleux, in charge of the service for Jewish affairs at the Prefecture of Police in Paris, whose men were major suppliers of foreign Jews for the camp at Drancy, but who, in July 1944, warned her of an imminent arrest.

Helen Berr, aged twenty-one, who was studying English at the Sorbonne but was unable to take the *agrégation* examination because of Vichy legislation, became a volunteer UG social worker. She was much like Lucienne Scheid-Haas; her diary[16] shows a powerful feeling of belonging to the French nation and a deep concern that the legal means of assis-

---

[14] Eyewitness account published in the appendix of my book *Juif dans la France allemande*, op. cit., pp. 385–91.
[15] Eyewitness account of Paul Lévy given to Lucienne Scheid-Haas, 1954, and repeated in 1995 to Professor Charles Haas, family archives.
[16] Michel Laffitte, *Juif dans la France allemande*, op. cit.

tance should be maintained intact. However, while being a volunteer social worker with the service for internees at the UGIF, Helen Berr became at the same time Denise Milhaud's secretary at L'Entraide Temporaire, side by side with her cousin Nicole Schneider.[17] L'Entraide Temporaire was an underground organization formed in February 1941 in the shadow of the Service Social d'Aide aux Emigrants (SSAE, Social Service for the Assistance of Emigrants). The SSAE, private and interdenominational, was run by Lucie Chevalley-Sabatier and gave assistance to the families of those incorporated into the Group of Foreign Workers, whilst passing on the mail for L'Entraide Temporaire under cover of official SSAE movements in the Southern Zone. Officially recognized, it created an underground rescue network for Jewish children. This network obtained a Parisian contact thanks to Doctor Alfred Milhaud, doctor at the apprentice centre of the Ecole Israélite du Travail at 4bis, rue des Rosiers in Paris, which became centre 32 of the UGIF. The monastery of Notre Dame de Sion, supervised by Théomir Devaux, rue Notre-Dame-des-Champs, Paris, served, according to the historian Lucien Lazare, as a pivot and a stop-off in the transit between legality and concealment for hundreds of Jewish children.[18] Fred Milhaud profited from the complicity of his wife Denise, who was René Cassin's cousin and chief social assistant of the Children's Homes of the UGIF, transferred on 28 April 1942 to the dispensary on rue Julien Lacroix in Paris, and from that of his father-in-law Frédéric Léon. Benjamin Weill-Hallé, UGIF administrative council member until the end of July 1944, was also a member of this underground network. His professional activities kept him in permanent contact with non-Jewish civilians. He was an old friend of Professor Calmette, whose wife was witness at his famous remarriage in Paris in February 1944; he continued to maintain a discreet consultancy at the children's hospital where he gave vaccinations against tuberculosis. At the same time, through his activities as head of the UGIF medico-social commission, he consolidated the work contacts between Jewish organizations and the municipal social services in the Parisian region.

---

[17] CDJC-DCXLI, 1 to 11.
[18] Lucien Lazare, *La Résistance juive*, Paris, Editions du Nadir, 2001, page 147; Madeleine Comte, *Sauvetages et baptêmes. Les religieuses de Notre-Dame de Sion face à la persécution des Juifs en France (1940–1944)*, Paris, L'Harmattan, 2001.

An organization that was plural in time and space

The ever-changing and uncertain situation south of the demarcation line was very different from the rigid codes imposed by the Germans which regimented the existence of Jews assigned to their *communes* and their homes in the Occupied Zone. The UGIF was geographically spread over seven management offices, which permitted former Jewish assistance groups that had been dissolved to survive behind a legal façade. One major difference from the situation in the Occupied Zone was that the dispersal and the mobility of assistance offices enabled the UGIF in the Southern Zone to assist the movement of Jewish refugees in their search for vital resources and their general movement towards the Italian refuge to the east of the Rhone. The presence of non-Jewish salaried workers in connection with rescue networks was an important asset. I showed this in a recent article about OSE which became, under the cover of the third management of the UGIF, a "nomadic organization"[19] whose headquarters, moving from Montpellier, reached Vic-sur-Cère in the Cantal at the very moment of the Wehrmacht's entry into the Southern Zone in November 1942, before its establishment from January 1943 at Chambéry, near the Swiss frontier.

Lambert's choice of Alain-Raoul Mossé for the position of UGIF delegate at Chambéry, following the advice of Maurice Brener, clearly showed a desire to capitalize upon the social and political contacts of this son of a former inspector general of the administrative services of the Ministry of the Interior, who had been, until January 1941, chief of personal staff for the Prefect of Chambéry. He was, amongst the upper ranks at the UGIF, the only former senior civil servant who was fully integrated in his former department. This was another major difference from the Occupied Zone; the UGIF managed to keep its non-Jewish staff, which anchored contacts with the civil society in these "Jewish deserts" of the Southern Zone. Seconded by a non-Jewish chief accountant, René Borel, Alain-Roaul Mossé immediately employed two non-Jewish sports teachers, Henri Montagne, appointed to the UGIF offices at Chambéry, and Roland Didier. This recruitment, which was presumed to offer additional security guarantees in the case of identity checks before the frontier, dis-

---

[19] "L'OSE de 1942 à 1944: une survie périlleuse sous couvert de l'UGIF" in "Les conseils juifs dans l'Europe allemande," *Revue d'Histoire de la Shoah*, 185, July/December 2006, pp. 65–86.

pleased Raymond-Raoul Lambert who, without opposing rescue activities, defended the principle of employing jobless Jews. Despite this, the presence of these non-Jewish paid members of staff was attested from the Massif Central to the Swiss border.

Roland Didier, born in Saint-Dié in the Vosges region in 1924, and living in Lyon, obtained a post at the former OSE children's home of Chabannes at Saint-Pierre-de-Fursac, one of three centers coming under the third management of the UGIF in the county of Creuse, and the first home to be disbanded in autumn 1943. Jules Félix Chevrier, his director since 1939, was also non-Jewish. It was precisely because Chevrier—a former printer and manager of the newspaper *Le Vosgien* in Epinal, a socialist and Freemason, aged fifty-nine—was not a Jew that he almost got arrested during a German police check in June 1943. Indeed, service cards could not be given to the non-Jewish staff of the UGIF, and Jules Félix Chevrier "had quite a lot of difficulty in justifying his position," as Joseph Millner pointed out to Raymond-Raoul Lambert on 23 June.[20] From 1 September 1942, Jules Félix Chevrier set about hiding ten foreign Jewish children from the men of Captain Chaumet, who was in charge of the gendarmerie of Guéret,[21] well before the rescue networks under the responsibility of the former sports teacher Joseph-Georges Loinger had been put in place, through contact with go-betweens and smugglers of the Annemasse region and the Burgundy Resistance network. Dotted here and there were the traces of the networks of dispersal and then escape routes across the Swiss border for these children.

The situation of the Jews in the internment camps in the Southern Zone was also ever changing and uncertain, offering rescue opportunities. At first, Raymond-Raoul Lambert's main concern was to free foreign Jews from the internment camps. For this policy there were contacts and complicity within the administrative apparatus of the Vichy French state, as can be seen in the case of the department of Indre on the demarcation line. Edmond Dauphin, general secretary at the prefecture of Châteauroux, was approached by Odette Schwob, the departmental delegate of the UGIF in August 1942, and managed to prevent the transfer to Drancy of hundreds of foreign Jews by agreeing to reopen the camp at

---

[20] CDJC YIVO 59–665.
[21] Israel Gutman (ed.), *Dictionnaire des Justes de France*, Paris, Fayard, 2003, p. 170.

Douadic. This camp, prepared in 1939, was a dozen kilometers from the town of Blanc and was a prisoner of war camp, before housing foreign refugees unfit for work and their families, as well as those who had been freed from camps and had chosen of their own free will to come to this center.[22] Doctor Gaston Lévy, who was the former director of the pediatric services of the departments of central France, found—through the UGIF, of which he was medical inspector of children's homes of the third management office—a post at a French law institution; this made it possible for him to be chosen by Edmond Dauphin[23] as collaborator in a plan to move Jewish children from Limoges in the direction of the Indre, placing them either with families or in religious institutions. Edmond Dauphin illustrates in this manner the predominance amongst the "Righteous" of those whom Patrick Cabanel called the "elite of vocation and of service."[24]

However, from 26 August 1942, Douadic was transformed into a sorting centre for foreign Jews aged from sixteen to sixty, who had been rounded up in the Indre and Cher departments. Edmond Dauphin allowed Gaston Lévy to enter the centre at Douadic in place of the departmental doctor, Dr Robini, in order to speed up releases for medical reasons. The other foreign Jews were regrouped at the camp at Nexon before being transferred to Drancy. Between the last days of August and 5 December 1942, the date of his report to the third management office, Gaston Lévy, who ran the day nursery at Limoges, managed to secretly place sixty-five Jewish children either with families or in Christian institutions in the Indre. In case of discovery, these children were systematically declared dependents of the public assistance of the department, following Edmond Dauphin's instructions to his services.[25] The centre at Douadic had once again been transformed, as Odette Schwab saw during a visit:

> The French children are kept there when their parents want it. The majority does not want to be separated from each other. The conditions under which they live are not too bad. The children go to the school in the village. The food at the cen-

---

[22] Samuel Pintel, "Les centres d'accueil du service social des étrangers sous Vichy (1941–1944)," *Revue d'Histoire de la Shoah*, 172, May-August 2001, p. 120.

[23] Israel Gutman (ed.), *Dictionnaire des Justes de France*, op. cit., p. 200.

[24] Jacques Fijalkow (ed.), *Vichy, les Juifs et les Justes. L'exemple du Tarn*, Toulouse, Privat, 2003, p. 201.

[25] Gaston Levy, *Souvenirs d'un médecin d'enfants à l'OSE en France occupée et en Suisse 1940–1945*, Paris-Jerusalem, 1978, pp. 24–5.

tre is not too bad for the children, who have a separate kitchen. We are principally asked for clothes, since many are left without any. Other families have moved into small villages where, through a lack of time, we have not yet been able to make enquiries. There also, we are asked essentially for clothes.[26]

In this report to her supervisor, dated 25 November 1942, Odette Schwob spoke of her almost daily contact with the services of the prefecture of Châteauroux where she always received "the best of welcomes," as with all public services. She also announced that she had managed to place, in the course of the same month, seven children in families in the department, one of whom had been passed to her by parents interned at the Douadic centre. Odette Schwob was also to make contact with Pierrette Poirier of L'Amitié Chrétienne at Châteauroux and allow her to make contact with Cardinal Gerlier. From January 1943, Pierrette Poirier, now in charge of a sub-branch of the network concerned with the underground placement of Jewish children, began receiving through Odette Schwob a part of the funding from the Joint, sent via Switzerland. Although there were these official and private channels, the UGIF bureau remained an essential mechanism for survival because of the policies pursued by the delegate of the Secours National who, acting independently from the Châteauroux Prefecture services, refused Jews access to its clothes supplies and its canteen. The historian is therefore forced to disabuse himself of the idyllic picture of the lands of welcome; the UGIF's assistance to impoverished people was vital right up to the last weeks preceding the Liberation.

Finally, the ever-changing situation that was particular to the Southern Zone was especially felt when the UGIF organization had to assess public opinion in the reception regions to find useful contacts and collusion. In the Southern Zone, even before the entry of the German troops, which would hasten the movements of the Jewish refugees there, the UGIF sent delegates to explore a veritable *Terra Incognita*. The first reports back were mixed. They sketched out a map of public opinion, a few examples of which I will give, revealing a true concern to preserve or to create links between the UGIF and the vocational or service elite. In May 1942, Raymond Geissmann, who was in charge of assistance to French Jews under the first management of the UGIF, signaled "certain refusals to help" by the Nice section of the Secours National. In the same way, from Septem-

[26] CDJC YIVO 68–500.

ber 1941 to May 1942, the section of the Secours National at Marseilles was discriminating in its assistance, refusing the local Jews a certain number of free soup coupons equal to a quarter of the coupons purchased. Raymond Geissmann noted regarding the relations between those being assisted and the rest of the population: "The racial prejudice that they frequently come up against, even for the most humble of jobs, appears more frequently and more obstinately at Nice than at Marseilles, and more at Marseilles than at Lyon."[27] UGIF salaried workers were sent prospecting at Alès in Huguenot country, where they were lodged by the pastor, less than two weeks before the entry of the Wehrmacht into the Southern Zone. They drew a picture of a population torn between practical considerations and religious and ideological convictions:

As it was an entirely working-class town, it will be difficult but possible to find rooms for everybody. The imminent arrival of the Germans gives us the chance to find lodgings with people who would not be renting if they were not scared of being requisitioned. [...] The Protestant population looks upon us most favorably. The town is said to be communist and it would appear that a part of the population and the police look upon us unfavorably.[28]

The choice of Alès paved the way for prospecting in the direction of the neighboring departments which had themselves become stepping stones on the way to the Italian refuge east of the Rhône. The story of these Jewish refugees in the provinces is a subject yet to be researched.

Plural in time and space, the UGIF was not the organization of which its creators had dreamed. In the Occupied Zone, the escape routes benefited from complicity or active involvement in all ways on the part of the Jewish organization, without any ideological motivations playing a decisive role, as I have shown through the example of Lucienne Scheid-Haas. In the Southern Zone, a nomadic assistance organization with no center, espoused the refugee movement, anticipating the different measures in a general movement of dispersal and immersion in non-Jewish civil society. Although the reason for the UGIF's existence was to isolate the Jews of the nation even more, the presence at its head of French Jews "of old stock" went against this objective, in as much as a good number of these men and women retained social foundations created before the war, and were able to capitalize upon powerful connections in civil society.

[27] CDJC YIVO70–257.
[28] CDJC YIVO67–45.

This decision to retain the traditional elite as efficient and credible agents for transmission of their orders was part of the general policy chosen by the Germans, at least until 1943. Whilst the Jewish leaders, confronted with the spiral of roundups, struggled to draw up a program for disbanding of charitable organizations because of the desperate needs of those seeking assistance, their participation in rescue activities, to varying degrees, is an unavoidable reality which reveals more improvisation than affirmed ideological choice.

25

ROUNDUPS, RESCUE AND SOCIAL NETWORKS IN PARIS (1940–1944)

Camille Ménager

Approaching the rescue of Jews in Paris by studying roundups and social networks involves taking an interest in individual behavior and decisions by the Paris population in face of the dangers hanging over the Jews during the occupation of the capital. Rescuing someone was by definition to save the person's life, so strictly speaking one cannot speak of rescuing except from the moment when Jews were in danger of being killed. This danger assumed two forms: *objective* danger—the result of measures taken by the Occupation authorities and the Vichy government—and *subjective* danger, awareness of this danger by the populations concerned. This danger was manifested in its most acute form during the roundups—mass arrests conducted publicly and in a brutal fashion. Did the population's reactions depend on the brutality of the arrests, or were they influenced by other parameters? Did they have an effect on the type of rescue that took place, that is, individual initiatives or systematized action?

The Paris roundups and growing awareness of the danger

On the eve of the war, two-thirds of France's 330,000 Jews, slightly over 200,000 individuals, were living in Paris.[1] In July 1944, 104,622 Jews were

[1] The number 330,000 is an estimate. Cf. Serge Klarsfeld in *Le Calendrier de la*

believed to be residing in the former Seine Department, which encompassed Paris at the time (cf. table 8). In August 1944, Chief Rabbi Jacob Kaplan reported 30,000 Jews in Paris and a similar number of Jews in hiding, or about 60,000 at the time of Liberation.[2] About 40,000 Jews thus appear to have left the Seine department sometime between October 1941 and July 1944, and 15,000 between October 1940 and October 1941.

Table 8: Estimate of voluntary departures in the Seine Department between 1940 and 1944

Seine Jewish population (October 1940)	Arrests in the Seine department (1941–1944)	Estimated Jewish population in Paris (August 1944)	Estimated voluntary departures
149,734	33,141	60,000	56,593

The 1941 roundups: a danger that went unnoticed?

The first mass arrests in Paris took place in 1941. On 14 May 3,710 Jews were arrested after being called in for an "examination of their situation." This mass arrest operation conducted by the French police[3] caught 3,430 Poles, 157 Czechs and 123 stateless persons off guard.[4] The second large-scale operation began on 20 August 1941: 4,232 Jews were arrested in four days. On 12 December 1941, in retaliation for a series of anti-German attacks, the Feldgendarmerie, assisted by the French police, arrested 743 Jewish men in Paris, almost all of them French nationals.[5]

---

persécution des juifs: 1940–1944, New York, Beate Klarsfeld Foundation, Paris, Fils et filles des déportés juifs de France, 1993, p. 1103.

[2] Jacob Kaplan, "French Jewry under the Occupation," in *The American Jewish Year Book 5706, 1945–1946*, Philadelphia (Pa.), The Jewish Publication Society of America, volume 47, 1945 [sic], pp. 71–118.

[3] i.e. the municipal police with the help of certain judicial police and Renseignements Généraux (police intelligence service) officials.

[4] The most affected *arrondissements* were the 11th (591), 20th (533), 10th (316), 18th (274) and 4th (268).

[5] Some foreigners were also arrested. To exceed the set goal of one thousand, the Germans chose 300 internees in Drancy. They were assembled at the École Militaire and then interned in Compiègne.

These first three roundups, although they took place in several Parisian *arrondissements*, had no specific impact on the population's behavior. The "Righteous" files make practically no mention of them.[6] They are more often mentioned in accounts of hidden children, and they seem to have convinced some Jews of the need to flee.[7] Out of the fifty-five cases of rescue to which hidden Parisian Jewish children bore witness, forty had the opportunity to determine the moment when their families became aware of the danger they faced. Out of seven of them in 1941, three realized the danger precisely after the arrest of the head of household during one of these roundups. And yet, in May 1941, individual summonses to report had generally "borne fruit." Answering a summons meant obeying the law, and people did not necessarily imagine beforehand that it would lead to arrest. For the Jews who were summoned, the situation was simple. If their papers were not in order, why throw themselves to the wolves by obeying the police summons? If they were in order, and if they were subject to the requirements of the October 1940 census, what did they fear by complying with a summons? Disobedience meant non-compliance with the law at a time when the danger was not necessarily felt. Not obeying a summons unequivocally brought about the need to go underground, and in that precise case, to flee. Changing procedures to conduct the arrests was a very clever move on behalf of the German authorities. The three methods used—summons, and then encirclement and arrest of the person at his home—were increasingly aggressive, and arrest became more and more inevitable.

Imposition of the yellow star: a trigger factor?

On 1 June 1942 the 8th German decree of 29 May 1942 was published, requiring Jews in the occupied zone to wear the yellow star.[8] This measure

---

[6] The research is based on individual files compiled to seek nomination for the "Righteous" medal, consulted at the Comité Français pour Yad Vashem (CFYV). 262 "Righteous" in Paris were recognized as of 1 September 2006 (this number is constantly but very slowly increasing). As the complete files are not all available at the CFYV, the data are drawn from 136 of them.

[7] Source: testimonies collected by Aloumim, on file at the CDJC. The association was founded by Rivka Avihail in 1993 to collect oral and written testimony of Jews hidden as children during the war.

[8] *Verordnungsblatt für die besetzten französischen Gebiete* (*VOBIF*), p. 383, in Claire Andrieu (ed.), *La Persécution des juifs de France 1940–1944 et le rétablissement de*

was an essential factor in the discrimination against Jews and the evolution of public opinion toward them. Even if the yellow star pertained exclusively to Jews, it also affected non-Jews in that it was to provoke a feeling of rejection toward the stigmatized individuals. A 6 June 1942 circular from the Paris Police Prefecture predicted possible forms of protest against this measure: Jews wearing several insignias, Jews in groups, non-Jews wearing the insignia, a special salute to someone wearing the insignia, the wearing of a fanciful insignia. In case of violation, Jews over eighteen years of age would be sent to Drancy, non-Jews handed over to the law and considered as "friends of the Jews."[9]

According to Renée Poznanski, it was against the star as a humiliation that some Jews reacted at first. The true consequences of the law did not appear to them until much later, when other measures ensued that were increasingly difficult to escape precisely because of the star.[10] Raymonde Mayer, a volunteer in the WIZO's department for the protection of Jewish children, recalls: "In 1942, we were required to wear the yellow star. I first refused to submit to this humiliation and then I realized that I had no right not to do as the others."[11] Was such sympathetic resignation shared by all of those who went to pick up their stars? According to André Kaspi, they started by wearing the stars with pride, but this gradually turned into resignation. It should nevertheless be kept in mind that going to pick up one's star did not necessarily mean wearing it, which further complicates our perception of the situation.

While Michael Marrus and Robert Paxton believe it is obvious that many Jews refused to submit to the law,[12] Renée Poznanski claims that "only a minority chose to ignore the new obligation placed on Jews."[13] The matter of obeying the law is essential. An initial reflex makes us pose

---

la légalité républicaine: recueil des textes officiels 1940–1999, Mission d'Etude sur la Spoliation des Juifs de France, Paris, La Documentation Française, 2000, p. 72.

[9] Police prefecture circular dated 6 June 1942, Préfecture de Police de Paris Archives (APP), BA 1813. On this issue, see Cédric Gruat and Cécile Leblanc, *Les Amis des juifs*, Paris, Tiresias-Michel Reynaud, 2005.

[10] Renée Poznanski, *Jews in France during World War II*, UPNE, 2001, pp. 247–8.

[11] Testimonial by Raymonde Mayer (WIZO), undated, CDJC, CMII-3.

[12] Michael Marrus and Robert Paxton, *Vichy France and the Jews*, Stanford University Press, 1981.

[13] Renée Poznanski, *Jews in France during World War II*, op. cit., p. 239.

the question in terms that have proven to be too simplistic: respect for the law or unawareness of the danger? Put that way, it does not take into account a variety of situations. A certain awareness of the danger did not necessarily mean immediately going underground, which involved having resources, making sacrifices and taking risks that in the short term were much more restrictive than what was involved in going to answer the census or pick up the yellow star. Annette Schmer, born in Paris in 1929 to parents who were tailors working at home and who had left Poland because of the persecutions, provides a good example of this type of situation: "There was the census of the Jews. As a law-abiding man, my father did what was required. He could not imagine that it meant a death sentence for Jews in extermination camps. Anyway, what could we have done against the anti-Jewish decrees? Leave? To go where? And with what?"[14]

The 16–17 July 1942 brutality

In the French collective memory, the Vélodrome d'Hiver roundup stands out as a symbol of the barbarity of the mass arrests targeting the Jews in France between 1940 in 1944. A closer examination of the number of arrests shows that in 1941, over 8,700 Jews were interned—12 per cent of the 75,721 French Jews deported during the war. Between 16 and 20 July 1942, this proportion was nearly 17 per cent, or 13,152 individuals arrested. More than the number of Jews arrested, it is the specific nature of the roundups that explains their profound symbolism in the collective memory. First of all, the mass effect was accentuated by the concentration in time (four days). Secondly, whereas the 1941 roundups had only affected men, the Vélodrome d'Hiver roundup also captured women and children.

The bi-monthly reports of the Paris Prefect were used to assess the influence of the roundup on people's behavior. Although the report dated 13 July 1942, under the section pertaining to public opinion and the Jews, emphasized that "a segment of the public seems inclined to display a sort of compassion toward them" after the anti-Jewish measures came into effect, the following report of 27 July 1942 is much more detailed:

> …the arrests of foreign Jews carried out on 16 and 17 July have given rise to considerable commentary from the public, the large majority of which believed that

---

[14] Testimonial by Annette Schmer, eleven pages, given in 2002, CDJC, Aloumim, 1510-4, testimonial no. 173.

these operations applied both to French Jews and foreign Jews. In general, these measures would have been fairly well received if they had only pertained to foreign adults, but many people were upset by the fate that awaited the children, rumors having quickly circulated that they had been separated from their parents. Though feeling little sympathy for the Jews, all inhabitants feel that these measures should not be inflicted on French Jews, particularly war veterans. Furthermore, many people did not hide their fears that such measures might be one day directed against the French.[15]

The Vélodrome d'Hiver roundup thus seems to mark the height of an awareness, until then very limited, that grew out of discriminatory measures, the most impressive of which had been the imposition of the yellow star. The scale of the measure provoked immediate reactions among Jews and non-Jews who had to face the urgency of the situation. Among accounts given by hidden children, the cases where awareness of the danger was directly linked to the Vélodrome d'Hiver roundup are more numerous (twenty cases) than those mentioning the 1941 roundups. Out of these twenty cases, six are related to the rumors surrounding the arrests of 16 and 17 July as opposed to fourteen where the extent of the danger and the need to react were asserted just after the roundup. Heightened awareness of the danger induced several types of reaction. Although some did not change their lifestyle in any way, remaining in Paris and leading an almost normal life, most Jews, whether French or foreign, decided to opt for a major change. Sometimes the danger was perceived but the families did not flee, for a variety of reasons. Some did decide to leave, whereas others chose to remain in Paris, in hiding or living in the open. Some placed their children in the care of religious institutions, others with relief organizations, and others in host families in rural areas.

A mass arrest seemed more serious, since they were more disturbing than scattered individual arrests that make the danger less apparent. But the 1941 roundups, which applied only to men, clearly show that the number of individuals affected by a roundup and physical brutality were not enough to generate strong reactions. Two other parameters must be taken into account: even though the Vélodrome d'Hiver roundup was carried out in several Parisian *arrondissements*, most of the Parisians still did not witness these mass arrests with their own eyes, as they were less visible than the yellow star and more spread out. In addition to these

---

[15] "Situation de Paris," Prefect's bi-monthly reports, 17 June–27 July 1942, APP.

external parameters in triggering action are social parameters that have to do with rescuers' personal motivations.

Individual motivations for deciding to act

It is very difficult to evaluate the number of people who came to the aid of Jews in Paris. Some of them have been recognized as "Righteous among the Nations," but many other operations on various scales helped to shield Jews from arrest. Whether it was rescuing someone in a single incident or arranging systematic aid to people in danger by participating in an organization, rescue was the outcome of individual initiatives. Is it possible, on the basis of statistics established by examining "Righteous" files, to establish the profile of a "Righteous Gentile" and, from there, draw up a general characterization of rescuers?

Resources conducive to aid. Membership in certain professions provided certain resources, habits or "mental tools" conducive to aid. In addition, some people's professions could concretely enable them to access information that they could then share. The jobs held by the "Righteous" were assorted and varied. Most of them were employees, artisans and tradesmen. Such people had contact and maintained professional social ties with neighborhood inhabitants. Members of religious organizations are also highly represented, which is not surprising given that solidarity and mutual aid are essential to their commitment. This hypothesis would also appear to hold in the case of the medical profession, social workers, and members of assistance organizations.

Eight *concierges*, all women, have been recognized as "Righteous." Their intermediary position between information—multiple contacts with the police—and the wanted Jews who were tenants in a building enabled them to warn about roundups. They could also open up vacant apartments in the building, thus permitting emergency rescue in the event of a roundup underway. Generalizations should however be avoided; Yvette Audo, for instance, has an entirely different recollection of the *concierge*'s role in her building during the war: "The building *concierge*, who opened the mail on the sly, had seen my father's CP membership card and rushed to denounce him to the Gestapo, who came to get my father and on checking his papers discovered that my mother was Jewish."[16]

---

[16] Testimonial by Yvette Audo, five handwritten pages, given in 1990, CDJC, Aloumim 1510–4, no. 96.

On 11 September 1942, the municipal police drafted a document marked "secret" and entitled "Instructions for the Teams in Charge of Arrests."[17] Written after July 1942, it sought to "perfect" roundup methods, since the Vélodrome d'Hiver roundup did not yield the results the Germans had hoped for. It is thus conceivable that the attitude of certain police officers was a cause of this, at least enough so for specific instructions to be imposed on them. They were at the heart of the law enforcement system, and received orders that they could disclose. They were in an uncomfortable position. They were certainly expected to obey orders, but did they also try to clear themselves of responsibility by warning certain families? Their office conferred on them possibilities to act in favor of the Jews: to warn them of roundups and/or not arrest them.

The variety of motives. This initial attempt at explanation is not entirely satisfactory: if membership in certain occupational categories and social circles was the only explanation for the deeds of certain individuals, why didn't all of those belonging to the same profession decide to act in the same way? Lack of self-interest is a criterion for awarding the "Righteous" medal. But although the case files by definition emphasize disinterested deeds, testimonials by those who were hidden children sometimes reveal less noble motives, sometimes financial ones, as the example of Suzanne Baron shows:

One day, my aunt's concierge's niece came to get us, saying that the concierge had been denounced and that she hid Jewish children in our country house. My uncle, still free thanks to his fake papers, asked the girl to go get us and bring us to Paris and above all to be very careful. The girl agreed because my uncle had promised to reward her.[18]

Sheltering children in the country, for a fee, during times of shortages could prove advantageous for a family looking for an extra pair of hands. Rivka Avihail has bad memories of this:

Our life as little farmers had begun [...]. Life quickly became hell for me. Maybe they had agreed to take us in without thinking about the fact that we were Jewish and what that meant. And they regretted it [...]. Until it was time to go back to

---

[17] Document entitled "Consignes pour les équipes chargées des arrestations," dated 11 September 1942, APP, BA 1813.
[18] Testimonial by Suzanne Baron, six pages, given in 1993, CDJC, Aloumim, 1510–1, no. 79.

school in October, I had really become the farm girl and did everything they required […]. I might've gotten used to their rude and cold behavior, but I couldn't bear their daily threats to denounce me as a Jew. I didn't realize that they couldn't do it without putting themselves in danger.[19]

How is it possible to know how many other host families took advantage of this unpaid labor?

The motivation leading to an act of rescue is mainly related to the nature of the ties between the rescuer and the person rescued. For instance, one theoretically comes to the aid of a friend, but alongside motives of friendship, there are also ideological or religious motives. A girl rescued by a woman remembers that "Madame Le Bris, who was very Catholic, had made a vow to rescue a Jewish child to bring her son back."[20] The sense of belonging to the same community of faith also sometimes came into play. For instance, the Dalian couple explained: "As for our motives, they were very simple. Since we ourselves came from the Armenian community, an ethnic minority which in other times had gone through comparable misfortunes, it was only natural and our duty to help those who would suffer and who on top of it were our friends."[21]

Selflessness in the act of rescue characterizes the "altruistic personality" as defined by Samuel and Pearl Oliner.[22] In their view, the deeds of the "Righteous" proved that individuals, seemingly powerless elements subject to the dominating structures that shape life in society, maintain a certain ability to act in violation of the rules. This notion of transgression is essential in thinking about rescue. In fact, how does one come to break the law simply by coming to the aid of someone else, *a fortiori* in an oppressive society dominated by the enemy? Samuel and Pearl Oliner use Auguste Comte's definition, which conceives altruism as devotion to the welfare of others, based on selflessness, which suggests that the action must be performed without any selfish considerations such as conceit or personal pleasure.

---

[19] Testimonial by Rivka Avihail, thirty pages, given in 1994, CDJC, Aloumim, 1510–2, not numbered.
[20] Le Bris file, no. 8743, CFYV.
[21] Dalian file, no. 6668, CFYV.
[22] Samuel and Pearl Oliner, *The Altruistic Personality: Rescuers of Jews in Nazi Europe*, New York, Free Press, 1988, p. 12.

Toward the decision to act: risk and the perception of danger

The risk run by rescuers adds interest to the question of their motives. I found no measure or law clearly directed against them, apart from a few mentions of punishment. First, the law of 22 July 1941 "concerning businesses belonging to Jews" states that "the same penalties will be inflicted on any person, even non-Jews, who, either in their own name or on behalf of a legal entity, intervenes to elude the provisions of the present law."[23] Later, the 6 June 1942 circular in application of the German decree making it mandatory to wear the yellow star stipulated that "any demonstration that could be construed as protest against the decree will be severely repressed."[24] People considered as "friends of the Jews" were interned in Tourelles prison for three months. No other law or decree mentioning more general punishment for helping Jews (apart from protests against the yellow star) could be found, except for a passing reference made in the 27 September 1942 issue of *La France Libre* to a "recent law" that "punishes any person who gives shelter to foreign Jews who appear on the lists and are wanted by the police by two months to five years in prison."[25]

It should however be mentioned that secrecy was not a *sine qua non* in the desire to give assistance to the Jews. In fact, some attempted to help them by going through the official channels of the Vichy authorities, as is shown by letters sent to those authorities. They manifest a desire to comply with the law, being signed and dated, while hoping to provide help to Jews known and liked. Even if replies from the Commissioner-General for Jewish Questions (CGQJ) were negative, it is important to highlight decisions to act taken by non-Jews who did not merely express their indignation.

The motives of the "Righteous" and other non-Jews who worked to rescue Jews finally depended on a number of parameters linked both to the specific nature of individuals and their personal history, the positions they occupied and the margin for maneuver that these allowed them. Realization of the danger was also an essential parameter, which should

---

[23] *Journal Officiel*, pp. 3594–5, in Claire Andrieu (ed.), *La Persécution des juifs de France 1940–1944...*, op. cit.

[24] Police prefecture circular dated 6 June 1942, APP, BA 1813.

[25] Article in *La France libre*, dated 27 September 1942, AIU, Archives OSE, XV (reel no. 6).

be allied with the circumstances of rescue that brought together rescuees and rescuers. The notion of network comes into play at several levels: in realization of the danger first of all, whether the aim was to warn families in danger or to spread the news, and then in the action itself, with the activation of networks existing before the war, formal ones in the case of (mainly religious) organizations and informal ones as regards to the social networks linking neighbors.

The multiple facets of rescue through pre-existing networks

The adaptation of formal networks. Pre-existing formal networks involved in rescue were mainly religious. Faith and membership, be it spiritual or concrete, in a community fueled the spirit of solidarity and a feeling that it was possible to do something—protest, help, hide, get involved—were all actions conditioned by the charitable principles of Christian morality. Thus in sermons, the Louvre Oratory pastor, Paul Vergara, urged his flock to put up resistance.[26] He also worked to rescue many children and was recognized as a "Righteous" person in 1988.

The primary vocation of the women's congregation of Notre-Dame-de-Sion, founded in France during the nineteenth century by converted Jews, apart from helping underprivileged Jews, was to convert them. Until 1942 its help was mainly given to people sent to them individually, foreign Jews or refugees from the Occupied Zone who could not return to their homes. Then groups of children began to pour in. The organization was thus not created *ad hoc* for the purpose of rescue, but some of its members worked together secretly to help persecuted Jews. We know the exact number of rescues organized from 68, rue Notre-Dame-des-Champs. Father Devaux kept a list of children who were offered sanctuary from March 1943 to 1945 with the name, age and place of refuge of each one, which he hid under the steps of his chapel altar. The *Bulletin des Enfants Cachés* published a list of 404 names.[27]

---

[26] *Voix chrétiennes dans la tourmente, 1940–1944. Sermons prêchés à l'église de l'Oratoire du Louvre par les pasteurs A.-N. Bertrand, P. Vergara et G. Vidal*, Paris, 150 copies published by the Église Réformée de l'Oratoire, 1945.

[27] *Bulletin des Enfants cachés, 1940–1944*, no. 12, September 1995, p. 9, and no. 13, December 1995, p. 10, cited by Madeleine Comte, *Sauvetage et Baptêmes. Les religieuses de Notre-Dame-de-Sion face à la persécution des juifs en France, 1940–1944*, Paris, L'Harmattan, 2001, p. 8.

Religious affiliation was not, however, the only trigger for a group rescue effort: a Paris-based network, Entraide Temporaire, was a secular group created by Lucie Chevalley, president of the Service Social d'Aide aux Émigrants (SSAE).[28] When war was declared, she got together a group of good-willed ladies to raise funds to come to the aid of families of foreign workers. She transported funds, including money allocated to pay the wages of paid SSAE employees, in balls of yarn. As pressure increased, prompting the organization to accelerate rescue measures, the funds raised went toward a priority: financing the rescue of Jewish children. The idea then came up to reactivate an existing children's charity founded in the 1920s called Sauvetage de l'Enfance, which for the circumstances was renamed Entraide Temporaire. So here was a case of a pre-existing structure that was adapted to the urgency of the situation of Jewish children, and, according to Katy Hazan, rescued 500 of them.[29]

Alongside such organized rescue, the most widespread action among the "Righteous" in Paris was individual, undertaken in emergency circumstances and motivated more by the immediacy of the danger. What social and personal networks were activated? All interpersonal relations—neighborhood, professional, friendly, and family—were involved in defining the characteristics of this form of rescue.

Activation of informal social networks: specific to Paris? Study of the "Righteous" files is a valuable but tricky exercise. In fact, the present research was based on the number of applications accepted, which necessarily indicates an external wish: the wish of the person who has requested recognition, the wishes of Yad Vashem which approved the application. Comparing the number of petitions filed in the main cities and the rest of France's regions, one notes that except for the greater Paris region, the "Righteous" were mainly recognized in villages around the main cities and in towns (cf. table 10). Thus, in the Center region, only one case was recognized in Orléans, as opposed to 131 in the rest of the region; in Burgundy, no "Righteous" has been recognized in Dijon, but sixty-four have been in the rest of the region. No case has been reported in Caen,

---

[28] Studied by Lucienne Chibrac in her doctorate dissertation entitled *Assistance et secours auprès des étrangers. Le service d'aide aux émigrants (SSAE), 1920–1945*, under the supervision of Yves Lequin, Lyon, Université Lumière-Lyon II, June 2004.

[29] Katy Hazan, *Les Orphelins de la Shoah*, Paris, Les Belles Lettres, 2000, p. 60.

but thirty-five in Lower Normandy. The only region that shows an exception is the greater Paris region. In fact, out of 443 files, 262 relate to the "Righteous" in Paris, as opposed to 181 in the smaller outlying towns.

Danger appears to have motivated rescuers in Paris to help evacuate the city, which had become a real trap, and undertake additional action afterward among host families in villages scattered throughout the provinces who provided rescue efforts at the other end of the chain. Another hypothesis has to do with the nationality of the Jews concerned: unlike the rest of France, Paris had a higher concentration of foreign Jews who needed help to flee since they had few or no relations outside the capital. Furthermore, perception of the danger in provincial towns was possibly less acute than in Paris.

The nature of the meeting between Jews and non-Jews was mainly a factor of the relations formed at various levels before the war. The most common tie was professional, slightly ahead of friendship and neighborhood ties. Family ties are the least represented. Regarding professional ties, cases where an employee rescued his boss or superiors were more numerous than the opposite. Other encounters were the product of a friendly relationship between colleagues or between customers and shopkeepers. According to Jacques Semelin, social networks of solidarity formed by concrete instances of assistance to the Jews represent a third "protective screen" against their arrest, the first two being defined as the opposition of a satellite state, such as Denmark or Finland, and by manifestations of public opinion.[30] Hiding potential victims or helping them to flee served as a sort of "social blanket that would wrap the Jews and thus make them invisible or inaccessible." As Annie Kriegel has pointed out, "it is at the grassroots level in the nature of the relationships and interpersonal relations between Jews and non-Jews at the level of everyday life that the secret of the most effective survival strategies is found."[31] It should be pointed out that people helped others in proportion to their ability. The situations were individually specific, depending on one's own history, occupation or acquaintances. One might or might not have relatives in the country willing to host one or more children, a flat big enough to offer a room, etc.

---

[30] Jacques Semelin, *Sans armes face à Hitler. La résistance civile en Europe, 1939–1943*, Paris, Éditions Payot, 1989, p. 207.

[31] Annie Kriegel, "De la résistance juive," *Pardès*, 2, Paris, Les Éditions du Cerf, February 1985, p. 202, cited by Jacques Semelin, *Sans armes face à Hitler…*, op. cit., p. 207.

Acts of rescue catalogued by reading the "Righteous" files pertain mainly to families (50 per cent of the cases), children (30 per cent) and single women (10 per cent). The nature of the act of rescue assumes various forms: rescued individuals were hidden and given accommodation (50 per cent of the cases), hidden and then evacuated (30 per cent) or evacuated immediately (15 per cent). Rescuers who hid and offered accommodation to the individuals they helped were mostly couples, closely followed by single women, as opposed to single men who did this rarely. Beate Kosmala, who has studied the rescue of Jews in Berlin, emphasized the importance of women's stewardship abilities, which are supposed to have made them more likely to hide and feed children in their homes.[32] The assumption of a more maternal sensitivity among women—whereas men, allegedly, were more oriented toward underground resistance activity such as providing false papers—is not borne out when another way of providing assistance is considered: that of evacuation. The proportions of single men, single women and couples who initiated this type of rescue act are virtually the same. Women thus both hid children and helped them to flee.

To see if there was something specific to Paris in forms of rescue, these figures were compared with data taken from the reading of Lyon's "Righteous" files, keeping in mind the differences between the two cities. Unlike Paris, Lyon was in the Unoccupied Zone until November 1942. It had a million inhabitants in May 1940,[33] and soon appeared as a safe city where the maze of old streets facilitated clandestinity. Just before the war, two-thirds of the Jews in France were concentrated in Paris, thirty times more than in Lyon where their number quadrupled between 1939 and 1942, going from 7,000 to 30,000, one-third of them foreigners.[34] Paris was the city one left, Lyon the city where one sought shelter or through which one transited before evacuation. This would appear to have been the case at least until the city, mythically labeled "capital of the Resistance," was occupied.

In Lyon, 39 per cent of the acts of rescue were carried out by men, just slightly more than the 36 per cent conducted by women, far more than

[32] Beate Kosmala, "Verbotene Hilfe. Rettung für Juden in Deutschland, 1941–1945," Bonn, Friedrich-Ebert-Stiftung, Historisches Forschungszentrum, 2004 (article from a symposium in Bonn on 28 September 2004).
[33] Erna Paris, *L'Affaire Barbie, analyse d'un mal français*, Paris, Ramsay, 1985, p. 89.
[34] Françoise Bayard and Pierre Cayez (eds), *Histoire de Lyon*, vol. 3, Lyon, Horvath, 1990, p. 398.

the 22 per cent undertaken by couples. These findings differ from those established for Paris, where single men rescued in 18 per cent of the cases, compared to 40 per cent for single women and 40 per cent for couples. These data would need to be compared with an analysis of the socio-occupational structures of Parisian women before and during the war. The question can indeed be raised as to the link between their involvement in rescue and their place in society, to which their power of decision and their influence were linked. As regards the nature of acts of rescue, it is virtually the same and occurred in similar proportions. More cases were noted in Paris of rescued individuals having been hidden before being evacuated, as opposed to Lyon where there were more cases of rescued individuals being evacuated directly, assuming less personal connection between the rescuer and rescuee(s).

More differences appear between the two cities when one looks into the individuals rescued. The "miscellaneous" category is much better represented in Lyon than in Paris, confirming the strong representation of organized, anonymous rescue. People helped individuals without worrying about who they were helping. In Paris, the predominance of cases in which individuals knew each other, compared with cases where the meeting was merely fleeting, indicates the highly individual and personal involvement of the rescuer. The rescuer would help a friend, neighbour or colleague, with or without a family. Feelings of solidarity, charity and friendship thus seem to dominate over ideology and the desire to institute some systematic form of rescue. Similarly, in Paris, families were rescued in greater numbers than individual men and women, a proportion that was reversed in the case of Lyon. A third element confirming that there was a specific form of rescue in Lyon was the help to men and women who had taken charge of themselves up to then, unlike children who depended on the good will of the people who crossed their paths. The importance of religious affiliation among rescuers in Lyon should moreover be pointed out, as shown by the large number of religious figures recognized as "Righteous," most of them working through Amitié Chrétienne.[35] In light of these elements, rescue in Paris appears as a

---

[35] Amitié Chrétienne was founded in late 1941, grouping leaders of Catholic and Protestant youth organizations united by a desire to fight the anti-Semitism all around. For the Catholics, it was led by the Jesuit priest Pierre Chaillet and Father Glasberg, a Jew converted to Catholicism, as well as Jean-Marie Soutou. Pastors Marc Boegner and Roland de Pury were its Protestant leaders.

gradually formed chain of help and mutual aid among various persons who for the most part had ties before the war and who, in emergency circumstances, found ways to face the looming danger. Three types of networks can finally be distinguished: informal social networks, pre-existing social networks, and aid networks formed specifically for this purpose.

The number of Jews who were helped by non-Jews during the war will never be known. Conversely, all those who rescued Jews have not been officially recognized: not all rescuers have been identified, particularly those who at the time aided children, who themselves do not necessarily recall the exact identity of the person who helped them. In some cases it is simply not possible to recognize the deeds of protagonists who died during or after the war. Furthermore, survivors have scattered throughout the world, making it very difficult to collect their testimony. Lastly, in cases of known rescue incidents in which the rescuers have been identified, some may wish not to be officially honored. Studying the "Righteous" thus raises the problem of reducing the field of analysis, in that only those who have been recognized are taken into consideration. Such institutionalization highlights the deeds of only some of those who helped the Jews and disregards many acts of complicity without which rescue, at least in some cases, would not have taken place. Thus, although all "Righteous" are rescuers, not all rescuers are "Righteous."

The "rescue chain," finally, is governed by certain criteria. First there is awareness of the danger, which prompts the act of mutual aid, an act that may or may not be rewarded in the end by success. To help someone flee, evacuate a child, supply a family with false papers, are all links in a chain that can be broken: there can be aid without rescue.[36] So it is after the fact, when the outcome of an action is known, that the notion of "rescue" is truly justified. The correlation between the rescue chain and the nature

---

All were recognized as "Righteous among the Nations." Specific, documented research should be conducted into the rescue operations undertaken by Amitié Chrétienne.

[36] A tragic example is the story of M. Marsat. He managed to get his co-worker and her sister into the Unoccupied Zone. They later wanted to return to Paris to see their mother, which he vehemently opposed. They both set off anyway but were denounced on 22 December 1942 at the demarcation line in Vierzon. After going through Drancy, they were deported to Auschwitz on 30 July 1943. Cf. Marsat file, no. 6793, CFYV.

of the arrests is situated in the influence of the latter on realization of the danger and the reactions it brings about. Thus, comparison between the 1941 and the July 1942 roundups, as well as the care with which operations to rescue children were set up, show that the nature of the individuals in danger was a more decisive factor than the number of persons targeted.

Table 9: Estimate of the evolution in the numbers of people considered as Jews in the Seine Department between October 1940 and July 1944

Date	Official figures (A)	Arrests (B)	(A-B)	Voluntary departures	Number given by the following census (C)	Difference between (A-B) and (C) = Estimated departures
19 October 1940	149,734[37]			nr[38]	139,979	−9,937
1st quarter 1941	139,979[39] / 135,721[40]			nr	135,721	−14,013
14 May 1941		3,710 (roundup)	132,011	nr		
20–24 August 1941		4,232 (roundup)	127,779	nr	126,181	−1,598
October 1941	126,181[41]			nr		
30 November 1941	125,992[42]			nr		
12 December 1941		743 (roundup)	125,249	nr	nr	
16–20 July 1942		13,152 (roundup)	112,097	nr	nr	
21 July to 31 December 1942		5,277[43] (roundups and individual arrests)	106,820	nr	nr	

1 January to 31 October 1943	3,829 (idem)	102,991	nr
1 November 1943 to 31 July 1944	2,198 (idem)⁴⁴	100,793	nr

---

[37] 19 October 1940 census, cited by Serge Klarsfeld, *Le Calendrier de la persécution des juifs en France, 1940–1944*, Paris, FFDJF and New York, The Beate Klarsfeld Foundation, 1993, p. 38. 19 October 1940 marked the day census-taking was completed in the Seine Department, which produced the police prefecture's Jewish registry. The Judicial Police was in charge of organizing it. The scale of this undertaking required the creation of a special administrative service, the "Tulard" service, named for its chief. 85,664 French Jews and 64,070 foreigners, or a total of 149,734 Jews, were thus registered in the Seine.

[38] Not reported.

[39] Dannecker Report dated 1 July 1941, cited by Serge Klarsfeld, *Le Calendrier de la persécution des juifs…*, op. cit., p. 95. A law passed on 2 June 1941 recommended another census (*JO*, p. 2476, in Claire Andrieu (ed.), *La Persécution des juifs de France 1940–1944…*, op. cit.) It is thus feasible that Dannecker used the results of this census for his report. However, the police prefecture report cited by Serge Klarsfeld, *Le Calendrier de la persécution des juifs…*, op. cit., pp. 162–3, indicates these results as dating from the "first quarter 1941."

[40] Dannecker Report dated 1 July 1941, cited by Serge Klarsfeld, *Le Calendrier de la persécution des juifs…*, op. cit., p. 95. Two different figures are given p. 95: 139,979 and 135,727; and p. 150: 139,981.

[41] Ibid., p. 150.

[42] Police prefecture report, 30 November 1941, cited by Serge Klarsfeld, *Le Calendrier de la persécution des juifs…*, op. cit., p. 162. It provides the following details: "A PP statistical report regarding the Jews inventoried specifies that in the Seine Department there were 110,992 Jews over the age of six. The number of children under six at that date has not been given to us, but it can be estimated at 15,000, and the total number of Jews in the Seine Department should have been adjusted from 150,000 in October 1940 to 125,000, to which should be added the 7,000 internees in the Loiret and Drancy camps, which makes a total of 132,000, a decrease of about 18,000 compared to the October 1940 census and of 7,000 with respect to the first quarter 1941 (Dannecker Report of 1 July)."

[43] Statistical assessment made by the municipal police on 31 December 1942 on its anti-Jewish activity for the year 1942, cited by Serge Klarsfeld, *Le Calendrier de la persécution des juifs...*, op. cit., p. 711. An attempt was made to determine the number of Jews arrested in roundups or individually: 208 Jews were arrested on 14 September 1942, 76 on 20 September 1,574 on 24 September and 1,060 on 5 November. 2,918 Jews were thus in all likelihood arrested individually.

[44] An attempt was made to determine the number of Jews arrested in roundups or individually: 275 Jews arrested the night of 25 to 26 November 1943, 635 in the night of 21 to 22 January 1944, sixty-two on 27 January 1944, twenty on 28 January 1944, 485 on 4 February 1944. 721 Jews were thus in all likelihood arrested individually.

Table 10: Distribution of French "Righteous" files between regions and main cities

Region	Number of "Righteous"	Detail: Number of "Righteous" by main city	Region	Main City
Rhône-Alpes	486	Lyon: 93	80	19
Île-de-France	443	Paris: 262	41	59
Midi-Pyrénées	257	Toulouse: 25	90	10
Aquitaine	218	Bordeaux: 14	93,5	6,5
PACA	197	Marseilles: 39	80	20
Auvergne	164	Clermont-Ferrand: 13	92	8
Center	132	Orléans: 1	99	1
Languedoc-Roussillon	125	Montpellier: 14	89	11
Limousin	117	Limoges: 25	79	21
Pays de la Loire	110	Nantes: 2	98	2
Nord-Pas-de-Calais	68	Lille: 27	60	40
Burgundy	64	Dijon: 0	100	0
Poitou-Charentes	64	Poitiers: 14	78	22
Lorraine	41	Nancy: 11	73	27
Lower Normandy	35	Caen: 0	100	0
Picardy	33	Amiens: 2	94	6
Franche-Comté	28	Besançon: 5	82	18
Champagne-Ardenne	26	Rheims: 4	85	15
Upper Normandy	16	Rouen: 1	–	–
Brittany	5	Rennes: 1	–	–
Alsace	1	Strasbourg: 0	–	–
Corsica	0	Ajaccio: 0	–	–

26

PROTESTANT MINORITIES, JUDEO-PROTESTANT AFFINITIES AND RESCUE OF THE JEWS IN THE 1940s

Patrick Cabanel

Amongst the 22,000 or so people who have been attributed the title of "Righteous amongst the Nations" for having rescued Jews in the course of genocide, two are civic groups, despite the fact that the Israeli law upon which the Yad Vashem Institute was founded prohibits this type of recognition. It concerns (in 1988) Chambon-sur-Lignon and its neighboring *communes* (municipalities), which form the "plateau du Vivarais-Lignon," bound by the Haute-Loire and the Ardèche; and the Dutch village of Nieuwlande, in the region of Drenthe, on the German border, honored in 1985 after 117 of its inhabitants received the title individually. The Yad Vashem Memorial honors each of these two "savior villages" with a monument: it is a unique privilege for two communities which, without it, would have remained well out of history and international fame. Both communities are Protestant, of the Calvinist Reformed Church to be exact, at least for the majority of the population. Those in charge of sheltering the Jews in the region of Chambon were pastors or prominent Protestants, the pastors Trocmé, Theis, Curtet, Bettex, etc., the laymen and women Roger Darcissac, Daniel Trocmé, Mireille Philip, etc. Also Protestant at Nieuwlande, the two main leaders were the farmer and municipal councilor Johannes Post and Arnold Douwes, son of a pastor, initially arrested for deliberately wearing the yellow star. Post persuaded Fredrik (Fritz) Slomp, pastor from 1927 to 1930, to return to the village in 1942, and he exhorted the inhabitants to fulfill their Christian duty and help the Jews.[1] Let us add a figure: the Protestants, who made up less than 2 per cent of the population of France in 1940, provided more than 10 per cent of the "Righteous" of this country.

What conclusion, made without haste, should be drawn from these few facts? The question is all the more complex since Protestantism is most diverse on a theological level and the dealings that its different churches have with their states and nations vary greatly. The Anglican Church and the majority of Lutheran Churches are "established," officially, with the sovereign of the state being their supreme head, the nation recognized within them. On the other hand, French Calvinists, the inheritors of the Hussites in Bohemia (around 2 per cent of the population), the Italian Vaudois or Waldensians (0.35 per cent of the population in 1911), but also churches created from dissidence or revival (from the Mennonites to the Methodists and Jehovah's Witnesses)—all these almost infinitesimal groups have, in their time, known persecution, dispersion, the rejection of institutionalization, and social solitude. This type of experience, united with a profoundly biblical religious and even Old Testament culture, serves to explain the affinity of minority Protestants with Jews and permits us to understand why their attitudes, faced with anti-Semitism and genocide, were different from those of Catholics and also "National" Protestants like the German Church.[2]

Protestants and Jews: a biblical reunion

If we want to understand why French Protestants and their pastors contributed so much to the rescue of Jews, we need to turn to four types of affinity: theological, cultural, historical and sociological. The first two types belong to Calvinism, if not Protestantism as a whole, while the last two are real specific features. From a theologico-cultural point of view—

---

[1] See Michel Fabréguet's contribution.
[2] I oversimplify this in such an extreme manner so as to underline the specificity of minority Protestantism; but let us remember that the Danish Lutheran Church, for example, despite being the official Church much like the German Church, was the spearhead of the spiritual resistance and help given to the Jews.

let us make no distinctions for now—it is a truism to recall that the Reformation brought about a (re)discovery of the entire Bible, a return to the Old almost as much as to the New Testament. Whilst their theologians were learning Hebrew again in order to read the Scriptures in their original language, the Protestants reclaimed this continent of history, of landscapes, of names of countries and of peoples, of literature, of poetry, of scent and of gestures, that make up the Jewish Bible which became, through its translation into the major European languages and by its infinitely large collective and individual readership, the Christian Bible. They henceforth shared a strange familiarity with the Jews—more exactly with the Hebrews. This tribe lives far from them, in space as in time, yet this is the tribe of their God; it is this Israel that fills their psalms and their prayers. The entire Reformation—Lutheran, Calvinist, Anglican—was involved in this. Everywhere, pastors and Christians were appropriating a Book that the Catholic Church had always carefully put out of the way of the uninstructed faithful, a Book which was none other than the Torah of the Jews. Everywhere, common and poetic languages found themselves enriched by biblical names and sayings, and a Hebraic "dialect" even appeared: "Pastors' German" (*pfarrerdeitsch*) in Alsace, the "Canaan dialect" in French speaking Protestantism.

On a strictly theological level—now is the occasion to introduce a first selection between Calvinism and the rest of Protestantism—Jean Calvin was most probably the first Christian theologian to have largely broken with Christian anti-Judaism. Luther had made a first attempt with his treatise *That Jesus was Born a Jew* (1523), in the Millenaristic hope of a general conversion of the Jews, before reversing his position and adopting a contempt and a hatred which would mark Lutheran culture until the 1940s. Calvin's main idea, which emanated from Saint Paul, rests upon the continuity and the similarity of the two Testaments (Chapter 10 of the second book of his *Institutes of the Christian Religion*): "The first of this point of resemblance brings the foundation of the other two, a lengthened proof is given of it. The first argument taken from a passage, in which Paul, showing that the sacraments of both dispensations had the same meaning, proves that the condition of the ancient church was similar to ours."[3] God not only promised to the Jews terrestrial happiness, but also eternal bliss. The truth can be found…in the misfortunes that

---

[3] Jean Calvin, *Institutes of the Christian Religion*, Second Book, Jean-Daniel Benoit (ed), Paris: Vrin, 1957, p. 207. See also p. 214.

the Hebrews have not ceased to encounter: "If these Holy Patriarchs expected a happy life from the Hand of God (and it is indubitable that they did), they viewed and contemplated a different happiness from that of a terrestrial life."[4] The same went for baptism: the crossing of the Red Sea baptized the Jews, as Saint Paul wrote in the First Letter to the Corinthians.[5] The apostle added that the majority of the Jews could not have been pleasing to God, since they died in the desert: he pointed out that they did not die because they were Jews, but because they were sinners. Though the Jews may have been rebels, concludes Calvin, "the Lord until the end will always save however many of them that remain, even though his vocation is without repentance."[6] Theodore de Bèze, Calvin's deputy and eventual successor, dispensed justice regarding the question of the "deicide" nation; neither the Jews nor Satan, neither Caiaphas nor Pilate killed Christ, but humanity. "It is we, say I, my brothers, that, after all those other sufferings, had him tied and garroted."[7] Afterwards, there were about-turns with, until the middle of the twentieth century, Reformed pastors steeped in anti-Judaism (and/or anti-Semitism), but Calvin brought about the decisive schism after 1,500 years: God saved the Jews, as Jews, and without conversion to Christianity; the Jews (or some Jews) belong to Him, and to attack them is to attack Him. One can imagine the possible consequences of this theological schism at a time when Nazism was about to hunt down the Jews of Europe.

Socio-historic affinities in a Europe of minorities and secularism

This, however, was not sufficient: a recent study has shown that the Swiss Reformed Churches remained largely impervious to the suffering of the Jews in the 1930s and 40s.[8] In order to reach understanding, it is neces-

---

[4] Jean Calvin, op. cit., *Institutes of the Christian Religion*, Book 2, Chapter 10, paragraph 13.
[5] I Corinthians; 10: 1–4, Louis Segond's translation. J. Calvin, *Institution...*, op. cit., p. 199.
[6] Jean Calvin's commentaries on the New Testament, Paris, Meyrueis, 1852, t, I, p. 23, quoted by Myriam Yardeni, "Juifs et judaïsme dans la théologie calviniste française du XVIIe siècle," *Foi et Vie*, CII, July 2003, p. 5. Our translation.
[7] *Sermons sur l'histoire de la passion et sépulture de Nostre Seigneur Jésus Christ descrite par les quatre Evangelistes*, 1590. Our translation.
[8] Nathalie Narbel, *Un ouragan de prudence. Les Eglises protestantes vaudoises et les réfugiés victimes du nazisme (1933–1949)*, Geneva, Labor et Fides, 2003.

sary to find other affinities, historical and sociological, between Protestant and Jewish minorities. I shall recall the fate of the Hussites of Bohemia, of the Waldensians of Italy after the Reformation, of the French Huguenots (Protestants), three groups to be distinguished clearly from the rest of European Protestantism. Their fate was marked by prohibition, popular and state persecution (pogroms and penal laws), the razing of temples, the creation of an underground, loyalty in the darkness, and dispersion (or Diaspora) to Europe and North America.[9] At this cruel school for minorities, these Protestants learned what it was to have neither state nor law nor police to protect you, what it was to see fanatical masses descending upon you since you were marked out to be a scapegoat or your presence alone conspired against all the gorgeous joy of the unity of souls; what it was to have to choose between abjuration and the tribulations of exile… Did that constitute a "Jewish style" experience? One might also suggest that the Huguenots and the Waldensians, drawing quite naturally from their Biblical culture, would describe their fate using categories and words taken from Hebrew history. Egypt, Pharaoh, Babylon, Desert all leapt from their quills. Claude Brousson, the lawyer from Nîmes martyred in 1698, entitled his collection of underground sermons *La Manne mystique du désert* (The Mystical Manna of the Desert). "Alpine Ghetto," "Israel of the Alps" were the names given in the nineteenth century to the Vaudois valleys of the Italian Alps.

Could minorities who had faced such struggles remain completely unmoved by the unleashing of similar attacks on the Jews? When the new laws appeared, when the forces of law and order came to arrest the innocent, these Protestants were confronted with their own story and some even suspected that the new regimes would finish by targeting them. Memory would seem to be the master word of this type of attitude. Every "Hussite," every "Huguenot," every "Waldensian," undoubtedly even today, is a walking encyclopedia of past persecutions, of loyalty safeguarded, of difference maintained, of pride shouldered. The degree of information and involvement may vary from one individual to the next, from a vague awareness to scholarly concern, from a smiling distance to fiery passion, but the certitude of a separate identity, and one worthy of its existence, persists even after observances and faith have disappeared. "The spiritual sons of the Huguenots quiver with emotion and affinity every time a reli-

---

[9] Historians speak of the Huguenot and Walloon Refuge.

gious minority is persecuted," wrote pastor Boegner to the Chief Rabbi of France on 4 April 1933, before adding in reference to the very first affinities discerned: "and they know only too well that Christianity and, more particularly, the Reformed Churches owe much to the Prophets who cleared the path to the Gospel, sparing them the wounds from the blows which struck the Children of Israel."[10] As for the Czech Josef Fisera, studying in France at the end of the 1930s and proclaimed "Righteous" for having saved children in the French Alpes Maritimes area, it is no coincidence that, when giving an address at a symposium in 1992, he immediately placed his involvement under the sign of the "Martyr Jean Hus and [of the] great exile and founder of modern education Jean-Amos Comenius, bishop of the Unity of Czech Brethren."[11]

It is equally important to observe the social experiments carried out by Protestants and Jews in modern societies on the path to social or official secularization from the end of the eighteenth century. These processes opened up new spaces and new opportunities to them: they occupied the first and seized the second with a sometimes uncanny success which could not have failed to irritate the Catholic majority, powerless or steeped with a feeling of loss and injustice. In France, as in Italy, Protestants and Jews were allowed citizenship at the same time: in 1789 then in 1791 in the French case, in 1848 for the Waldensians and some of the Italian Jews, thanks to Article 24 of the Constitution of Piedmont, the *Statuto Albertino*. In both cases, the legislator did not necessarily consider the two minorities together, but attempted to place the Catholic Mass and non-Catholic rites on the same footing in the eyes of the law. Once this unity had been achieved, the Kingdom of Italy had to pass through a legal revolution whose consequences were for the Jews ever-increasing integration based on the European model of Israeliticism, and for their Waldensian fellow-countrymen, hitherto confined to their valleys, departure from their sanctuary and the constitution of a middle class. Protestants and

---

[10] Message from the Council of the French Protestant Federation to the chief Rabbi of France, 4 April 1933, quoted by Michel Leplay, *Les Eglises protestantes et les Juifs face à l'antisémitisme au vingtième siècle*, Lyon, Editions Olivetan, 2006, p. 36.

[11] Account in André Encrevé and Jacques Poujol, *Les protestants français pendant la seconde guerre mondiale*, proceedings of the Paris symposium of November 1992, supplement to the *Bulletin de la Société de l'Histoire du Protestantisme Français*, 3–1994, p. 645–7.

Jews clearly emerged as members of the state and modern society elites in both France and Italy.[12]

Obviously, Catholic opinion, or at least some of its sectors, fought violently against this modernization that translated itself by the weakening of the Church, the pluralism of the religious countryside, and advances by minorities. Anti-Semitism, which blossomed at the time, was almost systematically mixed with an anti-Protestantism that is forgotten today[13]—wrongfully so if one wants to understand "hyphenated" hates (against Judeo-Protestantism, against the Judeo-Masonry…) and Judeo-Protestant solidarity, both objective and subjective. In the 1940s, Protestant minorities remembered that they had been hated along with the Jews during the preceding decades. The Dreyfus Case belongs to them almost as much as the Jews. Rather than return to the works of Drumont, Maurras, or Barrès, or even of the pioneer Toussenel, I will quote Mgr Alphonse Kannengieser, an Alsatian pastor who wrote a book entitled *Juifs et Catholiques en Autriche-Hongrie* (Jews and Catholics in Austria-Hungary) in 1896. The second part of this book deals with the situation in Hungary and with the very lively struggles surrounding mixed and civil marriages. It was as though all the contemporary history of Hungary and its secularization were seen the wrong way up…in some kind of Jewish-Calvinist plot. Kannengieser affirmed that a sort of sacred union could be seen amongst Catholics, Lutherans (who were Saxons of German origin) and the Rumanian and Serbian Orthodox and, on the other hand, amongst the government of the Calvinist Koloman Tisza (1875–90), the Jews and "Unbelieving Calvinists," both groups being often members of Masonic lodges. It would appear that Tisza planned the death of Catholicism, and then of Christianity as a whole. "He placed in the hands of his creatures all public posts and, in the formidable scramble that he organized, Jews and Calvinists avidly divided up the spoils of Hungary's patrimony. […] Did not the kingdom of Saint Stephen become a stronghold of Calvinism and of Judaism?"[14]

---

[12] Rainer Liedtke and Stephan Wendehorst, *The Emancipation of Catholics, Jews and Protestants. Minorities and the Nation State in Nineteenth-century Europe*, Manchester University Press, 1999; Patrick Cabanel and Chantal Bordes-Benayoun (eds), *Un modèle d'intégration. Juifs et Israélites en France et en Europe XIXe-XXe siècles*, Paris, Berg International, 2004.

[13] Jean Baubérot and Valentine Zuber, *Une haine oubliée. L'antiprotestantisme avant le « pacte laïque » (1870–1905)*, Paris, Albin Michel, 2000.

[14] A. Kannengieser, *Juifs et Catholiques en Autriche-Hongrie*, Paris, Lethielleux, 1896, pp. 224 and 250.

"A policy of occupation by religious confession," an "enterprise of de-Christianization of the State," the "replacement of Catholic influence by Judeo-liberalism," "Jewish and Calvinist invasion": all readers of the literature of the contemporary French far right will recognize in these expressions the heart of its argument. And yet, even though there has obviously never been a plot of this type in France or in Hungary, the historian cannot help but observe that in many of the groups working for the objectives and aims of secularization—the right of religious freedom, neutrality in education, family rights, emancipation of women, etc.—one finds members of religious minorities working in the forefront, and that the affinities between Protestants and Jews have proved to have real social effectiveness, as much in the joy of pluralist modernization as in the terrible ordeal of Catholic and Nationalist hatred (from the Dreyfus Case to the 1940s). This is more than a hypothesis: I would willingly refer to an ideal-type of Judeo-Protestant affinities based initially upon the French example, and one which needs to be confronted with other concrete historical situations, notably in Bohemia and Hungary.

The ideal type[15] of Judeo-Protestant affinity: the Waldensian example

Let us attempt to verify the relevance of such an ideal type with a detour via the Waldensians of Italy. In the second half of the 1930s, certain organs of the Fascist press and others subject to the regime published articles hostile to Italian Protestants, often with thinly veiled threats. *Liguria del Popolo*, at Genoa on 12 December 1936, described them as "blisters filled with pus" (*bolle piene di marciume*), exhorting that the blisters should rapidly be burst to get rid of them. Similarly, the literary journal *Quadrivio* published an article entitled "Religious cross-breeding" ("*Metticiato religioso*") which expressed the hope that measures similar to those against the Jews should be applied to all Protestants.[16] The official racist journal founded in 1938, *La difesa della razza*, published two articles in July and in October 1940, aimed at proving the collusion of values and interests between Jews and Protestants; this closely echoed Toussenel or Proudhon, and intersected with the anti-Semitisms of both the far left and the far right.[17]

---

[15] In the Weberian sense.
[16] Giorgio Spini, "Gli evangelici italiani di fronte alle leggi razziali," Il Ponte, n° 11–12, 1978, *La difesa della razza*, pp. 1353–8.
[17] A.M. De Giglio, "Il giudaismo, fomentatore del protestantesimo," 5 July 1940,

However, when the regime imposed its anti-Semitic legislation in 1938, the Waldensian Church showed, to say the least, a cautious reserve and voiced no protest. Only one article, published on 3 August 1938 in the Church's official weekly, *La Luce*, dared however to make its dissent heard. Its author, Mario Falchi, born in Genoa in 1869, was a mathematics teacher at the Vaudois college of Torre Pellice, and was to die in 1944 in a Salò Republic gaol. "*Quello che l'umanità gli deve. Vale a dire: quelle di cui essa, l'umanità, fu e rimane debitrice as Israel*"[18] is a vibrant homage to what the Jews contributed to humanity.[19] On the following 14 August the daily newspaper in Cremona, *Il regima fascista*, retaliated curtly under the title "*Anch'essi!*" ("Them as well!"—the Protestants) and concluded that a closer eye would have to be kept on the Waldensians. The Church understood the threat and kept silent. Even though the elite of its young Pastors, Barthians, as in France, followed with a painful passion the troubles with the German Confessing Church and Nazism[20]—the Waldensian magazine *Gioventù Christiana* dedicated a quarter of its space to this struggle—the Waldensian Church was not a Confessing Church,[21] no more than the Reformed Churches of France and Holland. It never even pronounced the least equivalent of the very strong words that the leaders of those other two churches wrote to condemn the deportation of the Jews.

---

pp. 42–4 and Gino Sottochiesa, "Lo spirito ebraico del puritanesimo," 20 Octobre 1940, p. 34–8, texts published with comments by Alberto Cavaglion and Gian Paolo Romagnani, *Le interdizioni del Duce. A cinquant'anni dalle leggi razziale in Italia (1938–1988)*, Turin, Albert Meynier, 1988, pp. 170–8.

[18] "What humanity owes to her. Exactly: the things that humanity did and will always owe to Israel."

[19] Text published with comments by Alberto Cavaglion and Gian Paolo Romagnani, *Le interdizioni del Duce*, op. cit., pp. 165–9, and by Giorgio Spini, "Gli evangelici…," op. cit., p. 1356–8. The French pastor Freddy Durrleman published a very similar text in April 1933, *Plaidoyer pour les Juifs*, Neuilly, La Cause, 1933.

[20] The Barthians are the disciples of the Swiss Karl Barth, a German language Calvinist theologian who spearheaded a spiritual opposition to Nazism and was expelled from the University of Bonn in 1935; there was, in the Confessional Church, a minority of pastors and laymen who were hostile to the regime and the support it was able to obtain from the Lutheran Church.

[21] In the sense of public acknowledgement of faith to the extent of martyrdom if necessary.

However, in no way did the attitude of the Church leaders influence that of the faithful, who were more often than not imbibed with a collective memory that could be instantaneously mobilized, to carry out the physical gestures of solidarity needed so much by the persecuted Jews. Moreover, eyewitness accounts agree that the Vaudois valley was an important land of refuge, no doubt comparable to the Cévennes, with the same type of landscape and rural economy—all fertile for runaways and for survival—the same type of religion, culture, memory. Jean-Pierre Viallet, who was most severe regarding the Church's silence, tells us that Jews had a text entitled *"Ringraziamento"* ("Thanks") published in the local Resistance journal, *Il Pioniere*, on 7 May 1945, referring to the population of the valleys.[22] Sandro Sarti recalled in an article in 1962 that the Vaudois communities of the region of Pignerol welcomed numerous Jewish families from Piedmont, and that very strong relationships were established at this point, over and above those that united young Jews and young Waldensians fighting shoulder to shoulder in the resistance.[23] The theology thesis of Maria Bonafede, presented in 1984, would appear to give further information about this, but I have been unable to gain access to it.[24] Perhaps the Waldensian theologian Giovanni Miegge's account, published from 1946 onwards, says the essential. This text could indeed offer a possible explanation for the existence of other Jewish refugees in Protestant countries, in Chambon-sur-Lignon, in the Cévennes, at Nieuwlande, etc.:

> There were also a great number of Jews [in the Vaudois valleys]: those persecuted today were seeking shelter from those who were persecuted yesterday, who offered them a most cordial and devoted hospitality. Nearly all of Italy, with very few exceptions, were welcoming to them, beginning with the priests. A most moving chapter of history could be written about this subject!

---

[22] Jean-Pierre Viallet, *La chiesa valdese di fronte allo stato fascista 1922–1945*, preface by Giorgio Rochat, Turin, Claudiana, 1985, p. 225.

[23] Sandro Sarti, "Il mondo protestante e la questione raziale: note sulla rivista Gioventu Christiana (1933–1940)," in Guido Valabrege (ed.), *Gli Ebrei in Italia durante il fascismo*, 2, 1962, p. 86.

[24] M. Bonafede, "Azione efavore degli Ebrei da parti di Pastori Metodisti e Valdesi in Italia dopo l'emanzione delle leggi razziali (1938–1945): una prima panoramica sulla dase delle testimonianze," *laurea* thesis, Facoltà Valdese de Teologia, Rome, 1984 (hitherto unpublished).

The Jews, however, were particularly drawn towards Protestants because of reasons of ancient affinity that were most understandable; were not both of them religious minorities? Did they not share in the Bible a communal treasure?[25]

One should note in this text, besides its parallel with the declaration of the Council of the French Protestant Federation in 1933, the allusions to each of the affinities I have attempted to define: theologico-cultural (the Biblical treasure), sociological (the minorities), historical (memory of persecutions), the word "affinity" which I have used all the way through this chapter. One finds this word used in the nineteenth century by the English thinker Matthew Arnold, to characterize the special link uniting "the genius and history" of the English nation and its American descendants to that of the Hebrews. It is also employed by…Charles Maurras, denouncing "deep fellow feelings of culture, indisputable mental and moral affinities (Bible and Talmud, English culture, German culture, Masonic ritualism), the natural position towards the conquerors, in the conquered people between Protestants and Jews."[26] When penal laws came, marking the persecutions of the 1930s and 40s, such affinities enabled the Jews to avoid isolation when rejected from the heart of the nations in which they had been led to integrate by the Israelite promise, and benefit from active solidarity.

Though the ideal-type based on the example of the Huguenots and the Waldensians has some validity, one could compare it profitably with the fate of the Hussites, and also with the Hungarian Calvinists of Transylvania (which was to become part of Romania in 1918), and suggest that there has been a Jewish refuge within their ranks. It is up to the historian to confirm or invalidate this hypothesis. It could also be used as an element of more general reflection regarding the capacity of religious or ethnic minorities to "understand" the misfortune that can swoop down on other minorities, and their capacity to give help to them. From this point of view, looking into the relations between Armenians and Jews since at least 1915 is promising.[27] As for the attitudes of Muslim minori-

---

[25] Giovanni Mieggi, "La Chrétienté au creuset de l'épreuve," in *L'Eglise sous le joug fasciste*, Geneva, Labor et Fides, vol. XI, 1946, p. 57.

[26] For references for these texts, I take the liberty of citing my work, *Juifs et protestants en France, les affinités électives XVIe-XXIe siècle*, Paris, Fayard, 2004.

[27] See several of the contributions in Jacques Adler, "Ailleurs, hier, autrement: connaissance et reconnaissance du génocide des Arméniens," *Revue d'Histoire de la Shoah*, 177–178, January to August 2003.

ties in the Balkans when faced with the deportation of the Jews, the question remains open. We must not, however, disguise the fact that the Huguenot-Jewish (or Waldensian-Jewish) model is exceptional in the sense that these groups shared both impregnation with the same Sacred Book and a history of experiencing the fate of being a minority. It also seems probable that the equation functioned even better in the case of Protestant "sects" that were, if possible, even more profoundly nourished with the Bible, and were the minorities amongst the minorities. The case of the Darbysts, who were so present in the region of Chambon-sur-Lignon and so generous regarding the Jews, stands out here. We would like to know more about them, as we would about the Arminians (Calvinist dissidents) in Holland and the Mennonites in the Germanic world, and even the Jehovah's Witnesses.[28] It would be necessary to seek answers in the Protestant communities of Germany, of Holland, of Switzerland, heirs of the Refuge of the Huguenots, since they have a supplementary trait in their identity: the exile and Diaspora experienced by their ancestors. We are aware, however, that the German Huguenots fully identified themselves with their new homeland from the end of the eighteenth century, and with its deliberately anti-Semitic nationalism:[29] there is Diaspora and Diaspora.

Let us finally add that the components of the ideal type and their association are not fixed: one amongst them can easily weaken and fade away, for another to appear and take over the entire scene. Thus, today, the French "Huguenots," who read the Bible less and less, appear to feel more affinities with the Palestinian minority than with the powerful State of Israel; whilst many American Protestant groups, with no experience of being a minority, support that same State in the name of a communion of a religious adventure of Jews and of Christians, and a more or less avowed millennialism. It would seem that the exceptional Judeo-Protestant conjunction seen in the nineteenth and twentieth centuries in most specific sectors of European Protestantism, which contributed to the

---

[28] The Baptists held much the same attitude as the Reformed and the Darbysts, see Sebastien Fath, *Une autre manière d'être chrétien en France. Socio-histoire de l'implantation baptiste (1810–1950)*, Geneva, Labor et Fides, 2001, pp. 425–39.

[29] Etienne François, "Du patriote prussien au meilleur des Allemands," in Michelle Magdelaine and Rudolf von Thadden, *Le Refuge huguenot*, Paris, Armand Colin, 1986, pp. 229–44.

reduction of Jewish mortality rates during the genocide, is being undone today. It is not certain that if such a thing as the genocide were to recur, new Chambon-sur-Lignons might appear in such a secular world—one that nowadays tends to muddle up the Jews with the State of Israel. Certain specific memories, whether theologico-cultural or socio-historical, have either weakened or been assimilated, and one can ask whether Europe has not lost, here, one guarantee of pluralism.

27

NIEUWLANDE, LAND OF RESCUE
(1941/1942–1945)

Michel Fabréguet

The village of Nieuwlande shares today with the French *communes* of the former *Consistoire de la Montagne* surrounding Chambon-sur-Lignon the privilege of having been collectively honored with the medal of the "Righteous amongst the Nations,"[1] a distinction which is usually only attributed by the state of Israel to individuals, on the basis of individual eyewitness accounts. We can query Yad Vashem's choice of Nieuwlande as a symbol of the Netherlands' civil resistance: Nieuwlande is not in fact an isolated case and there were many other "Nieuwlandes" in the Netherlands under German occupation, such as Ede in the province of Guelder, Enschede and Ommen in the Overijessel or Heerenveen and Steenwijk in the province of Friesland.

Questioning sources

The core of this chapter does not lie in the analysis of political memory, but in history. Like all histories of the underground, we discover what happened in Nieuwlande principally through the accounts of those who

---

[1] Yad Vashem: dossier 1148/2, Nieuwlande Honores, 13 March 1985 Ceremony, letter from David Kool dated 12 May 1985 and aerotelegram from R. Norden dated 14 July 1985.

played a part in it: rescuers and runaways—accounts that were all reconstructed retrospectively. We only really have one source available in the archives, which is the diary of Arnold Douwes, written during his time in action and preserved at the state Institute of War Documents in Amsterdam. This important document describes in particular the great difficulties the rescue network members met with in convincing the local inhabitants to shelter runaways, as well as the often less than diplomatic methods to which the rescuers had to resort.

When looking at all existing accounts, it is helpful to group together those given by the rescuers, who were inhabitants of Nieuwlande and its suburbs, and "Aryan" network members, and then those given by Jewish refugees, who either were *onderduikers*[2] or in turn became members of rescue networks. In 1985, Lammert Huizing published a first brochure entitled *Zij konden niet anders. Herinneringen aan het verzet in Nieuwlande 1940–1945*,[3] with a preface written by the mayor of Oosterhesselen in homage to resistance members and their help to the refugees. At the same time, the "Nieuwlande 1940–1945" Working Group organized an exhibition.[4] In 1988 a first version was published, entitled *Nieuwlande, dorp met vijf burgermeesters*,[5] of the work done by Jo Schonewille, J. Engels and J. van der Sleen who financed themselves the publication two years later of the definitive work entitled *Nieuwlande 1940–1945, een dorp dat sweeg.*[6] This book was put together using material from interviews with survivors, carried out by the authors half a century after the events. The works of Lammert Huizing and of Jo Schonewille combined prove to be of far more use than any history book. The main criticism that a researcher could make on encountering these two publications is that the subject matter's presentation is based on a quite specific format and little heed is paid to the chronology of events: the years 1940–45 do not make up a compact and homogenous block of time, either in Nieuwlande or in any

---

[2] This term, used to describe those working with the underground movement, signifies literally "those who have plunged under water," an aquatic metaphor which is most explicit in a Netherlands context.

[3] They had no other choice. *Memories from Resistance in Nieuwlande, 1940–1945*, Stichting Het Drentse Boek, Zuidwolde, 1985.

[4] Beit Lohamei Haghetaot: dossier 1262, Guide to temporary exhibition "Nieuwlande 1940–1945."

[5] "Nieuwlande, a village with five town councils."

[6] "Nieuwlande 1940–1945, A village where everyone kept quiet."

part of Europe under German occupation. It makes it hard for the researcher to realize with clarity that it was only in the spring of 1943—that is to say, relatively late in relation to the start of deportations towards the extermination camps in the East of Europe—that all the inhabitants of Nieuwlande acted together to save the runaways.

Eyewitness accounts from Jewish escapees make up another source that presents specific problems to researchers. These accounts were written up or gathered between the beginning of the 1970s and the end of the 1990s, that is to say a longer period of investigation than in the documenting of interviews by Lammert Huizing and by Jo Schonewille's team, and one could suppose that this was motivated by the collective commemorations organized by Yad Vashem from 1985 to 1988. Accounts given by Jewish *onderduikers*, especially those who became members of the rescue teams, were given by participants who were, at the time of the events, still adolescents or young adults, from large cities in the west of the Netherlands—Amsterdam, Rotterdam and The Hague. Their upbringing had, in general, brought with it abandonment of religious practice.[7] However, due to the tragic circumstances of war, these young people found themselves immersed in a rural society that was totally different from the urban civilization in which they had grown up until then: prayers before meals, daily Bible readings and regular church attendance on Sundays, a religious practice which punctuated the lives and the work of these most fervent orthodox Reformed Church people, who were also the most active of resistance members. Moreover, in sharing the perilous experience of underground resistance activities, they all developed very strong feelings of esteem and even affection for each other. Consequently, accounts given by Jewish escapers concerning their rescuers sometimes, tend towards hagiography, and only add to the stuff of legend, heady with the intense emotion that will always be connected with that feeling of solidarity amidst danger, and softened by time that has passed between what one went through and the moment, much later, when one thinks back. The passage of time helps to smooth out if not completely eradicate thoughts of difficulties encountered in the past. The accounts paint in this manner a touching picture, though a somewhat naïve and minimal one, of a monolithic moral and religious elite; this, of course, is problem-

---

[7] Bob Moore, Victims & Survivors. *The Nazi Persecution of the Jews in the Netherlands 1940–1945*, Arnold, London, New York, Sydney, Auckland, 1997, pp. 24–5.

atic for the researcher who is trying to gain a more rigorous insight into the more complex and sometimes less edifying motivations of the local people.

From rejection of the Occupation to the reorganization of civil resistance (May 1940—April/May 1943)

In the night of 9 May 1940, the Wehrmacht pushed back the Dutch line of defense opposite the town of Coevorden.[8] The Blitzkrieg rapidly got the better of Dutch resistance. On 18 May Arthur Seyss-Inquart was named head of the civil occupation authority by Hitler with the title of Commissioner of the Reich. The choice of the man who was the last Chancellor of Austria during the Anschluss led to speculation that the Führer was thinking of annexing the Netherlands to the Reich. However, the military capitulation did not formally put an end to the sovereignty of the Netherlands and Seyss-Inquart allowed a civil service under the direction of ministries' general secretaries to exist. The method was skilful since it encouraged the development of a civil service whose policy was one of working with the occupier, a policy intended to reassure the civil population, but which in fact favored opportunism, the traditional sense of discipline and a respect for authority which were traits fairly spontaneously displayed by Dutch people. In the disarray of consciences brought about by defeat and by the hasty departure to London of the legal authorities, the summer of 1940 was, as summed up by Christopher de Voogd, "a season of the duped" under the auspices of a policy of compromise. Heindrik Colijn, a right-centre politician and leader of the anti-revolutionary party, affirmed his conviction in a fitting pamphlet, *At the Frontier of two Worlds*, that Germany would definitely win the war and that it was therefore necessary to collaborate with the power that would, in the future, rule over the European continent.[9]

Faced with the ambiguity of the politics of compromise, the development of civil resistance was lengthy and difficult. The example of Nieuwlande, however, proves that there were, from May 1940 onwards, forerunners who refused to compromise with the occupiers and became

[8] Lammert Huizing, op. cit., pp. 10–14.
[9] Horst Lademacher, *Geschichte der Niederlande. Politik. Verfassung. Wirtschaft*, Darmstadt, Wissenschaftliche Buchgesellschaft, 1983, pp. 379–440. Christophe de Voogd, *Histoire des Pays-Bas*, Paris, Hatier, 1992, pp. 216–20.

quite naturally the main organizers of the civil resistance movement afterwards. As soon as the Germans arrived, Johannes Post tried to motivate a few peasants to join the Dutch army in order to carry on the fight, but he came up against the opposition of the pastor who enjoined the population to submit to the new authorities. Johannes Post was a minor local notable: this orthodox Calvinist countryman, a member of Colijn's Anti-revolutionary party, had been deputy mayor of Oosterhesselen since 1935.[10] Head of a large family, respected as much for his moral character than for his business acumen, a fine public speaker and administrator, he was held in esteem by his fellow citizens, but this in itself was not sufficient to convince the latter to follow him immediately in the resistance effort. Whilst the population felt humiliated by the brutality of the aggression by the Germans, a people to whom they had hitherto felt linguistically and culturally close, negative effects upon daily life were not immediately felt. By order of the Führer, Dutch prisoners of war who had been interned in Germany were rapidly released. Moreover, the economic climate was now showing favorable development.[11] The material conditions for a certain form of accommodation with the occupier were created.

In May 1941, Johannes Post welcomed to his farm Arnold Douwes, introduced as the first of the *onderduikers* of Nieuwlande. The son of a Calvinist pastor, a landscape artist by trade, Arnold Douwes had migrated before the war to the United States, where he had participated in the struggle against racial discrimination. Having returned to his country, he chose, just like Johannes Post, the path of resistance to the Nazis, a decision made on the very day of the capitulation of the Netherlands, and one that would rapidly condemn him to go underground.[12] Frits Slomp, a pastor at Heemse in the neighboring province of Overijessel, who had worked at Nieuwlande from 1927 to 1930, also belonged to the group of precursors of the civilian resistance, traveling the length and breadth of the country in search of hideouts for the very first runaways.[13]

---

[10] Article "Johannes Post" in *The Encyclopaedia of the Righteous among the Nations. Rescuers of Jews during the Holocaust*, The Netherlands, volume 2, Yad Vashem, Jerusalem, 2004, pp. 607–8. Lammert Huizing, op. cit., pp. 14 and 47.

[11] Jo Schonewille, J. Engels and J. van der Sleen, op. cit., pp. 35–6. Christophe de Voogd, op. cit., pp. 206–7.

[12] Article "Arnold Douwes" in *The Encyclopaedia of the Righteous*, op. cit., volume 1, pp. 223–4.

[13] Lammert Huizing, op. cit., p. 36.

Halfway between the small towns of Hoogeveen and Coevorden, Nieuwlande is in the southern part of Drenthe. This province in the north of the Kingdom of the Netherlands was the least densely populated, with only eighty-three inhabitants per square kilometer in the 1930s, and was also less urbanized and less powerfully industrialized than the rest of the country, with sand and marshland offering little of value. Nieuwlande (literally meaning "new land") was a village of pioneers, founded in the last decade of the nineteenth century, and lacked any specific administrative identity, having been founded on territories belonging to five communes: Oosterhesselen, Hoogeveen, Coevorden, Gramsbergen and Dalen. A pioneer village in the form of a chessboard, Nieuwlande gave more the impression of a "road village" which stretched for 2.7 kilometers around its one paved street, the Nieuwlandse Straatweg, prolonged by the Dwarsgat, and doubled by a canal which other canals and sandy pathways intersected at right angles. Isolated farmhouses were often built at a distance from lines of communication, and often simple planks would replace bridges for crossing the canals.[14] The manner in which the houses were dispersed, with certain parts even more isolated so that access was possible only via bridges and narrow pathways, offered favorable conditions for runaways in search of isolated hideouts. On the eve of World War II, agriculture had become Nieuwlande's principal activity, with predominance of crops over livestock. The land gave wheat, potatoes, vegetables, sugar beet and rapeseed, meat, milk and eggs.[15]

Nieuwlande counted around 800 inhabitants, mainly peasants, laborers and small business merchants. In the religious and political mixture, through the coexistence of Catholics, Protestants and a few freethinkers, there was a predominant "pillar" of Protestantism, which was, in fact, a double pillar: for, side by side with the faithful of the "moderate" Reform Church, the Hervormde Kerk, linked with the secular authorities, there were the Orthodox Reformed of the Gereformeerde Kerk, founded in 1885 by Abraham Kuyper, who, inspired by their faith in coming to help the persecuted, were to play the role of catalyzers in organizing the sheltering of *onderduikers*. Orthodox Calvinists, descendants of the Reawakening of anti-liberal inspiration in the nineteenth century, an electoral

---

[14] Jo Schonewille, J. Engels and J. van der Sleen, op. cit., pp. 14–16. Yad Vashem, dossier 1148/1, account given by Max Nico Leons, p. 18.
[15] Lammert Huizing, op. cit., p. 8. Jo Schonewille, J. Engels and J. van der Sleen, op. cit., pp. 14–15 and 108–10.

clientele of the Anti-revolutionary party of Kuyper and Colijn, represented a mere 8 per cent of the total population of the Netherlands. Though relatively numerous in the north-east provinces, they remained a minority.[16] In fact, recognition of diversity in the institutionalization of the political and social system of the *verzuiling* (pillarization)[17] assisted the compartmenting of different social groups in daily life. The *verzuiling* legitimized the particularities of Dutch society which had a tendency to retreat behind traditions and differences. It also meant that, within each pillar, individuals were submitted to a very strong form of social group control, which encouraged connivance amongst the elite of different *zuilen*[18]—factors that were essential in the success of the collective rescue of those on the run. Moreover, a natural tendency toward collective social cohesion encouraged by the *verzuiling* system found support, in the case of Nieuwlande, in the much-affirmed sense of solidarity found among laborers and peasants, brought together by the collective experience of the harsh conditions of existence in pioneer regions.[19] The favorable conjunction of different factors—demographic, geographic, topographic, economic, social, political and religious—explains the success of the development of civil resistance in Nieuwlande.

The first runaways welcomed at Nieuwlande at the beginning of 1941 were people evading forced labor for the Greater Reich, which the occupiers were imposing on unemployed Dutch people from October 1940 onwards. A similar measure of internment in work camps in the Netherlands was drawn up regarding unemployed Jews from January 1942. The camp of Wasterbork, in which all Jews not possessing Dutch nationality were interned from the beginning of 1942, was, moreover, situated

---

[16] Bob Moore, op. cit., p. 165.

[17] See more on this subject: Horst Lademacher, op. cit., pp. 338–42 and Christophe de Voogd, op. cit., pp. 201–5. The word *verzuiling* is difficult to translate. It designates the pillarized political and social system that regulated Dutch life during the first half of the nineteenth century, based on three or four pillars (Catholic, Protestant, Liberal, Socialist). Schools, trade unions, political parties, hospitals and the media were "pillarized" and daily life was marked by such partitioning. This social organization that favoured diehard particularisms in the Dutch society was largely inspired by the theory of "sphere sovereignty" defended during the nineteenth century by Abraham Kyper (1837–1920), founder of the Anti-revolutionary party.

[18] Christophe de Voogd, op. cit., p. 204.

[19] Lammert Huizing, op. cit., p. 9.

not far from Nieuwlande, in the territory of the province of Drenthe.[20] A precursor in the organization of help for fugitives, Johannes Post did not originally display any particular interest in the fate of the Jews: there were no Jews in Nieuwlande, and in addition, this Calvinist was not indifferent to the influence of a certain Christian anti-Judaism, which nourished within him fairly ambivalent feelings regarding Jews. But his judgment was to change completely in the summer of 1942, under the influence of Arnold Douwes and one of the first Jewish runaways, Dr. Cohen, who both presented him with a number of facts relating to the persecution of the Jews.[21] From this moment on, Johannes Post implicated himself personally, with the support of his family, in the organization of the rescue of persecuted Jews. He also invited the former pastor Frits Slomp to speak in front of a congregation of some 150 faithful, including a large number of youths. In his sermon, Frits Slomp encouraged the faithful to take in the Jews and did not stint in his denunciation of the rise of anti-Semitism in the heart of even the Reformed Church.[22] Frits Slomp's fiery sermon at Nieuwlande certainly won over a good part of opinion to the themes of civil resistance. The first Jewish fugitives, initially very few, who were on the run from the work camps of the ghettos in the large towns to the west of the country, arrived in Nieuwlande in the second half of 1942, as the process of deportations was beginning. This fledgling civilian resistance movement, limited initially to sporadic private family initiatives, could not offer an appropriate response to the tragedy of which the camp at Westerberg, transit centre for the deportations from the Netherlands towards the death centers of Auschwitz and then, from March 1943, of Sobibor, had become the pivot.

Saving the runaways (April/May 1943—April 1945)

In the spring of 1943, the Führer went back on his decision to free Netherlander prisoners of war taken after the victory of May 1940. General Christiansen, commandant in chief of occupation troops, therefore gave the order on 29 April 1943 to imprison the former prisoners of war anew

---

[20] Bob Moore, op. cit., pp. 85–8.
[21] "Johannes Post" in *The Encyclopaedia of the Righteous among the Nations*, op. cit., volume 2, p. 607.
[22] Lammert Huizing, op. cit., pp. 36–7.

in the Greater Reich.²³ However, his proclamation immediately brought about, much to the surprise of the Germans, a rash of strikes of which the epicenter was in the east of the province of Overijessel, around the industrial poles of Hengelo and of Twente, but which rapidly spread into the Dutch countryside, particularly in the north-east of the country, on 30 April and 1 May 1943. The population of Nieuwlande actively joined the movement, against the advice of Johannes Post who even condemned following a strike that might end in a bloodbath.²⁴ The general commissioner for security, the HSSPF (Höhere SS und Polizeiführer) Hermann Rauter declared a state of siege and undertook to break the strike by terror, using arrests, the taking of hostages and summary executions, demanding from students a declaration of loyalty.²⁵ From 3 May, work resumed in the majority of urban regions but the strike went on for several days more in Friesland and in Brabant. In the rural regions, the strikes of spring 1943 gained considerable importance, comparable to the strike of February 1941, which had been sustained in part by communist and socialist militants in the larger urban areas of Holland. The strikes represented the indignation and frustration felt by rural Catholics and Protestants against the occupation regime and the weight of the agricultural requisitions imposed upon them. This leap of patriotism was the definitive point of departure in the shift in opinion regarding the occupiers: they had revealed their true faces and the politics of accommodation no longer appeared acceptable to the patriots.²⁶

The turn in public opinion made possible an increase in the number of runaways. From spring 1943, most diverse categories of the population flowed toward Nieuwlande in proportion to the development of repression and persecution by the occupiers: the Jews, children and adults, dispersed in the countryside, hidden from the round-ups in the ghettos were but one category of fugitives amongst many, from forced labor escapees to students, from policemen and railway workers and laborers to Soviet,

---

[23] Louis de Jong, "Anti-Nazi Resistance in the Netherlands" in *European Resistance Movements 1939–1945*, New York, Pergamon Press, 1960, pp. 140–1. Werner Warmbrunn, *The Dutch under German Occupation 1940–1945*, Stanford University Press, 1963, pp. 113–18
[24] Lammert Huizing, op. cit., p. 39.
[25] Christophe de Voogd, op. cit., p. 39.
[26] Werner Warmbrunn, op. cit., pp. 117–18

French and Belgian prisoners of war on the run from Germany.[27] The considerable increase in the flow of refugees necessitated in particular the abandoning of private initiatives, which had been sufficient until then in favor of the structuring of a veritable rescue network, organized by the precursors of the civil resistance movement. Johannes Post remained in everyone's eyes the "big boss" whose legitimacy and moral weight guaranteed the successful welcome of the *onderduikers*: faced with his personal involvement in the saving of dissidents and the persecuted, those whose sympathies lay with the occupying authorities found themselves under an obligation to remain silent, or ran the risk of social exclusion in the village and even from church. However, after his arrest and temporary imprisonment at Apeldoorn on 16 July 1943, Johannes Post was forced, in turn, to go underground. He moved into the armed, military resistance of the Knokploegen, for which he became supervisor for the provinces of Drenthe, Groningen and Friesland at the beginning of March 1944.[28] After Johannes Post's arrest and definitive departure from Nieuwlande at the end of October 1943, the local head of the action group (KP) was Hemke van der Zwaag and then the schoolteacher Seine Otten, but the responsibility for the organization of the rescue of the *onderduikers* fell to Arnold Douwes, whom the fugitives considered their "father." Arnold Douwes was assisted by a young Jew from Rotterdam hiding in Nieuwlande in the spring of 1943, Max Léons, who was known by his middle name, Nico.

The creation of a rescue network meant division and specialization of tasks, showing a real professionalization of civil resistance. Next to the local heads, whose priority task was to find new hideouts for runaways and to convince the inhabitants to accept the sheltering of *onderduikers*, were the couriers, very often women like Thea van Zuylen, who died in deportation, Betsy Trompetter, Hennie Winkel and Frederika van der Zwaag, who all played an essential role. Whilst underground, it was important to maintain contacts between those in charge. It was also necessary to accompany the children during train journeys from the west of the country towards Drenthe, a task which more often than not fell to the urban network members, and to take charge of the runaways as they

---

[27] Jo Schonewille, J. Engels and J. van der Sleen, op. cit. pp. 79–80.
[28] Article "Johannes Post" in *The Encyclopaedia of the Righteous among the Nations*, op. cit., volume 2, p. 608.

arrived—usually by train at Hoogeveen station—and then go with them on bicycles to the homes of the people willing to shelter them, to check upon the distribution of letters between these families who were so often spread far apart, and provide ration books, false papers, money for lodgings, and even, in certain cases, transport arms for the Action Group.[29] While a very clear distinction was immediately established between the fugitive rescue organization and the development of the armed resistance movement, the rescue network and the Action Group at Nieuwlande rapidly came to cooperate and complement each other's work: from June 1943, raids upon offices of population registers and ration book distribution by the KP, under the command of Hemke van der Zwaag,[30] furnished the materials necessary for forging of identity papers and ration cards which were indispensable to the survival of the runaways. Two characteristic traits therefore become evident in the structure of the rescue network run by Arnold Douwes: women played an essential role in the civil resistance movement, and Jewish *onderduikers* were integrated into posts of responsibility in the organization.

The false papers service acquired considerable importance in the organization of the network and permitted underground Jews to survive thanks to the protection of a false identity. Two young Jewish typographers, Ish Davids and Lou Gans, who were themselves living under identities borrowed from Peter and Herman, were in charge of the falsification of identity cards that had either been stolen or been fortuitously abandoned by locals who then claimed to have lost them. Having acquired a typewriter and a roneo-typewriter, Peter and Herman brought out a little newsletter that was both satirical and hostile to the occupier, *De Duikelaar*,[31] and Herman even made his own postcards, which were then sold for the benefit of the resistance. In the spring of 1944, they had to hide with their material, without the pastor's knowledge, in a dugout underneath the Temple of the Gereformeerde Kerk, where they survived for several months before being finally discovered by a detachment of the Dutch SS in December 1944.[32]

---

[29] Lammert Huizing, op. cit., p. 23. Yad Vashem: dossier1148/1, account given by Max Nico Leons, p. 14.
[30] Article "Hemke & Frederika van der Zwaag" in *The Encyclopaedia of the Righteous among the Nations*, volume 2, pp. 865–6.
[31] Satirical term formed from the noun *onderduikers*.
[32] "Jan van den Bos" entry in *The Encyclopaedia of the Righteous among the Nations*,

The local rescue network began to lean toward the creation of national organizations, which gave the decisive push towards the development of the Dutch resistance movement. Arnold Douwes was helped in this by his contacts with the Trouw group, a Calvinist resistance network that was built around an underground newspaper distributed from the beginning of January 1943 and specialized most particularly in the rescue of Jewish children.[33] Pastor Frits Slomp was responsible for the creation, at the end of 1942, of the Landelijke Organisatie voor Hulp aan Onderduikers (LO),[34] later coupled with a national organization of the action groups, the Landelijke Knockploegen (LKP), of which Johannes Post became responsible on a national level, from March 1944 until his execution by the Germans on 16 July 1944. The LO would not become a force to be reckoned with until autumn 1943. It was now able, on a national scale, to bring assistance to some 300,000 fugitives including a minority of Jews.[35] The organization of the civil resistance movement on a national scale also ensured the financing of the help given to them. The networks needed money in order to buy false papers, or, where this was not possible, to assist the families sheltering the runaways, families that were often in need themselves. Initially, it was the victim who had to pay the costs, and he or she was frequently exposed to veritable extortion. From the end of 1943, however, the creation of a National Assistance Fund, financed by the Dutch government in exile in London, permitted a monthly allowance of seventy-five florins for the upkeep of each fugitive, increased to 100 florins in 1944.[36]

---

    op. cit., volume 1, pp. 143–4. Beit Lohamei Haghetaot: dossier 1266, Guide to temporary exhibition "Nieuwlande 1940–1945." Yad Vashem dossier 1148/1, accounts given by Lou Gans and Max Nico Leons, p. 17.

[33] *The Encyclopaedia of the Righteous among the Nations*, op. cit., volume 1, p. XLV. Yad Vashem: dossier 1148/2, aerogram from R. Norden dated 14 Nov. 1985.

[34] The National Organization for Help to Fugitives.

[35] Bob Moore, op. cit., pp. 171–2. The personal investment of the precursors of the civil resistance in Nieuwlande in the creation of the organizations of national resistance during the second part of the war, and the execution of Johannes Post, who was celebrated as a national hero after the war and as a martyr of the national resistance movement, certainly contributed to the choice of Nieuwlande by Yad Vashem in the 1980s as a symbol of the Netherlands civil resistance movement

[36] *The Encyclopaedia of the Righteous among the Nations*, op. cit., volume 1, p. XXVI. Under the German occupation, the florin was worth 1.32 Reichsmark.

With the flow of runaways, the territory covered by the network, the rescuers' "hunting ground" as Max Léons would have it, largely exceeded the bounds of the village of Nieuwlande. Within 10 kilometers around Nieuwlande, fugitives were housed in Elim, in Nieuw Zwinderen, in Nieuw Krim, in Nieweroord, in Hollandscheveld/Moskou, in Noordseschut, in Hoogeveen and in Dalen, and within a range of 10 to 20 kilometers, in Zuidwolde, in Pesse, in Dedensvaart, and also in Nieuw Amsterdam. Runaways were placed further away at Dorkwerd, 45 kilometers from Nieuwlande. All of these places in the province of Drenthe could be reached by bicycle from Nieuwlande. The towns of Wageningen and DeSteeg in the province of Gueldre, more than a hundred kilometers from Nieuwlande, were visited by train.[37] It would seem, then, that the term "rescue village" is inaccurate in view of the geographic extension of a phenomenon that was once dependent upon a tiny area of less than a thousand square kilometers in southern Drenthe.[38] The rescue movement organized itself around a centre, the village of Nieuwlande, where the main leaders lived and where the infrastructure and the means of action of the network were located, toward which the *onderduikers* were directed upon their arrival and from which they were sent out amongst the different lodging zones organised by the centre.

The accounts given by Arnold Douwes and Max Léons show us that apart from a few orthodox Calvinist families, who were always willing to shelter runaways, the permanent search for new rescue addresses was a particularly harassing and thankless task, especially when it concerned the hiding of Jews.[39] According to Max Léons, those in charge of the network tried to approach "patriotic families" known for "their anti-German sentiments." After a brief introduction, they outlined their requests,

---

[37] Yad Vashem: dossier 1148/1, account given by Max Nico Léons, p. 15.

[38] Arnold Douwes' network ensured the rescue of 120 to 200 Jewish children and adults in this geographic region according to estimates by Yad Vashem, but it does not seem to have been the only active rescue organization in the interior of this zone: R. Norden, a fugitive in Nieuwlande and then in Nieuw Amsterdam, notes that the resistance movement was not limited to a single Calvinist Trouw movement, but that his friends' rescuer belonged to a "more socialist" organization. Yad Vashem: dossier 1148/2, aerogram from R. Norden, dated 14 Nov. 1985.

[39] Rijkinstituut voor Oorlogsdokumentatie, Journal d'Arnold Douwes pp. 105–8 (25–28 February 1944). Yad Vashem: dossier 1148/1, account given by Max Nico Léons, pp. 16–17.

backed up by explicit guarantees concerning the attribution of ration cards and, if necessary, money. Generally, the prospective rescuers brought up complaints concerning a lack of space, the problem of the children, dangers about the neighborhood and the risk of being betrayed. It was then necessary to engage upon long and delicate discussions to wrench an agreement from them, which would always remain temporary as to the number of people taken in and the length of time that they would stay. Arnold Douwes adopted a method of direct confrontation which consisted in imposing upon them obligations that were even heavier than those to which they had agreed,[40] a method which would inspire lively criticism. Thus, the placing of people was more often forced upon than accepted by the local inhabitants. Moreover, the pressure placed upon them by the repressive policies of the occupier, felt more and more from spring 1943, increased the fragility of their situations and led to continual moving of fugitives within the country of rescue in a permanent search for new hiding places. Lou Gans, who arrived in Nieuwlande in the autumn of 1943, had to change hideouts six times, before returning to Amsterdam during the winter of 1944, not counting the two occasions when he was forced to hide in the forests around the village and hiding in the shelter under the Temple.[41] David Kool, who for his part arrived in July 1943, was sheltered in succession by four families in Nieuwlande and in Nieuw Krim before being arrested and interned in the camp of Westerbork.[42]

These rescue operations, whether spontaneous or forced, display the essence of a popular resistance movement. In the list of the "Righteous" honored by Yad Vashem, where the different occupations are specified in the volume of *The Encyclopedia of the Righteous Among the Nations* dedicated to the Netherlands, one can count ten peasants, two craftsmen, a gardener, four teachers, one soldier and three involved in liberal and medical professions. The presence of a pastor and two beadles shows proof of ecclesiastic intervention, which always took place on a personal level so as not to implicate the Churches as institutions—which remained, as such, very cautious in their dealings with the occupier at Nieuwlande. Arnold Douwes never wished to refuse aid to a victim of the persecu-

---

[40] Rijkinstituut voor Oorlogsdokumentatie, Journal d'Arnold Douwes, entry for 26 February 1944.
[41] Yad Vashem: dossier 1148/1, account given by Lou Gans.
[42] Yad Vashem: dossier 1148/2, letter from David Kool dated 12 May 1985.

tions, whatever the consequences might be. The orthodox Calvinist families, who willingly sheltered runaway Jews, also showed this sense of duty with a willingness to save human lives that would prevail over an acceptance of what was happening, as if it was an expression of divine will to which the notion of predestination could lead. These families were equally able to identify the persecuted Jews with the Israel of the Old Testament, a reference used by both religions.[43] Many families who sheltered Jews did so, however, less spontaneously and more under the pressure of strong moral and psychological constraints. Their motivations were not restricted to religious considerations or higher moral values. Pastor Frits Slomp suggested that the rescuing of the fugitives offered the opportunity to convert the Jews, even if it appears that the number of Jewish *onderduikers* who converted to the Gereformeerde Kerk was very limited.[44]

Certain host families had great need of the material aid and finance given by the resistance, without which they would not have been able to shelter runaways. The harboring of runaways procured for families undeniable material advantages in the form of extra laborers in the fields or even financial aid. As Bob Moore underlines, the motivations behind help given to the *onderduikers* make up a most diverse pattern, from the purest altruism to the most barefaced search for personal gain. The northeastern provinces, whose role was primordial concerning the rescue of the Jews, were not immune from these excesses, even if they remained less prevalent than in the rest of the country.[45] Most of all, altruism directly benefited the children, who were seen as innocent victims.

In all, the entirely accidental coming together of the rescuers and the runaway Jews was a veritable collision of two worlds that differed profoundly in their ways of life, mentalities and political and religious convictions. Immersed through circumstance in the homes of their hosts whom they knew nothing about, often separated from their parents or their children, sometimes condemned to a strict seclusion, the Jewish *onderduikers* had to deal with very difficult physical and psychological conditions of survival. It was usually only older people who had their own rooms in the homes; younger adults, on the other hand, often had to spend the night in makeshift shelters away from the homes or in hideouts

---

[43] *The Encyclopaedia of the Righteous*, op. cit., volume 1, p. XXV.
[44] Bob Moore, op. cit., p. 166.
[45] Bob Moore, op. cit., pp. 167 and 178.

dug out of the sandy earth under the floorboards of the houses. Such oppressive survival conditions, coupled with ignorance about how one's loved ones were faring, and the ever-present threat of round-ups or denunciation by neighbors, often resulted in emotional breakdowns and depression.[46]

The persistent reticence of the local population was due, of course, to the risks linked with the repression of the civil resistance movement. The occupying forces and the Dutch who collaborated held a position of strength in the province of Drenthe—on the frontier with the Greater Reich—until liberation, which came about relatively late, in April 1945. In a process that was related to the flow of runaways to Nieuwlande, the round-ups began in mid-June 1943 with the intervention of a pro-Nazi Dutch militia, the NSKK. In the month of August 1943, the village was taken over by fifty German police.[47] From spring 1944, the raids in search of runaways and their rescuers became even more frequent and an ever-increasing number of rescuers were forced, in their turn, to go underground. Because of this, at the end of summer 1944, the resistance movement in Nieuwlande was by and large in a state of disorganization due to the extent of the repression. However the harshest part was yet to come. At the beginning of September 1944 the Dutch believed that liberation was soon to come, but the failure of Operation Market Garden, the great airborne operation launched by the Allies, left the control of the Dutch territories to the north and east of the delta of the rivers in the hands of the Wehrmacht.

To ensure the maintenance of order and the search for runaways behind the lines whilst reinforcing troops on the front, the German authorities armed the members of the Dutch national-socialist party, the NSB. In and around Nieuwlande, NSB militia action was reinforced by the arrival of a detachment of Dutch SS who set up barracks in a school in Hollandscheveld. Henceforth, it was no longer a question of political accommodation, and the civil population of the Netherlands was now treated as an enemy population. On 18 September 1944, the mayor of Oosterhesselen, who was in close contact with the resistance, was killed by the Germans.[48] Property of those suspected of sheltering runaways or those

---

[46] Yad Vashem: dossier 1148/1, account given by Max Nico Léons, p. 21.
[47] Lammert Huizing, op. cit., p. 41.
[48] Lammert Huizing, op. cit., p. 46.

who refused forced labor to aid the occupying forces was seized by NSB militants. Healthy members of the male population were mobilized by the Todt organization to build up a new line of defense. All were gripped by an arbitrary reign of terror.[49] On 19 October 1944, Arnold Douwes was arrested by the Gestapo and transferred to the headquarters of the SD in Assen, capital of the province of Drenthe. Miraculously, he escaped capital punishment on 11 November 1944 following the armed intervention of a resistance action group.[50] In Nieuwlande, the SS made Pastor Jan van den Boos and some peasants dig under the temple to search for arms caches. The unleashing of the repression forced a certain number of *onderduikers* to distance themselves from the village in search for new hideouts in the surrounding forests, or even to leave the region indefinitely. They were replaced in the last weeks of the war by Catholic refugees from Limburg or by urban populations to the west who were fleeing the towns and cities with the appalling misery of the last winter of the war, the winter of hunger.

---

[49] Jo Schonewille, J. Engels and J. van der Sleen, op. cit., pp. 120–2.
[50] Article "Arnold Douwes" in *The Encyclopaedia of the Righteous*, op. cit., volume 1, p. 224.

28

SURVIVING UNDETECTED
THE "BUND," RESCUE AND MEMORY IN GERMANY[1]

Mark Roseman

When in April 1942 Marianne Strauss first encountered Artur Jacobs, she barely noticed him. Artur, a Gentile and leader of the "Bund"[2], a little known life-reform group, was paying a farewell call on David Krombach, an influential representative of Essen Jews, before the Krombach family's scheduled deportation to Poland the following day. The eighteen–year-old Marianne Strauss was spending the last hours with her fiancée, David's son. With Jacobs and Krombach senior closeted in the backroom, Marianne could not know that Jacobs' visit was merely part of the Bund's

[1] I am very grateful to the Alexander Humboldt Foundation for funding my research into the Bund, and to my co-researcher Norbert Reichling for the fruits of his analysis evident in many parts of this chapter. References here are kept to a minimum but Norbert Reichling and I are completing a book on the Bund. See also Mark Roseman, "Gerettete Geschichte. Der 'Bund'. Gemeinschaft Für Sozialistisches Leben Im Dritten Reich," *Mittelweg* 36 16, 2007, pp. 100–21; Mark Roseman, "Gespräche Und Lektüren Zum Körper," BIOS 20 (no.) Sonderheft: "Kritische Erfahrungsgeschichte und grenzüberschreitende Zusammenarbeit. The Networks of Oral History," 2007, pp. 75–81. All translations are my own.
[2] The full title of the group, which of course bore no connection to the more famous Polish Bund, was "Bund: Gemeinschaft für sozialistisches Leben" or "The League: Community for Socialist Life."

larger effort to maintain contact with the Jewish community and assist it where possible. Nor was she aware that on that very day, the first of the Bund's Jewish members had gone into hiding, to survive the rest of the war underground. But in the course of 1942 Marianne's acquaintance with Artur would deepen. Remarkably, in an era in which Jewish-Gentile contact was almost unheard of, Bund members made regular visits to the Jewish community offices where Marianne worked, proffering any assistance they could to Essen's beleaguered Jews. Bereft of her fiancée, Marianne too sought out the social contact and intellectual inspiration of the Bund. One day, Artur made her a more personal offer: should her own family be in danger he would help. And so it was on 31 August 1943, when the Gestapo finally came to round up the Strausses for deportation to Theresienstadt, Marianne slipped out of the house and ran, waiting till evening to seek out a prearranged Bund member and put Artur's word to the test. For the next twenty months she would move from place to place, family to family under the Bund's protection.[3]

Stories of rescue from the Holocaust have long excited compassionate interest more than they have generated serious historical research. The academic literature on the subject has been dominated by analyses of the rescuers' personality and by the search for the particular moral, psychological or other emotional characteristics that explain such active commitment.[4] Most of the work has been carried out by psychologists and moral theorists, hoping to offer contemporary societies a way to identify and encourage the formation of altruism and moral commitment.[5] Whilst

---

[3] Marianne Ellenbogen nee Strauss's story in Mark Roseman, *The Past in Hiding*, London, Allen Lane, 2000.

[4] Eva Fogelman, *Conscience and Courage: The Rescuers of the Jews During the Holocaust*, 1st ed., New York, Anchor Books, 1994; Eva Fogelman and Valerie Lewis Wiener, *The Few, the Brave, the Noble*, Washington, Psychology Today, 1985; Ellen Land-Weber, *To Save a Life: Stories of Holocaust Rescue*, Urbana, University of Illinois Press, 2000; Kristen R. Monroe, *The Hand of Compassion: Portraits of Moral Choice During the Holocaust*, Princeton University Press, 2004; Samuel P. Oliner and Pearl Oliner, *The Altruistic Personality: Rescuers of Jews in Nazi Europe*, New York, London, Free Press of Glencoe, Collier Macmillan, 1988; Nechama Tec, *Dry Tears: The Story of a Lost Childhood*, 1st ed., Westport, Conn., Wildcat Pub. Co., 1982; Nechama Tec, *Resilience and Courage Women, Men, and the Holocaust*, Yale University Press, 2004.

[5] Both Samuel Oliner and Kristen Monroe, for example, pursued their work on rescue in the wake of larger research projects on altruism. Cf. Kristen R. Mon-

such work has been of great importance, it cannot satisfy the historian, since it downplays the structures, contexts, ideological climate and material circumstances within which rescue actions took place. Recent historical studies by Bob Moore in France and the Netherlands, or by Gunnar S. Paulsson in Warsaw, have shown that particular communication structures, informal and semi-organized networks, and the tacit moral economy of larger subgroups were often just as important as the psychological propensities of heroic individuals.[6] It will be argued here that the example of Jacobs, and the Bund, shows how certain kinds of group structures and ideological assumptions could foster a climate that lifted quite ordinary individuals into the class of rescuers.

Marianne Strauss was not the only Jew sheltered by the Bund. The group's long-term member Lisa Jacob went into hiding in April 1942. Later in the war, Artur's Jewish wife, Dore Jacobs née Marcus, would also slip into clandestine existence. Half a dozen other Jews owed their lives to similar interventions. Given that only 3,000 or so Jews survived in Germany as a whole, a good half of those in the anonymity of big-city Berlin, this was a striking achievement. It was particularly remarkable that an organized political grouping should have taken on this work and managed to do so undetected: undetected by the Gestapo and, until very recently, by the post-war world. In later life, Marianne sought to have the Bund's members recognized as "Righteous Gentiles" at Yad Vashem, failing repeatedly. The records reveal that the officials in Yad Vashem could not quite credit her story, and received little confirmatory information from their contacts in West Germany.[7]

The present paper, then, has a double objective. On the one hand it seeks to understand the Bund's achievement—what motivated it, what were the sources of its courage and cohesion, how did it escape detection? On the other hand, it asks why the group has enjoyed so little resonance since the war. It will be argued here that the conventional emphasis on

---

roe, *The Heart of Altruism: Perceptions of a Common Humanity*, Princeton University Press, 1998.

[6] Bob Moore, *The Rescue of Jews in Nazi-Occupied Belgium, France and the Netherlands*, Blackwell Publishing Asia, 2004; Gunnar S. Paulsson, *Secret City: The Hidden Jews of Warsaw, 1940–1945*, New Haven, Yale University Press, 2002.

[7] Information based on conversations with Mordechai Paldiel at Yad Vashem and from seeing the Yad Vashem files on Marianne's case.

the moral choices of the upright individual not only hinders us from understanding the experience of an organization like the Bund, but is also characteristic of a postwar landscape of memory that prevented the group from achieving proper acknowledgement. Caught between post-war definitions of resistance to Nazism that emphasized military or overtly anti-regime political action, and understandings of rescue that were non-political and individually based, the Bund's engagement slipped through the cracks of postwar recognition.

The making of the Bund

The Bund was formed in Essen in 1924 by Artur Jacobs and graduates of his adult education classes. Jacobs, born in 1880, a former grammar school teacher who was caught up in the revolutionary tide after World War 1 and subsequently ushered into early retirement, was an inspiring teacher and mentor. A former student of Herman Cohen at Marburg, he was influenced by the Neokantians, and sought to harness Marxist insights into social contradictions with Kant's notions of objective ethical laws. Jacobs' wife Dore, born 1894, daughter of a distinguished, acculturated German-Jewish family, was also a pivotal figure in the new grouping. During the 1920s she began to pioneer her own approach to *Körperbildung* (physical training) and opened a school for gymnastics in 1925. Many later Bund members entered the Bund's orbit through first training with Dore.[8] Most of the Bund's members were a generation younger than Jacobs, having been born between 1900 and 1914. A large number of the Bund's members had come through the youth movement—in several cases left-wing youth groups like the Naturfreunde. Many were from working class backgrounds, some having succeeded in attainting professional qualifications as teachers. There was also a smattering of progressive minded bourgeois members, many of them women, as well a number of middle-class Jewish members of both sexes.

The Bund anticipated feminist movements in 1960s and 1970s in believing that the personal was the political. Lofty rhetoric which had no underpinning in day-to-day life was so much hot air to them. "He who puts the most modest idea into practice," Jacobs declared in 1929, "is

---

[8] Mark Roseman, "Ein Mensch in Bewegung. Dore Jacobs, 1894–1978," *Essener Beiträge. Beiträge zur Geschichte von Stadt und Stift Essen*, 114, 2002, pp. 73–109.

closer to the truth than someone who only researches or proclaims the most sublime."⁹ The Bund's members were as likely to discuss marital relationships or a group member's work problems as the development of the world economy. The "socialist life" in the Bund's title was thus meant to convey a dual program of campaigning for a better society and experimenting with new ways of living, or "life reform" in Weimar German parlance. The Bund's aspiration was not to be a utopian community withdrawn from the world, but, as they put it, "a socialist life and struggle-community in the industrial heartland."¹⁰

Like some other *Bündisch* and youth movements, the Bund thus bridged conventional gaps between public and private, organized and informal activity. It was a circle of friends rather than a formal organization. At the same time it was a very tight-knit group of people who spent much time together, in some cases lived together, who discussed everything and who swore a solemn oath or "commitment" to one another. The group's excursions provided an opportunity for members from further afield to bond with the core members and absorb the group's atmosphere. The Bund's strongholds were in Essen, Wuppertal and Remscheid, but there were satellites as far away as Brunswick, Hamburg and Göttingen. At its high point the group had between 100 and 200 core members and much larger group of occasional participants.

During the 1920s, Bund members bought, built or rented so-called "Bund houses." The "Blockhaus" in Essen was completed in 1927, and there was also a second Essen house, in the Dönhof, and a further one in Wuppertal. Some of the Bund members lived in them as collectives. Complementing these experiments in group living, the Bund engaged in extensive educational work. In another strand of the Bund's activity, Dore Jacobs led the members in physical training and so-called "movement ensembles" (*Bewegungschore*) that enacted organic community life in semi-choreographed steps. Finally, public events—lectures, cultural meetings, festivals other opportunities to invite new participants into the group—took up considerable time and energy.

---

⁹ "Wer die bescheidenste Erkenntnis ins Leben umsetzt, ist der Wahrheit näher, als wer die erhabenste nur erforscht und verkündet," in (No author) *Der Bund. Orden für sozialistische Politik und Lebensgestaltung*, Essen-Stadtwald, Verlag des Bundes, 1929, p. 41.

¹⁰ Archives of the Dore Jacobs School (ADJS), *Pamphlet, Der Bund. Eine sozialistische Lebens-und Kampfgemeinschaft im Industriegebiet*, no place, no date.

From life reform to rescue

After the Nazi's rise to power in January 1933 most left-wing circles collapsed. Some underestimated the regime and took part in foolhardy protest actions. Many were torn apart from within by Nazi infiltration. Others opportunistically "switched" themselves into line or fearfully went into liquidation. By and large the Bund did not engage in open resistance. But its various local groups managed to maintain their regular meetings, something that demanded courage enough. The groups developed elaborate systems, whereby members would turn up singly or in pairs, at staggered intervals, so that there would be no suggestion of a meeting. These were crucial in breaking through each individual's sense of isolation and finding the right balance between personal safety and activism.[11] In a number of cases during the 1930s, when the Ruhr had become too risky, Bund members moved elsewhere and began offering classes in *Körperbewegung*, in this way forming new networks away from the Ruhr. Even in 1944, the Bund held not just local group meetings but also at least one national get-together in the Sauerland, where not only group members but at least three of the endangered Jews hidden by the group took part.[12]

In the early years, Bund members protected individuals on the run from political persecution, and helped them get out of the country. In contrast to many other left-wing opponents of Nazism, the Bund recognized early on that the Nazi movement's anti-Semitism was at the heart of the problem. However critical they had been on aspects of the German-Jewish milieu (the Bund was zealously hostile to organized religion), they now recognized the victims of state persecution.[13] Particularly after *Kristallnacht* the Bund showed its true colors. One member, Tove Gerson, remembered, for example, having to run the gauntlet of a baying mob to visit a wealthy Jewish family in their destroyed flat on the day after *Kristallnacht*.[14]

---

[11] ADJS, Essen, unpublished Bund Manuscript "Zum Gedenken an Artur Jacobson."

[12] Roseman, *Past in Hiding*, op. cit., chapter "Underground Chronicles."

[13] Lisa Jacob, for example, rejoined the Jewish community in 1933 out of solidarity. HStAD NW1005–G.34–1011 Lisa Jacob [19.4.47].

[14] Interview, Tove Gerson, 8 Jan. 1997; Video by Jochen Bilstein with Frau Briel, Herr Jost, 9.11.1990.

When the deportations started, the Bund gave those slated for Lublin, Minsk or Riga any assistance it could, helping them carry their luggage, providing psychological support and sending parcels to the ghettos. In 1983, the German Radio Station WDR broadcast a moving selection of letters between Trude Brandt, who had been deported from Posen (then German) to Poland in 1939, and Lisa Jacob who, with the assistance of other Bund members, regularly sent her parcels of food and clothing.[15] Later parcels were sent to Theresienstadt. As Marianne Strauss witnessed, the Bund also reached out to community offices in the localities, providing dried food and other items that did not require ration cards.[16]

Most of the group's Jewish members managed to leave the country before the war. Tove Gerson, married to a half-Jew, left Germany for the USA in 1939. Erna Michels went into hiding in Holland. Dore Jacobs, living in a "privileged mixed marriage," was for the moment safe from deportation. April 1942 brought the group's biggest challenge yet when Lisa Jacob was put on the list for deportation to Izbica. But the Bund had long prepared for this eventuality. Lisa was hidden, fed and supported by the other Bund members in a variety of locations for three years. As well as Marianne Strauss, hidden by the group for twenty months, a woman named Eva Seligmann hid in the so-called Blockhaus, the Bund's headquarters, for a while. A half-Jewess, Hannah Jordan, was protected by Bund contacts. Dore Jacobs came under threat after September 1944, when the regime began deporting Jews in mixed marriages. In all, perhaps some eight Jews and half-Jews were saved by the group.[17]

For the most part those protected were not actually hidden, but rather slipped out of their previous lives and locations and "passed" under alternative identities. The small size of the Bund members' dwellings and the frequent need to leave their apartments during air raids made it in fact impossible to actually hide someone. So Lisa, Marianne and others would stay for a few weeks at a time with temporary hosts. Having a visible but ostensibly innocent visitor then required, if possible, new identity cards to be issued, or at least plausible stories to be created for neighbors and officials. Lisa Jacob for example obtained an identity card with the name and details of her non-Jewish colleague Else Bramesfeld but with her

---

[15] "Sie wußten was sie taten," WDR broadcast 1983.
[16] Interview Marianne Ellenbogen, née Strauss, 10 September 1996.
[17] Author's interviews with Hannah Jordan; Ellen Jungbluth; Video by Jochen Bilstein with Frau Briel, Herr Jost, 9 Nov. 1990.

own photo, after Else claimed to the authorities that her own card had been lost.[18] Artur Jacobs had in his house a series of bogus franked letters, so that in the event of a search the authorities would conclude that Lisa Jacob had fled to her former domiciles in Berlin and Ratibor.[19] To explain the presence of strangers in their hosts' homes, and, indeed, of healthy young women who were not at work or in uniform, cover stories had to be found to present to neighbors. They might be of a distant cousin bombed out of their own home and seeking shelter for a few weeks—that was a story that Änne Schmitz once offered the mayor of her little village when Marianne Strauss came to stay.[20] Or in another instance the child of a Bund member was borrowed for a week, to enable Marianne to visit as a young mother. Whatever the story it was usually not possible to spend too long in any one address, for fear of arousing suspicions. Only toward the end of the war did Dore, Lisa and one or two others set up home in a little guest house belonging to the sister of a Bund member, hidden away near Lake Constance. Here, if a wry retrospective poem is to be believed, the biggest danger arose from the stress of all sharing a single kitchen.[21]

Such kitchen conflicts are a reminder that saving lives required not just cover stories but also material resources. Most of the Bund members had very modest incomes. Artur's pension had been cancelled by the regime as a result of his earlier political activities; Dore and Lisa had officially not been allowed to teach since the mid-1930s. Food supplies for Germans held up well for most of the war, but rations so meagre that it was not easy to feed an extra mouth, and going to the black market was usually too expensive or too risky. Thus Bund members who were not directly involved in hosting provided a whole week of their ration cards every so often, to help feed those in hiding.

Despite the group's caution, Gestapo records reveal that there were many denunciations from neighbors and others. In the early Nazi years, the educational authorities openly elicited denunciations, hoping to prove

---

[18] ADJS, Unpublished manuscript, Lisa Jacob, "Der Bund," p. 112.
[19] Lisa Jacob, "Freundestreue," in Dore Jacobs and Else Bramesfeld, *Gelebte Utopie: Aus Dem Leben Einer Gemeinschaft*, 1. Aufl. ed., Essen, Klartext, 1990, pp. 129–33.
[20] Interview, Änne Schmitz, Wuppertal.
[21] Stadtarchiv Remscheid, NW417, Walter Jacobs poem "In der Küche! (Im Haus auf dem Fohrenberg!)," 1944.

that Artur was a Communist and strike his pension. Several neighbors responded to the call, one fantasizing about having seen photos of naked dancing between Jews and non-Jews (sadly the Third Reich's loyal snitch had mislaid the alleged images). The SD got involved in 1936, and there were to be Gestapo interrogations and reading of mail at various times during the war. In 1939 the Bund member and teacher Emmi Schreiber, standing in a line at the grocer's, expressed her sympathy for Jewish victims of persecution, which led to a denunciation and a lengthy and unnerving investigations. Many other Bund members were the subject of inquiries, checks on their mail and interrogations. In 1943 a major denunciation almost exposed the group. But in the end neither the Bund nor those who depended on its care were discovered.[22]

Engagement and success

How should we explain the Bund's engagement and its success? It clearly helped that a number of Jews were prominently involved, alerting the organization to the dangers of *völkisch*-racist thought well before the Nazis came to power. After 1933, Bund members' friends and relatives experienced Nazi policy at first hand. Studies have consistently emphasized the importance of prior social contact between rescuers and rescued.[23] But, of course, prior connections could be severed and people could choose, as so many did, not to look. The Bund, by contrast, sought actively to inform itself of what was happening.[24] Not only did the group maintain connection with local Jewish community leaders, and carefully read between the lines of every government announcement, but it also took every opportunity to question returning soldiers about what was happening at the front.[25]

The Bund's anti-racism was in any case far from being just an empathetic response to the plight of friends and family. As early as 1919, Jacobs had contrasted his pursuit of a people's university (*Volkshochschule*)

---

[22] HStAD Gestapo Files: Erna Michels RW58 1808; Artur Jacobs RW58 19223 and 71703; Emma Schreiber RW 58–41452; Lisa Jacob RW 58–58105; Grete Ströter RW58 47025; Ernst Jungbluth RW58, 1595.
[23] Oliner, *The Altruistic Personality*, op. cit., p. 115.
[24] Stadt-Archiv Essen (StAE), Bestand 626 Nachlass Jacobs, Artur Jacobs diary, 13 June 1942.
[25] Ibid. Jacobs diary entries, 18 September 1942, 30 October 1942, 13 December 1942.

with racist-ethnic ideas about education (*völkische Hochschule*).[26] Racism, *völkisch* ideology and nationalism were so alien to the Bund's ideology that even the term "nation" never figured in the group's programmatic statements. After 1933 the Bund rejected not only the Nazis' nationalism and anti-Semitism but also almost every aspect of their philosophy. Study sessions and texts exposed the misuse of terms like Honor, Performance, Courage, Socialism and People's Community.[27]

Central to the Bund's self-understanding was its belief in a continuum between political principles and habitual behavior. The Bund always conceptualized its task in Nazi Germany as being not merely trying to survive the regime but to live the better society according to the group's principles. Circumstances were more challenging but this only made the test of creating a robust, humane community all the more valuable. After the war, the Bund would write to foreign friends, "In those years we were constantly preoccupied with the great Kantian question of what man must do to fulfill his mission in creation, and what he must do to be a real human being (*Mensch*). That question mobilized and imbued our loves even down to the practical details of everyday existence."[28] This practical approach by the Bund anchored its principles and equipped it to act. For one thing, members were used before 1933 to taking moral risks in their everyday lives, notably imposing friends and family with unconventional choices. It was not easy to explain to one's church-going extended family why one was leaving the church, for example, or to a more conventional husband why the terms of the marriage had to be renegotiated. To be sure, the shock of terror after 1933 was absolutely unprecedented, causing the Bund to rethink many of its tenets; it took Artur Jacobs over a year after 1933 to regain his nerve and find his feet. But the point was that standing up and being counted was not something Bund had to invent in 1933.

Equally important was the fact that everyday actions were viewed with the same moral seriousness as programmatic goals of political change. Well before the Bund knew that it would be facing Nazi threats, it articu-

---

[26] Monika Grüter, "Der Bund. Gemeinschaft für sozialistisches Leben: Seine Entwicklung in den 20er Jahren und seine Widerständigkeit unter dem Nationalsozialismus," Staatsexamensarbeit Universität Essen, 1988, p. 57.

[27] "Ein Auslandsbrief" in Jacobs and Bramesfeld, *Gelebte Utopie: Aus Dem Leben Einer Gemeinschaft*, p. 116.

[28] Ibid., p. 117.

lated as a core element of its philosophy that "no task, including seemingly the most mechanical exercise, is too small to be done with full commitment and all one's capacities."[29] After 1933, small steps that might only temporarily lighten the load for a single victim of persecution were thus taken absolutely seriously, and enjoyed the same standing as measures targeted against the regime as such (which the Bund realistically recognized were largely out of its reach). That gave the group the urgency and conviction to save individual lives. We might add that for those under the Bund's protection it also offered an inspiring and heartening moral model that was as valuable as the material content of particular gestures.[30]

Other works on rescue have, as noted, drawn attention to the importance of networks, and it is clear that the Bund as a group achieved much more than its members could have done individually, however well intentioned. By pooling resources of time, accommodation, food and so on, networks enabled lives to be saved without over-taxing any given individual. In a network the members could also offer each other reassurance and moral support when things were tough. In the Bund's case, at least until the war years, communication within the network was facilitated by the existence of two or three *Bundeshäuser* wholly inhabited by Bund members.

But the Bund added to the generic virtues of the informal network a very distinctive cohesion and discipline, which proved essential in ensuring mutual trust and in galvanizing often quite ordinary, fearful individuals to undertake steps of great courage.

The Bund here profited from the fact that its utopianism was from the start accompanied by a Kantian sense of human weakness and a commensurate emphasis on the community "policing" required to help the individual fulfill his potential. A programmatic statement published in the 1920s devoted a whole chapter to the Bund as "*Erziehungsgemeinschaft*," that is, as a community whose task it was to educate its members to independence, responsibility and purposeful lives.[31] Members had to learn that only when the guiding hand of the collective will was fully accepted could the fetters and distractions of egocentricity, basic urges

---

[29] *Der Bund. Orden für sozialistische Politik und Lebensgestaltung*, p. 78.
[30] See Trude Brandt, in Jacobs and Bramesfeld, *Gelebte Utopie: Aus Dem Leben Einer Gemeinschaft*, p. 124. StAE, Bestand 626 Nachlaß Jacobs, Artur Jacobs diary, Entry 8 November 1941.
[31] *Der Bund. Orden für sozialistische Politik und Lebensgestaltung*, pp. 76–7.

and cowardice be banished and the individual find true freedom.[32] In the interest of group discipline individuals were expected to bow to collective decisions even if, in the first instance, they had not yet fully accepted their validity.[33] Reinforcing this discipline was a strong internal hierarchy. The group was avowedly anti-democratic, arguing that the "organic" emergence of truth within the hierarchy was a better server of truth than "parliamentary debating battles."[34] "A really purposeful organization should never overpower the superior leader," Dore Jacobs argued in 1928. "It is after all, not a democratic organization run by majority decisions. Nothing is more alien to its essential character."[35]

A tightly organized group, then, could enlist and deploy human and material resources with much greater effectiveness than individuals acting independently. Yet unlike loose networks of friends, which had a chance of slipping through the net, organized groups were vulnerable in the Nazi system, and few collectives that sought to act against the regime survived it. In this sense the Bund proved to be the almost accidental beneficiary of its own hybridity. The Bund's notion of an organic hierarchy and of a community living its principles led it to emphasize patterns of association and ties of friendship and loyalty that were not governed by formal organizational structures. Like many elements of the German youth movement it had evolved into a deliberately non-party structure, as a *Gemeinschaft* not an organization. After 1933 the blurring of the private and the political, and the absence of the obvious paraphernalia of a formal association or political party, would turn out to be vital in protecting the Bund. The fact that so many women were active in the Bund, particularly after many of the husbands were called up to the army during the war, made the group look even less like a traditional political party. Strikingly, the Bund was able—particularly via *Körperbildung* classes—to reach out and draw in new members even during the Nazi years.[36] The group thus combined the diffuseness and elusiveness of unorganized civil society with the discipline, cohesion and trust of a conspiratorial organization.

Or even that of a sect. For behind a number of these other characteristics, the Bund might be said to have enjoyed the strengths of a religious

---

[32] *Der Bund. Orden für sozialistische Politik und Lebensgestaltung*, p. 83.
[33] *Der Bund. Orden für sozialistische Politik und Lebensgestaltung*, p. 86.
[34] "Redegefechten" and "demokratische Gleichmacherei"—see *Der Bund. Orden für sozialistische Politik und Lebensgestaltung*, p. 84.
[35] Dore Jacobs, in *Sozialistische Jugend*, 1928, pp. 13 ff.
[36] Interviews with Ellen Jungbluth and Hilde Machinek.

sect without being quite so visibly defined to the outside world as, say, the Jehovah's Witnesses. The roots of the *Bündisch* model derived, after all, partly from the notion of "Bund" as biblical covenant. Even when avowedly anti-church, most *Bündisch* movements manifested some kind of affinity to religious experience.[37] Far more than Jacobs' Bund itself would have cared to acknowledge, his group drew on the terminology and missionary fervor of the pious pietistic or reform-church environment from which Jacobs and the group's strong Wuppertal contingent came. Witness the group's sense of an elite core proving itself by works, guided by inner enlightenment. The Bund's programmatic statements in 1929 spoke of "ethic instinct to purity (*ethischer Reinlichkeitsinstinkt*), an intuitive recognition of the spiritual-human situation" by which members would know the right course of action.[38] This was the old pietistic claim, dressed up in new clothing, that members of the covenant would be able indirectly to receive God's revelation. God's voice, according to Pietists, could be discerned only by those in a state of grace—and here one thinks of the Bund's constant self-monitoring for signs of straying from the path.[39] The language of the group's pre-Nazi writings was full of references to "demonic forces"; after the Third Reich one of their favorite phrases was the "*Abgrund*" or abyss into which man might fall. It is hard to know how to quantify this religious quality, or delineate its direct influence on Bund members as against the indirect way in which Christian teachings were in any case filtered through Kant's ideas and the generic characteristics of the *Bündisch* tradition. But one cannot help feeling that the Bund's mixture of missionary zeal and constant monitoring of self and other drew powerfully on the pieties of parental households.

The Bund and post-war memory

The Bund survived the Nazi era without losing a single member. Understandably, and with considerable justification, the members felt that

---

[37] Hermann Schmalenbach, "Die soziologische Kategorie des Bundes" in *Die Dioskuren. Jahrbuch für Geisteswissenschaften*, Munich 1922, vol. 1, pp. 35–105, here p. 41 ff. Cited from unpublished chapter by Norbert Reichling, "'Bund,' 'Orden' und sozialistische Lebensgestaltung" (2004), pp. 41 ff.

[38] *Der Bund. Orden für sozialistische Politik und Lebensgestaltung*, p. 85.

[39] I am very grateful to Martin Bauer for conversations on the pietistic parallels and roots in the Bund.

history had proved them right. Surely, they reasoned, this wartime achievement proved how vital the Bund was for the challenges that lay ahead. Yet by 1947 post-war optimism was giving way to despondency. "Our flock has dwindled," Jacobs informed former group members now living abroad, "one often feels very lonely. We are swimming against the tide just like during the twenty years [of Nazi rule]."[40] Private correspondence between members in the late 1940s and early 1950s is full of anguished soul-searching over the lack of a new generation of followers. Whilst the young people in the friends' circle maintained contact with one another, they did not move closer to the Bund. Not a single one of the generation of Bund children now in their teens and early twenties was drawn to join their parents.

The roots of the Bund's success were paradoxically the sources of its lack of recognition in post-war Germany. The seeming "everydayness" of its activities (though great courage and discipline had been required) was unwelcome proof to contemporaries of what was possible even under a totalitarian regime. The Bund's achievement raised too many painful questions about why others had not done more. The Bund also made the most unwelcome discovery that many of its own *Bündisch* characteristics had ironically become discredited by the downfall of its Nazi adversary. The ritual, subordination to the group, and quasi-religious missionary spirit that characterized Bund life were anathema to the once-burned-twice-shy young adults of the post-war years. Interviews with a number of those who came into contact with the group at this time show that many youngsters had been enormously impressed by what Artur Jacobs and his friends had achieved, but could not cope with the Bund's hierarchical character, its "inner circle," its ethereal rituals, its veneration for Artur Jacobs and the way youngsters were supposed to sit at his feet. They found the Bund leadership over-sensitive to criticism. Though extremely cautious about being quoted and feeling guilty about their own rejection, the children of the founding Bund generation tended to express similar sentiments. Many felt damaged by the invasion of the political into their private lives.[41]

---

[40] ADJS, Bund 'Dritter Auslandsbrief' (1947), p. 7.
[41] Interviews with Helmut and Helga Lenders, Düsseldorf; Kurt und Jenni Schmit, Wuppertal; Alisa Weyl, Meckenheim; Ursul Jungbluth, Wuppertal; Friedl Speer, Wuppertal.

In a sense, the Bund also paid for the very terms of its success: for making an impact on the post-war period, the politics of the personal was too unheroic. The Bund had mercifully survived without martyrs. The very approach which had ensured its survival also meant that it did not have the obvious symbols for heroic commemoration. For left-wing German historians participating in the 1970s rediscovery of left-wing resistance to Hitler, the Bund did not look like political resistance as they understood it. The saving of Jews was marginalized as localized, small-scale activity; its moral weight, the nature of the group's solidarity, its status as a friendship group rather than political party, all made it look not serious.[42] In short, what had helped the Bund elude the Gestapo now caused the historian to pass it over too.

When Marianne and others sought to have the Bund recognized at Yad Vashem, they enjoyed no success there either. At Yad Vashem, the model is the "Righteous" and heroic individual. The authorities in Jerusalem thus could not recognize the group as such, needed to be exactly sure which of the members were Gentiles, and wanted to know who exactly had done what, so that they could be precise about whom to recognize. This was divisive and difficult to establish. In any case the group seemed so unlike the model of the rescuer as they knew it that the Yad Vashem officials were uncertain how to act. It was to be many decades before the group obtained public recognition and almost sixty years before some of its members came to be honored as "Righteous among the Nations" by Yad Vashem.[43]

---

[42] See the single dismissive footnote on the Bund in Hans-Josef Steinberg, *Widerstand Und Verfolgung in Essen, 1933–1945*, Hanover, Verlag fur Literatur und Zeitgeschehen, 1969.

[43] Thanks to recent interventions a number of Bund members, Fritz und Maria Briel, Hedwig Gehrke, Meta Kamp-Steinmann, Karin Morgenstern, Änne Schmitz and Grete Ströter were finally recognized as "Righteous Gentiles" in 2005.

29

SOCIAL COHESION AND STATE OF EXCEPTION
THE MUSLIMS OF MABARE DURING THE GENOCIDE IN RWANDA (APRIL 1994)

Emmanuel Viret

All extreme experience reveals the constituents and the conditions of the "normal" experience.[1]

Rising in the hollow of the hill, in the shadow of the bank that descends towards the lake, the mosque of Mabare in Rwanda, is a little ruin of brown walls, slowly being overtaken by vegetation. On the evening of 13 April 1994, some 300 people who had sought refuge there, Tutsis, mainly women and children, of all denominations, were killed by assailants who had come from the neighboring sector of Rubona. All day, the inhabitants of the hill, without ethnic distinction, had defended themselves with the aid of stones, lances and spears, against a hostile mass of about 7,000 people.[2] Pitched battles took place at two different sites.

The facts laid out here do not tell the story of a "rescue," but rather that of an active and violent resistance to the killings. In other places, rescue

---

[1] Michael Pollak, *L'expérience concentrationnaire, Essai sur le maintien de l'identité sociale*, Paris, Editions Métailié, 1990, p. 15.
[2] This is an approximate estimate of the number of eyewitnesses (interview, Mabare, 19 June 2006).

initiatives often involved individuals against groups, marginals against the norm, anomalies in the public space. Not so in Mabare, where the resistance to the massacres was the reverse, not the opposite. For in both cases, the same plans of action, the same methods of mobilization and the same local hierarchical channels were used to protect the hill or assure its capture, to defend the threatened populations or aid in their murder.

The genocide of the Rwandan Tutsis, which engulfed the entire country for about three months, accompanied by the elimination of all opposition to the faction installed in power in Kigali, was carried out in about ten days in the region of Mabare. The day after the assassination of Juvénal Habyarimana, which marked the beginning of the genocide, the commune's principal authorities had the territory combed for Tutsis in Bicumbi, gave orders to the gangs of killers, and had the designated victims brought to public places in order to facilitate the task. In Bicumbi, the number of victims is estimated to be more than 15,000.[3]

It has often been said that, in the course of the genocide, the Rwandan Muslims helped the populations under threat escape from their killers;[4] that one religion was massively opposed to the massacres at the very moment when priests and pastors sometimes became the instruments of murder. Nothing here is aimed at contributing to this idea: all of the inhabitants of Mabare, and not just the Muslims, took part in its defense, while just a few miles to the north, the Muslims of Gahengeri, who were far more numerous, did not protect the Tutsis under threat there. The Muslims of Rwanda had no single design, nor did they adopt a general and coherent policy. The same went for Mabare, where it would be impossible to find shared, profound reasons within those who, faced with the ever-increasing massacres, put their lives on the line. However, the fact that the Muslims were the last ones fighting, the last on the battlefield at the very moment when retreat was becoming the only sane option, indicates the existence of bonds revealed during these few days outside time and space, which, in daily life, remain hidden. We will not dwell here

---

[3] République du Rwanda, Ministère de l'Administration Locale, du Développement Communautaire et des Affaires Sociales, *Recensement des victimes du génocide*, 2003.

[4] Stephen Smith, "L'Islam au Rwanda, un îlot préservé de haine," *Libération*, 8 September 1995, Emily Wax, "Islam attracting many survivors of Rwanda genocide," *Washington Post*, 23 September 2002, Marc Lacey, "Ten years after horror, Rwandans turn to Islam," *The New York Times*, 7 April 2004.

upon the history of Islam in Rwanda,[5] which made its appearance following nineteenth century colonization, in the baggage of the colonizers' servants, translators and kitchen staff, tied to the Swahili language and remaining essentially an urban phenomenon. Let us point out, however, that the way in which the Muslims were marginalized in cities[6] did not occur in the same manner in rural zones, since the implantation of Islam was recent and not coupled with trade as it was in Kigali.

Anxiety and then fear, the feeling of urgency, and the excitement which makes these feelings bearable can create, during crises, an open space where all the qualities that make up daily life are cancelled: fear blends in easily and can even, when fancy takes it, replace—in much the same way as the crowd's jubilation[7] does—all the places and moments that make up the normal experience of society. But despite affecting everything, fear just sheds light on itself. In Mabare, fear was evoked in order, on the one hand, to justify participation[8] in the massacres, and on the other, to justify opposition to them. However thick the veil might be, we cannot know why fear reduces itself to the choice of flight, opposition, or joining the assailant.[9] We shall focus on the social circuits that fear

---

[5] See José Kagabo, *L'Islam et les 'swahilis' au Rwanda*, Paris, Editions de l'Ecole des Hautes Etudes en Sciences Sociales, 1988.

[6] Illustrated by the following joke which appeared in a national newspaper close to the MDR—see below—at the beginning of the 1990s: "Four deadly sins. A man shows up on a site asking for work. Bad luck: he is Tutsi, Muslim, a member of the PL and he is from Gitarama," in *Rukukoma* n° 1, 15 September 1991, p. 3.

[7] Nicolas Mariot, "Les formes élémentaires de l'effervescence collective, ou l'état d'esprit prêté aux foules," *Revue Française de Sciences Politiques*, vol. 51, n° 5, October 2001, pp. 707–38.

[8] Scott Strauss, *The Order of Genocide, Race, Power and War in Rwanda*, Ithaca and London, Cornell University Press, 2006, p. 225

[9] Albert O. Hirschman, *Exit, Voice and Loyalty: Responses to Decline in Firms, Organisations, and States*, Harvard University Press, 1970. Those three dispositions, three possibilities of action in response to the crisis that was taking place, were proposed to the inhabitants of Mabare. This had nothing in common with the idea of "regression towards habitus" (see Michel Dobry, *Sociologie des crises politiques*, Paris, Presses de la Fondation Nationale des Sciences Politiques, 1992, pp. 239–59), which evoked, regarding the different players, the tendency towards a reduction of behaviour, in times of crisis, not to limited possibilities but to sketches of perception, of appreciation and of interiorized action by the individual in the course of his existence.

Mabare region (Bicumbi commune)

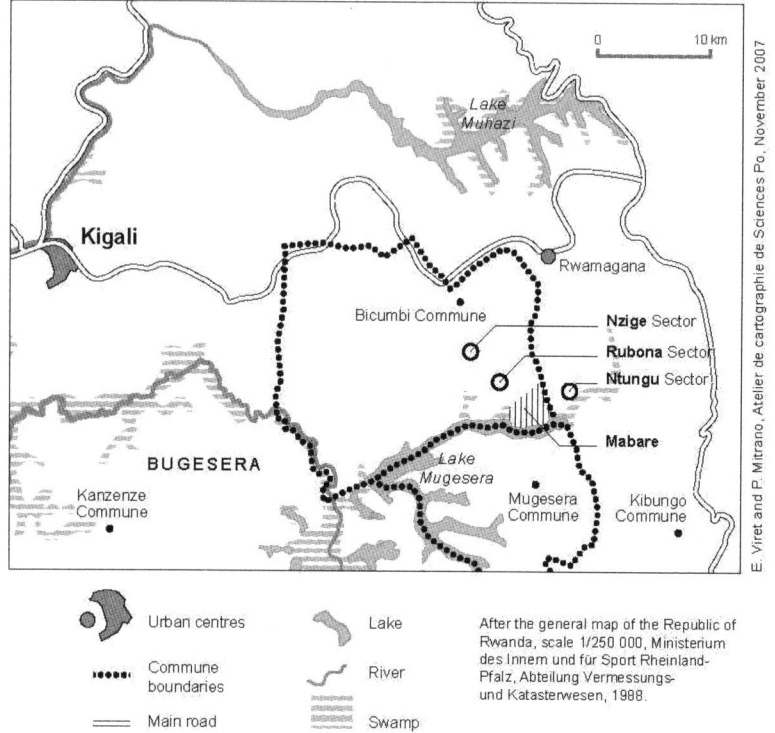

took, attempting to establish the continuity[10] of the interactions that founded it, that maintained it, that perpetuated it alongside those found in the normal course of existence.

The circles of conversion

The three hills of Mabare on the edge of Lake Mugesera converge at a point nestling in the east of the commune of Bicumbi to form its smallest sector[11] (7 km²) where according to the meticulous census carried out by

---

[10] See Pierre Favre, "Y a-t-il un rapport ordinaire au politique?" in *L'ordinaire. Mode d'accès et pertinence pour les sciences sociales et humaines* (ed. Jean-Louis Marie, Philippe Dujardin, Richard Balme), Paris, Editions L'Harmattan, 2002, pp. 275–305, and Michel Dobry, op. cit., pp. 13–46.

[11] Until the administrative reforms of 2000 and 2005, the Rwandan territories

Rwandan administrative authorities, in 1991 lived 2,257 people, 467 of whom were Tutsi. The lake's bounty is meager—few people fish there, and almost all of the population of Mabare live by growing bananas, sorghum, maize and tomatoes. Though there is a Protestant church and an Adventist temple, there is no Catholic church. Even though they are the majority in Mabare, the Catholics go to pray in Rubona.

In 1991, the communal report showed that there were 187 Muslims in Mabare,[12] not counting those who came to worship from Gisaka, a neighboring commune situated on the other side of the lake. It is uncertain exactly when Islam appeared here. At the end of the 1940s, four Muslim families came from Rwimicinya, in the region of Byumba to the north of the country, to take advantage of the larger amounts of land available. However, they were not proselytes, and went to pray at the mosque of the neighboring centre of Rwamagana.[13] In 1982, four young Protestants from Mabare, on an erratic quest for fortune,[14] went to Rwamagana and converted to Islam. The mosque in Rwamagana was a member of the Association des Musulmans du Rwanda (AMUR), an umbrella institution of which all believers were supposed to be members

---

were split into eleven *préfectures* and 146 *communes*. The latter were in their turn divided into sectors (it is often said that a sector corresponds to a hill), and then into cells. The smallest unit, the *nyumbakumi*, comprised on average ten families.

[12] The Second Rwandan Republic (1973–94) was keen on figures. Communal reports sent to the prefectures were full of censuses—related either to a close surveillance of the territory or to development, the national ideology at the time: details on people entering and leaving the *commune*, religious groups, places of worship, but also the number of concrete buildings, the number and nature of livestock, details of crops and volume of production, anti-erosion activities, literacy rate, number of radio sets… These censuses depended on the zeal of the sector's *conseillers* who quite often contented themselves with copying the previous year's report. Many surprising elements arose from unpublished inventories: for the Mabare sector alone Catholicism lost more than half its believers between 1986 and 1988 without necessarily adding to the ranks of other faiths; in 1989, not only did the Catholic Church manage to reconquer all those people it had lost during the past years, but it also attracted 164 new converts without taking them from the other religions in Mabare. Though the evolution in the number of Muslims seems coherent and relatively moderate, this should only be considered as affirmation.

[13] Interview, Mabare, 25 July 2006.

[14] "We were vagrants," interview, Mabare, 19 June 2006.

and whose legal representative was named by presidential decree.[15] Having heard the news, a man named Asmani, a Muslim from Gisaka, came to Mabare between 1982 and 1983 in order to convert its inhabitants, proselytizing door to door.[16] He was a member of Ansar Allah, an association that appeared at the beginning of the 1980s at the Islamic Cultural Centre in Kigali, under the rule of a Libyan *mwalimu*[17] whose objective was the conversion of the rural world to Islam, and in order to do this it leant heavily on *dawa*, preaching.[18] The association took its name from the last verse of the 61st *sura* (chapter) in the Qu'ran, called "The Ranks," which says: "We gave power to those who believed, against their enemies, and they became the ones that prevailed." Ansar Allah proposed a stricter interpretation of the Qur'an than that of the AMUR.

At first, the four young converts prayed at home, going to Rwamagana for the *juma* Friday prayer. The conversions progressed in concentric circles: first the family, then the neighbors, before targeting the Protestants,[19] then finally the Catholics. In 1983, they built a small house in which to pray and receive a larger number of the faithful. Rachid Bagabo, one of the four young men, became the Imam. In 1986, the communal report indicated thirty practicing Muslims in Mabare. Commune correspondence remains mute on the subject of Islam, not worthy of note, it seems, unless involved in charitable actions. Two years later, a new mosque was built a few dozen meters from the home of the Imam, thanks to payments by the faithful and help from Rwamagana.

The Muslim families' homes were dispersed about the sector, but the majority, and the most influential, lived in Rusanza, near the location where the mosque was built. There are no figures relating to the ethnic origins of the Muslims of Mabare.[20] Conversion in a rural setting did not

---

[15] République Rwandaise, *Journal Officiel*, 15 August 1987, AP n°799/05, p. 968.

[16] Interview, Mabare, 28 July 2006.

[17] A *mwalimu* is an educated person, whose deep knowledge of the Qu'ran is well known and who teaches religion.

[18] For a general study of the behavior of the Muslim community during the genocide in Rwanda and of the national rivalry between the AMUR and Ansar Allah, see Christin Doughty and David Moussa Ntambara, *Resistance and Protection: Muslim Community Actions during the Rwandan Genocide*, Case Study, Cambridge (Mass.), CDA-STEP, 2005.

[19] "Protestants were the most fragile," interview, Mabare, 27 July 2006.

[20] The Muslim interviewees generally said that there were equal numbers of

imply the rupture that went with turning to Islam and moving to the towns, but it did redefine the position a person held and the life he or she lived on the hill: learning some Arabic, changing one's name, and above all, a change in what kinship meant in everyone's eyes. Each convert had a sponsor who, if he did not replace the father, would certainly be a substitute for the second generation, becoming the equivalent of a grandfather for the children of the convert. This shift is not insignificant in as much as it redefines the very contours of the most basic family unit, the *rugo*, or nuclear family. In the same manner that a home is held together with dried saplings that protect and define it, the *rugo* is found in a larger space that is not wholly reliant upon lines of kinship (*umulyango*). Being a member of the *umulyango*—having one's place within the whole—is one of the ways to access influence, authority, and importance. Nevertheless, everyone is equally involved, bound by the obligations of the times and by the power of the guardians.

In the shifting of such basic relationships, conversion to Islam redefined the meaning of allegiance, turned it in another direction and held it there. We can see this shift in a statement by the former sector authorities regarding the Muslims: "They would take action themselves and would make sudden decisions." In 1992, the sector's *conseiller* had to give protection to the family of an adolescent who had stabbed a young Muslim following an argument about cows, this despite the fact the boy was going to be tried in Rwamagana.[21] In the event of a conflict between two Muslims, the Imam settled the matter, as opposed to what happened among people of other faiths, who would alert the representatives of the state. These episodes and their repetition reinforced the Muslims' image as "bad boys" in the eyes of the inhabitants of Mabare.

At the beginning of the 1990s, the economic crisis, the stifling regime, and the general discontent toward its elites forced the president to accept the principle of the multiparty system. The principal political parties appeared in 1991 and immediately set to work gaining supporters in the

---

Hutus and Tutsis practicing their religion. Members of other religions sometimes told me that Tutsis were proportionally more numerous within Islam than within other religions.

[21] The former sector *conseiller* gave several examples of conflicts between Mabare inhabitants and Muslims, some of which needed local police intervention (interview, Mabare, 25 July 2006).

rural zones;[22] each day, they had to compete with the former ruling party[23] of which all Rwandan citizens had been members from birth. Three of the most powerful new parties made their way to Mabare: the MDR, the PL and the PSD.[24]

Recruitment by the parties was favored by the economic crisis and the context of war that was going through the country. Their appearance on the hills started a trend of factions looking for a good pair of hands more than votes, muscles rather than voices. The state itself was under scrutiny, being entirely assimilated into the formerly single party system. Recruitment took place in the bars,[25] the two main bars displaying the flags of their affiliation to the MDR and the MRND. Cards, emblems and colored hats (*ingofera*) were distributed, which laborers even wore to work the fields.[26] The monotony of life on the hills conspired with anxiety for the future within the same movement. People could drink a beer together and buy beer to one another which permitted an escape from the mundane and the (re)forging of relationships that could be useful in the future.[27] In the rural political headquarters, joining the parties' ranks had become an obsession.

At the mosque, however, the Imam formally forbade membership in a political party. The short-lived Parti Démocratique Islamique (Islamic

---

[22] 95 per cent of Rwanda is rural.

[23] The Mouvement Révolutionnaire National pour le Développement (MRND) was the single political party created in 1975, whose apparatus was almost entirely intermingled with the state's and was reconstituted during the transition to a multi-party system, being renamed then the Mouvement Révolutionnaire National pour la Démocratie et le Développement (MRNDD).

[24] The Mouvement Démocratique Républicain (MDR), the former single party of the First Republic (1959–73) was recreated in July 1991 and was the main opponent to the MRND; the Parti Libéral was created in July 1991; the Parti Social Démocrate was created in July 1991, but had no representative in Mabare (though it had members there).

[25] "The mill was a meeting place and a place for social relations in a world most often closed and static. It was also a place where ideas could circulate, just as in inns and shops." We translated from Carlo Ginzburg, *Le Fromage et les Vers. L'univers d'un meunier du xvie siècle*, Paris, Aubier, 1980, p. 169.

[26] This was the normal activity of political parties. Their youth movements were transformed into militias and were not established in Mabare.

[27] Drinking beer is a central element of socialization in Rwanda. See Danielle de Lame, *A Mill among a Thousand. Transformations and Ruptures in Rural Rwanda*, Madison (Wis.), The University of Wisconsin Press, 2005, pp. 303–40.

Democratic Party) was unable to set up in Mabare because it emanated from the AMUR. Since alcohol was forbidden for Muslims, they did not go to the bars where beer and banana wine were the most popular drinks.

Instead, they frequented a small shop opened by an elderly woman who offered them guaranteed alcohol-free fruit juice. Their own headgear differentiated them from the other peasants and indicated their primary allegiance in an almost physical manner, whilst around them, political competition was deforming and reforming allegiances and multiplying fault lines. Moreover, whilst the parties were fighting over members, confronting each other physically to erect their flags over public buildings, and humiliating those who wished to stay out of the debate,[28] not one of them attacked Muslims.

The days of the attack

Ramadan had already started when the news of the assassination of President Juvénal Habyarimana reached the region on the morning of 7 April. Several Mabare inhabitants went to the home of Sekimonyo,[29] *conseiller* (councilor) for the sector, to ask for news.[30] Around 8 am, the commune's ambulance came to inform Sekimonyo of the holding of a communal council meeting. He refused to go because of a fit of diabetes. In Rubona, the weekly market to which the inhabitants of Mabare regularly went was suspended, and the communal police advised everyone to stay at home. The next day, Mugemanyi, the MRNDD's representative in Mab-

---

[28] *Kubohoza* is a Kinyarwanda verb meaning "liberate," used ironically to designate the forced recruitment of members organized by the MDR (but not only by it) mainly against the former sole party, the MRND; see Alison Des Forges (ed.), *Leave None to Tell the Story: Genocide in Rwanda*, Human Rights Watch, Fédération Internationale des Droits de l'Homme, 1999, p. 149. Another interpretation of the verb links it to its etymology *kuboha*, i.e. link, tying freshly cut straw or the arms of a criminal. Thus, *kubohoza* would mean cutting former links, for instance former patronage links (Danielle de Lame, personal communication).

[29] Froduard Sekimonyo, sector *conseiller*, farmer, member of the MRNDD, Hutu, Catholic.

[30] "People were not talking about what could happen to them, they were only talking about the President's death: who shot down the plane? Why? Who would take over from Habyarimana?" (Interview, Mabare, 25 July 2006).

are, a Tutsi, informed Sekimonyo of the arrival of refugees from the other sectors of Bicumbi and from neighboring communes. Emanating from several centers, usually local seats of power, the front line of the massacres was spreading out and gaining ground.

As surprising as it might seem, it does not seem that the inhabitants of Mabare were aware of the fact that only the Tutsis were targeted. "As the refugees were talking about Interahamwe, I thought it was a problem to do with political parties, I thought that the gendarmerie would intervene to calm down the situation."[31] Mabare had not been spared from the waves of violence which, at almost regular intervals, had devastated the country since its independence. Three people had been murdered on All Saints' Day 1959, whilst in 1973, cattle had been taken from Tutsis, killed and eaten. In the beginning of the 1990s, however, the sector had remained calm, unaffected by the pogroms that shook neighboring regions.[32]

On 8 April Sekimonyo forbade the inhabitants to leave the sector,[33] and organized patrols of east Mabare, having learned that the militia of Ntungu had threatened to pursue the refugees. On the 11 April, he learned that the massacres had reached Rubona and, seeing the danger approaching, organized a meeting the next day for the entire population. Everything that could be used for defense was amassed. The men were split into four groups to build barricades at all access points of the sector.[34] Nobody contested him. The women and children, regardless of their ethnic origin, formed groups in and around the mosque, which,

---

[31] Interview, Mabare, 25 July 2006.

[32] These were massacres organized in Bugesera (*communes* of Kanzenze, Ngenda and Gashora) during March 1992; cf. Alison Des Forges (ed.), *Leave None to Tell the Story*, op. cit., pp. 87–9.

[33] "Massacres took place at Mugesera, on the other side of the lake. I did not want people from Mabare to go there, start looting and that Interahamwe from there would follow them home and start killing over here" (interview, Mabare, 25 July 2006).

[34] In Gatare, under the leadership of Pierre Rutayisire, former chief of the cell, farmer, manager of the MRNDD cabaret, Tutsi and Catholic; at Mobuga, under the leadership of Froduard Sekimonyo; at Kagina, led by Étienne Sekamana, member of the Gasharu cell, MRNDD, Hutu, Protestant; and in front of the house of a man who had made it the party's cabaret, without any leader having been named. The defense system established by Sekimonyo in Mabare was identical to the system used by those in charge of massacres in the other sectors of the *commune*. The words that were used in the local archives to justify

being central within the sector, was easy to rally around. In the evening, a van belonging to the commune with two main merchants and members of the military aboard pulled up to the barricades. Sekimonyo was threatened and shot at. The assailants warned: "We are going to warn the burgomaster. We will be back tomorrow with reinforcements."[35] Filled with fear and hiding in his home, Sekimonyo explained to his neighbors that henceforth each one of them was free to do as he or she saw fit, to fight or to run away.[36]

On the morning of 13 April the main body of the assailants from Rubona moved toward the barricades. The shopkeepers of Nzige and Rubona had their vehicles available, which now bent under the weight of men. The fighting began in Gatare where, initially, people thought it was an attack by the *Kiga*. The term *Kiga* designates the inhabitants of northern Rwanda (Gisenyi and Kuhengeri, up to northern Kigali). The region of Bicumbi was sparsely populated, and so a policy of settlement had been organized by the government of the First Republic (1961–73), and numerous families came from the north,[37] spreading out into the neighboring countryside. Gradually, the new arrivals had elevated themselves to the heads of the commune: Laurent Semanza, its burgomaster for more than twenty-five years, and the principal organizer of the genocide in the region, was *Kiga*, as was his successor, Juvénal Rugambarara, as well as nearly half of the communal staff. This social advancement was the counterpoint of the domination wielded by the North over the rest of Rwanda from 1973 onwards.[38] The institutions in their hands, their

---

the arrest of Tutsis in 1992–93 were the same as those pronounced by Sekimonyo on 12 April: it was a question of "security" and of "defense of citizens."

[35] Interview, Mabare, 25 July 2006.

[36] "I told Nzaramba and the others: those who want to stay and fight can do so. But those who want to flee have the right to. I am leaving" (interview, Mabare, 25 July 2006). The same day, Sekimonyo's house in Rubona was destroyed and looted; it was publicly announced that he would be the first killed the next day.

[37] See François Bart, *Montagnes d'Afrique, terres paysannes. Le cas du Rwanda*, Bordeaux, Presses Universitaires de Bordeaux, 1993, and Victor Silvestre, "Différenciations socio-économiques dans une société à vocation égalitaire: Masaka dans le paysannat de l'Icyanya," *Cahiers d'Etudes Africaines*, 14(53), 1974.

[38] One-third of the eighty-five most important positions within the state were given to people originating from the same region as President Habyarimana,

numerous officers,[39] and the late incorporation of the North into the central kingdom had given the *Kiga* a reputation of brutality.

When, in March 1992, news of the massacres in Bugesera had reached Mabare, rumor said it was almost certainly the work of northern killers.

"At Gatare, we did not know that the assailants were coming to kill the Tutsis. I cannot accept that the Muslims were defending society. Everyone was fighting. We were fighting against the *Kiga*. And many of them had gone to live in Rubona, where the attackers came from."[40]

In Gatare, in the middle of fighting, the assailants, shouting through cupped hands, explained to the inhabitants that it was only the Tutsis that they were after. A powerful businessman in the area,[41] whose interests were located nearby,[42] decided to join them. He was a powerful man whose opinion mattered, not only because he was rich but also because of the influence of his extended family (*umuryango munini*) in Mabare.[43] Following his example, several hundred people changed sides.[44]

This changing of sides entirely disrupted the face of the battle. The Imam took over the leadership of the defenders in the middle of a crowd that was blurring the lines of confrontation. They had to retreat, abandoning terrain and wounded, in order to regroup. The outcome became evident and the core was breaking up. In Mobuga, where other battles had started around midday, the attackers were gaining ground. Amongst them, only one man, a retired corporal of the Rwandan Armed Forces, possessed a weapon. Having run out of ammunition not far from the mosque, he

---

Gisenyi. See Filip Reyntjens, *L'Afrique des Grands Lacs en crise. Rwanda Burundi: 1988–1994*, Paris, Karthala, 1994, p. 33.

[39] The sentence attributed to colonel Théoneste Bagosora, main organizer of the genocide, during the formation of the interim government following the assassination of Juvénal Habyarimana, "La guerre aux bakiga, la politique au banyaduga" ("War for Bakigas, politics to Banyadugas"), illustrates the overrepresentation of men from the northern region within the Rwandese army. See André Guichaoua, *Rwanda 1994. Les politiques du génocide à Butare*, Paris, Karthala, 2005, p. 63.

[40] Interview, Mabare, 28 July 2006.
[41] MRNDD, Hutu, Adventist.
[42] Interview, Mabare, 19 June 2006.
[43] Interview, Mabare, 28 July 2006.
[44] "There was even a Tutsi youngster. He hadn't realized, and was killed later on, on the other side" (interview, Mabare, 28 July 2006).

halted the attack to allow time to fetch more bullets from the communal office. The Imam, wounded, had designated another Muslim to take control of the last group. Reduced to a few, the defenders of Mabare were unable to withstand the last assault.

As the attackers surrounded the mosque, those who were able to run away fled[45] to hide among the papyrus on the banks of Lake Mugesera, or toward Ntungu and Rwamagana. The following day, the systematic massacres began under the orders of a manager of the MDR of the sector who had been nominated *conseiller* in place of Sekimonyo (now deposed).

Social cohesion and the emergency

The organization of the resistance in Mabare went far beyond the confines of the Muslim community and revealed numerous other factors: the relative isolation of the sector, the presence of Tutsi personalities in the heart of the civil service and in the MRNDD, doubts as to the identity of the assailants, the decision made by Sekimonyo to organize the area's defense, the wise loyalty of the merchants and local party leaders in this context of uncertainty. The Muslims, like the rest of the inhabitants of Mabare, were confronted with these pressures and doubts, but acted as a group. What guaranteed their cohesion during the emergency that was the genocide rested upon the same foundations that had hitherto marginalized them: the rupture induced by conversion, the concurrent grammar of authority, the inclusive circle in which its adepts were held, and the manner in which it was extended daily through religious observances.

The diversity of the networks and the reasons given in the defense of Mabare do not make it possible to assign a unanimous intention; the intention here was the fear of the *Kiga*, there the defense of the Tutsis, of the mosque, or of oneself. We are not trying to reduce intention to silence, to bring people's descriptions and their discourse to the level of justification. The history of identity and of observance seem to follow two parallel courses, yet they reflect each other. The Muslims we met, when questioned about the reasons behind this collective attitude, obtruded the *sura* of the Qur'an quoted above. They did so discreetly, under the haughty eye of the Imam, since that cohesion did not survive the genocide. The

---

[45] "Those who stayed in the mosque had already accepted to die" (interview, Mabare, 19 July 2006).

AMUR took over the mosque from Ansar Allah in 1996. The situation of cohabitation between the members of the two associations, which prevailed during the first few years, turned into frank hostility: two Imams nominated for the same mosque, clashes between the faithful, etc. A court order was sought and, pending judgment, all use of the mosque was suspended. In 2003–4, thanks to funds from Rwamagana, the AMUR built a new mosque in flamboyant turquoise a few hundred meters away from the old one. The members of Ansar Allah pray at home and use public land for important events. This apparent *status quo* is not protected from the conflicts that occur every time the Qur'an is used in public.[46]

The story told by the Muslims of Mabare is the product of these current conflicts. The irony is that the very moment of their recognition, of their social integration, was also that of their internal rupture. The AMUR, a national structure, received media dividends for its commitment during the genocide, which became a reason for conversion. An open, peaceful and tolerant Islam is given prominence, itself part of a global discourse which demotes it, in its turn, to the ranks of exoticism. Yet the *sura* of the Qur'an which gave its name to Ansar Allah already evokes enemies, a combat, even a state of siege. If the descriptions given are the object of permanent negotiation, they nonetheless articulate themselves around perennial themes. To really be aware of their power to stir people to action, we would need to see evidence of changes in direction, of adjustment of discourse. Not merely during moments of crisis, but, on the contrary, in the face of the decay of daily life, of the birth and slow death of religious observances, and the manner in which they decline and fall.

---

[46] On 28 August 2005, during the wedding of two members of Ansar Allah, AMUR interrupted the ceremony and police had to intervene to end the fight that started.

CONCLUSION
RESCUE, A NOTION REVISITED

Claire Andrieu

Until now, the history of rescue acts in genocidal situations has been studied far less than that of genocidal processes. Perhaps this is because these, being state undertakings, have produced archives, whereas by definition, a secret act leaves little or no trace. The historiography of genocidal periods is thus tilted toward the abysses into which humanity can sometimes sink.

A new meaning for the word 'rescue'

The rescue phenomenon is so little understood that we do not know how to quantify it. Some have written that rescuers have been much fewer in number than perpetrators, but can such dissimilar categories be compared? Genocide is triggered by a state that has an army and a large administration, and has the tactical advantage of initiative. Conditions for success are thus met. But most of all, since individuals generally tend to obey a regime in power, or at least allow it to act, it makes little sense to compare the number of perpetrators and their accomplices with the number of rescuers and their helpers. There will always be followers: that is the norm. Resistance is not expected, and thus constitutes an exception. If an attempt is nevertheless made to count perpetrators and rescuers, then the problem of definition arises. If the perpetrator is the one who actually kills or allows a victim to die from ill-treatment, then the numbers filling that category are not very high, at least regarding the Armenian and Jewish genocides. It took comparatively few armed soldiers to transport and kill hundreds, even thousands of civilians, whereas to rescue a family, a chain of individual actors was often involved together and ended up exceeding the number rescued in some cases. The scope given to the category considered can also alter the meaning of the assessment. The scale of the genocide, estimated as the number of victims, actually provides little information on the scale of rescues. A genocidal state will achieve its objective anyway, since it has the initiative as well as armed force. Among victims, however, it is impossible to identify those who at some point in time were given some sort of help before they fell into the killers' trap. Failed rescues are obliterated by successful killings.

In seeking to identify the parameters that define rescuers, we began by discarding the psychoeducational explanations that played an important role in the 1980s when an attempt was made to define the "altruistic personality," to borrow from the title of the emblematic book representing this school (*The Altruistic Personality. Rescuers of Jews in Nazi Europe*).[1] Drawing from psychology, sociology and education sciences, the book's authors, Samuel and Pearl Oliner, founded in 1982 the Altruistic Personality and Prosocial Behavior Institute at Humboldt State University. We have however sought a new approach to aid and rescue by straying from the moral and psychosociological register to draw on another trio of disciplines: history, sociology and political science. Instead of focusing the investigation on subjects and their qualities, we chose to examine the external constraints they faced, such as geography, closeness to the victims, presence of other minorities, precise details of the genocidal policy. And in order not to overgeneralize from a single case of genocide, we relied on the comparison of three genocides. These switches in focus, from subjective to objective determinants and from the Jewish genocide alone to a set of three cases, have enabled us to progress in defining acts of rescue.

As Jacques Semelin indicated in the introduction to this book, the traditional meaning of the words "rescue" and "rescuer" may seem ill-suited to deeds that accompanied a refusal of genocide. The limited, one-off, unique and critical nature of rescue at sea by a life-saving team is inap-

---

[1] Samuel P. Oliner and Pearl M. Oliner, *The Altruistic Personality. Rescuers of Jews in Nazi Europe*, foreword by Rabbi Harold M. Schulweis, New York, The Free Press, 1988.

propriate to describe a chain of individual acts, sometimes performed with no visibility of the overall situation, and in which the various actors were usually unaware of the links that preceded or followed them. The segmented and temporally extended nature of the rescue of people threatened by genocide lends new meaning to rescue. Taken in this new, other meaning, the term is more suitable than "help," too weak, or "savior," too religiously connoted. We thus opted for this new meaning.

Putting the notion of rescue into perspective

Almost every chapter in this volume follows a dual process of deconstruction and reconstruction of the notion of rescuer. This approach ends up placing the notion in perspective, but also extends it. The resulting concept nevertheless remains so heterogeneous that one may wonder if the task of categorization required by scholarly inquiry does not prove impossible. The often very individual nature of what is nevertheless a widespread and thus socially significant act makes its inclusion as one of the usual determinants of social analysis problematic. What, finally, is essential to rescue?

The first restriction to place on rescue has to do with the fact that it does not suffice to account for victims' survival. This issue is rooted in the comparison of Jews' survival rates in the various occupied countries. So it happens that France and Italy are the countries in which the survival rate was the highest (two-thirds to three-quarters of survivors in France, four-fifths in Italy). France's size and the existence of a "Free Zone" until November 1942 certainly facilitated the escape of the persecuted, as did the lesser brutality of Nazi oppression in Western than in Eastern Europe. But in addition to the structural effects, the Jews' own initiatives, as well as the strategies they used to hide and rescue themselves, must also be taken into account. Gunnar Paulsson has shown that even in Warsaw about one-third of the Jews surviving in 1943, prior to the ghetto uprising, lived in the "Aryan" part of the city.[2] The situation reveals the role of victims' initiative in their own survival. Restoring to the victims their autonomy of action means altering the widespread image of impotence or complete passivity attributed to them. It also makes analysis of the

---

[2] Gunnar S. Paulsson, *Secret City: The Hidden Jews of Warsaw, 1940–1945*, New Haven (Conn.), Yale University Press, 2002.

rescuer, who is not necessarily outside the persecuted community, more complex. We are beginning to learn more about the action of Jewish children's rescue networks in France and groups of Jewish partisans in the forests of Byelorussia, but the self-rescue of Armenians and Tutsis has yet to be studied. There also remains an entirely unexplored field of research: the decision-making process that leads to calling for help. Not all victims asked for help, for a variety of reasons. Some underestimated the danger, others were unable to detach themselves from the system of values that ruled their lives and that they would have to shelve in order to act. Principles as diverse as respect for the law, the sacredness of the family, or an identity reflex hampered decisions to act in self-rescue. One had to be clearly aware of the risk of death to take the inhuman decision of separating from one's children. Moreover, usually one had to agree to place them in the "other's" care, the family of another ethnocultural group, Turkish, Christian or Hutu. From this standpoint, we can make the assumption that in France, the universalistic and assimilationist culture of the Third Republic facilitated the expression of requests for help.

"Rescuees" may not be totally powerless, but rescuers are not all-powerful either. Their intervention takes place in conjunction with the protected person. The success of a rescue entails the notion of co-responsibility. In a paper given during the December 2006 symposium that was not selected for this volume, Mateusz Szpytma analyzes the murder by the German gendarmerie of sixteen residents on a farm in the Polish village of Markowa on 24 March 1944.[3] Eight hunted men and women had found shelter with a couple of tanners on a farm. Following a tip-off, the farmer, his pregnant wife and their six children were murdered on the spot with their eight guests. The informer, a Polish police officer, had previously hidden some of the Jews on that farm: a one-time rescuer had gone over to the killers. His act was made possible by the fact that his former protégés had kept in touch with him after he had driven them away as the danger of punishment increased. He was executed by the Polish Resistance in September 1944. On the other hand, the persecuted were dependent on the rescuer and his skill at hiding his new household. How could the increase in food purchases required by the secret guests be kept

---

[3] Mateusz Szpytma, "The Concealment of Jews in Markowa during the Second World War and the Tragic Consequences Thereof for the Polish Ulma Family and the Szal and Goldman Families, Whom the Former Attempted to Save," paper given for the *Pratiques de sauvetage en situations génocidaires. Perspectives comparatives* symposium, Sciences Po, Paris, December 2006.

a secret? Markowa villagers had certainly noticed the larger quantities of food purchased by the farmer's wife, not to mention the rise in the number of hides tanned by the farmer. Did these witnesses keep quiet? For the seventeen other Jews in the village who survived in hiding (out of an initial Jewish population of about 120 people), the answer is yes.

This example suggests both a possible restriction and an extension of the category of rescuers. First of all, the perpetrator/rescuer dichotomy is not absolute. In the context of the Armenian genocide, especially in Mardin, cases of behavior reversal were also noticed. Denunciation and murder can follow on the heels of benevolence and protection, under the pressure of events or even a precise threat, and sometimes even for no identified reason. It may be the Rwandan genocide, often perpetrated by civilians against other civilians, that gave rise to the most rescuer-killers. Rescuers therefore do not necessarily have a stable "personality." Conversely, someone who was a perpetrator by his position, such as any German in uniform in occupied Europe, did not necessarily act in the expected way. Gunnar Paulsson reports many cases of rescue performed by Germans in Poland. Not all magistrates or civil servants, with or without authority, can be placed automatically in the perpetrator category either. Their position enables them to warn victims of imminent arrest and delay or limit the execution of orders on various pretexts. In the *vilayet* of Diyarbekir in 1915, nearly half the sub-prefects were killed or dismissed from office for resisting orders to execute or deport Armenians. In Vichy France as well, policemen, prefects and mayors tried to limit the number of deported. In Nancy, in July 1942, a team of police officers warned the city's 400 Jews of an imminent roundup. The head of the police office for foreigners and his deputy were awarded the title of "Righteous among the Nations" from Yad Vashem. Even in Rwanda, where genocide swooped down like a hurricane, burgomasters and at least one prefect tried to step in. Their resistance only lasted a few days, either because they were killed, like the prefect of Butare and several burgomasters, or because they fled, or because they gave in and eventually took part in the wave of violence.[4]

---

[4] Cf. chapters 11, 20 and 23 in this volume as well as François Boulet, "Préfets et gendarmes face aux montagnes-refuges des Cévennes au Vercors (1940–1944)," in Patrick Cabanel and Laurent Gervereau (eds), *La Deuxième Guerre mondiale, des terres de refuge aux musées*, Chambon-sur-Lignon, Sivom Vivarais-Lignon, 2003, pp. 153–205.

Expand the notion

The story of Markowa also highlights the importance of the bystanders' role. One of the achievements of this book is to break with the accepted notion that the "perpetrator-victim-bystander" triad provides the key to comprehending genocides, placing co-responsibility for the crime on the "bystander." In this frame of thought, the entire population that was not a victim of genocide ends up being seen as bystanders. This oversimplification may come from the misuse of the title of Raul Hilberg's book, *Perpetrators, Victims, Bystanders*.[5] Yet among bystanders, Hilberg includes rescuers. In fact, rescue can be analyzed in a quadrangular relationship between perpetrator, victim, rescuer and bystander. A bystander is one who knows—which already restricts this category—without taking an active part in the events. He has seen people hunted or knows that a given house harbors some of them. Depending on whether he talks or remains silent, he places himself in the perpetrator camp or the rescuer camp. Here a sociopolitical given comes into play that varies according to country: the propensity to go to the authorities to report noted violations. The act of denunciation that is valued in certain national cultures is devalued in others. Traditions of contraband or fraud, various habits of civil disobedience can facilitate a certain law of silence that comes to the aid of the persecuted and their helpers. Since bystanders thus hold decisive power in the rescue process, the social circle rescue is involved in is considerably expanded. The border between rescuers and silent bystanders is not clear.

This volume has resolved to expand the notion of rescue by removing various limits once placed on its definition. For instance, rescue is not necessarily a high-risk activity conducted illegally. An illustration is provided by the many kidnappings of Armenian women and children that occurred on the death marches to the Syrian desert. These abductions were legal in that they were tolerated by the Ottomans. The victims, forced to convert and enslaved, nevertheless had their lives saved. In 1940–42 in France, the many steps taken by the American Varian Fry and then OSE to obtain visas for the United States constituted legal rescue attempts. The same is true of OSE's work to obtain permission to have children released from the internment camps for foreign Jews.

---

[5] Raul Hilberg, *Perpetrators, Victims, Bystanders*, New York, HarperCollins, 1992.

Another restriction on describing an act as rescue that this book seeks to remove lies in the disinterested nature of the action. The Israeli law defining the "Righteous among the Nations" in 1953 imposed the condition that rescue acts must be selfless, but it is difficult to limit rescue to unpaid help. Sheltering a family or children naturally incurred expenses. In France at least, many children were hidden for pay in homes that were accustomed to receiving them in the framework of child welfare programs. This was the case in Chambon-sur-Lignon, in particular. This village of 3,000 inhabitants hid several hundred Jewish children during the Occupation. Furthermore, even when accompanied by blackmail or extortion, hiding people remained a form of rescue. Placing selfless rescuers, exploiters and profiteers in the same category may seem paradoxical, but if a rescuer is one who saves lives, his intentions and methods of acting are only of secondary importance. On the other hand, a rescuer-profiteer who ends up killing his guests to finish stripping them of their belongings or because they have no more money, which happened in all the three cases of genocide studied, are placed in the rescuer-perpetrator category.

The question was also posed as to whether to extend the notion of rescue to events before or after the genocide. Such extension being more problematic, we chose to restrict rescue to the genocide period. Expanding the definition to what happened prior to the genocide immediately poses the problem of historical determinism. Were the combination of the Young Turk revolution in 1908 and the effects of World War I on the Ottoman Empire destined to produce the genocide of the Armenians? Did Hitler's rise to power irreversibly pave the way to genocide, or was it even the German *Sonderweg* already in place during the nineteenth century that (according to some historians) inexorably produced this result? Was the Rwandan genocide written into the country's history back in 1916 when Belgium imposed a colonial system that favored the Tutsi ethnic group over the Hutus? Only in the framework of a teleological vision of history can one date the start of rescue to before a genocide began, by including among rescue acts displays of opposition to the rise of such and such a form of government. The degree of interpretation and anachronism that the approach would imply invalidates it from the start.

It must be admitted that even the Convention for the Prevention and Punishment of the Crime of Genocide, adopted by the UN in 1948, defined no other "preventive" measures than punishment of the crime, probably banking on the dissuasive effect of the penalty. The Tutsi genocide has pointed up the shortcomings of the process. At the other end of genocide, after the fact, is the question of survival after genocide. In the Ottoman Empire, as soon as the great deportation ended in August 1915, Syriac Catholics and even Muslims began purchasing the new Armenian slaves to give them back their freedom. Were they rescuers? Another possible expansion of the notion of rescue: survivors of the three genocides, especially those in charge of OSE children homes, have attested to the "poison of pain" and rescues of another type that had to be implemented to help the victims live.

Rescue, the product of an ordinary society?

Clearly the "essence" of rescue is elusive. As a multifactorial and multifarious phenomenon involving many actors, some of them unstable, can rescue nevertheless find its place in the ordinary determinants of historic and social analysis? Can a few major parameters be identified with the help of the usual tools of social science analysis?

Attempts to study the socio-occupational makeup of rescuers are at present too fragmentary to be entirely convincing. Either they are based on limited knowledge of the corpus or the number of cases examined is too small.[6] The most thorough study remains that conducted by Nechama Tec.[7] Limited to altruistic rescuers in Poland, her analysis concludes that they are diverse in terms of social class, educational level, political commitment, religious belief and even their degree of anti-Semitism. She found none of the usual parameters used to predict social behavior to be decisive. In the current state of knowledge, this avenue of understanding leads nowhere, and the extreme diversity of rescuers encountered in this volume seems to confirm this.

Could the economics of rescue build more solid knowledge? The funding of rescue networks has been hardly studied until now, but systematic inquiry would reveal the social forces, local or international, that worked to protect persecuted persons. Churches and religious orders played a

---

[6] Lucien Lazare, *Le Livre des Justes. Histoire du sauvetage des juifs par des non-juifs en France, 1940–1944*, Paris, Hachette Pluriel, 1996; Samuel P. Oliner and Pearl M. Oliner, *The Altruistic Personality*, op. cit., p. 279 and 325.

[7] Nechama Tec, "Who Dared to Rescue Jews, and Why?," Chapter 6 in this volume, and *When Light Pierced the Darkness: Christian Rescue of Jews in Nazi Occupied Poland*, Oxford, Oxford University Press, 1986.

particular role. In the Ottoman Empire, Beatrice Rohner, a Swiss missionary from a German Protestant organization, started an orphanage and a service to assist Armenians in Aleppo despite extreme adversity. She received funds from her organization as well as from the Protestant American Board of Commissioners of Foreign Missions, the recently founded Near East Relief and the Relief Committee in Basel. All these organizations had solid financial backing in their respective societies. One could also look into how shelters provided by the Church and certain religious orders in France were funded during World War II. For instance, did the diocese of Nice use its own funds when Monsignor Rémond ordered the Catholic institutions under his supervision to hide some 500 children of the Abadi network? Approaching the question from the financial standpoint reintegrates the analysis of rescue into the preexisting society. For example, the Joint, the American Jewish Joint Distribution Committee that had been in existence since 1914 as an organization to help foreign Jews, contributed considerably to the funding of sheltering Jews in France. Similarly, the American Friends Service Committee, a Quaker charity that had already worked in Europe during World War I, supplied significant material and moral aid to the Jews hiding or interned in the Southern Zone.

Periodization, that essential tool of history as a discipline, also sheds light on the conditions of rescue. Each genocide takes place in a particular time frame. The Armenian genocide began with the killing of men where they were or near their place of residence, and continued with the deportation of women and children by forced march. Each of these situations spawned a different type of rescue. The speed with which men were massacred hampered the organization of rescues, whereas death marches left a few opportunities open, as did the parking of victims in the Ras ul-Ayn and Der Zor concentration camps in the Syrian desert. In 1942–44 in France, the time it took to round up victims and organize deportation also aided rescuers. It was the large-scale roundups of summer 1942 that awoke public opinion, provoked the first public protests and triggered rescue operations among circles outside those of the persecuted people. But if genocide is committed on site, rescue becomes extremely difficult. From this perspective, the cases of the Nazi-occupied USSR and Rwanda are similar. Due to the swiftness with which it was performed, killing on site or in roundup points close to the victim's homes left little leeway for rescuers to act.

These social, economic and chronological data help comprehend rescue, but they are not enough to draw up a typical rescuer profile or even describe the typical rescue operation. Does the attempt at categorization turn out to be impossible? Other rescue factors can be listed as well, but they often work both ways. For instance, rescue can correspond to the continuation of an activity prior to genocide but in different circumstances. This is the case for smugglers across border zones in particular. Or for certain local practices that contrast with the national environment: for instance, the work of the Yezidi Kurds, a remote Muslim sect living in the Sinjar area—a mountain region above the Mesopotamian desert—is consistent with their tradition of welcoming Christians. In 1915, escape routes were organized to help Armenians reach this mountain; the Yezidi Kurd Sheik Hamo Shero harbored and fed several thousand refugees. But the continuation of customary behavior can also work in favor of genocide, such as civil servants' and soldiers' obedience to orders, even murderous ones. Membership of a minority group is no guarantee of solidarity with the persecuted minority. The example of the Yezidi Kurds' welcome to Armenians was an exception among Kurds who usually took part in the massacre of Armenians. Similarly, during the Nazi occupation, Belarusian Tatars protected Jews; they were often mistreated by the occupying force, which sometimes likened them to Jews.[8] But Tatar collaborationist groups also formed, thereby invalidating the theory that minorities have a propensity to help one another. The cases of French Protestants and Rwandan Muslims, very much minorities in these countries, is probably less ambivalent.

The rescue society, a risk society

It remains to be examined what might be the rescuer's specificity: the willingness to take risks that are sometimes or often deadly for him and his family. The risk incurred was life-threatening and flagrant during the Rwandan genocide, which was at times committed door-to-door by militias and the armed forces with the complicity of local informers. The danger was also mortal and patent in Nazi-occupied Eastern Europe. It

---

[8] Sergey A. Kizima, "If One Minority Helps the Other One. The Example of Tatars and Jews during the Nazi Occupation in Belarus," paper given for the *Pratiques de sauvetage en situations génocidaires. Perspectives comparatives* symposium, Paris, Sciences Po, December 2006.

grew serious in the Netherlands when rescuers were threatened with six months in a concentration camp during the second half of 1943. It was less in France, except in places such as the Dauphiné region between September 1943 and March 1944 during Brunner's operation. And it was often deadly for subjects of the Ottoman Empire. But even when the risk was not life-threatening or was not perceived as such, violating state policy by "harboring" fugitives was a significant transgression, which involved others so as to feed and care for the hidden persons. The risk dimension is probably what the greatest number of rescuers had in common, with the fear it provoked being overcome with a variety of behavior ranging from accepting remuneration to selflessness and sacrifice.

It would be excessive to speak of a "rescue society" or a "risk society" if the word "society" was to evoke a stable and established milieu. But, including rescuers and the persecuted, the rescue society is also a risk society in another way. Risk is not confined to risk-taking by rescuers or the persecuted. Both have knowledge, foresight, or a mere premonition of the major risk that threatens them: the active destruction of the principle of humanity. A clear or vague perception of the ongoing catastrophe unites them at a time when their far-sightedness or sensitivity is not shared by all. There is a risk to society in a dual sense of the term.

This collective and comparative research undertaking has reasserted the rescuer's social role and historical depth. The model rescuer, the one sometimes called a "Righteous" person, is clearly not alone in his category, far from it. The point is not, however, to "deconstruct the myth of the rescuer," for if a myth indeed exists, it is based on the actual repetition of a phenomenon, the sacrifice of individuals who preferred to risk death rather than allow the principle of humanity to be destroyed. Exemplary cases of this abound in the three genocides. The case of Sula Karuhimbi is already known, but it is mentioned here as an illustration of the universality of the principle of rescue, beyond national, economic, social or cultural borders. This elderly seventy-five-year-old woman, a humble healer in Musamo, a hamlet in Rwanda, managed to hide some twenty Tutsis in her stable during the entire genocide despite repeated threats from gangs of killers. She chased them away by threatening to raise evil spirits against them. Even offers of money didn't sway her.[9] Although the number of victims of punishment for rescue operations is unknown and

---

[9] See Lee Ann Fujii, "Rescuers and Killer-Rescuers during the Rwanda Genocide," Chapter 9 in this volume.

the large majority of rescuers in the three genocides probably survived, there is no doubt that the ideal rescuer, selfless and human to the point of sacrificing his or her life, has indeed existed. He or she represents civilization, whether it is archaic or modern, rural or industrial.

But the conclusion must be drawn that the rescuer equation has yet to be found. Neither basically good, since he can suddenly change roles or shamelessly take advantage of the situation, nor the only one responsible for his action, since rescue is performed in a complex social configuration, nor socially predetermined, does the rescuer remain indefinable? Rather than a category, rescue resembles what statisticians called a stochastic phenomenon—one that is not subject to absolute determinism, that arises partly out of chance. Although no rescuer's gesture can be entirely governed by chance, the factors contributing to his or her deeds are so numerous and their interactions so complex that one cannot hope to construct a single coherent explanatory system of rescue. On the other hand, on the scale of each genocide, the appearance of a rescue society, segmented and unstable, but constant, can be observed. However random it may seem in detail, this disparate and fragmented society nevertheless represents a historical phenomenon.

BIBLIOGRAPHY

Documents

Andrieu, Claire (ed.), *La Persécution des juifs de France, 1940–1944, et le rétablissement de la légalité républicaine. Recueil des textes officiels, 1940–1999*, Paris: La Documentation Française, 2000.
Documents diplomatiques suisses, Volume 14 (1 Jan. 1941–8 Sep. 1943) and Volume 15 (8 Sep. 1943–8 May 1945), Berne: Benteli, 1997, and 1992.
Gust, Wolfgang (ed.), *Der Völkermord an den Armeniern 1915–1916: Dokumente aus dem politischen Archiv des deutschen Auswärtigen Amts*, Springe: Zu Klampen, 2005.
Lepsius (Johannes), *Archives du génocide des Arméniens: recueil de documents diplomatiques allemands, extraits de Deutschland und Armenien (1914–1918)*, Paris: Fayard, 1986.
Milton, Sybil and Bogin, Frederick D. (eds), *American Jewish Joint Distribution Committee, New York, Archives of the Holocaust. An International Collection of Selected Documents*, 10, New York: Garland Publishing Inc., 1995.
International Criminal Tribunal for Rwanda (ICTR)—UN, Online publications and compendium of ordinances, decisions, and judgments, printed volumes for 1995–1997 and 1998.

Dictionaries

Gutman, Israel (ed.), *Dictionnaire des Justes de France*, prepared by Lucien Lazare, Jerusalem, Yad Vashem, Paris: Fayard, 2003.
Gutman (Israel) (ed.), *I Giusti d'Italia. I non ebrei che salvarono gli ebrei 1943–1945*, prepared by Bracha Rivlin, Milan: Mondadori, 2006 [1st ed. Jerusalem: Yad Vashem, 2004].
Gutman, Israel (ed.), *The Encyclopedia of the Righteous Among the Nations: Rescuers of Jews during the Holocaust—The Netherlands*, prepared by Jozeph Michman and Bert Jan Flim, Jerusalem: Yad Vashem, 2004;—*Belgium*, prepared by Dan Michman, Jerusalem: Yad Vashem, 2005;—*Poland*, prepared by Sara Bender and Shmuel Krakowski, Jerusalem: Yad Vashem, 2004.

Gutman, Israel (ed.), *Lexikon der Gerechten unter den Völkern: Deutsche und Österreicher*, prepared by Daniel Fraenkel, Jerusalem: Yad Vashem, 2005.
Gutman, Israel (ed.), *The Encyclopedia of the Righteous Among the Nations: Rescuers of Jews During the Holocaust, Europe and Others*, 2 volumes, Jerusalem: Yad Vashem, 2007.
Poujol, Jacques, *Protestants dans la France en guerre, 1939–1945. Dictionnaire thématique et biographique*, Paris: Les Éditions de Paris, Max Chaleil, 2000.

Testimonies and diaries

Bedoukian, Kerop, *Some of Us Survived*, New York: Farrar, Straus and Giroux, 1979.
Boegner, Philippe, *Carnets du Pasteur Boegner, 1940–1945*, Paris: Fayard, 1992.
Bryce, Viscount James, *The Treatment of Armenians in the Ottoman Empire, 1915–1916: Documents Presented to Viscount Grey of Fallodon by Viscount Bryce*, London: HMSO, 1916; new, uncensored edition, Princeton, NJ: Gomidas Institute, 2000, p. 470.
Cavaliere, Alberto, *I campi della morte in Germania: nel racconto di una sopravvissuta*, Milan: Sonzogno, 1945.
Davis, Leslie, *The Slaughterhouse Province: An American Diplomat's Report on the Armenian Genocide of 1915–1917*, New York: Aristide D. Caratzas, 1988.
Debenedetti, Giacomo, *16 ottobre 1943*, Rome: OET, 1945.
———, *Otto ebrei*, Rome: Atlantica, 1944.
Errera, Anna, *Vita del popolo ebraico*, Milan: Garzanti, 1947.
Ertürk, Hüsamettin, *İki Devrin Perde Arkası*, Istanbul: Hilmi, 1957.
Fiorentino, Luigi, *Cavalli 8 uomini...: pagine di un internato*, Milan: La Lucerna, 1946.
Fittko, *Escape Through the Pyrenees*, Evanston (Ill.): Northwestern University Press, 1991.
Hautval, Adélaïde, *Médecine et crimes contre l'humanité*, Paris: Éditions du Félin, 2006 [new ed.].
Hirschmann, Ira, *Life Line to A Promised Land*, New York: Jewish Book Guild of America, 1946.
———, *Caution to the Winds*, New York: David McKay, 1962.
Jernazian, Ephraim, *Judgment Unto Truth: Witnessing the Armenian Genocide*, New Brunswick: Transaction Publishers, 1990.
Kerr, Stanley, *Lions of Marash: Personal Experiences with American Near East Relief*, Albany: State University of New York Press, 1973.
Karangwa, Abbé Hildebrand, *Le Génocide au centre du Rwanda. Quelques témoignages des rescapés de Kabgayi (le 2 juin 1994)*, no publisher named, 2000.
Künzler, Jakob, *Im Lande des Blutes und der Tränen. Erlebnisse in Mesopotamien während des Weltkriegs, 1914–1918*, Zurich: Chronos, 2004.

BIBLIOGRAPHY

Lambert, Raymond-Raoul, *Carnet d'un témoin 1940–1943. Présenté et annoté par Richard Cohen*, Paris: Librairie Arthème Fayard, 1985.

Leitner, Isabella, *Fragments of Isabella: A Memoir of Auschwitz*, New York: Thomas Y. Crowell, 1978.

———, *Saving the Fragments: From Auschwitz to New York*, New York: New American Library, 1985.

Lepsius, Johannes, *Le Rapport secret du Dr Johannes Lepsius, président de la Deutsche Orient-Mission et de la Société germano-arménienne, sur les massacres d'Arménie*, Paris: Payot et Cie., 1918.

Levi, Primo, *Se questo è un uomo*, Turin: De Silva, 1947.

Mazour-Ratner, Jenny, *Mes vingt ans à l'OSE, 1941–1961*, Paris: FMS/OSE-Le Manuscrit, 2006.

Millu, Liana, *Il fumo di Birkenau*, Milan: La Prora, 1947.

Misul, Frida, *Fra gli artigli del mostro nazista*, Leghorn: Stabilimento Poligrafico Belforte, 1946.

Momigliano, Eucardio, *40 000 fuori legge*, Rome: Carboni, 1944.

———, *Storia tragica e grottesca del razzismo fascista*, Milan: Mondadori, 1946.

Morgenthau, Henry, *Ambassador Morgenthau's Story*, Detroit (Mich.): Wayne State University Press, 2003 [new ed.].

Morpurgo, Luciano, *Caccia all'uomo! Vita sofferenze e beffe. Pagine di diario 1938–1944*, Rome: Dalmatia, 1946.

Mujawayo, Esther and Souâd Belhaddad, *SurVivantes, Rwanda, dix ans après le génocide, suivi d'un entretien croisé entre Simone Veil et Esther Mujawayo*, La Tour-d'Aigues: Éditions de l'Aube, 2004.

Nesimi, Abidin, *Yılların İçinden*, Istanbul: Gözlem, 1977.

Nissim, Luciana and Pelagia Lewinska, *Donne contro il mostro*, Turin: Ramella, 1946.

Papanek, Ernst, *Out of the Fire*, New York: William Morrow, 1975.

———, *Die Kinder von Montmorency*, Vienna-Munich-Paris: Europa Verlag, 1980.

Rechid, Mehmed, *Sürgünden İntihara Dr Rechid Bey'in Hatıraları* [Memoirs of Dr Rechid Bey, from Exile to Suicide], Izmir: no publisher named, 1992.

Riggs, Henry H., *Days of Tragedy in Armenia. Personal Experiences in Harpoot, 1915–1917*, Ann Arbor (Mich.): Gomidas Institute, 1997.

Svazlian, Verjine, *The Armenian Genocide: Testimonies of the Eyewitness Survivors*, Erevan: Guitoutiun, 2000.

Tedeschi, Giuliana, *Questo povero corpo*, Milan: Editrice Italiana, 1946.

Valech Capozzi, Alba, *A 24029*, Sienne: Soc. An. Poligrafica, 1946.

Vierbücker, Heinrich, *Armenia 1915: What the German Imperial Government Concealed from Its Subjects. The Slaughter of a Civilized People at the Hands of Turks*, Arlington (Mass.): Armenian Cultural Foundation, 2006.

Wegner, Armin, *Armin T. Wegner and the Armenians in Anatolia, 1915: Images and Testimonies*, Milan: Guerini E Associati, 1996.

Weil, Joseph, *Le Combat d'un Juste*, Saumur: Cheminement, 2002.
Zaroukian, Andranik, *Men Without Childhood*, New York: Ashod Press, 1985.

Reports

African Rights, *The History of the Genocide in Sector Gishamvu. A Collective Account*, Kigali: African Rights, 2003.
———, *Rwanda: Death, Despair, and Defiance*, London: African Rights, 1995 [rev. ed.].
———, *Tribute to Courage*, Kigali and London, 2002 (also published in French as *Hommage au Courage*, Kigali, 2002).
Centre de documentation juive contemporaine, *L'Activité des organisations juives sous l'Occupation*, Paris: CDJC, 1947.
Commission indépendante d'experts suisse—Seconde Guerre mondiale, *La Suisse, le national-socialisme et la Seconde Guerre mondiale. Rapport final*, Zurich: Pendo, 2002.
———, *Die Schweiz und die Flüchtlinge zur Zeit des Nationalsozialismus*, Zurich: Chronos, 2001.
Human Rights Watch, "The Rwandan Genocide: How It Was Prepared," *Human Rights Watch Briefing Paper*, 1, April 2006.
OSE, *Une mémoire pour le futur, 90 ans de l'OSE / A Legacy for the Future*, Paris: OSE, 2003.
Penal Reform International, *Gacaca Research Report n°5: Cell-level Preparations*, Sept. 2003. Available online: http://www.penalreform.org/gacaca-research-report-no. 5–cell-level-preparations.html
Rwanda, Republic of, *Commune de Bicumbi. Rapports communaux annuels*, 1980, 1981, 1983, 1984, 1985, 1986, 1987, 1988, 1989, 1990, 1991, 1992, 1993.
———, *Recensement général de la population et de l'habitat au 15 août 1991. Résultats provisoires*, Kigali: Service National du Recensement, 1991.
Rwanda, République du, *Rapport préliminaire d'identification des sites du génocide et des massacres d'avril-juillet 1994 au Rwanda*, Kigali: Commission pour le Mémorial du Génocide et des Massacres au Rwanda, 1996.
———, Ministère de l'Administration Locale, du Développement Communautaire et des Affaires Sociales, *Recensement des victimes du génocide*, 2003.

Comparative Studies, General Studies

Bartov, Omer and Phyllis Mack (eds), *In God's Name. Genocide and Religion in the Twentieth Century*, Oxford: Oxford University Press, 2001.
Chorbajian, Levon and George Shirinian (eds), *Studies in Comparative Genocide*, New York: St. Martin's Press, 1999.
Kieser, Hans-Lukas and Dominik J. Schaller (eds), *Der Völkermord an den Armeniern und die Shoah*, Zurich: Chronos, 2002.
Melson (Robert), *Revolution and Genocide: On the Origins of the Armenian Genocide and the Holocaust*, Chicago: University of Chicago Press, 1992.

BIBLIOGRAPHY

Radice, Ulianova and Anna Maria Samuelli (eds), *There is Always an Option to Say "Yes" or "No." The Righteous Against the Genocides of Armenians and Jews*, Padua: Cooperativa Libraria Editrice Universita di Padova, 2000.

Semelin, Jacques, *Purifier et Détruire. Usages politiques des massacres et génocides*, Paris: Seuil, 2005.

The Genocide of the Armenians

Akçam, Taner, *From Empire to Republic: Turkish Nationalism and the Armenian Genocide*, London: Zed Books, 2004.

Balakian, Peter, *The Burning Tigris: The Armenian Genocide and America's Response*, New York: HarperCollins Publishers Inc., 2003.

Bardakjian, Kevork, *Hitler and the Armenian Genocide*, Cambridge (Mass.): Zoryan Institute, 1985.

Dadrian, Vahakn, *The History of the Armenian Genocide: Ethnic Conflict from the Balkans to Anatolia and the Caucasus*, Oxford: Berghahn Books, 1995.

Hovhannisian, Richard G. (ed.), *The Armenian Genocide in Perspective*, New Brunswick (NJ): Transaction Books, Rutgers University, 1986.

Hovhannisian, Richard G. (ed.), *The Armenian Genocide: History, Politics, Ethics*, New York: St. Martin's Press, 1992.

Hyman, (Paula), *From Dreyfus to Vichy. The Remaking of French Jewry, 1906–1939*, New York: Columbia University Press, 1979.

Kaiser, Hilmar, *At the Crossroads of Der Zor. Death, Survival, and Humanitarian Resistance*, Princeton (NJ): Taderon, 2001.

Kévorkian, Raymond H., *Le Génocide des Arméniens*, Paris: Odile Jacob, 2006.

Kieser, Hans-Lukas (ed.), *Die armenische Frage und die Schweiz / La question arménienne et la Suisse, 1896–1923*, Zurich: Chronos, 1999.

Meyer, Karl, *L'Arménie et la Suisse*, Villeurbanne: no publisher named, 1974.

Miller, Donald and Lorna Touryan Miller, *Survivors: an Oral History of the Armenian Genocide*, Berkeley (Calif.): University of California Press, 1993.

Peterson, Merrill, *Starving Armenians: America and the Armenian Genocide, 1915–1930 and After*, Charlottesville (Va.): University of Virginia Press, 2004.

Slide, Anthony, *Ravished Armenia and the Story of Aurora Mardiganian*, Lanham (Md.): Scarecrow Press Inc., 1997.

Tachjian, Vahé, *La France en Cilicie et en Haute-Mésopotamie*, Paris: Karthala, 2004.

Ternon, Yves, *Mardin 1915. Anatomie pathologique d'une destruction*, Paris: Geuthner, 2007.

Ussher, Clarence, *An American Physician in Turkey*, Astoria: J.C. and A.L. Fawcett Inc., 1990.

Walker, Christopher, *Armenia: The Survival of a Nation*, London and New York: Croom Helm and St. Martin's Press, 1990.

Werfel, Franz, *The Forty Days of Musa Dagh*, New Brunswick: NJ and London, 1999 [originally published in Germany in 1933 as *Die vierzig Tage des Musa Dagh*]

The Genocide of the Jews

Adler, Jacques, *The Jews of Paris and the Final Solution: Communal Response and Internal Conflicts, 1940–1944*, New York and Oxford: Oxford University Press, 1987.

Anciens de la Résistance juive en France, *Organisation juive de combat: Résistance-sauvetage, France 1940–1945*, Paris: Autrement, 2002.

Avni, Haïm, "The Zionist Underground in Holland and France and the Escape to Spain," in Yisrael Gutman and Efraim Zuroff (eds), *Rescue Attempts During the Holocaust. Proceedings of the Second Yad Vashem International Historical Conference. Jerusalem, April 8–11, 1974*, Jerusalem: Yad Vashem, 1977, pp. 555–90.

Bankier, David and Israel Gutman (eds), *Nazi Europe and the Final Solution*, Jerusalem: Yad Vashem, 2003, pp. 449–453.

Bauer, Yehuda, *My Brother's Keeper: A History of the American Jewish Joint Distribution Committee 1929–1939*, Philadelphia (Pa.): The Jewish Publication Society, 1974.

———, *American Jewry and the Holocaust: The American Jewish Joint Distribution Committee, 1939–1945*, Detroit (Mich.): Wayne State University Press, 1981.

———, *Out of the Ashes: The Impact of American Jews on Post-Holocaust Jewry*, Oxford: Pergamon Press, 1989.

———, *Jews for Sale: Nazi-Jewish Negotiations, 1933–1945*, New Haven (Conn.): Yale University Press, 1994.

Becker, Annette, Danielle Delmaire and Frédéric Gugelot, *Juifs et chrétiens: entre ignorance, hostilité et rapprochement, 1898–1998*, Villeneuve d'Ascq: Université de Lille-3, 2002.

Ben-Tov, Arieh, *Facing the Holocaust in Budapest. The International Committee of the Red Cross and the Jews in Hungary, 1943–1945*, Geneva: Henry Dunant Institute, Dordrecht, Martinus Nijhoff Publishers, 1988.

Benz, Wolfgang and Julianne Wetzel (eds), *Solidarität und Hilfe für Juden während der NS-Zeit*, volume 2, Berlin: Metropol, 1998, pp. 193–280.

Berenbaum, Michael and Abraham J. Peck (eds), *The Holocaust and History: The Known, the Unknown, the Disputed, and the Reexamined*, copublished with the United States Holocaust Memorial Museum, Bloomington (Ind.): Indiana University Press, 1998.

Bidussa, David, *Il mito del bravo italiano*, Milan: Il Saggiatore, 1993.

Block, Gay and Malka Drucker, *Rescuers*, New York: Holmes and Meier Publishers Inc., 1992.

BIBLIOGRAPHY

Blom, J.C.H., *Crisis, Bezetting en Herstel. Tien Studies over Nederland 1930–1950*, Rotterdam: Nijgh & Van Ditmar Universitair, 1989.

Bolle, Pierre (ed.), *Le Plateau Vivarais-Lignon. Accueil et Résistance, 1939–1944*, Le Chambon-sur-Lignon: Société d'Histoire de la Montagne, 1992.

Bolle, Pierre and Jean Godel, *Spiritualité, théologie et résistance. Yves de Montcheuil, théologien au maquis du Vercors*, Grenoble: Actes du Colloque de Biviers de 1984, 1987.

Boulet, François, *Les Alpes françaises, 1940–1944: des montagnes-refuges aux montagnes-maquis*, Bordeaux: Les Presses Franciliennes, 2008.

———, *Histoire de la montagne-refuge aux limites de la Haute-Loire et de l'Ardèche, de la réforme protestante à la seconde guerre mondiale*, Polignac: Ed. du Roure, 2008.

Braham, Randolph L., *Politics of Genocide: The Holocaust in Hungary*, 2 volumes, New York: Columbia University Press, 1981.

Braham, Randolph L. (ed.), *Nazis' Last Victims: The Holocaust in Hungary*, published in association with the United States Holocaust Memorial Museum, Detroit (Mich.): Wayne State University Press, 1998.

Breitman, Richard, *American Refugee Policy and European Jewry: 1933–1945*, Bloomington (Ind.): Indiana University Press, 1987.

———, *Official Secrets: What the Nazis Planned, What the British and Americans Knew*, New York: Hill and Wang, 1998.

Brustein, William I., *Roots of Hate: Anti-Semitism in Europe before the Holocaust*, Cambridge: Cambridge University Press, 2003.

Cabanel, Patrick, *Juifs et protestants en France, les affinités électives xvie-xxie siècle*, Paris: Fayard, 2004.

——— and Chantal Bordes-Benayoun (eds), *Un modèle d'intégration. Juifs et israélites en France et en Europe, xixe-xxe siècle*, Toulouse: Berg International, 2004.

Cabanel, Patrick and Laurent Gervereau, *La Deuxième Guerre mondiale, des terres de refuge aux musées*, Le Chambon-sur-Lignon: Sivom Vivarais-Lignon, 2003.

Caron, Vicki, *Uneasy Asylum: France and the Jewish Refugee Crisis, 1933–1942*, Stanford University Press, 1999.

Cavaglion, Alberto and Gian Paolo Romagnani, *Le interdizioni del duce. A cinquant'anni dalle leggi razziale in Italia, 1938–1988*, Turin: Albert Meynier, 1988.

Cesarani, David (ed.), *Genocide and Rescue: The Holocaust in Hungary, 1944*, Oxford: Berg, 1997.

Chessa, Pasquale and Francesco Villari (eds), *Interpretazioni su Renzo De Felice*, Milan: Baldini e Castoldi, 2002.

Cohen, Asher, *Persécutions et Sauvetages. Juifs et Français sous l'Occupation et sous Vichy*, Paris: Éditions du Cerf, 1993.

Cohen, Richard I., *The Burden of Conscience: French Jewish Leadership during the Holocaust*, Bloomington (Ind.): Indiana University Press, 1987.

Collotti, Enzo, *Il fascismo e gli ebrei. Le leggi razziali in Italia*, Bari: Laterza, 2003.

Comte, Madeleine, *Sauvetage et Baptêmes. Les religieuses de Notre-Dame de Sion face à la persécution des juifs en France, 1940–1944*, foreword by Étienne Fouilloux, Paris: L'Harmattan, 2001.

Croes, Marnix, "Gentiles and the Survival Chances of Jews in the Netherlands 1940–1945: A Closer Look," in Beate Kosmala and Feliks Tych (eds), *Facing the Nazi Genocide: non-Jews and Jews in Europe*, Strasbourg/Berlin: European Science Foundation/Metropol Verlag, 2004, pp. 41–72.

———, "The Dutch Police and the Persecution of Jews in the Netherlands during the German Occupation, 1940–1945," in Bruno de Wever, Herman van Goethem and Nico Wouters (eds), *Local Government in Occupied Europe (1939–1945)*, Ghent: Academia Press, 2006, pp. 67–82.

——— and Peter Tammes, *"Gif laten wij niet voortbestaan." Een onderzoek naar de overlevingskansen van joden in de Nederlandse gemeenten, 1940–1945*, Amsterdam: Aksant, 2006 [2nd ed.].

De Felice, Renzo, *Storia degli ebrei italiani sotto il fascismo*, Turin: Einaudi, 1961.

Douwes, Arnold, *Belevenissen van een verzetsman in de periode 1940–1945*, Stegeman: Heiloo, 2002.

Favez, Jean-Claude, *Une mission impossible? Le CICR, les déportations et les camps de concentration nazis*, in collaboration with Geneviève Billeter, Lausanne: Payot, 1988.

Fein, Helen, *Accounting for Genocide. National Responses and Jewish Victimization during the Holocaust*, Chicago: University of Chicago Press, 1979.

Fijalkow, Jacques (ed.), *Vichy, les Juifs et les Justes. L'exemple du Tarn*, Toulouse: Privat, 2003.

———, *Les Enfants de la Shoah*, Actes du Colloque de Lacaune, September 2005, Paris, 2006.

Focardi, Filippo, *La guerra della memoria. La Resistenza nel dibattito politico italiano dal 1945 a oggi*, Bari: Laterza, 2005.

Fogelman, Eva, *Conscience and Courage: The Rescuers of the Jews During the Holocaust*, New York: Anchor Books, 1994.

Forti, Carla, *Il caso Pardo Roques, un eccidio del 1944 tra memoria e oblio*, Turin: Einaudi, 1998.

Gensburger, Sarah, *Les Justes de France. Politiques publiques de la mémoire*, Paris: Presses de Sciences Po, 2010.

Gerlach, Christian and Gotz Aly, *Das letzte Kapitel: Realpolitik, Ideologie und der Mord an den ungarischen Juden, 1944–1945*, Munich: Deutsche Verlagsanstalt, 2002.

Gilbert, Martin, *The Righteous: The Unsung Heroes of the Holocaust*, Basingstoke: Macmillan, 2003.

Goschler, Constantin, Philipp Ther and Claire, Andrieu (eds), *Spoliations et restitutions des biens juifs. Europe, xxe siècle*, Paris: Autrement, 2007.

BIBLIOGRAPHY

Gruat, Cédric and Cécile Leblanc, *Amis des Juifs. Les résistants aux étoiles*, Paris: Éditions Tirésias, 2005.

Gutman, Israel and Efraim Zuroff (eds), *Rescue Attempts During the Holocaust. Proceedings of the Second Yad Vashem International Historical Conference. Jerusalem, 8–11 April 1974*, Jerusalem: Yad Vashem, 1977.

Grynberg, Anne, *Les Camps de la honte. Les internés juifs des camps français 1939–1944*, Paris: La Découverte, 1991.

Hallie, Phillip, *Lest Innocent Blood Be Shed*, New York: Harper and Row, 1979.

Hanyok, Robert, *Eavesdropping on Hell: Historical Guide to Western Communications Intelligence and the Holocaust, 1939–1945*, Washington: National Security Agency, 2004.

Hazan, Katy, *Les Orphelins de la Shoah, les maisons de l'espoir, 1944–1960*, Paris: Les Belles lettres, 2000.

——— and Eric Gozlan, *À la vie! Les enfants de Buchenwald du shtetl à l'OSE*, Paris: FMS/OSE-Le Manuscrit, 2005.

Hellman, Peter, *Avenue of the Righteous*, New York: Atheneum, 1980.

Hilberg, Raul, *Perpetrators, Victims, Bystanders: The Jewish Catastrophe, 1933–1945*, New York: Aaron Asher Books, 1992.

———, *The Destruction of the European Jews* Chicago (Ill.): Quadrangle Books, 1961.

Hilbrink, C., *De Illegalen. Illegaliteit in Twente en de aangrenzende Salland, 1940–1945*, The Hague: SDU, 1989.

Hyman (Paula), "*From Dreyfuss to Vichy. The Remaking of French Jewry, 1906–1939*," New York: Columbia University Press, 1979.

Iranek-Osmecki, Kazimierz, *He Who Saves One Life*, New York: Crown Publishers, 1971.

Isnenghi, Mario, *Le guerre degli italiani*, Milan: Mondadori, 1989.

Isnenghi, Mario (ed.), *I luoghi della memoria: strutture ed eventi dell'Italia unita*, Bari: Laterza, 1997.

Jacobs, Dore and Bramesfeld Else, *Gelebte Utopie: Aus Dem Leben Einer Gemeinschaft*, Essen: Klartext, 1990 [1st ed.].

Joly, Laurent, *Vichy dans la "Solution finale." Histoire du Commissariat général aux questions juives, 1941–1944*, Paris: Grasset, 2006.

Joutard, Philippe, Jacques Poujol and Patrick Cabanel (eds), *Cévennes, terre de refuge, 1940–1944*, Montpellier: Presses du Languedoc, 2006 [1st ed. 1987].

Katzburg, Nathaniel, *Hungary and the Jews: Policy and Legislation, 1920–1943*, Ramat-Gan: Bar-Ilan University Press, 1981.

Katznelson, Ira, *Desolation and Enlightenment: Political Knowledge after Total War, Totalitarianism and the Holocaust*, New York: Columbia University Press, 2003.

Klarsfeld, Serge, *La Shoah en France*, 4 volumes, Paris: Fayard, 2001.

Knout, David, *Contribution à l'histoire de la résistance juive en France, 1940–1944*, Paris: Centre de Documentation Juive Contemporaine, 1947.

Kochavi, (Arieh J., *Post-Holocaust Politics: Britain, the United States, and Jewish Refugees, 1945–1948*, Chapel Hill: University of North Carolina Press, 2001.

Laborie, Pierre, *L'Opinion française sous Vichy*, Paris: Seuil, 1990.
Laffitte, Michel, *Juif dans la France allemande. Institutions, dirigeants et communautés au temps de la Shoah*, Paris: Tallandier, 2006.
——, *Un engrenage fatal, l'UGIF face aux réalités de la Shoah 1941–1944*, Paris: Liana Levi, 2003.
Lagrou, Pieter), *Mémoires patriotiques de l'occupation nazie*, Brussels: Complexe, 2003.
Land-Weber, Ellen, *To Save a Life: Stories of Holocaust Rescue*, Urbana (Ill.): University of Illinois Press, 2000.
Laqueur, Walter, *The Terrible Secret: Suppression of the Truth about Hitler's Final Solution*, Londres: Penguin Books, 1982.
—— and Breitman, Richard, *Breaking the Silence*, New York: Simon and Schuster, 1986.
Lasserre, André, *Frontières et camps. Le refuge en Suisse de 1933 à 1945*, Lausanne: Payot, 1995.
Latour, Anny, *La Résistance juive en France*, Paris: Stock, 1970.
Lazare, Lucien, *La Résistance juive en France*, Paris: Stock, 1987.
——, *Le Livre des Justes, histoire du sauvetage des juifs par des non-juifs en France, 1940–1944*, Paris: Hachette, 1996.
Le Bot, Florent, *La Fabrique réactionnaire. Corporatisme, antisémitisme et spoliations dans le monde du cuir en France, 1930–1950*, Paris: Presses de Sciences Po, 2007.
Lemalet, Martine (ed.), *Au secours des enfants du siècle. Regards croisés sur l'OSE*, Paris: Nil, 1993.
Leplay, Michel, *Les Églises protestantes et les juifs face à l'antisémitisme au vingtième siècle*, Lyon: Éditions Olivetan, 2006.
Liedtke, Rainer and Stephan Wendehorst, *The Emancipation of Catholics, Jews and Protestants. Minorities and the Nation State in Nineteenth-century Europe*, Manchester: Manchester University Press, 1999.
Liempt, Ad van, *Kopgeld. Nederlandse premiejagers op zoek naar joden 1943*, Amsterdam: Balans, 2002.
Loinger, Georges and Hazan, Katy, *Aux frontières de l'espoir*, Paris: FMS/OSE-Le Manuscrit, 2006.
London, Louise, *Whitehall and the Jews, 1933–1948: British Immigration Policy, Jewish Refugees, and the Holocaust*, Cambridge: Cambridge University Press, 2000.
Ludwig, Carl, *La Politique pratiquée par la Suisse à l'égard des réfugiés de 1933 à nos jours*, Berne: report to the Federal Council, 1957.
Mächler, Stefan, *Hilfe und Ohnmacht. Der Schweizerische israelitische Gemeindebund und die nationalsozialistische Verfolgung 1933–1945*, Zurich: Chronos, 2005.
Maesschalk, Walter de, *Gardes in de oorlog. De Antwerpse politie in WO II*, Antwerp-Rotterdam: C. de Vries-Brouwers, 2004.
Matard-Bonucci, Marie-Anne, *L'Italie fasciste et la persécution des juifs*, Paris: Perrin, 2007.

BIBLIOGRAPHY

Meershoek, Guus, *Dienaren van het Gezag. De Amsterdamse Politie tijdens de Bezetting*, Amsterdam: van Gennep, 1999.

Miccoli, Giovanni, *I dilemmi e il silenzio di Pio XII*, Milan: Rizzoli, 2000.

Michman, Dan (ed.), *Belgium and the Holocaust*, Jerusalem: Yad Vashem, 1998.

Monroe, Kristen Renwick, *The Hand of Compassion: Portraits of Moral Choice During the Holocaust*, Princeton University Press, 2004.

———, *The Heart of Altruism: Perceptions of a Common Humanity*, Princeton University Press, 1996.

Moore, Bob, *Victims and Survivors. The Nazi Persecution of the Jews in the Netherlands 1940–1945*, London: Arnold, 1997.

Narbel, Nathalie, *Un ouragan de prudence. Les Églises protestantes vaudoises et les réfugiés victimes du nazisme, 1933–1949*, Geneva: Labor et Fides, 2003.

Neufeld, Michael J. and Michael Berenbaum (eds), *The Bombing of Auschwitz: Should the Allies Have Attempted It?*, published with United States Holocaust Memorial Museum, New York: St. Martin's Press, 2000.

Nissim, Gabriele, *Il tribunale del bene. La storia di Moshe Beskj dalla lista di Schindler al Giardino dei giusti*, Milan: Mondadori, 2003 (translated as *Le Jardin des Justes*, Paris, Payot, 2007).

Novick, Peter, *L'Holocauste dans la vie américaine*, Paris: Gallimard, 2001 [1999].

Oliner, Samuel P. and Pearl M. Oliner, *The Altruistic Personality: Rescuers of Jews in Nazi Europe*, foreword by Rabbi Harold M. Schulweis, New York: The Free Press, 1988.

Paggi, Leonardo (ed.), *Le memorie della Repubblica*, Florence: La Nuova Italia, 1999.

Paldiel, Mordechai, *Saving the Jews, Amazing Stories of Men and Women who Defied the "Final Solution,"* Rockville (Md.): Schreiber Publishing, 2000.

———, *The Path of the Righteous: Gentile Rescuers of Jews During the Holocaust*, Hoboken: NJ, KTAV-JFCR-ADL, 1993.

Paulsson, Gunnar S., *Secret City: The Hidden Jews of Warsaw, 1940–1945*, New Haven (Conn.): Yale University Press, 2002.

Pavan, Ilaria and Guri Scharz (ed.), *Gli ebrei in Italia tra persecuzione fascista e reintegrazione postbellica*, Florence: Giuntina, 2001.

Phayer, Michael and Eva Fleischner, *Cries in the Night, Women who Challenged the Holocaust*, Kansas City (Mo.): Sheed and Ward, 1997.

Picard, Jacques, *La Suisse et les Juifs, 1933–1945. Antisémitisme suisse, défense du judaïsme, politique internationale envers les émigrants et les réfugiés*, translated from German, Lausanne, Éditions d'En Bas, 2000 [1re éd. 1997].

Picciotto-Fargion, Liliana, *Il libro della memoria*, Milan: Mursia, 2002.

Plas, Pascal and Michel C. Kiener (eds), *Enfances juives, Limousin-Dordogne-Berry, 1939–1945*, Saint-Paul: Souny, 2006.

Poliakov, Léon, *La Condition des Juifs en France sous l'occupation italienne*, Paris: Éditions du Centre, 1946.

——— and Jacques Sabille, *Jews under Italian Occupation*, Paris: Éditions du Centre, 1955.

Poznanski, Renée, *Être juif en France pendant la Seconde Guerre mondiale*, Paris: Hachette, 1994.
Prost, Antoine, Rémy Skoutelsky and Sonia Étienne (eds), *Aryanisation économique et restitutions*, Mission d'étude sur la spoliation des juifs de France, Paris: La Documentation Française, 2000.
Ramati, Alexander, *The Assisi Underground: The Priests Who Rescued Jews*, New York: Stein and Day, 1978.
Ranki, Vera, *The Politics of Inclusion and Exclusion: Jews and Nationalism in Hungary*, New York: Holmes and Meier, 1999.
Regard, Fabienne, *La Suisse, paradis de l'enfer? Mémoires de réfugiés suisses*, Geneva: Cabédita, 2002.
Reviriego, Bernard, *Les Juifs en Dordogne, 1939–1944, De l'accueil à la persécution*, Périgueux: Édition Fanlac, 2003.
Reymond, Bernard, *Une Église à croix gammée?*, Lausanne: L'Âge d'Homme, 1980.
Rodogno, Davide, *Il nuovo ordine mediterraneo. Le politiche di occupazione del'Italia fascista in Europa, 1940–1943*, Turin: Bollati Boringhieri, 2003.
Romijn, Peter, *Burgemeesters in Oorlogstijd. Besturen onder Duitse besetting*, Amsterdam: Balans, 2006.
Roseman, Mark, *The Past in Hiding*, London: Allen Lane, 2000.
Rubinstein, William D., *The Myth of Rescue: Why the Democracies Could Not Have Saved More Jews from the Nazis*, London: Routledge, 1997.
Rusconi, Gian Enrico, *Resistenza e postfascismo*, Bologna: Il Mulino, 1995.
Saerens, Lieven, *Vreemdelingen in een Wereldstad*, Tielt: Lannoo, 2000.
Samuel, Vivette, *Sauver les enfants*, Paris: Liana Levi, 1995.
Sarfatti, Michele (ed.), *Il ritorno alla vita: vicende e diritti degli ebrei dopo la seconda guerra mondiale*, Florence: Giuntina, 1998.
Sarfatti, Michele, *Gli ebrei nell'Italia fascista. Vicende, identità, persecuzione*, Turin: Einaudi, 2000.
Schenkel, M. J., *De Twentse Paradox. De lotgevallen van de joodse bevolking van Hengelo en Enschede tijdens de Tweede Wereldoorlog*, Zutphen: Walburg, 2003.
Schwarz, Guri, *Ritrovare se stessi. Gli ebrei nell'Italia postfascista*, Bari: Laterza, 2004.
Seaton, Jean and Ben Pimlott (eds), *The Media and British Politics*, Aldershot: Avebury, 1987.
Semelin, Jacques, *Unarmed Against Hitler. Civil Resistance in Nazi Europe (1939–1943)*, Westport (CT): Praeger, 1994 (French original *Sans armes face à Hitler. La résistance civile en Europe, 1939–1943*, Paris: Payot, 1996 [1989]).
Shulman, Holly Cowan, *The Voice of America: Propaganda and Democracy, 1941–1945*, Madison (Wis.): University of Wisconsin Press, 1990.
Snoek, J.M., *De Nederlandse Kerken en de Joden*, Kampen: Kok, 1990.
Soley, Lawrence C., *Radio Warfare: OSS and CIA Subversive Propaganda*, New York: Praeger, 1989.
Stárk, Tamas, "Hungary's Human Losses in World War II," *Uppsala Multiethnic Papers*, 33, Uppsala: Centre for Multiethnic Research, Uppsala University, 1995.

BIBLIOGRAPHY

Steinberg, Maxime, *L'Étoile et le Fusil*, tome 2: *1942. Les cent jours de la déportation des juifs de Belgique*, 4 volumes, Brussels: Vie Ouvrière, 1984.

Steinberg, Hans-Josef), *Widerstand Und Verfolgung in Essen, 1933–1945*, Hanover: Verlag für Literatur und Zeitgeschehen, 1969.

Tec, Nechama, *Dry Tears: The Story of a Lost Childhood*, Oxford: Oxford University Press, 1984 [1982].

―――― *When Light Pierced the Darkness: Christian Rescue of Jews in Nazi-Occupied Poland*, Oxford: Oxford University Press, 1986.

―――― *In The Lion's Den: The Life of Oswald Rufeisen*, Oxford: Oxford University Press, 1990.

―――― *Defiance: The Bielski Partisans*, Oxford: Oxford University Press, 1993.

―――― *Resilience and Courage: Women, Men, and the Holocaust*, New Haven (Conn.): Yale University Press, 2003.

Tranfaglia, Nicola, *Un passato scomodo. Fascismo e postfascismo*, Bari: Laterza, 1999 [1996].

Toscano, Mario (ed.), *L'abrogazione delle leggi razziali in Italia, 1943–1987. Reintegrazione dei diritti dei cittadini e ritorno ai valori del Risorgimento*, Rome: Senato della Repubblica, 1988.

Toscano, Mario, *La "porta di Sion." L'Italia e l'immigrazione clandestina ebraica in Palestina, 1945–1948*, Bologna: Il Mulino, 1990.

―――― *Ebraismo e antisemitismo in Italia. Dal 1848 alla guerra dei sei giorni*, Milan: Angeli, 2003.

Van Dongen, Luc, *La Suisse face à la Seconde Guerre mondiale, 1945–1948. Émergence et construction d'une mémoire politique*, Geneva: Société d'Histoire et d'Archéologie, 2000.

Verheyde, Philippe, *Les Mauvais Comptes de Vichy. L'aryanisation des entreprises juives*, Paris: Perrin, 1999.

Viallet, Jean-Pierre, *La chiesa valdese di fronte allo stato fascista 1922–1945*, foreword by Giorgio Rochat, Turin: Claudiana, 1985.

Wasserstein, Bernard, *Britain and the Jews of Europe, 1939–1945*, London: Leicester University Press, 1999.

Weinberg, David H., *A Community on Trial. The Jews of Paris in the 1930s*, Chicago: University of Chicago Press, 1977.

Weill, Joseph, *Contribution à l'histoire des camps d'internement dans l'Anti-France*, Paris: CDJD, 1946.

Welch, David, *The Third Reich: Politics and Propaganda*, London: Routledge, 1993.

Wieviorka, Annette, *Déportation et génocide: entre la mémoire et l'oubli*, Pari: Plon, 1992.

Wieviorka, Annette (ed.), *Justin Godart, un homme dans son siècle*, Paris: Éditions du CNRS, 2004.

Wulmann, Dr L. (ed.), *In Fight for the Health of the Jewish People (50 years of OSE)*, 2 volumes, New York: World Union OSE, 1968.

Wyman, David S., *The Abandonment of the Jews: America and the Holocaust, 1941–1945*, New York: Pantheon Books, 1984.

Wyman, David S. (ed.), *War Refugee Board: Special Problems*, volume 9: *America and the Holocaust*, New York: Garland Publishing, 1990.
Yagil, Limore, *Chrétiens et Juifs sous Vichy, 1940–1944. Sauvetage et désobéissance civile*, Paris: Éditions du Cerf, 2005.
Yahil, Leni, *The Holocaust: The Fate of European Jewry*, Oxford: Oxford University Press, 1990.
Zasloff, Tela, *A Rescuer's Story. Pastor Pierre-Charles Toureille in Vichy France*, Madison (Wis.), University of Wisconsin Press, 2003.
Zeitoun, Sabine, *Ces enfants qu'il fallait sauver*, Paris: Albin Michel, 1989.
―――― *L'Œuvre de secours aux enfants sous l'Occupation en France*, Paris: L'Harmattan, 1990.
Zunino, Pier Giorgio), *La Repubblica e il suo passato*, Bologna: Il Mulino, 2003.

The Genocide of the Tutsis

Adelman, Howard and Astri, Suhrke (eds), *The Path of A Genocide: The Rwanda Crisis from Uganda to Zaire*, New York: Transaction Publishers, 1999.
Angelucci, Maria Augusta, et al., *C'est ma taille qui m'a sauvée. Rwanda: de la tragédie à la reconstruction*, Johannesburg: Colorpress, 1997.
Bart, François, *Montagnes d'Afrique, terres paysannes: le cas du Rwanda*, Bordeaux: Presses Universitaires de Bordeaux, 1993.
Broch-due, Vigdis (ed.), *Violence and Belonging. The Quest for Identity in Post-Colonial Africa*, London: Routledge, 2005, pp. 195–213.
Crummey, Donald (ed.), *Banditry, Rebellion and Social Protest in Africa*, London: James Currey, 1986.
Des Forges, Alison, *Leave None to Tell the Story: Genocide in Rwanda*, New York: Human Rights Watch, 1999.
Doughty, Christin and David Moussa Ntambara, *Resistance and Protection: Muslim Community Actions during the Rwandan Genocide*, Cambridge (Mass.): Case Study, CDA-STEP, 2005.
Fierens, Jacques (ed.), *Femmes et Génocide: le cas rwandais*, Brussels: La Charte, 2003, pp. 75–112.
Guichaoua, André, *Rwanda 1994. Les politiques du génocide à Butare*, Paris: Karthala, 2005.
Hatzfeld, Jean, *Une saison de machettes*, Paris: Seuil, 2003.
Kagabo, José, *L'Islam et les "Swahili" au Rwanda*, Paris: Éditions de l'École des Hautes Etudes en Sciences Sociales, Paris, 1988.
Kayimahe, Vénuste, *France-Rwanda: les coulisses du génocide. Témoignage d'un rescapé*, Paris: Dagorno, 2002.
Lame, Danielle de, *A Hill among a Thousand, Transformations and Ruptures in Rural Rwanda*, Madison (Wis.): University of Wisconsin Press, Tervuren: Musée Royal de l'Afrique Centrale, 2005.
Mamdani, Mahmood, *When Victims Become Killers, Colonialism, Nativism, and the Genocide in Rwanda*, Princeton: Princeton University Press, 2001.
Melvern, Linda, *Conspiracy to Murder. The Rwandan Genocide*, London: Verso, 2004.

BIBLIOGRAPHY

Minear, Larry and Philippe Guillot, Soldiers to the rescue: Humanitarian lessons from Rwanda (also in French, *Soldats à la rescousse: Les leçons humanitaires des événements du Rwanda*), Paris: Organisation for Economic Cooperation and Development, 1996.

Nduwayo, Léonard, *Giti et le génocide rwandais*, Paris: L'Harmattan, 2002.

Neuffer, Elizabeth, *The Key to my Neighbor's House: Seeking Justice in Bosnia and Rwanda*, New York: Picador, 2001.

Quémener, Jean-Marie and Éric Bouvet, *Femmes du Rwanda. Veuves du génocide*, Paris: Catleya, 1999.

Reyntjens, Filip, *L'Afrique des Grands Lacs en crise. Rwanda, Burundi, 1988–1994*, Paris: Karthala, 1994.

Straus, Scott, *The Order of Genocide: Race, Power and War in Rwanda*, Ithaca: Cornell University Press, 2006.

Uvin, Peter, *Aiding Violence: The Development Enterprise in Rwanda*, Hartford (Conn.): Kumarian Press, 1998.

Articles

Adler, Jacques, "The 'Sin of Omission'? Radio Vatican and the Anti-Nazi Struggle, 1940–1942," *Australian Journal of Politics and History*, 50 (3), 2004, pp. 396–406.

"Ailleurs, hier, autrement: connaissance et reconnaissance du génocide des Arméniens," special issue, *Revue d'Histoire de la Shoah*, 177–178, Jan.-Aug. 2003.

Barozzi, Federica, "I percorsi della sopravvivenza: salvatori e salvati durante l'occupazione nazista di Roma (8 settembre 1943–4 giugno 1944)," *La Rassegna Mensile di Israel*, 64 (1), 1998, pp. 95–144.

Bensoussan, Georges and Michel Laffitte, "Les conseils juifs dans l'Europe allemande," *Revue d'Histoire de la Shoah*, 185, July–Dec. 2006.

Blom, J.C.H., "Gescheidenis, sociale wetenschappen, bezettingstijd en jodenvervolging. Een besprekingsartikel," *Bijdragen en Mededelingen betreffende de Geschiedenis der Nederlanden (BMGN)*, 70, 2005, pp. 562–80.

Bourgeois, Daniel, "La Suisse, les Suisses et la Shoah," *Revue d'Histoire de la Shoah*, 163, 1998, pp. 132–51.

Bruttmann, Tal, "L'action Brunner' à Grenoble (February–March 1944)," *Revue d'Histoire de la Shoah*, 174, January–April 2002, pp. 18–43.

Cole, Tim, "Constructing the 'Jew', Writing the History of the Holocaust: Hungary 1920–1945," *Patterns of Prejudice*, 33 (3), July 1999, pp. 19–27.

———, "Writing 'Bystanders' into Holocaust History in More Active Ways: 'Non-Jewish' Engagement with Ghettoisation, Hungary 1944," *Holocaust Studies: A Journal of Culture and History*, 11 (1), Summer 2005, pp. 55–74.

Croes, Marnix, "The Netherlands 1942–1945: Survival in Hiding and the Hunt for Hidden Jews," *The Netherlands' Journal of Social Sciences*, 40 (2), 2004, pp. 157–75.

———, "De zesde fase? Holocaust en geschiedschriving," *Bijdragen en Mededelingen betreffende de Geschiedenis der Nederlanden*, CXXI, 2006, pp. 292–301.

———, "The Holocaust in the Netherlands and the Rate of Jewish Survival," *Holocaust and Genocide Studies*, 20 (3), 2006, pp. 474–99.

Encrevé, André and Poujol, Jacques), "Les protestants français pendant la Seconde Guerre mondiale," *Bulletin de la Société de l'Histoire du Protestantisme Français*, 3, 1994.

Feingold, Henry, "'Courage First and Intelligence Second': The American Jewish Secular Elite, Roosevelt and the Failure to Rescue," *American Jewish History*, 72 (4), 1983, pp. 424–60.

Felstiner, Mary, "Commandant de Drancy: Aloïs Brunner et les juifs de France," *Le Monde Juif*, 128, 1987, pp. 143–72.

Fivaz-Silbermann, Ruth, "Refoulement, accueil, filières: les réfugiés juifs à la frontière franco-genevoise entre 1942 et 1944," *Revue Suisse d'Histoire*, 51, 2001, pp. 296–317.

Focardi, Filippo, "La memoria della guerra e il mito del 'bravo italiano'. Origine e affermazione di un autoritratto collettivo," *Italia Contemporanea*, 220–221, 2000, pp. 393–9.

Fogelman, Eva and Valerie Lewis Wiener, "The Few, the Brave, the Noble," *Psychology Today*, 19, 1985, pp. 60–5.

Garel, Georges, "L'OSE sous l'occupation allemande en France," in *L'activité des organisations juives en France sous l'Occupation*, Paris: Éditions du centre, 1983, pp. 117–79.

Gensburger, Sarah, "L'émergence de la catégorie de Juste parmi les nations comme paradigme mémoriel. Réflexions contemporaines sur le rôle socialement dévolu à la mémoire," in Carola Hähnel-Mesnard, Marie Liénard-Yeterian and Cristina Marinas (eds), *Culture et Mémoire*, Paris: Éditions de l'École Polytechnique, 2008, pp. 25–32.

———, "Les figures du 'Juste' et du résistant et l'évolution de la mémoire historique française de l'Occupation," *Revue Française de Science Politique*, 52 (2–3), 2002, pp. 291–322.

———, "La création du titre de Juste parmi les nations, 1953–1963," *Bulletin du Centre de Recherche Français de Jérusalem*, 15, 2004, pp. 15–35.

———, "La sociologue et l'actualité. Retour sur 'l'Hommage de la Nation aux 'Justes' de France'," *Genèses*, 68, Sept. 2007, pp. 116–31.

——— and Agnieszka Niewiedzial-Bédu, "Figure du Juste et politique publique de la mémoire en Pologne: entre relations diplomatiques et structures sociales," *Critique Internationale*, 34, January–March 2007, pp. 27–148.

Gerlach, Christian, "The Wannsee Conference, the Fate of the German Jews, and Hitler's Decision in Principle to Exterminate All European Jews," *Journal of Modern History*, 70, 4, December 1998, pp. 759–812.

Griffioen, Pim and Ron Zeller, "The Persecution of the Jews: Comparing Belgium and the Netherlands," *The Netherlands' Journal of Social Sciences*, 34 (2), 1998, pp. 126–64.

Herf, Jeffrey, "The 'Jewish War': Goebbels and the Antisemitic Campaigns of the Nazi Propaganda Ministry," *Holocaust and Genocide Studies*, 19 (1), Spring 2005, pp. 51–80.

BIBLIOGRAPHY

Jefremovas, Villia, "Acts of Human Kindness: Tutsi, Hutu and the Genocide," *Issue: A Journal of Opinion*, 23 (2), 1995, pp. 28–31.

Jefroykin, Jules, Dika, "Témoignage de Jules Jefroykin," *Echanges: Périodique Consacré aux Oeuvres Juives de Santé, d'Assistance Sociale et d'Education*, 20, 1964, pp. 22–4.

Lammers, Cornelis J., "Persecution in the Netherlands during World War Two. An Introduction," *The Netherlands' Journal of Social Sciences*, 34 (2), 1998, pp. 111–25.

Marrus, Michael R. and Robert O. Paxton, "The Nazis and the Jews in Occupied Western Europe 1940–1944," *Journal of Modern History*, 54, 1982, pp. 687–714.

Matard-Bonucci, Marie-Anne, "L'antisémitisme en Italie: les discordances entre la mémoire et l'histoire," *Hérodote*, 89, 1998, pp. 217–38.

Miccoli, Giovanni, "Tra memoria, rimozioni e manipolazioni: aspetti dell'atteggiamento cattolico verso la Shoah," *Qualestoria*, 19 (2–3), 1991, pp. 161–88.

———, "Cattolici e comunisti nel secondo dopoguerra: memoria storica, ideologia e lotta politica," *Studi storici*, 38 (4), 1997, pp. 951–91.

Milland, Gabriel, "The BBC Hungarian Service and the Final Solution in Hungary," *Historical Journal of Film, Radio and Television*, 18 (3), 1998, pp. 353–73.

Mironko, Charles, "*Igitero*: Means and Motive in the Rwandan Genocide," *Journal of Genocide Research*, 6 (1), 2004, pp. 47–60.

Moore, Bob, "The Rescue of Jews from Nazi Persecution: A Western European Perspective," *Journal of Genocide Research*, 5 (2), 2003, pp. 293–308.

———, "The Rescue of Jews in Nazi-Occupied Belgium, France and the Netherlands," *Australian Journal of Politics and History*, 50 (3), 2004, pp. 385–95.

Newbury, David), "Understanding Genocide," *African Studies Review*, 41 (1), April 1998, pp. 73–97.

Pavone, Claudio, "La Resistenza oggi: problema storiografico e problema civile," *Rivista di Storia Contemporanea*, 21 (2–3), 1992, pp. 456–81.

———, "La Resistenza in Italia: memoria e rimozione," *Rivista di Storia Contemporanea*, 23–24 (4), 1994–1995, pp. 484–92.

Peck, Sarah, "The Campaign for an American Response to the Nazi Holocaust, 1943–1945," *Journal of Contemporary History*, 15 (2), 1980, pp. 367–400.

Penkower, Monty, "Jewish Organizations and the Creation of the U. S. War Refugee Board," *The Annals*, 450, 1980, pp. 122–39.

Poliakov, Léon, "Mussolini and the Extermination of the Jews," *Jewish Social Studies*, 11 (3), 1949.

Poznanski, Renée, "A Methodological Approach to the Study of Jewish Resistance in France," *Yad Vashem Studies*, 18, 1987, pp. 1–39.

Roseman, Mark, "Ein Mensch in Bewegung. Dore Jacobs, 1894–1978," *Essener Beiträge. Beiträge zur Geschichte von Stadt und Stift Essen*, 114, 2002, pp. 73–109.

———, "Gerettete Geschichte. 'Der Bund'. Gemeinschaft Für Sozialistisches Leben Im Dritten Reich," *Mittelweg*, 36 (16), 2007, pp. 100–21.

———, "Gespräche Und Lektüren Zum Körper," BIOS 20, (no.) Sonderheft: "Kritische Erfahrungsgeschichte und grenzüberschreitende Zusammenarbeit. The Networks of Oral History," 2007, pp. 75–81

Sarafian, Ara, "The Disasters of Mardin during the Persecutions of the Christians, Especially the Armenians, 1915," *Haigazian Armenological Review*, 18, 1998, pp. 261–92.

Shulman, Holly Cowan, "The Voice of America, US Propaganda and the Holocaust: 'I Would Have Remembered'," *Historical Journal of Film, Radio and Television*, 17 (1), 1997, pp. 91–105.

Spini, Giorgio, "Gli evangelici italiani di fronte alle leggi razziali," *Il ponte*, 11–12, 1978.

Varese, Frederico and Meir Yaish, "The Importance of Being Asked. The Rescue of Jews in Nazi Europe," *Rationality and Society*, 12 (3), 2000, pp. 307–34.

Verwimp, Philip, "An Economic Profile of Peasant Perpetrators of Genocide. Micro-level Evidence from Rwanda," *Elsevier*, 77 (2), Aug. 2005, pp. 297–323, available online: http://ideas.repec.org/s/eee/deveco.html/.

Vidal, Claudine, "Questions sur le rôle des paysans durant le génocide des Rwandais Tutsi," *Cahiers d'Etudes Africaines*, 38 (150–152), 1998, pp. 331–45.

Wagner, Michele D., "All the Bourgmestre's Men: Making Sense of Genocide in Rwanda," *Africa Today*, 45 (1), January–March 1998.

Weill, Georges, "Le sauvetage des enfants juifs en France," *Revue des Etudes Juives*, 163 (3–4), July–Dec. 2004, pp. 507–16.

Weill, Georges, Katy Hazan and Ruth Fivaz-Silbermann, "Joseph Weill," in *Nouveau Dictionnaire de Biographie Alsacienne*, 48, pp. 5011–16.

INDEX OF NAMES

Abdulhamid: 44, 212, 385
Abdülhalik (Mustafa): 191, 372
  German Military Administration (Militärbefehlshaber in Frankreich): 58
Ador (Gustave): 225–226
Aga Azaizoglu (Mustafa): 192
Jewish Agency for Palestine: 305
Akayesu (Jean-Paul): 333, 339–341
Akçam (Taner): 165, 196, 511
Ali (Batti): 390
Ali (Fuad): 374
Ali (Suad): 198
Ali Bey (Mehmed): 184, 191, 195
Allied forces: 48, 52, 55, 179, 301
American Committee for Armenian and Syrian Relief (Near East Relief): 168, 179–180, 373, 382, 503, 508
American Friends Service Committee (see Quakers): 98, 253, 503
American Jewish Joint Distribution ("Joint") Committee (JDC): 132, 160, 242, 246–247, 249–250, 253–255, 257, 261, 293–311, 401, 407, 503, 507, 512
Amitié Chrétienne (Christian Friendship): 54, 60, 97, 98, 365, 407, 425–426
Andry (Georges): 401

Antirevolutionnary Party (Netherlands): 453
Araxia: 380–381
Armalé (Father): 388
Armée Juive (La Main Forte, B'nei David, Organisation Juive de Combat): 300–301, 303, 310
Arnold (Matthew): 443
Aron (Raymond): 86
Atıf Bey: 193
Azéma (Vincent): 271

Baerwald (Paul): 294–295, 307
Bagh Effendi: 173
Baghdad: 190, 192, 392
Baghdad Railway: 372, 390, 392
Bahaeddin (Sakir): 39, 188
Bajyanama (Augustin): 351
Barrès (Maurice): 439
Bauernfeind (Hans): 192–193
Baur (André): 399–400
BBC (British Broadcasting Corporation): 11, 89, 92, 94, 162, 216, 313–329, 523
Bedreddin (Ibrahim): 387
Bejski (Moshe): 3, 164
Berr (Hélène): 402–403
Bethmann-Hollweg (Theobald von): 208, 376
Bettex (Pastor): 433

525

INDEX OF NAMES

Bèze (Théodore de): 436
Blank (Karl): 370
Bloch (Marc): 86
Blum (Léon): 93–94, 304
Boegner (Pastor Marc): 425, 438, 508
Boos (Pastor Jan van den): 463
Borel (René): 404
Born (Frédéric): 227
Bousquet (René): 60, 117, 254, 272
Bramesfeld (Else): 471–472, 474–475, 515
Brandt (Trude): 471, 475
Braun (Father Roger): 28–29
Braunschweig (Saly): 235
Brener (Maurice): 301–302, 304, 308–309, 401, 404
British Political Warfare Executive (PWE): 317, 321
Brooks (Howard): 97,
Broughey (Peter): 323–324
Brousson (Claude): 437
Brull (Colonel): 402
Brunner (Alois): 61, 161, 280–283, 285, 287–290, 505, 522
Brunswick (Joseph): 257
Büll (Hedwig): 378
Bund: Gemeinschaft für sozialistisches Leben: 465, 474, 524
Bunel (Lucien, Father Jacques): 61
Burckhardt (Carl J.): 224, 235

Calvin (Jean), calvisim: 30, 79–80, 274, 364, 433–436, 439–441, 443–444, 451–452, 454, 458–459, 461
Cantoni (Raffaele): 136
Cassin (René): 87, 403
Cemal Sagiroglu (Sabit): 191
Çetin (Fethiye): 213, 216
Cevdet Bey: 187, 189, 197

Chah (Ibrahim): 194
Chaigneau (Jean): 122
Chaillet (Reverend Father Pierre): 60, 365, 425
Chaumet (Captain): 405
Chevalley-Sabatier (Lucie): 403
Chevrier (Jules Félix): 405
Cohen (Herman): 468
Colijn (Heindrik): 450–451, 453
Combat: 91–93, 96
Comenius (Jean-Amos): 438
Comète: 54
Comité Amelot: 54, 98, 252, 269
Comité d'action pour le sauvetage des enfants: 258
Committee for Refugee Children in unoccupied France: 250
Comité d'assistance aux réfugiés: 302
Comité de défense des juifs (CDJ— Jewish Defense Committee): 269
Comité de Nîmes: 250, 254, 256, 298,
Search Committee for Deported Jews (CRDE, Italy): 131, 137
Committee for the Care of European Children: 255,
Comité français pour Yad Vashem (CFYV): 413, 419, 426
Comité National des Unions Chrétiennes des Jeunes de France: 283
Free France Committee: 315
Amerose (OSE committee in the United States): 253, 262–263
Committee for the celebration of the 10th anniversary of Liberation: 139
Committee for Jewish Refugees: 269
CUP (Committee of Union and Progress): 40, 41, 43–48, 173, 183,

INDEX OF NAMES

186, 188–190, 193–194, 196, 203, 205, 209, 211, 213, 377, 383, 386
Commissariat-General for Jewish Questions (CGQJ): 116, 118–120, 122, 401, 420
Commission des Camps des Oeuvres Israélites d'Assistance aux Réfugiés: 256
Memorial Commission: 335
Committee for the Gardens of the Righteous Worldwide: 180
Communist Party of Italy (PCI): 134, 141
Compagnons de France: 283
Conseil National de la Résistance: 55
Conseil Représentatif des israélites de France (CRIF): 261
Consistoire central israélite de France: 301, 302, 395
Croux (Paul): 290
Curtet (Pastor): 433

Darcissac (Roger): 60, 433
Dauphin (Edmond): 405–406
Davids (Ish, known as Peter): 457
Davis (Leslie): 166, 192, 508
Deltour (Yvonne): 27–28
Christian Democratic Party (CD): 134, 141
Desbons (Jean): 121, 125
Devaux (Reverend Father Théomir): 403, 421
Didier (Roland): 404–405
Dink (Hrant): 165
Djevdet Bey: 169
Donati (Angelo): 281–282
Douwes (Arnold): 433, 448, 451, 501, 454, 456–460, 463, 514
Drumont (Edouard): 439

Éclaireurs Israélites de France (EIF): 241, 286, 400
Éclaireurs Unionistes de France: 283
Edinger (Georges): 399
Education physique: 282
Eichmann (Adolf): 3, 21, 22, 128, 130, 143, 280–282, 291, 326
Einsatzgruppen: 314
Einstein (Albert): 246, 250, 262–263
Elia (Raoul): 140
Entraide temporaire: 403, 422
Enver Pacha: 169
Escarra (Jean): 87–88
Eskijian (Hovhannes): 368, 374, 378

Faik Ali Bey: 195
Falchi (Mario): 441
Falkenhausen (Alexander von): 270
Federation of Young Italian Jews (FGEI): 141
Fédération des Sociétés Juives de France (FSJF): 300–302, 304
Fehmi Bey: 196
Ferik Bey: 191
French Protestant Federation: 438, 443
Fisera (Josef): 438
Fisher (Ariel, Joseph): 295, 303, 310
Jehovah's Witnesses: 434, 444, 477
Jewish National Fund (KKL): 303
Foreign Affairs Ministry (Italy): 134–136
Foreign Office (British): 315–317, 324–325
(German): 371
Franc-Tireur: 58, 91–92
Frenay (Henri): 89, 92
Fresco (Raymond): 282

Gaillard (Philippe): 229
Gamzon (Robert): 400–401

INDEX OF NAMES

Gans (Lou, known as Herman): 457–458, 460
Garabed: 374, 379–380
Garel (Georges): 256–257, 522
Gaudefroy (Pauline): 27
Gaulle (Charles de): 88, 94, 238
Geissmann (Raymond): 407–408
Gereformeerde Kerk (Dutch Reformed Church): 452, 457, 461
Gerlier (Cardinal Pierre): 90, 275, 407
Gerson (Tove): 470–471
Grand Seminary of Nyakibanda: 351, 353
Guiolet (Jean): 120–121
Gurvic (Lazare): 249, 251
Gutmann (Claude): 282–283

Habyarimana (Jean-Baptiste): 347
Habyarimana (Juvénal): 149, 152, 333–334, 346–347, 482, 489, 492
Haguenau (Marc): 285–286
Haidar (Ali): 390
Haig: 380
Hakkı Bey (Ibrahim): 191
Hakkı Bey (Ismail): 196
Halide (Edib): 377
Hamdi Bey (Mehmed): 191
Hamon (Léo): 88–89
Hauben (Herta): 285
Hautval (Adelaide): 61, 508
Helpers: 51–59, 356–357, 495, 500
  (paid): 105–107
Hermann (Nahum): 303
Hervormde Kerk (Dutch Protestant Church): 452
Hillesum (Etty): 181
Hilmi Bey: 190, 388
Hilmi Filibeli (Ahmed): 188
Hitler (Adolf): 9, 54, 85–86, 91–92, 125, 164, 224, 236, 247, 253, 282, 313, 318, 450, 479, 501, 513, 516, 518, 523
Hocazâde Rasık (family): 195
Hoffnung (Marthe): 83
Horthy (Admiral): 325
Huber (Max): 225–226
Hülfsbund für christliches Liebeswerk im Orient: 364, 367, 369
Hus (Jean): 438

Institut d'étude des questions juives et ethnoraciales (IEQJ—Institute for Jewish and Ethnoracial Studies): 118
Interahamwe: 149–151, 155–156, 337, 339, 347–348, 357, 490
International Committee of the Red Cross (ICRC): 160, 219, 222, 224, 229, 234, 248, 512
International Criminal Tribunal for Rwanda: 333, 339–340, 507
Israel (State of): 2–4, 16, 20, 22–23, 26–31, 56–57, 130–131, 135–139, 247, 262, 304, 435, 441, 444–445, 447, 501
Israelowicz (Leo): 398

Jackson (Jesse): 168, 185, 373
Jacob (Lisa): 467, 470–473
Jacobites: 385–388, 390–391
Jacobs (Artur): 465, 467–468, 470, 472–475, 478
Jacobs (Dore): 468–469, 471–473, 476–478, 515, 524
Jarblum (Marc): 304, 306–307, 309
Jefroykin (Israel): 301
Jefroykin (Jules): 160, 293, 298–304, 307–311, 523
Jelal Bey: 372
Jemal Pasha: 367, 372
Jensen (Anna): 373

INDEX OF NAMES

Jewish committee for children coming from Germany and Central Europe: 253
Jezler (Robert): 237
Jordan (Hannah): 471
Judenrat: 320, 326, 396–398

Kahn (Madeleine): 285
Kaiser (Hilmar): 168, 368, 371–372, 511
Kállay (Miklós): 324
Kâmil (Mahmud): 187–188
Kannengieser (Monsignor Alphonse): 439
Kant (Immanuel): 468, 474–475, 477
Karuhimbi (Sula): 505
Kemal Bey: 376
Kermiyanzâde (family): 195
Khalil Agha: 390
Klein (Théo): 83–84
Knochen (Helmut): 280
Knokploegen: 456
Kress von Kressenstein (General Friedrich): 372
Krombach (David): 465
Kuciukian (Pietro): 180–181
Künzler (Jakob): 368, 370, 377, 382, 508
Kuyper (Abraham): 452–453

L'Avant-garde: 90
Labarthe (André): 92–93
Lambert (Raymond-Raoul): 302, 398, 401, 404–405, 509
Lambert (Ruth): 258–260
Landelijke Knockploegen (LKP): 458
Landelijke Organisatie voor Hulp aan Onderduikers (LO): 458
Lauterborn (Felix): 273

Law (Derek): 316
Lazard (Didier): 401
League of Nations: 232
Léon (Frédéric): 403
Léons (Max Nico): 452, 456–459, 462
Lepsius (Dr Johannes): 164, 369, 507, 509
Lévy (Gaston): 406
Lévy (Paul): 402
Liberal Party of Italy (PLI): 141
Liberal Party of Rwanda (PL): 483, 488
Libération: 90–92, 482
Liman von Sanders (general Otto): 196
Loinger (Georges): 257–258, 405, 516
Lowrie (Donald): 98, 250
Lutz (Carl): 382

Macartney (Carlisle Aylmer): 321–323, 327
Manughian (Sisag): 372, 378
Margolis (Laura): 309
Maritain (Jacques): 87
Martenot (Ginette): 401
Maurras (Charles): 439, 443
Mayer (Raymonde): 414
Mayer (Saly): 242, 249, 257, 299, 303–304, 307–308, 310
Mazhar Bey (Hasan): 190
Meir (Golda): 21, 23
Memduh (Koranli): 387
Ménard (Abbey Armand): 401
Menthonnex (family): 289
Meyer (Germaine): 282–283
Meyer (Karl): 226, 377–378, 511
Michels (Erna): 471, 473
Miegge (Giovanni): 442
Milhaud (Denise): 403

INDEX OF NAMES

Milhaud (Dr Alfred alias Fred): 403
Military Intelligence: 54
Millner (Joseph): 400
Minas (from Bunduk): 379
Minassian (John): 374, 378
Minkowski (Dr Eugène): 251–252
Monbrison (Hubert de): 251
Monika (network): 286–287
Montagne (Henri): 404
Morgenthau (Henry): 164, 194, 197, 371, 509
Mosdorf (Jan): 108
Mossé (Alain-Raoul): 285, 404
Moulin (Jean): 89–90
Mouvement démocratique républicain (MDR): 483, 488–489, 493
Mouvement révolutionnaire national pour le développement (MRND): 488–489
Mouvement Révolutionnaire National pour la Démocratie et le Développement (MRNDD): 333–335, 337, 341, 488–490, 492–493
Moynier (Gustave): 222–223, 225
Murray (Ralph): 321–322
Murtula beg: 189
Muslim Association of Rwanda (Association des musulmans du Rwanda-AMUR): 485–486, 489, 494
Mustapha Bey: 215

Nadji Bey: 190
Namier (Lewis B.): 325
National Association for Reconstruction (Karen Hayessod): 303
Near East Relief: *see* American Committee for Armenian and Syrian Relief
Nesimî (Abidin): 44

Nesimî (Hüseyin): 41–49, 190–191
Nissim (Gabriele): 3, 23, 164, 181, 517
Nowodworski (Leon): 108
NSB (National socialist movement in the Netherlands): 462–463
NSKK (pro-Nazi Netherlands militia): 462
Ntahiganayo (Pascal): 351
Nuri Bey (commandant): 196
Nusret Bey (Mehmed): 189
Nyandwi (Charles): 336–337, 339, 341

O'Leary (Pat): 54
Oeuvre de Secours aux Enfants (OSE): 27, 54, 160, 161, 241, 245–253–262, 281, 285, 301–302, 304, 309, 400, 404–406, 420, 500, 502, 509, 515–516, 520, 522
Oeuvres Sociales Israélites d'Alsace et de Lorraine: 255
Organisation, Reconstruction, Travail (ORT): 248, 260
Otten (Seine): 456
Ottoman War Academy: 156
OZANIAN (Andranik), General Andranik: 168, 180

Papanek (Ernst): 251, 253, 509
Paulsson, (Gunnar S.): 467, 497, 499, 517
Peet (William): 185, 371, 373
Pehle (John W.): 326
Permilleux (Charles): 402
Philip (Mireille): 433
Pineau (Christian): 91
Piperno (Sergio): 139, 143
Platteau (Léon): 28
Pleven (René): 87–88
Poirier (Pierrette): 407

INDEX OF NAMES

Poliakov (Léon): 136, 138, 142–143, 396, 517, 524
Police for Jewish Questions (PQJ): 116, 125
Post (Johannes): 364, 433–434, 451, 454–456, 458
Protestant American Board of Commissioners of Foreign Missions (ABCFM): 371, 503
Proudhon (Pierre-Joseph): 440
Pulver (Édith): 286
Pury (Pastor Roland de): 425

Quakers (American Friends Service Committee): 250, 253–254, 305

Rabaut (Jean): 97
Rahmi (Mustafa): 196
Randall (Walter): 325
Rauter (Hermann): 455
Ravished Armenia or Auction of Saints: 168, 511
Rechid Bey(Dr Mehmed): 509
Renault (Odette): 123–125
Renda (Abdulhalik Mustafa): 372
Rhétoré (Jacques): 190, 387, 389
Riegner (Gerhart): 136, 235, 238, 306, 314
Riggenbach (Emanuel): 376
Righteous among the Nations: 2–4, 8, 10, 13, 15–33, 37, 49, 53, 55–57, 61–62, 101–102, 106, 108, 112, 121, 128, 130, 138–139, 143, 163–63, 169, 171, 176, 181, 203–204, 265, 329, 366, 368, 406, 413, 417–426, 431, 433–434, 438, 447, 451, 460, 479, 499, 501, 505, 508, 511, 514–515, 517
Riggs (Henry): 174, 192, 509
Robini (Doctor): 406
Roey (Monsignor van): 275

Rohner (Beatrice): 168, 363–365, 367–82, 503
Roos (Joseph): 282
Roosevelt (Eleanor): 255
Roosevelt (Franklin D.): 305, 317, 326
Rosenman (Samuel): 326
Rössler (Walter): 168, 255, 370, 373, 374–76,
Röthke (Heinz): 279–83, 289
Rothmund (Heinrich): 233, 235–40, 258
Rothschild (Germaine de): 251
Rothschild (Guy de): 253
Rwandan Patriotic Front (FPR): 6, 147–148, 150–152, 335–336, 338, 340–42, 346, 352–353, 355, 358

Şahingiray: *see* Rechid (Dr Mehmed)
Said Bey: 195
Saint-Vincent (General): 60
Salamon (Andrew): 319
Salih Zeki: 374
Salomon (Andrée): 256–257, 319
Sariac (René de): 401
Sasson (David): 391
Schäfer (Paula): 372
Scheid-Haas (Lucienne): 400–402, 408
Schendel (Kurt): 398
Schindler (Oskar): 3–4, 23, 517
Schmitz (Änne): 472, 479
Schneider (Nicole): 403
Schreiber (Emmi): 473
Schuchardt (Friedrich): 370–372, 378
Schüepp (Conrad): 373
Schwartz (Dr Joseph): 250, 293, 298–311
Schwartz (Lotte): 260
Schwarzenberg (Jean-Étienne de): 234

531

INDEX OF NAMES

Schweizerische Israelitische Gemeinschaft (SIG): 249–250, 257
Schwob (Odette): 405, 407
Sebashongore (Augustin): 353
Sebushumba (Édouard): 334–335, 337, 339, 341
Seligman (Eva): 471
Selim Agha: 171
Service de Contrôle des Administrateurs Provisoires (SCAP): 115, 118, 121, 123
  Department for Restitution of Property of Victims of the Legislation and Spoliation Measures: 116
Service social des jeunes (SSJ—Youth social service): 285–286
Service Social d'Aide aux Emigrants (SSAE): 403, 422
Setrag: 380
Seyss-Inquart (Arthur): 270, 450
Shakir: 188, 387
Shepard (Fred): 371
Shero (Hamo): 391–93, 504
Sicherheitspolizei (Sipo-SD): 273, 280–281, 283–284, 287, 463
Sindahuga (Alexis): 351
Sinder (Henri): 86
Sindikubwabo (Isaie): 354
Sindikubwabo (Théodore): 349
Sixième (La): 282, 400
Slomp (Frits): 364, 434, 451, 454, 458, 461
Social-Democratic Party of Italy (PSDI): 141
Socialist Party of Italy (PSI): 141
  OZE (Russian Jewish Welfare Association): 245–248
Soulier (Cyprien): 289, 290
Spears (M.J.A.): 324

Special Operations Executive (SOE): 317, 323, 324
Special Organization (Turkey): 44, 45, 48, 167, 171, 186, 191–193
Spolianski (Grégoire): 282
SS: 58–61, 68–69, 80, 161, 254–55, 266, 270, 272–71, 282, 285–89, 326, 399–400, 457, 462–63
Steiger (Eduard von): 233, 235–236, 239
Stern (Juliette): 399–400
Stimson (Henry L.): 316–317
Stockmayer (Otto): 369
Strauss (Marianne): 465–67, 471–472
Streicher (Julius): 236
Stülpnagel (General von): 58
Suhard (Cardinal Emmanuel): 399
Swiss Red Cross: 233

Tahsin Bey (Hasan): 187–188, 195, 388
Talât (Mehmed): 191, 195
Tappouni (Monsignor Gabriel Tappouni): 387–89
Terroine (Émile): 116, 119, 123
Tevfik Bey: 196
Theis (Pastor): 60, 433
Tissier (Pierre): 87
Tisza (Koloman): 439
Toussenel (Alphonse): 439–440
Towarzystwo Ochrony Zdrowia (TOZ): 248–249
Trocmé (André, Pastor): 439, 440
Trocmé (Daniel): 60–61, 433
Troper (Morris): 299
Trouw (network): 458–459
Tschlenoff (Dr Boris): 247–250, 258–259, 262
Tulp (Sybren): 272
  Italian Union of Israelite Communities (UCII): 131

INDEX OF NAMES

Union des Juifs pour la Résistance et l'entraide (Jewish Union for resistance and mutual help, dedicated to the situation in Nice—UJRE): 282, 288
Union Générale des Israélites de France (UGIF): 252, 269, 281, 298, 365, 395, 399
Universal Israelite Alliance: 246
Unitarian Service Committee: 97
United Jewish Appeal (UJA): 294

Vaad Hatzalah: 304–305
Valabrègue (Alfred): 401–402
Vallat (Xavier): 122, 401
Valobra (Lelio): 140
Vatican: 129, 133, 135, 137, 386, 521
Vergara (Paul): 421
Vichy (government): 9–10, 58–61, 63, 83, 85–89, 95, 97–98, 117, 119, 125, 161, 237–239, 245, 250, 254–256, 270–273, 279–280, 284–285, 288, 295–296, 298, 301, 311, 365, 395–400, 402, 405–406, 411, 414, 420, 499, 511, 513–515, 519–520
Vischer (Andreas): 370, 373

War Refugee Board: 294, 305, 326, 520, 524

Wegner (Armin): 164, 509
Weill (Dr Joseph): 248, 256–258, 260, 304, 519, 524
Weill-Hallé (Benjamin): 400, 403
Weintrob (Jacques): 282–283
World Jewish Congress: 87, 98, 132, 136, 234–235, 238, 304–305, 307, 310–311, 314

Yad Vashem: 2, 4–5, 7, 19–27, 29, 31–32, 49, 57, 61, 72, 76, 89, 101–102, 108, 112, 120, 128, 138–139, 146, 163–164, 268, 296, 304, 413, 422, 433, 447, 449, 451–452, 457–460, 462, 467, 479, 499, 507–508, 512, 515, 517
Youth Men Christian Association (YMCA): 98, 250, 253

Zeki (Salih): 44, 374
Zitter (Prosper de): 273
Ziya Bey (Yusuf): 197
Zionist Youth Movement (ZYM): 241
Zollinger (Emil): 373, 377
Zuylen (Thea van): 456
Zwaag (Frederika): 456–457
Zwaag (Hemke van der): 456–457
Zygielbojm (Shmuel): 314

INDEX OF PLACES

Adana: 196–197, 219
Africa, North: 44, 255, 296, 301, 316–317
Ainteb: 371
Akanyaru: *see* Kanyaru (river, Rwanda/Burundi)
Aleppo (Syria): 168, 179, 184–186, 194–195, 198, 210, 363, 367–368, 370–381, 388, 390, 503
Alpes-Maritimes (France): 122
Amsterdam (Netherlands): 214–215, 239, 269, 272, 448–449, 459–460, 516
Angora (Ottoman Empire): 193, 195
Antwerp (Belgium): 241, 268, 272, 516
Assen (Netherlands): 461
Auschwitz (Poland): 6, 60–62, 108, 115, 234, 240–241, 280, 283, 286, 288, 300, 321, 327–328, 426, 454, 509, 517
Austria: 67, 319, 327, 439, 450

Baghdad (Ottoman empire): 190, 192, 372, 390, 392
Basel (Switzerland): 132, 136, 367–371, 376, 378, 503
Basel (Switzerland): 132, 136, 367–368, 370, 376, 503
Bayazed (Ottoman Empire): 173

Bayburt (Ottoman Empire): 189
Belgium: 66–67, 161, 224, 261, 265–272, 275, 277, 305, 365, 395, 399, 467, 501, 507, 517, 523
Berlin: 6, 11, 39, 246–248, 270, 281, 283, 290, 298, 324, 424, 467, 472
Birkenau (Poland): 131, 234, 509
Bitlis (Ottoman Empire): 187, 189, 191, 216, 383, 386
Bohemia (Czech republic): 434, 437, 440
Brussels: 241–242, 268,
Buchenwald (Germany): 247, 262, 515
Budapest (Hungary): 1, 222, 227, 234, 318, 320, 327–328, 382, 512
Butare (Rwanda): 336, 339, 347, 354–355, 360–361, 492, 499, 520

Cévennes (France): 12, 442, 499, 515
Chambéry (France): 285, 404
Châteaubriant (France): 115
Constance (Lake, Switzerland/Germany): 472
Constantinople: 42, 166–167, 184–186, 188, 190, 192–197, 214, 371, 377, 387

Den Haag (Netherlands): 72

INDEX OF PLACES

Der-el-Zor: *see* Der Zor (Syria) / Deir ez Zor: Deir al-Zaafaran (Ottoman Empire)
Der Zor (Ottoman Empire): 207, 368, 370, 374–375, 377, 379–380, 503, 511
Dersim (Ottoman Empire): 192
Diarbekir (Ottoman Empire): 45, 187, 189–191, 212–216, 384–387, 390, 499
Dink (Hrant): 165
Diyarbekir: *see* Diarbekir (Ottoman Empire)
Djezireh (Ottoman Empire): 385, 390
Drancy (France): 62, 114–115, 239, 280, 282–283, 290–291, 399, 402, 405–406, 412, 414, 426, 429, 522
Drenthe (Netherlands): 433, 452, 454, 456, 459, 462–463
Dspni, Kars (Ottoman Empire): 168

Erzerum (Ottoman Empire): 187–187, 190, 214, 383
Erznka (Ottoman Empire): 173
Essen (Germany): 363, 465–466, 468–470, 472–474, 479, 515, 519, 524

France: 3, 9–10, 12, 15–16, 18, 24–32, 35, 51, 53–63, 66–67, 75, 78, 83–93, 95, 97–99, 113, 116, 119–122, 128, 136, 143, 159–161, 191, 212, 238–242, 245–258, 260–262, 265, 267–276, 279–283, 286–290, 293, 294–311, 315, 358, 363, 365–366, 391, 393, 395–403, 405–406, 411–415, 420–424, 428, 434, 438–441, 443–444, 467, 497–503, 505, 507–508, 511–520, 522–524

Friesland (Netherlands): 447, 455–456

Geneva (Switzerland): 98, 219–220, 225–227, 234–235, 239–240, 242, 246–250, 255, 257–258, 260–261, 303, 401
Germany: 2–3, 6, 10, 22, 35, 53, 58, 66–67, 75, 83, 85, 90, 95, 99, 125, 137, 191, 224, 228, 232, 237–238, 251, 253, 262, 276–277, 315, 317–318, 321–322, 324–326, 363–364, 374, 376–377, 382, 399, 444, 450–451, 456, 465, 467, 471, 474, 478, 512
Gikongoro (Rwanda): 347–348, 354
Gishamvu (Rwanda): 345–355, 358–361, 510
Giti (Rwanda): 147, 333–341, 521
Göttingen (Germany): 469
Grenoble (France): 60, 83, 161, 280–281, 285–291, 521
Gueldre (Netherlands): 459
Gulia (Ottoman Empire): 390

Hakkâri (Ottoman Empire): 385, 391
Hamburg (Germany): 469
Harpoot: *see* Kharpert (Ottoman Empire)
Hungry: 177, 179, 227, 231, 314–324

Ismit (Ottoman Empire): 195
Israel: 2–5, 16, 20, 22–23, 26–31, 56–57, 94, 128, 130, 136–139, 247, 262, 304, 435, 437–438, 441, 444–445, 447, 461, 521
Istanbul: 40, 48, 187, 190, 192–193, 204, 209, 212, 214, 216–217, 304, 367, 369–371, 377
Izbica (Ottoman Empire): 471

INDEX OF PLACES

Jabour (Ottoman Empire): 392
Jerusalem: 2, 22, 27, 85, 128, 188, 190, 246, 298, 304, 370, 479, 512, 515, 522

Kanyaru (river, Rwanda/Burundi): 351, 353
Kars (Ottoman Empire): 168, 180
Kessab (Ottoman Empire): 171
Kharpert (Ottoman Empire): 166, 171, 174, 192, 509
Kharput: *see* Kharpert (Ottoman Empire)
Kigali (Rwanda): 3, 147–149, 155, 335–337, 339, 341, 349, 353, 361, 482–483, 486, 491, 510
Kigembe (Rwanda): 345–351, 354, 355, 356, 358–361
Konya (Ottoman Empire): 194–195, 199, 370
Kurdistan (Ottoman Empire): 384, 391
Kütahya (Ottoman Empire): 195

Le Chambon-sur-Lignon (France): 4, 12, 98, 246, 363, 365, 433, 442, 444–445, 447, 499, 501, 513
Lisbon (Portugal): 136, 250, 254–255, 257, 299, 303, 307–310
London: 39, 51, 54, 87–93, 135–136, 239, 314–315, 317, 325, 329, 402, 450, 458
Lublin (Poland): 471
Lyon (France): 60, 91, 275, 305, 365, 405, 408, 424, 425, 431

Mabare (Rwanda): 363, 364, 481–494
Majdanek (Poland): 61, 234
Malatia (Ottoman Empire): 192–193
Malines (Belgium): 241, 275

Mamuret ul-Aziz (Ottoman Empire): 187, 191, 383
Marash (Ottoman Empire): 367–372, 374, 377–380, 382, 508
Marburg (Germany): 468
Mardin (Ottoman Empire): 190, 363, 383–393, 499, 511, 524
Marseille (France): 2, 255, 279, 283, 295, 298, 301, 305, 408, 431
Marsovan (Ottoman Empire): 175
Mauritius Island: 319
Megève (France): 241
Mesopotamia: 166, 179, 185–186, 369, 386
Metz Yeghern (Ottoman Empire): 164–165
Minsk (Former USSR): 111, 247, 471
Montauban (France): 90
Mosul (Ottoman Empire): 190, 385, 390–391
Mush (Ottoman Empire): 172
Mparamirundi (Burundi): 352
Mubuga (Burundi): 347
Mugesera (Lake, Rwanda): 484, 490, 493
Mureke (Burundi): 352
Musa Dagh (Ottoman Empire): 168, 512
Musambira (Rwanda): 333, 335–342
Mush (Ottoman Empire): 172

Netherlands (The): 24–25, 30, 57, 62, 66–70, 72, 77–78, 80–81, 110, 161, 239, 265–277, 363–364, 395, 447–455, 458, 460, 462, 467, 505, 507, 514, 517, 522–523
New York (United States of America): 235, 247, 249–250, 252–253, 255, 262, 295, 308–310
Ngoma (Rwanda): 348, 351, 361

INDEX OF PLACES

Nice (France): 61, 280–283, 285, 288, 302, 407–408, 503
Nieuwlande (Netherlands): 363–364, 433, 442, 447–463
Nisibe (Ottoman Empire): 390, 392
Nkomero (Rwanda): 346, 348, 350
Nord-Pas-de-Calais (France): 431
Nyakizu (Rwanda): 348, 354, 356
Nyumba (Rwanda): 346, 348–349, 351

Palestine: 30, 42, 87, 135, 248, 258, 262, 303, 305, 316
Paris (France): 4, 27, 39, 58, 62, 86, 88–91, 93–94, 118, 120, 123, 125, 138, 246–247, 249, 251–252, 269, 289, 298, 300, 365–367, 369, 400, 402–403, 411–418, 422–426, 429, 431, 512, 519
Pignerol (Italy): 442
Poland: 6–7, 11, 18, 24–25, 57, 62, 67, 74–75, 102, 108, 127, 161, 247–249, 254, 262, 274, 319, 397, 415, 465, 471, 499, 502, 507, 519
Portugal: 161, 250, 253
Posen (Poland): 471

Ras ul-Ain (Ottoman Empire): 390, 392
Ras ul-Ayn: *voir* Ras ul-Ain (Ottoman Empire)
Ratibor (Poland): 472
Reich: 6, 11, 57, 142, 161, 208, 224, 226, 270, 450, 453, 455, 462, 465, 473, 477, 519, 524
Remscheid (Germany): 469, 472
Riga (Latvia): 471
Rome (Italy): 130, 132, 139, 141–142, 385
Rotterdam (Netherlands): 449, 456
Runyinya (Rwanda): 348, 353, 360

Russia: 44, 116, 214, 245, 246–247, 324, 329, 383
Rwanda: 3, 18–20, 23, 145, 147, 150–151, 160, 222, 228–229, 314, 331, 332–343, 345–350, 352–358, 363–366, 481–483, 485–486, 488–489, 491–492, 499, 503, 505, 507–510, 520–521, 523–524

Sasoun (Ottoman Empire): 171–173
Savour (Ottoman Empire): 389
Sebastia (Ottoman Empire): 176–177
Sinjar (Ottoman Empire): 363, 383, 388, 390–393, 504
Sivas (Ottoman Empire): 175–176, 184, 187, 214, 383–384
Smyrna/Izmir (Ottoman Empire): 167, 195–196, 374
Sobibor (Poland): 106, 454
Spain: 56, 161, 208, 224, 253, 271, 304–305, 308, 512
Stanoz (Ottoman Empire): 194

Taba (Rwanda): 333, 335–337, 339–341
Taron (Ottoman Empire): 180
Theresienstadt (Czech Republic): 77, 226, 466, 471
Torre Pellice (Italy): 441
Tortum (Ottoman Empire): 187–188
Toulouse (France): 90–91, 431
Trabzon (Ottoman Empire): 187
Tur Abdin (Ottoman Empire): 385–386, 391

United Kingdom: 56
United States of America: 254, 371, 471
Uganda: 148, 319, 520

INDEX OF PLACES

Urfa (Ottoman Empire): 370–371, 377

Valais (Switzerland): 239
Van (Ottoman Empire): 42, 169, 187, 189, 197, 212, 383–385

Waldensian (valleys, Piedmont, Italy): 437, 441–442
Vichy (France): 87, 119, 250, 254–255, 499, 511
Voves (France): 115
Walzenhausen (Switzerland): 382

Warsaw (Poland): 108, 314, 329, 467, 497
West Germany: 467
Westerbork (Netherlands): 460
Wuppertal (Germany): 469, 477
Wüstenroth (Germany): 378, 382

Zeytun (Ottoman Empire): 370, 379
Free Zone/Southern Zone (France): 59–60, 83, 119–120, 159–160, 250, 252–256, 260, 279, 281, 284, 298, 301, 364, 396, 398, 400–401, 403–405, 407–408, 497, 503